Catholic
High School
Entrance Exams
FOR
DUMMIES®

Catholic High School Entrance Exams

FOR DUMMIES®

by Lisa Zimmer Hatch, MA, and
Scott A. Hatch, JD

WILEY

Wiley Publishing, Inc.

Catholic High School Entrance Exams For Dummies®

Published by
Wiley Publishing, Inc.
111 River St.
Hoboken, NJ 07030-5774
www.wiley.com

Copyright © 2010 by Wiley Publishing, Inc., Indianapolis, Indiana

Published by Wiley Publishing, Inc., Indianapolis, Indiana

Published simultaneously in Canada

For general information on our other products and services, please contact our Customer Care Department within the U.S. at 877-762-2974, outside the U.S. at 317-572-3993, or fax 317-572-4002.

For technical support, please visit www.wiley.com/techsupport.

Wiley also publishes its books in a variety of electronic formats. Some content that appears in print may not be available in electronic books.

Library of Congress Control Number: 2010921237

ISBN: 978-0-470-54873-8

Manufactured in the United States of America

10 9 8 7 6 5 4 3 2

WILEY

About the Authors

Lisa Zimmer Hatch, MA, and **Scott A. Hatch, JD,** have prepared teens and adults for college and careers since 1987. They were owners of The Center for Legal Studies for more than 20 years, during which time they created and administrated standardized test preparation and legal career courses offered online and in live-lecture format through more than 300 universities nationwide. Currently, Lisa is an Independent College Counselor and president of College Primers, where she applies her expertise to guiding high school and college students through the admissions process. She dedicates herself to helping clients gain admission to the colleges or programs that fit best with their goals and personalities. Scott is President of Hatch Education, a company that provides career training courses and continuing legal education for attorneys.

Lisa graduated with honors in English from the University of Puget Sound and received a master's degree in humanities with a literature emphasis from California State University. She is currently completing the UCLA College Counseling Certificate Program. She is a member of the Higher Education Consultants Association (HECA) and the Rocky Mountain Association of College Admissions Counselors (RMACAC).

Scott received his undergraduate degree from the University of Colorado and his Juris Doctorate from Southwestern Law School in Los Angeles. Scott is listed in *Who's Who in California* and *Who's Who Among Students in American Colleges and Universities* and was named one of the Outstanding Young Men of America by the United States Jaycees. He was a contributing editor to *The Judicial Profiler* and the *Colorado Law Annotated* series and has served as editor of several award-winning publications.

Scott and Lisa have coauthored numerous career training and standardized test preparation books, including *Paralegal Procedures and Practices,* 2nd Edition (Cengage/Delmar Publishing); *Paralegal Career For Dummies; GMAT For Dummies,* 5th Edition; *SAT II U.S. History For Dummies; SAT II Biology For Dummies;* and *SAT II Math For Dummies* (all from Wiley Publishing).

Dedication

We dedicate *Catholic High School Entrance Exams For Dummies* to Alison, Andrew, Zachary, Zoe, Dan, and Paige. Our family demonstrated patience, understanding, and assistance while we wrote this book, and we're very blessed to have them in our lives.

Authors' Acknowledgments

This book wouldn't be possible without the contributions of Zachary Hatch, Zoe Hatch, Bryan Gomez, and Morgan Burrows, who provided practice test material and helpful input, as well as Barbara Zimmer, who provided lots of moral support. We also acknowledge the input of the thousands of students who've completed our test preparation courses over the last 30 years. The classroom and online contributions offered by these eager learners have provided us with lots of information about what areas require the greatest amount of preparation.

Our project organization and attempts at wit were greatly facilitated by the editing professionals at Wiley Publishing. Our thanks go out to Alissa Schwipps and Mike Baker for their patience and guidance throughout the process and to Jen Tebbe, Cindy Kaplan, Masahiko J. Taniguchi, and Alexsis Venter for their attention to detail and helpful suggestions during the editing process.

Finally, we wish to thank our literary agent, Margo Maley Hutchinson, at Waterside Productions in Cardiff for her support and assistance and for introducing us to the innovative *For Dummies* series.

We thrive on feedback from our students and encourage our readers to provide comments and critiques at info@hatchedu.com.

Publisher's Acknowledgments

We're proud of this book; please send us your comments at http://dummies.custhelp.com. For other comments, please contact our Customer Care Department within the U.S. at 877-762-2974, outside the U.S. at 317-572-3993, or fax 317-572-4002.

Some of the people who helped bring this book to market include the following:

Acquisitions, Editorial, and Media Development

Senior Project Editor: Alissa Schwipps

Senior Acquisitions Editor: Mike Baker

Copy Editor: Jennifer Tebbe

Assistant Editor: Erin Calligan Mooney

Editorial Program Coordinator: Joe Niesen

Technical Editors: Cindy Kaplan, Masahiko J. Taniguchi, Alexsis Venter

Senior Editorial Manager: Jennifer Ehrlich

Senior Editorial Assistant: David Lutton

Editorial Assistants: Rachelle Amick, Jennette ElNaggar

Cover Photo: © Getty Images

Cartoons: Rich Tennant (www.the5thwave.com)

Composition Services

Project Coordinator: Patrick Redmond

Layout and Graphics: Carl Byers, Carrie A. Cesavice, Nikki Gately, Mark Pinto, Christine Williams

Proofreaders: Rebecca Denoncour, Shannon Ramsey

Indexer: Potomac Indexing, LLC

Special Help: Megan Knoll

Publishing and Editorial for Consumer Dummies

Diane Graves Steele, Vice President and Publisher, Consumer Dummies

Kristin Ferguson-Wagstaffe, Product Development Director, Consumer Dummies

Ensley Eikenburg, Associate Publisher, Travel

Kelly Regan, Editorial Director, Travel

Publishing for Technology Dummies

Andy Cummings, Vice President and Publisher, Dummies Technology/General User

Composition Services

Debbie Stailey, Director of Composition Services

Contents at a Glance

Table of Contents

Introduction

1f you're reading this book, you're probably planning to attend a Catholic high school. Congratulations on your dedication to an excellent education! But before you can don your uniform and complain about your class schedule, you have to take one of three possible entrance exams. The test you take — whether that's the HSPT, the TACHS, or the COOP — will tell your chosen high school a little bit about how prepared you are for the next step in your education. High school administrators evaluate your score and use it to determine what classes to put you in and even whether to give you a little scholarship money. We don't want to put undue pressure on you, but you do have to get ready for the challenge. How do you prepare for a test you've never seen? Sure, you can read through your notes from English and math classes (if only you'd taken any). Or you can watch a lot of *Jeopardy!* But we have a better way. . . .

Catholic High School Entrance Exams For Dummies puts at your fingertips everything you need to know to conquer the exam required by your future Catholic high school. We give you a complete review of the language, reading, math, quantitative relationship, and logic concepts the various entrance exams test. We also provide insight into how to avoid the pitfalls that standardized test-takers sometimes encounter.

About This Book

If you're like most 13- and 14-year-olds, studying for your Catholic high school entrance exam is the absolute last thing you want to do. We get that. Really, we do. That's why we've filled *Catholic High School Entrance Exams For Dummies* with clearly written advice presented in an easy-to-swallow, casual tone. The other great thing about this book is that you can get in and get out to find what you need quickly. You don't have to read this book from cover to cover. If you have an extra hour before basketball practice or clarinet lessons, you can devour a chapter or even a particular section within a chapter. If you just want to brush up on your grammar skills or perfect your analogy-deciphering ability, you can gobble up the relevant chapter or section and forget about the rest. (If these eating metaphors are making you hungry, then by all means take a snack break.)

Note: Some of the sections in this book are applicable to only one or two tests. For instance, if you're taking the TACHS exam, you won't encounter any of the question types covered in the chapter on verbal reasoning. You may want to refer to the table of contents at the front of this book to see which sections apply to the particular test required by the high school you're planning to attend.

The sample questions we sprinkle throughout each chapter in Parts II and III read like the actual test questions. Because the best way to gear up for any standardized test is to practice, practice, practice on lots of test questions, we give you well over 1,000 opportunities to answer questions and get familiar with the way your exam phrases questions and presents answer choices. Then there's the pièce de résistance of the book: two full-length practice tests for each of the three Catholic high school entrance exams (complete with full-length answer chapters to explain the answers to each and every test question).

Ultimately, we want you to succeed on whichever exam you're taking, so we're dedicated to giving you time-tested techniques for improving your score. In the following pages, you discover how to quickly spot incorrect answer choices, make educated guesses based on what you know, and manage your time wisely for the best possible score. With *Catholic High School Entrance Exams For Dummies,* you have all you need to ace the HSPT, TACHS, or

COOP so you can move on to more important matters — arranging to get the cute classmate sitting next to you in science class to be your lab partner without seeming too interested.

Conventions Used in This Book

To help you find your way through this book — as in all *For Dummies* books — we've used the following basic conventions:

- *Italics* highlight new words and terms that we're defining. They also point out individual words or short phrases that we want to draw your attention to.
- **Boldfaced** text indicates the actions in numbered steps and keywords in bulleted lists.
- Monofont alerts you to the presence of a Web address.

You'll also notice that some of the chapters contain sidebars (a paragraph or two in a shaded box). Sidebars contain quirky bits of information that we think may interest you but that aren't essential to your performance on any of the Catholic high school entrance exams. Skip over 'em if you'd prefer; you won't hurt our feelings — too much.

Finally, some words may appear in *this font*. These are vocabulary words we've chosen to shine a spotlight on to help you prep for your exam.

Foolish Assumptions

Here's the most important assumption we're making about you: You're most likely an eighth-grader planning on attending a Catholic high school, and you've been told you must take an entrance exam. (Yes indeed — we've been praised for our startling ability to recognize the obvious!) Generally, students who attend parochial schools make learning a top priority, so we're also thinking that you're a pretty motivated student. And it's likely that your grade and middle school years have been spent in a parochial environment too, which means you've had an awesome education already. Good for you!

Most of the concepts you'll encounter on the Catholic high school entrance exam you're facing aren't new to you, but the way they're presented can be downright weird for some question types. So, even if you're a math whiz with a college-level vocabulary, you should expose yourself to the question types ahead of time just so you know what to expect. What if you're at the other end of the spectrum and are wishing you paid a little more attention in Miss O'Brien's algebra class? No worries; we're ready for you, too. Inside these pages are thorough math and English reviews just in case you've been napping in class.

How This Book Is Organized

Catholic High School Entrance Exams For Dummies is divided into five parts that are packed with important information to get you ready for exam day. We organized these parts so you can easily navigate through the book to find whatever topic you're looking for. Following is a quick look at what each part covers.

Part I: Providing Perspective on Catholic High School Entrance Exams

This part tells you how to figure out which exam you're supposed to take, how Catholic high schools use each of the exams, and what each exam looks like. It also helps you get super-organized for your test-taking adventure. It features information on registering for your exam, assembling everything you need to take with you to the testing site, and developing a tried-and-true strategy for moving successfully and efficiently through the test questions.

Part II: Vanquishing the Verbal Questions

Here's where you discover what kinds of language and reading questions appear on the entrance exams. Get ready to encounter all sorts of ways to play with vocabulary words, find out how to approach analogies in words and pictures, train your brain to think logically, and create a plan for working through reading comprehension passages and their questions. This part also includes pithy reviews of proper grammar, usage, punctuation, spelling, and sentence construction.

Part III: Mastering Math and Conquering Quantitative Questions

The third part of the book is more than just an exciting overview of every math class you've had since kindergarten. In addition to reviews of the traditional math concepts of arithmetic, geometry, algebra, and word problems, you discover how to tackle other inventive quantitative question types. The Catholic high school entrance exams present you with creative questions that ask you to complete number and picture sequences, evaluate shapes and figures, balance squares and triangles on scales, and figure out strange-seeming hole-punch problems.

Part IV: Practice Makes Perfect

As promised, after you feel comfortable with your increased vocabulary, memorized math formulas, and that hole-punch question type, you can put your skills to the test tackling the full-length exams contained in this part. For your testing enjoyment, we include two HSPTs, two TACHSs, and two COOPs. Each exam comes complete with a sample bubble answer sheet so you can practice filling in circles, as well as thorough explanations of all the answers.

Part V: The Part of Tens

No *For Dummies* book is complete without The Part of Tens, and this book is no different. Here, we include ten important test-taking strategies you should apply to master the exam you're facing. We also include a chapter for you to share with your parents so they know their role in helping you do your best. (They didn't think they could just buy you this book and ditch you, did they?)

Icons Used in This Book

One exciting feature of *Catholic High School Entrance Exams For Dummies* is the icons that highlight especially significant portions of the text. These little pictures in the margins alert you to areas where you should pay particularly close attention.

This icon is pretty self-explanatory. When you see it, you know you're going to get to practice the particular area of instruction covered in that section with a question like one you may see on the test. Our examples include detailed explanations of how to most efficiently answer exam questions and avoid common pitfalls.

Information tagged with this icon relates specifically to one (or all) of the entrance exams. It highlights facts you should know about each exam that'll help you perform your best.

This icon points out those general concepts, such as math formulas and grammar rules, that you should keep in mind as you tackle the test questions.

Throughout the book, we give you insights into how you can enhance your performance on the entrance exam you're facing. Text featuring the Tip icon presents you with juicy test-taking timesavers.

Where to Go from Here

Wondering where to get started? Well, if you're a test-taking whiz or straight-A student who only needs to brush up on a few areas, you can go right to the chapters and sections that cover those areas. (Use the table of contents and index as your guides.) Then again, if you really want to ace the HSPT, TACHS, or COOP, we suggest you take a more thorough approach to preparing. Familiarize yourself with the general test-taking process in Chapter 2 and then work through the complete verbal and math reviews. You can skim through sections that you know a lot about by just reading the Tip, Remember, and Heads Up paragraphs and working through the Example questions.

If nothing else (and after you've done some preparatory work), we encourage you to take at least one of the practice exams in Part IV. Taking a practice test shows you which questions you seem to cruise through and which ones you need more work on. One way to use the practice tests is to take the first practice test for your exam and calculate your score. Then read through the verbal and math reviews in Parts II and III. After that, take the second practice test and compare your new score to the one you got on the first test so you can see just how much you improved with a little practice.

Wherever you begin, be confident that you're making a giant contribution to bettering your future by working through this book. Now, get ready to pass that Catholic high school entrance exam with flying colors!

Part I

Providing Perspective on Catholic High School Entrance Exams

The 5th Wave
By Rich Tennant

"I always get a good night's sleep the day before a test so I'm relaxed and alert the next morning. Then I grab my pen, eat a banana, and I'm on my way."

In this part . . .

Here's where you really get to know your Catholic high school entrance exams. First, you discover just what your school of choice might do with your scores. Then you spend time becoming familiar with the formats of the HSPT, TACHS, and COOP, as well as how they're scored. (Here's a hint: You really only need to review the section for the test you're taking. How's that for speed reading?)

Next, we introduce you to the nitty-gritty details of taking a Catholic high school entrance exam, including registering and requesting testing accommodations if you need them. We also share helpful tips for achieving a stellar score, organizing your time, and relaxing if you get nervous. Do yourself a favor and spend the 20 or so minutes it takes to read through these two informative chapters. You won't regret it!

Chapter 1

Getting to Know You: Meet the HSPT, TACHS, and COOP

- -

In This Chapter
▶ Figuring out why you have to take a Catholic high school entrance exam in the first place
▶ Familiarizing yourself with the format and scoring of the HSPT, TACHS, and COOP

- -

1 f you're planning to attend a Catholic high school, you need to be prepared to pass a special entrance exam. Just what is a Catholic high school entrance exam? And why on earth do you have to take one aside from the fact that most Catholic high schools require it? We enlighten you on that and more in this chapter. Prepare to discover why Catholic high schools want you to take an entrance exam, how they use your scores, and what the particular exam you're facing looks like.

Understanding How Schools Use Your Score

What a Catholic high school does with your entrance exam score really depends on the policies of that particular school. Many schools consider the exam a way to weed out applicants for the incoming freshman class, but some schools also use your score to determine what classes you should be placed in and whether you deserve a scholarship. The following sections delve into these uses of Catholic high school entrance exams in greater detail.

The entrance exam as an admissions requirement

Before you apply to any Catholic high school, you and your parents should research its admissions requirements. You can usually find the most up-to-date information by browsing the high school's Web site or by calling the admissions office or school official in charge of admissions. Read the admissions requirements carefully to find out what entrance exam the high school requires and how the school uses your score. *Note:* Most Catholic high schools require an entrance exam for new freshmen only; transfer students are usually exempt.

Here are some of the degrees to which Catholic high schools may consider your entrance exam for admissions purposes:

✔ Some actually don't consider your entrance exam score at all. (They do, however, use it as a placement tool for honors classes; see the next section.)

✔ Some may consider your entrance exam score with the same weight as they do your sixth-, seventh-, and eighth-grade report cards.

✔ Other schools put more emphasis on your previous grade point average but do use your entrance exam score for additional admissions consideration (along with letters of recommendation and lists of extracurricular activities).

Most Catholic high schools require more than just your entrance exam score and grade records from the previous three years. Depending on the school, you may also have to submit letters of recommendation, write an essay (some schools even ask your parents to write an essay, too), and participate in an interview. So, there's a good chance your entrance exam score is just one of several admissions requirements you must fulfill to be considered.

Find out how your high school of choice evaluates your entrance exam score by calling the admissions office. Knowing just what's at stake when you walk into the exam is always a good idea.

The entrance exam as a placement tool

Some Catholic high schools actually use your entrance exam score to figure out what classes to place you in during your freshman year. For instance, your score may indicate that you're qualified to take honors courses, such as an advanced math class, or it may let the school's faculty know that you should stick with basic algebra to start.

The number of Advanced Placement (AP) or honors classes you take in high school may influence your chances of being accepted to certain colleges. Some colleges give you college credit as a result of your successful completion of AP courses and AP exams, which means qualifying for and taking AP courses could lessen your college course load and tuition payments down the road. So, scoring your best on your Catholic high school entrance exam can result in big-time future benefits. (See Chapter 2 for tips on how to maximize your entrance exam score.)

The entrance exam as a source of scholarships

Your entrance exam score may also make you eligible for scholarship money, which no doubt would make your parents happy. This extra help toward tuition can be based on your overall score or on how well you do in a specific test section. Perhaps a generous donor who has made a fortune in selling top-of-the-line hole punches has allocated funds designed specifically for freshmen who excel at figuring out those clever holes-in-the-folded-paper questions on the TACHS. Hey, it could happen!

Covering Most of the Country: The HSPT

HSPT stands for High School Placement Test. The exam is produced by the Scholastic Testing Service and is designed for eighth-graders interested in attending a Catholic high school practically anywhere in the country (the New York City area and parts of New Jersey have their own tests, as you find out later in this chapter). The individual high schools that require the HSPT have a lot of control over when it's given, but the test is often held on a Saturday in early December. Usually, you take the test at the high school you're applying to. (**Note:** If you're considering more than one school, it's best to take the test at the high school you like the most.) Whether you're charged a fee to take the exam is up to the high school that administers it. Contact the school official in charge of admissions to get more information on fees and other exam administration policies.

The sections that follow introduce you to the ins and outs of the HSPT, from format to scoring.

Figuring out the format of the HSPT

The HSPT has nearly 300 multiple-choice questions that you're expected to answer in just over two hours. The questions are numbered from 1 to 298, which is nice because you'll never see a question with the same number as one in a different section. To see what a full-length HSPT test looks like, check out the two practice tests in Chapters 17 and 19.

The content of the HSPT is broken down into five sections called Verbal Skills, Quantitative Skills, Reading, Mathematics, and Language. The different sections have roughly 60 questions each, but the time allotted for each section varies. Except for a few questions in the Verbal Skills and Mathematics sections, each question has four answer choices designated (A), (B), (C), and (D).

Even though we're pretty sure the question types won't change from HSPT to HSPT, make sure you read the directions for each section just to be safe.

The creators of the HSPT have also made available to Catholic high schools three optional multiple-choice tests in the specific areas of Catholic religion, mechanical aptitude, and science. High schools choose whether to require one of these tests in addition to the HSPT, and only a few use them. To find out whether you have to take one of the optional exams, contact the official who's in charge of admissions at the school where you plan to take the HSPT.

The Verbal Skills section

The HSPT's Verbal Skills section contains 60 questions that you must answer in 16 minutes. If you just did the math on that one, you realize that you have about 15 seconds to answer each question. Relax! That should be enough time because you don't have to do a bunch of reading to answer these questions. Here's what you find in the Verbal Skills section:

- **Synonyms and antonyms:** These questions give you a word and ask you to choose the answer that's either most similar to it or most opposite. We explain how to answer synonym and antonym questions in Chapter 3.

- **Grouping words questions:** Expect to see two question types that ask you to categorize words. One type is the analogy question, which we cover in Chapter 4; the other is the type that asks you to find the word that doesn't belong, which we cover in Chapters 3 and 8.

- **Verbal reasoning:** This question type gives you some statements as well as a conclusion based on those statements. You have to determine whether the conclusion is true, false, or uncertain, which means there are only three answer choices. We show you how to answer these babies in Chapter 8.

The Quantitative Skills section

The Quantitative Skills section features 52 questions that ask you to complete a sequence, compare values, and create equations. You have 30 minutes to answer all the questions, which means you should spend no more than about 30 seconds per question. Three kinds of questions appear in this section:

- **Sequence questions:** The HSPT gives you a sequence of numbers and tells you to find the answer that completes the missing number or numbers in the sequence. Flip to Chapter 14 for help answering these questions.

- **Comparing values:** These questions give you three values and ask you to figure out their relationship. One may be greater than another, or they may all be equal. You choose the answer that describes the correct relationship. See Chapter 15 for insight into how to answer these questions.

- **Creating equations:** This question type expresses a quantity in words. Your mission is to translate the problem into an equation and solve it. You can find the mathematical equivalents to words in Chapter 13.

The Reading section

The HSPT's Reading section provides you with 62 questions to answer in 25 minutes, which gives you less than 30 seconds per question. Approximately 40 of the questions are based on a series of about five or six reading passages. The remaining questions are more vocabulary questions. To discover how to answer reading comprehension questions, head to Chapter 5. You can improve your performance on vocabulary questions with the pointers in Chapter 3.

Because reading comprehension questions take more time to answer than vocabulary questions, you may want to jump ahead and answer the vocabulary questions at the end of the Reading section before you answer the reading comprehension questions. Just make sure you mark the answers in the proper places on your answer sheet!

The Mathematics section

The Mathematics section is broken down into two subsections: Concepts (with 24 questions) and Problem Solving (with 40 questions). The problem-solving questions are mostly word problems (which you can find out more about in Chapter 13). To improve your score in both sections, be sure to review Chapters 10, 11, and 12.

The Language section

The 25 minutes the HSPT gives you to complete the Language section should be sufficient to answer all 60 questions. Those 60 questions are broken down into 50 questions that ask you to find errors in punctuation, capitalization, usage, and spelling and 10 questions that test your knowledge of sentence construction and written composition. Help for how to recognize punctuation and spelling errors lies in Chapter 6. Chapter 7 offers a refresher on basic grammar, and Chapter 5 helps you figure out how to answer written composition questions.

Scoring the HSPT

The Scholastic Testing Service (STS) computes how many questions you answer correctly on your HSPT and converts that score to a scaled score that ranges anywhere from 200 to 800. (Yes, you get 200 points just for taking the test. How awesome is that?) The STS then compares you to all the other HSPT test-takers and gives the high school you're applying to a report that shows where you rank both nationally and locally. From there it's up to the high school to figure out what to do with that information. If you have questions, talk to the admissions office at your high school of choice. And if you want to find out your HSPT score, ask the school about that as well, but be prepared for it to pass on sharing your score with you.

HSPT-takers beware: The optional essay

Some Catholic high schools like to see how you write without outside help from parents, siblings, teachers, or your best friend's cousin. So on test day they may ask you to write an essay before taking the HSPT. The topic will be fairly general, along the lines of "Why do you want to attend our school?" Ask a school official in charge of administering the HSPT whether or not you're expected to write an essay. If the answer is yes, prepare ahead of time by coming up with three reasons that you want to attend that particular high school, such as the school athletic program, its academic reputation, acting opportunities, or other areas that interest you. Just make sure your answer doesn't include the phrase "because my parents are forcing me" and take care to spell the name of the school correctly.

For New Yorkers Only: The TACHS

The TACHS is more formally known as the Test for Admission into Catholic High Schools, and it's exclusively required of eighth-graders who want to go to Catholic high schools in the Diocese of Brooklyn/Queens and the Archdiocese of New York. It's usually given on a November morning at Catholic high schools in the New York City area.

When you sign up for the TACHS, you have to pay an examination fee (which is currently $49, although that can change), which includes the registration materials, a student handbook, test materials, and score reports to three high schools of your choice and the Catholic elementary school you attend (or your home if you don't go to a Catholic elementary school). The TACHS has a very informative Web site (www.tachsinfo.com) where you can download a handbook and see a sample practice test. Or you can just head to Chapters 21 and 23 for the two TACHS practice tests you already have right here in your hot little hands.

Following is some information on the format of the TACHS's various sections and how the exam is scored.

Deciphering the format of the TACHS

The TACHS varies a bit from year to year, but generally it contains around 200 multiple-choice questions. Plan for a total testing time of around three or four hours, including the time it takes for you to fill in the preliminary test sections and for the proctor to explain the directions. The odd-numbered questions designate the answers as (A), (B), (C), and (D), and the even-numbered questions mark the answer choices as (J), (K), (L), and (M). Each section of the test begins with question number 1, so make sure you're marking your answers on the right section of your answer sheet.

Most of the four sections of the TACHS break down into subcategories. The Reading section has subsections on vocabulary and comprehension. The Language section has one part for spotting errors in usage and mechanics and another for testing your knowledge of written composition. The Math section features standard math problems and an entire section dedicated to estimating. Finally, the unusual questions in the Ability section test your reasoning skills. The creators of the TACHS change the test's format a little bit every year, so the number of questions of each type vary.

The Reading section

The approximately 10 to 20 vocabulary questions in the TACHS's Reading section are mere synonym questions (find out more about these in Chapter 3). You have about 5 to 10 minutes to answer them all. Standard reading comprehension passages and questions make up the rest of this section. Expect to encounter around 20 to 30 questions based on several passages and have about 25 minutes to answer them. (We cover how to answer reading comprehension questions in Chapter 5.)

The Language section

To study for the approximately 40 capitalization, spelling, punctuation, and usage questions in the Language section, read Chapters 6 and 7. Assistance for the remaining 10 questions (which, by the way, deal with written composition) can be found in Chapter 5. The TACHS gives you about 23 minutes to spot the errors and around 7 minutes to correct the sentence composition.

The Math section

The first 30 questions or so in the TACHS's Math section ask you standard math questions about numbers, basic operations, charts and graphs, and problem solving. The remaining questions (approximately 18) ask you only to estimate the answers to simple math problems. Brushing up on your math by reading Chapters 10, 11, 12, and 13 will help you fly through this section in the approximately 40 minutes you're given.

The Ability section

The TACHS presents you with a few question types you may not have seen before. Depending on the whims of the test-makers, the TACHS's Ability section features about 10 to 30 questions that you must answer in roughly 5 to 15 minutes. The majority of them have you evaluate the similarities and differences in shapes and figures. Reading Chapter 15 on quantitative comparisons and Chapter 4 on analogies can help you answer these questions. The last approximately 10 questions in this section provide you with pictures of a folded piece of paper with holes punched in it. Your charge? To use your powers of reasoning to choose the answer choice that displays the proper pattern of holes when the page is unfolded. (We share tips for answering this very distinct question type in Chapter 15.)

Scoring the TACHS

The TACHS administrators calculate your score based on how many of the questions you answer correctly. They then report your score to up to three high schools of your choosing and to your Catholic elementary school if you attend one. If you don't, they send your scores directly to you. Scores are usually sent to the high schools in December, but you won't receive your report until January. From there the high schools can interpret and use your score as they see fit. To get more information on how the high school you're interested in attending uses your TACHS score, contact its admissions office.

Strictly for the Garden State: The COOP

The COOP exam (or the Cooperative Admissions Examination Program) is administered to eighth-graders who want to attend a Catholic high school in New Jersey's Archdiocese of Newark or Diocese of Paterson. The test is usually held in November at participating Catholic high schools. The COOP test changes a little bit every year, but the tested concepts remain the same. To find out exactly what questions will appear on your exam, visit the helpful COOP Web site at coopexam.org. In the summer before the exam date, the COOP powers-that-be present a practice test there that gives a sampling of the question types they'll use that year. In the meantime, check out the two practice COOPs we include in Chapters 25 and 27.

The COOP charges an application fee (which is currently $40). It reports your score to up to three high schools of your choice in January; it also sends a score report to your Catholic elementary school (you'll receive your report at your home if you're home-schooled). Want to find out more about the COOP's format and scoring? Check out the following sections.

Walking through the COOP's format

Though the format varies a little bit, the nearly 200 test questions on the COOP usually have four answer choices designated (A), (B), (C), and (D) for odd-numbered questions and (F), (G), (H), and (J) for even-numbered ones. The roughly two-and-a-half-hour test covers sequences, analogies, quantitative reasoning, verbal reasoning, reading and language arts, and mathematics.

The Sequences section

The approximately 20 sequence questions in the first section of the COOP involve figures, shapes, numbers, and letters. You have about 15 minutes to evaluate the given information and find the answer choice that completes the sequence. Chapter 14 gives you tips on how to cruise through this section on exam day.

The Analogies section

The 20 analogy questions on the COOP are a little different from some of the others you may have seen — they compare pictures rather than words. To find out how to work through these questions in the approximately 7 minutes allotted, read through Chapter 4.

The Quantitative Reasoning section

The Quantitative Reasoning section gives you 15 minutes to answer about 20 questions that ask you to deal with numbers in unusual ways. Following is a rundown of the question types (find out how to answer them in Chapter 15):

- **Finding the quantitative relationship:** These questions feature a series of three number relationships joined by the same mathematical operation. Your job is to find the operation and use it to pick an answer choice that completes the last relationship.

- **Calculating shaded areas:** Several questions present you with a shape that has a shaded portion. Your must choose the fraction that indicates how much of the shape is shaded.

- **Balancing the scale:** This unusual question type tells you what quantity of squares equals a certain number of triangles. Based on this information, you have to choose an answer that balances the scale.

The Verbal Reasoning sections

A glutton for your punishment, the COOP boasts two Verbal Reasoning sections: One deals with word relationships, and the other deals with logic problems. Each section has around 20 questions for you to answer within 15 minutes. The first Verbal Reasoning section features several different question types:

- **Finding the necessary part:** These questions give you a word and then ask you to choose the answer that's necessary to the given word. In other words, they want you to pick the answer that conveys something that must be present for the given word to exist. For instance, a necessary part of the word *dentist* is *teeth*. Without teeth, dentists wouldn't exist. See Chapter 8 for more on this question type.

- **Examining series of analogies:** You may see a question that gives you two rows of words. The words in the top row have a relationship to one another, and the words in the bottom row are related similarly. After you've figured out the relationship in the top row, you must choose the answer that properly completes the analogy in the second row. Chapters 4 and 8 can help you with series-of-analogies questions.

- **Eliminating the word that doesn't belong:** Yes, technically you want the word that doesn't fit with the others, but the way to find it is to find the words in the answer choices that *are* alike. Check out Chapter 8 for more on this question type.

- **Choosing the word that *does* belong:** Just when you get comfortable eliminating words that don't belong, the COOP asks you to pick a word that *does* belong. It gives you three words that are similar, and you have to choose the answer that has a similar meaning. These are really just fancy synonym questions; head to Chapters 3 and 8 for tips.

The second Verbal Reasoning section requires you to examine a bunch of statements and draw the most logical conclusion. Expect to face about 20 of these questions. We show you how to pick the best answer (and avoid the wrong ones) in Chapter 8.

Introducing the ISEE and SSAT

Not all Catholic high schools require the HSPT, COOP, or TACHS. A few may examine your scores on tests you've already taken in elementary or middle school, such as the Iowa Basics or SRA tests, or they may rely on other standardized entrance exams, such as the ISEE (Independent School Entrance Exam) and SSAT (Secondary School Admission Test). Private schools generally rely on these two tests for admitting freshmen and placing them in classes, but neither test is used specifically by Catholic high schools. Some Catholic high schools, however, may require you to take one of them, or you may wind up deciding to apply to a private high school that isn't Catholic. In either case, you should know that both of these exams test concepts that are very similar to those found on the HSPT, TACHS, and COOP. In fact, preparing for the three tests covered in this book gives you an excellent preparation for the ISEE and SSAT too.

You'll see questions on math, reading, verbal reasoning, and vocabulary on all five exams, but one of the big differences between the ISEE and SSAT and the three tests covered in this book is that the ISEE and SSAT require you to write an essay. (That makes your Catholic high school entrance exam seem lots better all of a sudden, doesn't it?) Another thing you don't have to worry about that SSAT test-takers do is a penalty for a wrong answer. The SSAT takes off a quarter of a point for every wrong answer, which gives you a whole guessing philosophy to master.

If you need to take one of these other tests, you can find out more about it by contacting the high school that requires it. The SSAT also has a very informative Web site; check it out at www.ssat.org. You can find information about the ISEE at www.erbtest.org; choose ISEE where it asks you to select the test you want to know about.

The Reading and Language Arts section

The COOP combines reading comprehension questions and questions about proper English usage and writing in the same section. The passages you see in this section draw on the concepts we review in Chapters 5, 6, and 7 to provide you with a combination of questions that test your ability to understand what you read and evaluate sentences for all sorts of errors. Luckily, the test gives you about 40 minutes to answer the 40 questions in this section, so you have a lot of time to take on this task.

The Mathematics section

You have 35 minutes to complete the approximately 40 questions in the COOP's Mathematics section. The variety of concepts tested in this section spans everything from basic operations and inequalities to geometry, charts, and graphs. Make sure you understand what's covered in Chapters 10, 11, and 12 if you want to ace this section.

Scoring the COOP

The COOP test-makers scale your raw score of total questions answered correctly and convert that scale to a percentage. They then send your report to the three (or fewer) Catholic high schools of your choice. The schools get to decide how to interpret and use your score. To find out just how your scores will be interpreted and used, contact the high school you're interested in attending.

Chapter 2

Executing a Plan for Success

● ●

In This Chapter

▶ Registering for the exam and other details

▶ Figuring out how to score the most points possible

▶ Picking up tips for using your precious time well

▶ Keeping your cool with tried-and-true relaxation techniques

● ●

Who in his or her right mind wants to spend an early morning crammed into a classroom with a bunch of other #2-pencil-wielding, half-awake-and-wanting-to-go-back-to-bed test-takers? No one, that's who. But most Catholic high schools won't admit you if you don't pass an entrance exam, so here you are. You may as well reward yourself with the best exam score you can get. This chapter contains the tools you need to pull together a winning strategy. You find out how to arrive at the testing site perfectly prepared, eliminate wrong answers, manage your time well, avoid a panic attack, and so much more in the following pages. But don't take our word for it. Dive on in!

Looking at What You Need to Do before the Exam

Part of preparing for your Catholic high school entrance exam is knowing how to register for the exam, where to take it, and what to bring with you. You can get most of this information from the high school you're applying to, but the next sections give you a general summary of what you need to know.

Registering for your entrance exam and picking a testing site

It's best not to walk into a testing site without giving officials prior notice that you're coming. This is one party you don't want to crash because there might not be a seat for you if you just walk in. Contact the high school(s) you want to attend to find out what procedures you need to follow to register for the exam.

Both the TACHS and COOP have online registration options on their official Web sites. You can find the TACHS information at www.tachsinfo.com and the COOP forms at coopexam.org. You register for the HSPT through the Catholic high school you want to attend.

The TACHS and COOP are usually offered in November each year, and registration is generally available beginning in September or October. The HSPT test dates are determined by the Catholic high schools that administer it. Most give it on the first Saturday in December, but some schedule the exam as late as January. Registration usually begins about one or two months before the test date.

The tests are intended to be taken only once, so make sure you're fully prepared for the exam on your scheduled date. Any makeup test dates are for those unable to take an exam on its original date — not people who aren't happy with their original scores.

As for where you take the test, most of the exams are offered at the Catholic high schools themselves. If you're considering several high schools that require the HSPT but prefer one over the others, we suggest you sign up to take the HSPT at your top choice of high school, if possible. Signing up to take an exam at a particular high school is a great way of telling the admissions personnel that you really want to go to their school. When they know you're eager to attend, they're more likely to accept you.

When you register for either the COOP or the TACHS, you get to choose where you want to take your exam (the location isn't necessarily related to what high school you want to attend). You also get to pick which schools you want your scores sent to. Both tests let you choose up to three schools.

Deciding what to bring to the exam (and what to leave at home)

Regardless of where you take your Catholic high school entrance exam, you need to bring certain items with you (and leave other items at home!).

The absolute essentials to bring with you to the exam are

- ✓ **Your registration confirmation:** When you register for the exam, you'll receive an admissions ticket or other form of confirmation receipt. Have it on you on test day because you may be asked to prove that you're registered for the exam.

- ✓ **A form of identification:** You may also have to prove that you're really you and not your neighbor with the borderline genius IQ and current *Teen Jeopardy!* champion status coming in to take the test for you. Here are the kinds of acceptable IDs (double-check with the school to make sure your ID is what it wants to see):

  - A government or state-issued identification card

  - A school identification card

  - A valid passport

  - A library card

- ✓ **A bunch of new and sharpened #2 pencils with good erasers:** Make sure they're #2s and that you have a few of them. Most importantly, the erasers on the end should be new and not the kind that create more marks than they eliminate (you know the kind we're talking about). Mechanical pencils (even if they contain #2 lead) aren't tradition-ally allowed for use on the entrance exams, so make sure the pencils you take with you are the kind that have to be sharpened.

Don't even think about bringing one of the following items with you on test day; just leave 'em at home:

- ✓ **Cellphones, calculators, watches that contain calculators, or MP3 players:** Any elec-tronic device is taboo at the testing site. Leave them at home, or else you may be asked to leave yourself.

  Watches of *any* kind aren't allowed on the TACHS, so leave your watch at home if you're taking this test. The COOP allows watches if they don't have built-in calculators or computers. The high schools that give the HSPT make determinations about whether or not watches are allowed, so contact the high school administrator in charge of admissions if you want to know whether you can have a watch at your HSPT site.

✔ **Scratch paper:** You aren't allowed to take in paper of any kind. You can, however, write anything you want in your test booklet. If a test administrator allows you to use scratch paper during the test, he or she will give it to you.

✔ **Highlighters, pens, or protractors:** Any kind of writing utensil or mechanical device other than your lucky #2 pencil is a no-go.

✔ **Books:** Even if you think you'll have time to read between test sections, you won't. You can't have a book with you. Period.

Requesting accommodations

Pretty much the only testing accommodation that the Catholic high school entrance exams make for students with documented learning differences is extended testing time. If you have an Individualized Education Program (IEP) or other documentation that shows that you require extra test-taking time, you can fill out an eligibility form to request accommodation. The test administrators need these eligibility forms before the regular registration forms, though, so get them in early. More information is available from the TACHS and COOP Web sites (see the earlier "Registering for your entrance exam and picking a testing site" section for the addresses) or from the individual high schools if you're taking the HSPT.

The nitty-gritty details regarding the administration of the HSPT are determined by the particular high school that requires it. Always contact the school administrator in charge of admissions to find out about exam specifics such as test dates, registration procedures, and items to bring with you and leave at home.

Maximizing Your Score on Test Day

You'll feel better on test day (and score better too) if you have a plan and stick to it. Your pretest plan should include studying the concepts and practice tests in this book, laying out all the stuff you need for the test the night before you take it, getting a good night's sleep, eating a breakfast with a balance of carbohydrates and protein for energy and sustenance, and arriving at the testing site with plenty of time to check in and get settled. Of course, your plan should also include strategies for tackling the test itself on exam day. The following sections present you with several key strategies for carrying out a plan during the test to achieve the best possible score on your Catholic high school entrance exam.

Before you start answering exam questions, the test administrator will go over testing procedures and walk you through completing the preliminary sections of the test (those parts that ask you to fill in your complete name and address so that they know the test is yours). Be sure to listen carefully and ask questions before the exam begins. When the clock starts running, you need to devote all of your attention to finishing the whole test in the time allotted.

Answer every question

To get the best score possible, you must provide one answer (and *only* one answer) for each question in every section. You can't get credit for a question if you don't answer it, and if you don't answer all the questions, you miss the points you receive just by being lucky.

None of the entrance exams penalizes you for wrong answers. Your raw score is just the total number of questions you answer correctly. You don't lose any points or a fraction of points for questions you answer incorrectly. So, never ever leave an answer bubble blank on your answer sheet and mark only one answer per question.

If you notice that you have only three or four minutes remaining in a section and more than five questions left, spend the remaining minutes marking an answer for every question — even if you don't have time to read them. For questions with four answer-choice possibilities, you have a 25 percent chance of randomly guessing the correct answer (which is way better than not answering the question at all).

If you have to guess randomly at the end of a section, mark the same bubble for each answer. Marking the same bubble saves you time because you don't need to choose which answer to mark for each question.

Manage your answer sheet

The answer sheets for the Catholic high school entrance exams, like those for most standardized tests, have a series of bubbles for each of the answer choices in the test booklet. The questions on the HSPT answer sheet are numbered from 1 to 298, but the TACHS and COOP start again with 1 for each new test section. When you mark the answer to Question 12 in the TACHS Reading section, be careful that you do so in the Reading section of the answer sheet and not in the Mathematics section.

One handy way to keep track of your answers is to move them from your test booklet to your answer sheet in chunks of five. After you've determined the answer to a question, circle the answer in the booklet and move on to the next question. When you've answered five questions, take a few seconds to transfer those answers to your answer sheet, making sure to mark the answer in the appropriate bubble for that question.

Before the proctor calls out the end of time on a section, check your answer sheet for the following issues:

- ✔ Your answer sheet shouldn't contain any stray marks; erase any that you see.
- ✔ Only one bubble should be filled in per question, and it should be filled in completely.
- ✔ The answers should correspond with the proper questions.

If you discover that you've been marking answers in the wrong places, go up and talk to the test administrator about it at the end of the test. Sometimes he or she will give you time to correct the problem. The best way to avoid this unfortunate occurrence, though, is to mark your answers carefully from the start.

Take advantage of extra time

You may finish a section or two before the time is up. Instead of using this time to investigate the ceiling pattern or practice balancing pencils on the side of your desk, use it to return to questions in that section that you aren't sure you answered correctly on the first try.

You can't use extra time at the end of a section to return to questions in an earlier section. Stick to the section you're in, or else you could be asked to leave the testing site and may have your test score canceled.

Following is a simple system you can use to help you organize your test booklet so you know which questions are most worthy of reexamination if you have some extra time at the end of a section:

1. **Read the question quickly but thoroughly.**

2. **Examine each answer choice (again, quickly but thoroughly).**

3. **Use your pencil to cross out answer choices that are obviously incorrect.**

   See the next section for great tips on eliminating incorrect answer choices.

4. **If you can eliminate three answer choices (and, therefore, know the correct answer), transfer that choice to your answer sheet.**

   Mark a big X next to the question in your test booklet and go on to the next one.

5. **If you can eliminate at least two of four answer choices, choose one of the remaining answer choices and fill in its bubble on the answer sheet.**

   Put a big 2 next to this question in your test booklet and move along.

6. **If you can eliminate only one of the four answer choices, choose one of the remaining answer choices and fill in its bubble on the answer sheet.**

   Write a large 3 next to the question and keep going.

7. **If you can't cross out any of the four answer choices, choose one of the answer choices and fill in its bubble on the answer sheet.**

   Write a large 4 by the question and go on to the next one.

8. **If you finish before the proctor calls time, first look at the questions with 2s by them, then those with 3s, and, only as a last resort and if you have lots of time, the 4s.**

9. **Change the answer you previously marked if you're pretty sure another answer is better.**

Try out this technique on the practice tests in Part IV. We bet you'll be glad you did!

Eliminate incorrect answer choices

Drawing a big fat line through the wrong answers in your test booklet is perhaps the biggest favor you can do for yourself when you want to achieve a stellar exam score. The next sections explain the value of tossing wrong answer choices aside and give you a strategy for figuring out when an answer is incorrect.

Getting the lead out

Concerned that crossing out wrong answers actually wastes what little time you have? Bah! You can push your pencil through a line of text in less than a second. And if you're worried about your pencil supply, take a bunch of them with you to the test. Here's why using your #2 pencil to cross out wrong answers is a good idea:

- ✔ You don't waste time rereading an incorrect answer choice.

- ✔ Crossing out answers gives you a psychological boost because when you look at the question, you see one or two possible answers rather than four.

Why doubling back is beneficial

Studies have shown that test-takers who reconsider their answers to previously answered questions and decide to change them often improve their scores. Two of the main reasons for this are that

- ✔ Your brain may be working on the question subconsciously while you're answering subsequent questions.

- ✔ Sometimes information you receive in later questions helps you answer questions you had trouble answering earlier.

If crossing out answer choices doesn't come naturally to you, practice at home. Use the practice tests in Part IV to not only practice your approach to the question types but also to train yourself to mark up your question booklet.

Knowing what to cross out

Some answers are obviously incorrect, but others aren't. By applying these techniques, you can more easily recognize incorrect answers and cross 'em out:

✓ **Use common sense.** Answer choices that don't make sense can't possibly be right; eliminate them. For instance, if the HSPT asks you how many marbles Derek has if he began with 50 and lost 20 of them to Jennifer, you can immediately eliminate an answer choice of 50 because Derek wouldn't end up with the same number of marbles he started with.

✓ **Rely on what you know.** Use simple stuff you know to narrow your choices. For example, if a math question asks for an absolute value, you know you can eliminate any negative answer choices because absolute values are positive. If you're looking for the answer to a reading comprehension question that asks for a passage's main point, you know you can eliminate answers that contain information that isn't discussed in the passage.

✓ **Avoid choices with debatable words.** Weed out answer choices by crossing out ones that contain *debatable words,* which are words that leave no room for exception. Some examples of debatable words are *all, always, only, completely, never, must, every,* and *none.* Unless a reading comprehension passage or question gives you a really good reason to choose an answer with such words, eliminate it.

Don't avoid choices with debatable words without thinking, though. If a question asks you to choose an answer that is *not* true, a choice that contains a debatable word may be your clue to the correct answer.

✓ **Pick the more specific choice.** When you've narrowed your choices down to two and can't decide between them, the one that's more specific is *usually* the best answer. (*Note:* The opposite is true when you're picking among three or more options. In this case, going with an answer just because it's the most specific answer isn't a good strategy.)

Manage your time wisely

Each of the Catholic high school entrance exams has roughly 200 to 300 questions for you to answer. On average, depending on the question type, you have about 30 to 60 seconds to answer each question. Now, before you panic, go grab a watch with a second hand. Take a deep breath and hold it for 30 seconds. Unless you're an underwater distance swimmer or a tuba player, you probably have a tough time holding your breath that long. A half a minute seems like forever now, huh?

Keep track of your timing while taking your test, but don't continually waste precious seconds glancing at the clock. Instead, check your progress as you go. In a section that has 60 questions, check your time every 20 questions or so. Depending on the section, you should be about 20 minutes into the exam when you hit Question 20. At Question 40, you should be about 40 minutes into the test.

If at any time you find yourself to be way off pace, say by five or more questions in either direction, you need to make adjustments.

✓ If you're behind, you're probably spending too much time on hard questions. Recall that an easy question and a hard one are both worth one point. Don't spend so much time on hard questions that you don't have time to answer the easy ones.

✓ If you're ahead, you may be moving through questions too quickly at the risk of reading carelessly. Slow down a little and read each question thoroughly.

You're much less likely to find yourself in either of these situations if you practice time management when you take the practice tests in Part IV.

Calm your nerves

Repeat this to yourself: I *will* be prepared for whatever the Catholic high school entrance exam dishes out, and I *will* score well. Sure, you may feel nervous on test day, but that feeling is normal. Heck, it's even a little beneficial. The extra shot of adrenaline keeps you alert. However, too much anxiety isn't good for you *or* your test performance. One important way to make sure you're relaxed and ready before the test begins is to get to the testing site a little early so you have time to get settled and comfortable.

To avoid becoming paralyzed by a frustrating question during the test, we suggest you develop and practice a relaxation plan. At the first sign of panic, take a quick time out. You'll either calm down enough to handle the question, or you'll get enough perspective to realize that it's just one little test question and not worth your anguish. Mark your best guess and move on. If you have time, you can revisit the question later. The sections that follow give you some additional practical ways you can combat anxiety.

Practice a quick relaxation routine in the days before you take the exam so that when you feel panicky on test day you know just what to do to calm your nerves.

Inhale deeply

Stressing out causes you to tighten up and take quick breaths, which doesn't do much for your oxygen intake. Restore the steady flow of oxygen to your brain by inhaling deeply. Feel the air go all the way down to your toes. Hold it and then let it all out slowly. Repeat this process again several times.

Stretch a little

Anxiety causes your muscles to get all tied up in knots. Combat its evil effects by focusing on reducing your muscle tension while breathing deeply. If you feel stress in your neck and shoulders, also do a few stretches in these areas to get the blood flowing.

The following quick stretches are quite soothing and should take you ten seconds tops:

- ✔ Shrug your shoulders toward your ears; hold this position for a few seconds and then release.
- ✔ Roll your head slowly in a circle.
- ✔ With your hands together, stretch your arms straight over your head as high as you can. Relax and then repeat.
- ✔ Stretch your legs out in front of you and move your ankles up and down (but don't kick the person in front of you!).
- ✔ Shake your hands vigorously as if you just washed your hands in a public restroom that's out of paper towels.
- ✔ Open your mouth wide as if to say "Ahhh." (But don't actually say it out loud.)

Think positive thoughts

Your Catholic high school entrance exam isn't the end-all, be-all of your life. Cut yourself some slack during test day. You probably won't feel comfortable about every question, so don't beat yourself up when you feel confused. If you've tried other relaxation efforts and you still feel frustrated about a particular question, fill in your best guess and mark the question in your test booklet in case you have time to review it at the end, but don't think about it until then. Put your full effort into answering the remaining questions. Focus on the positive, congratulate yourself for the answers you feel confident about, and force yourself to leave the others behind.

Take a little vacation

Create a place in your imagination that makes you feel calm and comfortable. Maybe you like the beach. Or perhaps a ski slope. Wherever your relaxation zone, sit back in your chair, close your eyes, and visit your happy place for a few seconds when you're really tense about a particular question. Just make sure you come back to reality!

Catholic saints to call on for help

Reviewing math concepts, vocabulary, and usage rules, as well as practicing with sample test questions, prepares you amply for taking a Catholic high school entrance exam, but enlisting the help of those saints who have a special interest in your situation certainly can't hurt. Following is a list of several Catholic saints to appeal to as you prepare for and take your exam:

✔ **St. Thomas Aquinas:** A great teacher in the medieval Catholic Church, St. Thomas Aquinas saw reason as a divine gift, and the ability to reason gets you through all question types, especially those nasty verbal reasoning ones. As the patron saint of students and Catholic schools, St. Thomas Aquinas may provide guidance throughout the process of deciding which Catholic high school to attend.

✔ **St. Ambrose:** If you have difficulty nailing down a concept, request assistance from the patron saint of learning, St. Ambrose, who was dedicated to gaining knowledge from many sources.

✔ **St. Catherine of Alexandria:** A woman with incredible wisdom and debating skills, St. Catherine of Alexandria is the patron saint of students.

✔ **St. Francis de Sales:** For assistance with written composition questions, call on St. Frances de Sales, who was a prolific writer and just so happens to be the patron saint of writers.

✔ **St. Teresa of Avila:** If all of your studying and test-taking result in justifiable pain, seek relief from St. Teresa of Avila, the patron saint of headaches.

Part II
Vanquishing the Verbal Questions

The 5th Wave   By Rich Tennant

"I hate the synonyms part of this test.
I always get stumped, stymied,
and puzzled."

In this part . . .

Vocabulary, synonyms and antonyms, analogies, punctuation, capitalization, usage, reading comprehension, written composition, and verbal reasoning. You face a combination of most (or all!) of these question types on your upcoming Catholic high school entrance exam. Never fear, though. In this part, we show you how to excel on all of these question types.

Chapter 3 helps you broaden your vocabulary. Chapter 4 offers insight into analogies. Chapter 5 prepares you for reading comprehension questions that rely solely on what you read in the related passage and written composition questions that test your knowledge of how sentences should be structured. Chapter 6 helps you brush up on your spelling and mechanics, and Chapter 7 serves as your refresher of basic grammar rules. Chapter 8 introduces you to the kinds of verbal reasoning questions that appear on the HSPT and COOP. Last, but certainly not least, Chapter 9 gives you the opportunity to put all of this knowledge together to solve a variety of verbal practice questions.

Chapter 3

Unlocking the Mysteries of Vocabulary, Synonyms, and Antonyms

- -

In This Chapter

▶ Pumping up your mental word bank

▶ Acing synonym questions

▶ Outsmarting antonym questions

- -

*W*hen you sit down to take your entrance exam, you'll suddenly realize why all the grown-ups in your life keep nagging you to work on your vocabulary. Words that you never knew existed are bound to show up on the test in one way or another. All three Catholic high school entrance exams give you an opportunity to show off your vocabulary. They may ask you to find an answer that means the same thing as a particular word (a *synonym*), or they may want you to come up with a word that has the opposite meaning (an *antonym*).

Regardless of whether you're looking for a synonym or an antonym, your level of success depends on how well you know the meaning of the word you have to duplicate or the words in the answer choices. But you knew that already! Sometimes a word's meaning is obvious. Other times you may wonder whether the word is even English. You probably don't need a bunch of help answering vocabulary questions about the words you know, so this chapter concentrates on how to answer questions about vocabulary that's not so familiar.

 The HSPT and TACHS test your vocabulary directly with questions that come right out and ask you to choose a synonym or antonym. The COOP sneaks a little vocabulary into its Verbal Reasoning section, which we cover in more detail in Chapter 8.

Improving Your Vocabulary

The more you expose yourself to new words, the better you'll do on vocabulary questions (and the more intelligent you'll sound). Don't worry. We're not suggesting you should memorize the dictionary. That's simply not practical. Besides, you have better things to do with your time. Instead, we show you how to play around with mysterious words in order to glean as much information about them as you can. (In case you're wondering, *glean* means "to pick up or gather.")

 Whenever you encounter an unfamiliar word, look it up. If you're social networking on your computer (and we bet you are) and you come across a word you don't know, use an online dictionary to discover what it means. Doing so takes about a minute. Keep a list of words and their definitions, and you'll be surprised at how many stick with you.

Noticing parts of speech

Sometimes the same word has a different meaning depending on whether it's used as a noun, adjective, or verb (to review the properties of different parts of speech, head to Chapter 7). For example, the noun form of the word *bark* can refer to the tough exterior of a woody stem or root (for example, "the bark on a tree"). But this word's verb form may refer to making the sound a dog speaks (for example, "to bark at the mail carrier"). Before you choose an answer to a vocabulary question, make sure you know how the word is being used. You can figure this out in one of two ways, depending on the kind of question you're answering:

- ✔ **Put the word in context.** In other words, note how the term is used in the question. Most of the vocabulary questions put the word you must define in a phrase with other words so you can more easily tell which part of speech the question wants.

- ✔ **Look at the answer choices.** Some of the vocabulary questions on the HSPT don't put the word in context. To figure out which part of speech the HSPT is dealing with for these questions, look at the answer choices. If all the answer choices are nouns, the test is looking for the noun form of the word.

Breaking up unfamiliar words

Vocabulary questions can be difficult if the words are unfamiliar to you, but sometimes you can get an idea of what a word means by breaking it up. Remember when you studied prefixes, suffixes, and roots in English class? If not, here's a refresher: A *prefix* introduces the word, the *root* conveys the main gist of the word, and the *suffix* rounds it out. For example, undoable is a word with a prefix (un-), a root (do), and a suffix (-able). *Un-* means "not," *do* means "perform," and *-able* means "having the necessary skill." Put all that together and you realize that **undoable** means "not having the necessary skill to perform."

Not all words contain all three parts. And many words don't have any recognizable prefixes, suffixes, or roots at all. Still, getting a little cozy with some of the more common word parts may help you understand some words you've never seen or even heard of before. Table 3-1 lists some prefixes, Table 3-2 contains a sampling of common roots, and Table 3-3 supplies some suffixes. Tons more exist, but we won't torture you by listing them all.

Strongly consider studying all three tables before exam day. If you can't tackle them all, skimp on the suffixes because they supply the least amount of info about a word.

Table 3-1	Common Prefixes	
Prefix	*Meaning*	*Example*
a-, an-	Lack of, not	Amoral, amorphous
ac-	To, toward	Accost
col-	With, together	Collate, collection
counter-	Against, opposite	Counterattack
di-	Not, away from, two, double	Digress, dichotomy
ig-	Not	Ignorance, ignoble
inter-	Between	Interject
ob-	Over, against, toward	Objective, observe, object
pan-	All	Panorama
re-	Back, again	Repeat, reverse, replay

Prefix	Meaning	Example
se-	Apart, away	Secede
sub-, suc-, suf-	Under, beneath	Submerge, succumb, suffocate
sys-	With, at the same time	System
tele-	Far	Telescope

Table 3-2   **Common Roots**

Root	Meaning	Example
acr	Bitter	Acrid, acrimonious
ali	Other	Alien
bell	War	Antebellum, belligerent
cap, capt, cept	Seize, take, hold	Capture, intercept
cas, cad, cid	Fall	Accident, cascade
cede, ceed	Go, yield	Proceed
cit	Summon, impel	Citation
cur, curr, curs	Run, course	Current, recurring
duc, duct	Lead	Conductor
ev	Time, age	Eventual
fac, fact, fect	Do, make	Manufacture
fer	Bear, carry	Conifer
fug	Flee	Fugitive, refugee
her, hes	Stick, cling	Adhere, adhesive
iso	Same, equal	Isosceles
ject	Throw	Project
lud, lus	Play	Ludicrous
miss, mit	Send	Mission
mon, monit	Warn	Monitor, admonish
orth	Straight, correct	Orthodontia
pet, peat	Seek	Repeat
phil	Love	Philanthropy
sed, sid, sess	Sit, seat	Sedentary, residence
sum, sumpt	Take	Assume
ten, tain, tent	Hold	Contain
ven, vent	Come	Convention

Table 3-3	Common Suffixes	
Suffix	*Meaning*	*Example*
-acious, -cious	Characterized by, having the quality	Conscious
-age	Sum, total	Advantage
-cy	Act, state, or position of	Urgency
-dom	State, rank, that which belongs to	Kingdom
-escent	Becoming	Convalescent
-fy	To make	Unify
-ious	Having, characterized by	Precious
-ism	Belief or practice of	Idealism
-ize	To act	Realize
-logue, -loquy	Speech or writing	Monologue
-ous	Full of, having	Delicious
-ship	Skill, state of being	Relationship, marksmanship
-tude	State or quality of	Attitude
-ward	In the direction of	Windward
-y	Full of, like, somewhat	Sleepy

Say, for instance, your exam gives you this phrase: a <u>tenacious</u> attitude. To choose a word that has a similar meaning to tenacious, you probably need to know what tenacious means. The word may sound vaguely familiar — perhaps you heard it in class or read it in a book — but you're not certain about its definition. If you remember your root and suffix lists (see Tables 3-2 and 3-3), you can analyze tenacious to see that it has a root of *ten* (which means "hold") and a suffix of *-cious* (which tells you the word describes a quality). So **tenacious** roughly means "the quality of having a hold on something." From that rough definition, you can conclude that a tenacious attitude is strong, fixed, or determined — it holds tight.

Even if you can't remember the meaning of a bunch of suffixes, roots, and prefixes, you can probably get a pretty good idea of what a word means by thinking of other words you know that contain the same prefixes, roots, or suffixes. Think of other words that have the root *ten* in them, words such as *attend, tension,* or *tentacle.* All of these words give you the feeling of strength. Knowing this little bit of information makes it easier for you to find the best synonym.

Although it's a handy trick, you should know that breaking a word into its parts isn't an exact science. It won't provide you with a precise definition of the word, and not all words can be divided into common prefixes, suffixes, and roots. But it does force you to begin thinking about words so you can have a plan of action. After all, the more confident and relaxed you are during your exam, the more access you'll have to your personal memory bank where you store words you don't even realize you know.

Scoring Points with Synonyms

Most of the vocabulary questions on the entrance exams ask you to find a word that has a similar meaning to the underlined word in a phrase. In other words, they ask you to identify the word's *synonym* from a list of choices. The HSPT also throws in some other types of synonym questions in its Verbal Skills section. The following sections walk you through the different kinds of synonym questions you may encounter.

Working out the meaning of words in context for the TACHS and HSPT

Vocabulary-in-context questions are a popular way the TACHS and HSPT try to test your knowledge of synonyms. These questions give you a word in the context of a short phrase. Your task is to

1. **Figure out the meaning of the underlined word and restate it in your own words.**

2. **Substitute the answer choices for the underlined word and eliminate answers that don't convey the same meaning.**

We walk you through these steps in the following vocabulary-in-context question.

a <u>bellicose</u> temperament

(A) moody

(B) hostile

(C) loud

(D) generous

The underlined word is bellicose, a word you probably don't use too much in everyday conversation. You know it's an adjective because it's describing a type of temperament (and because all the answer choices are adjectives). Try figuring out what it means by analyzing its parts (if you don't know how to do that, see the earlier "Breaking up unfamiliar words" section). The root of the word is *bell,* which, according to the root list in Table 3-2, means "war." The suffix *-ose* means "full of," so you can think of *bellicose* as roughly meaning "full of war." With this information at your disposal, glance at the answer choices. Choice (D), generous, doesn't relate to being warlike, so you can eliminate it. Moodiness doesn't relate to war either, so cross out Choice (A). Choice (B), hostile, and Choice (C), loud, remain. War is definitely hostile, and it can be loud. Which choice fits best? It makes less sense to describe a temperament as loud, and hostile more clearly relates to war than loud does. The best answer is Choice (B).

Handling other types of synonym questions on the HSPT

The HSPT features two special kinds of synonym questions, both of which appear in its Verbal Skills section. One comes right out and asks you what a word means; the other asks you to find which of the four answer choices doesn't belong with the others.

"Most nearly means" questions

When the HSPT asks you what a word most nearly means, think of the word's definition. Then look at the answer choices to see which one comes closest to the meaning you've thought of. Eliminate any obviously incorrect answers, such as opposites or words that are way off the mark. *Remember:* You're looking for the *best* answer of the four choices, not the *perfect* one. Try your hand at this question.

Oppressive most nearly means

(A) sad

(B) burdensome

(C) light

(D) controversial

You may not know exactly what oppressive means, but you do know that it has the word *press* in it. What image comes to mind with the word press? Push down. Heavy. Hmm. You can probably eliminate Choice (C). As an adjective, light means having little weight, so its meaning is opposite.

The HSPT may include an antonym in the list of possible answers. If one of the answer options has a different meaning than the others, it just may be the opposite of the word you have to define. Watch for this word because it may give you a clue as to the question word's meaning. (Be careful with this strategy, though, because an obvious opposite can't always be found among the answer choices.)

In this example, light is different from the other three answer choices, so it may be the opposite of oppressive. You can therefore conclude that *oppressive* means "heavy." You may be tempted to pick Choice (A), but sad is better related to depressed. Something that's oppressive may make you sad, but sad isn't the best definition. The word that relates best to heavy or pressing is Choice (B), burdensome.

"One of these things is not like the others" questions

Remember when you used to watch *Sesame Street* and it had that game where one of the characters had to choose which object didn't fit with the others? Some of the HSPT questions are like that game. These questions ask you to choose which of the four answer choices doesn't belong with the other three. They're synonym questions because you have to eliminate the three words that mean relatively the same thing (the three synonyms) and then pick the remaining choice. Following is an example of this type of tricky HSPT problem.

Which of these words does *not* belong with the others?

(A) energetic

(B) lively

(C) leisurely

(D) active

The three words with relatively the same meaning are Choice (A), energetic; Choice (B), lively; and Choice (D), active. Cross out those choices and pick Choice (C). *Leisurely* means "relaxed and unhurried," which is the opposite of the pace suggested by the other answers.

Outwitting the Ever-Tricky Antonym

Some of the HSPT's Verbal Skills questions direct you to pick an *antonym,* a word with an opposite meaning. You approach antonyms pretty much the same way you do synonyms — which can make them tricky. When you're facing an antonym question and you've defined the question word, make sure you choose an answer that has an opposing meaning rather than the same meaning.

Here are a few ways to avoid being tricked by antonym questions:

✔ **Establish the meaning of the question word and then eliminate any answer choices that have a similar meaning.** So if the question asks for the opposite of *right,* eliminate answer choices such as *correct, unmistaken,* and so on.

✔ **After you determine what the question word means, think of a word that's its opposite and look for an answer choice that's a synonym of the antonym you're thinking of.** For example, if you're supposed to find the opposite of *good,* think of its opposite, *bad.* Then look for an answer that means bad.

✔ **Check every answer choice, even if you think you know the right answer.** Another answer choice may be a better opposite than the one you first picked.

The best way to show you how to approach antonym questions is by giving you an example.

Avoid is the *opposite* of

(A) evade

(B) devoid

(C) confront

(D) solidify

You probably know what *avoid* means, but we're going to remind you anyway. It means "to stay away from something." Before you check the answer choices, come up with an antonym for avoid, something like *go toward* or *approach.* Now look for an answer that means the same thing as going toward. The best synonym for going toward something is Choice (C), confront. You may have picked Choice (B) because it has the same root as avoid, but *devoid* means "lacking," which isn't the opposite of staying away. Choice (A), evade, is a synonym for avoid, and Choice (D) isn't really related to avoiding something. It's neither a synonym nor an antonym of avoid.

Chapter 4

Analyzing Analogy Questions

. . . .

In This Chapter

▶ Contrasting COOP picture analogies with HSPT word analogies

▶ Seeing how to solve any analogy question

▶ Looking at the six types of relationships you may encounter

. . . .

COOP and HSPT analogy questions test your ability to recognize the relationship between things and thoughts by presenting you with three words or images. The first two words or images are somehow related. Your job is to find the word or image that demonstrates the same relationship when paired with the third word or image. To accomplish this task, you must first figure out the nature of the relationship between the first set of words/images. We show you how to do just that in this chapter.

Comparing COOP and HSPT Analogy Questions

Two of the entrance exams, the COOP and the HSPT, contain analogies, but they present them quite differently. The HSPT uses words, and the COOP uses pictures. Even though they look different, the analogy questions in both tests require the same approach. They set you up with a *primary relationship* (the relationship between the first two words/images), give you a third word or image, and ask you to find the answer that relates to that third element in the same way as the primary relationship. The COOP has about 20 analogy questions, which is twice as many as the HSPT has. The COOP puts its analogies in a completely separate section; the HSPT includes them throughout its Verbal Skills section.

Before you can tackle analogies on either test, you need to know what they look like. Here are two examples that present the same analogy. The first example shows the way analogies appear on the HSPT, and the second gives you a preview of how they look on the COOP.

Cat is to yarn as baby is to

(A) woman

(B) crib

(C) knitting needle

(D) rattle

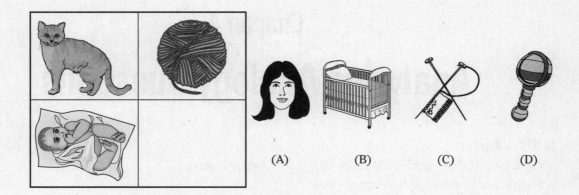

(A)   (B)   (C)   (D)

Because the COOP relies on drawings rather than words, its analogies must be pretty concrete, like the one in the example. The only tricky thing about the COOP analogies is that you first have to figure out exactly what the images are picturing. You may initially think a picture of a clock represents a clock, but when you examine the relationship, you may discover that the clock is really intended to represent time. The HSPT version of analogies presents easy-to-picture analogies, too, but it also tests more abstract concepts, such as impoverishment or ease. What does that mean for you? If you're taking the HSPT, be prepared to face slightly more complex analogies than you would if you were taking the COOP.

Working Your Way through Analogies

Analogies can be fun if you know what you're doing. To make sure you enjoy every last one of them, follow this tried-and-true approach to tackling any analogy question you may encounter. (We work through the question from the preceding section to show you how it's done.)

1. **Examine the primary relationship and determine what kind of relationship it is.**

   The *primary relationship* is the relationship between the first two words or pictures. Cats play with yarn, so the primary relationship in the sample question is that the second word/image is a toy for the first word/image.

2. **Create a sentence that links together the two words or images in the primary relationship and shows how they're related.**

   Depending on the words/images, the sentence can be pretty general: A *cat* plays with *yarn*. Or it can be more specific: The purpose of the *rib cage* is to protect the *lungs*.

3. **Apply the sentence you've created to the second relationship and choose the answer that best completes the second relationship.**

   The *second relationship* is the relationship between the third word/image and the answer choices. Plug in the answer choices to see which one fits best. The third word/image in the sample question is baby. Which of the answer choices is a toy for a baby? Well, babies sleep in cribs, and we certainly hope that babies don't play with knitting needles! Choices (B) and (C) are clearly incorrect. And although a woman may play with a baby, her primary purpose isn't to be a baby's toy. You can safely eliminate Choice (A). This means that the best answer is Choice (D), a rattle, which makes a fine toy for a baby.

If no answer seems to fit, you've made your analogy sentence too specific. Go ahead and make it more general. If, however, more than one answer works in your sentence, the sentence is too general, and you have to make it more specific.

If you can't figure out the primary relationship or you don't know what one of the words means, concentrate on the second relationship. See whether the third word/image forms any of the possible relationship types (covered later in this chapter) with any of the answer choices. Eliminate choices that don't form a logical relationship with the third word/image and make your best guess from the remaining answers. (To improve your vocabulary, study the tips in Chapter 3.)

By categorizing the primary relationship and making a sentence, you should have little trouble defeating COOP or HSPT analogies.

Recognizing the Types of Relationships Featured in Analogy Questions

Analogies are all about relationships, but how do you know what type of relationship to look for out of the hundreds of possibilities? Well, lucky for you both the COOP and the HSPT have a staple of six relationship types they commonly test for:

- ✔ Functional
- ✔ Degree
- ✔ Part-of-a-whole
- ✔ Developmental
- ✔ Characteristic
- ✔ Uncharacteristic

If you're taking the COOP, expect to see the relationships that deal primarily with nouns, (functional, part-of-a-whole, and degree) because these relationships are usually easier to illustrate than relationships relying on verbs or adjectives.

The following sections explain how to figure out which relationship type you're dealing with so you can ace every analogy question you face. Don't worry too much if you can't classify every analogy question you see into one of the six categories. The purpose for giving you these possible relationships is simply to help you do better on analogy questions. Neither test actually asks you to state the type of relationship an analogy has.

Functional relationships

A *functional relationship* describes what something (or someone) does, as well as how and where that thing or person does it. Some of the sentences you can create for a functional relationship are as follows:

- ✔ **Something is used to . . .** An example of this noun-to-verb relationship is "knife is to cut." A *knife* is used to *cut* things.

- ✔ **Something or someone uses another thing for . . .** An example of this relationship, where a noun is associated with a noun, is "lumberjack is to axe." A *lumberjack* uses an *axe* to do his or her job. In fact, the axe is an essential part of the lumberjack's job.

- ✔ **Something is used to do something to another thing . . .** This is a noun-to-noun relationship. For instance, "knife is to bread." A *knife* is used to cut *bread*.

- ✔ **Something or someone belongs or works in . . .** Here's yet another noun-to-noun relationship, like "teacher is to classroom" or "bird is to cage." A *teacher* works in a *classroom,* and a *bird* belongs in a *cage.*

Here's an example of a COOP analogy question that's looking for a functional relationship.

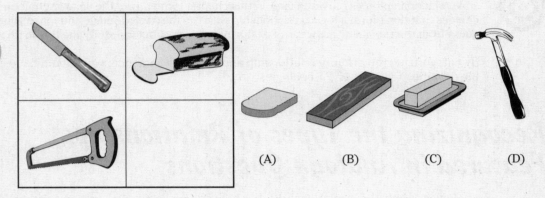

(A)   (B)   (C)   (D)

The primary relationship in this question is "knife is to bread." Ask yourself what the relationship is between a knife and bread. Well, a knife is used to cut bread. Use this sentence to figure out the second relationship. The third picture is of a saw. A saw is used to cut what? Try the possible answers. Using a saw to cut a piece of bread or a stick of butter is overkill. Eliminate Choices (A) and (C), which are there to lure you down the wrong path. But you aren't fooled! You know you're looking for an answer that completes the relationship, not one that looks similar to one of the words in the primary relationship. Choice (D) is another distraction. Saws and hammers are both tools, but that's not what the primary relationship in this question is all about. Only Choice (B), a piece of wood, shows you something that you use a saw to cut through. Therefore, it's the best answer.

Degree relationships

A *degree relationship* shows objects or concepts that are basically similar except that one's bigger, smaller, taller, shorter, older, newer, more intense, less intense, and so on than the other. The words in a degree relationship are usually adjectives or abstract nouns, like emotions or thoughts. But sometimes they can be concrete nouns, like boats or houses, that are larger or smaller than other similar concrete nouns.

The sentences you create for degree relationships can be fairly general. For instance, "*Rage* is a more intense degree of emotion than *anger*." Or they can be pretty darn specific: A pair of *shorts* is an item of clothing with two legs that are shorter than the length of the two legs in a pair of *pants*.

Following are two examples of degree analogies. The first one is more abstract and therefore in the HSPT format because you can't show abstract terms using pictures. The second one is more concrete and therefore the type of degree analogy you may find on the COOP.

Fond is to infatuated as enthusiastic is to

(A) fanatical

(B) apathetic

(C) cautious

(D) realistic

To be *fond* of something is to have a warm feeling toward it. To be *infatuated* with something is to be so fond of it as to be obsessed. Therefore, to be infatuated is to have a much more intense feeling of liking than to be fond. Apply this sentence to the third word: To be _____ is to have a more intense feeling of excitement than to be enthusiastic. Check out the choices to see which one fills in the blank the best.

Choice (A), *fanatical*, means "to be enthusiastic to the point of obsession." This answer seems pretty good. Obsessive enthusiasm is a much more intense feeling than everyday, garden-variety enthusiasm. Look over the other choices just to make sure no other word conveys overenthusiasm even better. Choice (B) expresses an emotion that's the opposite of enthusiastic, and Choices (C) and (D) have unrelated meanings. They don't come close to showing a more intense degree of enthusiasm. Choice (A) is the best answer.

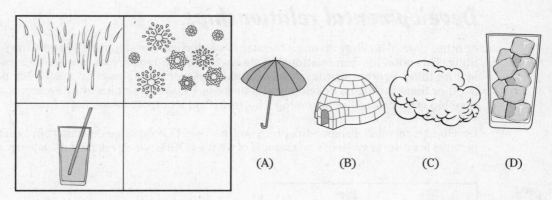

The primary relationship in this question is "rain is to snow." What's the difference between a rain shower and a snow shower? The temperature of the precipitation. Snow is colder than rain, so you can phrase your sentence this way: A rain shower isn't as cold as a snow shower. The third image is a glass of water. Which of the answers is colder than a glass of water? You don't think of an umbrella or a cloud as being hot or cold, so Choices (A) and (C) don't apply. You're down to an igloo and a glass of ice, both of which are colder than a glass of water. To choose the better answer, try modifying your sentence: A rain shower is like a snow shower, but a snow shower is colder. A glass of ice cubes is more like a glass of water than an igloo. Choice (D) is the better answer.

Part-of-a-whole relationships

Another relationship you see quite often is the *part-of-a-whole relationship*. This relationship is usually of the noun-to-noun variety and has two types:

- **One thing is an individual unit in a larger whole made up of a bunch of the same kind of unit.** An example of this type of part-of-a-whole relationship is that a *flower* is part of a *bouquet* (which is the name for a group of flowers).

- **Something is a specific type of a more general grouping.** For instance, you can say that *rice* is a type of *grain*. Rice is one type of a general classification called grain. (**Note:** You rarely see this type of part-of-a-whole relationship on the COOP because general categories [such as grain] are usually too generic to show in pictures.)

The first type of part-of-a-whole relationship is pretty easy to spot, but the second type may be a little more difficult. Here's an example of the second type for your viewing pleasure.

Baseball is to sport as biology is to

(A) microscope

(B) school

(C) plant

(D) science

If you don't examine the primary relationship first, you may be tempted to pick either Choice (A) or Choice (B) because a microscope and a plant have something to do with biology. But a glance at the primary relationship tells you that you're looking for a part-of-a-whole relationship. Baseball is one of many kinds of sports. Biology is one of many kinds of sciences. It isn't a type of school. Choice (D) is your answer.

Developmental relationships

Another type of analogy involves the stages of physical development of someone or something. This noun-to-noun relationship shows that something grows into another, more mature thing. In other words, a *developmental relationship* shows that something becomes another thing through a developmental process. Classic examples of a developmental relationship are a caterpillar becoming a butterfly and a tadpole becoming a frog.

Developmental relationships work pretty well for the COOP because depicting physical traits with pictures is rather easy. Here's an example of what a COOP-style developmental analogy looks like.

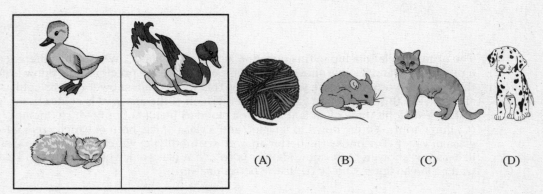

The primary relationship is that between a duckling and a duck. Specifically, the duckling is the less mature version of the duck, so your sentence may be that the duckling grows up to be a duck. The third image is a kitten. The kitten doesn't grow up to be a mouse or a dog, so Choices (B) and (D) are wrong. Kittens play with yarn, but they don't become a ball of yarn; eliminate Choice (A). If you've thought carefully about the primary relationship, then you know that the only fitting option is Choice (C), a cat. A kitten grows up to be a cat.

Characteristic relationships

If two words have a *characteristic relationship,* then one of the words is an essential feature of the other. The sentences you create for this noun-to-noun relationship show that something is a primary feature or characteristic of another thing. The relationship "liar is to dishonesty" is an example of a characteristic relationship because a fundamental characteristic of a liar is dishonesty. Following is an example of how this type of analogy appears on the HSPT.

Shortage is to paucity as surplus is to

(A) army

(B) abundance

(C) knowledge

(D) underperformance

Figuring out the primary relationship in this question is tough if you're not familiar with the meaning of paucity. So stop and consider what you do know: Paucity is paired with shortage, a *shortage* is a state of scarcity, and a *surplus* is a state of oversupply. Because Choice (A), army, and Choice (C), knowledge, have absolutely nothing to do with scarcity and oversupply, you can safely eliminate them. The remaining answers are Choice (B), abundance, and Choice (D), underperformance. You may think you need to know what paucity means in order to pick between Choices (B) and (D), but you can use what you know about analogy relationships to find the right answer.

The analogy types that might be appropriate in this situation are either degree or characteristic. A degree relationship would mean that the sentence for the primary relationship would be "Shortage is a lesser (or greater) limit of resources than paucity," which would make the sentence for the second relationship "Surplus is a lesser or greater degree of resources than _____." A characteristic relationship would mean that "Paucity is a fundamental feature of a shortage" and that "_____ is a fundamental feature of a surplus." Choice (D) doesn't work for either relationship. Underperformance is neither a lesser nor greater degree of resources; it's not a fundamental feature of a surplus either.

Indeed, *paucity* means "scarcity," so a fundamental characteristic of a shortage is paucity, and a fundamental characteristic of a surplus is abundance, Choice (B). See? You really can figure out the answer even when you don't know the definition of one of the words in the question.

Uncharacteristic relationships

An *uncharacteristic relationship* is the opposite of a characteristic relationship. It's expressed as *not* having a particular characteristic. The sentence that results from this type of analogy may be "A fundamental characteristic of something is that it is *not* another thing" or "This thing is *not* something that this other thing would do." For instance, your exam may present you with this primary relationship: exception is to rule.

Consider the relationship between exception and rule. It's uncharacteristic of an exception to go along with a rule. The second relationship will therefore be two nouns that are uncharacteristic of each other, something like "conformist is to rebellion." It's uncharacteristic of a conformist to go along with a rebellion.

Try this example of an HSPT question featuring an uncharacteristic analogy.

Sloth is to activity as bee is to

(A) importance

(B) idleness

(C) hive

(D) buzz

A *sloth* is a slow, inactive mammal, so "Activity is uncharacteristic of a sloth." Apply this sentence to the answer choices, substituting each answer for activity and bee for sloth.

✔ **Importance is uncharacteristic of a bee.** Bees aren't particularly unimportant. In fact, their distribution of pollen is pretty crucial to the environment. Choice (A) is wrong.

✔ **Idleness is uncharacteristic of a bee.** We're guessing you know the expression "busy as a bee," which hints that bees probably aren't characterized by sitting still. Choice (B) has a lot of potential.

- ✔ **Hive is uncharacteristic of a bee.** This sentence makes little sense. Bees live in hives, so a hive is more characteristic of a bee than not. Eliminate Choice (C).

- ✔ **Buzz is uncharacteristic of a bee.** Buzzing is what bees do; it also means hum, as in "the hive was a buzz of activity." Like hive, buzz is more beelike than not. Choice (B) has to be the right answer because Choice (D) sure isn't.

Chapter 5

Two out of Three "Rs": Reading and Writing Questions

. . . .

In This Chapter

▶ Examining the ins and outs of reading and writing questions on all three tests

▶ Sharing the process for answering reading comprehension questions accurately

▶ Providing pointers for success on the various written composition questions

. . . .

All three Catholic high school entrance exams want to know what you know about reading and writing. Consequently, all three contain questions that quiz you on how well you comprehend material that you read and how well you put together sentences and paragraphs. Get ready to ace any reading comprehension and written composition questions you face with the advice we provide in this chapter.

Distinguishing among the Different Reading and Writing Question Formats

The HSPT, TACHS, and COOP present reading comprehension and written composition questions similarly, but there are some distinctions that you should be aware of before you take your seat on test day.

On each test, the reading comprehension portion presents you with a passage that you're supposed to read and questions about that passage that you're supposed to answer. The questions can be about the main point of the passage, information covered in the passage, the meaning of words used in the passage, or the author's point of view.

Written composition questions on all three tests are primarily concerned with how sentences and paragraphs should be constructed. For these question types, you evaluate individual sentences and whole paragraphs to make sure they're put together clearly.

Here's how reading comprehension and written composition questions appear on each exam:

✔ **HSPT:** The Reading section of the HSPT bestows upon you 40 reading comprehension questions that it spreads out among approximately five to six passages that can be anywhere from two to six (or more!) paragraphs long. Its Language section contains ten written composition questions that may ask you to choose the best way to show transition, begin or complete a sentence, express ideas clearly, position sentences in a paragraph, or deal with paragraph topics.

✔ **TACHS:** The TACHS's Reading section presents you with four or five passages that have around four or five reading comprehension questions each for a total of approximately 20 questions. Its ten written composition questions chill out in the second part of the Language section, where you find four or five paragraphs with two to three questions each that test you on how to express sentences clearly and correctly.

✔ **COOP:** This exam combines reading comprehension and written composition questions in its 40-question Reading and Language Arts section. Expect to see about four to six fairly lengthy passages with anywhere from six to ten questions that ask you about the information in the passage. Also included are several paragraphs with two to three questions about anything from sentence structure and clear transitions to topic sentences and paragraph organization.

How Not to Get Stumped by Reading Comprehension Questions

Reading comprehension questions are designed to find out how much you understand about what you read. Just about every standardized test has a section with reading passages and questions about those reading passages. If you're like many test-takers, you may not be too fond of reading comprehension questions, but the following sections may just change your outlook. There we show you how to follow what you're reading, move swiftly through a passage, indentify the types of questions you're facing, narrow down your answer options, and handle the occasional exception question.

Comprehending what you read regardless of the subject matter

The range of topics covered in reading comprehension passages includes natural sciences (think plants and animals), social sciences (think history and politics), literature and the arts, and personal stories of everyday life. Fortunately, reading comprehension questions don't assume you've had any previous training on the subject of a passage. The answer to every question is based on information located somewhere in the related passage. All you have to do is find it.

Reading comprehension questions test your reading skills, not the multitude of details tucked away in your long-term memory. When you come across a passage on a subject that you're pretty familiar with, avoid turning to your outside knowledge. Answer the questions based only on information that's in the passage — not what's in your head.

Don't let a perplexing sentence (or paragraph) rattle you. Mark it with an exclamation point and keep reading. If you're actually asked a question about the frustrating text, then you can easily find where it's located in the passage because you've marked it. You can try to figure out the puzzling text when you're asked the question, or you can mark your best guess for the question and come back to it after you've answered the other questions in the section.

To give you an idea of what a reading comprehension passage might look like on any of the entrance exams, here's a short sample passage. This one falls under the social sciences category. We refer to this passage throughout the sections that follow.

Under the United States Constitution, persons accused of crimes have an absolute right to trial by jury. Parties to most civil lawsuits, like ones involving automobile accidents, may choose to have their cases heard by a judge and a jury or by just a judge.

At trial, the function of the jury and judge are significantly different. The judge decides questions of law, such as how a specific statute should be interpreted and applied. The jury has the duty to decide questions of fact, such as whether a person acted reasonably in driving through a yellow caution light. Therefore, at trial, the judge decides questions of law, and the jury applies the law to the facts of a particular case.

Most parties in civil suits choose to have a jury hear their cases. This is because they think that a "jury of their peers" is more likely to sympathize with a <u>party's</u> experience than a judge. Plus, a jury consists of many members, so parties have more personality types to empathize with them than if their cases were heard by just one judge with one viewpoint. Usually the only civil cases that are presented to just a judge without a jury are cases that involve complicated contract matters, like divorce cases, because a jury would have a hard time understanding the legal complexities of a contract.

Moving quickly by knowing what to focus on

Time is of the essence when you're tackling reading comprehension questions. Generally, you shouldn't spend more than a couple minutes reading a passage before you answer the questions that follow it (spending only a minute or so per question, we might add). This time crunch means you need a plan for getting through each passage in a way that allows you to answer the questions quickly *and* correctly.

When you read a passage, focus on these important aspects of it:

- ✔ The passage's main point
- ✔ The author's tone
- ✔ The way the author organizes information in the passage
- ✔ Commonly tested details

Unless you have a photographic memory, you won't be able to remember all of a passage's details long enough to answer the questions without referring back to the passage. Because you'll probably need to refer to the passage later anyway, don't spend time trying to figure out every little thing the passage talks about while you're reading it. If you come across a question that asks you about one of those little details, you can go back and reread the relevant section.

Identifying the main point

Authors usually write passages for one of two reasons: to inform or to persuade. Most of the passages on the entrance exams are informative rather than argumentative (and even the argumentative ones are pretty tame). You can probably identify an author's main point — whether he or she is trying to inform you about a topic or persuade you to think/do something — in the first few seconds of reading a passage. If the main point isn't clear in the first couple paragraphs, then head to the end of the passage because the author has likely summarized his or her point there.

So that you don't forget the author's main point shortly after figuring it out, write a word or two about it in your test booklet. Your notation gives you something to refer to when you come across the inevitable question that asks you to summarize the passage's main point.

For the sample passage (see the earlier "Comprehending what you read regardless of the subject matter" section), you could write down *diff judge/jury* to signify that the passage primarily discusses the differences in jury trials versus trials by just a judge.

Deciphering the author's tone

In addition to understanding the author's point, you need to know how the author feels about the issue. You get clues as to the author's tone or mood by noticing the kinds of words he or she uses. Informative passages are often more objective than persuasive ones, so the author's tone is usually neutral in a passage whose main point is to inform you of something. Authors of persuasive passages may use more emotion to get their points across. In these passages, you may sense that an author is critical, sarcastic, pessimistic, optimistic, or supportive.

When you figure out how the author feels about the topic, write down a short description of the tone in your test booklet, something like *objective* (like the tone of the sample passage), *enthusiastic,* or *critical.* Knowing the tone of a passage helps you choose answers that have the same type of tone.

Regardless of the author's mood, don't let your personal opinions about a passage's subject matter decide the answer choice you pick. Getting emotionally involved with the content of a passage may hurt your ability to answer questions objectively because you may subconsciously rely on your own opinions to answer the questions. Remind yourself to stay objective by asking yourself what's true "according to the passage" or "according to the author."

Outlining so you can see the organization clearly

Knowing how a passage is organized is much more important than understanding its details. Instead of trying to understand everything being covered in a passage, focus on how the author organizes the information.

As you may have learned in English class, a standard essay has an introduction with a thesis statement, two or three supporting paragraphs, and a conclusion. Many passages on the various Catholic high school entrance exams are excerpts from larger works, so they may not be in standard essay form, but they *will* contain evidence of an introduction, body, and conclusion.

As you read a passage, determine its overall point as well as the main points of each individual paragraph. You may find it helpful to create an outline of the passage as you read it. Underneath the passage's main point, jot down a word or two that describes the type of information contained in each paragraph.

So under the main theme of *diff judge/jury* that you jotted down for the sample passage in this chapter, you'd list a short summary of each of the supporting paragraphs — *what each decide* for the second paragraph and *why choose jury/judge* for the third. When you look at your outline while trying to answer a question, you can recall that the second paragraph contains information about what a jury and judge are responsible for deciding and that the third paragraph explains why a party would choose a jury to hear his or her case and what cases are appropriate for a judge only.

Although a quick read of a passage may not give you a complete understanding of all the fascinating details surrounding the author's description, thanks to your outline you know where to go in the passage when one of the questions asks you about a detail. For instance, if a question asks you about what a jury is responsible for deciding, your outline tells you to look in the second paragraph of the sample passage for that information.

Even though you don't need to read and understand every detail of a passage before you answer its questions, don't try to answer a single question without reading the passage first. You need to read the passage to get an idea of what it's about and how it's organized before you look at the questions. Any minutes you save by skipping a passage and jumping into the questions will be lost because you won't know where information is located or what the passage is about.

Noting commonly tested details

Although details shouldn't be your primary focus as you read through a passage, you should circle, underline, or otherwise mark a few common types of details that the reading comprehension questions are usually interested in. These commonly tested details include the following:

✔ Dates and other indicators of time, such as the phrase *twenty years ago*

✔ Numbers, such as the quantity of people who prefer orange soft drinks over grape ones

✔ Names of people and places

✔ Topic sentences of paragraphs if they're pretty obvious

✔ Information in a series, such as "most people prefer orange, grape, root beer, and sassafras soda"

✔ Transition words, such as *however* and *furthermore,* that reveal the author's thought process

You don't have colored pencils to clarify what type of information you're marking, so use different kinds of marks to distinguish information. For instance, circle numbers, put boxes around people's names, and surround transition words with fluffy clouds.

Answering questions by first pinning down the question type

The first step in answering a reading comprehension question correctly is to figure out what type of question you're dealing with. We've found that most reading comprehension questions fall into one of these five categories:

✔ Main-point questions

✔ Details questions

✔ Vocabulary-in-context questions

✔ Inference questions

✔ Tone questions

Each of the five question types requires a slightly different approach. Main-point, tone, and some inference questions ask you about the passage as a whole, whereas details, vocabulary-in-context, and other inference questions ask you about particular portions of a passage. When you know, for example, that a question is about specific details in a passage, you can focus your attention on the part of the passage that covers that information. The next sections break down each of these question types and explain how to answer them correctly.

Main-point questions

When you're asked to identify the primary purpose of an entire passage, you're dealing with a *main-point question.* Almost every reading comprehension passage has at least one main-point question, and many times it's the first in the set of questions for a passage.

This question type tests your ability to distinguish the main idea from its supporting evidence. You can usually find the main idea of a passage in the opening and closing paragraphs of the passage. In fact, more often than not, the main point is set forth in the first sentence of the opening paragraph.

You can easily identify main-point questions by noting the language that they use. Main-point questions are often worded in one of three ways:

- ✔ The passage deals mainly with . . .

- ✔ What is a good topic sentence for this passage?

- ✔ Which of these is a good title for this passage?

The best answer to a main-point question is general rather than specific. If an answer choice for a main-point question involves information that's covered in just one part of the passage, it probably isn't the best answer. Here are some other ways to eliminate answer choices for main-point questions:

- ✔ **Avoid answer choices that contain information that comes only from the middle paragraphs of the passage.** These paragraphs probably deal with specific points rather than the main theme.

- ✔ **Cross out any answer choices that contain information that isn't covered in the passage.** These choices are irrelevant.

- ✔ **See whether you can eliminate answer choices based on just the first words.** For example, if you're trying to find the author's main point in a natural science passage with an objective tone, you can eliminate answers that begin with more subjective words, like *argue* or *criticize*.

Here's a sample main-point question for the passage presented in the earlier "Comprehending what you read regardless of the subject matter" section.

The best title for this passage would be

(A) Applying the United States Constitution

(B) Defending a Civil Lawsuit

(C) The Different Roles of a Judge and Jury

(D) The Personality Types of Jury Members

A good title summarizes the main point of the passage, which means you can safely eliminate titles that deal with information not covered in the passage. The passage mentions the Constitution in the first sentence, but it doesn't go on to describe how one applies it to any area other than a right to a jury trial. Choice (A) is too general to be the right answer. Likewise, Choice (B) is irrelevant. The passage mentions that jury trials are often chosen for civil lawsuits, but it says nothing about how someone defends a lawsuit in general. The subject of jurors' personality types is mentioned only briefly in the last paragraph. It isn't discussed enough to be a main point of the passage, so eliminate Choice (D). The best answer is Choice (C) because the passage covers the differences between what juries and judges do at trial and shows how the differences affect whether a party would choose to have a jury trial.

Details questions

Details questions, which (no surprise here) ask you about specific details in a passage, are potentially the easiest type of reading comprehension question because everything you need to answer them is right there in the passage. The information may be about numbers, such as years, dates, and figures, or it may be about ideas, emotions, or thoughts. The key to answering details questions is knowing where the information is located in the passage so you can get to it quickly. (Here's where noting the main point of each paragraph as you read comes in handy; see the earlier "Outlining so you can see the organization clearly" section for more.)

Pinpointing the wording of details questions is tough because they're worded in different ways depending on the specific facts of the passage. However, we decided to give it a go just for you. Often (but not always!) details questions contain a reference to the passage. Here are some examples:

> ✔ The passage states that . . .
>
> ✔ Which of the following is true about . . .
>
> ✔ In the passage, the author indicates that . . .

To succeed on a details question, read the question carefully and refer to the outline of the passage that you wrote in your test booklet to remind you where information is found in the passage. And keep in mind that the right answer may paraphrase the passage instead of repeating it word for word.

A details question for the earlier sample passage might look like the following.

According to the passage, parties to civil lawsuits may choose to have their cases heard by which of these?

(A) a jury made up of judges

(B) only a jury

(C) a jury and judge or only a judge

(D) only a judge because there is no right to a jury in civil lawsuits

Eliminate obviously incorrect answers. Choice (D) contradicts the information in the second sentence that says that parties in civil lawsuits can have their cases heard by a jury. The same sentence also tells you that parties can have their cases heard by a judge, so Choice (B) is wrong too. Nowhere does the passage suggest that juries are made up of judges, so Choice (A) must be wrong. Choice (C) is the correct answer; it paraphrases the information provided in the second sentence.

Vocabulary-in-context questions

Questions that ask you for the meaning of a word contained in the passage are known as *vocabulary-in-context questions.* They're pretty easy to answer correctly because you can use the passage to figure out what the word in question means. The only potentially tricky part about these questions is that they may test you on a word that you know the meaning of but whose usage in the passage is slightly different from what you're familiar with. Make sure the answer you choose matches the meaning of the word as it's used in the passage.

Vocabulary-in-context questions are easy to spot; they're most often phrased like this:

> ✔ As it is used in the passage, the word *genuine* most nearly means . . .
>
> ✔ The word *genuine* is used in the passage to mean . . .
>
> ✔ Which of these answers best captures the meaning of *genuine?*

The key to finding the best answer for a vocabulary-in-context question is to substitute the answer choices for the word in the passage. The answer choice that replaces the vocabulary word and makes sense is the right answer.

Here's a vocabulary-in-context question you could reasonably expect to see following the earlier sample passage.

As it is used in the passage, <u>party</u> most nearly means

(A) festivity

(B) participant

(C) victim

(D) event

If you answer this question too quickly, you may be tempted to pick Choice (A) or Choice (D) because the definition of *party* that you're probably used to is *festivity* or *event,* as in a birthday party. But if you substitute either of these words for *party* in any of the places that it's used in the passage, you see that these definitions don't make sense. Saying that "most *festivities* in civil suits choose to have a jury hear their cases" would be silly. Now just Choices (B) and (C) remain. Not every person involved in a lawsuit is a victim, so Choice (B) is a better answer than Choice (C). Substitute *participant* in the sentence: Most *participants* in civil suits choose to have a jury hear their cases. It makes sense! Choice (B)'s your answer.

Inference questions

Inference questions ask you about information that a passage implies rather than states directly; they test your ability to draw conclusions that aren't directly mentioned in the passage. For instance, suppose you read a passage about hummingbirds. Information in one paragraph may state that hummingbirds fly south for the winter. Information in another paragraph may say that the Speckled Rufus is a kind of hummingbird. From this information, you can infer that the Speckled Rufus flies south for the winter.

You can spot inference questions pretty easily because they often contain the words *infer* or *imply*.

> ✔ It can be *inferred* from the passage that . . .
>
> ✔ The author *implies* that . . .
>
> ✔ The author brings up southern migration patterns to *imply* which of the following?

When facing an inference question, look for the choice that extends the information in the passage just a little bit. Answer choices that make inferences that aren't covered by what's stated in the passage are usually incorrect. Don't choose an answer that requires you to come up with information that isn't somehow covered in the passage. Also, be sure to use *only* what's provided in the passage — not what's in your head. Sometimes knowing a lot about a passage's topic can throw you off because you may be tempted to answer questions based on your own knowledge rather than what's provided in the passage. Make sure anything you infer can be justified by information in the passage.

Following is an inference question (based on the earlier sample passage, of course) for you to try your hand at.

The author of the passage implies which of the following?

(A) A jury may be able to relate to a party's situation better than a judge.

(B) A judge is more important than a jury in the U.S. system of justice.

(C) Juries are more crucial to maintaining justice than judges are.

(D) The duties of judges and juries are very similar.

Good news! You don't actually have to do a lot of inferring to answer this question. The author doesn't reveal any indication that either the judge or jury is more important in promoting justice, so you can't infer either Choice (B) or Choice (C). Choice (D) contradicts the author's statement in the first sentence of the second paragraph that the roles of judge and jury are different; toss it out. The best answer is Choice (A). The last paragraph tells you that juries are made up of different personality types, so you can infer that the author thinks the chances of someone on the jury relating to a party are better than they are for just one judge.

Tone questions

Questions that ask you to figure out the author's attitude or complete the logical flow of the author's ideas are *tone questions*. Your job is to discover the author's feeling from the way he or she presents the passage. With practice, you can discover how to distinguish between an enthusiastic author and one who's faking enthusiasm to make fun of the passage's subject.

Tone questions stand out thanks to the way they're worded. Watch for verbiage such as

- ✓ The author's attitude appears to be one of . . .
- ✓ With which of the following statements would the author most likely agree?
- ✓ The tone of the passage suggests that the author is most skeptical about which of the following?

As you read through the passage, get to know the author. Pay attention to the vocabulary she uses and the way she advances the main point. Objective authors tend to use more formal language and apply traditional essay structure. Authors who tell a story or offer a subjective opinion often rely on informal language and first-person narratives.

Here's an example of a question about the author's tone in the sample passage.

Which of the following best describes the author's tone?

(A) critical of the U.S. jury system

(B) enthusiastic about the importance of juries

(C) disappointed that more people do not choose to have a jury trial

(D) descriptive about the differences between the roles of judge and jury

Reading the passage is your chance to get a handle on the author's tone. Because you did that earlier, you already determined that the author's tone in the passage is relatively neutral. Consequently, you can forget about Choices (A), (B), and (C). *Critical, enthusiastic,* and *disappointed* are subjective terms that don't convey the author's objectivity. The only neutral option is Choice (D); the author is primarily descriptive in the passage.

Eliminating answer choices

One of the most effective ways of moving speedily through reading comprehension questions is to eliminate incorrect answer choices. That's because you're looking for the best answer choice, not necessarily the perfect answer choice. Sometimes you have to choose the best choice out of three pretty great choices; other times you must choose from four really crummy options. Because the definitive answer doesn't always jump right out at you, knowing how to eliminate obviously wrong choices is essential.

Common wrong answers to reading comprehension questions include the following:

- ✓ **Choices that contain information that isn't covered in the passage:** Even if the information in these choices is true in real life, you can't pick them because the passage isn't the source of the information. Eliminate these choices no matter how tempting they may be.
- ✓ **Choices that contradict the passage's main point, author's tone, or specific details:** After you've read the passage, you should be able to quickly eliminate most of the

choices that contradict what you know from the passage (without having to refer back to the passage).

✔ **Choices that don't answer the question:** Paying careful attention to the wording of each question can help you narrow down your answer options. For example, a question may ask about a disadvantage of something discussed in the passage. If one of the answer choices lists an advantage rather than a disadvantage, you can eliminate that choice without thinking twice.

Sometimes you need to think twice about eliminating an answer option, as in the case of choices containing *debatable words,* words that leave no room for exception. Examples of debatable words are *all, always, complete, never, every,* and *none.* An answer choice that contains a debatable word is probably wrong, but you shouldn't automatically throw it out the window. If information in the passage justifies the presence of a debatable word in an answer choice, that choice may be right. For instance, if a passage tells you that all hummingbirds travel south in the winter, a choice that has *all* in it may in fact be okay.

Dealing with exception questions

Most questions ask you to choose the one correct answer, but some questions are cleverly disguised to ask for the one answer that isn't true. We call these beauties *exception questions;* you can recognize them by the presence of a negative word (usually *except* or *not*) in the question. When you see questions worded this way, you know you're looking for the one answer choice that isn't true.

Exception questions aren't that difficult if you approach them systematically. Determining which answer choice isn't touched on in the passage takes time because you may think you have to look in the passage for the choice and not find it. But there's a better way. Instead of determining whether an answer *isn't* true, just eliminate the three true answers. Doing so leaves you with the one false (and therefore correct) answer. Identifying choices that are true according to the passage is much easier than determining the one choice that isn't. Take your time, and you'll do exceptionally well on exception questions.

See how the process works by trying this exception question based on the earlier sample passage.

Each of these is true about judges and juries *except*

(A) Juries are better at making decisions in complex contract cases.

(B) Judges interpret statutes.

(C) Juries apply laws to the facts of the case.

(D) Juries decide questions about facts.

Reword the question so that it's clear what you're looking for: Which of these statements says something false about judges and juries? The second paragraph tells you it's true that judges interpret statutes and that juries deal with facts and how the law applies to the facts. Eliminate Choices (B), (C), and (D) because all of them say something true, and you're looking for the choice that states something false. The passage says that judges, not juries, are better at deciding complex contract cases. Choice (A) is false and therefore correct.

Tackling Written Composition Questions

You don't jot down one sentence of your own creation on any of the Catholic high school entrance exams, but you're still tested on how clearly you write sentences and organize ideas in paragraphs.

All three Catholic high school entrance exams feature written composition questions, but they present them in slightly different ways, as you can see from the following information:

- **HSPT:** This exam has the most thorough approach to written composition questions. You may be shown four different ways of expressing something and asked to choose the answer choice that does the best job of getting the message across. However, you may also be asked to fill in the blank in a sentence in the way that offers the best transition from one thought to another. Other HSPT written composition questions look for the group of words that best completes or starts a sentence, and still others test your ability to determine what ideas go best with particular topics.

- **TACHS:** The TACHS's written composition questions follow several paragraphs with numbered sentences. The focus of these questions is less on paragraph construction and topic sentences and more on proper word use, such as whether the tense of a verb is correct or whether a sentence is complete.

- **COOP:** Some of the COOP's written composition questions are also related to specific paragraphs containing numbered sentences. The COOP usually picks out one of the sentences and asks you to figure out which of the answer options does the best job of expressing the idea in the sentence. Other written composition questions on the COOP ask you to evaluate how a passage is organized by having you pick a good topic sentence for it or determine which sentence doesn't belong in it.

The next sections help you tackle written composition questions effectively without getting bogged down in how awful some of the answer options can be.

Clarifying sentences

Questions that ask you to choose the best or clearest way to write a sentence usually concentrate on three specific elements of good writing — sentence structure, transitions, and usage. Throw out answer choices that contain any of these problems:

- Poor sentence structure
- Inappropriate transition words
- Faulty word usage

The sections that follow give you practice spotting these errors so you can make a sentence crystal clear on a moment's notice.

Arranging sentences clearly

As a rule, simple, straightforward sentences are clearer than complex ones. So when you have to choose the clearest way to write a sentence, pick the option that states the message in the simplest way possible and eliminate choices that use passive voice. (For more on avoiding unnecessary wordiness, as well as a general review of grammar rules, head to Chapter 7.)

Following are two examples of written composition questions about recognizing clear sentence structure. The first one is in the HSPT format; the second is a COOP-style question.

Which choice expresses the idea most clearly?

(A) After doing homework, playing the guitar, reading science fiction, and running around the block are things I like to do.

(B) Things I like to do are running around the block, playing the guitar, and reading science fiction after doing homework.

(C) After I do my homework, I like to play the guitar, read science fiction, and I also enjoy running around the block.

(D) After doing homework, I like to run around the block, play the guitar, and read science fiction.

Eliminate answer choices that contain serious grammar problems (such as misplaced modifiers, unparallel structure, and passive voice). Choice (A) expresses the thought in passive voice ("playing, reading, and doing are things I like" instead of "I like playing, reading, and doing"), plus it has a modifier problem. The way it's phrased makes it sound like "playing," "reading," and "running" did the homework. Choice (B) is better, but it still has a modifier problem. Putting "after doing homework" right after "reading science fiction" makes it sound like the thing I like is reading science fiction only after doing homework, not at any time. Choice (C)'s addition of "I do" to the beginning phrase makes it clear who's doing the homework, but there's a lack of parallel structure in the last part of the sentence. All the things I like should be listed in a similar way: I like to play, read, and run. Choice (D) corrects all of these problems. The subject of the sentence is "I," so it's clear who's doing the homework mentioned in the beginning phrase, and the list of things I like to do after I do my homework maintains parallel structure. (Notice how the right answer in this case is also the shortest sentence?)

The shortest sentence isn't always the correct answer to a written composition question, but if one sentence is significantly shorter than the other answer options, that's a good indication that the sentence isn't using unnecessary words to make its point.

[1]On Sunday mornings, my father reads the paper, walks the dog, and eats breakfast. [2]He also goes to church every Sunday morning. [3]He thinks these activities are very relaxing.

What is the best way to combine Sentence 1 and Sentence 2?

(A) On Sunday mornings, my father reads the paper, walks the dog, eats breakfast, and goes to church.

(B) On Sunday mornings, my father reads the paper, walks the dog, eats breakfast, and he also goes to church.

(C) My father reads the paper, walks the dog, eats breakfast, and goes to church on Sundays during the mornings.

(D) During the morning hours of a Sunday, reading the paper, walking the dog, eating breakfast, and going to church are what my father does.

Choice (A) is the only option that doesn't contain a modification problem, lack of parallel structure, or wordiness issue. The second part of the sentence in Choice (B) doesn't apply parallel structure in the list of things my father does. The placement of the phrase "on Sundays during the mornings" in Choice (C) doesn't make it clear that that the activities other than going to church also occur on Sunday mornings. "Sunday during the mornings" also uses more words than is necessary; saying "Sunday mornings" is better and more straightforward. Choice (D) is a real mess. It uses too many words to mean "Sunday mornings," and it uses passive rather than active voice in the second part of the sentence.

Providing clear transitions

Transition words and *transition phrases* are signals that tell the reader how ideas are related. Using the wrong transition word can completely change the meaning of a sentence. Table 5-1 introduces you to common transition words/phrases and their purpose in a sentence.

Table 5-1	The Purpose of Common Transition Words & Phrases
Transition Words/Phrases	**Purpose**
Similarly, in fact, likewise, also	To show that one idea is similar to another
But, however, although, on the contrary	To reveal a dissimilarity between ideas
Therefore, for this reason, because	To show that one element results in or causes another
Finally, formally, after, first	To show the time relationship between elements in a sentence
For instance, for example	To indicate that part of a sentence is providing an illustration of another part

To answer written composition questions regarding transition words/phrases, examine the sentence to figure out how its elements are related. Here's an example from the HSPT to show you how to do just that.

Choose the word or words that best join the thoughts.

Stanley has never enjoyed watching baseball; _____ he didn't join us at the baseball league championship game.

(A) but,

(B) therefore,

(C) finally,

(D) none of these

Use what you know about the purpose of transition words to answer this question. The first part of the sentence supplies a reason for the second part of the sentence: Stanley didn't go to the championship game because he has never liked watching baseball. The answer that shows cause or reason is Choice (B), therefore. Choice (A) shows contrast, so it's not right. No time element is involved in the sentence, which makes Choice (C) incorrect. Because Choice (B) works, you know that Choice (D) is wrong.

Transitions also apply to linking ideas in paragraphs. To show how paragraphs are related, use transition words/phrases the same way you would in a sentence.

Using words correctly

Some written composition questions are there to test you on whether you know the rules of standard written English. To be prepared for all the usage rules you might be tested on, review the information in Chapter 7 on how to recognize sentence fragments, proper verb tenses, standard English expressions, subject-verb agreement, appropriate use of adverbs, and so on.

When you're ready, check out this example of a TACHS-style written composition question that concerns proper word usage.

(1)Poodles make great pets for kids with allergies. (2)Studies have shown that poodle hair is similar to the kind of hair that humans had.

In Sentence 2, which word is in the wrong tense?

(A) shown

(B) kind

(C) had

(D) is

All the verbs in both sentences are in the present tense except *had*, Choice (C). To maintain consistent verb tense, you must change *had* to the present tense *have*. Choice (A), shown, is the proper form to follow *have*. Choice (D), is, is also properly in present tense. As it's used in Sentence 2, Choice (B), kind, is a noun, and nouns don't have tenses. The answer you're looking for is Choice (C).

Organizing paragraphs

Most of the questions on the HSPT, TACHS, and COOP that ask you about organizing paragraphs concern how to stick to a topic. Here are some facts to remember about the topics of paragraphs:

- ✔ Each paragraph should have no more than one main topic.
- ✔ Usually the first sentence of a paragraph introduces the topic (and may hint at what topic was covered in the prior paragraph).
- ✔ The rest of the sentences in the paragraph give more detailed information about the topic.
  - • The sentences should be arranged in a logical order.
  - • The sentences shouldn't mention things that have nothing to do with the topic.
- ✔ The last sentence of the paragraph usually gives you a little hint about what the topic of the next paragraph will be.

Some paragraphs may arrange their information in a format that contradicts the standard paragraph organization you're taught in English class. Some logical, nonstandard ways a paragraph can be organized are chronologically, from general topics to more specific ones, and from the least important fact to the most important fact (or vice versa).

Only the HSPT and COOP have questions that deal with paragraph organization. Here's an example to show you what this type of question looks like on either exam.

Which title works best for a matter that can be discussed in one paragraph?

(A) The Effects of World War II on the European Economy

(B) The Big Cats of Africa

(C) The Reason That Poodles Make Good Pets for Kids with Allergies

(D) None of these

Because you know that a paragraph should discuss only one main idea, you can eliminate Choices (A) and (B). You could probably write a whole book about the effects of World War II on the European economy, and supplying complete information about all the big cats that live in Africa would require at least several chapters. Choice (C) suggests that it discusses just one reason why a specific dog breed, poodles, makes a good pet for specific types of kids, those with allergies. Because Choice (C) is so specific, it could be covered in one paragraph. Choice (C) is a good answer, which means Choice (D) must be wrong.

Chapter 6

Acing Spelling and Mechanics Questions

....

In This Chapter

▶ Brushing up on spelling rules so you can identify spelling errors

▶ Refreshing your memory of punctuation and capitalization rules

▶ Picking up tricks for recognizing mistakes in writing mechanics

....

Spelling is one of those things that some people are good at and others just aren't. If you're among the ace-speller crowd, you'll do great on this question type. If you're not, take comfort in knowing that spelling questions make up just a tiny part of the TACHS and HSPT (the COOP doesn't have spelling questions). You can improve your spelling proficiency by familiarizing yourself with a few rules (and their exceptions).

Of course, spelling is only one component of good writing. You also need to be able to show your proficiency at writing mechanics — punctuation and capitalization. The HSPT and TACHS have separate sections dedicated to writing mechanics questions; the COOP includes these types of questions in its Reading and Language Arts section. Consider this chapter your go-to guide for all kinds of spelling- and mechanics-related tips and tricks.

Spelling 101: 1 before E except after C and All That Other Stuff

English doesn't have hard-and-fast spelling rules like, say, Spanish does. A lot of words you just have to know. One of the best ways to improve your spelling is by reading — a lot. Another way is to pay attention to the spell-check feature on your word-processing program to see which words you commonly misspell. Keep a running list of those words and their correct spellings and study it from time to time to refresh your memory. You can also ask your English teacher for a list of problem words and review that periodically. However you choose to go about improving your spelling, we suggest you take some time to memorize the rules, tricky words, and tips we present in the following sections.

 To really get serious about improving your spelling, search for "commonly misspelled words" in your favorite Internet search engine. Read through the lists that appear on the Web sites you find and write down the words that give you trouble on 3-x-5 cards. Then use the cards as flashcards to help you memorize the correct spellings.

Following the rules

English words have very few spelling restrictions, which means you must memorize both the rules *and* the exceptions to them. Table 6-1 lists the most important spelling rules and the exceptions you may be tested on. Study this list closely because knowing which words *don't* follow the rules is just as important as knowing which ones do.

These rules and exceptions don't tell you how to spell every word in the English language, but they do give you enough information so you can spot most of the incorrectly spelled words on the TACHS and the HSPT.

Table 6-1	The Top 15 Spelling Rules & Their Exceptions	
Rules	**Examples**	**Exceptions**
To form the plural of a noun, add -*s*.	Dogs, cats, trains, thoughts	See the next three rules.
To form the plural of a noun that ends in *o*, add -*es*.	Tomatoes, heroes, potatoes	Pianos, radios, studios, zoos, kangaroos
To form the plural of a noun that ends in *y*, change the *y* to *i* and add -*es*.	Skies, tries, babies, families	None
To form the plural of some nouns that end in *f* or *fe*, change the *f* to *v* and add -*es*.	Elves, wolves, lives	Beliefs, proofs, reefs
To add -*ed* or -*ing* to a base word that ends in a consonant and is stressed on the preceding vowel, double the consonant before adding the ending.	Swimming, stopped, occurred, preferred, excellent	None
To add -*ed* or -*ing* to a base word that ends in a consonant and has either an unstressed preceding vowel or two preceding vowels, do *not* double the consonant before adding the ending.	Reading, visited, developed, shouting, canceled, traveled	None
To add -*ed* or -*ing* to a base word that ends in *c*, add -*k* before adding the ending.	Panicked, picnicking	None
To add -*ed* or -*ing* (or other suffixes that begin with a vowel) to a word that ends with a silent *e*, drop the *e* before adding the ending.	Making, saved, diving, defensive, oration	One-syllable words that end in *ye* or *oe* keep the final *e* before adding -*ing*. Examples are dyeing and hoeing.
To add -*ed* to a word that ends in *ee* or *ie*, drop the *e* before adding -*ed*.	Tied, agreed	None
To add -*s* to a verb that ends in *s*, *z*, *x*, *sh*, or *ch*, add -*e* before adding -*s*.	Passes, buzzes, coaxes, crashes, catches	None

Rules	Examples	Exceptions
To add -s to a verb that ends in y, change the y to ie before adding -s.	Marries, cries	None
To add -ed to a verb that ends in y, change the y to i before adding -ed.	Married, cried, lied, fried	If a vowel comes before the y, keep the y and add -ed. Examples are stayed and toyed.
To add -ing to a verb that ends in ie, change the ie to y before adding -ing.	Tying, dying, lying	None
Put i before e except after c unless ei is pronounced with a long a sound.	Achieve, receive, neighbor, conceited, believe, feint, reign	Either, neither, deity, feisty, foreign, forfeit, height, heir, heist, leisure, caffeine, protein, weird, science, seize, sheik, seismic, seizure
Adding a prefix to a word doesn't usually change its spelling.	Mis + spelling = misspelling Un + necessary = unnecessary	None

Honing in on some commonly confused homophones

Homophones are words that sound alike but have different meanings and may be spelled differently. The test you take may ask you to distinguish between or among homophones to determine which spelling is appropriate in a particular sentence. To help you out with this task, we list some of the commonly tested (and confused!) homophones in Table 6-2.

Table 6-2	Commonly Confused Homophones	
Homophones	**Proper Use**	**Examples**
too, two, to	*Too* means *also* or *more than enough*.	Shelly is going to the park; I want to go *too*. I ate *too* much.
	Two refers to the number 2.	We ate *two* hot dogs for lunch.
	Use *to* in all other circumstances: as a preposition, as a part of the infinite form of verbs, and so on.	We like *to* go *to* the park and eat hot dogs.
it's, its	*It's* is the contraction of *it is*.	*It's* sort of fun to study spelling rules.
	Its is the possessive form of *it*.	The company completed *its* financial reports before the deadline.
they're, their, there	*They're* is the contraction of *they are*.	*They're* coming to visit us in one week.
	Their is the possessive form of *they*.	I hope they remember to bring *their* dog.
	There is mostly used as an adverb showing location or as an indefinite pronoun.	*There* is no way to know whether or not they lived *there* in October.

(continued)

Table 6-2 *(continued)*

Homophones	Proper Use	Examples
you're, your	*You're* is the contraction of *you are*.	*You're* the best friend I've ever had.
	Your is the possessive form of *you*.	I value *your* friendship.
who's, whose	*Who's* is the contraction of *who is*.	*Who's* coming to the party tomorrow?
	Whose is the possessive form of *who*.	*Whose* purse is that?

As you can see, most of the commonly misused homophones involve confusion between a pronoun's contracted form and its possessive form. Here's an example of how the HSPT may test you on homophones.

Choose the answer than contains the spelling error. If there is no error, pick Choice (D).

(A) The man walked into the building.

(B) The dog chased it's tail.

(C) Have you seen my sister?

(D) No mistakes

Did you notice the pesky homophone in Choice (B)? ***Remember:*** *It's* is the contraction of *it is*. To figure out whether this homophone is used correctly, ask yourself this question: If I change the homophone (it's) to a pronoun plus *to be* verb (it is), does the sentence still make sense? If the answer is "yes," the contraction is proper; if the answer is "no," the possessive form is probably correct. Lengthen the contraction to see whether the sentence still makes sense: The dog chased it is tail. Whoops! You must need the possessive form instead: The dog chased its tail. Now you know that Choice (B) contains a spelling error, which makes it the correct answer.

Approaching spelling questions on the TACHS and HSPT

Both the TACHS and HSPT test your spelling ability in their Language sections. You can expect to see a series of three sentences that may or may not contain a misspelled word. The fourth answer choice gives you the option to claim that none of the sentences contains a mistake. Because the misspelled words appear in sentences, you must read carefully in order to spot them. Here's what you can do to make sure you're checking the sentences as thoroughly possible:

✔ If you spot a misspelled word immediately, go ahead and mark it on your answer sheet but still review the rest of the sentences to make sure you haven't missed something.

✔ Skim the words in the sentences to see whether any of them involve any of the rules listed in Table 6-1 or the homophones listed in Table 6-2. If you find any such words, make sure they properly follow the rules (and exceptions).

✔ Scan each of the first three answer choices to see whether any of the words seem to belong to the list of commonly misspelled words that you've compiled from your research. If you spot one from the list, double-check its spelling.

✔ If your initial skimming doesn't reveal any misspellings, carefully read through each word in each sentence to make sure you haven't glanced over a problem word.

✔ If you really can't find a thing wrong with any of the words in any of the sentences, pick Choice (D).

About two of the ten spelling questions on the TACHS and HSPT have no spelling mistakes at all, so don't hesitate to pick Choice (D) if you scanned the sentences carefully and didn't find any spelling errors.

Following is an example of what a spelling question on the TACHS or HSPT looks like.

(A) She maintained a high grade throughout the semester.

(B) Mary was happy to recieve the top score on the spelling test.

(C) You have to commend Mary on her awesome performance.

(D) No mistakes

To answer this question, first look for words that involve any of the many spelling rules. Choice (B) contains *recieve* (which concerns the *i*-before-*e*-except-after-*c* rule) and *spelling* (which has an -*ing* ending). *Spelling* adds the ending properly, but *recieve* violates its rule. The vowel combination follows a *c,* which means it should be *ei* rather than *ie. Recieved* should therefore be spelled *received.* Choice (B) is probably the answer, but check the other sentences just in case. *Commend* is sometimes misspelled with only one *m,* but Choice (C) properly spells it with two *m*'s. All the words in Choice (A) are spelled correctly. The problem word is definitely *recieved* in Choice (B).

Recalling Writing Mechanics

Writing mechanics — punctuation and capitalization — are the foundation of a well-written sentence or paragraph. Without them, even the best grammar is practically useless. After all, a paragraph can be pretty hard to decipher if the punctuation is sloppy. That's why all three Catholic high school entrance exams devote precious space to questions that test your knowledge of punctuation rules. And beCause Sentences just Look siLlY when THEY'RE capitalizEd incorrectly (case in point!), the exams also test your ability to properly capitalize words depending on the context in which they're being used.

Unless you write a lot, remembering every little punctuation and capitalization rule is tough, so we help refresh your memory of these rules in the following sections. We also share some helpful strategies for spotting writing mechanics errors in sentences.

Punctuation rules for every persuasion

You use periods, commas, semicolons, and other forms of punctuation all the time when you write. But are you using them correctly? Punctuation rules are pretty straightforward, so after you have them down, you can be sure you're practicing proper punctuation. (**Note:** Understanding the rules of punctuation is much easier when you know the rules of grammar. If your handle on grammar is a little shaky, be sure to review Chapter 7.)

The entrance exam you're facing probably isn't going to ask you directly about a punctuation rule, but it *is* going to expect you to know how to the follow the rules in order to spot punctuation errors and choose properly punctuated sentences.

Get ready to review everything from commas and semicolons to apostrophes and quotation marks in the sections that follow.

Placing periods and question marks

The two simplest types of punctuation to use properly are periods and question marks. Periods end sentences that aren't questions (like this one). Periods also follow initials, as in *J. K. Rowling,* and abbreviations, such as *etc.* But you don't use periods for initials in agency names, such as *ROTC* and *YMCA,* or for commonly used shortened forms, such as *ad* or *memo.*

Question marks end direct questions, like "When will dinner be ready?" However, you should never put a question mark at the end of indirect questions, such as "Pam asked me when dinner would be ready."

Conquering commas

The comma is perhaps the most-often-misused punctuation mark in the English language. When you're dealing with commas in sentences, always know what purpose they serve. Don't just place a comma in a sentence because you think it needs a pause.

Knowing these comma rules takes the guesswork out of placing commas:

- ✔ **Series:** In a series of three or more expressions joined by one conjunction, put a comma after each expression except the last one, as in the sentence "Rachel, Bryan, and Tyler bought sandwiches, fruit, and doughnuts for the picnic." Notice that there's no comma after *Tyler* and no comma before *doughnuts.*

  Commas should never separate a subject from its verb or a verb from its complement. (See Chapter 7 if you need to know more about the parts of a sentence.)

- ✔ **Omitted words:** Use a comma to replace words omitted from a sentence. In the second clause of the sentence "I studied with Jerry yesterday, with Pam today," the comma replaces the *and.*

- ✔ **Separation of clauses:** Put a comma before the conjunction when you're joining two independent clauses with a conjunction (flip to Chapter 7 for the definitions of independent and dependent clauses). Here's an example of what we mean: The polka-dot suit was Sammie's favorite, but she didn't wear it when she was feeling shy.

  You should also use a comma to set apart a beginning dependent clause from the rest of a sentence, as in "Because Sammie was feeling shy, she didn't wear her polka-dot suit." But don't put in a comma when the dependent clause comes after the independent clause. So the revised sentence looks like this: Sammie didn't wear her polka-dot suit because she was feeling shy.

  Run-on sentences appear when a sentence with a bunch of independent clauses is improperly punctuated. Here's an example: I had an interview that morning and I combed my hair and wore my best suit. Both "I had an interview that morning" and "I combed my hair and wore my best suit" are independent clauses. You can't stick a coordinating conjunction between them to make a sentence, but you do have three other options: put a comma before the first *and* (I had an interview that morning, and I combed my hair and wore my best suit), eliminate the first *and* and add a semicolon (I had an interview that morning; I combed my hair and wore my best suit), or create two separate sentences by putting a period after *morning* and taking out the first *and* (I had an interview that morning. I combed my hair and wore my best suit).

- ✔ **Nonessentials:** When a sentence includes information that's important but not crucial to the meaning of the sentence, that information gets set off with commas on both sides (unless the nonessential info begins or ends a sentence — then you just use one comma). Sometimes determining whether an expression is essential is difficult, but following these guidelines should help:

  - **Asides** consist of words such as *however, in my opinion,* and *for example* and are set apart from the rest of the sentence. Here's an example: In my opinion, Sammie looks smashing in her polka-dot suit.

  - **Appositives** provide additional information about a noun that isn't critical to understanding the main idea of the sentence. In the sentence "The science teacher, Ms. Paul, scheduled a meeting with her top students," *Ms. Paul* lets you know the science teacher's name. Yet without that information, the sentence still retains its meaning. When a name is part of a title, as in the sentence "Professor Paul requested a meeting," don't use commas.

  - **Titles and distinctions** that follow a name are always enclosed in commas. Case in point: Georgia White, RN, is the first speaker for career day.

- **Abbreviations** such as *etc., e.g.,* and *i.e.,* are enclosed in commas. Here's an example: Tyler pulled out the sandwiches, drinks, doughnuts, etc., from the picnic basket.

- **Dates and place names** contain what can be considered nonessential information and are therefore punctuated with commas. For example, "Mike attended school in Boulder, Colorado, from September 1, 2008, to May 23, 2009." Notice that there are commas on both sides of the state name and both sides of the year in the date.

- **Nonrestrictive clauses** are by definition nonessential (as you can see from the nearby sidebar). Because nonrestrictive clauses always provide information that doesn't affect the meaning of a sentence, commas always set them apart from the rest of a sentence. The second clause in the sentence "The meeting took place in Ms. Paul's classroom, which is just down the hall from the library" provides important information, but the meaning of the sentence wouldn't change if that information wasn't there.

Only important information that isn't essential to the sentence is included in a nonessential phrase or clause. Information that's interesting but not important shouldn't be included in the sentence at all.

Improving sentence clarity with semicolons

A semicolon looks like a period placed over a comma (;). The break made by a semicolon is more definite than that made by a comma but less final than that made by a period. Here are the times when using semicolons is appropriate:

- **To join two independent yet closely related clauses without a conjunction:** For example, the sentence "It's almost the weekend; I can finally relax" has two independent clauses that are closely related, so they appear together in the same sentence separated by a semicolon.

- **To begin a second clause with a conjunctive adverb:** Clauses that begin with conjunctive adverbs (such as *accordingly, also, besides, consequently, furthermore, hence, however, indeed, likewise, moreover, nevertheless, otherwise, similarly, so, still, therefore,* and *thus*) use a semicolon to separate them from another clause. Here's an example: I should relax this weekend; otherwise, I'll be tired all week. Note that a comma comes after the conjunctive adverb.

- **To provide clarity in compound-complex sentences:** Semicolons appear in sentences that have a numbered series or when using commas would be confusing. See what we mean in this sentence: The secretary's duties include (1) creating, sending, and filing documents; (2) making and organizing appointments; and (3) scheduling and planning meetings.

Classifying clauses

Dependent clauses can be classified as either *restrictive* or *nonrestrictive*. Distinguishing between the two can be tricky unless you know the following:

- **Restrictive clauses are vital to the meaning of a sentence.** Without them, the sentence is no longer true. For example, in the sentence "Susan never wins long-distance races that are held in the afternoon," the restrictive clause "that are held in the afternoon" provides essential information about the particular type of long-distance races Susan never wins. The point of the sentence is that she never wins *afternoon* long-distance races.

- **Nonrestrictive clauses provide clarifying information, but they don't have to be there for the sentence to**

make sense. In the sentence "Susan never wins long-distance races, which are held in the afternoon," the nonrestrictive clause "which are held in the afternoon" makes a "by the way" statement. It provides additional information about when Susan's long-distance races are held. The main point of the sentence is that she never wins a long-distance race, period.

Tip: In these examples, the restrictive clause begins with *that* and the nonrestrictive clause begins with *which*. You don't use a comma before the clause that begins with *that* because it's a restrictive clause and an integral part of the sentence. However, you should use commas to set the nonrestrictive clause apart from the rest of the sentence.

Understanding the many purposes of colons

Colons have several functions. You can use them in place of periods to separate two independent clauses (although usually semicolons fill this role). You can also use them to introduce a list of specifics, long appositives and explanations, or quotations that relate to the clause that came before.

The main rule to remember regarding colons is twofold: A colon should always follow an independent clause, and it should never separate a verb from its complement or a preposition from its object. (If all that sounds like grammar mumbo jumbo to you, definitely read through Chapter 7.)

The words that come before a colon form a complete sentence, as in "Megan will be finished with her homework when she completes three assignments: a rough outline for an essay, a worksheet of math problems, and the final draft of her chemistry report." If the words before the colon don't form a complete sentence, then you've used the colon incorrectly, like this: Megan will be finished with her homework when she completes: a rough outline for an essay, a worksheet of math problems, and the final draft of her chemistry report.

Another hint that the preceding sentence is incorrect is the fact that the colon separates the verb *completes* from its complements — the objects outline, worksheet, and draft. An example of a sentence containing a colon that improperly separates a preposition from its object is "After finishing her assignments, Megan went to: the store, the deli, and the movie theater." If you want to use a colon in this sentence, you have to keep the preposition and its object together, as in "After finishing her assignments, Megan went to these places: the store, the deli, and the movie theater."

Colons also serve a few other purposes. They separate the hour and minutes when indicating clock time (for example, 10:28 a.m.), and they separate a main title from its subtitle, as in *The Big Book of Punctuation: Everything You Ever Wanted to Know About Colons.* Last but not least, colons end the salutation of a business letter (think along the lines of "Dear Dr. Lawrence:").

Using dashes to shake up a sentence's flow

Dashes typically appear in less formal writing. In addition to introducing long appositives, they separate a beginning series from the rest of a sentence and signal abrupt breaks in the continuity of a sentence. Here's an example: A state championship, a college scholarship, and a Super Bowl ring — such were the dreams of the high school quarterback.

A dash isn't the same as a hyphen, which is a punctuation mark used to join words. Hyphens have two specific purposes (although because most of the rules regarding when you use hyphens aren't hard and fast, the exams likely won't test you on 'em):

- Joining written-out compound numbers, such as *seventy-two* and *twenty-four*

- Linking two or more words that are used as a single adjective right before a noun, such as *well-known celebrity*

Knowing when (and when not) to add apostrophes

Apostrophes have two purposes: creating contractions and forming possessives. The apostrophe takes the place of the missing letter or letters in a contraction (think *they're* [they are], *can't* [cannot], *here's* [here is], and so on). If you can show ownership of one noun by another, you show that possession by using an apostrophe. For example, a dog owned by a girl is "the girl's dog" and an opinion of a judge is "a judge's opinion." Here are some rules for forming possessives:

- **Most possessives are formed by adding *'s* to the end of a singular noun.** This statement is true even if the noun ends in s. Here are three examples: "Mrs. Roger's car," "the committee's decision," and "Charles's surgery."

  ✓ **If the possessive noun is plural and ends in *s*, only add the apostrophe.** Some examples include "the four boys' bikes" and "the Smiths' front porch."

  ✓ **Plural nouns that don't end in *s* become possessive when you add *'s*.** *Women's, children's,* and *men's* are some examples.

Of course, not all possessive forms use apostrophes. Specifically, the possessive forms of proper pronouns have no use for apostrophes whatsoever. We strongly suggest you memorize the following list of apostrophe-avoiding possessive pronouns:

  ✓ **Possessive pronouns that come before other nouns:** *My, his, her, your, its, our,* and *their*

  ✓ **Possessive pronouns that occur at the end of a clause or are used as a subject:** *Mine, his, hers, yours, its, ours,* and *theirs*

None of the possessive proper pronouns contains an apostrophe. (*It's* is a contraction of *it is,* not the possessive form of it, as in "The dog wagged its tail.") But indefinite pronouns *do* contain apostrophes, as in the sentence "Somebody's dog chewed my carpet."

Qualifying quotation marks

Quotation marks have three specific jobs that are tested on the various entrance exams. Here's a brief breakdown:

  ✓ **They indicate exact phrasing of another person's spoken or written words.** Direct quotes are separated from any introductions or embellishments by a comma, like this:

  Jeffrey shouted, "All hands on deck!"

  "But my hands will get dirty," replied Steve, "and I won't be able to stand."

  ✓ **They mark words that are used ironically or in a "so-called" sense.** If someone tells you not to count on Dave's offer of "help" because he rarely comes through, that person is using quotation marks ironically.

  ✓ **They set off certain titles of short works, such as songs, short stories, essays, short poems, chapters, and newspaper or magazine articles.** "Let It Be" (a classic song by The Beatles) and "The Raven" (a famous poem by Edgar Allan Poe) are two examples of this quotation mark function.

Whether a punctuation mark appears inside or outside a set of quotation marks depends almost entirely on what the punctuation mark is. Periods and commas always go inside a set of quotation marks (When she called him a "lazy bum," Missy didn't mean that Larry was homeless). Colons and semicolons, on the other hand, appear outside of quotation marks. Finally, if an exclamation point or question mark is part of the quoted material, it goes inside the quotation marks (Susan asked, "Where did you put your wallet?"); otherwise, it appears after the last quotation mark (Have you ever listened to "Let It Be"?).

Putting it all together with an example

The entrance exam you're facing may test several rules of punctuation in one question, like the following HSPT-type question does.

Choose the sentence that contains an error. If no sentence has an error, select Choice (D).

(A) It's not enough to want to win the race; you have to work hard, too.

(B) When you arrive at school, check in with the office before you go to class.

(C) Before he went to sleep, Sam wanted to: finish his homework, brush his teeth, and straighten up his room.

(D) No mistakes

Each of the three choices has punctuation considerations. Choice (A) includes a semicolon that separates two complete thoughts; okay, there's no problem here. It also has a word with an apostrophe. Because *it's* is a contraction of *it is,* that's also fine. Looks like Choice (A) has no punctuation errors. Choice (B) properly uses a comma to separate the beginning clause from the rest of the sentence; that one's okay too. Choice (C) contains a colon. Check the words that come before the colon: Sam wanted to. Is that a complete sentence? Nope, which means the colon is used improperly. The correct answer to this question is Choice (C). (Although the question doesn't ask you to correct the sentence, you could fix it by making a complete sentence with the words before the colon, as in "Before he went to sleep, Sam wanted to do three things: finish his homework, brush his teeth, and straighten up his room.")

Capitalization issues, large and small

Don't expect to get out of the testing room without first tackling a few verbal questions that ask you to spot capitalization errors. The first word of any sentence, as well as the first word of a quotation that's a complete sentence, is always capitalized. Capitalization rules get trickier beyond that, so make sure you know the ones regarding

- ✔ **Proper names:** Capitalize the name of a particular person (Sally), place (Canada), event (Cherry Creek Arts Festival), language (Latin), or thing (U.S. Supreme Court). Don't capitalize nouns that aren't specific. So in the sentence "Many states hold festivals throughout the year," *festivals* shouldn't be capitalized.

  If you struggle with remembering when and when not to capitalize names, repeat this to yourself a few times: If a noun is the proper name of a specific entity, it should be capitalized; if it names a generality, it should appear in lowercase. The sentence "The senators will meet with Governor Stanton next week" demonstrates both parts of this rule.

- ✔ **Family relationships:** Capitalize them when they're used like a name, as in "You know, Dad, you're the best father a guy could ask for" or "Uncle Steve is my favorite uncle."

- ✔ **Titles of people:** Capitalize titles that come before a person's name, as in Professor John Hill, Senator June Grey, or President Hammond. Generally, professional titles that follow a name or stand alone should be in lowercase. For example, "John Hill, a professor of geology, will speak tonight" and "The senator and the president will attend." Degrees and distinctions that follow a person's name are capitalized, though, as in the case of Stephanie Stephens, MD.

- ✔ **Titles of literary works, songs, articles, and so on:** Capitalize the first word and all major words in the title, such as *A Tree Grows in Brooklyn* (a novel by Betty Smith).

- ✔ **Days of the week, months of the year, and holidays:** Always capitalize 'em. Here's an example of what we mean: Next Friday, April Fool's Day, Ms. Hammond will post the schedule of classes for the Fall semester. Notice how *Fall* is capitalized in that sentence? That's because it's part of a title. If a season isn't part of a title, it should be in lowercase, as in "I'm glad we'll know the schedule before summer begins in June."

- ✔ **Directions:** Capitalize the words *east, west, north,* and *south* only when they name a section of the United States. For example, "People who live in the Northwest tend to travel south to California for their vacations."

Quite a few questions in the exams' Verbal sections include capitalization issues, so be on the lookout for the proper use of upper- and lowercase letters when you see questions like this one (which is in the HSPT format).

Choose the answer that contains the error. If there is no error, pick Choice (D).

(A) Aunt Cathy scheduled a party for my cousin, Jerry, on Friday, March 21st, a day after spring begins.

(B) Professor Roberts decided against reading *War and Peace* aloud to the English class.

(C) The group of homesteaders traveled west to the area of the United States that is now considered to be the Midwest.

(D) No mistakes

Every sentence is capitalized (and punctuated) correctly, so the answer is Choice (D). In Choice (A), *Aunt* is part of Cathy's name, so it's capitalized. The reference to *cousin* isn't part of Jerry's name, so it shouldn't be capitalized. The names of days and months are always capitalized, so *Friday* and *March* are right. In this sentence, *spring* isn't part of a title, so it should be lowercase. *Professor* is used as a title in Choice (B), so it's properly capitalized. The book title is capitalized and so is *English* because languages are capitalized. In Choice (C), *west* refers to the direction the homesteaders traveled, not a place they traveled to, so it correctly appears in lowercase. *Midwest* refers to an actual location name, so the capitalization is right there too.

Strategies for spotting errors in punctuation and capitalization

Even when you master the rules, finding errors in sentences can be difficult. Both the HSPT and the TACHS give you several sentence constructions that you must check for errors. Sometimes no errors exist, so you have to be able to recognize perfection, too. Other times the questions may include all kinds of errors to look for. Finding them all can get a little overwhelming! Curb your frustration by developing a system for handling these questions. We suggest you

- ✔ Analyze each answer choice one at a time.
- ✔ Look for error clues as you read through the choices.
  - • If the sentence contains a punctuation mark, such as a comma, semicolon, or colon, make sure it's used properly.
  - • If the commas check out, look for how possessives are formed to make sure an apostrophe isn't misplaced or missing.
  - • Confirm that quotations are properly marked and punctuated.
  - • Look at uppercase letters to check for proper capitalization. Make sure every word in a place or organization name is capitalized and that there's a good reason for every uppercase letter in the answer choices.
- ✔ Stop looking for errors after you find one. Mark the answer with the error (or "No mistakes," if that's the answer) on your answer sheet and move on to the next question.

Here's a sample question for you to try. This one is in the TACHS format, where each of the first three answer choices is one part of one sentence.

Choose the last answer if none of the first three contains an error.

(A) So I wouldn't lose my dog, spot,

(B) I added an address tag

(C) to its collar.

(D) No mistakes

The comma placement in Choice (A) is correct. *Spot* renames the dog, so you can set the name off with commas. The second comma works for separating the beginning clause from the rest of the sentence, too. But because it's a proper name, *spot* should be capitalized. The answer is Choice (A). If you picked Choice (C), you may have thought that *its* should be *it's*. But the possessive form of *it* is *its*, so that part of the sentence is fine. There's nothing wrong in Choice (B).

Chapter 7

Getting a Grip on Grammar and Usage

• •

In This Chapter

▶ Solidifying your grasp on grammar basics

▶ Sharing commonly tested usage errors so you can spot them when you need to

• •

*W*e bet you were so excited to see a chapter on grammar and usage in this book that you raced right here as soon as you could! Well, maybe not. In fact, you may be asking yourself why you have to study these questionably interesting topics in the first place. After all, don't you speak English every day? The cold hard facts are that all three entrance exams test your knowledge of standard written English, and most of us don't follow all the rules when we speak. When you enter that testing room, you need to be able to evaluate sentences and find errors (and sometimes even correct them!). You can't rely on sounding things out to catch grammar and usage errors; you must have a plan instead. Never fear. This chapter reviews the rules you need to know and points out the most commonly tested errors.

Building a Solid Foundation: Grammar Basics

After you understand the basic rules regarding the parts of speech and the elements of a sentence, you pretty much have the hang of grammar. The following sections cover what you need to know to do well on grammar and usage questions.

Reviewing the parts of speech

Most of the usage questions ask you to evaluate sentences. Every word in a sentence has a purpose, known as its part of speech. The parts of speech in the English language that are important to know for your Catholic high school entrance exam are nouns, pronouns, verbs, adjectives, adverbs, conjunctions, and prepositions.

Obtaining information from nouns

You've undoubtedly heard *nouns* defined as persons, places, or things. They provide information about what's going on in a sentence and who or what is performing or receiving the action, such as the italicized nouns in the sentence "The social studies *teacher* gave the *students* five *pages* of *homework* regarding *countries* in *Europe*."

Avoiding repetition with pronouns

Pronouns rename nouns and provide a way to avoid too much repetition of nouns in a sentence or paragraph. You should be familiar with the three types of pronouns:

✔ **Personal pronouns rename specific nouns.** They take several forms: subjective, objective, possessive, and reflexive.

- The subjective personal pronouns are *I, you, he, she, it, we, you* (plural), and *they*. No surprise here, but they serve as the subjects of sentences.

- The objective personal pronouns are *me, you, him, her, it, us, you* (plural), and *them*. They appear as objects in sentences.

- Possessive pronouns, such as *my, mine, your, yours, his, her, hers, its, our, ours, their,* and *theirs,* are used to show possession of other nouns.

- Reflexive pronouns — *myself, yourself, himself, herself, itself, ourselves, yourselves,* and *themselves* — indicate that the doer and the receiver of an action are the same.

✔ **Indefinite pronouns refer to general nouns rather than specific ones.** Some common examples are *everyone, somebody,* and *anything.*

✔ **Relative pronouns connect descriptions to nouns.** Examples include *that, which,* and *who* (the subjective form), *whom* (the objective form), and *whose* (the possessive form).

Taking action with verbs

A sentence must have a verb to be complete. There are three types of verbs:

✔ **Action verbs state what's going on in a sentence.** For example, "Sam *runs.*"

✔ **The verb *to be* (conjugated as *am, is, are, was, were, been,* and *being*) links one part of a sentence to another, sort of like an equal sign in an equation.** So the sentence "Zach is a student" really means "Zach = student."

✔ **Linking verbs, like the verb *to be,* join the parts of a sentence together but give a little more information than the verb *to be* does.** Common linking verbs are *feel, seem, appear, look, sound, taste,* and *smell.*

Verbs appear in a variety of tenses. Table 7-1 outlines the verb tenses that are tested most frequently on the Catholic high school entrance exams and gives you examples.

Table 7-1	Commonly Tested Verb Tenses	
Verb Tense	*Purpose*	*Examples*
Present	To express an action or a condition occurring right now	Steve *studies* grammar every day. The dog *is* asleep.
Past	To express an action or a condition that happened at a particular time and has been completed	Steve *studied* grammar in high school. The dog *was* asleep when I *came* in.
Future	To express an action or a condition that hasn't happened yet but will happen	Steve *will study* grammar in college, too. The dog *will be* asleep when the guests arrive.
Present perfect	To express an action or a condition that has started already and may continue or that happened at an undefined time	Steve *has studied* grammar for the exam. The dog *has been* sleeping for several hours.

Verb Tense	Purpose	Examples
Past perfect	To express an action or a condition that happened before another one did	Steve *had studied* grammar for many weeks before he took the exam.
		The dog *had been* sleeping for several hours when the cat awakened him.
Future perfect	To express an action or a condition that will happen before another one does	Steve *will have studied* grammar thoroughly by the time he takes the exam.
		The dog *will have been* sleeping for several hours before his owner awakens him for a walk.

Occasionally the COOP and the HSPT may include a test question that requires you to recognize the irregular construction of verb tenses. You usually form the past and perfect tenses by adding *-ed* to the present-tense form of a verb, but like all things in the English grammar world, exceptions do exist. For example, the past tense of *bring* isn't *bringed* or even *brang* — it's *brought*. If you need a refresher of irregular verb tenses for the rare occasions when you'll face them on your exam, type "irregular verbs" into an Internet search engine and review the lists that appear.

Filling in the details with adjectives

Adjectives describe and clarify nouns. In the sentence "The putrid odor in the lab resulted in a bunch of sick students," *putrid* defines the kind of odor, and *sick* describes the condition of the students. Without the adjectives, the sentence takes on a different and silly meaning: The odor in the lab resulted in a bunch of students.

When you check a sentence on your exam for errors, make sure the adjectives are positioned correctly so each adjective describes the word it's supposed to.

Describing verbs with adverbs

Adverbs give extra information about verbs, adjectives, and other adverbs. They include all words and groupings of words (called *adverb phrases*) that answer the questions where, when, how, how much, and why. In the sentence "The chemistry students gradually recovered from smelling the very putrid odor," *gradually* explains how the students recovered.

Many adverbs end in *ly,* but not all of them do. If you can't figure out whether a word is an adverb because it doesn't end in *ly,* ask yourself whether it addresses where, when, how, how much, or why in the sentence.

Connecting with conjunctions and prepositions

Conjunctions and *prepositions* link the main elements of a sentence.

✔ **Conjunctions join words, phrases, and clauses.** The three types of conjunctions are *coordinating, correlative,* and *subordinating.* Don't worry about memorizing these terms; just know that they exist.

- The seven coordinating conjunctions — *and, but, for, nor, or, so,* and *yet* — are the ones you probably come up with when you think of conjunctions.

- Correlative conjunctions always appear in pairs: *either/or, neither/nor, not only/ but also.*

- Subordinating conjunctions introduce dependent clauses and connect them to independent clauses. *Although, because, if, when,* and *while* are common examples of subordinating conjunctions. (For more on clauses, see the later "Figuring out phrases and clauses" section.)

✔ **Prepositions join nouns to the rest of a sentence.** We'd need several pages to list all the prepositions, but common examples are *about, above, for, over,* and *with.* Prepositions always appear in prepositional phrases, which also include a noun. Prepositional phrases usually modify nouns (as in "the students *in the band*") or verbs (as in "the football player ran *down the field*").

Piecing together the parts of a sentence

The parts of speech described earlier in this chapter work together to form sentences. Every sentence has at least a subject and a verb, but most add a little (or a lot) more information.

Identifying the subject and the predicate

Every sentence has two parts: the subject and the predicate. The *subject* is the main actor in the sentence; it's the noun that's doing the action in the sentence or whose condition the sentence describes. The *predicate* is the verb and pretty much everything else in the sentence that isn't part of the subject. Subjects and predicates can be simple, complete, or complex. Table 7-2 shows you examples of each kind.

Table 7-2	Types of Subjects & Predicates	
Type	*Sample Subject*	*Sample Predicate*
Simple (one word only)	Cats	Nap
Complete (includes more description)	Lazy cats	Nap all day
Compound (includes more than one subject or verb)	Lazy cats and sleepy dogs	Nap all day and sleep all night

Comprehending complements

Complements are parts of the predicate that add to the meaning of the sentence. You should be able to recognize the following complements in a sentence:

✔ **Predicate adjectives:** Adjectives that follow linking verbs and describe something about the subject. An example is "The dog is *brown* and looks *furry.*"

✔ **Predicate nouns and pronouns:** Nouns that follow the verb *to be* and name the subject in a new way. "The dog is a *collie*" is one example of a predicate noun. In the sentence "It was *she* who arrived late," *she* is a predicate pronoun.

✔ **Direct objects:** Nouns and pronouns that receive the action of action verbs. Examples include "Dogs eat *meat*" and "The dog licked *her* and *me.*"

✔ **Indirect objects:** Nouns and pronouns that receive the action of the verb when there's also a direct object in the sentence. For example, "The dog gave *Julia* the stick" and "The dog gave *her* the stick."

Your entrance exam won't ask you to locate complements in sentences, but if you know what they are, you'll be able to spot them and the errors that may accompany them.

Figuring out phrases and clauses

A sentence usually contains single words, phrases, or clauses that convey more information about the sentence's main message. Phrases and clauses are groups of words that work together to form a single part of speech, like an adverb or adjective. The difference between phrases and clauses is that clauses contain their own subjects and phrases don't.

There are two types of clauses: independent and dependent. Understanding the difference between the two helps you recognize sentence fragments and reference errors as well as punctuation errors (see Chapter 6 for more about punctuation).

✔ **Independent clauses express complete thoughts and can stand as sentences by themselves.** The sentence "Jeff opened the door, and the cat slipped out" contains two independent clauses.

✔ **Dependent clauses express incomplete thoughts and are therefore sentence fragments if left by themselves.** "Although the cat slipped out" is an example of a dependent clause. To convert any dependent clause into a complete sentence, you must add an independent clause, as in "Although the cat slipped out, Jeff caught him before he could run away."

Knowing the rules of grammar and usage helps you spot errors, but the entrance exam you're facing may also test you directly on recognizing parts of speech. Here's an example of how one of these questions may appear on the TACHS. (For additional grammar- and usage-related questions, flip to Chapter 9.)

What is an adverb in this sentence?

The crafty burglar in the black cape slipped away silently.

(A) crafty

(B) in

(C) burglar

(D) silently

Adverbs answer the questions where, when, how, or why. *Silently* tells you how the burglar slipped away, so the answer is Choice (D). (**Note:** *Away* is also an adverb because it answers the question of where, but it isn't one of the possible answers.) Choice (B) is a preposition, and Choice (A) is an adjective that describes the noun *burglar*. Because *burglar* is a noun, it can't be an adverb, making Choice (C) incorrect.

Spotting Mistakes: Commonly Tested Errors

The TACHS, HSPT, and COOP test a bunch of English usage rules. The next sections highlight the errors that appear pretty frequently so you're prepared to spot 'em without breaking a sweat.

Picking up on pronoun errors

All three entrance exams test you on how to use pronouns correctly. A pronoun's job is to rename a noun, so it should refer clearly to the noun it renames. A pronoun also needs to be in *agreement* with the noun it represents, meaning it must keep the same number (singular or plural) and appear in the proper form (subjective or objective).

Recognizing unclear pronoun references

If you can't tell which noun a pronoun refers to, something's wrong with the sentence. *It, that, this, these,* and *which* are some of the more common pronouns involved in this type of error, but no pronoun is immune to this issue. For example, the pronoun reference in the sentence "Bob and Tom went to the store, and he purchased a candy bar" is unclear. Because the subject of the first clause is plural, the pronoun *he* could refer to either Bob or Tom.

Finding faulty pronoun references

A pronoun must agree in number with the noun (or other pronoun) it refers to. In other words, plural nouns take plural pronouns, and singular nouns take singular pronouns. So the sentence "You can determine the ripeness of citrus by handling them and noting their color" has improper noun-pronoun agreement. *Citrus* is a singular noun, so using plural pronouns to refer to it is wrong. To correct this sentence, you'd say, "You can determine the ripeness of citrus by handling it and noting its color."

Noticing improper pronoun forms

A pronoun needs to be in the same form (objective or subjective) as the noun it's substituting for. (See the earlier "Avoiding repetition with pronouns" section for a list of pronoun forms.) That makes sense, doesn't it? The problem is that some of the rules about pronoun forms have been violated so often in general speech that errors may not seem wrong to you when you see them.

Make sure you know these pronoun rules:

- **Use the subjective form when a pronoun is the subject of a clause.** This construction is incorrect: Amy is taller than me. Why? Because *me* is the subject of an understood clause, and you can't use an objective pronoun as a subject. The correct construction is "Amy is taller than I (am)."

- **Use the subjective form of pronouns in compound subjects.** The construction "Him and me saw a movie last night" is wrong. *Him and me* is the compound subject of the sentence, so you have to use subjective forms. The correctly written version of the example sentence is "He and I saw a movie last night."

- **Use the objective form of pronouns that serve as objects.** Writing "Jessie eats lunch with Dave and I every day" is inaccurate. *I* is the object of the preposition *with,* so it has to be in the objective form, as in "Jessie eats lunch with Dave and me every day."

- **Use reflexive pronouns only when the receiver and the doer of an action are the same.** The sentence "Please return the forms to the secretary and myself" is wrong because you're not the one returning the forms; you're telling someone else to give the forms to you and your secretary. The correct version of this sentence is "Please return the forms to the secretary and me." (Note that a sentence such as "He came up with the idea all by himself" is accurate because the doer and the receiver of the action are the same person.)

- **Use *who* to refer to people, *which* to refer to animals and things, and *that* to refer to both.** You can't say, "There's the police officer which pulled me over yesterday." But you can say, "There's the police officer who pulled me over yesterday." (You can also say, "There's the police officer that pulled me over yesterday.")

Getting subjects and verbs to agree

Okay, so subjects and verbs don't actually fight, but they do sometimes disagree. To bring peace to the situation, you must pair plural subjects with plural verbs and singular subjects with singular verbs. To find errors in subject-verb agreement, locate the subject and the verb that goes with it.

When the subject isn't simple or obvious, finding it may be difficult. Just take a look at this sentence: Terry's continual quest to embellish his truck with a ton of amenities make it hard for him to stick to a budget. The subject is *quest* (a singular noun), but the interjection of "to embellish his truck with a ton of amenities" between the subject and verb may confuse you into thinking that *amenities* (a plural noun) is the subject. However, amenities can't be the subject of the sentence because it's the object of a preposition, and a noun can't be an object and a subject at the same time.

To spot subject-verb agreement errors in a complex sentence, focus on the main elements of the sentence by crossing out words and phrases that aren't essential to the point. Then you can check the subjects and verbs to make sure they agree. When you remove all the fluff from the sentence "Terry's continual quest to embellish his truck with a ton of amenities make it hard for him to stick to a budget," you get "Terry's quest make it hard." Now the problem is obvious! The singular noun *quest* requires the singular verb *makes*.

Calling out sentence fragments

Sentence fragments are incomplete sentences. They usually show up on the various entrance exams either as dependent clauses that pretend to convey complete thoughts or as a bunch of words with something that looks like a verb but doesn't act like one.

Always keep the following points about sentence fragments in mind:

- ✔ Dependent clauses that appear by themselves are sentence fragments because they don't provide complete thoughts. Case in point: "Although the stairs are steep" is far from a complete thought.

- ✔ Phrases with a verb phrase rather than a verb can appear complete if you don't read them carefully. In the sentence "The peacefulness of a morning warmed by the summer sun," *warmed* looks like a verb but doesn't act like one. The lack of a verb in this "sentence" leaves you hanging. You're not told what you're supposed to know about "the peacefulness of a morning warmed by the summer sun."

Having trouble spotting sentence fragments? Try reading the words under your breath. That way you should be able to tell whether they express a complete thought.

Dealing with verb tense issues

Verb forms must be in the proper tense for a sentence to make sense. Review the purposes for each verb tense in Table 7-1 in the earlier "Taking action with verbs" section so you can be better prepared to spot incorrect tenses. For example, you know that using future perfect tense in the sentence "Yesterday, I will have read 300 pages" is incorrect because *yesterday* is in the past, and the future perfect tense isn't used to refer to past events.

Also, the other verbs in a sentence give you clues as to what tense a particular verb should be in. All verbs in a sentence should be in the same general tense. So the sentence "I had read 300 pages in the book when my friends invite me to see a movie" must be incorrect because it mixes tenses. *Had read* is past perfect tense, so the other verb in the sentence should be changed from present tense, *invite*, to past tense, *invited*.

Whenever you see a verb in a usage question, check to make sure it agrees with its subject and that it's in the proper tense.

Identifying problems with parallelism

All phrases joined by conjunctions should be constructed in the same manner. For example, this sentence has a problem with parallelism: Ann spent the morning taking practice tests, studying word lists, and she read a chapter in a novel. Not all of the elements joined by the *and* in this sentence are constructed in the same way. The first two elements are phrases that begin with a *gerund* (or *-ing* form); the last element is a clause. Changing *read* to a gerund and dropping *she* solves the problem: Ann spent the morning taking practice tests, studying word lists, and reading a chapter in a novel.

When you see a sentence with a list of any sort, check for a lack of parallelism.

Eliminating redundancy and wordiness

Sentences that exhibit awkward, wordy, redundant, or unclear constructions can be grammatically correct but still need fixing. The good news is that the right answer often just sounds better.

> ✔ **Passive rather than active voice makes a sentence seem weak and wordy.** Passive voice beats around the bush to make a point. The passive voice in this sentence hides who's doing the action: The speech was heard by most of the students. The sentence isn't technically incorrect, but it's better said this way: Most of the students heard the speech. Notice also that the active-voice sentence uses fewer words. When given the chance, choose active voice over passive voice.

> ✔ **Repetitive language adds unnecessary words.** A sentence shouldn't use more words than it needs to. Saying "The custodian added an additional row of desks to accommodate the large class" is silly. The construction of "added an additional" is needlessly repetitive. This is better: The custodian added a row of desks to accommodate the large class.

A sentence that uses an excessive amount of words to convey its message probably has construction problems. Think of how you can tighten it up and make it active.

Sticking to standard expressions

English speakers use certain words in certain ways for no particular reason other than because that's the way it is. But sometimes even native English speakers fail to use standard expressions correctly. It's common to hear people use *further* rather than *farther* when they mean distance or *less* rather than *fewer* when they refer to a number of countable items.

The only way to know the proper construction of standard expressions is to study them, but you probably know many of them already. To help you along, Table 7-3 lists some commonly tested expressions and how to use them correctly.

Table 7-3	Proper Use of Commonly Tested Words & Expressions	
Word or Expression	*Rule*	*Correct Use*
among/between	Use *among* for comparing three or more things or persons and *between* for comparing two things or persons.	*Between* the two of us there are few problems, but *among* the four of us there is much discord.
as . . . as	When you use *as* in a comparison, use the construction of *as . . . as.*	The dog is *as* wide *as* he is tall.
different from	Use *different from* rather than *different than.*	This plan is *different from* the one we implemented last year.
either . . . or/ neither . . . nor	Use *or* with *either* and *nor* with *neither.*	*Neither* Nellie *nor* Isaac wanted to go to *either* the party *or* the concert.
less/fewer	Use *less* to refer to quantity (things that can't be counted) and *fewer* to refer to number (things that can be counted).	That office building is *less* noticeable because it has *fewer* floors.

Word or Expression	Rule	Correct Use
more/most	Use *more* to compare two things and *most* to compare more than two things.	Of the two girls, the older is *more* generous, and she is the *most* generous person in her family.
less/least	Use *less* to compare two things and *least* to compare more than two things.	He is *less* educated than his brother is, but he isn't the *least* educated of his entire family.
better/best, worse/worst	Use *better* and *worse* to compare two things; use *best* and *worst* to compare more than two things.	Of the two actors, the first is *better* known, but Jeff is the *best* known of all 20 actors in the movie.
like/as	Use *like* before nouns and pronouns; use *as* before phrases and clauses.	*Like* Ruth, Steve wanted the school's uniform policy to be just *as* it had always been.
many/much	Use *many* to refer to number and *much* to refer to quantity.	*Many* days I woke up feeling *much* anxiety, but I'm better now that I'm reading *Catholic High School Entrance Exams For Dummies.*
effect/affect	Generally, use *effect* as a noun and *affect* as a verb.	No one could know how the *effect* of the lengthened class periods would *affect* the students.
farther/further	Use *farther* to refer to distance and *further* to refer to time or quantity.	Carol walked *farther* today than she did yesterday, and she vows to *further* study the benefits of walking.
lay/lie	Use *lay* and its irregular verb tense constructions *(laid, has laid, is laying)* to mean the act of putting or placing and to refer to what hens do.	I always *lay* a plastic cloth over the table to protect it. Grandma *is laying* out the silverware on the counter to see what requires polishing. The hen *laid* a dozen eggs last week, which is more eggs than it *has laid* in any other one-week period this year.
	Use *lie* and its irregular verb tense constructions *(lay, has lain, is lying)* to mean the act of reclining or the state of resting or reclining. **Note**: To further confuse matters, the present tense of *lay* and past tense of *lie* are both *lay*.	My uncle *lies* down on the couch every afternoon for a nap. Yesterday, he *lay* there for three hours. I couldn't find my hat in the closet because it *was lying* on the floor. I think it *has lain* there for several weeks and would be *lying* there still if I hadn't seen it when I dropped my gloves.

Recognizing misplaced modifiers

The entrance exam you're facing may test how well you can spot errors in modification. *Modifier* is a fancy term for words or phrases, such as adjectives and adverbs, that give more information about other words, usually nouns. Errors occur when modifiers are too far away from the words they modify and when what they're modifying is unclear.

✔ **Modifiers should be as close to the words they modify as possible.** This sentence is incorrect because of a misplaced modifier: Sam set down the speech he wrote on the desk. It sounds like Sam wrote the speech on the desk. Writing "Sam set down his speech on the desk" is much better.

✔ **Beginning phrases must have a clear reference.** A beginning phrase in a sentence always modifies the subject of the sentence, so the sentence has to be constructed in a way that relates the phrase to the subject. Consider this sentence: Driving down the road, a deer darted in front of me, and I had to swerve to miss it. If you read that literally, you may believe the deer drove down the road because the beginning phrase "driving down the road" refers to the subject of the sentence, which is *deer*. To make it clear that the driver drove down the road and not the deer, you'd need to rewrite the sentence as follows: As I was driving down the road, a deer darted in front of me, and I had to swerve to miss it.

Beginning clauses don't have to modify the subject of the sentence because they have a subject in them, so often the best way to correct the sentence is to make the phrase a clause. (For more on clauses, see the earlier "Figuring out phrases and clauses" section.)

Because the test-makers tend to focus on modification errors involving beginning phrases, you should check for this error every time you see a sentence with a beginning phrase.

Here's a sample TACHS-style question that tests your ability to find a usage error. Chapter 9 features additional practice questions you can try.

Choose the part of the sentence that contains an error, if any.

(A) Much of the work performed by teachers,

(B) like completing paperwork and creating lesson plans,

(C) go unnoticed by their students.

(D) *(No mistakes)*

Read each part of the sentence together as a whole. Is there a problem? Isolate the main elements of the sentence:

✔ The subject is *work*.

✔ The main verb is *go*.

✔ The complement is *unnoticed*.

The essential sentence states that "work go unnoticed." Well, that doesn't sound right! You know there's an error, so cross out Choice (D). The problem is in Choice (C). To correctly construct the last part of the sentence, *go* should be changed to the singular verb *goes* to make it agree with the singular subject *work*. The rest of the sentence is fine. (You may have thought there was a parallel structure error in Choice (B), but both duties have the same *-ing* form.)

Chapter 8

Solving the Puzzle of Verbal Reasoning Questions

In This Chapter

▶ Getting to know the four kinds of verbal reasoning questions

▶ Discovering the essential elements of informal logic

▶ Figuring out how to approach logic questions on the COOP and the HSPT

If you're taking the HSPT or COOP, get ready to encounter *verbal reasoning questions,* problems that specifically test your critical reasoning skills. (That's right, TACHS-takers; you don't have any of these babies on your test, so feel free to skip this chapter!) These questions are kind of like the logic puzzles you might find in a book of brainteasers. Most of them appear on the COOP in its Verbal Reasoning—Words and Verbal Reasoning—Context sections (how appropriate). The HSPT has a few of them spread throughout its Verbal Skills section. The COOP features a few different types of verbal reasoning questions; the HSPT has but a couple. In this chapter, we give you everything you need to know to answer every last verbal reasoning question on both tests.

 There's one COOP question type that we don't cover here. Within the COOP's Verbal Reasoning—Words section, you'll see some questions where you're given three underlined words and asked to find a fourth word that has a similar meaning. These verbal reasoning questions are essentially synonym questions, so you should approach them by following the guidelines for answering synonym questions (presented in Chapter 3).

Introducing the Types of Verbal Reasoning Questions

Verbal reasoning questions on the COOP and HSPT come in four different types:

✔ What element does the question word need to make it what it is?

✔ What's the missing word in the row?

✔ Which word doesn't belong?

✔ What must be true?

 All four types of verbal reasoning questions appear on the COOP; the HSPT contains questions that are similar to the third and fourth types.

Deciding what's necessary

On the COOP, you may be shown an underlined word followed by four answer options and then asked to pick the answer that describes a "necessary part" of the word in the question. Sounds like mumbo jumbo, we know, but take a minute to hear us out.

For an answer option to be absolutely essential to the question word's definition or purpose (in other words, for it to be the "necessary part"), you must be able to answer "yes" to the following questions:

- ✔ Does the answer choice describe the real meaning of the word in the question?
- ✔ Does the answer choice tell me the overriding purpose of the word in the question?
- ✔ Does the answer choice describe an element of the word in the question that's so important that the word wouldn't exist without it?

Getting a "no" answer to one or more of these questions should help you eliminate incorrect answers for a necessary-part question. Following are a couple examples of necessary-part questions; we walk you through the thought process so you can feel confident when you face these questions on the COOP.

mystery

(A) novel

(B) detective

(C) secrecy

(D) solution

Think about the nature of a mystery. If there's a mystery, something is unknown. Eliminate choices that don't describe the essential element of not knowing. What about Choice (A)? Mystery novels exist, but a mystery doesn't have to be told in a novel to be a mystery. A mystery without a novel would still be a mystery. Toss out Choice (A). A detective, Choice (B), tries to solve a mystery, but even if no detective showed up to figure out the mystery, the mystery would still exist. A mystery doesn't require a solution. In fact, after there's a solution, a mystery is no longer a mystery. So Choice (D) actually describes something that's an *unnecessary* part of a mystery. Now you're left with Choice (C), secrecy. If a mystery didn't contain an element of secrecy, would it still be a mystery? No, the very nature of a mystery is that something is unknown, hidden, or secret. Choice (C) is the correct answer.

parka

(A) fashion

(B) comfort

(C) snow

(D) warmth

Eliminate answer choices that don't state the primary reason for wearing a parka. Sure, you can wear a parka to make a fashion statement, but a parka isn't necessarily fashionable. Choice (A) isn't right. A cozy parka may offer comfort, but comfort isn't the main reason you wear a parka. (You may want to leave Choice (B) alone until you read through the rest of the choices, though.) Snow isn't the only condition that necessitates wearing a parka; you could need a parka because it's supercold out without a trace of precipitation. Eliminate Choice (C). You wear a parka for warmth in all sorts of chilly conditions. The primary reason for a parka — its essential purpose for existing — is to provide warmth, which means Choice (D) is a better answer than Choice (B).

Filling in the blank

If you enjoyed Mad Libs as a child, as in the story game where you got to fill in the blanks to your heart's content, then you're going to love this second type of verbal reasoning question (found only on the COOP, we might add). The fill-in-the-blank question type provides you with two rows of three words. The words in the top row are related to each other, and the words in the bottom row are related in the same way. However, one of the words in the bottom row is missing. Your mission? To find the answer choice that fills in the blank by keeping the proper relationship.

Fill-in-the-blank verbal reasoning questions are really just another way that the COOP tests you on analogies. (We guess the COOP test-makers feel their pretty picture analogies just aren't enough relationship training for you.) Fortunately, the COOP doesn't give you very many of them — only about four or five. To do your best on these questions, head to Chapter 4 to review our technique for solving analogy questions.

Try this sample fill-in-the-blank question for practice.

quick   intellectual   genius
       stupid   obtuse

(A) slow

(B) acute

(C) insensitive

(D) smart

The relationship among the three words in the first row shows greater degrees of intelligence from the first word to the third. The second row has the same type of relationship as the first, which means it also moves toward a greater degree of its topic from the first word to the third one. The first word in the second row is missing, but you know the second and third words. Both have to do with a lack of intelligence. The third word is a greater degree of stupidity than the second, which tells you you're looking for a word that shows a little lesser degree of stupidity than stupid.

Eliminate Choice (D) immediately because it's the opposite of stupid. Choice (B) is also an opposite; acute is the opposite of obtuse (as we explain in Chapter 12). The process of elimination leaves you with Choices (A) and (C). Insensitivity isn't the same as stupidity, so the best answer is Choice (A). To be slow is to be unintelligent to a lesser degree than stupid.

Selecting the word that isn't like the others

Both the COOP and the HSPT contain questions that ask you to choose a word from among the answer choices that doesn't belong with the other options. These questions may fall under the verbal reasoning category, but they're essentially vocabulary questions. Three words are synonymous or analogous; one word isn't. (Read Chapter 3 for tips on how to recognize synonyms and Chapter 4 for advice on spotting analogies.)

The word that doesn't belong can be an antonym, but it doesn't have to be. As long as it doesn't relate to the other three words in some way, it doesn't belong.

The COOP and HSPT questions that ask for the word that doesn't belong look almost identical. Here's an example.

Which word does *not* belong with the others?

(A) coat

(B) shoe

(C) sock

(D) slipper

Examine the answer choices carefully to uncover a relationship. All four options are articles of clothing, which means you need to find a more specific relationship among three of them. Choices (B), (C), and (D) are all items of clothing worn on the feet, whereas Choice (A) covers the upper body. Therefore, Choice (A) doesn't belong with the others and is the correct answer. See how easy and fun this question type can be?

Determining truth for logic questions

Some verbal reasoning questions on the COOP and HSPT ask you to use informal logic. On the COOP, you evaluate a series of two or more statements and choose the answer that must be true based on the statements. The HSPT provides you with a few statements followed by a conclusion; it then asks you to determine whether the conclusion is true, false, or uncertain.

A fair number of logic questions appear on the Catholic high school entrance exams (20 on the COOP and about 10 on the HSPT, to be exact). That's why we devote the rest of this chapter to telling you how to perform your best on this question type.

Grasping the Basics of Informal Logic

You can do well on the COOP's and HSPT's logic questions without knowing anything about informal logic, but understanding a few of the basic terms and concepts makes logic questions easier to answer. For starters, you should know that a logical argument has two basic components and two main types of reasoning.

A logical argument consists of premises and a conclusion. The *premises* give the supporting evidence that you can draw a conclusion from. For example, here's an argument with two premises and a conclusion: All cheerleaders are strong. Amy is a cheerleader. Therefore, Amy is strong. The premises in the argument are that "all cheerleaders are strong" and "Amy is a cheerleader." Because these statements provide supporting evidence for the third statement, you have no logical choice but to conclude that Amy is strong.

The sections that follow introduce you to the types of reasoning you can use to solve logic questions as well as ways of spotting faulty logic.

Drawing conclusions

Every logical argument has premises and a conclusion, but not every argument reaches a conclusion in the same way. Some require deductive reasoning, and others require inductive reasoning. (You use a combination of both types of reasoning to answer COOP and HSPT logic questions.)

Moving from the general to the specific: Deductive reasoning

With *deductive reasoning,* you come up with a specific conclusion from general premises. The great thing about deductive reasoning is that if the premises are true, the conclusion must be true. We used deductive reasoning in the previous section to determine that Amy is strong. Here's another example of deductive reasoning:

- **All zebras have stripes.** This is the general premise about all zebras.
- **Butch is a zebra.** This is the more specific premise about a particular zebra.
- **Therefore, Butch has stripes.** This is the specific conclusion about a particular trait of a particular zebra.

If it's true that all zebras have stripes and that Butch is a zebra, it absolutely must be true that Butch has stripes.

In order to apply deductive reasoning properly, the more specific premise of an argument must share an element of the general premise. That's the only way the resulting conclusion can be true without the shadow of a doubt.

Going from specific to general: Inductive reasoning

Inductive reasoning develops a general conclusion from specific premises. So the conclusion of an argument that uses inductive reasoning can be false — even if all the premises are true. With inductive reasoning, the conclusion is really your best guess based on what you have to work with. That's because an inductive-reasoning argument relies on less complete information than a deductive-reasoning argument does.

Consider the following example of an inductive-reasoning argument:

- **Butch is a zebra and has stripes.** Specific premise about one zebra.
- **Sydney is a zebra and has stripes.** Specific premise about one zebra.
- **Koda is a zebra and has stripes.** Specific premise about one zebra.
- **Shadow is a zebra and has stripes.** Specific premise about one zebra.
- **Therefore, it is likely that most zebras have stripes.** General conclusion about most zebras.

Because an inductive-reasoning argument derives general conclusions from specific examples, you can't come up with a statement that absolutely must be true. In this case, you can't say that every single zebra has stripes. The best you can say, even if all the premises are true, is that the conclusion can be or is likely to be true. The truth of the conclusion is uncertain.

Recognizing faulty logic

When you evaluate conclusions for any logic question — whether it's a deductive-reasoning-based one or an inductive-reasoning-based one — watch for these flaws in logic:

- **Conclusions that assume too much:** Don't choose conclusions that make assertions about stuff that isn't clearly stated in the premises. For example, if you're told that high school girls receive better grades in science courses than high school boys, you can't automatically conclude that high school girls are smarter than high school boys. The premises don't tell you what the grade differences in other subjects may be, nor do they tell you that good grades are a proper indicator of intelligence.

> ✔ **Irrelevant conclusions:** Avoid choosing conclusions that are off topic. If the premises state that Jack creates paper airplanes, it isn't logical to conclude from this bit of information that Jack would make a good pilot. Being a good pilot has nothing to do with making paper airplanes.
>
> ✔ **Conclusions that state that what's true for some or many must be true for all:** A bunch of specific examples doesn't justify a general conclusion about the whole. So even though you know that most people leave the office at 5 p.m. and that Jack works in an office, you can't say for sure that Jack goes home at 5 p.m.
>
> ✔ **Conclusions that are based on premises that aren't linked with a common reference:** If you're told that Cosmo is south of the North Star and north of the sky station and that the rocket is north of Cosmo, you know nothing about the relationship of the rocket and the North Star. Why? Because no common element links the rocket and the North Star to clarify their relationship.

Puzzling Out Logic Questions

Thinking straight on logic problems requires some practice, especially when you take into account that the approach for solving the COOP's logic questions is a little different than the approach for solving the HSPT's logic questions.

Coping with the COOP's logic questions

Logic questions on the COOP give you the premises and ask you to find the most logical conclusion from four options in the answer choices. Follow these steps to keep focused on the task at hand:

1. **Analyze the premises to define exactly what they state without making assumptions.**

2. **Eliminate answer choices that require faulty logic.**

3. **Unless you're told otherwise, choose the conclusion that *must* be true according to the statements.**

Now we show you how to put these steps into action.

Find the statement that is true based on the information provided.

Sophie lives in Scooterville, a small town outside of the city of Livingston. Every weekend she and her mother travel to Livingston to shop for groceries.

(A) Livingston is the closest city to Scooterville.

(B) Most of the residents in Scooterville shop for groceries in Livingston.

(C) Scooterville is boring.

(D) Livingston has a store that sells groceries.

First, figure out what you know from the premises. You know that Scooterville is a small town and that Livingston is a city. Scooterville is located outside of Livingston. Sophie lives in Scooterville. She has a mother. She goes with her mother to Livingston every weekend. She buys groceries in Livingston.

Then think about what you *don't* know based on the premises. The information in the question doesn't tell you anything about the characteristics of Scooterville other than its size. Nor does it reveal any details about the activities of the other Scooterville residents. It doesn't state exactly when Sophie and her mother shop, why they shop in Livingston, or how long it takes them to travel from Scooterville to Livingston. It also says nothing about any other towns or cities.

Great. Now you can immediately eliminate answer choices that rely on any of the details you've established that you don't know. You don't know about other towns or cities, so you can't assume that there's no other city closer to Scooterville than Livingston. Cross out Choice (A). *Remember:* What's true for some isn't necessarily true for all, so just because Sophie and her mother shop in Livingston doesn't mean others do too. Toss Choice (B). Choice (C) is irrelevant. The premises don't discuss the characteristics of Scooterville, so you can't make assumptions about whether it provides stimulating activity or not. The best answer is Choice (D). Because Sophie and her mother shop for groceries in Livingston, you know that there must be some place there that sells groceries.

Handling the HSPT's logic questions

Logic questions on the HSPT consist of premises, a conclusion that you must evaluate, and three (that's right, only three) possible answers — true, false, and uncertain. If you decide that a conclusion is uncertain, then you're admitting that there's not enough information in the premises to say whether the conclusion is true or false.

The HSPT tosses its logic questions into its Verbal Skills section. All the other questions in this section have four answer options, which means you need to pay extra attention when you hit the three-answer-option logic questions. Even though the questions have only three answer options, the answer sheet may have bubbles for four. If you mistakenly mark Choice (D) for one of these questions, you're harming your score for no good reason.

Many of the HSPT's logic questions are easy enough to figure out in your head, but sometimes you may want to visualize them by drawing a helpful diagram. *Venn diagrams* use circles to show how things are related. They work best for the few questions that classify information according to groups or characteristics; these questions usually begin with the word *all.* Line diagrams work well for questions that compare and position people, places, or things.

This next question is an example of one that's easily solvable with the aid of a Venn diagram.

All prupel rocks are smooth. The rock I found is not smooth. The rock I found is prupel. If the first two statements are true, the third statement is

(A) true

(B) false

(C) uncertain

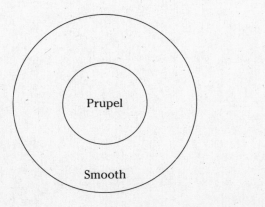

The diagram shows that you have enough information to determine whether the conclusion is true; eliminate Choice (C). Because all pruple rocks are smooth, the entire pruple circle fits in the smooth circle. The rock I found isn't smooth, which means it doesn't intersect with the smooth circle at all. If it doesn't intersect with the smooth circle, it can't intersect with the pruple circle. Consequently, the rock can't be pruple, which means the conclusion is false, Choice (B).

The HSPT uses nonsense words (like, say, prupel) in its logic questions so you won't use your own knowledge about things to answer them. Silly, we know; giggle to yourself at the test-makers' ridiculousness and move on.

Try your hand at this HSPT logic question to see how using line diagrams can be helpful.

The Brown Building is taller than the Nelson Building. The Stephens Building is shorter than the Nelson Building. The Brown Building is the tallest of the three. If the first two statements are true, the third statement is

(A) true

(B) false

(C) uncertain

As you read through the premises, create a line diagram that orders the buildings by decreasing size: Brown → Nelson → Stephens. Brown is the tallest of the three buildings, so the conclusion is true, Choice (A).

Chapter 9

Giving Your Verbal Skills a Workout with Practice Questions

In This Chapter

▶ Getting your fill of vocabulary, analogy, and language questions

▶ Giving reading comprehension and written composition questions a go

▶ Preparing for the COOP's and HSPT's verbal reasoning questions

The HSPT, COOP, and TACHS feature a wide variety of verbal question types. This chapter gives you a sampling of all of them in one place. Each section contains several practice questions and explanations of the correct answers. Answer the questions on your own before you read the explanations — that means no looking ahead! And be sure to review all the answer explanations, even for the questions you answered correctly. Something you read there may help you with a future question.

Sampling a Mix of Vocabulary Questions

The questions in this section test your vocabulary skills. We give you two HSPT/TACHS-style vocabulary-in-context questions, one HSPT most-nearly-means question, two HSPT/COOP-style doesn't-belong questions, and one HSPT antonym question. If after checking your answers you find you need a vocabulary refresher, see Chapter 3.

1. a <u>fruitless</u> gesture

   (A) peachy

   (B) futile

   (C) cheery

   (D) hopeful

When a plant bears fruit, it's productive. So, a gesture that's fruitless is unproductive or ineffective. Look for the answer that has a negative connotation. Don't be tempted by Choice (A); *peachy* is a slang term that means "wonderful or groovy." Because Choices (A), (C), and (D) have positive meanings, you can eliminate them and pick Choice (B). *Futile* means "ineffective or wasted." *Correct Answer:* Choice (B)

2. a daring <u>feat</u>

   (A) journey

   (B) memento

   (C) limb

   (D) accomplishment

Immediately cross out Choices (B) and (C) because using daring to describe a memento or limb doesn't make sense. You're down to a daring journey or a daring accomplishment. A *feat* is an act or achievement, which means Choice (D) is a better answer than Choice (A). *Correct Answer:* Choice (D)

3. Puzzle most nearly means

   (A) brainteaser

   (B) explanation

   (C) jigsaw

   (D) sport

Both a puzzle and a brainteaser, Choice (A), require you to figure out the answer to a mystery. Choice (B) is the opposite of puzzle, Choice (C) is a tool you use to create some types of puzzles, and Choice (D) is unrelated. *Correct Answer:* Choice (A)

4. Which word does *not* belong with the others?

   (A) glove

   (B) shirt

   (C) hat

   (D) ring

Choices (A), (B), and (C) are articles of clothing. Choice (D) is jewelry and therefore doesn't belong with the other words. *Correct Answer:* Choice (D)

5. Which word does *not* belong with the others?

   (A) notice

   (B) spot

   (C) drop

   (D) observe

It's probably clear to you that Choices (A), (B), and (D) have similar meanings. They're all ways of saying to become aware or to see. The answer that doesn't fit is Choice (C), drop, because it isn't related to seeing. *Correct Answer:* Choice (C)

6. Bliss is the *opposite* of

   (A) enjoyment

   (B) misery

   (C) kiss

   (D) confusion

This particular question is asking for the antonym. *Bliss* is a positive word that means "delight or heaven," so the right answer will have a negative meaning. Choices (A) and (C) are positive; get rid of them. The remaining answers are Choices (B) and (D). Confusion is the opposite of understanding, and misery is the opposite of delight. *Correct Answer:* Choice (B)

Testing Yourself on COOP- and HSPT-Style Analogies

Analogy questions appear in one of two forms, depending on the Catholic high school entrance exam you're taking. Two of the questions in this section appear in the COOP's picture-analogy style, and the other two questions are word analogies like the kind you find on the HSPT. Refer to Chapter 4 if you need assistance solving analogy questions of either type.

1.

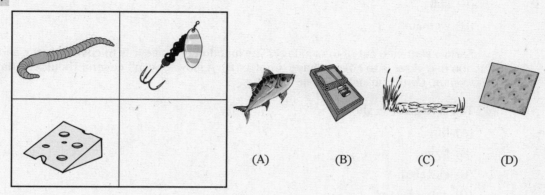

Your first inclination may be to think that a worm belongs on a hook. When you apply this sentence to the second analogy, you have these options:

- ✔ Cheese doesn't belong on a fish. Eliminate Choice (A).
- ✔ Cheese could belong on a mousetrap.
- ✔ Cheese doesn't belong on a lake; it'd get soggy. Cross out Choice (C).
- ✔ Cheese could belong on a cracker.

Looks like you have two possible answer choices. To pick the right one, make your sentence more specific. When a worm is on a hook, it's being used as bait to catch fish. When cheese is on a mousetrap, Choice (B), it's being used as bait to catch mice. You don't think of cheese on a cracker, Choice (D), as bait. *Correct Answer:* Choice (B)

2.

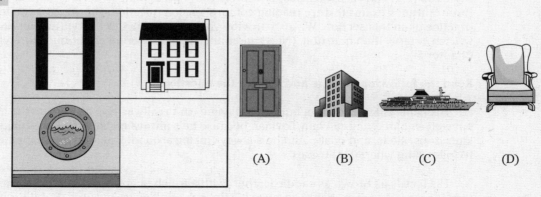

This part-of-a-whole analogy may be a little easier for you to figure out. A window is the part of a house that lets in light, just like a porthole is the part of a ship that lets in light. Some doors have windows, but they don't have portholes, which means Choice (A) can't be right. Skyscrapers don't have portholes, and thinking of a chair with a porthole is ridiculous. *Correct Answer:* Choice (C)

3. Sleeve is to arm as glove is to

   (A) shoulder

   (B) hand

   (C) shirt

   (D) woman

Form a sentence out of the analogy. The function of a sleeve is to cover an arm, and the function of a glove is to cover a hand, Choice (B). A glove doesn't cover a shoulder, shirt, or woman. *Correct Answer:* Choice (B)

4. Tall is to giant as short is to

   (A) tiny

   (B) large

   (C) elevated

   (D) unimportant

This is a degree relationship; tall and giant both mean big, but giant is the larger version of tall. Tall has a similar meaning to giant but to a lesser degree. Short isn't a lesser degree of large because short and large don't mean roughly the same thing. The same goes for elevated. Short is unrelated to Choice (D), unimportant. The best answer is Choice (A). Short and tiny both mean small, but tiny is a greater degree of smallness than short. *Correct Answer:* Choice (A)

Trying Your Hand at Reading and Writing Questions

Reading comprehension and written composition questions test your ability to understand what you read and recognize proper sentence and paragraph structure, respectively. All three entrance exams feature reading comprehension questions, so we give you four to practice on in this section. We also provide you with both a COOP-style and an HSPT-style written composition question. (Need additional help answering either question type? Flip to Chapter 5.)

Read the following passage and answer the questions.

His name is Frank Clarke, but his real name isn't really as real as the one the children have given him. They call him Toyman because he's always making the kids things, such as kites, tops, sleds, and boats. And he's always joking around. Laughter and happiness seem to follow him wherever he goes.

His face is as brown as saddle leather, with a touch of apple red in it from the sun. His face is creased, too, probably because it's forever crinkled up in a grin. But it's when Toyman appears to be <u>solemn</u> that you want to laugh most, for he's only pretending. And, best of all, if you hurt yourself or if your pet dog hurts himself, Toyman knows how to fix it to make it all well again.

My first experience with Toyman was when I was nine years old. I had competed in a local spelling bee and had missed first place by one lousy word. I spelled "misspell" with just one *s*. I was mortified, but hours after the competition, I received a package wrapped in shiny gold paper and trimmed with a rainbow-striped bow. I opened the box and pulled out a hand-carved wooden sailboat. It was the most beautiful toy I'd ever seen. An attached card simply said, "Congratulations!" It was signed "Toyman."

1. A good title for this passage would be

   (A) The Art of Hand-Carved Toys

   (B) How I Lost a Spelling Bee

   (C) My Friend the Toyman

   (D) Toys I Will Always Remember

Eliminate answers, such as Choice (B), that focus on only one part of the passage. The title has to be about the passage as a whole. Choices (A) and (D) are far too general. The focus of the passage isn't on toys but a description of Toyman as seen through the author's eyes. *Correct Answer:* Choice (C)

Questions that ask you for a good title are main-point questions. Look for the answer that summarizes the main topic of the passage and don't be concerned if the best answer isn't the cleverest of titles.

2. As it is used in the passage, <u>solemn</u> most nearly means

   (A) ill

   (B) serious

   (C) merry

   (D) jovial

This vocabulary-in-context question asks for the answer that has the same meaning as *solemn*. The word appears in the second paragraph where the author describes Toyman's face. First, the author talks about his smile. The next sentence begins with *but*, which means it contains a contrasting idea. The answer that contrasts with or is opposite to smiling or grinning is Choice (B), serious. Plug Choice (B) into the passage to see whether it fits: But it's when Toyman appears to be *serious* that you want to laugh most, for he's only pretending. Choices (C) and (D) have the same meaning. They can't both be right, so they must both be wrong. Choice (A) would be cruel; the children wouldn't want to laugh at Toyman if he looked ill — even if he were pretending! *Correct Answer:* Choice (B)

3. Frank Clarke received his nickname because he was always

   (A) fixing toys

   (B) making toys for the children

   (C) telling stories about toys

   (D) playing with toys

This is a details question, which means you can find the answer right there in the passage. The first paragraph in the passage explains that the children gave Frank the nickname of Toyman because he makes toys for them. The passage doesn't mention the activities in the other choices. *Correct Answer:* Choice (B)

4. Which of these best expresses the attitude of the author?

   (A) The author is suspicious of Toyman.

   (B) The author thinks that the children should be nicer to Toyman.

   (C) The author wishes Toyman had helped him study for the spelling bee.

   (D) The author is fond of Toyman.

   The tone of the passage is light-hearted and positive, which means you can eliminate Choices (A) and (B) because they imply that the author has a negative attitude. Concluding that the author wanted spelling help from the Toyman is illogical because the passage doesn't contain enough information about the spelling bee. In fact, the passage suggests that the author didn't even know the Toyman until after the spelling bee. *Correct Answer:* Choice (D)

   Answer Question 5 based on this paragraph.

   Medieval guilds were similar to modern-day labor unions. These groups of merchants or craftspeople set rules regarding economic activity in order to protect themselves. Some guilds held considerable economic power, but even small guilds protected members. Guilds also served a social purpose.

5. What might you expect the next paragraph to be about?

   (A) a description of how medieval guilds fulfilled a social purpose

   (B) a critique of modern-day labor unions

   (C) a comparison of the economic power held by medieval guilds and by groups of merchants

   (D) an account of the ways medieval citizens protected themselves

   Look for clues to what comes after a paragraph in its last sentence. The last sentence says that the guilds served a social purpose, so it makes sense that the next paragraph would be about that topic. The paragraph is about guilds rather than labor unions, Choice (B), which means the next paragraph likely wouldn't switch gears so suddenly without notice. Medieval guilds and groups of merchants are the same, so comparing their economic power doesn't make sense. Choice (D) is wrong because there's no indication of why the next paragraph would stop discussing guilds and begin talking about citizens in general. *Correct Answer:* Choice (A)

6. Which of these fits best under the topic of "Knitting a Scarf"?

   (A) A hand-knit scarf makes a beautiful gift, and it's easy to create.

   (B) The yarn produced in South America is denser than the yarn produced in England.

   (C) One of America's most famous seamstresses is Betsy Ross.

   (D) None of the above

   Look for a sentence that relates to the title; it should contain both the act of knitting and the scarf. Choice (B) talks about yarn, but it doesn't talk about knitting, and it certainly doesn't mention a scarf. Choice (C) is even further off track. A seamstress isn't one who knits. This sentence would fit better under the topic of "Famous Seamstresses" or in a piece about Betsy Ross. Choice (A) includes knitting and the scarf, so it's a good sentence for the topic. Because one of the sentences fits, you can eliminate Choice (D). *Correct Answer:* Choice (A)

Looking at All the Different Language Questions

All three Catholic high school entrance exams test your ability to spot errors in punctuation, capitalization, spelling, grammar, and usage of the English language. The TACHS and HSPT include more of these questions than the COOP, which mixes its language questions with its reading comprehension questions. The first two practice questions are in the COOP style, the next two are like the ones you see on the TACHS, and the last two are the kind that show up on the HSPT. See Chapters 6 and 7 for pointers on answering these types of questions.

This paragraph has a few mistakes that need correcting. Read the paragraph and answer Questions 1 and 2.

[1]Good leaders get involved in their subordinates' careers. [2]People merely obey arbitrary commands and orders, but they respond quickly and usually give extra effort for leaders who genuinely care for them. [3]A neglected leadership principle in today's environment of technology and specialization is knowing the workers and showing sincere interest in their problems career development and welfare. [4]Leadership is reflected in the degree of efficiency, productivity, morale, and motivation demonstrated by subordinates. [5]Leadership involvement is the key ingredient to maximizing worker performance.

1. What is the best way to write Sentence 1?

   (A) Good leaders get involved in their subordinates careers.

   (B) Good leaders get involved in their subordinates's careers.

   (C) Leaders, who are good, get involved in their subordinate's careers.

   (D) Best as is.

There are many subordinates, and the careers belong to them; the proper form for a plural possessive is to add an apostrophe after the ending *s*. Choice (A) neglects to make subordinates a possessive. Choice (B) forms the possessive improperly. Choice (C) forms the singular possessive of subordinate rather than the plural form, and it improperly makes *good* a nonessential part of the sentence, which changes the sentence's meaning. *Correct Answer:* Choice (D)

2. Which of the sentences contains a punctuation error?

   (A) Sentence 2

   (B) Sentence 3

   (C) Sentence 4

   (D) Sentence 5

Sentence 2 contains two independent clauses that are joined by the conjunction *but*. It properly separates the clauses with a comma before the conjunction, so eliminate Choice (A). Sentence 4 has a series of nouns that are separated by commas, which means it's correct and Choice (C) is wrong. The only punctuation in Sentence 5 is the ending period; no other punctuation is necessary. The incorrectly punctuated sentence is Sentence 3, Choice (B), because it contains a series that should be separated by commas like this: interest in their problems, career development, and welfare. *Correct Answer:* Choice (B)

Find the error in spelling.

3. (A) Sam wasted a significant amount of time

   (B) running in the lengthy marathon because

   (C) he was continually tieing his shoes.

   (D) No mistakes

Read carefully through the part of the sentence in each answer choice and watch for any problems in spelling. Everything seems to be fine until you get to Choice (C). When you add *-ing* to tie, you change the *ie* to *y*. Choice (C) should be "he was continually *tying* his shoes." *Correct Answer:* Choice (C)

Find the error in capitalization.

4. (A) Escaping to the Appalachian Mountains

   (B) last weekend was a perfect way to celebrate

   (C) Valentine's Day.

   (D) No mistakes

Appalachian Mountains is properly capitalized in Choice (A), and weekend is properly formatted with lowercase letters in Choice (B). Valentine's Day is a holiday, which means the capitalization is also appropriate in Choice (C). *Correct Answer:* Choice (D)

Choose the answer that has an error in punctuation, capitalization, or usage. If there is no error, select Choice (D).

5. (A) Marcie drove to Fort Worth on Tuesday.

   (B) Because Jeff could not attend the dinner, we brought him a snack.

   (C) Gary could of come with us if he had wanted to.

   (D) No mistakes

The capitalization, punctuation, and usage all look good in Choice (A). Choice (B) correctly separates the beginning dependent clause from the independent clause with a comma. Choice (C), however, has a problem with usage. The proper construction of the verb is *could have. Could of* is never right. *Correct Answer:* Choice (C)

The HSPT doesn't always tell you what specific kinds of errors to look for like the TACHS does, which means you must consider all sorts of issues when you approach an HSPT language question.

6. Which of these answers expresses the idea most clearly?

   (A) Before making breakfast, I relax in the warm sunshine streaming in from the window.

   (B) Relaxing in the warm sunshine streaming in from the window, it is before I make breakfast.

   (C) Before making breakfast in the warm sunshine streaming in from the window, I cause myself to relax.

   (D) Before making breakfast, the warm sunshine streaming in from the window causes me to relax.

Whenever you see a sentence that starts with a beginning phrase, check to make sure the subject of the sentence relates to the action in the phrase. In Choice (B), *it* doesn't do the relaxing; I do. However, the way the sentence is constructed makes it seem as if *it* is engaged in relaxing. The same problem occurs in Choice (D). The way that sentence is worded makes it sound like the sunshine makes breakfast. Now that's something we'd like to see! The sentence in Choice (C) has *I* making the breakfast, but it changes the meaning. The warm sunshine isn't where I make breakfast; it's where I relax. The clearest sentence is Choice (A). It states that *I* make the breakfast and clarifies that the relaxing takes place in the sunshine. *Correct Answer:* Choice (A)

Facing Verbal Reasoning Questions on the COOP and HSPT

If you're taking the COOP or the HSPT, you need to be prepared to face verbal reasoning questions that test your ability to draw reasonable conclusions. Fortunately, this section contains four for you to try out. The first two are in the COOP style, and the second two are in the HSPT style. Chapter 8 can get you better acquainted with verbal reasoning questions if you need additional help with 'em.

For Questions 1 and 2, find the statement that is true based on the information provided.

1. Kelly is typing a paper. Kelly is perspiring. She often perspires when she is hot.

    (A) Kelly's paper consists of many pages.

    (B) Kelly hates to type papers.

    (C) Kelly is probably hot.

    (D) Kelly is sitting at a desk.

    You don't know that Kelly's perspiration is related to the paper she's typing, so you can't say that her paper is long or that she hates to type papers. You don't even know that she's sitting at a desk; she could be typing at the kitchen table. All you know is that Kelly is perspiring and that she often perspires when she gets hot. Therefore, Kelly's probably hot. *Correct Answer:* Choice (C)

2. The Michaels family plays board games together every Wednesday. They watch movies together every Friday. They eat dinner at a restaurant together twice a week.

    (A) The Michaels family goes out to dinner before they watch movies.

    (B) The Michaels family eats dinner at a restaurant on Mondays and Tuesdays.

    (C) The Michaels family spends time together at least twice a week.

    (D) The Michaels family does not spend time together every night.

    Consider what you do and don't know. The Michaels family definitely plays board games together on Wednesdays and watches movies together on Fridays, which means they spend time together at least twice a week. You know that the family eats dinner together twice a week, but you don't know which days they eat dinner together. So, you can't select Choice (A) or Choice (B). Just because the statements don't reveal that the Michaels family does other things together doesn't mean they don't; Choice (D) is wrong too. *Correct Answer:* Choice (C)

3. Jane is taller than Stan. Stan is taller than Greta. Jane is taller than Greta. If the first two statements are true, the third statement is

(A) true

(B) false

(C) uncertain

Chapter 8 shows you how to prepare a diagram to answer these kinds of logic questions. The diagram for this question, in order of tallest to shortest, is Jane → Stan → Greta. Looks like the third statement is true. *Correct Answer:* Choice (A)

4. All dwezzles are haps. Some haps are jovial. Some dwezzles are jovial. If the first two statements are true, the third statement is

(A) true

(B) false

(C) uncertain

When you draw a Venn diagram like the following one, you see that you don't know whether some dwezzles are jovial or not because the jovial circle could fit in a couple different spots. The statement is therefore uncertain. *Correct Answer:* Choice (C)

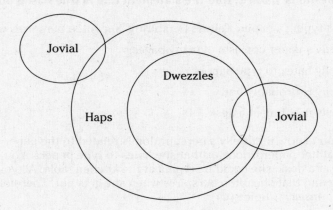

Part III
Mastering Math and Conquering Quantitative Questions

The 5th Wave   By Rich Tennant

Sherlock Holmes Takes His Entrance Exam

Hmm...ELEMENTARY!
Ah, yes...ummm...AHA!
ELEMENTARY! ELEMENTARY!
Now, let's see. Ahhh HA!
ELEMENTARY INDEED!

Gimme a break.

In this part . . .

Here it is — the long-awaited math review! In the next 80 or so pages, we provide you with a thorough run-through of all the important and most commonly tested math concepts on the Catholic high school entrance exams. We start with the basics (think fundamental operations, averages, percentages, fractions, and exponents) in Chapter 10 and then dive right into algebra essentials in Chapter 11. Chapter 12 gets you in good "shape" for the geometry problems on the entrance exams, and Chapter 13 helps you figure out just what math word problems are asking for.

Now, your entrance exam may feature some quantitative question types you haven't seen before. These questions may ask you to complete a sequence of numbers or pictures or compare the shaded areas of shapes and the values of several equations. The COOP even has you balance a scale using squares and triangles. Rest assured that after you review Chapters 14 and 15 to see how to approach these unusual question types, you may find you actually enjoy them! Of course, that joy may be short-lived when you tackle the math practice questions in Chapter 16. C'est la vie!

Chapter 10

Acing Arithmetic Problems

They crop up everywhere: grade school math tests, those dreaded achievement tests, and now on your high school entrance exams. We're talking about multiple-choice math questions. Because the various Catholic high school entrance exams test what you've learned so far, most of the math questions you'll face cover the basics, such as adding numbers and finding averages. This chapter reviews the fundamentals in case some of the concepts have grown fuzzy for you since you first learned them.

Delving into the Details of Numbers

It's probably no surprise to you that the math problems on the entrance exams involve numbers, but it's also probably been a while since you thought about the properties of numbers. That's why we're offering you a fairly complete number review. (You can thank us later.)

Keeping it real: Types of numbers

The math problems on the Catholic high school entrance exams deal primarily with *real numbers* — also known as all the numbers that you normally think of and deal with in everyday life. Think of real numbers as those numbers represented by all the points on a number line (see the next section if you're not familiar with this handy tool), either positive or negative. Real numbers are also those numbers you use to measure length, volume, or weight. In fact, almost any number you can think of is a real number.

Real numbers include integers, rational numbers, and numbers that can't be written as fractions (called *irrational numbers*) — all of which you'll see on your entrance exam.

✔ **Integers** consist of all positive and negative whole numbers, as well as zero. Integers aren't fractions, decimals, or portions of a number, so they include –5, –4, –3, –2, –1, 0, 1, 2, 3, 4, 5, and continue infinitely on either side of zero. Integers greater than zero are called *natural numbers* or *positive integers;* integers less than zero are called *negative integers*.

Tread carefully when working with zero because it's neither positive nor negative.

✓ **Rational numbers** include all positive and negative integers, zero, and fractions and decimal numbers that either end or repeat. For example, the fraction ⅙ can be expressed as 0.16666. . . .

✓ **Numbers that can't be written as fractions** (such as π and $\sqrt{2}$) round out the set of real numbers.

Visualizing the lineup: The number line

If you're a visual person, you may have an easier time picturing numbers if you see them on a number line. The *number line* is a device used to show all real numbers. Zero sits at the middle of the line. All positive numbers extend infinitely to the right of zero, and all negative numbers extend infinitely to the left of zero. The numbers increase in value as you move to the right and decrease in value as you move to the left. Here's what a number line looks like:

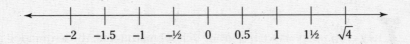

$$-2 \quad -1.5 \quad -1 \quad -\tfrac{1}{2} \quad 0 \quad 0.5 \quad 1 \quad 1\tfrac{1}{2} \quad \sqrt{4}$$

Numbers can be expressed in a variety of ways on the number line as long as they have the same value. For instance, the space between 0 and 1 can be shown as either 0.5 or ½. Likewise, $\sqrt{4}$ is the same as 2.

Working in absolutes: Absolute value

No review of numbers would be complete without covering the concept of absolute value. The *absolute value* of any real number is that same number without a negative sign. It's the value of the distance a particular number is from zero on a number line (see the preceding section). The symbol for absolute value is $|\ \ |$, so the absolute value of 1 is written mathematically as $|1|$. And because 1 sits one space from 0 on the number line, $|1| = 1$. The absolute value of –1 is also 1, because –1 also hangs out one space away from 0 on the number line. So, $|-1| = 1$.

Absolute value relates only to the value inside those absolute value bars. If you see a negative sign outside the bars, the value of the result is negative. That means $-|-1| = -1$; the negative sign outside the bars makes the end value a negative number.

Absolute value problems can drag down your math score on your entrance exam if you're not careful. Here's a sample one so you know what to watch for.

What is the value of $|-16|$?

(A) –16

(B) –4

(C) 4

(D) 16

You know by the $|\ |$ symbol that this question is asking you to find the absolute value of –16. Remember that the absolute value of a number equals the number of spaces that number extends from zero on the number line. You know that –16 is 16 spaces away from zero, so the answer is 16, Choice (D). You can eliminate Choices (B) and (C) because you can't have a different number as your answer for an absolute value problem. Finally, you know Choice (A) is wrong because absolute value is always a positive number.

Factoring it all in: Prime numbers

Whichever entrance exam you're taking, be prepared to see a question or two involving *prime numbers,* which are all the positive integers that can be divided only by themselves and 1. Here are some of the other facts you should know about prime numbers:

- ✔ **One** isn't a prime number.
- ✔ **Two** is the smallest of the prime numbers, and it's also the only number that's both even and prime.
- ✔ **Zero** can never be a prime number because you can divide it by every number in existence.

You don't need to memorize a bunch of prime numbers for your test, but do keep in mind that the lowest prime numbers are 2, 3, 5, 7, 11, 13, 17, 19, 23, and 29.

When you know how to recognize prime numbers, you can use *prime factorization,* which is just a fancy way of saying that you can break down a number into all of the prime numbers (or *factors*) that go into it. For instance, 50 factors into 2×25, which factors into 5×5, giving you $2 \times 5 \times 5$ for the prime factors of 50.

Questions on your entrance exam that test you on prime factorization may simply ask you for the factors of a particular number, or they may be less obvious, like this one.

Which of the following answers contains prime numbers that when multiplied together equal 60?

(A) $2 \times 2 \times 3 \times 5$

(B) $2 \times 2 \times 15$

(C) $2 \times 3 \times 3 \times 5$

(D) $2 \times 3 \times 5$

The question says that all the multiplied numbers must be prime numbers, so cross out any answers containing a number that isn't prime. Even though the multipliers equal 60, Choice (B) is wrong because 15 isn't a prime number. You can also eliminate any answers that don't equal 60 when you multiply them. Choice (C) equals 90, and Choice (D) comes out to 30; they're both out. The correct answer must be Choice (A) because it contains only prime numbers that equal 60 when you multiply them together.

You can also solve this question by using prime factorization to create a diagram called a *factor tree*. To find the prime factors of 60, think of numbers that equal 60 when multiplied together. Do the numbers 30 and 2 come to mind? (We hope so, because that's what we're going with.) You can break 30 into 2 and 15, which gives you factors of $2 \times 2 \times 15$. Ah, but 15 can be broken down again into 3 and 5. Therefore, the prime factorization of 60 is $2 \times 2 \times 3 \times 5$, which is — drumroll please — Choice (A).

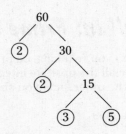

Minor Surgery: Reviewing Basic Mathematical Operations

Performing the basic mathematical operations — addition, subtraction, multiplication, and division — is a little like performing surgery on numbers, only you don't have to be a brain surgeon to do it right. All you have to do is refresh your memory of the rules once in a while. Consider the following sections your basic-math refresher.

Adding up the properties of addition

Addition — the act of combining two or more numbers to get an end result called the *sum* — just may be the simplest of all the mathematical operations. Your basic addition problem looks like this: $2 + 3 + 4 = 9$.

Addition also has two important properties that we bet you use pretty frequently in math class. Burning these properties into your mind will help you greatly on your exam:

- **The associative property:** This one means that the grouping you use to associate numbers doesn't matter in addition. Regardless of whether you add 2 and 3 together first and then add 4, which looks like $(2 + 3) + 4$, or you add 3 and 4 together followed by 2, which looks like $2 + (3 + 4)$, you still get 9.

- **The commutative property:** Thanks to this property, it doesn't matter what order you use to add the same numbers. Regardless of what number you list first in a set of numbers, those numbers always produce the same sum. So $2 + 3 = 5$ is the same as $3 + 2 = 5$.

Cutting down the properties of subtraction

Subtraction is the opposite of addition. When you subtract one number from another, you're taking away a value from another value and ending up with the *difference* (the answer to a subtraction problem). So if $4 + 5 = 9$, then $9 - 5 = 4$.

Unlike addition, grouping *does* matter in subtraction. You get completely different answers for the problem $20 - 7 - 4 = ?$ depending on how you associate the values. Here's what we mean: $(20 - 7) - 4 = 9$, but $20 - (7 - 4) = 17$. The order of the values counts in subtraction, too. The problem 2 – 3 isn't the same as the problem 3 – 2. The first one gives you a difference of –1, but the second one gives you a difference of +1.

None of the entrance exams lets you bring in a calculator, so the actual calculations that you have to perform on your test won't be so complex that you can't do them in your head or work them out quickly in the space in your test booklet. So, an entrance exam subtraction question may be pretty straightforward, like this one.

What is the difference between 18 and 30?

(A) 12

(B) 48

(C) –12

(D) 0.6

First off, you should recognize that the question is asking for the answer to a subtraction problem. (Why? Because you know that *difference* is defined as the answer to a subtraction problem.) Don't forget that order matters in subtraction; keep the proper order: 18 – 30 = –12. The correct answer is Choice (C). If you picked Choice (A), you switched the order of the numbers. Choice (B) is the answer you'd get if you added the two numbers, and Choice (D) is the quotient rather than the difference (see the later "Splitting hairs with properties of division" section for an explanation of the term *quotient*).

Increasing greatly through properties of multiplication

Think of *multiplication* as repeated addition with an end result called the *product*. The multiplication problem 3×6 is therefore the same as the addition problem $6 + 6 + 6$. Both problems equal 18.

Multiplication is also like addition in that the order of the values doesn't matter. It too obeys the commutative property, which means $2 \times 3 = 3 \times 2$, and the associative property, which means $(2 \times 3) \times 4 = 2 \times (3 \times 4)$. Check out the earlier "Adding up the properties of addition" section for the definitions of these two properties.

Another property associated with multiplication is the distributive property over addition. Say you encounter a multiplication problem like $2(3 + 4) = ?$ You can solve this problem by adding the numbers in parentheses ($3 + 4 = 7$) and then multiplying that sum by 2 (as in $7 \times 2 = 14$). But you can also do a little *distribution*, which means you multiply the value outside the parentheses (the 2 in this case) by each of the values within the parentheses (the 3 and the 4). So, you multiply 2 by 3 and 2 by 4 and then add the products together. You get the same answer: $(2 \times 3) + (2 \times 4) = 6 + 8 = 14$. And because subtracting is really just adding a negative, you can use the distributive property even when you have a minus sign inside the parentheses.

The distributive property comes in handy when you multiply variables in algebra problems. (You find out more about that in Chapter 11.)

Your entrance exam may use several different signs to represent the multiplication operation. A multiplication sign can be designated simply with a dot ($\cdot$) or by $\times$. And in many instances, especially when variables are involved (refer to Chapter 11), multiplication can be indicated by just putting the factors right next to each other. So, *ab* means the same thing as $a \times b$, and $2a$ is the same as $2 \times a$.

Splitting hairs with properties of division

Division is taking your total number of items and breaking them up into equal groups. The result (the number of items in each group) is called the *quotient.* You may also consider division to be the opposite of multiplication, so because $4 \times 6 = 24$, $24 \div 6 = 4$ and $24 \div 4 = 6$.

Just so you're prepared in case your test throws some math terminology at you, you should know that the number at the beginning of any division problem (24 in the preceding expression) is called the *dividend,* and the number that goes into the dividend is called the *divisor* (that's 4 in the preceding expression).

Order is just as important in division as it is in subtraction. The quotient of $10 \div 2$ (which is 5) is a much different answer than the quotient of $2 \div 10$ (which is ⅕ or 0.2).

Performing basic operations with odds and evens and positives and negatives

Basic math operations are pretty simple, but some elements can make them a bit trickier. Know the rules for dealing with odd/even and positive/negative numbers.

Rules for odds and evens

The number line (depicted earlier in this chapter) gives you an easy way to visualize even and odd numbers. We're pretty sure you know that *even numbers* are numbers that are evenly divisible by 2 (2, 4, 6, 8, 10, and so on) and that *odd numbers* are numbers that aren't evenly divisible by 2 (1, 3, 5, 7, 9, and so on).

You're probably with us so far, but what's important to remember for the math questions is what happens to even or odd numbers when you add, subtract, multiply, or divide them by one another.

Here are the rules regarding the addition and subtraction of odd and even numbers:

- ✔ When you add or subtract two even numbers, your result is an even number.
- ✔ When you add or subtract two odd numbers, your result is also even.
- ✔ If you add or subtract an even number and an odd number, your result is an odd number.

When it comes to multiplying even and odd numbers, don't forget the following:

- ✔ When you multiply an even number by an even number, you get an even number.
- ✔ When you multiply an odd number by an even number, you also get an even number.
- ✔ The only time you get an odd number for your product is when you multiply an odd number by another odd number.

The division rules for odd and even numbers are as follows:

- ✔ When you divide an even number by an odd number, you get an even number.
- ✔ An odd number divided by another odd number results in an odd number.

Knowing the rules for performing operations with odds and evens can be a big timesaver when it comes to eliminating answer choices. For instance, if you have a problem that multiplies only large even numbers, you know you can eliminate any odd-number answer choices without even doing the math!

Rules for positives and negatives

Positive and negative numbers have their own set of rules regarding operations, and those rules are even more important to remember than the ones for even and odd numbers. When you multiply or divide

- ✔ Two positive numbers, the answer is positive

- ✔ Two negative numbers, the answer is also positive

- ✔ A negative number by a positive number, you get a negative answer

You also have to know a thing or two (or four, actually) about adding and subtracting positives and negatives:

- ✔ When you add two positive numbers, your answer is positive: 3 + 5 = 8.

- ✔ Adding two negative numbers gives you a negative answer: –3 + –5 = –8. You may have to add two negative numbers even though the sign between them is a minus sign. For example, –3 – 5 is the same as saying –3 + –5, which is –8. (Subtracting 5 is the same thing as adding –5.)

- ✔ When you add a negative number to a positive number, your answer can be positive or negative: –3 + 5 = 2, and 3 + –5 = –2.

  If adding positive and negative numbers is confusing for you, think of the number line. Start at the point of the first number and move right for positive numbers and left for negative numbers. To solve the first equation, you'd find –3 on the number line and move right 5 spaces to 2. For the second equation, you'd find 3 on the number line and move left 5 spaces to –2.

- ✔ If you subtract a negative number from another number, you end up adding the second number to the first, and your answer can be either positive or negative: 3 – (–5) is the same as 3 + 5, so the answer is 8; –5 – (–3) is the same as –5 + 3, so the answer is –2.

This sample question gives you a chance to test what you know about subtracting negative numbers.

–24 – (–23) is equal to _____?

(A) –47

(B) –1

(C) 1

(D) 47

To subtract a negative number, change it to a positive number and add. So to subtract –23 from –24, you must change –23 to +23 and add the numbers: –24 + 23 = –1 (start at –24 on the number line and move right 23 spaces). The answer is Choice (B). Choice (A) results from adding –23 to –24 rather than subtracting it. If you picked Choice (C), you changed –23 to +23 but subtracted it *and* neglected the negative sign in front of 24. Choice (D) doesn't recognize that the difference is a negative number rather than a positive one.

Climbing Up the Complexity Ladder: More Advanced Arithmetic

Hey, wouldn't it be great if simple addition, subtraction, multiplication, and division were all you had to know for your entrance exam's math questions? Sadly, you must master more advanced concepts, including fractions, ratios, and averages, before you can say you're completely ready for test day. No fear! It's all right here.

Breaking a whole into parts: Fractions, decimals, and percentages

Fractions, decimals, and percentages all represent parts of a whole. *Fractions* are really answers to division problems. If you divide 3 by 4, you get the fraction ¾ (so 3 ÷ 4 = ¾). *Decimals* show fractions as tenths, hundredths, thousandths, and so on. *Percent* literally means "something per 100" or "something divided by 100." The following sections detail the specifics of these three ways to cut a whole into separate parts.

Converting fractions, decimals, and percentages

Because fractions, decimals, and percentages are different ways of showing similar values, you can change pretty easily from one form to another (and you may even be required to by some test problems).

- To convert a fraction to a decimal, you just divide: ¾ = 3 ÷ 4 = 0.75.

- To convert a decimal to a fraction, you first count the digits to the right of the decimal point and then divide the number over a 1 followed by the same number of zeros as there were digits to the right of the decimal. So 0.75 = ⁷⁵⁄₁₀₀. Be sure to reduce your fraction, though! ⁷⁵⁄₁₀₀ = ¾.

- Changing a decimal to a percent is really pretty easy. Just move the decimal two places to the right and add a percent sign. To change 0.75 to a percent, simply move the decimal two places to the right and add a percent sign: 0.75 = 75%.

- To turn a percent back into a decimal, you follow the preceding procedure in reverse. You just move the decimal point two to the left and get rid of the percent sign, like so: 75% = 0.75

Defining fraction terminology

Fractions tell you what part a piece is of a whole. The *numerator* is the top number in the fraction and represents the piece; the *denominator* is the bottom number of the fraction and indicates the value of the whole.

Picture a delicious apple pie sliced into eight equal pieces and a hungry family of seven, each of whom has a slice after dinner (or before dinner if they're sneaky). That pie looks a little something like this:

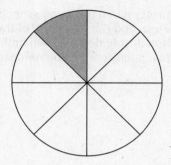

The unshaded pieces of pie show how much of the dessert the family gobbled up. The shaded piece shows what's left of the pie when the family is finished. The number of pieces in the pie to begin with (the whole) represents the denominator, and the number of pieces that were eaten up (the part of the whole) represents the numerator. In this case, the number of devoured pieces makes up ⅞ of the total pie, so 7 is the numerator, and 8 is the denominator.

Proper fractions are those fractions where the numerator is less than the denominator, like ⅔. *Improper fractions* are those fractions where the numerator is either greater than or equal to the denominator, like ½ or ⅗. You can also show an improper fraction as a *mixed number* (sometimes called a *mixed fraction*), which is made up of a whole number and a fraction, like 1⅓.

Simplifying fractions

When you're dealing with fractions, it helps to know that ⁶⁄₁₈ has the same value as ⅓. Actually, ⅓ is ⁶⁄₁₈ in its *simplest* (or smallest) terms. Usually answers to math questions that involve fractions show the fractions in simplest terms. So if you come up with an answer of ⁶⁄₁₈, you may not find that answer in the list of available choices, which means you have to simplify. To do that, find a number that goes into both the numerator and the denominator and divide both by that number.

To simplify ⁵⁄₁₀, find a number that goes into both 5 and 10. That number is 5 because 5 and 10 are evenly divisible by 5. Dividing both the numerator and the denominator by 5 allows you to simplify ⁵⁄₁₀ as ½.

Multiplying and dividing fractions

Multiplying fractions is easy. Just multiply the numerators by each other and then do the same with the denominators. Then simplify if you have to.

$$\frac{1}{5} \times \frac{5}{8} = \frac{1 \times 5}{5 \times 8} = \frac{5}{40} = \frac{1}{8}$$

When working with larger numbers, you may want to simplify first to make life easier (and the numbers smaller) before you multiply straight across. Here's an example:

$$\frac{5}{21} \times \frac{14}{3} = \frac{5}{3} \times \frac{2}{3} = \frac{5 \times 2}{3 \times 3} = \frac{10}{9}$$

Dividing fractions is pretty much the same as multiplying them except for one very important additional step. First, find the *reciprocal* of the second fraction in the equation (that is, turn the second fraction upside down). Then multiply (yes, you have to multiply when dividing fractions) the numerators and denominators of the resulting fractions. Here's how:

$$\frac{1}{3} \div \frac{1}{2} = ?$$

$$\frac{1}{3} \div \frac{1}{2} = \frac{1}{3} \times \frac{2}{1}$$

$$\frac{1}{3} \times \frac{2}{1} = \frac{2}{3}$$

Adding and subtracting fractions

You can bet your Catholic high school entrance exam will ask you to add or subtract a few fractions. This task can be as easy as simply adding and subtracting the numerators and putting the answer over the original denominator, as you can see from the following:

$\frac{2}{5} + \frac{4}{5} = \frac{6}{5}$

$\frac{6}{5} - \frac{4}{5} = \frac{2}{5}$

You can only add and subtract fractions if they have the same denominator. Simply adding or subtracting numerators doesn't work if the denominators are different.

No sweat, right? But what if you see something like this on your exam: $\frac{1}{3} + \frac{1}{4} =$ _____?

To answer this problem, you must find the smallest number that both of the denominators go into; in other words, you must find the *lowest common denominator.* Because your denominators in this problem are 3 and 4, you need to find a number that both 3 and 4 go into evenly. If you multiply 3 by 4, you get the number 12, so you know that both 3 and 4 go into 12. Actually, that just so happens to be the lowest common denominator here. Convert $\frac{1}{3}$ to $\frac{4}{12}$ by multiplying $\frac{1}{3}$ by $\frac{4}{4}$. Convert $\frac{1}{4}$ to $\frac{3}{12}$ by multiplying $\frac{1}{4}$ by $\frac{3}{3}$. Add the numerators of the two new fractions and keep the same denominator to get your answer: $\frac{4}{12} + \frac{3}{12} = \frac{7}{12}$.

Adding and subtracting decimals

You add and subtract decimal numbers just like you do integers (see the earlier "Keeping it real: Types of numbers" section for a definition of integers). The only special thing about decimals is that you have to line them up when you add or subtract them, which means if your exam asks you to add 0.53 and 7, you need to arrange the problem like this:

$$\begin{array}{r} 0.53 \\ \underline{+7.} \end{array}$$

When you add the numbers, you get 7.53.

Figuring percentages

Usually the exams ask you to find a percentage of another number: What is 30% of 60? When you get a question like this, evaluate the language like so:

- **What** means ? or x (the unknown), or what you're trying to find out.
- **Is** means = (equals).
- **Of** means × (multiply).

Your job is to multiply: ? = 30% × 60. To do so, just convert 30% to a decimal (0.30) and multiply by 60. Tada! The answer is 18.

Sometimes they may ask you to figure out what percent one number is of another, like "The number 20 is what percent of 80?" Just apply a little translation to the question to get a math equation you can work with.

The number 20 is, of course, 20. You know that *is* means =. *What* gives you the unknown, or *x*, and *of* means ×. Put it all together and you get this expression: $20 = x\% \times 80$. All that's left is to solve for *x*. (See Chapter 11 if you need to find out how to go about solving for *x*.) Divide both sides by 80, and you get this equation: $0.25 = x\%$. Convert 0.25 to a percent by multiplying by 100, and you have your answer: $0.25 \times 100 = 25\%$.

Drawing comparisons: Ratios and proportions

Ratios and proportions share a similar purpose: They both allow you to draw comparisons between two things. A *ratio* shows a relationship between two like numbers or two like values. A ratio may be written as a fraction (⅛), as a division expression (1 ÷ 8), with a colon (1:8), or as a statement (1 to 8).

So how exactly will your entrance exam test you on ratios? Probably like this.

The ratio of 8 to 14 is _____?

(A) ½

(B) ¹⁴⁄₈

(C) ⁴⁄₇

(D) ²⁄₇

Because you know that ratios express division, you can solve this problem by dividing 8 by 14. Take a quick glance at the answer choices before you engage in a tedious long division problem. Notice that all the answer choices are fractions? That means you can just set up a fraction to show the ratio, like so: ⁸⁄₁₄.

Looks like ⁸⁄₁₄ isn't one of the answer choices, so you need to simplify the fraction (the earlier section "Simplifying fractions" shows you how). Turns out ⁸⁄₁₄ is the same as ⁴⁄₇, so the correct answer is Choice (C). Choice (B) is wrong because it shows the ratio of 14 to 8; order definitely matters in ratios. Choice (D) results from simplifying the fraction incorrectly. And if you picked Choice (A), you probably just hazarded a guess.

Your entrance exam may toss in a few proportion problems, too. A *proportion* is a relationship between two ratios where the ratios are equal. Just like with fractions, multiplying or dividing both numbers in the ratio by the same number doesn't change the value of the ratio. So, for example, these two ratios make up a proportion: 2:8 and 4:16, which you may also see written as 2:8 = 4:16.

To test your knowledge of proportions, your entrance exam may give you a couple of equal ratios with a missing term and ask you to figure out the missing value. To solve these problems, you *cross multiply*, which means you multiply the terms that are diagonal from each other and solve for *x*.

Here's how you solve for *x* when you see a proportion problem like $\frac{1}{8} = \frac{2}{x}$:

1. **Find the terms that are diagonal from each other.**

   Pair up 1 with *x* and 2 with 8.

2. **Multiply each set of diagonal terms and set the products equal to each other.**

   So $1 \times x = 1x$, and $2 \times 8 = 16$. You're left with $1x = 16$.

3. **Solve for x.**

   Chapter 11 explains how to solve algebraic equations, but know that in this problem $x = 16$.

Sizing things up: Rounding and estimating

Knowing how to round numbers and estimate calculations is important on any multiple-choice math test, but if you're taking the TACHS, expect to see a whole math section devoted to estimation. Fortunately, the rules for rounding are pretty simple.

1. **Figure out which digit (or place value) in the number you need to round to.**

2. **Look at the digit next to it on the right.**

3. **If the digit to the right is a 5 or higher, round up to the next number. If the digit to the right is a 4 or lower, keep the digit the same.**

4. **Substitute zeros for all of the places to the right of the digit you started with.**

If you're asked to round 1,345 to the nearest hundred, you'd go to the hundreds place (for a list of the names of decimal places, see Chapter 13); in this case, that's 3. Look at the digit next to 3, which is 4. Keep 3 the same and replace the 4 and 5 with zeros to get 1,300. To round to the nearest ten, look at the tens place, which is 4. Check out the digit to the right, which is 5; because that digit is 5, you have to round up. Add 1 to the 4 and replace the 5 with a zero to round 1,345 to 1,350.

You can use rounding to make estimates. For example, if you have 4,589,734 marbles and you want to have at least 5 million marbles in your collection, you can use estimation to determine about how many marbles you need to collect to reach your goal. First, round 4,589,734 to the nearest hundred-thousandth to get 4,600,000. Now you can easily subtract your rounded figure from 5 million to determine that you need to collect about 400,000 more marbles to make you happy.

Here's a sample rounding problem for you to try.

What do you get when you round 42,653 to the nearest hundred?

(A) 42,000

(B) 43,000

(C) 42,600

(D) 42,700

The hundreds place is represented by the 6. Look to the immediate right of the 6, and you find a 5. A value of 5 or more means you must round up, so add 1 to the 6 and replace the 5 and 3 with zeros. Your answer is Choice (D). If you picked Choices (A) or (B), you were working with the thousands place rather than the hundreds. If you selected Choice (C), you didn't round up.

Covering your bases: Exponents and roots

You may see a few questions on your exam that require you to know about exponents and roots, especially if you're taking the HSPT. To keep you from getting bogged down in all the info out there about exponents and roots (which we pair together because finding a root is basically like finding the base of an exponent), we cover only what you need to know for your exam within the following sections.

Working with exponents

Exponents represent repeated multiplication, much like multiplication itself represents repeated addition. This means that 5^3 is the same as $5 \times 5 \times 5$, or 125. You call the big number, the 5, the *base*. The little number, the 3, is the *exponent,* and it tells you how many times you multiply the base by itself. (By the way, another name for exponent is *power.*) So the expression 2^5 tells you to multiply 2 five times, like this: $2 \times 2 \times 2 \times 2 \times 2$, or 32.

Bases with an exponent of 2 are called *squares.* You should be familiar with the value of the squares of the numbers 1 through 12. Bases with an exponent of 3 are called *cubes.* If you're taking the HSPT, we suggest you memorize the cubes of 2, 3, 4, and 5.

Whichever entrance exam you're facing, you should know how to add, subtract, multiply, and divide numbers with exponents. The best way to perform any basic mathematical operation with bases and exponents is to figure out the values of the terms and solve. For example, to find the product of 3^2 and 2^3, figure out the value of each term and multiply: $3 \times 3 = 9$; $2 \times 2 \times 2 = 8$; $9 \times 8 = 72$.

Don't try to add numbers with exponents by simply adding the bases together and then adding the exponents together. That definitely doesn't work.

Your entrance exam may not require you to perform operations completely to answer an exponent question like the following one.

What is $2^2 \times 3^3$?

(A) $5 \times 5 \times 5 \times 5 \times 5$

(B) $2 \times 2 \times 3 \times 3$

(C) $2 \times 2 \times 3 \times 3 \times 3$

(D) $2 \times 2 \times 2 \times 3 \times 3$

Remember that an exponent indicates how many times you multiply the base by itself. An exponent of 2 means you multiply the base of 2 twice (2×2). The expression 3^3 means 3 multiplied by itself 3 times ($3 \times 3 \times 3$). Multiply the two expressions together and you get Choice (C). If you picked Choice (A), you mistakenly added the numbers and exponents together. Choices (B) and (D) are what you get if you read the question too quickly and mistake the number of exponents.

Powering up by 10

Multiplying or dividing a number by a power of 10 just requires moving around the decimal point. To multiply a number by a power of 10, move the decimal point of the number to the right as many times as the value of the exponent: $0.1234 \times 10^5 = 12{,}340$.

When you divide by a power of 10, you simply move the decimal point to the left as many times as indicated by the exponent and add zeros if you need to: $0.1234 \div 10^5 = 0.000001234$.

People use powers of 10 to make humongous and teensy-weensy numbers more manageable. They also give this simple action a fancy-sounding name: *scientific notation.* You express a number in scientific notation by dividing the entire number so that the decimal point moves to the left and all the digits except one are to the right of the decimal point. Then you use an exponent to show how many places you moved the decimal point, like this: 20 million $(20,000,000) = 2.0 \times 10^7$.

Digging into roots

Various mathematical roots exist, but for your entrance exam, you just need to worry about square roots. The *square root* of a particular number is the number you have to square to get that number. Because the square of 3 is 9 $(3^2 = 9)$, the square root of 9 is 3 $(\sqrt{9} = 3)$.

You can often use prime factorization to simplify square roots and make them easier to handle (see the earlier "Factoring it all in: Prime numbers" section if you need help with this technique). For example, if you're asked to find the square root of 225, don't panic! Just calculate the factors of 225 to find values that you *can* determine the square root of.

To factor $\sqrt{225}$, think of squares that go into 225. You know that 5^2 is 25. Is 25 a factor of 225? Yep! It goes into 225 nine times: $25 \times 9 = 225$. The number 9 is also a perfect square (3^2) — pretty neat, huh? Put the two factors under the square root sign: $\sqrt{25 \times 9}$. The square root of 25 is 5, and the square root of 9 is 3. Because $5 \times 3 = 15$, the square root of 225 is 15.

If you're feeling a little bewildered by square roots, don't despair. You'll see very few of them on the HSPT and nearly none on the TACHS or COOP.

Meeting in the middle: Average, median, and mode

Don't be surprised if your entrance exam asks you a few basic statistic questions. Most of these will be about averages, but you may see a few that deal with medians and modes. We prepare you to face all three in the next sections.

Doing better than average on averages

To perform above average on questions about averages, you need to know how to apply the following formula for finding the average value of a set of numbers:

$$Average = \frac{Sum\ of\ the\ numbers\ in\ the\ set}{Amount\ of\ numbers\ in\ the\ set}$$

To find the average of 23, 25, 26, and 30, apply the formula

$$Average = \frac{23 + 25 + 26 + 30}{4} = \frac{104}{4} = 26$$

You can use given values in the average formula to solve for the other values. For instance, if your exam gives you the average and the sum of a group of numbers, you can figure out how many numbers were in the set by using the average formula.

Check out the following example.

Justin tried to compute his average score out of 8 tests. He mistakenly divided the correct sum of all of his test scores by 7 and got an average of 96. What is Justin's actual average test score?

(A) 76

(B) 80

(C) 84

(D) 106

You know Justin's average score when the sum is divided by 7, so you can use the formula to figure out the sum of Justin's scores. Then you can use the average formula to determine his average over 8 tests. Here's how:

1. Apply the average formula to Justin's incorrect calculation.

$$96 = \text{Sum of scores}/7$$

$$96 \times 7 = \text{Sum of scores}$$

$$672 = \text{Sum of scores}$$

2. Use the sum of Justin's test scores to figure out the correct average score.

$$\text{Average} = {}^{672}\!/_{8}$$

$$\text{Average} = 84$$

Eliminate Choice (D) right away because Justin's average can't possibly increase when he divides by 8 rather than 7. Any answer greater than 96 has to be wrong. If you picked either Choice (A) or Choice (B), you probably just guessed. The correct answer is Choice (C).

Mastering medians

The *median* is the middle value in a list of several values or numbers. To find out the median, list the values or numbers in order, usually from low to high, and choose the value that falls exactly in the middle of the other values. If you have an odd number of values, just select the middle value. If you have an even number of values, find the two middle values and average them. The outcome is the median.

Managing modes

The *mode* is the value that occurs most often in a set of values. For example, you may be asked what income occurs most frequently in a particular sample population. If more people in the population or sample have an income of $45,000 than any other income amount, the mode is $45,000. Every now and then, you may have a question with more than one mode, so don't panic if you get a set of values with two or more numbers that fit the bill. For example, in the set {2, 2, 3, 3, 3, 4, 5, 5, 5}, both 3 and 5 are modes.

Following the Order of Operations

Because test-makers like to throw you off your game every now and then, you may see one equation that requires you to perform a bunch of operations. It's going to look a little messy, but we promise you can solve it fairly easily by following this specific order of operations:

1. Start with the parentheses.

2. Move on to the exponents (and roots).

3. **Then multiply and divide, from left to right.**

4. **Finally, add and subtract, again from left to right.**

You can use a handy phrase to help you remember the proper order. The traditional phrase is "Please Excuse My Dear Aunt Sally," but we've come up with a different one just to keep things interesting. Are you ready for it? Here it is: **P**olly **E**lf **M**akes **D**olls **A**nd **S**hoes. Use whichever phrase you think is easier to remember (although we're willing to bribe you to tell all of your friends about our version).

Enough talk. Here's a sample equation, just for you.

$2(7 - 4)^3 - 15 \div 3 + 1 = ?$

The first word of the catchphrase (**Polly**) tells you to solve what's in the parentheses first.

$2(3)^3 - 15 \div 3 + 1 = ?$

The next word (**Elf**) tells you to deal with the exponents.

$2 \times 27 - 15 \div 3 + 1 = ?$

The next two words (**Makes** and **Dolls**) tell you to multiply and divide.

You don't necessarily multiply before you divide; you just move from left to right. But do always multiply and divide before you add and subtract.

$54 - 15 \div 3 + 1 = ?$

$54 - 5 + 1 = ?$

The final words (**And Shoes**) tell you to do the addition and subtraction from left to right.

$49 + 1 = ?$

Looks like the final answer is 50. That wasn't too hard now, was it?

Chapter 11

Venturing into the Unknown
with Variables

Algebra's really just a form of arithmetic with symbols, usually letters, standing in for numbers. You use algebra to solve equations and to find the value of a variable. Whenever you're asked to solve an equation for *x*, you're working with algebra.

The various Catholic high school entrance exams test elementary algebra, so you're not at a disadvantage if you've never taken an advanced algebra course. As long as you have a good understanding of the basics, you'll be just fine. We provide a little refresher on those basics in this chapter.

Variables 101: Flashing Back to the Basics

As you probably recall, you encounter a lot of variables in algebra problems. *Variables* are merely symbols that stand in for numbers. Usually the symbols take the form of letters and represent specific numeric values. True to their name, variables' values can change depending on the equation they're in.

Think of variables as stand-ins for concrete things. For example, if a store charges a certain price per apple and a different price for each orange and you buy two apples and four oranges, the clerk can't just ring up your purchase by adding 2 + 4 to get 6 and then applying one price. That would be incorrectly comparing apples and oranges! In algebra, you use variables to stand in for the price of apples and oranges, something, for instance, like *a* for apple and *o* for orange. When you include variables, the equation to figure out the total price of your order looks something like this:

$(2 \times a) + (4 \times o)$ = Total cost of apples and oranges

Instead of using the × sign to show multiplication, algebra equations indicate multiplication by simply placing the number right next to the variable, like so:

$2a + 4o$ = Total cost

The combination of a number and a variable multiplied together is called a *term*. In the case of your fruit shopping spree, $2a$ and $4o$ are both terms. The number part of the term has a fancy name; it's called the *coefficient*. When you have a collection of these terms joined by addition and/or subtraction, you've got yourself an *algebraic expression*.

Terms that have the same variable (and the same exponents on those variables), even if they have different coefficients, are called *like terms*. For example, you may see an expression that looks something like this:

$$5x + 3y - 2x + y = ?$$

$5x$ and $-2x$ are like terms because they both contain an x variable; $3y$ and y are also like terms because they both contain the y variable and only the y variable.

To combine like terms, add or subtract their coefficients. In this example, you combine the x terms by adding 5 and -2. To combine the y terms, you add the coefficients of 3 and 1 (because y is really $1y$). Your original expression with four terms simplifies to $3x + 4y$.

If a variable doesn't have a coefficient next to it, its coefficient is 1.

Coming to Terms with Basic Algebraic Equations

You use the same tools to solve algebraic equations that you use to solve basic arithmetic problems. But where arithmetic uses numbers with clear values, such as $4 + 5 = 9$, in its operations (flip to Chapter 10 for more on basic arithmetic operations), algebra problems deal with unknowns, such as $x + y = z$. You can't find a definite answer to this problem because you don't know what values x and y represent, let alone what z represents. But venturing into the unknown shouldn't stop you from solving algebra problems as best you can with the given information. Just rely on your old friends — the basic arithmetic operations. That's right. You can still add, subtract, multiply, and divide even when an expression contains a bunch of variables. The following sections show you how to do just that and more.

Adding and subtracting by keeping like with like

Adding and subtracting expressions with variables is pretty simple as long as you remember that you can only add and subtract like terms. Your exam may try to trick you into thinking you can combine terms with different variables in this same manner. Don't fall for it. If you have the expression $3x + 5y$, you can't do any more adding or subtracting unless you know the actual value of either x or y.

Pretend for a moment that you're in charge of buying doughnuts for your annual class Groundhog Day party. To feed the crowd, you purchase 4 dozen chocolate doughnuts and 7 dozen jelly doughnuts for a total of 11 dozen. You know that 1 dozen equals 12 doughnuts, so you use the basic operations of addition and multiplication to write an equation that shows how many doughnuts you purchased.

$$(4 \times 12) + (7 \times 12) = (11 \times 12)$$

But you can also write this equation by using a variable, like x, to stand in for one dozen.

$$4x + 7x = 11x$$

And you can subtract to get the opposite result.

$$11x - 7x = 4x$$

Don't forget to combine positive and negative numbers according to the rules of arithmetic. If you add two or more numbers in an expression, they keep the positive sign. If you add a positive number to a negative number, you may as well be subtracting. (See Chapter 10 for an additional refresher on the rules of arithmetic.)

Here's a sample question to show you how the entrance exams may test you on adding and subtracting terms.

What is equal to $10x - 5x + 3x$?

(A) $8x$

(B) 18

(C) 8

(D) $2x$

To answer this question, focus on the coefficients. You know you can add the two positive numbers (10 and 3) and subtract the negative number (5). Well, $10 + 3 = 13$, and $13 - 5 = 8$. Remember to tack on the variable to come up with the right answer of $8x$, which is Choice (A). If you picked Choice (C), you jumped the gun and chose your answer before you included the x variable. Choice (B) is wrong for two reasons: It adds 5 instead of subtracting it, and it ignores that all-important x variable. Choice (D) includes the x variable but adds and subtracts incorrectly.

Adding and subtracting like terms is a piece of cake, you say? Hold on just a second because your entrance exam may also make you simplify expressions that contain unlike terms. Take a look at this problem.

What is the value of $3x - 2y + 5x - 4y$?

(A) $2xy$

(B) $8x - 2y$

(C) $8x - 6y$

(D) $x + y$

If you tried to add and subtract all the terms, you'd come up with Choice (A), and your answer would be marked wrong. Instead, you have to separate the terms with the x variable from the terms with the y variable and *then* add and subtract. So in this problem, you realize that the $3x$ and the $5x$ hang out together and the $-2y$ and $-4y$ keep each other company. Add the x terms: $3x + 5x = 8x$. Combine the y terms: $-2y - 4y = -6y$. Put it all together and voilà! You get $8x - 6y$, which is Choice (C). That's it. You're done. You can't do any more because there are no more like terms. (***Note:*** If you went for Choice (B), you added $2y$ instead of subtracting it; if you picked Choice (D), you weren't paying attention to like terms when you tackled the problem.)

You can't combine terms with different symbols or variables the way you can when the symbols or variables are the same. When adding and subtracting, like terms must always be kept together; unlike terms should stay far, far away from each other, never to be mixed.

Multiplying and dividing terms with variables

Not only can you add and subtract expressions with variables (as explained in the preceding section) but you can also multiply and divide them. The rules you need to know for your entrance exam are pretty simple.

✔ To multiply like variables, add the exponents and keep the variable the same:

$$x \times x = x^2$$
$$y^2 \times y^3 = y^5$$

✔ Divide like variables by subtracting the exponents and keeping the variable the same:

$$w^4 \div w^7 = w^{-3}$$
$$b^5 \div b^3 = b^2$$

You can apply the distributive property of multiplication over addition to variables, too. (Flip to Chapter 10 for more on this property.) For instance, when you multiply a number by two terms added together, you multiply the number by each term in the parentheses. So $2(x + y) = 2x + 2y$.

Mastering multiple operations with variable expressions

Problems that ask you to add, subtract, and multiply terms with variables don't crop up too often on the various Catholic high school entrance exams, but when they do, you'll congratulate yourself for knowing how to answer them. Here's a sample question that gives you a chance to do all three operations.

Simplify $2x(x + 3) - 3x$.

(A) $6x$

(B) $2x^2 + 3x$

(C) $2x^2 - 3x$

(D) 3

The word *simplify* in a math problem means you must add, subtract, multiply, or divide terms until there's nothing more you can do.

According to the order of operations (abbreviated as PEMDAS; see Chapter 10 for the full scoop), you solve what's going on in the parentheses first. But you can't simplify $(x + 3)$ any further because x and 3 aren't alike, meaning they don't have the same variables.

The problem doesn't have any exponents, so the next operation to look at is multiplication. Turns out you can use the distributive property to multiply $2x$ by $(x + 3)$. Here's how:

1. **Multiply $2x$ and x.**

   The variable in the two terms is the same (x), so you can multiply them. Add the exponents and keep the number and variable the same: $2x \times x = 2x^2$.

2. **Multiply $2x$ and 3.**

   2×3 is 6, so you get $6x$.

3. **Add the resulting terms.**

   The sum is $2x^2 + 6x$. You can't simplify that any further because you can't add variables with different exponents.

So far your simplification gives you this expression: $2x^2 + 6x - 3x$. Now you just need to subtract the like terms ($6x - 3x$) to get $3x$. Tada! You're done! The simplified expression is $2x^2 + 3x$, which looks an awful lot like Choice (B), the correct answer. If you picked Choice (A), you just added and subtracted without considering that you need to work with like terms. You got Choice (C) if you mistakenly found $-3x$ when you subtracted $3x$ from $6x$. If you picked Choice (D), you distributed $2x$ incorrectly.

Most of the math questions on the Catholic high school entrance exams aren't terribly complex. (But if you're still concerned, we suggest you head to Chapter 16 for some additional practice using the various arithmetic operations with variable expressions.)

Isolating variables to figure out what they are

A few math questions on your exam will contain an unknown variable (usually x) that you must solve for. Here are two things to keep in mind when you're solving for a variable:

✔ Isolate the variable in the equation you're trying to solve by getting it all alone on one side of the equal sign.

✔ Whatever operation you perform on one side of the equal sign, you also have to perform on the other side.

A math question that asks you to solve for a variable may look like the following problem.

Where $2x + 10 = 20$, solve for x.

(A) 20

(B) 10

(C) 0

(D) 5

You can only solve for x by getting it all by itself on one side of the equal sign. Fortunately, here you can isolate x in just two simple steps:

1. **Eliminate 10 from the picture by subtracting it from both sides of the equation.**

   Here's what happens when you subtract 10 from the left and right sides of the equation:

$$2x + 10 = 20$$
$$2x + 10 - 10 = 20 - 10$$
$$2x = 10$$

2. **Divide both sides by 2 to find out what x is.**

$$\frac{2x}{2} = \frac{10}{2}$$
$$\frac{\cancel{2}x}{\cancel{2}} = \frac{10}{2}$$
$$x = 5$$

Because $x = 5$, the correct answer is Choice (D). If you wound up with any of the other answers, you performed the operations incorrectly.

To test your answer, plug it back into the original equation in place of the variable and see whether both sides are in fact equal. Here, $2(5) + 10 = 10 + 10 = 20$, so you're in the clear. If your answer doesn't match up, however, you need to recheck your work.

Tackle division problems the same way. So, if you're asked to solve for x in this problem, $\frac{x}{4} = 5$, you know what to do. Isolate x to the left-hand side of the equal sign by multiplying both sides of the equation by 4.

$$\frac{x}{4} = 5$$
$$\frac{x}{4} \times 4 = 5 \times 4$$
$$\frac{x}{4} \times 4 = 20$$
$$x = 20$$

Substituting to solve equations

It doesn't happen often, but every now and then the HSPT, TACHS, and COOP throw out an equation with two different variables and ask you to solve for one of 'em. You can solve an equation that contains two different variables as long as you have another equation that contains at least one of the variables. Then all you have to do is substitute the value of one of the variables into the equation and solve for the other variable. The following sample question shows you what that substitution looks like.

If $4x + 5y = 30$ and $y = 2$, solve for x.

(A) 2

(B) 5

(C) 10

(D) 15

Perhaps you're wondering how you can possibly solve for one unknown when you have yet another unknown. Never fear. The second equation gives you the value of one of the unknowns, so you're actually ready to start solving! The problem tells you that $y = 2$, so all you have to do is put 2 in the place of y and solve for x, like so:

$$4x + 5y = 30$$
$$4x + 5(2) = 30$$
$$4x + 10 = 30$$
$$4x + 10 - 10 = 30 - 10$$
$$4x = 20$$
$$\frac{4x}{4} = \frac{20}{4}$$
$$\frac{4x}{4} = \frac{20}{4}$$
$$x = 5$$

Choice (B) is the answer you're looking for, but any of the other choices may seem right if you mess up while performing the operations.

Sometimes substitution problems take the form of age problems. Trust that these complex-sounding word problems are really just asking you to perform simple substitution. Also, age questions show up rarely on the Catholic high school entrance exams, so don't keep yourself up at night expecting you'll have to face one.

Knowing More Than Enough about Inequalities

Mathematical expressions don't always have to show equal sides. You may in fact see a few *symbols of inequality,* signs that mean values aren't equal to each other or that one value is greater or less than another.

In addition to the symbols for addition, subtraction, multiplication, and division, mathematics also applies standard symbols to show how the two sides of an equation are related. You're probably pretty familiar with these symbols, but a little review never hurts. Table 11-1 gives you a rundown of the more common symbols used in algebra to signify inequality. Expect to see them on your entrance exam.

Table 11-1	Mathematical Symbols for Inequality
Symbol	**Meaning**
≠	Not equal to
>	Greater than
<	Less than
≥	Greater than or equal to
≤	Less than or equal to

When you use the greater than or less than symbols, always position the wide side of the arrow toward the bigger value, like this: 5 > 2 or 2 < 5. If it helps, you can think of the greater than and less than symbols as sharks and the numbers as fish. The shark always goes for the bigger fish, which just so happens to be the bigger value.

You can solve for x in simple inequalities just like you do in equations by adding or subtracting the same number to or from both sides of the inequality, as well as multiplying and dividing both sides by the same number.

$$x + 6 \leq 0$$
$$x + 6 - 6 \leq 0 - 6$$
$$x \leq -6$$

When you multiply or divide both sides of an inequality by a negative number, you have to reverse the direction of the inequality symbol. For example, when you simplify $-2x < 6$ by dividing both sides by -2 to isolate x, you switch the symbol so that the final answer is $x > -3$.

You can also use inequalities to show a range of numbers as opposed to one single value. For instance, your entrance exam may show the range of integers between -3 and $+2$ as an inequality, like this: $-3 < x < 2$. This expression, called a *compound inequality,* means that x could be any of these numbers: $-2, -1, 0,$ and 1.

To show the range of -3 and $+2$ including -3 and $+2$, you'd use the ≤ sign: $-3 \leq x \leq 2$. Now integers represented by x include all of these possibilities: $-3, -2, -1, 0, 1,$ and 2.

Note that you can separate compound inequalities into two separate inequalities, using the variable in each of the new inequalities. Saying $-3 \leq x \leq 2$ is the same as saying $x \geq -3$ and $x \leq 2$.

The following example problem shows you how inequalities generally appear on the Catholic high school entrance exams.

If $3 > x > -1$, and x is an odd integer, what does x equal?

(A) 2

(B) 0

(C) 1

(D) –1

Use the process of elimination to narrow your choices. The problem says that x is odd, so you know that Choices (A) and (B) are wrong. Neither 2 nor 0 are odd (for more about odd and even integers, see Chapter 10). Because x is greater than –1, it can't equal –1. Consequently, Choice (D) is out. The answer must be Choice (C) because you know that x is between 3 and –1. Therefore, the possible integers for x are 2, 1, and 0. The only odd integer in that list is 1.

Chapter 12

Getting the Right Angle on Geometry Problems

*B*ecause most students don't take a geometry class until they hit high school, you're probably wondering what you're going to do about these questions on your Catholic high school entrance exam. Well, geometry questions on the HSPT, TACHS, and COOP cover the basics, things like measuring angles and working with basic shapes. We're pretty sure you've seen most of these fundamental concepts in the math classes you've had so far, but in case you've missed (or forgotten) something important, this chapter is here to help. (*Note:* Some of the geometry problems require you to use basic math and algebra to solve them, so make sure to refer to Chapters 10 and 11 if you need refreshers in these areas.)

Walking the Straight and Narrow (And Sometimes Wide) of Lines and Angles

Lines and angles form the foundation of geometry, but perhaps it has been a while since you've thought about the properties of lines or contemplated the elements of angles. Fortunately, the following sections present some important definitions and vital rules you need to know before you tackle geometry questions on test day.

Defining lines and angles

You don't need to make flashcards and memorize the following definitions for your entrance exam, but you do need to be familiar with them. Here are the common terms about lines and angles that may pop up on your test:

✔ **Line:** A straight path of points that extends forever in two directions. Arrows sometimes show that the line goes on forever in either direction. See Line *AB* in Figure 12-1.

✔ **Line segment:** The set of points on a line between any two points on that line. Basically, it's just a piece of a line from one point to another that contains those points and all the points in between. See Line Segment *CD* in Figure 12-1.

Figure 12-1:
A line
and line
segment.

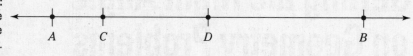

✔ **Midpoint:** The point halfway (an equal distance) between two endpoints on a line segment. In Figure 12-1, Point D is the midpoint between Points A and B.

✔ **Intersect:** To cross. Two lines can intersect each other much like two streets cross each other at an intersection.

✔ **Vertical line:** A line that runs straight up and down. Figure 12-2 shows you an example of this and the three other kinds of lines.

✔ **Horizontal line:** A line that runs straight across from left to right. Check one out in Figure 12-2.

✔ **Parallel lines:** Lines that run in the same direction and keep the same distance apart. Parallel lines never intersect one another, as illustrated in Figure 12-2.

✔ **Perpendicular lines:** Two lines that intersect to form a square corner. The intersection of two perpendicular lines forms a right, or 90°, angle (see Figure 12-2).

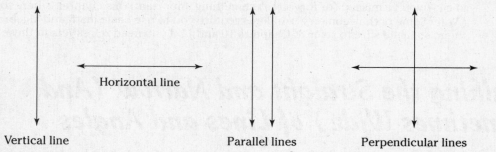

Horizontal line

Figure 12-2:
Types of
lines.

Vertical line   Parallel lines   Perpendicular lines

✔ **Angle:** The intersection of two line segments that share an endpoint (called a *vertex*). An angle is usually measured in degrees or radians.

✔ **Acute angle:** Any angle measuring less than 90°. Like an acute, or sharp, pain, an acute angle has a sharp point. Another way of looking at it is that acute angles are small and therefore "cute." See Figure 12-3.

✔ **Right, or perpendicular, angle:** An angle measuring exactly 90°. It makes up a square corner. If an angle on your entrance exam has a little square like the one in Figure 12-3, you know it's a right angle.

✔ **Obtuse angle:** An angle that measures more than 90° but less than 180°. The opposite of an acute angle, an obtuse angle is dull rather than sharp. Figure 12-3 shows what an obtuse angle looks like.

✔ **Straight angle:** An angle that measures exactly 180°. A straight angle looks just like a straight line, as shown in Figure 12-3.

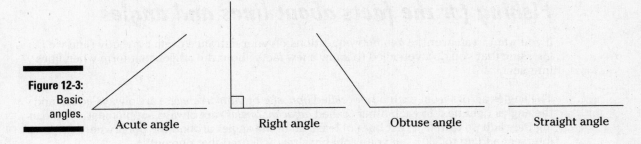

Figure 12-3:
Basic
angles.

Acute angle   Right angle   Obtuse angle   Straight angle

✔ **Complementary angles:** Angles that add together to total 90°. When you put them together, they create a right angle like the one in Figure 12-4.

✔ **Supplementary angles:** Angles that add together to total 180°. Together they form a straight angle (see Figure 12-4).

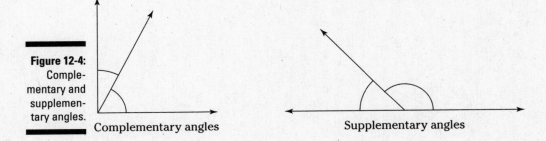

Figure 12-4:
Comple-
mentary and
supplemen-
tary angles.

Complementary angles   Supplementary angles

Knowing these definitions is important because your entrance exam may ask direct questions about them, much like this sample question.

This angle measures 123°. What type of angle is it?

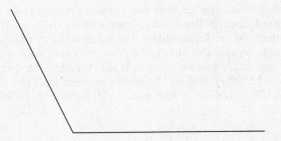

(A) obtuse

(B) right

(C) acute

(D) perpendicular

Without even looking at the figure, you can eliminate Choices (B) and (D). Right and perpendicular refer to the same type of angle, and you can't have two right answers. So, the angle is either obtuse or acute. Remember that acute angles are sharp and little. The angle on the figure is dull and wide — the measure of the angle is more than 90°, which makes it obtuse. The answer is Choice (A).

Fishing for the facts about lines and angles

If you want to answer the geometry questions on your entrance exam correctly (and we're guessing that you do), you need to know a few facts about the angles that form when lines intersect.

The angles across from each other (called *opposite* or *vertical angles*) are always equal, and the angles right next to each other (called *adjacent angles*) are always supplementary (meaning they add up to 180°). Last but not least, all of the angles around the point where the lines intersect add up to 360°, but you probably already figured that one out!

Your entrance exam may refer to an angle by using the symbol that means angle, ∠, and listing its three points. The *vertex* is the middle point.

In Figure 12-5, ∠ABD and ∠EBC are equal, and ∠EBA and ∠CBD are equal. ∠ABD and ∠CBD form a straight line, which makes them supplementary. All the other angles that form straight lines are also supplementary.

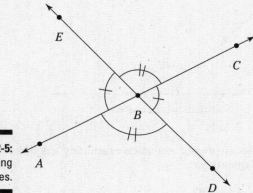

Figure 12-5:
Intersecting
lines.

When you see parallel lines that are crossed by another line (called a *transversal*), you know a lot about the angles that are formed. Each of the small angles is equal to each other, and the large angles are also equal to each other. Additionally, the measurement of any small angle added to that of any large angle equals 180°. In Figure 12-6, the small angles are marked with one short line, and the large angles are marked with two short lines. All the angles marked with one line are equal to each other, and all the angles marked with two lines are equal to each other. (So ∠ACB = ∠ADE = ∠HCF = ∠GDF, and ∠ACH = ∠BCF = ∠ADG = ∠EDF.) Pretty simple, huh?

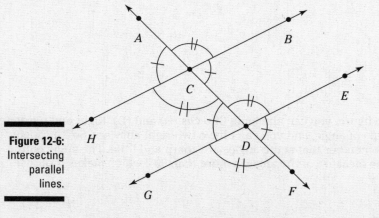

Figure 12-6:
Intersecting
parallel
lines.

Following is a sample question that tests your ability to use what you know about the angles formed by intersecting lines.

In the following figure, Line *m* and Line *n* are parallel, and Line *t* crosses both lines. Given the information contained in this figure, what is the value of *e*?

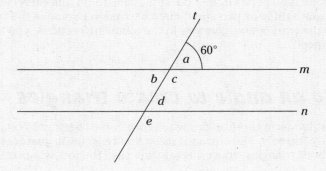

(A) 30°

(B) 60°

(C) 100°

(D) 120°

(E) None of the above

Attention all COOP-takers: In the math portion, you may occasionally see an extra answer tacked on that gives you the option to bow out of any of the other answer choices. Don't fret too much about it. Just solve the question like you would any other math problem. If you don't see the right answer among the first four choices, the correct answer is probably "None of the above."

At first it may look like the picture doesn't give you enough information to answer the question, but when you apply the facts about intersecting parallel lines, you find that you already know everything you need to to uncover the right answer. Here's what you know (get ready; it's an impressive amount):

- Lines *m* and *n* are parallel.

- Angle *a* is 60°.

- Angle *a* + Angle *c* = 180° because *a* and *c* form a straight line and angles on a straight line add up to 180°.

- Angle *c* must be 120° because 180 − 60 = 120.

- Angle *c* is equal to *e* because they're both large angles formed by the parallel lines and the intersecting line.

- The value of *e* is 120° because *c* = *e* and *c* = 120°.

The correct answer is Choice (D). If you picked any of the other answers, you either subtracted incorrectly or you didn't recognize that *a* and *c* are supplementary angles and that *c* and *e* are equal.

Getting into Basic Shapes

Lines and angles (covered in depth earlier in this chapter) are the building blocks of most of the shapes you'll see on your entrance exam. The general term for closed shapes made of lines and angles is *polygon*. Three connected line segments form a *triangle;* connect four lines together, and you get a *quadrilateral*. You can create shapes with a larger number of lines, but the various entrance exams generally focus on triangles and quadrilaterals.

However, they also spend a bit of time on circles. When you think about it, even circles can result from lines and angles. If you connect a bunch of lines that end in points an equal distance away from a center point, you get a circle. You won't have to do this exercise for your test, but you will have to know a thing or two about circles to answer some of the geometry problems. Never fear. With the workout we give you in the following sections, you'll be in good shape for tackling shapes!

Adding a line to an angle to create triangles

What shape has three sides that form three angles when they come together? You guessed it: a *triangle* (with *tri* meaning "three"). The entrance exam you're facing is guaranteed to test how much you know about triangles, so we suggest you read the following sections carefully.

Presenting your personal crash course in triangle properties and types

Time to get into the nitty-gritty of triangles. First things first: understanding how triangles are named. The points where the three sides of a triangle come together form angles. Triangles are named by the points where the three lines come together, so a triangle with points labeled *A*, *B*, and *C* is called $\triangle ABC$.

One of the most important facts to know about triangles is that for every kind of triangle, the measurements of the three angles always add up to 180°.

It also helps to know that triangles have great proportions. The opposite sides of angles are proportionate to those angles, which means the smallest angle faces the shortest side, and the largest angle is opposite the longest side. If two or more angles have the same measurement, their opposite sides are equal.

Finally, you should be able to recognize the following special triangles at a glance:

- An **equilateral triangle** has three equal sides and three equal angles, like the one in Figure 12-7. Because the three angles add up to 180°, the value of each of the angles in an equilateral triangle is 60° (180 ÷ 3 = 60).

- An **isosceles triangle** has two equal sides, and the values of the angles opposite those two sides are also equal. An example is shown in Figure 12-7.

- A **right triangle,** like the one in Figure 12-7, has one angle that measures 90°. The side opposite the right angle is called the *hypotenuse*. The other two sides are called the *legs* (but no, triangles can't walk).

Figure 12-7:
Equilateral,
isosceles,
and right
triangles.

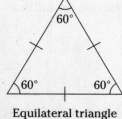

Equilateral triangle

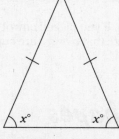

Isosceles triangle

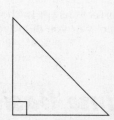

Right triangle

Calculating the area and perimeter of a triangle

Be prepared for the entrance exam you're facing to include questions about the perimeter or area of a triangle. The *perimeter of a triangle* is the measurement around the outside of the triangle. To find it, just add the lengths of all three sides together. So the perimeter of a triangle with side lengths of 2 feet, 3 feet, and 4 feet would be 9 feet (2 + 3 + 4 = 9). Perimeter questions are usually pretty easy, but they may throw in some extra work like this sample question does.

The long side of an isosceles triangle measures 8 inches, and one of the two short sides measures 5 inches. What is the perimeter of the triangle?

(A) 5 inches

(B) 10 inches

(C) 18 inches

(D) 40 inches

The question tells you that the triangle is isosceles, so you know that two of the sides are equal. There's one long side and two shorter sides, which means the two shorter sides must be the equal ones. Therefore, the three side lengths, in inches, are 8, 5, and 5. Add the sides together to get a perimeter of 18 inches, Choice (C). If you picked Choice (A), you probably got so excited about figuring out the other side length that you forgot to add it to the two other sides. Choice (D) is the result of multiplying the two known side lengths, which isn't how you figure out perimeter. If you came up with Choice (B), you either didn't add correctly or didn't understand how to calculate the perimeter.

The *area of a triangle* is the measurement of all the space inside the triangle. To find a triangle's area, you must use this formula: $A = \frac{1}{2}bh$. *A* stands for (what else?) area, *b* is the length of the base (often — but not always — the bottom) of the triangle, and *h* stands for the height (or *altitude*) of the triangle, which is the distance that a perpendicular line runs from the base to the angle opposite the base. Check out Figure 12-8 for a helpful visual.

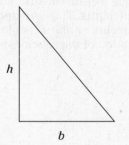
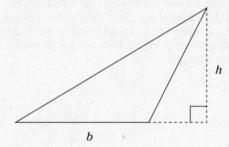

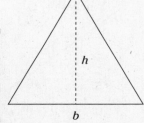
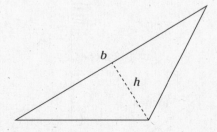

Figure 12-8: The base and height of various triangles.

The height of a triangle is always perpendicular to the base, and it can be shown either inside or outside the triangle.

Care to try your hand at a triangle area question? Be our guest.

A triangle with an area of 6 square centimeters has a base of 4 centimeters. What is the triangle's height in centimeters?

(A) 3

(B) 4

(C) 10

(D) 24

Test-takers who have no idea what to do may just multiply 4 and 6 and pick Choice (D). But you're better prepared. Attack this question by substituting information into the formula for finding the area of a triangle. Insert 6 in the place of *A* and 4 in the place of *b*. Then solve for *h*, like so:

$$A = \frac{1}{2}bh$$
$$6 = \frac{1}{2}(4)(h)$$
$$6 = 2h$$
$$\frac{6}{2} = \frac{\cancel{2}h}{\cancel{2}}$$
$$3 = h$$

The answer is pretty clearly Choice (A). Guessing is the only way to come up with Choice (B) or Choice (C).

Seeing the resemblance in similar triangles

Triangles are *similar* when they have exactly the same angle measurements. Similar triangles have the same shape, but their sides can be different lengths. The corresponding sides of similar triangles are in proportion to each other. The heights or altitudes of the two triangles are also in proportion. Figure 12-9 provides an illustration of the relationship between two similar triangles.

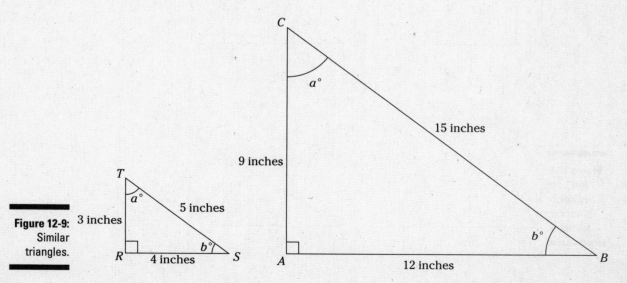

Figure 12-9: Similar triangles.

In Figure 12-9, △*ABC* and △*RST* are similar and have a *scale factor* of 3 (meaning one triangle is three times as large as the other one). Side *AB* is three times as long as Side *RS*, Side *BC* is three times as long as Side *ST*, and Side *AC* is three times as long as Side *RT*. Also, the area of △*ABC* is 9 (or 3^2) times as great as that of △*RST*.

Knowing about similar triangles helps you answer questions like this one.

△*RTS* and △*ACB* are similar right triangles. What is the measurement, in inches, of Line *AB*?

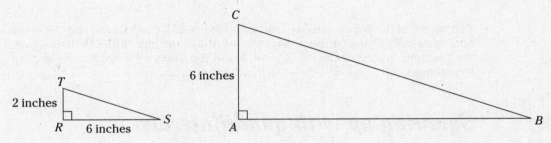

(A) 10 inches

(B) 12 inches

(C) 18 inches

(D) 24 inches

Because the two triangles are similar, you can use what you know about △*RTS* to find the base measurement of △*ACB*. *CA* is three times greater than *TR*, so *AB* must be three times greater than *RS*. The measurement of *RS* is 6 inches, and 6×3 is 18. So the measurement of *AB* must be 18 inches, Choice (C). If you picked any other choice, you didn't grasp the concept of similar triangles.

Theorizing with Pythagoras

An important triangle rule that applies only to right triangles is the *Pythagorean theorem*, which states that $a^2 + b^2 = c^2$, where *c* is the measure of the hypotenuse and *a* and *b* are measures of the legs. The *hypotenuse* is always the longest of the three sides and is across from the right angle. Here's an example of a Pythagorean theorem question you may encounter.

The following triangle is a right triangle, and the two legs (shorter sides) are 6 inches and 8 inches. What is the measurement, in inches, of the hypotenuse?

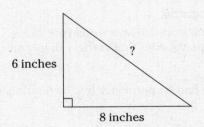

(A) 10 inches

(B) 14 inches

(C) 24 inches

(D) 48 inches

The two legs, *a* and *b*, are 6 inches and 8 inches respectively, so all you have to do is substitute those values into the formula and solve.

$$a^2 + b^2 = c^2$$
$$6^2 + 8^2 = c^2$$
$$36 + 64 = c^2$$
$$100 = c^2$$
$$10 = c$$

The length of the hypotenuse is 10 inches, Choice (A). Choices (B) and (D) result from adding or multiplying (respectively) the lengths of the legs rather than plugging them into the theorem. If you got Choice (C), you found the triangle's area, not the length of the hypotenuse.

Squaring up with quadrilaterals

Quadrilateral is just a fancy term for a closed shape that has four sides and four angles. Squares and rectangles are two classic examples of quadrilaterals. For your entrance exam, you may need to know a little bit about the properties of quadrilaterals and how to find their areas and perimeters. The next sections are here to help.

Examining parallelograms

The kinds of quadrilaterals you'll see on your entrance exam are usually parallelograms.

Parallelograms have several properties that are good to know for solving math problems:

- The opposite sides are parallel and equal in length.
- The measurements of the opposite angles are equal to each other.
- The measurements of the two angles next to each other add up to 180°.
- The measurements of the four angles always add up to 360°.

Several types of parallelograms exist, but here are the two that appear most frequently on the HSPT, TACHS, and COOP:

- A **rectangle** is a parallelogram with four right angles.
- A **square** is a rectangle with four equal sides.

Finding the perimeter and area of parallelograms

The *perimeter of a parallelogram* is the measurement all the way around the shape's sides. To find the perimeter of any parallelogram (or any polygon for that matter) simply add up the measurements of all four sides.

Because a square has four equal sides, you can find its perimeter just by multiplying the length of one side by 4.

The *area of a parallelogram* is the value of the space inside the parallelogram. Here's the formula you use to find it: $A = bh$. In this case, *b* stands for the base (or bottom) of the figure, and *h* stands for the height.

Another way of stating the formula for the area of a rectangle (which, as you're well aware, is a parallelogram) is this: *Area = length × width*. In rectangles and squares, the base and height are referred to as the length and width, where the length is always the longer side and the width is always the shorter side. Of course, in a square, both the length and the width are equal to one another. Figure 12-10 gives you the visual.

Figure 12-10: Area of a rectangle.

w

l

Because a square has four equal sides, you can easily find its area if you know the length of only one side. The area of a square can be expressed as $A = s^2$ or $A = s \times s$, where s is the length of a side.

Handling polygons with more than four sides

Just to make life interesting, your entrance exam may throw some polygons with more than four sides into the mix. No set formula exists for determining the area of a polygon with more than four sides. Instead, you need to focus on creating quadrilaterals and triangles within the polygon, finding their areas, and adding them together to get the total area of the polygon.

You may recall that the sum of the angles of a triangle is 180° and that the sum of the angles of a quadrilateral is 360°. Are you starting to detect a pattern here? Just add another 180° and you have the sum of the angles in a five-sided polygon — 540°. But if you had to add the angles up like this every time, you'd soon run out of fingers to count on. So here's a formula for determining the sum of the interior angles of any polygon:

Sum of the angles = $(n - 2) \times 180°$, where n is equal to the number of sides

If the polygon is *regular* (meaning all the sides and angles are equal), you can also determine the measure of the individual angles by dividing the sum of the angles by the total number of angles. Therefore, each angle in a regular pentagon measures 540 ÷ 5, or 108°.

Following is a sample question that tests your knowledge of angles in polygons.

What is the sum of the interior angles of a polygon that has seven sides?

(A) 180°

(B) 900°

(C) 360°

(D) 1,260°

First, apply the formula — $(n - 2) \times 180°$ — and substitute 7 for n. 7 − 2 is 5, and 5 × 180 is 900, so the answer is Choice (B). As for the other options, Choice (A) would be correct if you were working with a triangle, whereas Choice (C) is the sum of the interior angles in a quadrilateral. If you selected Choice (D), you forgot to subtract 2 from the number of sides in the polygon.

Piecing together circles

A *circle,* by technical definition, is a set of points in a plane that are at a fixed distance from a given point (called the *center*). Your entrance exam may include a few questions about the measurement of circles, so make sure you know all the info presented in the next three sections.

Circling 'round the basics: Radius and diameter

The *radius* of a circle is the distance from the center of the circle to any point on the circle. Think of it as a ray going out from the center to the edge of the circle. The radius is usually indicated by the letter *r*, as shown in Figure 12-11.

The *diameter* of a circle is the length of a line that goes from one side of the circle to the other and passes through the center. The diameter is twice the length of the radius, and it's the longest possible distance across the circle. Diameter is usually indicated by the letter *d*, as you can see in Figure 12-11.

If you know the radius of a circle, you can figure out the diameter simply by multiplying the radius by 2: $d = 2 \times r$.

Figure 12-11: The radius and diameter of a circle.

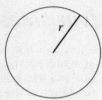 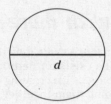

Calculating specific circle measurements: Circumference and area

The *circumference* of a circle is the distance around the circle. To figure out circumference (*C*), you can use one of two formulas:

- ✔ $C = 2\pi r$
- ✔ $C = \pi d$ (This is an option because $d = 2r$.)

The *area of a circle* is the value of the space within it. Here's the formula for calculating the area of a circle: $A = \pi r^2$. See the following section for more on π.

Getting acquainted with π

To find other measurements of a circle besides radius and diameter (such as area and circumference, discussed in the preceding section), you must be familiar with a little symbol called *pi* (π). π is a math value that's usually used in figuring out measurements involving circles and is approximately equal to 3.14. Following is a sample question that shows you how the entrance exams expect you to work with π.

What is the circumference of a circle with a radius of 4?

(A) 8π

(B) 16π

(C) 8

(D) 4π

You know that the formula for circumference is $2\pi r$, so just plug in 4 for r. 2×4 is 8, so the answer is Choice (A). If you picked Choice (B), you used the formula for area. Choice (C) neglects the presence of π, and Choice (D) forgets to multiply by 2.

Welcome to the 3-D World of Solid Figures

Solid geometry doesn't appear frequently on any of the Catholic high school entrance exams, so we don't go into a lot of detail about it. The following sections contain just enough information so that you won't be surprised by a question about rectangular solids, cubes, or cylinders on your exam.

Working with rectangular solids and cubes

You make a *rectangular solid* by taking a simple rectangle and adding depth. Good examples of rectangular solids are bricks and boxes of your favorite cereal. A rectangular solid has three dimensions: length, height, and width. The volume (V) of a rectangular solid takes all of these dimensions into account. It's a measure of how much space a rectangular solid occupies or, to put it in terms everyone can appreciate, how much cereal a cereal box holds.

The volume of an object is measured in cubic units. The formula for the volume of a rectangular solid is simply length (l) × width (w) × height (h). The short form looks like this: $V = lwh$.

A cube is a solid made of squares. Because the length, width, and height of a cube have the same measurement, the formula for the volume of a cube is even simpler: $V = s^3$, where s equals the measure of any of the cube's sides.

You can see what a rectangular solid and cube look like in Figure 12-12.

Rectangular solid   Rectangular cube

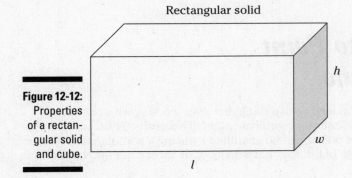

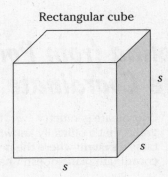

Figure 12-12: Properties of a rectangular solid and cube.

In case a solids question should appear on your exam, we want you to be prepared, so here's a sample one for your solving pleasure.

The side of a square box measures 2 feet. What is its volume in cubic feet?

(A) 4

(B) 2

(C) 8

(D) 16

You only need to know the measure of one of the sides of a cube to determine its volume because volume is the measure of the side cubed. $2 \times 2 \times 2 = 8$, so the answer you're looking for is Choice (C). Choice (A) is the area of a square with a side measurement of 2, not the volume of a similar-sided cube. If you opted for Choices (B) or (D), you probably didn't know the formula for the volume of a cube and simply guessed.

Summing up cylinders

A *cylinder* has a radius, a diameter, and a circumference, just like a circle, but it also has a third dimension — its height (or *altitude*). To get an idea of what a cylinder looks like, think of the shape of a soda can or just check out Figure 12-13.

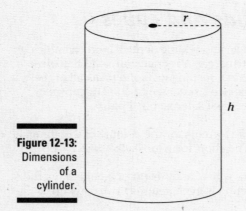

Figure 12-13: Dimensions of a cylinder.

To calculate the volume of a cylinder, you must first find the area of the base (a circle), which is πr^2, and multiply by the height (h) of the cylinder. Here's the formula: $V = \pi r^2 h$.

Traveling from Point to Point on the Coordinate Plane

Coordinate geometry (yes, there is indeed such a thing) involves working with points on a graph that's officially known as the *Cartesian coordinate plane*. This perfectly flat surface contains a system where the position of points can be identified by using a pair of numbers. The coordinate plane doesn't have wings, but it does have points that spread out into infinity.

Following are some of the coordinate geometry terms that show up from time to time on the various Catholic high school entrance exams:

- ✔ **x-axis:** The *x*-axis is the horizontal axis on a coordinate plane, where values or numbers start at the intersect point that has a value of 0. Numbers increase in value to the right of this point and decrease in value to the left of it. The *x* value of a point's coordinate is always listed first. All points along the *x*-axis have a *y* value of 0.

- ✔ **y-axis:** The *y*-axis is the vertical axis on a coordinate plane, where values or numbers start at the intersect point that has a value of 0. Numbers increase in value going up from this point and decrease in value going down from it. The *y* value of a point's coordinate is always listed second. All points along the *y*-axis have an *x* value of 0.

✔ **Origin:** The origin is the point (0,0) on the coordinate plain. It's where the *x*- and *y*-axes intersect.

✔ **Quadrant:** The intersection of the *x*- and *y*-axes forms four quadrants on the coordinate plane, which just so happen to be named Quadrants I, II, III, and IV.

✔ **Ordered pair:** An ordered pair is made up of two *coordinates,* which describe the location of a point in relation to the origin. The horizontal (*x*) coordinate is always listed first, and the vertical (*y*) coordinate is always listed second.

You can identify any point on the coordinate plane by its coordinates, which designate its location along the *x*- and *y*-axes. For example, the ordered pair (2,3) is a point that's located two places to the right of the origin along the horizontal (*x*) number line and three places up on the vertical (*y*) number line. In Figure 12-14, Point A is at (2,3). Pretty simple, huh?

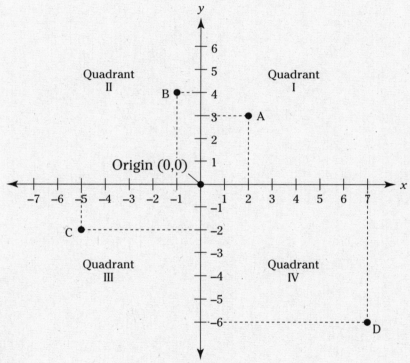

Figure 12-14:
Points on the coordinate plane.

When it comes to quadrants, Quadrant I starts to the right of the *y*-axis and above the *x*-axis. In other words, it's the upper-right portion of the coordinate plane. As shown in Figure 12-14, the other quadrants move counterclockwise around the origin.

Here's a short overview of what you can find in each quadrant (refer to Figure 12-14 to see where each specific point is located):

✔ **All points in Quadrant I have a positive *x* value and a positive *y* value.** Point A is in Quadrant I and has coordinates (2,3).

✔ **All points in Quadrant II have a negative *x* value and a positive *y* value.** Point B is in Quadrant II and has coordinates (−1,4).

✔ **All points in Quadrant III have a negative *x* value and a negative *y* value.** Point C is in Quadrant III and has coordinates (–5,–2).

✔ **All points in Quadrant IV have a positive *x* value and a negative *y* value.** Point D is in Quadrant IV and has coordinates (7,–6).

You may be asked to identify what quadrant a particular point belongs in, so know how to find where a given set of coordinates "flies" on the coordinate plane.

Chapter 13

Making Sense out of Math Word Problems

*N*ot all of the math questions on your Catholic high school entrance exam will contain one sentence or request that you simply "Solve for *x*." In fact, some of the math questions get downright wordy. They ask you to sift through bunches of information to figure out just what the real question is. These word problems require you to translate words into numbers and then arrange them in a way that makes mathematical sense. You know what we're talking about — those problems that tell you how fast Train A travels and what speed Train B moves along at and then expect you to figure out exactly what hour the two trains will collide. Yikes!

Don't worry; there's a system to all of this. Several words translate nicely into mathematical expressions; certain types of word problems, like work and rate problems, lend themselves perfectly to specific formulas or strategies; and graphs and maps can be downright fun to work with — all of which you discover in this chapter.

Translating English into Math

When you see a word problem on a math test, you may feel a little lost. Straightforward math equations seem so much more, well, straightforward. Even though they're written in English, word problems may read like a foreign language to you. To help you with the translation, Table 13-1 provides you with some of the more common words you'll encounter in word problems and tells you what they mean (and look like!) in math terms.

Table 13-1	Common Words & Their Math Counterparts
Plain English	**Math Equivalent**
More than, increased by, added to, combined with, total of, sum of	Add (+)
Decreased by, diminished by, reduced by, difference between, taken away from, subtracted from, less than, fewer than	Subtract (−)
Of, times, product of	Multiply (×)
Ratio of, per, out of, quotient	Divide (÷ or /)
Percent	÷ 100
Is, are, was, were, becomes, results in	Equals (=)
How much, how many, what, what number	Variable (usually *x* or *y*)

Subtraction phrases such as "taken away from," "subtracted from," "less than," and "fewer than" require you to switch the order of the quantities you're subtracting. For example, "Ten decreased by six" means 10 − 6 (which equals 4), but "Ten subtracted from six" is 6 − 10, or −4.

As you read through a word problem, analyze its language to determine what math operations it involves. First, figure out what you're supposed to solve for, specifically what the *x* is in the equation. Then analyze the rest of the information to figure out how you arrange the equation to solve for *x*.

Many of the word problems on the various entrance exams concern percentages, like this one.

To pay for college expenses, Ms. Bond takes out a loan in the amount of $650 with a simple interest rate of 8%. What is the total amount of the loan with interest?

(A) $658

(B) $52

(C) $702

(D) $1,170

The problem asks for the total amount (that's the *x*) of Ms. Bond's loan with (which means +) interest, so you have to add what she owes in interest to the original amount of the loan. Before you add the interest amount, you must find out what the amount of interest is. The language tells you that there's an interest rate *of* (meaning ×) 8% (which means you divide 8 by 100). Written with numbers rather than words, the problem would look something like this: $x = (8 \div 100) \times \$650 + \$650$. When you do the operation in parentheses first (as explained in Chapter 10), you find that 8 ÷ 100 is 0.08. Next, multiply $650 by 0.08: $650 × 0.08 = $52. Ms. Bond therefore pays $52 in interest. Add the interest amount to the loan amount to get your final answer: $650 + $52 = $702. The correct answer is Choice (C). If you picked Choice (A), you added 8 to $650, which isn't the proper way to determine interest. Choice (B) is the correct interest amount but not the total amount of the loan plus the interest. If you opted for Choice (D), you incorrectly divided 8 by 10 rather than 100 to come up with the interest amount.

Naming numerical place holders

The kind of place holders we're talking about are most definitely not the ones your grandmother uses to show where each family member sits at the Thanksgiving table! Instead, these place holders are the names you use to refer to the place each digit holds in a number. Here's a little chart that shows the name of each digit from millions to millionths for the rather unwieldy number 7,654,321.123456:

7	6	5	4	3	2	1	.	1	2	3	4	5	6
Millions	Hundred Thousands	Ten Thousands	Thousands	Hundreds	Tens	Ones	Decimal Point	Tenths	Hundredths	Thousandths	Ten Thousandths	Hundred Thousandths	Millionths

Punching the Clock: Work Problems

Work problems ask you to find out either how much work two or more workers get done in a certain amount of time or how long it takes two or more workers to complete a task together or individually. Following is the standard formula for algebra work problems:

Total production = (Rate of work × Time)Worker 1 + (Rate of work × Time)Worker 2

Total production refers to the amount of work that gets done. When you encounter work problems, find the information in the story that fills in the formula. Then solve. Here's an example of how you can apply this formula on an entrance exam work problem.

There are two furniture movers, Andy and Barbara. Andy can move 16 pieces of furniture per day, and Barbara can move 24 pieces per day. If they each work 8-hour days, how many pieces of furniture can the two of them move in 1 hour, assuming they maintain a steady rate?

(A) 2

(B) 5

(C) 40

(D) 160

This question asks you to find the amount of production and gives you the rate and the time. But to calculate the rate properly, you must state the hours in terms of days. Because a day is eight hours, one hour is ⅛ of a day. Figure out how much Andy loads in one hour (⅛ of a day) and add that to what Barbara loads in one hour:

> Total production = Andy's (work rate × time) + Barbara's (work rate × time)
>
> Total production = (16 × ⅛) + (24 × ⅛)
>
> Total production = 2 + 3
>
> Total production = 5

You now know that Andy and Barbara can load 5 pieces of furniture in 1 hour (⅛ of a day), which is Choice (B). If you picked Choice (C), you figured out the total production for 1 day rather than 1 hour. And if you selected one of the other two choices, well, that was just guessing.

Another type of work problem gives you the amount of time two workers take to complete a job alone and then asks you to find the amount of time they need to complete the job when they work together. For these types of questions, time is the unknown. Let the job (or total production) equal 1 because there's just one job to complete. Here's the formula:

$$1 = \frac{\text{Time spent on job working together}}{\text{Time spent on job working alone}} + \frac{\text{Time spent on job working together}}{\text{Time spent on job working alone}}$$

The first fraction represents the effort of the first worker, and the second fraction represents (not surprisingly) the effort of the second worker. An exam question of this type looks a little something like the following.

Sally can finish sewing a quilt in 3 days; Meg completes a quilt in 9 days. How many days does it take for the two women to sew a quilt if they work together?

(A) 6 days

(B) 4.5 days

(C) 1 day

(D) 2.25 days

Apply the formula. The unknown for both women is how much time each spends when they work together, so make that the x for both of them. You know the amount of time each woman spends alone, so enter those figures into the formula:

$$1 = \frac{x}{3} + \frac{x}{9}$$

To add the fractions, make the denominators the same (flip to Chapter 10 if you need a refresher on how to do this) and solve:

$$1 = \frac{3x}{9} + \frac{x}{9}$$
$$1 = \frac{3x + x}{9}$$
$$9 = 3x + x$$
$$9 = 4x$$
$$2.25 = x$$

It takes the women 2.25 days working together to sew one quilt, which is the answer in Choice (D). You can eliminate Choices (A) and (B) because it wouldn't take longer for the two women working together than it takes for Sally to sew a quilt alone. If you picked Choice (C), you probably just guessed.

Work problems are fairly rare on the Catholic high school entrance exams, so don't worry too much if you're not terribly fond of them. Who likes work, anyway?

Going the Distance: Rate Problems

Any problem involving distance, *rate* (just a fancy name for speed), or time spent traveling can be boiled down into the formula for computing distance: *Distance = Rate × Time*. Sure, that looks easy, but you can mess up quickly if you don't have your variables and numbers plugged in properly. With that in mind, check out this sample rate problem.

Paige can run a mile in 8 minutes. How long does it take her to run $\frac{1}{10}$ of a mile at the same rate?

(A) 30 seconds

(B) 48 seconds

(C) 60 seconds

(D) 480 seconds

The problem tells you that Paige's distance is $\frac{1}{10}$ of a mile. You can figure her rate to be $\frac{1}{8}$ because she runs 1 mile in 8 minutes. But because the problem is asking how long she runs, you need to solve for time. Plug the numbers into the distance formula:

$$\text{Distance} = \text{Rate} \times \text{Time}$$
$$\tfrac{1}{10} = \tfrac{1}{8} \times t$$

To find time, you need to isolate *t* on one side of the equation, so divide both sides by $\frac{1}{8}$ or multiply both sides by 8. (Here's a hint: Multiplying is faster.)

$$(\tfrac{1}{10}) \times 8 = t$$
$$\tfrac{8}{10} = t$$

So Paige runs $\frac{1}{10}$ of a mile in $\frac{8}{10}$ of a minute. Because $\frac{8}{10}$ isn't an answer choice, you must convert minutes to seconds. One minute equals 60 seconds, so $\frac{8}{10} \times 60$ seconds is 48 seconds. The correct answer must be Choice (B). Choice (D) is obviously wrong because 480 seconds is 8 minutes, and you know that it takes Paige less time to run $\frac{1}{10}$ of a mile than it does for her to run a whole mile. Guessing is the only way you can come up with one of the other two answers.

Always check the possible answer choices for options that don't make any sense in the problem. You can toss those out right away and save your time for doing the math.

The Ins and Outs of Graphs and Charts

Whether you're taking the HSPT, TACHS, or COOP, expect to encounter some math questions containing graphs or charts that you have to evaluate. Several different kinds of graphs and charts exist, and some are better than others at depicting specific kinds of information. The following sections show the various types of graphs and charts and tell you the type of information each one portrays best. (*Note:* Pictographs and maps also tend to appear on the various Catholic high school entrance exams. They're pretty self-explanatory, though, so we don't spend time covering them.)

Chart and graph questions appear most frequently on the TACHS.

Reporting values with tables

Tables (like the one shown in Figure 13-1) are good for reporting values. For instance, a table is good for displaying the results of a science experiment, reporting the average daily high and low temperatures for a city, or listing a band's top ten hits. On the other hand, tables aren't great for showing percentages or trends. You can use tables to compare data, but that usually isn't their primary purpose.

Average Daily Temperatures (°F) in Tourist Cities				
City Name	January		July	
	High	Low	High	Low
Acapulco	87	72	89	77
Calcutta	80	55	89	79
Madrid	50	34	89	61
Stockholm	31	23	70	55
Tokyo	48	31	84	71

Figure 13-1: Sample table.

Depicting range and comparing data with bar graphs

Bar graphs are good for showing a range of values or how often values occur in a specific data set. For example, you can use a bar graph to show the number of high school students employed in specific summer jobs. With two or more types of bars, you can show comparisons between, say, the types of jobs seniors hold and those held by juniors. The bar graph in Figure 13-2 not only shows the range of test scores in an algebra course but it also compares them by class period.

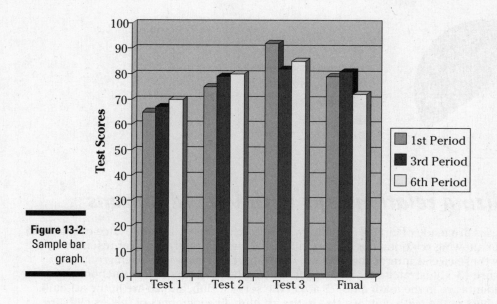

Figure 13-2:
Sample bar
graph.

Looking at things over time with line graphs

Line graphs are good for observations made over time. Time almost always lies on the *x*-axis; what's being measured usually resides on the *y*-axis. Line graphs are especially useful for showing trends, peaks, or lows, as you can see in Figure 13-3.

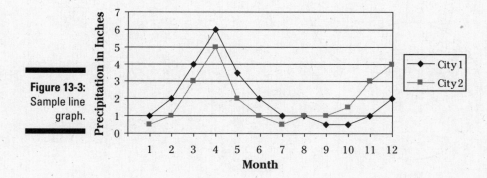

Figure 13-3:
Sample line
graph.

Piecing together the whole with pie charts

Pie charts, also known as *circle graphs,* are very handy for showing values that are parts of a whole, such as percentages. They show how much there is of one thing compared to how much there is of another. The chart in Figure 13-4 presents a clear picture of the percentage of students employed in a variety of summer jobs.

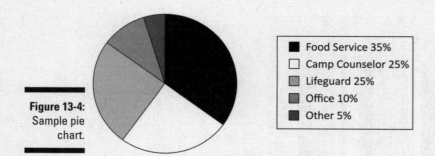

Food Service 35%

Camp Counselor 25%

Lifeguard 25%

Office 10%

Other 5%

Figure 13-4:
Sample pie
chart.

Visualizing relationships with Venn diagrams

Venn diagrams are made of circles (usually two or three on the various entrance exams) and are good for showing relationships among things. Each entity or group is represented by a circle. How these circles intersect shows how the different members of each group are related. Figure 13-5 illustrates the relationship among the members of three school clubs. Twelve students are in the math club, 15 are in the service club, and 20 are in the art club. Three members of the math club are also in the art club, five members of the art club are also in the service club, and two students are members of all three clubs.

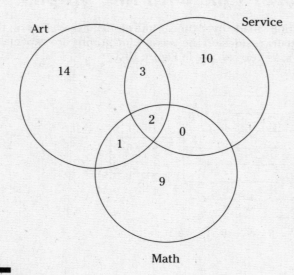

Figure 13-5:
Sample
Venn
diagram.

Total in Art: 14 + 1 + 2 + 3 = 20
Total in Math: 9 + 1 + 2 = 12
Total in Service: 10 + 2 + 3 = 15

Approaching chart and graph questions

Some exam questions present data on some type of chart or graph and then ask you to evaluate said data. Your particular test may even ask more than one question about a particular graph. When you see such questions, follow these steps to answer them:

1. **Look over the chart or graph to determine its type.**

2. **Read the question.**

3. **Figure out what you need from the graph.**

4. **Solve the problem.**

Here's a sample problem that shows you how to apply these four simple steps.

This bar graph shows how many students received high school scholarships at four different schools. Which of the four high schools presented just about twice as many scholarships as the school that gave the fewest number of scholarships?

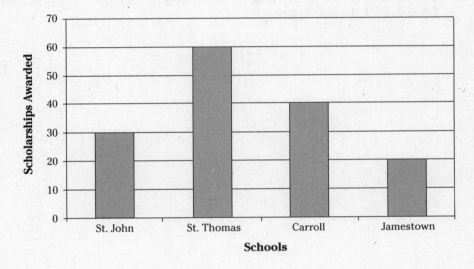

(A) St. John

(B) St. Thomas

(C) Carroll

(D) Jamestown

The graph presents four bars, one for each high school. The numbers on the *y*-axis of the graph show the number of students who received scholarships. The highest bar represents the school that gave out the greatest number of scholarships; the lowest bar is the school that distributed the fewest. Jamestown has the lowest bar, so you can eliminate Choice (D). Look on the *y*-axis to determine about how many scholarships Jamestown gave out. The Jamestown bar ends at the number 20, but you're looking for the school that gave out twice as many scholarships as Jamestown. Well, 2×20 is 40, so find 40 on the *y*-axis and note which bar ends at the 40 mark. Carroll is the one! Choice (C) is your answer. St. Thomas has the highest bar, but it ends at 60, which means it gave out at least three times as many scholarships as Jamestown. Choice (B) is therefore wrong. St. John gave out 30 scholarships, which isn't twice the number of Jamestown scholarships; eliminate Choice (A).

Your entrance exam may also ask you to choose which chart is best at showing a particular type of data, so make sure you know which charts and graphs are best for showing which types of information. Following is a sample of this question type.

Which of these diagram methods would be the best way to show what specific percentages of total middle school student athletes participate in baseball, football, tennis, golf, and basketball?

(A) Table

(B) Line graph

(C) Venn diagram

(D) Pie chart

Usually the best chart for showing parts of a total is a pie chart, Choice (D). A table reports data nicely, but it doesn't show percentages well; cut Choice (A). A line graph is better for showing trends over time, but that's not what you're looking for, so Choice (B) is wrong. A Venn diagram would be good to show how many athletes participate in one sport, two sports, or more, but it's not so great at showing percentages. Choice (C) isn't right, so Choice (D) is the logical answer.

Chapter 14

Sifting through Sequence Problems

In This Chapter

▶ Seeing sequences in pictures and symbols

▶ Finding numerical patterns in number sequences

▶ Picturing and counting letters to solve letter sequences

Sequence problems give you a pattern and ask you to complete a missing part of it. The patterns come in three varieties: pictures, numbers, and letters. The approach to these questions is pretty much the same regardless of the type of pattern.

Sequence questions appear only on the COOP and HSPT, so if you're taking the TACHS, you don't have to worry about them. The COOP has a completely separate section for these babies, whereas the HSPT just sprinkles a few number sequence questions into its Quantitative Skills section.

Discovering the Design in the Picture Sequence

The picture sequence appears only in the COOP exam's Sequences section. Previous tests have had only about six of these questions, and there's no reason to believe that the COOP-powers-that-be will add too many more to future tests. The patterns seem to get more complex as you move through the picture sequence questions, so usually the first questions are easier than the last ones.

Defining picture sequences

The *picture sequence* is a list of two to four related figures usually arranged in four groups in some sort of logical pattern. The questions can distinguish the figures by shape, shading, size, position, or any number of differentiations. At the end of the sequence is a blank. Your job is to find the answer choice that logically completes the pattern.

We could spend paragraphs talking about what a picture sequence looks like, but because a picture is worth a thousand words, here's a visual example of one:

Notice that the sequence is a set of four groups of three figures. A logical pattern exists within the group of three figures and among the set of four groups. From your analysis of this pattern, you must choose which of the figures in the answer choices completes the pattern.

Strategizing your approach to picture sequence questions

Don't be overwhelmed by picture sequences! They're not worth it. If you use a strategy to answer these questions, you'll figure them out pretty easily. Here's how to do just that with the sample question from the preceding section:

1. **Look at the sequence briefly to get a general idea of the types of features it uses to distinguish each figure.**

   When facing picture sequences, it may help to write down a one-word description of each figure type in the sequence.

   The sequence in question includes four groups of three figures. There are four different shapes, and all four shapes are circles. One is completely shaded (shaded), one contains a circle within a circle like a doughnut (doughnut), one looks like a NO sign (NO), and the other is plain (plain).

2. **Examine the groups to see whether you can find an obvious pattern.**

   Note: In the first question or two, a pattern may jump out at you, but usually clear patterns don't readily emerge in picture sequences.

   There are no duplicate figures in each group, and at least two of each figure appear in the whole sequence. There's a plain in every group, and the doughnut appears in each of the first three groups.

3. **Scan the answer choices to gauge whether you can eliminate any containing figures that don't belong.**

   Usually, you can eliminate at least two obviously wrong answer choices by looking over all the options. In this case, you can eliminate Choice (C), the smiley face, because the pattern doesn't introduce new shapes into the third position within the groups. Also cross out Choice (B), because no figure appears twice in one group, which means the pattern doesn't justify two plains. You're now left with Choice (A), shaded, and Choice (D), doughnut.

4. **Express the pattern in words to determine which of the remaining answer choices fits best.**

   The pattern goes shaded, plain, doughnut; NO, doughnut, plain; shaded, doughnut, plain; NO, plain. . . . The first and third groups start with a shaded circle, and the second and fourth groups start with a NO sign. Consequently, it doesn't make sense for the last group to end with a shaded. You can probably cross out Choice (A). Check Choice (D), though. Could the last group use a doughnut in the last spot? Yes, all groups have a doughnut, and the doughnut appears in either the second or third spot of each group. Putting Choice (D) at the end of the last group makes more sense than any of the other answer choices.

5. **If you think you're spending too much time (like more than a minute) on one question, mark your best guess from the remaining answer choices and move on.**

   As we explain in Chapter 2, marking something on your answer sheet is always better than leaving a question blank.

Picture sequences always have a logical pattern, even if it doesn't seem like that at first. Concentrate and you'll get it!

Try this picture sequence question for yourself.

@@##   ##@@   @#@#   #@ ___

(A) #@   (B) @@   (C) @#   (D) ##

The pictures in this question are actually symbols. Odd, perhaps, but this still counts as a picture sequence. You have four groups of @s (which we'll call "and") and #s (which we'll name "pound"). Each group has two @s and two #s. That's all you need to know to eliminate Choices (B) and (D) because both of those choices give the last group three of one of the symbols, which just isn't consistent with the rest of the sequence. You've now narrowed the possibilities to Choice (A) and Choice (C). Look at the sequence again. The pattern is and, and, pound, pound; pound, pound, and, and; and, pound, and, pound; pound, and. . . . Notice that the second group is the opposite of the first. You can safely guess that the fourth group is the opposite of the third, which is Choice (A). That makes much more sense than picking Choice (C).

Noticing the Pattern in Number Sequences

Some sequence problems ask you to recognize the patterns in groups of numbers. The pattern can be about repeating numbers or combinations of numbers, like 4, 5, 6, 4, 5, 6. Or it can be a result of adding, subtracting, multiplying, or dividing in a set manner, like a pattern of adding 2 to each number to get a sequence of 2, 4, 6, 8, 10, 12. Or it can be a little of both: 2, 2, 4, 4, 6, 6.

Two of the entrance exams contain number sequence questions. The HSPT sticks a few in its Quantitative Skills section, and the COOP includes them in its Sequences section, along with the picture and letter sequences. The following sections offer advice for solving both tests' number sequence problems.

Solving the HSPT number sequence questions

The patterns of the HSPT number sequence questions result from performing one or more mathematical operations. Usually the HSPT presents you with a sequence of numbers and asks you to figure out what comes next. But sometimes it asks you to come up with a number in the middle of the sequence.

The HSPT patterns are pretty easy to spot if you ask yourself what math operation you must perform to move from number to number. Be sure to write the operation in your test booklet as you examine the sequence so you don't lose track.

Basically, if an HSPT number sequence question wants you to provide the next number in this sequence — 44, 48, 52, 56 — just do the math. Look at the first number, 44. What operation do you perform to 44 to get the second number, 48? You add 4. Write +4 in your test booklet in between 44 and 48. Then look at 52. It's 4 more than 48, so you perform the same operation. A quick glance at the next number, 56, tells you that you solved the mystery. Just add 4 to 56 to determine that 60 is the next number in the sequence.

Of course, not all patterns are as simple as that. Some require more than one operation, and some call for you to rethink the pattern entirely. Check out this example.

Consider the following sequence: 2, 4, 6, 12, 14, . . . What number comes next?

(A) 16

(B) 18

(C) 28

(D) 21

At first you may look at the 2 and the 4 and think your first operation is +2. Then the second operation would be to add 2 to 4 to get 6. You may think you're on to something, add 2 to 14 to get 16, and hastily pick Choice (A), but you'd be wrong. Take the pattern a step further, and you notice that you don't add 2 to 6 to get 12. Instead, 12 results from multiplying 6 by 2. You have to rethink the pattern to get this question right.

Go back and consider the first two numbers of the sequence, 2 and 4. You can also move from 2 to 4 by multiplying by 2. Erase the +2 you undoubtedly wrote between 2 and 4 in your test booklet and write in ×2 instead. You still add 2 to 4 to get 6, so keep the +2 between those two numbers. Write ×2 in between 6 and 12. The next number is 14, which is 2 more than 12. Write in +2 and check out the pattern: ×2, +2, ×2, +2. The next operation in the pattern is to multiply by 2: 14 × 2 is 28, which is Choice (C). (If you answered Choice (B) or Choice (D), you were probably sleeping!)

Cracking the COOP number sequence questions

The COOP's number sequences look similar to its picture sequences (described earlier in this chapter). They usually consist of three sets of three numbers. Patterns appear within the individual sets of numbers and are maintained throughout the entire sequence of numbers. One of the numbers in the last set in the sequence is missing. Your mission (should you choose to accept it — and we advise that you do) is to uncover its identity. Search for clues in the first sets of numbers. Following is an example of what a COOP number sequence may look like.

17 20 40   11 14 28   33 _____ 72

(A) 35

(B) 36

(C) 30

(D) 69

Like the HSPT number sequence questions, the COOP number sequences usually apply mathematical operations to the numbers to create patterns. (We reveal how to apply basic operations to number sequences in the preceding section.) Unlike those on the HSPT, however, the COOP questions may also include other operations (such as squares and cubes of numbers) and different types of number patterns (like repeating a certain number in each set) that aren't as obvious as patterns that are based solely on addition, subtraction, multiplication, and division.

Here's how to approach a COOP number sequence question like the earlier sample one:

1. **Examine the first two numbers in the first set of the sequence and determine what mathematical operation relates them.**

   The difference between 17 and 20 is 3, so the operation is probably +3.

2. **Check out the first two numbers in the second set of the sequence to see whether their relationship is the same as the relationship of the first two numbers in the first set.**

   You add 3 to 11 to get 14, so the operation is very likely +3.

3. **If the relationships are the same, write that relationship in your test booklet.**

   Write +3 in your booklet and add 3 to 33 (which is 36). Look for 36 in the answer choices. It's there! Just to be safe, though, check the rest of the sequence to make sure you haven't missed something.

4. **Examine and compare the second and third numbers in the first two sets in a similar way and write down the appropriate operation in your booklet.**

   You add 20 to 20 to get 40, so the operation could be +20. You don't add 20 to 14 to get 28, but you can multiply 14 by 2 to get 28. Hmm. 20 × 2 is 40, so the operation must be ×2. 36 × 2 is 72. You've completed the pattern. Well done!

5. **If a pattern that applies to all sets isn't obvious, scan the answer choices for clues.**

   Eliminate choices that have nothing to do with the pattern. Then try replacing the blank with the remaining choices; doing so may reveal the proper pattern.

Feeling good about how to tackle the COOP's number sequence questions? Then apply the steps we just walked you through to this potentially tricky sample question.

4 9 8   3 9 6   7 ____ 14

(A) 21

(B) 15

(C) 9

(D) 12

No consistent operation exists that can get you from 4 to 9 *and* from 3 to 9, so something else must be going on in this sequence. The first two sets have a middle number of 9. You don't know about the middle number of the third set because that's the one you have to find. The pattern may simply repeat 9 as the middle number with no related math operation at all! (Note that there *is* a related math operation between the first and third number of each set; you multiply the first number by 2 to get the third number.) Look at the answer choices. 9 is an option in Choice (C). That's the only logical answer.

If you picked Choice (A), you may have looked at the second set of numbers and thought the pattern was to multiply the first number by 3 to get the second. But that doesn't work for the first set of numbers. If you opted for Choice (D), you may have added 5 to 7 based on your observation in the first set that adding 5 to 4 gives you 9. The second set of numbers doesn't follow this operation, though. If you decided to concentrate on the last two numbers of the first set, you probably picked Choice (B). You may have decided that the operation between the last numbers in the set was −1 and filled in the missing number with 15. That just doesn't work for the second set of numbers, so it can't be right.

What's true about a pattern for one of the sets of numbers in the sequence has to be true for all the sets, so check each set before you settle on a solution to the mystery of the missing number.

Looking Closely at Letter Sequences on the COOP

The COOP's Sequences section ends with several questions that ask you to find a pattern in sets of letters (sometimes with a few numbers thrown in for sport). The COOP groups the letters in several sets that typically have three or four letters each. Your task? Examine the sets of letters to determine a pattern and eliminate answers that don't fit.

Solving letter sequences requires you to combine the skills you need for solving picture and number sequences (which we present earlier in this chapter). Think of each letter as a kind of figure (like you find in the picture sequences) and consider the numerical properties of letters as you move up and down the alphabet. The letter sequences on the COOP often involve both properties. The next sections get you acquainted with letter sequences and how to solve them.

Picturing letters as figures

Be prepared for the COOP to use the appearance of letters to create a pattern in one of these ways:

- ✔ It may create sequences from a combination of lowercase and uppercase letters, such as RrRr SsSs TtTt _____.
- ✔ Patterns can emerge from combinations of vowels and consonants similar to something like this: MOMA NONA POPA _____.

Sometimes the easiest way to solve sequences that focus on the appearance of the letters is to eliminate answer choices that don't fit.

Counting letters like numbers

When attempting to solve letter sequence problems, we suggest you look at the alphabet as a sort of number line. The COOP forms patterns based on the amount of spaces between letters up and down the alphabet. For example, you can consider the set of {A,C,E} as moving up the alphabet 2 spaces (+2). Here's how this pattern could develop:

ACE BDF CEG DFH

If you're not particularly familiar with the position of each letter in the alphabet, you may want to quickly write it out at the top of your test booklet before you tackle the letter sequences. Although this step seems time consuming, it may actually save you time because you won't have to continually recite the alphabet song in your head while you're taking the exam.

Some of the letter sequences may contain actual numbers, usually in the form of exponents or subscripts. So you may see a sequence like this one on the COOP:

$A_1B_2C_3$ $A_2B_3C_4$ $A_3B_4C_5$ $A_4B_5C_6$

The letters stay the same, and the numbers increase by 1 within each set. The beginning number of each set is 1 more than the beginning number of the previous set.

Use the following sample letter sequence question to jump right in!

SaTa   UaVa   WaXa   _____

(A) YaZA

(B) XaYa

(C) YaZa

(D) TaSa

Each set of this sequence contains an alternating repetitive lowercase *a*. That means you can immediately eliminate Choice (A) because it contains a nonconforming uppercase *A*. (Choice (A) is such a rebel!) All the remaining answers present the lowercase *a* in the proper position, so you need to dig into the pattern more deeply to find the answer.

The consonants of each set move up the alphabet one space from *S* to *X*. The next consonant after *X* is *Y,* so the next set should be YaZa, which is Choice (C). Choice (B) duplicates *X,* which isn't part of the pattern, and Choice (D) presents a tricky little reversal of the first set, which isn't justified by the rest of the sequence.

Chapter 15

Comprehending Comparisons and Other Quantitative Relationships

• •

In This Chapter

▶ Balancing values

▶ Decoding the relationship among numbers for the COOP

▶ Visualizing relationships among shapes, symbols, and sets

• •

Quantitative questions test your ability to work out logic problems by using quantitative concepts such as space and measure.

Even though all three Catholic high school entrance exams test essentially the same mathematics concepts, each exam has a quantitative question type that's a little out of the ordinary.

✔ The HSPT includes a question in its Quantitative Skills section that asks you to evaluate and compare three different values.

✔ The COOP not only devotes an entire section to three distinctive types of quantitative reasoning questions but also throws in a few questions about sets.

✔ The TACHS gets really original with its ability questions; one of its question types may remind you of arts-and-crafts hour as you mentally fold and punch paper.

Although these question types look different from one another, they test the same concepts and are actually pretty fun. In fact, you may find yourself doing some of these problems just for grins!

Weighing the Values for Comparison Questions

Some quantitative questions test your ability to compare values. The HSPT accomplishes this goal with a few quantitative comparison questions scattered throughout its Quantitative Skills section, whereas the COOP has you weigh symbols on a scale to come up with an equal balance. We help you figure out how to handle both kinds of questions in the following sections.

Sizing up HSPT comparisons

The quantitative comparison questions on the HSPT test a variety of math concepts (so check out Chapters 10, 11, and 12 if you need a review of the basics). What makes these questions different from other math questions is that they give you three values in the form of equations, geometric values, or inequalities and ask you to compare and contrast them.

The questions start by asking you to evaluate three problems, (a), (b), and (c). Here's how you do that:

1. **To effectively compare the three values, you first have to figure them out, so determine the value of (a) and write it down in your test booklet and then do the same for (b) and (c).**

   If the three problems contain variables, you may not be able to come up with a clear value for each option because the values depend on what the variables are. For these questions, focus on what you know about the relationship among the three problems.

2. **Give a quick consideration to the relationships among the three values before you check out the answer choices; assess which value is greater, which is lesser, and which values are equal.**

   Always try to figure out the three values *before* looking at the answer choices. If you skim the answer choices first, you may swerve off track or miss something.

3. **Look through the answer choices and eliminate those that don't match the relationships you've come up with.**

   The remaining choice is the right answer!

Try this approach on the following practice question that asks you to evaluate equations.

Look at (a), (b), and (c) and choose the best answer.

   (a) $(2 \times 3) + 11$

   (b) $(7 \times 3) - 3$

   (c) $(6 \times 2) + 6$

(A) (b) is less than (a) and less than (c).

(B) (b) is equal to (c) and less than (a).

(C) (a) is equal to (c) and greater than (b).

(D) (c) is greater than (a).

To find the values of (a), (b), and (c), you perform simple operations. Solve (a) first: $2 \times 3 = 6$, and $6 + 11 = 17$. Write 17 next to (a) and move on to (b): $7 \times 3 = 21$, and $21 - 3 = 18$, so write 18 next to (b). Finally, calculate the value of (c): $6 \times 2 = 12$, and $12 + 6$ is 18. Write 18 next to (c). Note that (b) is equal to (c) and (a) is less than (c) or (b). Read through the answer choices. The only one that works is Choice (D). If you picked any of the other choices, you probably didn't figure out the values before you looked at the answer choices. You may have quickly glanced at (a), (b), and (c) and thought that (a) was greater than the other two values because more was added to (a) than to the other two. Or perhaps you thought that (b) had a lesser value because it included subtraction rather than addition.

Balancing COOP symbol relationships

The problems described in this section, which only appear on the COOP, feature a scale that shows equal measures of combinations of two different shapes (usually squares and triangles), like this:

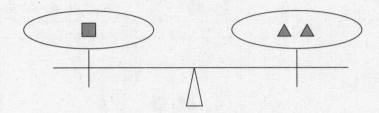

Based on the information provided by the scale, you must choose an answer that shows equal measures of the two shapes. The answer choices look a little something like this:

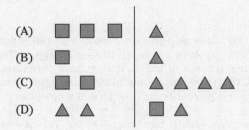

 You can balance the scales using substitution just like you would for an algebra problem with two variables (see Chapter 11). So, for example, if the problem tells you that one square equals two triangles, you can substitute two triangles for every square in the answer choices to find the right answer.

When you combine that advice with our ongoing example, you find that you can rewrite the answer choices in your test booklet like so:

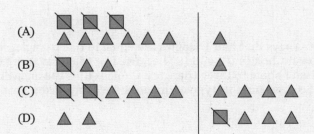

After you change all the shapes to triangles, all you have to do is compare the triangles. A quick glance shows you that Choice (C) balances the scale: Four triangles are equal to four triangles. The other answers don't balance the scale: Neither six triangles nor two triangles are equal to one triangle; similarly, two triangles aren't equal to three triangles. Make sense? Great. Now give this sample question a whirl.

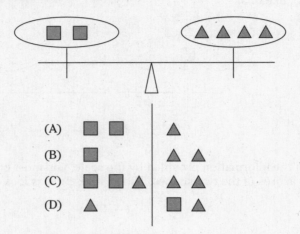

This question requires an additional math step before you do your substitution. The scale tells you that two squares are equal to four triangles. That's great, but you still need to know what one square is equal to. It's probably obvious to you that if two squares equal four triangles, then one square equals two triangles. If not, simply set up a proportion and solve: ²⁄₄ = ¹⁄ₓ. (For a refresher on how to solve a proportion, head to Chapter 10.)

Because one square equals two triangles, you replace every square with two triangles.

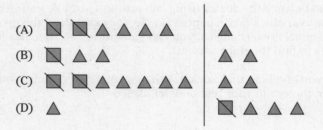

Choice (A) says that four triangles are equal to one triangle, so eliminate that answer. You can also cut Choices (C) and (D) because five triangles aren't equal to two triangles and one triangle isn't equal to three triangles. Choice (B) is the answer: Two triangles equal two triangles. See how fun this type of quantitative comparison problem can be?

Deciphering Numerical Relationships on the COOP

The COOP's Quantitative Reasoning section contains a question type that's a lot like number sequence questions (see Chapter 14 for more on sequences). Each question presents you with three series consisting of a number that points to a box that points to another number, except that the last number of the last series is missing. (Got all that?) Your job is to find the value of the missing number by using clues from the first two series.

To accomplish this task, evaluate the first two series to determine what operation belongs in the box. For example, examine this relationship: $2 \rightarrow \square \rightarrow 3$. The operation you use to move from 2 to 3 is +1, so the relationship between the numbers — in other words, the stuff that fills the box — is +1. Most relationships you're asked to find on the COOP aren't as obvious. Here's an example: $2 \rightarrow \square \rightarrow 6$. The relationship between 2 and 6 could be +4, but it could also be ×3. That's why you need another series to help you out. If the next series is $7 \rightarrow \square \rightarrow 21$, you know that the relationship in the box is ×3; if it's $7 \rightarrow \square \rightarrow 11$, you know the relationship is +4.

The COOP's numerical relationship questions can be a little frustrating, so here's a tip that should make solving them easier: If the first number in each series is smaller than the second, the operation is probably + or ×. If the first number in each series is larger than the second, the operation is probably − or ÷. Just remember that you're not finished when you discover the numerical relationship. You still have to apply it to the last series to find the answer that fills in the blank.

Here's what a complete COOP numerical relationship question looks like.

$8 \rightarrow \square \rightarrow 4$
$4 \rightarrow \square \rightarrow 0$
$6 \rightarrow \square \rightarrow \underline{}$

(A) 4 (B) 2 (C) 3 (D) 1

When you examine the first relationship, you see that you move from a larger number, 8, to a smaller number, 4. However, you don't know whether the operation that gets you there is subtraction or division because you either subtract 4 from 8 or divide 2 into 8 to get 4. Look at the second relationship; it moves from 4 to 0. You subtract 4 from 4 to get 0, so the operation is −4. Apply the operation to the last series: 6 − 4 = 2, Choice (B). If you picked Choice (A), you were thinking of the operation rather than the missing value. If you went with Choice (C), you probably decided that the operation was ÷2 and failed to double-check by looking at the second relationship. Choice (D) is the result of a miscalculation.

Evaluating Shapes, Symbols, and Sets

The TACHS and COOP contain unique questions that test your ability to assess shapes and symbols. They're all pretty easy to manage after you're familiar with their format.

The TACHS calls the section that contains these types of questions the Ability section. One of the three question types in the Ability section gives you three figures; you must evaluate them and then choose a similar figure from among the answer options. Another question type in this section looks for the end result of an imaginary paper-folding exercise (pretty creative of those TACHS test designers, huh?). The third question type in the Ability section involves shape analogies. The approach to that question type is the same as for other analogy questions; we cover analogies in Chapter 4, so head there for tips.

The COOP brings shapes into the picture (so to speak) with yet another question type in its Quantitative Reasoning section. It shades parts of figures and expects you to determine what fraction of the shape is shaded.

Last but not least, you may be called upon to work with sets. *Sets* are just groups of objects where the order doesn't matter. These kinds of questions sometimes pop up on the exams' Math sections, so we give you a little crash course here.

Making the connection among similar shapes, TACHS-style

If you're taking the TACHS, you need to be able to recognize similarities among a series of three shapes. The test presents you with three shapes. Using your sharp powers of observation, you then choose an additional shape that belongs with the others. For some reason we can't explain, the TACHS provides you with five answer choices rather than four, so you have more to choose from.

To answer similar-shapes questions correctly, you need to know what you're looking for. Following are some common elements that make shapes similar. It's not a complete list (those tricky test-makers can always come up with something new), but it's a good way to begin your focus.

- ✔ **Number of sides:** The figures can be alike because they each have the same number of sides.

- ✔ **Sharp corners and rounded edges:** The shapes may all have sharp corners where the lines meet, or they may contain some rounded edges. Who knows? They may even contain a similar combination of both.

- ✔ **Direction:** The shapes may point in the same direction. On the other hand, they may all be upside down or right side up.

- ✔ **Shading:** The shapes may share a common shading pattern or amount of shading.

After you've determined the element that the shapes have in common, look at the answer choices to find one that shares the same element. If you get stuck coming up with a similarity, jump into the answer choices and eliminate shapes that are definitely different. Then choose from the remaining possibilities. Something in the answer choices may point you to the element that makes the group of shapes alike.

The similar-shapes questions on the TACHS aren't sequence questions. The figures don't build along a pattern, so their order doesn't matter. You're not trying to find the next figure in a series; you're just looking for one that fits in with all the others.

Try to find the similarities in the following sample question.

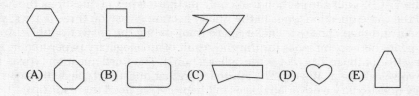

(A) (B) (C) (D) (E)

Count the sides of the three figures in the problem. Each figure has six sides, so the common element of the three shapes is that they all have six sides. Eliminate any answers that don't have six sides, specifically Choices (B) and (D). Choice (C) looks promising, but it only has five sides. Choice (A) is an octagon, which means it has eight sides. The correct answer is Choice (E), the six-sided houselike shape.

Unveiling the approach to TACHS fold-and-punch questions

The TACHS's fold-and-punch questions are some of the most unique questions we've ever seen (and we've seen a bunch of test questions in our lifetimes). This question type allows you to engage in a little mental paper folding and hole punching. Understanding the format of these babies takes a little getting used to. The question shows you a series of paper folds with arrows that point out in the direction the paper gets folded. The last figure in the series supplies the position where this folded paper receives a hole punch. Here's the visual:

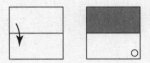

The answer choices give you a selection of unfolded pages, like this:

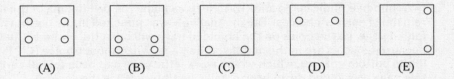

(A)   (B)   (C)   (D)   (E)

You must choose the figure that correctly reflects the position of the holes in the paper after it has been punched and unfolded.

The key to answering fold-and-punch questions correctly is to know how many holes will appear in the paper when it's unfolded. The final number of holes depends on how many times the paper is folded.

- ✔ If the paper is folded once (two pictures in the question), the unfolded page will have twice the number of holes punched in the folded picture. So if the folded page is punched once, the unfolded page will have two holes.

- ✔ If the paper is folded twice (three pictures in the question), the unfolded page will have four times the number of holes punched in the folded picture. Therefore, a folded page with one punch will result in an unfolded page with four holes.

- ✔ A paper that's folded three times (four pictures in the question) will have six times as many holes when it's unfolded.

- ✔ We doubt you'll see too many of these, but a paper folded four times (five pictures in the question) has eight times as many holes when it's unfolded.

After you eliminate any answer choices that don't have the proper number of holes for the number of folds, your next concern is placement. Where will the holes appear on the page when it's unfolded? Check the position of the remaining choices and determine which is the most logical. Punches in the corners on the folded page will end up in the corners of the unfolded page. Punches closer to the fold will appear in the middle of the unfolded page.

If you're having a hard time visualizing this problem, cut out some squares of paper and fold them and punch them as directed by the practice questions. Then unfold them to see what they look like.

Give this sample fold-and-punch problem a shot.

First things first: Observe how many times the paper is folded for a clue as to how many holes the unfolded paper will have. The paper in this question is folded once, which means the unfolded page will have twice as many holes as the folded page. The folded page has one hole, and 2 × 1 is 2. Eliminate answer choices that have any number of holes other than two (buh-bye Choices (A) and (B)!). Next, examine the positioning of the holes in the remaining answer choices. The original hole was punched in the bottom-right corner of the folded page, so the holes on the unfolded page will be in the corners. Cut Choice (D) because its holes are in the middle of the page. What about Choice (C)? It places the holes in the bottom corners, which would work if the page had been folded vertically. However, this page was folded down horizontally, so Choice (E) is the answer.

Finding shades of meaning in shaded figures on the COOP

Questions that ask you to determine the part of a figure that has been shaded appear in the Quantitative Reasoning section of the COOP. These questions should be pretty easy for you to answer. All you have to do is count the number of equal parts inside the figure, count how many parts are shaded, and create a fraction. The number of shaded parts is the numerator, and the total number of parts is the denominator. If you have a circle divided into four equal parts and two are shaded, the fraction is ²⁄₄. When you reduce ²⁄₄, you get ½. One half of the circle is shaded.

The answers to shaded-figure questions are usually presented in simplified form, so you have to reduce the fraction before you check the answers. For more about fractions and how to reduce them, flip to Chapter 10.

The only way these questions get tricky is when the shaded area cuts through one of the shaded portions of the shape, as you can see here.

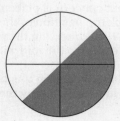

Just make sure you count the number of shaded and total parts correctly. The total number of equal parts in the circle is four. The shaded area cuts two of those parts in half, so the total shaded area is one part + ½ part + ½ part, which makes a total of two shaded parts out of four. Even though there appear to be three dividing lines, the total number of equal parts is *not* six. Here's another shape for you to evaluate.

(A) ½

(B) ⅓

(C) ¼

(D) 1

This shape has four equal parts, and only one of them is shaded. Make the number of shaded parts the numerator and the total number of parts the denominator to get ¼. That's all there is to it! Choice (C) is your answer. If you picked Choice (B), you made the shaded part the numerator but put the total number of unshaded parts in the denominator. Choice (D) takes into account only the shaded part and doesn't consider the total number of parts. If you opted for Choice (A), you may have looked at only one half of the square.

Memorizing a little set terminology

None of the Catholic high school entrance exams has a separate section devoted to sets, but one or more of them may include questions that deal with sets in their math sections. For those few questions, it helps to know a little bit of set terminology.

A *set* is a collection of objects, numbers, or values that belong to the set and are called its *members* or *elements*. Here are some symbols related to sets that you should know:

- ✔ ∈ means "is a member of a set."
- ✔ ∉ means "is not a member of a set."
- ✔ ∅ indicates a set with nothing in it.
- ✔ ∪ shows the union of two sets.
- ✔ ∩ shows the intersection of two sets.

Union and *intersection* are ways of stating how two or more sets can be combined, with union being the most inclusive and intersection being the least inclusive. The *union* of two sets (A and B) is the set of all values that are members of either Set A or Set B or both. For example, the union of Sets $A = \{1, 2, 3, 4, 5\}$ and $B = \{3, 4, 5, 6, 7\}$ is the Set $A \cup B = \{1, 2, 3, 4, 5, 6, 7\}$.

The *intersection* of two sets (A and B, written as $A \cap B$) is the set of the values that appear in both sets but doesn't include the values that are in one set but not the other. For example, the intersection of Sets $A = \{0, 1, 2, 3, 5, 6, 7, 8, 9\}$ and $B = \{2, 4, 6, 8\}$ is $\{2, 6, 8\}$.

After you know all the symbols, set questions are pretty easy. Following is what one may look like on your entrance exam.

If A = {0, 1, 2, 3, 4, 5} and B = {2, 4, 6, 8, 10}, what is $A \cap B$?

(A) {0, 1, 2, 3, 4, 5, 6, 8, 10}

(B) {2, 4}

(C) $\varnothing$

(D) {0, 1, 2, 3, 4, 5}

The question is asking for the intersection of Sets A and B. Because the intersection of two sets includes only those members that show up in both sets, the correct answer is Choice (B). If you selected Choice (A), you misread the symbol and picked the answer that gave you the union of the two sets. Choice (D) ignores Set B altogether. If you went for Choice (C), you probably forgot what the intersection symbol means.

Chapter 16

Everything but the Kitchen Sink: A Hodgepodge of Math Practice Questions

• •

In This Chapter

▶ Warming up your basic math skills

▶ Taking on COOP-style sequence problems

▶ Analyzing relationships with quantitative questions

• •

There's nothing like practice to make you a better test-taker. That's why we know you're absolutely thrilled about taking on this chapter! Following are sample math problems in a variety of categories designed to give you the practice you need to help you do your best on the math portions of your Catholic high school entrance exam. Each section features questions and answer explanations. Answer the questions on your own before you read the explanations — no cheating allowed! And be sure to review the explanations even for the questions you answered correctly. Something you read there may help you with a future question. Ready? Set. Go!

Mastering a Little Math

The following 18 questions test your knowledge of math concepts. Among other delightful topics, they include a little arithmetic, algebra, and geometry. In other words, they're the kinds of questions you can expect to see in the math section of any Catholic high school entrance exam. Have fun!

1. What happens when you add an odd number to another odd number?

(A) Your answer is an odd number.

(B) Your answer is an even number.

(C) Your answer could be either odd or even depending on the value of the numbers being added together.

(D) Your answer is zero.

If you've memorized the rules about odds and evens presented in Chapter 10, you can just pick Choice (B) and move on. If you've forgotten them, use real numbers to figure out the answer. Pick two random odd numbers, say, 3 and 5. 3 + 5 = 8, and 8 is an even number. It looks like Choice (B) is the answer, but go ahead and try another set of odd numbers just to be sure. How about numbers in the name of a popular convenience store, 7 and 11? 7 + 11 = 18, an even number. Looks like you're on a roll. *Correct Answer:* Choice (B)

2. How many integers come between 2^2 and $\frac{11}{2}$?

   (A) 1

   (B) 2

   (C) 0

   (D) 5

   To ace this problem, determine the value of the first number: $2^2 = 2 \times 2$, which is 4. The second number equals $11 \div 2$, which is 5½. So you're looking for the number of integers that come between 4 and 5½. The set of integers doesn't contain fractions, so 5 is the one and only integer between 4 and 5½. *Correct Answer:* Choice (D)

3. If $\frac{3}{4} = \frac{x}{12}$, what does x equal?

   (A) 9

   (B) 3

   (C) 12

   (D) 10

   Solving this problem is easy when you recognize that it's a proportion. (And if you didn't, we suggest you flip back to the proportion section in Chapter 10 for a quick refresher.) You can eliminate Choice (C) right away. If x were 12, the fraction would be $\frac{12}{12}$, which is equal to 1. It doesn't make sense that $\frac{x}{12}$ would equal 1. Cross multiply and solve for x: $4x = (3 \times 12)$; $4x = 36$; $x = 9$. If you picked Choice (B), you probably figured out that you can multiply $\frac{3}{4}$ by $\frac{3}{3}$ to find the value of x, but you didn't perform the multiplication properly. *Correct Answer:* Choice (A)

4. $\frac{3}{10} - \frac{4}{15} =$

   (A) $\frac{1}{5}$

   (B) $-\frac{6}{75}$

   (C) $\frac{8}{9}$

   (D) $\frac{1}{30}$

   Do you know how to subtract fractions? We hope so because that's what this question is testing. If you picked Choice (A), you subtracted the numerators and the denominators to get $\frac{1}{5}$, but you can't subtract fractions that way. Instead, you must make the denominators the same and *then* subtract the numerators. Ask yourself what the lowest common denominator of 10 and 15 is. Both numbers go into 30; 10 goes in 3 times, and 15 goes in twice. Change the first fraction by multiplying it by $\frac{3}{3}$: $\frac{3}{10} \times \frac{3}{3} = \frac{9}{30}$. Change the second fraction by multiplying it by $\frac{2}{2}$: $\frac{4}{15} \times \frac{2}{2} = \frac{8}{30}$. Subtract 8 from 9 and keep the denominators the same to get $\frac{1}{30}$. *Correct Answer:* Choice (D)

5. Round 3,486,245 to the nearest million.

   (A) 3,500,000

   (B) 4,000,000

   (C) 3,000,000

   (D) 3,490,000

   The millions place is the first digit of the number, so look at the number to the right of the 3 to see whether you can round up. The digit to the right of the 3 is 4. Because 4 is less than 5, you don't round up to 4, ruling out Choice (B). Keep the 3 and replace all the other digits with zeros. (If you selected Choices (A) or (B), you rounded properly but to the wrong place. Better luck next time.) *Correct Answer:* Choice (C)

6. What percent of 40 is 8?

(A) 0.2%

(B) 5%

(C) 20%

(D) 25%

Ah, the dreaded percentage problem. If you remember to translate it into the language of math, it really isn't so bad. *What* is the unknown (x), *percent* means %, *is* means =, and *of* is the same as ×. Set up the equation and solve for x: $x\% \times 40 = 8$. Divide both sides by 40: $x\% = \frac{8}{40}$ (or 0.2). At this point, you've solved for $x\%$ not x, so don't pick Choice (A). (It's a trap!) Instead, multiply 0.2 by 100 to change it to a percentage: 8 is 20% of 40. If you picked Choice (B), you mistakenly divided 40 by 8; if you selected Choice (D), you probably tried to figure this one out by guessing. *Correct Answer:* Choice (C)

7. Evaluate $\dfrac{2(5-2)^2-(3-9)}{-4(4-6)^3}$.

(A) $-\dfrac{24}{32}$

(B) $\dfrac{3}{4}$

(C) $\dfrac{21}{256}$

(D) $\dfrac{15}{16}$

To solve this problem, you have to know the order of operations (Polly Elf Makes Dolls And Shoes; see Chapter 10). Work with the stuff in the parentheses (P for Polly) first: $5 - 2 = 3$; $3 - 9 = -6$; and $4 - 6 = -2$. Now the fraction looks like this: $\dfrac{2(3)^2-(-6)}{-4(-2)^3}$. Next, solve the exponents (E for Elf): $\dfrac{2(9)-(-6)}{-4(-8)}$. Then multiply (M for Makes) the stuff in the numerator and the stuff in the denominator: $\dfrac{18+6}{32}$. Add the numerator (A for And) to get $\dfrac{24}{32}$. You may be tempted to pick Choice (A) at this point, but the answer isn't negative, and $\dfrac{24}{32}$ isn't simplified. Go ahead and simplify the fraction by dividing the numerator and denominator by 8 to get $\dfrac{3}{4}$. If you selected Choices (C) or (D), you performed the operations incorrectly or in the wrong order. *Correct Answer:* Choice (B)

8. Which of the following demonstrates the associative property of addition?

(A) $(4 \times 5) \times 6 = 4 \times (5 \times 6)$

(B) $4 + 5 + 6 = 6 + 4 + 5$

(C) $4(5 + 6) = (4 + 5) + (4 + 6)$

(D) $(4 + 5) + 6 = 4 + (5 + 6)$

Cross off Choice (A) first because it involves multiplication rather than addition. Also, Choice (C) is incorrect because it demonstrates the distributive property. Now remember the two common properties of addition: the associative property and the commutative property. The commutative property says that when you're adding numbers, you can swap their positions and still get the same result. An example of this is Choice (B). The associative property says that when you're adding three numbers, you can either add the first and second together and then add the third or you can add the second and third together and then add the first. An example of this is Choice (D). *Correct Answer:* Choice (D)

9. What is the square root of 196?

   (A) 98

   (B) 7

   (C) 14

   (D) 16

   You're looking for the number that equals 196 when you multiply it by itself. You know that's not Choice (A) because 98×98 is a huge number, much bigger than 196. Choice (B) is obviously wrong because 7×7 is only 49. Calculate 14×14 on your scratch paper: $14 \times 14 = 196$. That's it! Of course, you can also determine that 196 is the product of two perfect squares: 4 and 49. The square root of 4 is 2, and the square root of 49 is 7. 2×7 is 14, so 14 is the square root of 196. *Correct Answer:* Choice (C)

10. What is the median of this set of numbers: 35, 42, 42, 50, 65, 65, and 65?

    (A) 65

    (B) 50

    (C) 52

    (D) 57.5

    Remember that the *median* is the middle number of a set. This particular set is made up of seven numbers, which is an odd number. All you have to do is find the number that comes in the middle. 50 has three numbers to the left of it and three numbers to the right, so that's the median of the set. If you selected Choice (A), you found the mode rather than the median. Choice (C) is the mean (average), not the median. Choice (D) is the average of 50 and 65, but it's not the median. *Correct Answer:* Choice (B)

11. If $4x + 3y = 31$ and $y = x + 1$, what does x equal?

    (A) 5

    (B) 3

    (C) 10

    (D) 4

    Don't be put off by the two different variables in this problem. Apply a little substitution, and this problem's a piece of cake! You're told that $y = x + 1$, so replace the y in the first equation with $x + 1$: $4x + 3(x + 1) = 31$. Distribute the 3: $4x + 3x + 3 = 31$. Add: $7x + 3 = 31$. Solve for x by subtracting 3 from both sides and then dividing both sides by 7: $7x = 28$; $x = 4$. *Correct Answer:* Choice (D)

TIP

If you really aren't sure what to do, try substituting each answer for x in the equations and see which one works.

12. What kind of triangle has two angles that measure 70°?

    (A) equilateral

    (B) isosceles

    (C) right

    (D) even

There's no such thing as an even triangle, so eliminate Choice (D). A triangle with two equal angles has two equal sides. The type of triangle that has two equal sides is an isosceles triangle, so the answer is Choice (B). The angles of an equilateral triangle measure 60°, so Choice (A) is wrong. The only way the triangle could be a right triangle is if the two equal angles measured 45°. This isn't the case, so Choice (C) can't be right. *Correct Answer:* Choice (B)

13. In the following figure, what is the measure of $\angle a$?

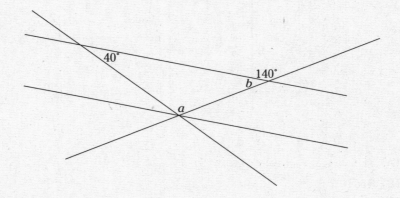

(A) 100°

(B) 40°

(C) 140°

(D) 60°

This problem isn't as hard as it looks. Use what you know about triangles and lines to find the answer (or flip to Chapter 12 if you need some reminders). You know that Angle b measures 40° because it and the 140° angle are supplementary angles that add up to 180° (180 − 140 = 40). Because Angles a and b are two angles in a triangle with another angle that measures 40°, and because the sum of angles in a triangle is 180°, you can just subtract to find the measure of a: 180 − 40 − 40 = 100. Angle a is 100°, which is Choice (A). If you picked Choice (C), you forgot to subtract the third angle. Choice (B) is the measure of Angle b, and Choice (D) is completely unrelated. *Correct Answer:* Choice (A)

14. What is the area of a circle with a diameter of 4?

(A) 16π

(B) 2π

(C) 4π

(D) 8π

The formula for the area of a circle is πr^2. Diameter is 2 times the radius, and the diameter of this circle is 4, so its radius is 2 (4 ÷ 2). 2^2 is 4, so the answer is 4π, Choice (C). If you opted for Choice (A), you squared the diameter of the circle rather than the radius. Choice (B) results from failing to square the radius, and if you got Choice (D), you incorrectly used a formula of 2πd. *Correct Answer:* Choice (C)

15. What is the perimeter of this figure?

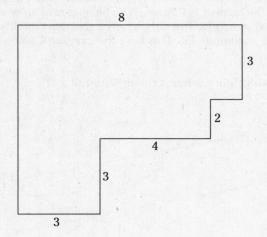

(A) 31

(B) 64

(C) 32

(D) 23

Find the perimeter of a polygon by adding up the values of the sides. This problem gives you the value of all the sides except for two: the entire left side of the figure and the small segment at the right side of the bottom. The left side of the figure is equal to the sum of the other vertical segments: 3 + 2 + 3 = 8. Mark 8 next to the left side. The small unknown segment is equal to the value of the top boundary minus the value of the sum of the rest of the horizontal segments: 8 – (3 + 4). 8 – 7 = 1, so write 1 next to the small unknown segment. Add up all the segments, and you get 32. If you picked Choice (A), you forgot about that little unknown segment. Choice (D) results from ignoring both unknown segments. If you selected Choice (B), you weren't sure how to figure out perimeter in the first place (perhaps you should revisit Chapter 12). *Correct Answer:* Choice (C)

In perimeter problems, never guess the values of unknown segments by looking at them. Always use math to determine their values, or else you'll fall for the trick answer the test preparers have inevitably included to trap you.

16. Emma went grocery shopping at the Colossal Supercenter. The store had a special on kumquats, 10 for $10, and a sale on artichokes, 2 for $5. Emma bought 6 kumquats and 5 artichokes. How much did she spend?

(A) $18.50

(B) $85.00

(C) $15.25

(D) $56.00

Because kumquats are 10 for $10, they're $1 each. Likewise, artichokes are 2 for $5, so they cost $2.50 a piece. Emma bought 6 kumquats at $1 each, so she spent $6 on kumquats. She also purchased 5 artichokes at $2.50 each, which is a total of $12.50. Add $12.50 to $6 to get a total purchase of $18.50. If you went with any of the other answers, you failed to correctly figure out the cost of each kumquat and artichoke. *Correct Answer:* Choice (A)

17. Dan ran the 5k Fun Run in 25 minutes. What was his average speed (in kilometers per hour)?

    (A) 0.2 km/hr

    (B) 2 km/hr

    (C) 12 km/hr

    (D) 5 km/hr

Apply Dan's results to the distance formula (*Distance = Rate × Time*, as explained in Chapter 13) to find how fast he ran. The unknown is Dan's speed (the rate at which he ran). The distance he ran is 5 kilometers, so substitute 5 for *Distance* in the formula. Dan's time was 25 minutes, so replace *Time* with 25. Here's your equation: $5 = r \times 25$.

To solve for *r*, divide both sides by 25: $5 \div 25 = r$; $0.2 = r$. This means that Dan's rate was 0.2 kilometers per minute. Don't pick Choice (A), though; the question asks for the rate in hours, not minutes. You therefore have to convert the rate from minutes to hours. You know that Dan can run 0.2 kilometers in 1 minute, and 60 minutes equals 1 hour, so to find out how many kilometers Dan runs in 60 minutes, set up a proportion: $\frac{0.2}{1} = \frac{x}{60}$. Cross multiply: $x = 0.2 \times 60$; $x = 12$. Dan runs an average of 12 km/hr.

If you immediately recognize that Dan's speed is 5 kilometers in 25 minutes, or ⁵⁄₂₅, you can quickly figure out the answer by setting up a proportion: $\frac{5}{25} = \frac{x}{60}$. Cross multiply and solve: $25x = 5(60)$; $x = 12$ km/hr. *Correct Answer:* Choice (C)

Always pay attention to what a question is asking. If you have to reread it two or three times to understand what you're solving for, that's okay.

18. A high school athletic director charted the rise in the average price of athletic shoes from 1985 to 2005. According to his graph, between what years did the average price increase most significantly?

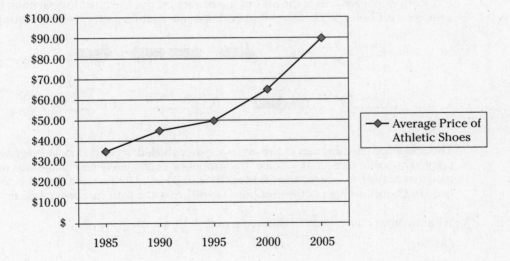

    (A) 1985 and 1990

    (B) 1990 and 1995

    (C) 1995 and 2000

    (D) 2000 and 2005

Sure, you can see just by looking at the graph that the biggest jump in price was from 2000 to 2005, but we recommend you analyze the data just to be certain. The price in 1985 was about $35; it went up to $45 in 1990 (a $10 rise). It went up about $5 more to $50 in 1995. Five years later the price was $65, a $15 increase. But the biggest increase was from 2000 to 2005 when the price went up $25 to $90. *Correct Answer:* Choice (D)

Sampling Some COOP Sequence Problems

The next six questions give you a little more exposure to the fairly unusual sequence questions found on the COOP. (Okay, so technically we threw in one practice question similar to the HSPT's number sequence problems. It's only because we have your best interests at heart.) See how well you do by checking the answers and reading through the explanations. If you find you need a little more help, check out Chapter 14.

1.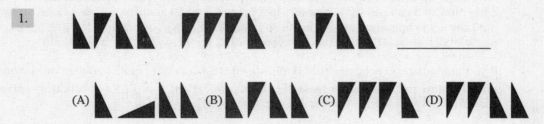

The sets contain four triangles in two types: One is resting on its small side, and one is standing on its tip. Each of the three initial sets of triangles has three of one kind and one of the other, so you can feel pretty good about eliminating Choice (D), which has two of each kind. Choice (A) has a triangle resting on its long side; it introduces a new position without any good reason, so you can probably eliminate it too. Now you're left with Choices (B) and (C). Both duplicate one of the sets in the sequence, but the most logical choice to finish the sequence is Choice (C) because it provides an alternating pattern. *Correct Answer:* Choice (C)

2.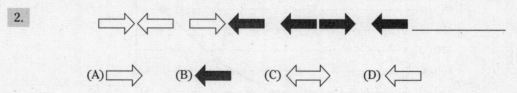

This sequence contains sets of two arrows, either shaded or unshaded. In every set, the arrows point in opposite directions. Choice (C) introduces a completely new shape, so you can eliminate that answer. The arrows in Choices (B) and (D) point in the same direction as the one in the last set. Choosing either of these options would break the pattern. *Correct Answer:* Choice (A)

3. What number comes next in this sequence: 7, 13, 19, 25, 31, . . . ?

(A) 6

(B) 37

(C) 41

(D) 35

This number sequence question is the kind you can expect to see on the HSPT. Start tackling it by analyzing the first two numbers in the sequence. To get from 7 to 13, you add 6. The next number is 19, which is 6 more than 13. Each of the following numbers is also 6 more than the previous number, so the pattern is +6. Add 6 to the last number, 31, and you get the answer, 37, Choice (B). If you picked Choice (A), you probably got so excited about finding the pattern that you selected the amount you add by rather than the last number in the series. The other two choices result from addition errors. *Correct Answer:* Choice (B)

4. 2 4 16   4 8 64   5 10 100   _____ 12 144

   (A) 6

   (B) 10

   (C) 7

   (D) 8

This number sequence of the COOP variety has four sets of three numbers. Your task is to find the first number of the last set. Notice how the second number of the other three sets is twice the first number? The second number in the last set is 12, and 12 divided by 2 is 6. That's all you need to know. *Correct Answer:* Choice (A)

5. $X_2Y^1Z_3$ $X_4Y^2Z_5$ _____ $X_8Y^4Z_9$

   (A) $X_3Y^3Z_5$

   (B) $X_6Y^3Z_7$

   (C) $X_3Y_3Z^5$

   (D) $X_6Y^3Z_8$

The letters in each set of this sequence are the same, so concentrate on the numbers. The first and third numbers of each set are subscript, and the second is superscript. Eliminate Choice (C) because it doesn't follow that pattern. The first numbers in each set increase by 2 as you move from set to set. That means the first number of the third set should be 6, so Choice (A) is incorrect. Choice (D) fits the pattern with the X numbers (as well as the Y numbers, which increase by 1 from set to set) but not with the Z numbers, which also increase by 2. *Correct Answer:* Choice (B)

6. ABCD   BBEF   CBGH   _____

   (A) DEFG

   (B) DBJK

   (C) DBIJ

   (D) IJKL

Notice that the second letter in each set is B. Eliminate Choice (D) because it doesn't have a B in the second position. All of the remaining choices begin with D, so concentrate on the pattern of the last two letters in each set. See how they move through the alphabet, CD EF GH? The next two letters should be IJ, which is the option provided in Choice (C). The other two choices don't complete the pattern of the last two letters. *Correct Answer:* Choice (C)

Quickening Your Quantitative Reasoning and Comparisons Skills

These six practice problems give you a sample of the question types that test your ability to use quantitative reasoning. Answers and explanations follow each question.

1. Based on the relationship between the numbers in the left column and the numbers in the right column, find the answer that completes the blank.

   $7 \rightarrow \square \rightarrow 12$
   $3 \rightarrow \square \rightarrow 8$
   $9 \rightarrow \square \rightarrow \underline{}$

   (A) 14

   (B) 5

   (C) 7

   (D) 13

   To go from 7 to 12, you add 5; similarly, you get 8 when you add 5 to 3. The number that goes in the box is +5. Wait a minute! 5 isn't the answer, so don't pick Choice (B). You're supposed to find out what number fills in the blank. 9 + 5 is 14. *Correct Answer:* Choice (A)

2. Determine what portion of the shape is shaded.

   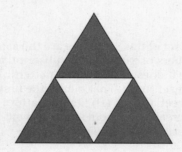

   (A) ¾

   (B) ⅔

   (C) ⅓

   (D) ¼

   The triangle contains four equal triangles. Because three of the four triangles are shaded, ¾ of the figure is shaded. If you chose any of the other answers, we're betting you guessed. Don't next time. Questions like this one are gimmies if you just take a minute to think 'em through. *Correct Answer:* Choice (A)

3. Given that the scale shows shapes that are equal in weight, choose an answer with shapes that are also equal in weight.

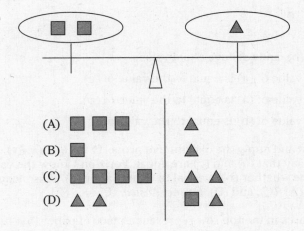

The scale shows you that two boxes equal one triangle. If two boxes equal one triangle, then neither three boxes nor one box can equal one triangle. Eliminate Choices (A) and (B). If one triangle is the same as two boxes, then two triangles are the same as four boxes. There aren't enough boxes on the other side of the scale to offset the two triangles, so Choice (D) can't be right. *Correct Answer:* Choice (C)

4. Study shapes (a), (b), and (c) to determine the correct answer.

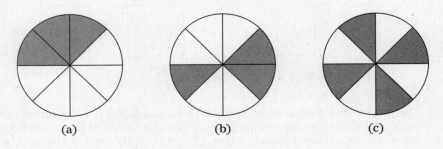

(A) (a), (b), and (c) are shaded equally.

(B) (a) has more shaded area than (b) but less than (c).

(C) The shaded area of (a) plus (c) is less than the shaded area of (b) plus (c).

(D) (c) has more shaded area than either (a) or (b).

All of these equal circles are divided into eight parts. Circle (a) and Circle (b) have three shaded parts, and Circle (c) has four shaded parts. That means two things: The shaded parts of Circle (a) and Circle (b) are equal, and Circle (c) has more shaded area. *Correct Answer:* Choice (D)

5. Study (a), (b), and (c) to determine which answer must be true.

  (a) $3(x + y)$

  (b) $3xy$

  (c) $3x + 3y$

(A) (a), (b), and (c) have equal values.

(B) The value of (a) is equal to the value of (c).

(C) The value of (a) is equal to the value of (b).

(D) The value of (b) is equal to the value of (c).

Go ahead and apply the distributive property to (a). $3(x + y)$ can be written as $3x + 3y$, so you can say that (a) and (c) are equal. You don't know the value of x and y, so you can't determine whether (b) is equal to either (a) or (c). This means that you can eliminate Choices (A), (C), and (D). *Correct Answer:* Choice (B)

6. The squares in the top row represent a piece of paper that has been folded and punched as shown. Select an answer that shows what the paper looks like when it is unfolded.

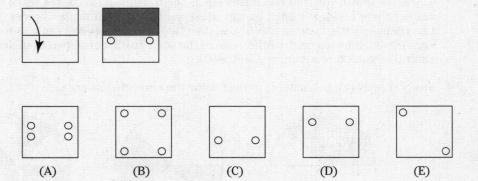

  (A)   (B)   (C)   (D)   (E)

The page is only folded once. With one fold, you multiply the number of holes on the folded page by 2 to find out how many holes are on the unfolded page. The folded page has two holes, so the unfolded page has four. Choices (C), (D), and (E) have only two holes, so cross them out. The holes on the folded page are close to the fold line, so they have to end up in the middle of the unfolded page. Choice (B) shows the holes in the corners, so it can't be right. *Correct Answer:* Choice (A)

Part IV
Practice Makes Perfect

In this part . . .

What better way to get ready for your Catholic high school entrance exam than to practice answering questions in the test's format? We certainly can't think of one, which is why this part provides you with six complete entrance exams — two for the HSPT, two for the TACHS, and two for the COOP. Before you sit down with your #2 pencil, though, make sure you have least two to three uninterrupted hours to devote (per test, that is) so you can get the full mind-numbing effect of plugging through a Catholic high school entrance exam.

The chapters immediately following each of the tests provide explanations of the answers for each of the questions. This is your chance to find out why the right answers are right and the wrong answers are wrong. We share a lot of valuable information in these explanations, so we suggest you read through all of them — even the ones for questions you answered correctly.

Chapter 17

HSPT Practice Test 1

• •

*T*he best way to get good at taking tests is by practicing taking them! So here's a full-length practice HSPT to help get you ready and raring to go on test day.

We've done all we can to make this practice test as close to the real HSPT as possible, but you never know when the test-makers may get it in their heads to change up the test a bit. The HSPT you take may have a different number of questions or slightly different time limits, but overall it'll be pretty much like the one in this chapter.

We strongly encourage you to make your practice test experience as much like the real thing as you can. Here's how:

✔ Find a place where you won't be distracted (step away from the video games!).

✔ Try to take this practice test at approximately the same time of day as your HSPT is scheduled (that means early in the morning, sorry).

✔ Tear out the answer sheet in this chapter and mark your answers on it by filling in the appropriate bubbles.

✔ Use the margins of the test pages to take notes and make computations (unless of course you're dealing with a question that wants you to estimate the answer).

✔ Use a timer to time yourself on each section and stop answering questions when the timer goes off. At that point, you have to move on; there's no going back to skipped questions.

✔ Give yourself a short (10- to 15-minute) break between the Reading and Mathematics sections, which is when you'll probably get a break on exam day.

After you've completed the last section, head to Chapter 18 to check your answers and review the answer explanations.

Answer Sheet for HSPT Practice Test 1

Section 1: Verbal Skills

1. Ⓐ Ⓑ Ⓒ Ⓓ
2. Ⓐ Ⓑ Ⓒ Ⓓ
3. Ⓐ Ⓑ Ⓒ Ⓓ
4. Ⓐ Ⓑ Ⓒ Ⓓ
5. Ⓐ Ⓑ Ⓒ
6. Ⓐ Ⓑ Ⓒ Ⓓ
7. Ⓐ Ⓑ Ⓒ Ⓓ
8. Ⓐ Ⓑ Ⓒ Ⓓ
9. Ⓐ Ⓑ Ⓒ Ⓓ
10. Ⓐ Ⓑ Ⓒ Ⓓ
11. Ⓐ Ⓑ Ⓒ Ⓓ
12. Ⓐ Ⓑ Ⓒ Ⓓ

13. Ⓐ Ⓑ Ⓒ
14. Ⓐ Ⓑ Ⓒ Ⓓ
15. Ⓐ Ⓑ Ⓒ Ⓓ
16. Ⓐ Ⓑ Ⓒ Ⓓ
17. Ⓐ Ⓑ Ⓒ Ⓓ
18. Ⓐ Ⓑ Ⓒ Ⓓ
19. Ⓐ Ⓑ Ⓒ Ⓓ
20. Ⓐ Ⓑ Ⓒ Ⓓ
21. Ⓐ Ⓑ Ⓒ Ⓓ
22. Ⓐ Ⓑ Ⓒ
23. Ⓐ Ⓑ Ⓒ
24. Ⓐ Ⓑ Ⓒ Ⓓ

25. Ⓐ Ⓑ Ⓒ Ⓓ
26. Ⓐ Ⓑ Ⓒ Ⓓ
27. Ⓐ Ⓑ Ⓒ
28. Ⓐ Ⓑ Ⓒ Ⓓ
29. Ⓐ Ⓑ Ⓒ Ⓓ
30. Ⓐ Ⓑ Ⓒ Ⓓ
31. Ⓐ Ⓑ Ⓒ Ⓓ
32. Ⓐ Ⓑ Ⓒ Ⓓ
33. Ⓐ Ⓑ Ⓒ Ⓓ
34. Ⓐ Ⓑ Ⓒ Ⓓ
35. Ⓐ Ⓑ Ⓒ Ⓓ
36. Ⓐ Ⓑ Ⓒ

37. Ⓐ Ⓑ Ⓒ Ⓓ
38. Ⓐ Ⓑ Ⓒ Ⓓ
39. Ⓐ Ⓑ Ⓒ Ⓓ
40. Ⓐ Ⓑ Ⓒ Ⓓ
41. Ⓐ Ⓑ Ⓒ Ⓓ
42. Ⓐ Ⓑ Ⓒ Ⓓ
43. Ⓐ Ⓑ Ⓒ
44. Ⓐ Ⓑ Ⓒ Ⓓ
45. Ⓐ Ⓑ Ⓒ Ⓓ
46. Ⓐ Ⓑ Ⓒ Ⓓ
47. Ⓐ Ⓑ Ⓒ Ⓓ
48. Ⓐ Ⓑ Ⓒ Ⓓ

49. Ⓐ Ⓑ Ⓒ Ⓓ
50. Ⓐ Ⓑ Ⓒ Ⓓ
51. Ⓐ Ⓑ Ⓒ Ⓓ
52. Ⓐ Ⓑ Ⓒ Ⓓ
53. Ⓐ Ⓑ Ⓒ
54. Ⓐ Ⓑ Ⓒ Ⓓ
55. Ⓐ Ⓑ Ⓒ Ⓓ
56. Ⓐ Ⓑ Ⓒ
57. Ⓐ Ⓑ Ⓒ Ⓓ
58. Ⓐ Ⓑ Ⓒ Ⓓ
59. Ⓐ Ⓑ Ⓒ Ⓓ
60. Ⓐ Ⓑ Ⓒ

Section 2: Quantitative Skills

61. Ⓐ Ⓑ Ⓒ Ⓓ
62. Ⓐ Ⓑ Ⓒ Ⓓ
63. Ⓐ Ⓑ Ⓒ Ⓓ
64. Ⓐ Ⓑ Ⓒ Ⓓ
65. Ⓐ Ⓑ Ⓒ Ⓓ
66. Ⓐ Ⓑ Ⓒ Ⓓ
67. Ⓐ Ⓑ Ⓒ Ⓓ
68. Ⓐ Ⓑ Ⓒ Ⓓ
69. Ⓐ Ⓑ Ⓒ Ⓓ
70. Ⓐ Ⓑ Ⓒ Ⓓ
71. Ⓐ Ⓑ Ⓒ Ⓓ

72. Ⓐ Ⓑ Ⓒ Ⓓ
73. Ⓐ Ⓑ Ⓒ Ⓓ
74. Ⓐ Ⓑ Ⓒ Ⓓ
75. Ⓐ Ⓑ Ⓒ Ⓓ
76. Ⓐ Ⓑ Ⓒ Ⓓ
77. Ⓐ Ⓑ Ⓒ Ⓓ
78. Ⓐ Ⓑ Ⓒ Ⓓ
79. Ⓐ Ⓑ Ⓒ Ⓓ
80. Ⓐ Ⓑ Ⓒ Ⓓ
81. Ⓐ Ⓑ Ⓒ Ⓓ
82. Ⓐ Ⓑ Ⓒ Ⓓ

83. Ⓐ Ⓑ Ⓒ Ⓓ
84. Ⓐ Ⓑ Ⓒ Ⓓ
85. Ⓐ Ⓑ Ⓒ Ⓓ
86. Ⓐ Ⓑ Ⓒ Ⓓ
87. Ⓐ Ⓑ Ⓒ Ⓓ
88. Ⓐ Ⓑ Ⓒ Ⓓ
89. Ⓐ Ⓑ Ⓒ Ⓓ
90. Ⓐ Ⓑ Ⓒ Ⓓ
91. Ⓐ Ⓑ Ⓒ Ⓓ
92. Ⓐ Ⓑ Ⓒ Ⓓ
93. Ⓐ Ⓑ Ⓒ Ⓓ

94. Ⓐ Ⓑ Ⓒ Ⓓ
95. Ⓐ Ⓑ Ⓒ Ⓓ
96. Ⓐ Ⓑ Ⓒ Ⓓ
97. Ⓐ Ⓑ Ⓒ Ⓓ
98. Ⓐ Ⓑ Ⓒ Ⓓ
99. Ⓐ Ⓑ Ⓒ Ⓓ
100. Ⓐ Ⓑ Ⓒ Ⓓ
101. Ⓐ Ⓑ Ⓒ Ⓓ
102. Ⓐ Ⓑ Ⓒ Ⓓ
103. Ⓐ Ⓑ Ⓒ Ⓓ
104. Ⓐ Ⓑ Ⓒ Ⓓ

105. Ⓐ Ⓑ Ⓒ Ⓓ
106. Ⓐ Ⓑ Ⓒ Ⓓ
107. Ⓐ Ⓑ Ⓒ Ⓓ
108. Ⓐ Ⓑ Ⓒ Ⓓ
109. Ⓐ Ⓑ Ⓒ Ⓓ
110. Ⓐ Ⓑ Ⓒ Ⓓ
111. Ⓐ Ⓑ Ⓒ Ⓓ
112. Ⓐ Ⓑ Ⓒ Ⓓ

Section 3: Reading

Comprehension

113. Ⓐ Ⓑ Ⓒ Ⓓ
114. Ⓐ Ⓑ Ⓒ Ⓓ
115. Ⓐ Ⓑ Ⓒ Ⓓ
116. Ⓐ Ⓑ Ⓒ Ⓓ
117. Ⓐ Ⓑ Ⓒ Ⓓ
118. Ⓐ Ⓑ Ⓒ Ⓓ
119. Ⓐ Ⓑ Ⓒ Ⓓ
120. Ⓐ Ⓑ Ⓒ Ⓓ

121. Ⓐ Ⓑ Ⓒ Ⓓ
122. Ⓐ Ⓑ Ⓒ Ⓓ
123. Ⓐ Ⓑ Ⓒ Ⓓ
124. Ⓐ Ⓑ Ⓒ Ⓓ
125. Ⓐ Ⓑ Ⓒ Ⓓ
126. Ⓐ Ⓑ Ⓒ Ⓓ
127. Ⓐ Ⓑ Ⓒ Ⓓ
128. Ⓐ Ⓑ Ⓒ Ⓓ

129. Ⓐ Ⓑ Ⓒ Ⓓ
130. Ⓐ Ⓑ Ⓒ Ⓓ
131. Ⓐ Ⓑ Ⓒ Ⓓ
132. Ⓐ Ⓑ Ⓒ Ⓓ
133. Ⓐ Ⓑ Ⓒ Ⓓ
134. Ⓐ Ⓑ Ⓒ Ⓓ
135. Ⓐ Ⓑ Ⓒ Ⓓ
136. Ⓐ Ⓑ Ⓒ Ⓓ

137. Ⓐ Ⓑ Ⓒ Ⓓ
138. Ⓐ Ⓑ Ⓒ Ⓓ
139. Ⓐ Ⓑ Ⓒ Ⓓ
140. Ⓐ Ⓑ Ⓒ Ⓓ
141. Ⓐ Ⓑ Ⓒ Ⓓ
142. Ⓐ Ⓑ Ⓒ Ⓓ
143. Ⓐ Ⓑ Ⓒ Ⓓ
144. Ⓐ Ⓑ Ⓒ Ⓓ

145. Ⓐ Ⓑ Ⓒ Ⓓ
146. Ⓐ Ⓑ Ⓒ Ⓓ
147. Ⓐ Ⓑ Ⓒ Ⓓ
148. Ⓐ Ⓑ Ⓒ Ⓓ
149. Ⓐ Ⓑ Ⓒ Ⓓ
150. Ⓐ Ⓑ Ⓒ Ⓓ
151. Ⓐ Ⓑ Ⓒ Ⓓ
152. Ⓐ Ⓑ Ⓒ Ⓓ

Vocabulary

153. Ⓐ Ⓑ Ⓒ Ⓓ   158. Ⓐ Ⓑ Ⓒ Ⓓ   163. Ⓐ Ⓑ Ⓒ Ⓓ   168. Ⓐ Ⓑ Ⓒ Ⓓ   173. Ⓐ Ⓑ Ⓒ Ⓓ
154. Ⓐ Ⓑ Ⓒ Ⓓ   159. Ⓐ Ⓑ Ⓒ Ⓓ   164. Ⓐ Ⓑ Ⓒ Ⓓ   169. Ⓐ Ⓑ Ⓒ Ⓓ   174. Ⓐ Ⓑ Ⓒ Ⓓ
155. Ⓐ Ⓑ Ⓒ Ⓓ   160. Ⓐ Ⓑ Ⓒ Ⓓ   165. Ⓐ Ⓑ Ⓒ Ⓓ   170. Ⓐ Ⓑ Ⓒ Ⓓ
156. Ⓐ Ⓑ Ⓒ Ⓓ   161. Ⓐ Ⓑ Ⓒ Ⓓ   166. Ⓐ Ⓑ Ⓒ Ⓓ   171. Ⓐ Ⓑ Ⓒ Ⓓ
157. Ⓐ Ⓑ Ⓒ Ⓓ   162. Ⓐ Ⓑ Ⓒ Ⓓ   167. Ⓐ Ⓑ Ⓒ Ⓓ   172. Ⓐ Ⓑ Ⓒ Ⓓ

Section 4: Mathematics

Concepts

175. Ⓐ Ⓑ Ⓒ Ⓓ   180. Ⓐ Ⓑ Ⓒ Ⓓ   185. Ⓐ Ⓑ Ⓒ Ⓓ   190. Ⓐ Ⓑ Ⓒ Ⓓ   195. Ⓐ Ⓑ Ⓒ Ⓓ
176. Ⓐ Ⓑ Ⓒ Ⓓ   181. Ⓐ Ⓑ Ⓒ Ⓓ   186. Ⓐ Ⓑ Ⓒ Ⓓ   191. Ⓐ Ⓑ Ⓒ Ⓓ   196. Ⓐ Ⓑ Ⓒ Ⓓ
177. Ⓐ Ⓑ Ⓒ Ⓓ   182. Ⓐ Ⓑ Ⓒ Ⓓ   187. Ⓐ Ⓑ Ⓒ Ⓓ   192. Ⓐ Ⓑ Ⓒ Ⓓ   197. Ⓐ Ⓑ Ⓒ Ⓓ
178. Ⓐ Ⓑ Ⓒ Ⓓ   183. Ⓐ Ⓑ Ⓒ Ⓓ   188. Ⓐ Ⓑ Ⓒ Ⓓ   193. Ⓐ Ⓑ Ⓒ Ⓓ   198. Ⓐ Ⓑ Ⓒ Ⓓ
179. Ⓐ Ⓑ Ⓒ Ⓓ   184. Ⓐ Ⓑ Ⓒ Ⓓ   189. Ⓐ Ⓑ Ⓒ Ⓓ   194. Ⓐ Ⓑ Ⓒ Ⓓ

Problem Solving

199. Ⓐ Ⓑ Ⓒ Ⓓ   207. Ⓐ Ⓑ Ⓒ Ⓓ   215. Ⓐ Ⓑ Ⓒ Ⓓ   223. Ⓐ Ⓑ Ⓒ Ⓓ   231. Ⓐ Ⓑ Ⓒ Ⓓ
200. Ⓐ Ⓑ Ⓒ Ⓓ   208. Ⓐ Ⓑ Ⓒ Ⓓ   216. Ⓐ Ⓑ Ⓒ Ⓓ   224. Ⓐ Ⓑ Ⓒ Ⓓ   232. Ⓐ Ⓑ Ⓒ Ⓓ
201. Ⓐ Ⓑ Ⓒ Ⓓ   209. Ⓐ Ⓑ Ⓒ Ⓓ   217. Ⓐ Ⓑ Ⓒ Ⓓ   225. Ⓐ Ⓑ Ⓒ Ⓓ   233. Ⓐ Ⓑ Ⓒ Ⓓ
202. Ⓐ Ⓑ Ⓒ Ⓓ   210. Ⓐ Ⓑ Ⓒ Ⓓ   218. Ⓐ Ⓑ Ⓒ Ⓓ   226. Ⓐ Ⓑ Ⓒ Ⓓ   234. Ⓐ Ⓑ Ⓒ Ⓓ
203. Ⓐ Ⓑ Ⓒ Ⓓ   211. Ⓐ Ⓑ Ⓒ Ⓓ   219. Ⓐ Ⓑ Ⓒ Ⓓ   227. Ⓐ Ⓑ Ⓒ Ⓓ   235. Ⓐ Ⓑ Ⓒ Ⓓ
204. Ⓐ Ⓑ Ⓒ Ⓓ   212. Ⓐ Ⓑ Ⓒ Ⓓ   220. Ⓐ Ⓑ Ⓒ Ⓓ   228. Ⓐ Ⓑ Ⓒ Ⓓ   236. Ⓐ Ⓑ Ⓒ Ⓓ
205. Ⓐ Ⓑ Ⓒ Ⓓ   213. Ⓐ Ⓑ Ⓒ Ⓓ   221. Ⓐ Ⓑ Ⓒ Ⓓ   229. Ⓐ Ⓑ Ⓒ Ⓓ   237. Ⓐ Ⓑ Ⓒ Ⓓ
206. Ⓐ Ⓑ Ⓒ Ⓓ   214. Ⓐ Ⓑ Ⓒ Ⓓ   222. Ⓐ Ⓑ Ⓒ Ⓓ   230. Ⓐ Ⓑ Ⓒ Ⓓ   238. Ⓐ Ⓑ Ⓒ Ⓓ

Section 5: Language

239. Ⓐ Ⓑ Ⓒ Ⓓ   251. Ⓐ Ⓑ Ⓒ Ⓓ   263. Ⓐ Ⓑ Ⓒ Ⓓ   275. Ⓐ Ⓑ Ⓒ Ⓓ   287. Ⓐ Ⓑ Ⓒ Ⓓ
240. Ⓐ Ⓑ Ⓒ Ⓓ   252. Ⓐ Ⓑ Ⓒ Ⓓ   264. Ⓐ Ⓑ Ⓒ Ⓓ   276. Ⓐ Ⓑ Ⓒ Ⓓ   288. Ⓐ Ⓑ Ⓒ Ⓓ
241. Ⓐ Ⓑ Ⓒ Ⓓ   253. Ⓐ Ⓑ Ⓒ Ⓓ   265. Ⓐ Ⓑ Ⓒ Ⓓ   277. Ⓐ Ⓑ Ⓒ Ⓓ   289. Ⓐ Ⓑ Ⓒ Ⓓ
242. Ⓐ Ⓑ Ⓒ Ⓓ   254. Ⓐ Ⓑ Ⓒ Ⓓ   266. Ⓐ Ⓑ Ⓒ Ⓓ   278. Ⓐ Ⓑ Ⓒ Ⓓ   290. Ⓐ Ⓑ Ⓒ Ⓓ
243. Ⓐ Ⓑ Ⓒ Ⓓ   255. Ⓐ Ⓑ Ⓒ Ⓓ   267. Ⓐ Ⓑ Ⓒ Ⓓ   279. Ⓐ Ⓑ Ⓒ Ⓓ   291. Ⓐ Ⓑ Ⓒ Ⓓ
244. Ⓐ Ⓑ Ⓒ Ⓓ   256. Ⓐ Ⓑ Ⓒ Ⓓ   268. Ⓐ Ⓑ Ⓒ Ⓓ   280. Ⓐ Ⓑ Ⓒ Ⓓ   292. Ⓐ Ⓑ Ⓒ Ⓓ
245. Ⓐ Ⓑ Ⓒ Ⓓ   257. Ⓐ Ⓑ Ⓒ Ⓓ   269. Ⓐ Ⓑ Ⓒ Ⓓ   281. Ⓐ Ⓑ Ⓒ Ⓓ   293. Ⓐ Ⓑ Ⓒ Ⓓ
246. Ⓐ Ⓑ Ⓒ Ⓓ   258. Ⓐ Ⓑ Ⓒ Ⓓ   270. Ⓐ Ⓑ Ⓒ Ⓓ   282. Ⓐ Ⓑ Ⓒ Ⓓ   294. Ⓐ Ⓑ Ⓒ Ⓓ
247. Ⓐ Ⓑ Ⓒ Ⓓ   259. Ⓐ Ⓑ Ⓒ Ⓓ   271. Ⓐ Ⓑ Ⓒ Ⓓ   283. Ⓐ Ⓑ Ⓒ Ⓓ   295. Ⓐ Ⓑ Ⓒ Ⓓ
248. Ⓐ Ⓑ Ⓒ Ⓓ   260. Ⓐ Ⓑ Ⓒ Ⓓ   272. Ⓐ Ⓑ Ⓒ Ⓓ   284. Ⓐ Ⓑ Ⓒ Ⓓ   296. Ⓐ Ⓑ Ⓒ Ⓓ
249. Ⓐ Ⓑ Ⓒ Ⓓ   261. Ⓐ Ⓑ Ⓒ Ⓓ   273. Ⓐ Ⓑ Ⓒ Ⓓ   285. Ⓐ Ⓑ Ⓒ Ⓓ   297. Ⓐ Ⓑ Ⓒ Ⓓ
250. Ⓐ Ⓑ Ⓒ Ⓓ   262. Ⓐ Ⓑ Ⓒ Ⓓ   274. Ⓐ Ⓑ Ⓒ Ⓓ   286. Ⓐ Ⓑ Ⓒ Ⓓ   298. Ⓐ Ⓑ Ⓒ Ⓓ

Section 1: Verbal Skills

Time: 16 minutes

Directions: Choose the best answer for Questions 1–60.

1. Conservative is to liberal as pepper is to
   - (A) soda
   - (B) salt
   - (C) seasoning
   - (D) spice

2. Which of these words does *not* belong with the others?
   - (A) restaurant
   - (B) house
   - (C) condominium
   - (D) apartment

3. Which of these words does *not* belong with the others?
   - (A) surrender
   - (B) yield
   - (C) relinquish
   - (D) object

4. Cryptic most nearly means
   - (A) mysterious
   - (B) basic
   - (C) frightening
   - (D) secure

5. Sommerville is closer to the lake than Derbyville is. Dillon is closer to the lake than Sommerville is. Dillon is closer to the lake than Derbyville is. If the first two statements are true, the third statement is
   - (A) true
   - (B) false
   - (C) uncertain

6. Which of these words does *not* belong with the others?
   - (A) wretched
   - (B) miserable
   - (C) glum
   - (D) happy

7. Patient is to hospital as student is to
   - (A) cave
   - (B) bus
   - (C) school
   - (D) clouds

8. Genial most nearly means
   - (A) intelligent
   - (B) amiable
   - (C) distant
   - (D) slow

9. A daft fellow is
   - (A) wise
   - (B) dexterous
   - (C) aged
   - (D) foolish

10. Which of these words does *not* belong with the others?
    - (A) advise
    - (B) apprise
    - (C) instruct
    - (D) reprimand

11. Incarcerate is to jail as deposit is to
    - (A) account
    - (B) store
    - (C) apartment
    - (D) prison

Go on to next page

12. Which of these words does *not* belong with the others?

    (A) simple

    (B) tenacious

    (C) persistent

    (D) obstinate

13. Maggie is younger than David. David is younger than Stuart. Stuart is younger than Maggie. If the first two statements are true, the third statement is

    (A) true

    (B) false

    (C) uncertain

14. An actor is a

    (A) stage

    (B) director

    (C) thespian

    (D) musician

15. Savory most nearly means

    (A) bitter

    (B) flavorful

    (C) unattractive

    (D) gutsy

16. Field is to wildflower as pond is to

    (A) stone

    (B) lily pad

    (C) frog

    (D) river

17. Sinister most nearly means

    (A) menacing

    (B) insipid

    (C) zesty

    (D) searing

18. Tepid most nearly means

    (A) enthusiastic

    (B) scalding

    (C) lukewarm

    (D) calm

19. Hour is to minute as year is to

    (A) century

    (B) clock

    (C) calendar

    (D) day

20. Which of these words does *not* belong with the others?

    (A) gregarious

    (B) sociable

    (C) introvert

    (D) outgoing

21. Which of these words does *not* belong with the others?

    (A) ludicrous

    (B) sensible

    (C) farcical

    (D) absurd

22. Micky has more trophies than Donald does. Donald has more trophies than Cal does. Cal has more trophies than Micky does. If the first two statements are true, the third statement is

    (A) true

    (B) false

    (C) uncertain

23. Colfax Avenue is longer than Speer Street. Speer Street is longer than Downing Drive. Downing Drive is longer than Mitchell Road. If the first two statements are true, the third statement is

    (A) true

    (B) false

    (C) uncertain

24. A shrewd investment is

    (A) naive

    (B) wise

    (C) classy

    (D) recent

Go on to next page

25. Which of these words does *not* belong with the others?
    (A) solace
    (B) destitution
    (C) desolation
    (D) ruin

26. Discipline is the *opposite* of
    (A) regulation
    (B) anarchy
    (C) evil
    (D) rebuke

27. All professors are teachers. All teachers are tenured. All professors are tenured. If the first two statements are true, the third statement is
    (A) true
    (B) false
    (C) uncertain

28. Tension is the *opposite* of
    (A) serenity
    (B) strain
    (C) security
    (D) potential

29. An irrevocable agreement is
    (A) definitive
    (B) displeasing
    (C) binding
    (D) flexible

30. Abundant is the *opposite* of
    (A) copious
    (B) meager
    (C) heavy
    (D) weak

31. Which of these words does *not* belong with the others?
    (A) narrow
    (B) swollen
    (C) puffy
    (D) distended

32. Contract is the *opposite* of
    (A) agree
    (B) dwell
    (C) enlarge
    (D) engage

33. Shift is the *opposite* of
    (A) alter
    (B) maintain
    (C) change
    (D) destroy

34. Cloud is to confusion as illuminate is to
    (A) shadow
    (B) combustion
    (C) consumption
    (D) clarification

35. Which word does *not* belong with the others?
    (A) dispute
    (B) argue
    (C) challenge
    (D) acquiesce

36. Green Mountain is higher than Smoky Hill. Smoky Hill is lower than Windy Peak. Green Mountain is higher than Windy Peak. If the first two statements are true, the third statement is
    (A) true
    (B) false
    (C) uncertain

37. Which of these words does *not* belong with the others?
    (A) trip
    (B) journey
    (C) sojourn
    (D) skirmish

38. Labor is the *opposite* of
    (A) struggle
    (B) rest
    (C) join
    (D) divide

Go on to next page

39. A provisional government is
    (A) temporary
    (B) tyrannical
    (C) unrestricted
    (D) democratic

40. Which word does *not* belong with the others?
    (A) blunt
    (B) dull
    (C) quick
    (D) rounded

41. Seismograph is to earthquake as speedometer is to
    (A) time
    (B) velocity
    (C) rotation
    (D) hurricane

42. Mow is to lawn as shave is to
    (A) fitness
    (B) energy
    (C) beard
    (D) garden

43. Daphne plays more sports than Angela. Angela plays more sports than Brittany but fewer than Trini. Trini plays more sports than Brittany. If the first two statements are true, the third statement is
    (A) true
    (B) false
    (C) uncertain

44. Which of these words does *not* belong with the others?
    (A) porch
    (B) parlor
    (C) veranda
    (D) terrace

45. Hypocritical most nearly means
    (A) legitimate
    (B) annoying
    (C) analytical
    (D) insincere

46. A satiated appetite is
    (A) satisfied
    (B) diminutive
    (C) voracious
    (D) hearty

47. Horse is to stable as airplane is to
    (A) sky
    (B) wing
    (C) runway
    (D) hangar

48. Talkative is most *opposite* of
    (A) chatty
    (B) reserved
    (C) garrulous
    (D) miserable

49. Which of these words does *not* belong with the others?
    (A) subordinate
    (B) sovereign
    (C) independent
    (D) autonomous

50. Which of these words does *not* belong with the others?
    (A) remiss
    (B) meticulous
    (C) careful
    (D) scrupulous

51. Engaged most nearly means
    (A) free
    (B) married
    (C) occupied
    (D) separated

Go on to next page

52. Emancipated is the *opposite* of
    (A) uncontrolled
    (B) open
    (C) restricted
    (D) sheltered

53. Hooterville is southwest of Jamestown. Marshdale is northeast of Kellysburg and southeast of Hooterville. Marshdale is north of Jamestown. If the first two statements are true, the third statement is
    (A) true
    (B) false
    (C) uncertain

54. Grounded most nearly means
    (A) established
    (B) dirty
    (C) scared
    (D) volatile

55. Major is the *opposite* of
    (A) foremost
    (B) substantial
    (C) civilian
    (D) trivial

56. The economy car is smaller than the full-size model. The luxury car is larger than the full-size model but not as big as the SUV. The SUV is not as large as the full-size model. If the first two statements are true, the third statement is
    (A) true
    (B) false
    (C) uncertain

57. An indigenous plant is
    (A) foreign
    (B) beautiful
    (C) dehydrated
    (D) native

58. Which of these words does *not* belong with the others?
    (A) celebrity
    (B) star
    (C) luminary
    (D) upstart

59. Ice cream is to caramel sauce as hot dog is to
    (A) ketchup
    (B) bun
    (C) hamburger
    (D) baseball

60. No tibbles are mammals. No mammals fly. All tibbles fly. If the first two statements are true, the third statement is
    (A) true
    (B) false
    (C) uncertain

STOP DO NOT TURN THE PAGE UNTIL TOLD TO DO SO. DO NOT RETURN TO A PREVIOUS TEST.

Section 2: Quantitative Skills

Time: 30 minutes

Directions: Choose the best answer for Questions 61–112.

61. What is the next number in this sequence: 33, 37, 41, . . . ?

(A) 44

(B) 47

(C) 45

(D) 43

62. What number is 5 less than 20% of 100?

(A) 5

(B) 10

(C) 15

(D) 20

63. What number is 10 less than the average of 40, 45, 50, 55, and 40?

(A) 46

(B) 36

(C) 45

(D) 35

64. Examine (a), (b), and (c) and choose the best answer.

(a)   (b)   (c)

(A) (a) is more shaded than (b).

(B) (b) is less shaded than (a) and more shaded than (c).

(C) (c) is less shaded than (a) and more shaded than (b).

(D) (a) is less shaded than (b) and more shaded than (c).

65. What is the next number in this sequence: 75, 69, 63, . . . ?

(A) 56

(B) 57

(C) 58

(D) 55

66. What number is 16 more than ½ of 32?

(A) 32

(B) 16

(C) 48

(D) 12

67. Examine (a), (b), and (c) and choose the best answer.

(a)   (b)   (c)

(A) (a) has fewer circles than (b).

(B) (b) has fewer circles than (a) or (c).

(C) (a), (b), and (c) have an equal number of circles.

(D) The number of circles in (a) plus the number in (b) equals the number in (c).

68. What are the next two numbers in this sequence: 3, 6, 12, 24, . . . ?

(A) 48, 96

(B) 36, 48

(C) 46, 92

(D) 30, 42

Go on to next page

69. What is the cube of 3 divided by 3?
    (A) 3
    (B) 1
    (C) 7
    (D) 9

70. What number is ⅕ of 30?
    (A) 6
    (B) 1
    (C) 7
    (D) 5

71. What is the missing number in this sequence: 56, 63, _____, 77, 84?
    (A) 69
    (B) 70
    (C) 91
    (D) 76

72. Examine (a), (b), and (c) and choose the best answer.
    (a) three quarters
    (b) two quarters, two dimes, and one nickel
    (c) one quarter, four dimes, one nickel, and five pennies
    (A) (a) is greater than (b) or (c).
    (B) (b) is greater than (a).
    (C) (c) is greater than (a).
    (D) (a), (b), and (c) are equal.

73. Examine (a), (b), and (c) and choose the best answer.
    (a) 30% of 90
    (b) 90% of 30
    (c) 30% of 90%
    (A) (a) is less than (b) or (c).
    (B) (a) is equal to (c).
    (C) (a) is equal to (b).
    (D) (c) is less than (b) and greater than (a).

74. What number added to 30 is ¼ of 124?
    (A) 1
    (B) 4
    (C) 6
    (D) 9

75. What is the next number in this sequence: 1,000, 500, 250, 125, . . . ?
    (A) 62
    (B) 63
    (C) 62.5
    (D) 60.5

76. What is the missing number in this sequence: 5, 10, _____, 40?
    (A) 15
    (B) 25
    (C) 30
    (D) 20

77. Examine (a), (b), and (c) and choose the best answer.
    (a) ⅞
    (b) 0.5
    (c) 4.2×0.65
    (A) (b) is greater than (a) and less than (c).
    (B) (a) is greater than (b) and less than (c).
    (C) (c) is less than (a) and greater than (b).
    (D) (a) plus (b) is equal to (c).

78. What number divided by 4 is ⅛ of 72?
    (A) 36
    (B) 9
    (C) 8
    (D) 288

Go on to next page

79. Examine the isosceles triangle *ABC* and choose the best answer.

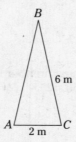

(A) *AB* is greater than *BC*.

(B) *AB* is twice as long as *AC*.

(C) The length of *AB* plus *AC* is equal to *BC* plus *AC*.

(D) *AC* is 1 m shorter than the length of *AB* less *BC*.

80. What is the next number in this sequence: 279, 275, 271, . . . ?

(A) 277

(B) 269

(C) 265

(D) 267

81. ⅓ of what number is 5 times 8?

(A) 150

(B) 120

(C) 40

(D) 39

82. Examine (a), (b), and (c) and choose the best answer.

    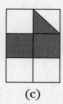

   (a)   (b)   (c)

(A) (a) is more shaded than (b) and less shaded than (c).

(B) (b) and (c) are equally shaded.

(C) (a) and (c) are equally shaded.

(D) (a) is shaded less than (b).

83. What is the missing number in this sequence: 5, 10, 6, 11, _____, 12?

(A) 7

(B) 10

(C) 13

(D) 6

84. What number subtracted from 50 is 3 times the quotient of 36 and 9?

(A) 40

(B) 12

(C) 38

(D) 4

85. ¼ of what number is 10 times 4?

(A) 80

(B) 160

(C) 40

(D) 120

86. Examine (a), (b), and (c) and choose the best answer.

   (a) ¼ of 12

   (b) ⅗ of 15

   (c) ½ of 10

(A) (b) and (c) are equal.

(B) (a) plus (c) is greater than (b).

(C) (c) is greater than (a) and (b).

(D) (b) is greater than (a) and (c).

87. What is the missing number in this sequence: 3, 6, 14, 28, _____, 72?

(A) 46

(B) 25

(C) 48

(D) 36

88. What is the next number in this sequence: V, 10, XV, _____?

(A) XX

(B) 20

(C) XVI

(D) XXV

Go on to next page

89. Examine (a), (b), and (c) and choose the best answer.

    (a) 8^2

    (b) $(8 \times 2)(2 \times 8)$

    (c) 2^8

    (A) (a) is equal to (c) and greater than (b).

    (B) (b) is equal to (c).

    (C) (a) is equal to (b).

    (D) (a) plus (b) is equal to (c).

90. 40% of a number plus 80% of the same number equals 144. What is the number?

    (A) 48

    (B) 96

    (C) 144

    (D) 120

91. What is the missing number in this sequence: 4, 8, 7, _____, 13?

    (A) 10

    (B) 14

    (C) 8

    (D) 12

92. Examine this triangle and choose the best answer.

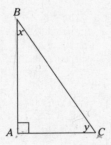

    (A) AB is equal to BC.

    (B) AB plus AC is equal to BC.

    (C) AC is less than BC.

    (D) The measure of $\angle x$ plus the measure of $\angle y$ is greater than the measure of the right angle.

93. What number is 7 less than 4 cubed?

    (A) 64

    (B) 55

    (C) 63

    (D) 57

94. What are the next two numbers in this sequence: 47, 43, 41, 41, 43, 47, . . . ?

    (A) 49, 42

    (B) 47, 53

    (C) 53, 61

    (D) 45, 43

95. Examine (a), (b), and (c) and select the best answer.

    (a) $(4 \times 7) + 2$

    (b) $(5 \times 7) - 7$

    (c) $(3 \times 9) + 1$

    (A) (c) is equal to (b).

    (B) (a) is greater than (b) plus (c).

    (C) (b) is equal to (c) and greater than (a).

    (D) (a), (b), and (c) are equal.

96. What number is 10 less than ⅛ of 112?

    (A) 88

    (B) 98

    (C) 16

    (D) 56

97. What is the next term in this sequence: A^1, B_2, C^3, . . . ?

    (A) C_4

    (B) C^4

    (C) D^4

    (D) D_4

Go on to next page ⇨

98. Examine this figure and select the best answer.

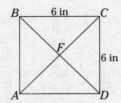

(A) The area of Triangle *AFB* is less than the area of Triangle *BFC*.

(B) *CD* is equal to *CF*.

(C) The area of Quadrilateral *ABCD* is 36 in².

(D) The measure of ∠*BAD* is greater than the measure of ∠*BFC*.

99. Examine (a), (b), and (c) and select the best answer.

   (a) $3^3 \times 10$

   (b) ⅔ of 150

   (c) ½ of 12^2

(A) (a) is greater than (b) plus (c).

(B) (b) is less than (a) and greater than (c).

(C) (b) is equal to (c).

(D) (c) is less than (b), which is less than (a).

100. What are the next three numbers in this sequence:
101, 102, 103, 118, 119, 120, 137, . . . ?

(A) 138, 139, 140

(B) 138, 156, 157

(C) 138, 139, 158

(D) 154, 155, 156

101. What is the missing number in this sequence: 5, 20, 6, 24, 10, _____, 26?

(A) 40

(B) 28

(C) 22

(D) 20

102. The number that is 5 more than 76 is the square of what number?

(A) 11

(B) 9

(C) 8

(D) 7

103. What number multiplied by 7 is 4 more than 80?

(A) 12

(B) 84

(C) 9

(D) 13

104. Examine (a), (b), and (c) and select the best answer.

   (a) $2(45 + 25)$

   (b) $(45 + 25)^2$

   (c) $45 + 2(25)$

(A) (c) is greater than (a).

(B) (a) plus (c) is greater than (b).

(C) (b) is more than 20 times greater than (a) plus (c).

(D) (b) minus (c) is less than (a).

105. What is the missing term in this sequence: L_3, N_5, _____, R_9?

(A) P^6

(B) Q_7

(C) Q_8

(D) P_7

Go on to next page

106. Examine the graph and select the best answer.

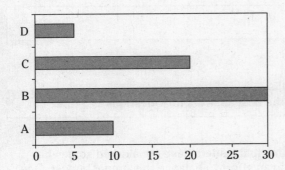

(A) D plus A is equal to C.

(B) B minus C is equal to A.

(C) A plus C is greater than B.

(D) A plus B is twice that of D plus C.

107. What are the next three numbers in this sequence:
20, 21, 25, 23, 24, 25, 26, 27, 25, . . . ?

(A) 30, 31, 33

(B) 28, 29, 25

(C) 29, 30, 25

(D) 26, 27, 28

108. What number added to 70 is a perfect cube?

(A) 125

(B) 100

(C) 50

(D) 55

109. What number decreased by 20% of itself is 72?

(A) 18

(B) 92

(C) 90

(D) 96

110. Examine (a), (b), and (c) and select the best answer.

(a) 3^3

(b) 4^2

(c) 2^4

(A) (b) = 2 × (c)

(B) (b) > (a) > (c)

(C) (b) + (c) > (a)

(D) (a) > (c) > (b)

111. Examine this figure and select the best answer.

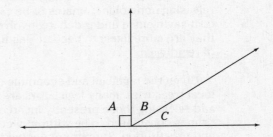

(A) ∠A plus ∠B is equal to 135°.

(B) ∠A plus ∠B equals an acute angle.

(C) ∠B is equal to ∠C.

(D) ∠B plus ∠C equals a right angle.

112. What number is 3 less than ⅗ of 15?

(A) 9

(B) 3

(C) 6

(D) 12

STOP DO NOT TURN THE PAGE UNTIL TOLD TO DO SO.
DO NOT RETURN TO A PREVIOUS TEST.

Section 3: Reading

Time: 25 minutes

Comprehension

Directions: Read the following 5 passages and choose the best answers for Questions 113–152.

Challenged by the recession, state and municipal leaders have considered somewhat novel methods to cut government spending in an effort to balance the annual budget. One of the cost-cutting ideas being bandied about involves shortening prison sentences and releasing nonviolent inmates to be cared for by neighborhood probation officers. Another cost-saving idea under debate involves teaching inmates <u>vocational</u> and career skills so that they are more likely to become gainfully employed once released, thereby reducing the rate of <u>recidivism</u>.

Given the financial and economic challenges currently confronting our federal, state, and local treasuries, many legislators are advocating for <u>decriminalizing</u> some current crimes and releasing those presently incarcerated for committing nonviolent "victimless" crimes. Crimes considered to be without victims commonly consist of drug possession, gambling, and prostitution. Studies conducted by the Federal Bureau of Prisons last year demonstrated that the government spends an average of $256 million per state to catch, prosecute, and incarcerate perpetrators of victimless crimes. Legalizing some victimless crimes and releasing those currently serving time for those crimes would result in a significant savings for taxpayers.

The second legislative proposal to teach vocational skills to prisoners will lead to significant annual tax savings along with a well-trained inmate population. Statistics demonstrate that an investment in vocational training saves money in the long run because inmates are less likely to commit crimes after they are released if they have been trained for a career. Contrary to those naysayers who believe that vocational programs represent a waste of taxpayers' money, vocational training would result in fewer criminals repeating their crimes, which means an overall savings in continually catching, prosecuting, and incarcerating past inmates.

113. The author of this article would most likely agree that
   (A) Victimless crimes should not be legalized.
   (B) Drug possession is the easiest victimless crime to prosecute.
   (C) One method of saving law enforcement costs is to cease prosecuting victimless crimes.
   (D) Society does not have a say about what should be considered criminal behavior.

114. The argument in favor of vocational and career training for inmates assumes which of the following?
   (A) that taxpayers do not mind spending money to create new jails
   (B) that the definition of "victimless crimes" will be expanded to include white-collar crimes
   (C) that inmates who have received vocational or career training will be hired when they are released
   (D) that many taxpayers do not believe that victimless crimes should be decriminalized

Go on to next page

115. The word <u>decriminalizing</u>, as it is used in the passage, most nearly means

    (A) legalizing

    (B) declaring unconstitutional

    (C) outlawing

    (D) prosecuting

116. According to the passage, about how many dollars would be saved per state if victimless crimes were decriminalized?

    (A) $256 million

    (B) $256,000

    (C) $2.56 million

    (D) $256 billion

117. The term <u>recidivism</u>, as it is used in the passage, most nearly means

    (A) progression

    (B) repetition of criminal behavior

    (C) improvement of career skills

    (D) deterioration

118. You would expect to find the information contained in this passage in

    (A) the editorial section of a newspaper

    (B) a professional journal for biology

    (C) a sports magazine

    (D) none of the above

119. The word <u>vocational</u>, as it is used in the passage, most nearly means

    (A) remedial

    (B) positive

    (C) job

    (D) detrimental

120. Which of the following is *not* a proposal for saving money provided by the passage?

    (A) releasing nonviolent prisoners

    (B) shortening prison terms

    (C) providing job training to prisoners

    (D) writing novels about prison life

121. People who are opposed to the author's proposal for vocational training would say what?

    (A) that drug possession is not a victimless crime

    (B) that the government spends too much money prosecuting criminals

    (C) that gamblers are more likely than other criminals to commit crimes after they have been released

    (D) that job training does not result in a reduction of future crimes

122. Which of the following statements can be logically inferred from the information presented in the passage?

    (A) Most inmates confess to wrongdoing and become successfully employed in executive positions once they are released from prison.

    (B) Career training programs offer hope for those criminals who wish to change their prior lifestyles.

    (C) It costs less to imprison perpetrators of victimless crimes than other criminals.

    (D) Because most prisoners are repeat offenders, they will never get jobs.

Go on to next page

It is commonly agreed that recycling is a critical step in both maintaining a clean and green environment and sustaining America's quest for energy independence. The secondary markets for recycled paper, cardboard, aluminum, asphalt, copper, plastic, and glass are at all-time highs. Public education regarding the moral and ethical responsibilities to keep the environment clean has increased. There is now a large supply of and an increasingly strong demand for recycled goods. But we still have problems in one area: the ability to collect and sort recyclables.

Recycle bins have seemingly become depositories for virtually any type of trash, recyclable or not, from a tattered mattress to last week's TV dinner. The recycle bins that newspaper publishers, grocery stores, and big-box department stores have traditionally placed in their parking lots have become trash magnets that produce increasingly <u>determined</u> complaints from patrons and neighbors. Neighbors frequently ask stores to remove their recycle bins largely because they become unsightly. Part of the reason that the stores are so willing to remove the bins is because of the significant expense involved in having to separate trash from newsprint and other recyclables, including aluminum, cardboard, plastic, and glass.

One solution to the problem has come from entrepreneurs who have begun charging for monthly pickups of recyclable materials, like paper, aluminum, plastic, and glass, from customers' curbsides. The monthly fee for this service usually pays for the costs associated with collection and separation of the materials. Additionally, these businesses sell the materials for a profit on the secondary recyclable market after they separate them. This practice is generally viewed as a "win-win" situation for the businesses and their <u>contented</u> customers, who have to pay only a small fee to contribute toward a cleaner, more energy-independent America.

123. As used in the passage, the word <u>determined</u> most nearly means

(A) bitter

(B) proven

(C) resolute

(D) weak

124. According to the passage, which group has been successful in collecting recycled materials from consumers?

(A) government agencies

(B) garbage companies

(C) entrepreneurs

(D) grocery stores

125. As used in this passage, the term <u>contented</u> most nearly means

(A) unselfish

(B) greedy

(C) relaxed

(D) satisfied

126. For what reason did neighbors of recycling bins wish to have them removed?

(A) They were opposed to the idea of recycling.

(B) The smell coming from the bins attracted wild animals.

(C) The bins were ugly.

(D) All of the above.

127. Which of the following is a lament of the author?

(A) Recycling is an important step for maintaining a clean and green environment.

(B) Recycling bins have become depositories for trash.

(C) Recycling assists in America's quest for energy independence.

(D) The secondary markets for reprocessed materials are at all-time highs.

Go on to next page

128. Which of the following items have been placed in recycle bins?

    (A) torn mattresses

    (B) newspapers

    (C) TV dinners

    (D) all of the above

129. Which of the following words best describes the author's attitude toward the businesses that pick up recycled materials for a fee?

    (A) grateful

    (B) naive

    (C) suspicious

    (D) uninterested

130. Which of the following is true given the information in the passage?

    (A) The biggest problem regarding recycling is that Americans do not care about the environment.

    (B) Consumers who participate in recycling contribute toward making America cleaner and more energy efficient.

    (C) Recycling bins in store parking lots have solved the problem of collecting and sorting recycled materials.

    (D) The pickup service provided by businesses is free.

131. Which of the following is *not* a practice of the businesses that pick up recycling?

    (A) They provide recycling bins in their store parking lots.

    (B) They charge a monthly fee.

    (C) They separate the recyclable materials.

    (D) They sell the materials on the secondary market.

132. Which of these is *not* a recyclable material?

    (A) plastic

    (B) newsprint

    (C) aluminum

    (D) bedding

Go on to next page

It is becoming increasingly obvious that the preoccupation with a liberal arts curriculum in higher education is misplaced as the unemployment rate and student loan delinquency rate reach new highs. The days when college students were virtually guaranteed immediate placement upon graduation are rapidly disappearing as our workforce competes for graduates with vocational training skills.

Statistics from the U.S. Department of Labor tell us that the demand for graduates trained in trades, like plumbers, electricians, mechanics, and other technicians, has never been greater in the last century. Similarly, unemployment rates for vocational grads, who often attend private trade schools rather than public state universities, are also at an all-time low. Based upon these facts, it is time for our state legislature to allocate more funding for vocational educational programs rather than schools that focus on a liberal arts curriculum.

133. Based on the information in the passage, which of these professions is probably *not* considered to be a trade?

(A) plumber

(B) psychologist

(C) automotive technician

(D) electrician

134. According to the article, vocational training is most commonly offered in which of the following settings?

(A) private liberal arts colleges

(B) public libraries

(C) large, public universities

(D) private trade schools

135. Which of the following is true?

(A) Graduates from liberal arts schools cannot work as technicians.

(B) The demand for plumbers, electricians, and mechanics is high.

(C) All plumbers, electricians, and mechanics have degrees from trade schools.

(D) Schools that offer a liberal arts curriculum will no longer exist in the next century.

136. Which of these would be the best title for this passage?

(A) Vocational Education Should Receive More Funding

(B) Learning a Trade Is the Only Way to Get a Job

(C) A Liberal Arts Education Is Useless

(D) How to Earn Top Dollar in Today's Job Market

Go on to next page

The First Amendment to the United States Constitution provides that "Congress shall make no law respecting or prohibiting the free exercise thereof; or abridging the freedom of speech, or of the press, or the right of the people peaceably to assemble, and to petition the Government for a redress of grievances." This amendment and nine others constitute the Bill of Rights, which is comprised of the first ten amendments to our Constitution. The Bill of Rights protects more than 30 liberties and rights. The Fourteenth Amendment made most of the Bill of Rights applicable to the states through a process called incorporation.

The origins of the Bill of Rights include the English Magna Carta of 1215, the English Bill of Rights of 1689, various other English precedents and acts, and the experience of people in England and America. Once our Bill of Rights was ratified by three-fourths of the fourteen states, virtually all opposition to the U.S. Constitution quickly disappeared.

The effect of the Bill of Rights is deeply <u>embedded</u> in our daily lives. For example, the Bill of Rights prohibits most attempts to censor certain types of art or music. It also protects speech, which means you can pretty much say whatever you want about a government official in the editorial section of a newspaper or in a blog on the Internet. The Bill of Rights protects our often heated debates on abortion, school prayer, and the death penalty. And the speech you hear police officers give on TV shows when they tell someone who has been arrested that he has "the right to remain silent" is also a Bill of Rights issue. This practice is known as reading someone the Miranda rights. The First Amendment protection of the rights of extremist groups to peacefully assemble means that any group can stage a protest as long as it is not violent. By protecting the civil liberties of even extreme groups, the police and courts seek to preserve the right to freedom of expression for all Americans.

137. Which of the following did *not* provide inspiration to the creators of the Bill of Rights?

(A) the U.S. Constitution

(B) the English Magna Carta of 1215

(C) the English Bill of Rights of 1689

(D) the experience of the English people

138. Which amendment made most of the U.S. Bill of Rights apply to the states?

(A) First Amendment

(B) Tenth Amendment

(C) Second Amendment

(D) Fourteenth Amendment

139. What is the name of the process that made most of the U.S. Bill of Rights applicable to the states?

(A) opposition

(B) reading the Miranda rights

(C) incorporation

(D) ratification

140. According to the passage, the Bill of Rights was ratified by approximately how many of the fourteen states?

(A) 8

(B) 9

(C) 7

(D) 11

141. Which of the following civil liberties would *not* be protected under the Bill of Rights?

(A) the right to stage a violent protest

(B) the right of an extremist group to assemble peacefully

(C) the right of an arrested person to be read the Miranda rights

(D) the right of a magazine to print an article that criticizes a government official

142. The U.S. Bill of Rights is made up of how many amendments?

(A) 30

(B) 10

(C) 9

(D) 14

Go on to next page

143. As is it used in the passage, <u>embedded</u> most nearly means

   (A) implied

   (B) rooted

   (C) respected

   (D) disregarded

144. This passage probably appeared in

   (A) a letter to a state senator

   (B) an impassioned speech to an extremist group

   (C) a science textbook

   (D) a pamphlet about the U.S. Constitution

   After a series of well-publicized failures by various inventors, Orville and Wilbur Wright succeeded in flying and controlling a heavier-than-air craft on December 17, 1903. The War Department, stung by its investment in a failed effort by Samuel Langley and troubled by the Wrights' secretiveness, initially rejected the brothers' requests for the government to buy the aircraft. <u>Prevailing</u> sentiments held that the immediate future still belonged to the balloon. In August 1908, the two brothers delivered the first Army aircraft to the U.S. government. That the U.S. government agreed to purchase an airplane was a minor miracle. For more than four years after the Wright brothers' successful flight at Kitty Hawk, North Carolina, the government refused to accept the fact that man had flown in a heavier-than-air machine.

145. Which of the following is true?

   (A) The Wright brothers were the first to attempt to fly a heavier-than-air craft.

   (B) The U.S. government agreed to purchase an airplane from the Wrights in 1903.

   (C) The Wright brothers approached the government with their proposal to sell it an airplane several years before 1908.

   (D) The Wright brothers successfully flew the heavier-than-air craft in 1903, but they were not able to control the craft until four years later.

146. For what purpose did the government purchase the first airplane?

   (A) to transport government officials across the country

   (B) to form the first private air transportation company

   (C) for use in the military

   (D) to completely replace balloons as a form of air transportation

147. As it is used in the passage, <u>prevailing</u> most nearly means

   (A) existing

   (B) triumphant

   (C) crushing

   (D) minority

148. Which of the following is *not* supported by the passage?

   (A) At the time of the Wrights' successful flight, balloons were already in existence.

   (B) The Wright brothers' secretiveness contributed to their problems in getting the government interested in their aircraft.

   (C) The historic flight took place on the East Coast.

   (D) It took more than six years for the Wright brothers to interest the U.S. government in their airplane.

149. A good title for this passage would be

   (A) Never Give Up

   (B) Famous Inventions

   (C) A History of Flight

   (D) The Wright Brothers' Minor Miracle

150. The author of this passage is most likely

   (A) a pilot

   (B) an Army officer

   (C) a historian

   (D) a U.S. senator

Go on to next page ➡

151. The reason that the author calls the Wright brothers' sale a minor miracle is

    (A) The government did not need an airplane.

    (B) The government did not believe that heavier-than-air craft could fly.

    (C) The government was more interested in Langley's invention.

    (D) Balloons were less expensive than and as effective as airplanes.

152. Which of the following terms describes the government's attitude toward the Wright brothers' invention?

    (A) ecstatic

    (B) agitated

    (C) confident

    (D) skeptical

Vocabulary

Directions: For Questions 153–174, choose the answer that is closest to the same meaning as the underlined word.

153. a <u>paltry</u> sum of money

    (A) substantial

    (B) insignificant

    (C) fat

    (D) clean

154. a <u>foul</u> smell

    (A) musty

    (B) repulsive

    (C) fresh

    (D) floral

155. a state of <u>tedium</u>

    (A) boredom

    (B) enthusiasm

    (C) agitation

    (D) tranquility

156. a <u>zealous</u> fan

    (A) ardent

    (B) uninterested

    (C) continual

    (D) fleeting

157. a <u>debilitating</u> disease

    (A) rapid

    (B) sudden

    (C) devastating

    (D) lengthy

158. to <u>mind</u> your manners

    (A) object to

    (B) pay attention to

    (C) worry about

    (D) ignore

159. a glowing <u>eulogy</u>

    (A) lamp

    (B) humiliation

    (C) interment

    (D) tribute

160. to <u>propose</u> a plan

    (A) end

    (B) marry

    (C) allow

    (D) suggest

Go on to next page

161. a <u>commemorative</u> plaque
    (A) dedicatory
    (B) wooden
    (C) ancient
    (D) contemporary

162. a <u>delightful</u> gathering
    (A) objectionable
    (B) brief
    (C) agreeable
    (D) dull

163. <u>abhorrent</u> morals
    (A) likeable
    (B) odious
    (C) pleasant
    (D) weak

164. a foreign <u>realm</u>
    (A) kingdom
    (B) tribe
    (C) tongue
    (D) technique

165. a <u>literal</u> interpretation
    (A) ambiguous
    (B) factual
    (C) symbolic
    (D) fictitious

166. a <u>congenial</u> disposition
    (A) irascible
    (B) sociable
    (C) cynical
    (D) reserved

167. to <u>vilify</u> an enemy
    (A) justify
    (B) compliment
    (C) disparage
    (D) dislike

168. a discourteous <u>heckler</u>
    (A) ally
    (B) companion
    (C) detractor
    (D) stranger

169. the <u>cantankerous</u> old woman
    (A) grumpy
    (B) affable
    (C) lethargic
    (D) ailing

170. an experienced <u>cosmopolitan</u>
    (A) sophisticate
    (B) manager
    (C) bragger
    (D) plebeian

171. to <u>discombobulate</u> the expert
    (A) execute
    (B) recognize
    (C) comfort
    (D) confound

172. an <u>obvious</u> truth
    (A) unknown
    (B) inconspicuous
    (C) flimsy
    (D) axiomatic

173. an unwanted <u>interloper</u>
    (A) hermit
    (B) intruder
    (C) citizen
    (D) affiliate

174. to <u>conjure</u> a memory
    (A) destroy
    (B) plan
    (C) summon
    (D) suppress

STOP   DO NOT TURN THE PAGE UNTIL TOLD TO DO SO.
DO NOT RETURN TO A PREVIOUS TEST.

Section 4: Mathematics

Time: 45 minutes

Directions: Choose the best answer for Questions 175–238.

Concepts

175. What is 54.673 written to the nearest tenth?

(A) 55

(B) 54.7

(C) 54.67

(D) 54.6

176. Which of the following is a type of angle?

(A) pythagorean

(B) rhomboid

(C) obtuse

(D) parallel

177. Simplify: $2(-5)^2$

(A) 50

(B) −50

(C) 25

(D) −25

178. $\{2, 4, 6, 7, 8, 9\} \cap \{1, 3, 4, 7, 10, 11\} =$

(A) {1, 3}

(B) {2, 3, 4}

(C) {11, 10, 7}

(D) {4, 7}

179. What is an example of a pair of consecutive numbers?

(A) 4, −4

(B) 2, 3

(C) 2, 2

(D) ¼, ½

180. What is 0.23 written as a fraction?

(A) ²³⁄₁₀₀

(B) ²³⁄₁₀

(C) ¹⁰⁰⁄₂₃

(D) ¹⁄₁₀₀

181. When multiplying a number by 100, how many places does the decimal place need to be moved?

(A) five places to the right

(B) four places to the right

(C) three places to the right

(D) two places to the right

182. What is the radius of the circle?

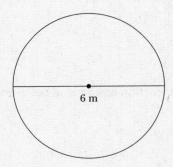

6 m

(A) 3 m

(B) 6π m

(C) 6 m

(D) 3π m

183. How many integers are between ³⁵⁄₉ and 17.4?

(A) 4

(B) 5

(C) 6

(D) 7

184. The square root of 95 is between which of these two numbers?

(A) 8 and 9

(B) 81 and 100

(C) 5 and 6

(D) 9 and 10

Go on to next page

185. How many centimeters are in 1 meter?

    (A) 10,000

    (B) 1,000

    (C) 100

    (D) 10

186. Which of the following is *not* true?

    (A) When adding a negative and a positive number, the answer is always negative.

    (B) Multiplying two negatives results in a positive number.

    (C) Multiplying a negative and a positive always results in a negative number.

    (D) None of the above.

187. The ratio of two numbers is 4:1. The sum of the two numbers is 60. What is the larger of the two numbers?

    (A) 60

    (B) 48

    (C) 5

    (D) 10

188. What fraction has a value between ⅛ and ⅜?

    (A) ½

    (B) ⅝

    (C) ¾

    (D) ¼

189. Which of the following is true?

    (A) $0.35 = 3.5 \times 10$

    (B) $0.032 = 3.2 \times (\frac{1}{10})^2$

    (C) $320 = 3.2 \times 10^3$

    (D) $3,200 = 3.2 \times 10^4$

190. The angle of the shaded area in the circle is $ABC = 40°$. What fraction of the circle is shaded?

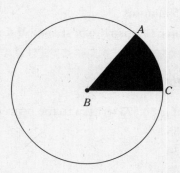

    (A) ⅔

    (B) ⅙

    (C) ⅑

    (D) ⅚

191. Royce spent 30% of his allowance on baseball cards. If Royce's allowance is $20, how much did he spend on baseball cards?

    (A) $6

    (B) $7

    (C) $8

    (D) $9

192. Which of the following numbers is one of the prime factors of 30?

    (A) 5

    (B) 30

    (C) 7

    (D) 4

193. At a recent re-election for a fire chief, 43% voted yes to keeping the old fire chief, 27% voted no, and the rest did not vote at all. What fractional part of the whole did not vote?

    (A) ⅓

    (B) ³⁄₁₀

    (C) ³⁄₁₀₀

    (D) ¹⁄₁₀

Go on to next page

194. Which of the following is a type of quadrilateral?

    (A) octagon

    (B) pentagon

    (C) rhombus

    (D) hexagon

195. What is the least common multiple of 3 and 5?

    (A) 5

    (B) 15

    (C) 12

    (D) 30

196. What proportions must be true if Triangle *XYZ* and Triangle *XVW* are similar?

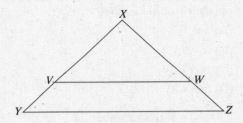

    (A) $^{XV}/_{XW} = {}^{VW}/_{XZ}$

    (B) $^{XY}/_{XZ} = {}^{VW}/_{YZ}$

    (C) $^{XY}/_{YZ} = {}^{XZ}/_{WZ}$

    (D) $^{XV}/_{XY} = {}^{VW}/_{YZ}$

197. Which of these is an example of the associative property of addition?

    (A) (¾ + ⅓) + 4 = ¾ + (⅓ + 4)

    (B) ¾ + ⅓ = 3⅓

    (C) ½ + ½ = 1

    (D) ⅓ + ¾ + 3 = 2 (⅓ + ¾)

198. What is the measure of Angle *x*?

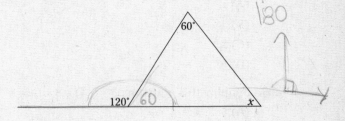

    (A) 30°

    (B) 60°

    (C) 90°

    (D) 120°

Problem Solving

199. Marsha bought 8 notebooks at $4.35 each and 5 folders at $3.78 each. How much did she spend?

    (A) $53.70

    (B) $52.38

    (C) $54.12

    (D) $50.47

200. Mr. Black uses the public transportation system and spends $630 a year on bus and subway tickets. Approximately how much does he pay, on average, each month (rounded to the nearest dollar)?

    (A) $50

    (B) $51

    (C) $52

    (D) $53

201. Solve for *x*: $15 + 4x = x + 30$

    (A) 10

    (B) 15

    (C) 5

    (D) 3

Go on to next page

202. What is the difference between 2½ and 1¾?

    (A) ¾

    (B) 1½

    (C) ¼

    (D) ⅕

203. Simplify this equation: $3 + (-4) + 8 + (-5) =$

    (A) 5

    (B) 4

    (C) 3

    (D) 2

204. The formula for converting temperature from Centigrade to Fahrenheit is $F = \frac{9}{5}C + 32$. What is the Fahrenheit temperature that is equal to 10° Centigrade?

    (A) 32°

    (B) 40°

    (C) 50°

    (D) 53°

205. Solve this equation: $(-6) + (-2) + 5 + (-2) =$

    (A) 5

    (B) -5

    (C) -3

    (D) 3

206. Wade has 5 fewer baseball cards than 3 times the amount Casey has. If Casey has 106 cards, how many does Wade have?

    (A) 313

    (B) 310

    (C) 527

    (D) 400

207. Solve this equation: $1\frac{2}{3} \times \frac{1}{2} =$

    (A) ½

    (B) ⅔

    (C) ⅚

    (D) ¾

208. If Kathy can do 15 math problems in an hour, how many can she do in 5 hours?

    (A) 60

    (B) 65

    (C) 70

    (D) 75

209. A butcher charges $3 per pound for select meats. What would be the cost for 1 pound 8 ounces of select meats?

    (A) $4.00

    (B) $4.50

    (C) $5.00

    (D) $5.50

210. The sum of two numbers is N. If one of the numbers is 3, then three times the other number would be what?

    (A) $3N$

    (B) $3 + N \times 3$

    (C) $3(N \times 3)$

    (D) $3(N - 3)$

211. If $2x - 3 > 5$, then x^2 must be

    (A) <5

    (B) 16

    (C) >16

    (D) >5

212. If $a + 3 = b + 8$, then

    (A) $a > b$

    (B) $a = b$

    (C) $a = 5b$

    (D) $b > a$

213. Katie has 6 shoes fewer than 2 times the number of shoes her best friend has. If her best friend has 48 shoes, how many shoes does Katie have?

    (A) 96

    (B) 48

    (C) 60

    (D) 90

Go on to next page

214. The cost of a bicycle includes a 4% tax that equals $8.60. How much does the bike cost excluding the tax?

   (A) $225

   (B) $215

   (C) $205

   (D) $250

215. If $x = 4$ and $y = \frac{1}{2}$, then what does $x^3 + 5y - 7$ equal?

   (A) 57

   (B) 59½

   (C) 61½

   (D) 59

216. Billy is going to put carpet in his room that will cover his whole floor. If carpeting is $5 per square foot, how much will the carpet cost if his room is 10 ft by 16 ft?

   (A) $800

   (B) $550

   (C) $120

   (D) $255

217. Find the volume of this rectangular solid.

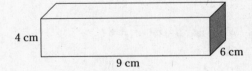

4 cm   9 cm   6 cm

   (A) 88 cm³

   (B) 156 cm³

   (C) 198 cm³

   (D) 216 cm³

218. In the first year that he held a loan, Mr. Caldwell paid $47.50 in interest. The simple interest rate was 4%. What was the original loan amount?

   (A) $1,187.50

   (B) $1,015.00

   (C) $1,137.50

   (D) $1,371.00

219. If $l = 3$, $m = 5$, and $n = 2$, then $3lmn =$

   (A) 45

   (B) 90

   (C) 110

   (D) 13

220. $5.29 + 0.649 + 1.19 =$

   (A) 7.245

   (B) 8.546

   (C) 7.129

   (D) 6.973

221. In the equation $4b - 8 = a$, what is the value of b if $a = 16$?

   (A) 6

   (B) 10

   (C) 12

   (D) 4

222. Solve for x: $5x + 6 = -x + 9$

   (A) ¼

   (B) ⅓

   (C) ⅔

   (D) ½

223. What is a possible value of z if z is an even integer and $-8 > z > -13$?

   (A) −9

   (B) −12

   (C) 0

   (D) 10

224. $36.43 \times 0.062 =$

   (A) 22.5866

   (B) 2.25866

   (C) 0.225866

   (D) 225.866

Go on to next page

225. Stan has lost 3 buttons in 10 days. If Stan keeps on losing buttons at the same rate for 30 days, how buttons will he have lost?

    (A) 6

    (B) 10

    (C) 9

    (D) 13

226. Jessie earns $40 a week doing chores for her parents. She puts 30% of her earnings in a bank account. How much does she put in this bank account every 4 weeks?

    (A) $48

    (B) $50

    (C) $52

    (D) $54

227. What is a possible value of x if $3x - 5 > 17$?

    (A) 2

    (B) 4

    (C) 7

    (D) 8

228. What is $2.5455\overline{)4.31}$?

    (A) 1.69

    (B) 59

    (C) 0.59

    (D) 0.69

229. Renting 4 movies costs $23.40. How much would it cost to rent 2 movies at the same price?

    (A) $11.00

    (B) $11.70

    (C) $12.35

    (D) $12.50

230. Solve for x: $\sqrt{x} + 6 = 11$

    (A) 95

    (B) 100

    (C) 110

    (D) 25

231. Find the value of $\frac{3}{4}x$ if $\frac{1}{2}x = 40$.

    (A) 60

    (B) 65

    (C) 70

    (D) 75

232. $436 \times 42 =$

    (A) 18,123

    (B) 18,312

    (C) 18,321

    (D) 18,100

233. Ten years ago, Sally's mother was 3 times as old as Sally. How old is Sally's mother today if Sally is 25?

    (A) 75

    (B) 35

    (C) 45

    (D) 55

234. What is the ratio of ¾ to ⅛?

    (A) ½

    (B) ⅜

    (C) ⅓

    (D) 2

235. What is x if $\sqrt{x+10} = 8$?

    (A) 65

    (B) 64

    (C) 54

    (D) 50

236. Andrew has twice as much money saved up as his older sister. If Andrew gives his sister $5, both Andrew and his sister will have equal amounts of money. How much money did Andrew save?

    (A) $35

    (B) $30

    (C) $25

    (D) $20

Go on to next page

237. If *y* is an even integer and 8 > *y* > 5, what is *y*?

    (A) 6

    (B) 8

    (C) 5

    (D) 7

238. What is the area of the following figure?

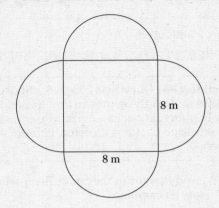

8 m

8 m

    (A) $(64 + 4\pi)$ m²

    (B) $(64 + 32\pi)$ m²

    (C) $(64 + 16\pi)$ m²

    (D) $(64 + 8\pi)$ m²

Section 5: Language

Time: 25 minutes

Directions: For Questions 239–278, choose the answer with the sentence that has an error in punctuation, capitalization, or usage. If no sentence contains an error, choose Answer D.

239. (A) Andy swims in the Snake River when we go camping.
   (B) Our school always has a party on Valentine's day.
   (C) My dad and I have seen *The Wizard of Oz* 20 times.
   (D) No mistakes

240. (A) Him and Mary bought several items.
   (B) "Have you see my gloves?" Helen asked.
   (C) The dog ran around the block.
   (D) No mistakes

241. (A) Jessica placed her textbook next to my glasses on the table.
   (B) Before she packed her suitcase, Marcia checked the weather.
   (C) Gerald remarked, "I think I'll set down on this bench and wait for the train."
   (D) No mistakes

242. (A) When we were growing up, our mother tells us that nothing is impossible.
   (B) Please note that I will be collecting exams at exactly 11:00 a.m.
   (C) Duke worked at the pizza counter every Sunday from 1:00 to 5:00 p.m.
   (D) No mistakes

243. (A) Peter commented, "I'm not sure whether or not I will go hiking tomorrow."
   (B) Daisies are my favorite flowers.
   (C) Dad takes my brother and me to school before he goes to work.
   (D) No mistakes

244. (A) Suzanne hardly never stops by our house to visit us.
   (B) The children wore makeup instead of masks for Halloween.
   (C) I love when the snow finally melts and the garden shows the first signs of spring.
   (D) No mistakes

245. (A) Get to bed without delay!
   (B) Terry has played the tuba in the marching band for three years.
   (C) We celebrated Passover on Thursday this year.
   (D) No mistakes

246. (A) Every year my family summered at the beach.
   (B) Belinda was born on October 21 1995.
   (C) Do you know the way to the airport?
   (D) No mistakes

247. (A) The cat has been licking its paw for hours.
   (B) On Saturdays and Sundays we visit our grandparents.
   (C) Neither my brother or I have any idea how to fly a kite.
   (D) No mistakes

248. (A) Missy asked her teacher to explain the assignment to her.
   (B) Matt is the younger of the five brothers.
   (C) He sits in his armchair and reads the newspaper every night.
   (D) No mistakes

Go on to next page

249. (A) Patsy melted butter in the microwave.
 (B) Christmas is the busiest season of the year for shoppers.
 (C) This year there have been less cases of flu than there were last year.
 (D) No mistakes

250. (A) Be sure to buy your ticket for the raffle by 3:00.
 (B) Gladys asked if I knew the way to the grocery store?
 (C) We had to travel through a long, dark tunnel to reach our destination.
 (D) No mistakes

251. (A) I refuse to believe that you haven't had a thing to eat all day.
 (B) Where did you get that shirt?
 (C) Sal broke his tooth when he bit into the apple.
 (D) No mistakes

252. (A) The band played 15 songs before it took a break.
 (B) I set the book on the desk.
 (C) When you get to Chicago, give my aunt a call.
 (D) No mistakes

253. (A) Jackie and Mannie have waited all of they're lives to travel to Europe.
 (B) Driving while talking on a cell phone is dangerous.
 (C) Ask Pat to help you with the cake.
 (D) No mistakes

254. (A) If you want your computer to run efficient, you must perform regular maintenance.
 (B) Only time will tell how effective the medication actually is.
 (C) In the autumn, we see herds of elk grazing in the fields behind our house.
 (D) No mistakes

255. (A) It mystifies me that such a large sleeping bag fits into such a tiny sack.
 (B) Paul couldn't eat dessert because he had eaten to much for dinner.
 (C) Nora decided to set the table with the good silverware.
 (D) No mistakes

256. (A) I didn't unload the dishwasher until the dishes were dry.
 (B) My fathers' coat is too big for me.
 (C) She and I have been arguing about this topic for years.
 (D) No mistakes

257. (A) Pretend that you don't see Margie.
 (B) We asked for directions at the gas station.
 (C) If we had known you were coming, we would of saved a place for you.
 (D) No mistakes

258. (A) If you follow the rules, you will be rewarded.
 (B) Please don't track mud into the house.
 (C) Dustin ordered a hot chocolate, because he was cold.
 (D) No mistakes

259. (A) Did the Cougars win the game?
 (B) The students will vote for either Bobbie or Jasmine.
 (C) Strawberry is the most popular of the three types of ice cream.
 (D) No mistakes

260. (A) The puppy ran away with it's tail between it's legs.
 (B) I have never been as embarrassed as I was last night!
 (C) Have you seen the Grand Canyon?
 (D) No mistakes

Go on to next page

261. (A) Gary doesn't understand why he can't attend the meeting.
    (B) Grandmother met us at Kennedy airport in her new car.
    (C) Gardening is my mother's favorite hobby.
    (D) No mistakes

262. (A) Joe's parents have lived in Reno for several years.
    (B) If you travel to Seattle, bring your umbrella.
    (C) Do you know who's book this is?
    (D) No mistakes

263. (A) I stop at the coffee shop after work.
    (B) Please don't tell no one about the secret I've told you.
    (C) Your secret is safe with me.
    (D) No mistakes

264. (A) Angel and Joshua have differing opinions on the effects of global warming.
    (B) Can't you stop talking and start listening for once?
    (C) The toddler learned how to climb the stairs by himself.
    (D) No mistakes

265. (A) The cat hissed at the whirling leaves as they fell from the tree.
    (B) There isn't a soul around.
    (C) The company makes their money by selling intricate widgets.
    (D) No mistakes

266. (A) The noise was deafening as we walked into the gymnasium.
    (B) Shouts and applause emanated from all four corners of the room.
    (C) We felt very privileged to be honored at the Lincoln Center last year.
    (D) No mistakes

267. (A) Zachary was meticulous about choosing the correct answer to the question.
    (B) Did you see how quick that cat chased after the mouse?
    (C) Rex hoped that his soccer coach would give Pete and him a break.
    (D) No mistakes

268. (A) Anthony based his opinion on something his father had said.
    (B) Carlos has been skiing for as long as I have known him.
    (C) Have you talked to Ruby lately?
    (D) No mistakes

269. (A) Kevin bought Agatha a diamond ring for their anniversary.
    (B) Don't you wish that we had more time to take the test?
    (C) After his run, Dad lied down on the couch and took a nap.
    (D) No mistakes

270. (A) Marco joined the Air Force when he graduated from college.
    (B) Carl and Cathy bought there snowboards through an online auction.
    (C) Jack hasn't been to Wyoming since he started working.
    (D) No mistakes

271. (A) Big things come in small packages.
    (B) If you can't beat them, join them.
    (C) Nellie is much better at softball than me.
    (D) No mistakes

272. (A) I expect wonderful news from my cousins today.
    (B) There has been breaking news in the developing story about the fire.
    (C) Kids of all ages enjoy the Circus.
    (D) No mistakes

Go on to next page

273. (A) After the party ended, Marty and Paul wash dishes.
    (B) I haven't heard from Dave, and I don't expect to until Friday.
    (C) Maria and he have been friends since third grade.
    (D) No mistakes

274. (A) I haven't been to Coney island since my brother was born.
    (B) We used to go there at least once each summer.
    (C) People are really mad about the highway closure.
    (D) No mistakes

275. (A) Sunshine on my shoulders makes me feel warm and cozy.
    (B) Roberta missed the bus, now she must walk home.
    (C) My experience at camp last summer was one of the best of my life.
    (D) No mistakes

276. (A) Mother has been wondering where you have been.
    (B) Correct me, if I'm wrong.
    (C) Isn't Bridget your sister?
    (D) No mistakes

277. (A) The tortoise married the hare, and they lived happily ever after.
    (B) There's no place like home.
    (C) I figured out where you were hiding.
    (D) No mistakes

278. (A) After waiting an hour, I simply gave up.
    (B) If you don't have to time to pick up Sarah and me, my mom can do it.
    (C) If you go East on Pennsylvania Avenue, you'll get there more quickly.
    (D) No mistakes

Directions: For Questions 279–288, choose the answer that has the spelling error. If no sentence contains an error, choose Answer D.

279. (A) The hospital recieved notice that the patients had not been admitted.
    (B) The passengers' families waited eagerly for the plane to land.
    (C) Nobody noticed that the thief had slipped out of the room.
    (D) No mistakes

280. (A) Stephanie stepped up to bat for the first time.
    (B) The physician was examinning the boy for any signs of illness.
    (C) She was covered from head to toe in spider webs and soot.
    (D) No mistakes

281. (A) Barry mastered his golf swing just in time for the tournament.
    (B) Please do not approach the counter without having your ticket ready.
    (C) The restaurant serves a wide variety of dishes.
    (D) No mistakes

282. (A) Until I met Sandy, I did not know that she was a sciencetist.
    (B) Melanie and Mitch met at the laundry room to wash their clothes.
    (C) We were told to use our best judgment in making the decision.
    (D) No mistakes

283. (A) Patty and Steve have skated together for more than forty years.
    (B) Traveling to Spain is something I want to accomplish before I graduate.
    (C) Don't you wish that teachers made their lectures more humorous?
    (D) No mistakes

Go on to next page

284. (A) Thanksgiving is a holiday that celebrates family and food.

    (B) Imediately after ordering the chicken sandwich, I wished I had ordered turkey instead.

    (C) The cherry blossoms make March a lovely time to visit Washington D.C.

    (D) No mistakes

285. (A) Business has been booming since we decided to open earlier in the morning.

    (B) No one really knows how long the expedition into the jungle will take.

    (C) Our forfathers constructed the Constitution to preserve our rights.

    (D) No mistakes

286. (A) Whenever I go to class, I make sure that I have pen and paper in my possession.

    (B) Grant thinks he will make the varsity soccer team next year.

    (C) I made my decision independant of others' opinions.

    (D) No mistakes

287. (A) Before you climb mountains, make sure you have the right equiptment.

    (B) The amount you spend on travel should not exceed the designated limit.

    (C) Peter was relaxing on the porch when we came by for a visit.

    (D) No mistakes

288. (A) The north wind brought a heavy snowstorm to the state.

    (B) Our house in Georgia had two gigantic columms at the front entrance.

    (C) I was not conscious of how much time my mother had spent sewing my costume.

    (D) No mistakes

Directions: Follow the given directions for Questions 289–298.

289. Choose the group of words that best completes the sentence.

    Gazing out the schoolroom window, _____.

    (A) a herd of grazing deer caught my eye

    (B) I spotted a herd of grazing deer

    (C) a herd of deer was spotted by me

    (D) I spotted a herd of deer grazing in a group

290. Choose the word that best joins the thoughts together.

    Visiting China has always been a dream of mine; _____ until now I have not had the funds to go there.

    (A) therefore,

    (B) additionally,

    (C) however,

    (D) none of these

291. Which of these sentences expresses the idea most clearly?

    (A) After graduating from high school, college seemed like the natural next step for Sam.

    (B) Sam graduated from high school, and then college naturally, for Sam, seemed like the next step.

    (C) After he graduated from high school, Sam considered college to then be the natural next step.

    (D) Sam considered college to be the natural next step after he graduated from high school.

Go on to next page

292. Which sentence does *not* belong in the paragraph?

    (1)Fantasy is the language of the imagination. (2)Therefore, I think it is appropriate to use fantasy to educate children. (3)I can make this statement with the support of the great poet, Shelly. (4)He stated, "The great instrument of moral good is the imagination." (5) Science fiction stories are based on fantasy.

    (A) Sentence 2

    (B) Sentence 3

    (C) Sentence 4

    (D) Sentence 5

293. Which of these sentences would fit best under the topic of "Finding a Summer Job"?

    (A) Review your resume and brush up on your interview skills.

    (B) The summer months are the hottest, so drink plenty of liquids when you are at the pool.

    (C) Summer and spring break are when most students go on vacation.

    (D) None of these

294. Choose the word or words that best join the thoughts together.

    Doug has run a four-minute mile in his last three races; _____ it is reasonable to conclude that he will run a four-minute mile in the race this weekend.

    (A) therefore,

    (B) nevertheless,

    (C) in contrast,

    (D) none of these

295. Which of these sentences expresses the idea most clearly?

    (A) I left the schedule for the meeting on my desk, and I had to go back to my office and get it.

    (B) Going back to get it, the meeting schedule was left on my desk by me.

    (C) The meeting schedule was left on my desk, and going back to get it was I.

    (D) I left the meeting schedule on my desk, and I had to go back to my office to get it.

296. Choose the group of words that best completes the sentence.

    After hearing how cold it was outside, _____.

    (A) putting on hats and mittens was required of the children by their teacher

    (B) hats and mittens were put on by the children at the request of their teacher

    (C) the teacher required the children to put on their hats and mittens

    (D) the teacher required that hats and mittens be put on by the children

297. Which of these sentences expresses the idea most clearly?

    (A) Again, I will never attempt to cross without my waders and snorkel the wide and treacherous river.

    (B) The wide, treacherous river I will again never attempt to cross without both my waders and snorkel.

    (C) Never again will I attempt to cross the wide, treacherous river without my waders and snorkel.

    (D) Attempting to cross the wide and treacherous river again without my waders and snorkel I will never do.

Go on to next page

298. Where is the best place for this sentence in the following paragraph?

Therefore, the federal government should permit private companies to take over transportation so that federal interstates and state-held roads and highways would run more efficiently and economically.

[1]It has been proven statistically that private companies do a better job of operating public transportation than the government does. [2]For instance, private companies could easily change state-maintained roads into toll roads, which would make it so only those who use the roads would be responsible for paying for them. [3]Instigating toll roads would save some citizens lots of money.

(A) Before Sentence 1

(B) Between Sentence 1 and Sentence 2

(C) Between Sentence 2 and Sentence 3

(D) The sentence does not belong in this paragraph.

Chapter 18

Answers to HSPT Practice Test 1

The following explanations are for HSPT Practice Test 1, which is in Chapter 17. Take your time reviewing them, making sure to read everything. We guarantee you'll pick up valuable pointers for eliminating wrong answers and choosing the right ones if you do. *Note:* If you don't have the time to read through each answer explanation, flip to the end of this chapter to check your answers using the short 'n' sweet answer key.

Section 1: Verbal Skills

1. **B.** Conservative is the opposite of liberal. The answer that's most opposite to pepper is salt, Choice (B). Seasoning and spice are more descriptive of pepper than opposites, and soda is unrelated.

2. **A.** The best answer is Choice (A), restaurant. All the other choices name places where people live. A restaurant is where they eat.

3. **D.** Choices (A), (B), and (C) are synonyms for giving in; Choice (D) isn't.

4. **A.** If you know that a crypt is a burial chamber, you may be tempted to pick Choice (C). But a tomb isn't called a crypt because it's frightening; *cryptic* means "hidden, secret, or mysterious," which is Choice (A).

5. **A.** Visualize this logic question by creating a line diagram that lists the cities in order of closest to farthest from the lake based on the information in the first two statements: Dillon → Sommerville → Derbyville. Dillon is the closest, which means the third statement is true, Choice (A).

6. **D.** *Wretched*, *miserable*, and *glum* are words that mean "sad." Choice (D) is an antonym.

7. **C.** For this analogy question, tell yourself that a patient belongs in a hospital. A student could belong in a school or on a bus, so you need to make your sentence more specific. A hospital is a structure that houses patients, and a school is a structure that houses students. A bus provides transportation for students, but it doesn't house them; Choice (C) is your answer.

8. **B.** This synonym question may be a little tricky because you may think that genial sounds sort of like genius. But *genial* actually means "friendly." Therefore, the best answer is Choice (B), *amiable*, which also means "friendly or agreeable."

9. **D.** To be *daft* is to be goofy or silly. The best answer is Choice (D).

10. **D.** *Advise*, *apprise*, and *instruct* mean "to inform"; *reprimand* means "to scold," which means it's not like the other words. Pick Choice (D).

11. **A.** To *incarcerate* is the act of placing someone in jail. To *deposit* is the act of placing something in an account (not a store, apartment, or prison). Go with Choice (A).

12. **A.** Simple doesn't belong with the other three choices, all of which mean to be determined or stubborn. Choice (A) is the best answer.

13. **B.** Create a line diagram from youngest to oldest: Maggie → David → Stuart. Stuart is older than Maggie, which means the third statement is false, Choice (B).

14. **C.** Look for the word that means the same thing as actor. An actor isn't a stage. Some actors can be directors, but an actor and a director don't do the same things. Playing music and acting aren't the same. The process of elimination shows you that the answer must be Choice (C); another word for actor is *thespian*.

15. **B.** Savory has to do with how something tastes; eliminate Choices (C) and (D). A savory taste is pleasant, so cross out Choice (A). Choice (B) is the best answer.

16. **B.** A field is a place where wildflowers grow just as a pond is a place where lily pads grow. You may be tempted to select Choice (C), frog, but the primary relationship involves plants, which makes the better answer Choice (B).

17. **A.** Something *sinister* is evil or threatening. The best synonym is Choice (A), menacing. Choice (B) may sound evil, but *insipid* just means "dull or bland."

18. **C.** *Tepid* water is neither hot nor cold; it's lukewarm, Choice (C). It can also describe a person's indifference. Choices (A) and (B) are antonyms, and Choice (D) is unrelated.

19. **D.** An hour is a whole made up of minutes. A year is a whole made up of days, Choice (D). If you picked Choice (A), you reversed the relationship. A year isn't made up of a bunch of centuries; a century is made up of 100 years.

20. **C.** Choices (A), (B), and (D) are synonyms for extrovert. Choice (C) is the opposite.

21. **B.** Sensible, Choice (B), is the opposite of *ludicrous*, *farcical*, and *absurd*, all of which mean "silly or ridiculous."

22. **B.** The line diagram from owning more trophies to fewer looks like this: Micky → Donald → Cal. Cal doesn't have more trophies than Micky, so the third statement is false, Choice (B).

23. **C.** From longest to shortest, the roads are Colfax Avenue → Speer Street → Downing Drive. There's no prior reference for Mitchell Road, which means the premises don't give you the information you need to determine whether Downing Drive is longer than Mitchell Road. The statement is therefore uncertain, Choice (C).

24. **B.** A *shrewd* investment is a smart one, which makes Choice (B) the best answer. Choice (A) is opposite, and Choices (C) and (D) are unrelated.

25. **A.** Choices (B), (C), and (D) show extreme lack and devastation. You may need solace or comfort if you find yourself in one of these states, but Choice (A) is different.

26. **B.** Discipline is obedience or control; regulation is a synonym. The word that means the opposite of obedience or control is Choice (B), anarchy.

When an HSPT question asks you for the *opposite* word, remember that you're looking for an antonym. Inevitably the synonym will be hiding among the answer choices; don't pick it.

27. **A.** Draw a Venn diagram of the first two statements to solve this logic question.

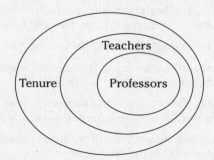

Because all professors are included with teachers, the professors are also tenured. Therefore, the statement is true, Choice (A).

28. **A.** The opposite of tension is peace or serenity, Choice (A). Choice (B), strain, is a synonym, and the other options aren't related.

29. **C.** An *irrevocable* agreement is one that can't be broken, which means it's binding, Choice (C).

30. **B.** Choice (B), *meager*, meaning "insignificant," is the opposite of *abundant*, which means "plentiful." Choice (A) also means plentiful, so it's a synonym rather than an antonym.

31. **A.** Choices (B), (C), and (D) are words that mean enlarged. Choice (A) doesn't belong because narrow conveys thinness rather than enlargement.

32. **C.** You must look for the opposite of the verb form of the word *contract*, which means to get smaller. Choice (C), enlarge, is the opposite of getting smaller.

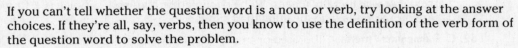

If you can't tell whether the question word is a noun or verb, try looking at the answer choices. If they're all, say, verbs, then you know to use the definition of the verb form of the question word to solve the problem.

33. **B.** To *shift* is to move or change. Eliminate Choices (A) and (C) because they have the same meaning. Shift doesn't mean build, so destroy isn't its opposite. The best answer is Choice (B); *maintain* means "to stay the same or continue in the same way."

34. **D.** Used as a verb, *cloud* means "to make unclear," which means that to cloud is to bring about confusion. To *illuminate* is to bring about clarification, Choice (D).

35. **D.** The first three choices are words that mean to disagree. Choice (D) means to give in or agree, which means it doesn't belong with the others.

36. **C.** The first two statements give you two possible diagrams: Green Mountain → Windy Peak → Smoky Hill or Windy Peak → Green Mountain → Smoky Hill. You don't know whether Windy Peak is lower or higher than Green Mountain, which makes the third statement uncertain, Choice (C).

37. **D.** Choices (A), (B), and (C) are ways to convey an excursion. Choice (D), a *skirmish*, is a minor battle, so it doesn't belong with the other words.

38. **B.** The opposite of labor or work is rest, Choice (B). Choice (A) is a synonym, and the other options are unrelated to work.

39. **A.** A *provisional* government is one that has power until the permanent government is established, which means it's temporary, Choice (A). Provisional doesn't have a political connotation, so Choices (B), (C), and (D) can't be right.

40. **C.** Blunt, dull, and rounded are words that describe something that's not sharp. Choice (C) isn't related to sharpness or dullness, so it doesn't belong.

41. **B.** A *seismograph* is a tool to measure the strength of earthquakes, and a *speedometer* is a tool to measure the velocity of a vehicle, Choice (B).

42. **C.** To mow is to cut a lawn, and to shave is to cut a beard, Choice (C).

43. **A.** There are two ways to order the girls from the one who plays the most sports to the one who plays the least: Daphne → Trini → Angela → Brittany or Trini → Daphne → Angela → Brittany. In both cases, Trini plays more sports than Brittany, so the third statement is true, Choice (A).

44. **B.** Porch, veranda, and terrace name outside sitting areas. A parlor, Choice (B), is inside, so it doesn't belong.

45. **D.** To be *hypocritical* is to say you have feelings or qualities that you don't really have, which makes the best synonym Choice (D), insincere. Although listening to a hypocritical person may be pretty annoying, hypocritical doesn't mean the same thing as annoying.

46. **A.** *Satiated* means "full." If you're full, you're satisfied, Choice (A). Choice (B) doesn't fit, and Choices (C) and (D) have pretty much the same meaning.

You can't have two right answers for one question, so anytime you see a pair of answer choices that have eerily similar definitions, you know neither can be right.

47. **D.** A horse is housed in a stable, and an airplane is housed in a hangar, Choice (D). Sure, an airplane travels on a runway or in the sky, but housing one in either location is unsafe.

48. **B.** Choices (A) and (C) are synonyms for talkative, so cross them out. Choice (D) is unrelated to talkative. The word that's most opposite is Choice (B), *reserved*, which means "shy."

49. **A.** Choices (B), (C), and (D) are synonyms for self-ruling. Choice (A), *subordinate*, means "inferior," so it's unrelated to the other words.

50. **A.** The last three answers have similar meanings; all of them refer to strict attention to detail. Choice (A) is an antonym. *Remiss* means "careless or lax."

51. **C.** Resist the temptation to pick Choice (B) here. To be engaged isn't the same as being married. *Engaged* literally means "to be occupied or involved," Choice (C). Choices (A) and (D) are more opposite in meaning than similar.

52. **C.** *Emancipated* means "liberated or freed." The opposite of freed is restricted, Choice (C). Choices (A) and (B) are more similar in meaning to emancipated, and Choice (D) doesn't show lack of freedom so much as lack of exposure.

53. **B.** The relationships in this logic question can't be expressed in a straight line, so your diagram will be crooked.

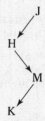

There's no way Marshdale can be north of Jamestown if it's south of Hooterville. The third statement has to be false, Choice (B).

54. **A.** To be *grounded* is to be firmly fixed or established, Choice (A). Although being grounded means that you have your feet placed firmly on the ground, it doesn't mean that your feet are dirty, Choice (B). The other choices are unrelated.

55. **D.** If something's major, it's important. The opposite is Choice (D), trivial. Stay away from Choices (A) and (B) because they're synonyms of major.

56. **B.** Arrange the vehicles from smallest to largest like this: Economy Car → Full-Size Car → Luxury Car → SUV. The SUV is the largest vehicle, so saying it's not as large as the full-size car is false, Choice (B).

57. **D.** An *indigenous* plant is one that's native to the area where it's growing. The best answer is Choice (D). Choice (A) is an antonym, and the other choices are unrelated.

58. **D.** Celebrity, star, and luminary are names for famous people. An *upstart*, Choice (D), is someone who's unknown and therefore doesn't fit in with the others, poor thing.

59. **A.** You top yummy ice cream with delicious caramel sauce, and you top a plump hot dog with thick ketchup. Buns may surround a hot dog, but they don't top them in the way caramel sauce tops ice cream. Choice (A) fits the best. (Feeling hungry yet?)

60. **C.** When you make a Venn diagram from the first two statements, you draw a circle for the ability to fly and a separate circle for mammals. You can put the circle for tibbles anywhere in relation to the ability to fly so long as it doesn't intersect with the mammal circle. This figure shows the possibilities.

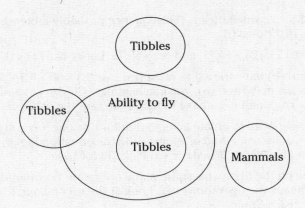

The tibbles circle could go completely inside the fly circle, completely outside the fly circle, or partially inside and out. What does that tell you? That how many tibbles fly is uncertain, Choice (C).

Section 2: Quantitative Skills

61. **C.** The sequence progresses by +4, which means the next number is 45, Choice (C).

62. **C.** First figure out 20% of 100. 20% is the same as 0.2 and *of* means ×, so take 0.2 × 100 to get 20. 5 less than 20 is the same as 20 – 5, which is 15, Choice (C).

63. **B.** 40 + 45 + 50 + 55 + 40 = 230; 230 ÷ 5 = 46. But don't stop there and pick Choice (A)! Remember to subtract 10: 46 – 10 = 36, Choice (B).

   The *average* is the sum of a set of numbers divided by the amount of numbers in the set.

64. **D.** Write down the shaded portion of each of the figures: (a) is ½ shaded, (b) is ¾ shaded, and (c) is ¼ shaded. Then eliminate answers. You know that (a) is less shaded than (b), so cross out Choice (A). Because (b) is more shaded than (a), you don't have to read any further to know that Choice (B) is wrong. (c) is less shaded than (a), which means so far so good for Choice (C). But (c) isn't more shaded than (b), so you can eliminate it. Choice (D) is correct: ½ is < ¾ and > ¼.

The HSPT questions that ask you to examine and evaluate aren't usually difficult, but they do require you to undergo a lengthier problem-solving process because you must consider and compare several values. If you notice you've spent more than 30 seconds trying to solve this question (and others like it), next time mark your best guess and move on. You can always go back to the question if you have time at the end of the section.

65. **B.** The numbers in this sequence decrease by 6. 63 – 6 = 57, which is Choice (B).

66. **A.** Half of 32 is 16. When you add 16 to 16, you're back at 32, Choice (A).

67. **A.** Count the circles in each picture (don't guess!) and write down the totals: (a) has 8 circles, (b) has 10, and (c) has 15. So (a) < (b) < (c). Choice (A) is right; (a) has fewer circles than (b). Don't waste your time checking the other options in this case because the answer's so obvious.

68. **A.** The operation from 3 to 6 could be +3 or ×2. 6 × 2 = 12, so the operation is ×2. 24 × 2 = 48. The only answer that lists 48 as the next number is Choice (A).

69. **D.** The cube of 3 is 3 × 3 × 3, which equals 27. 27 ÷ 3 = 9, Choice (D).

70. **D.** ⅙ × 30 = ³⁰⁄₆, or 5, which is Choice (D).

71. **B.** 63 – 56 = 7, which means the sequence probably increases by 7. What do you know? 63 + 7 = 70, Choice (B).

72. **D.** (a) = \$0.75, (b) = \$0.75, and (c) = \$0.75. Looks like (a) = (b) = (c), Choice (D).

73. **C.** (a) and (b) have the same value because $0.3 \times 90 = 0.9 \times 30$. Both equal 27. Based on the information in (a) and (b), you can eliminate Choice (A) and pick Choice (C) as the correct answer. You don't even have to figure out that the value of (c) is $0.3 \times 0.9 = 0.27$.

74. **A.** You may need to create an equation for this one. Let x stand for "what number." *Added* means +, *is* means =, and *of* means ×. So the equation looks like this: $x + 30 = \frac{1}{4} \times 124$. Solve for x: $x + 30 = \frac{124}{4}$; $x + 30 = 31$; $x = 1$. Pick Choice (A).

75. **C.** Based on the first two numbers, the operation is either –500 or ÷2. $500 \div 2 = 250$, which means the operation is ÷2. Look at the second and third numbers in the sequence. $125 \div 2 = 62.5$, Choice (C).

76. **D.** This sequence is a little trickier because you don't have a third number to test the first operation with. 10 is either 5 more than 5 or twice 5. If the operation were +5, the third number would be 15, and the fourth would be 20. But the fourth number isn't 20, which means the operation is ×2. The missing number is 20, Choice (D).

77. **B.** Change (b) to ½. ½ < ⅞, which means (a) > (b). You can eliminate Choice (A). Without computing the value of (c), you can guess that 4.2×0.65 is > 1. So you know that (c) > (a) > (b). This is the answer in Choice (B).

78. **A.** Set up the equation: $x \div 4 = \frac{1}{8} \times 72$; $x \div 4 = \frac{72}{8}$; $x \div 4 = 9$; $x = 36$, which is Choice (A).

79. **C.** Because the triangle is isosceles, which means $AB = BC$, cross out Choice (A). $AB = 6$ and $AC = 2$, so AB isn't twice as long as AC; Choice (B) is wrong. Consider Choice (C). Because $AB = BC$, it makes sense that $AB + AC = BC + AC$ (6 + 2 = 6 + 2). The answer is likely Choice (C), but you should check Choice (D) just to be sure: $AB – BC = 0$, and $AC = 2$, which means AC isn't 1 m shorter than $AB – BC$.

80. **D.** The numbers decrease by 4. The next number is $271 – 4 = 267$, Choice (D).

81. **B.** The equation is $\frac{1}{3} \times x = 5 \times 8$. Solve for x: $\frac{1}{3} \times x = 40$; $x = 40 \times \frac{3}{1}$; $x = 120$. Pick Choice (B).

82. **A.** Each of the three figures has 6 boxes, which means you just have to compare the value of the shaded boxes. (a) has 2 shaded boxes, (b) has 1.5 shaded boxes, and (c) has 2.5 shaded boxes. So (c) > (a) > (b), Choice (A).

83. **A.** This sequence features more than one operation. The first operation is +5 followed by –4. $5 + 5 \rightarrow 10 – 4 \rightarrow 6 + 5 \rightarrow 11 – 4 \rightarrow 7$. The missing number is 7, Choice (A).

84. **C.** Create an equation and solve for x: $50 – x = 3(36 \div 9)$; $50 – x = 3(4)$; $50 – x = 12$; $–x = –38$; $x = 38$. Choice (C) is the answer.

85. **B.** The equation is $\frac{1}{4} \times x = 10 \times 4$. Solve: $\frac{1}{4} \times x = 40$; $x = 40 \times 4/1$; $x = 160$. Pick Choice (B).

86. **D.** Find the value of the three products. The value of (a) is 3, the value of (b) is 9, and the value of (c) is 5, which means (b) > (c) > (a). Eliminate Choices (A) and (C). Choice (D) is right, so you don't have to figure out Choice (B).

87. **D.** This sequence alternates between ×2 and +8: $3 \times 2 \rightarrow 6 + 8 \rightarrow 14 \times 2 \rightarrow 28 + 8 \rightarrow 36 \times 2 \rightarrow 72$. The missing number is 36, Choice (D).

88. **B.** This sequence alternates between regular numbers and Roman numerals, which means the missing number *isn't* a Roman numeral. Eliminate Choices (A), (C), and (D). The answer is Choice (B), and the operation is +5.

89. **B.** The value of (a) is 8×8, or 64, and the value of (b) is 16×16 (or 16^2). Without calculating the value of (b), you know that (b) > (a) and can eliminate Choices (A) and (C). That leaves you with Choices (B) and (D). Choice (B) states that (b) = (c). Is that true? 2^8 is the same as $2 \times 2 \times 2 \times 2 \times 2 \times 2 \times 2 \times 2$. $2 \times 2 \times 2 \times 2 = 16$, which means 2^8 is the same as 16×16. Therefore, (b) = (c) — Choice (B).

90. **D.** Here's the equation: $0.40x + 0.80x = 144$. Solve for x: $1.2x = 144$; $x = 120$, Choice (D).

91. **B.** The operations for this sequence are either +4 then –1 or × 2 then –1. If you apply the first set of operations, the missing number would be 11 ($7 + 4 = 11$). But $11 - 1$ doesn't equal 13, which means the second set of operations must be correct. $7 \times 2 = 14$; $14 - 1 = 13$. 14, Choice (B), is the missing number.

92. **C.** The triangle is a right triangle because it contains a 90° angle. The line opposite the right angle is called the hypotenuse and is the longest of the three sides. All of that tells you Choice (A) is incorrect and Choice (C) is right. Based on the Pythagorean theorem, you know $AB^2 + AC^2 = BC^2$, which isn't the same as $AB + AC = BC$; Choice (B) can't be right. Choice (D) isn't right because the sum of the other two angles is equal to the right angle: $180° - 90° = 90°$.

93. **D.** The equation is: $x = 4^3 - 7$. $x = 64 - 7$, and $x = 57$. Pick Choice (D).

94. **C.** Say the pattern to yourself: –4 then –2 then 0 then +2 then +4. The pattern appears to decrease by even numbers and then increase by even numbers. The even number after 4 is 6. Add 6 to 47, and you get 53. Choice (C) begins with 53, and its second number is $53 + 8$ (61). The only answer that follows the pattern is Choice (C).

95. **A.** The value of (a) is $28 + 2$, or 30; (b) is $35 - 7$, or 28, and (c) is $27 + 1$, or 28. So (a) > (b) = (c). The best answer is Choice (A).

96. **A.** You know that 10 less than $\frac{7}{8}$ of 112 isn't 16 or 56 because those numbers are half of 112 or less, and $\frac{7}{8}$ is much more than half. Eliminate Choices (C) and (D). Figure out $\frac{112}{1} \times \frac{7}{8}$. You can factor out 8 from 112 on top and 8 on the bottom to create this problem: $\frac{14}{1} \times \frac{7}{1}$. $14 \times 7 = 98$. When you subtract 10 as instructed, you get 88, Choice (A).

97. **D.** The letters progress alphabetically, so the next letter must be D. Cross out Choices (A) and (B). The even numbers are subscript, which means the answer is Choice (D).

98. **C.** Look through the answers to see which ones are the easiest to evaluate. You know that the figure is a square because its sides are equal in length. The area of a square is s^2, and the side length is 6. That means the area of this square is 36 in^2, Choice (C). Go ahead and check the other answers to be certain. The diagonals of a square form right angles, which means the four triangles formed by the diagonals are equal right triangles. Choice (A) is therefore wrong. CA is the hypotenuse of the right triangle, which makes it longer than the other sides; cross out Choice (B). $\angle BAD$ and $\angle BFC$ are right angles and equal, which means Choice (D) isn't right.

99. **A.** First things first: Solve (a), (b), and (c). (a) is 27×10, or 270; (b) is $\frac{2}{5} \times \frac{150}{1}$, or $\frac{300}{5}$, or 60; (c) is $\frac{1}{2}$ of 144, or 72. You now know that (a) > (c) > (b), which means you can eliminate Choices (B), (C), and (D). Choice (A) is the answer because it's true that $270 > 60 + 72$ (or 132).

100. **C.** The sequence has a set of three consecutive numbers then +15 followed by a sequence of three consecutive numbers and +17. The next two numbers should be 138 and 139 to complete the pattern of three consecutive numbers, so cut Choices (B) and (D). Choice (A) can't be right because it has a fourth consecutive number. Choice (C) is the best answer.

101. **A.** Say the pattern to yourself as you read through the sequence: +15 then –14 then +18 then –14 and so on. Hmm. That doesn't make sense, does it? The first operation could be ×4: $5 \times 4 = 20$, $6 \times 4 = 24$. That means the missing number is 40 because $10 \times 4 = 40$. Tada! That's the option in Choice (A).

102. **B.** Your equation looks like this: $5 + 76 = x^2$. $5 + 76 = 81$. 81 is 9^2. $x = 9$, Choice (B).

103. **A.** Create the equation and solve: $7x = 4 + 80$; $7x = 84$; $x = 12$. Pick Choice (A).

104. **C.** You know that the value of (b) is greater than (a) because a number squared is greater than that same number times 2 (unless of course that number is 2, which isn't the case here). (c) has to be less than (a) because the value of twice the total of 45 and 25 is greater than 45 plus twice the value of 25. So, (b) > (a) > (c), and Choices (A) and (B) are wrong.

45 + 25 = 70, which means the value of (b) is 70 × 70, or 4,900. The value of (a) is 140, and the value of (c) is 95. 4,900 is much greater than 140 and 95, so the answer has to be Choice (C).

105. **D.** The sequence of letters is every other letter in the alphabet, and the numbers are all odd. Eliminate Choices (A) and (C) because they have even numbers. Skip O and you find that the next letter in the sequence is P. The answer is Choice (D).

106. **B.** The graph tells you that the value of D is probably 5, C is 20, B is 30, and A is 10. Choice (A) is wrong because 5 + 10 ≠ 20. Cross out Choice (C) because 10 + 20 isn't greater than 30. And 10 + 30 isn't 2(5 + 20), which means Choice (D) is wrong. 30 – 20 = 10; Choice (B) is the correct answer.

107. **C.** At first the numbers seem to be consecutive, but the pattern isn't strictly consecutive. You may need to try plugging in the answer choices to see the pattern. The only number that repeats is 25, so you can cross out Choice (D). In fact, 25 seems to repeat every two numbers. The last number in the sequence is 25. To follow the pattern of introducing 25 every two numbers, the correct answer must end in 25. That leaves you with Choices (B) and (C). Choice (B) begins with 28, 29, and Choice (C) starts with 29, 30. Choice (C) makes the most sense because it maintains the pattern of adding 2 to the number before 25 to get the number that comes after 25.

108. **D.** The next perfect cube that comes after 70 is 125. 125 – 70 = 55, which is the option in Choice (D). 55 + 70 = a perfect cube (125).

109. **C.** Solve this equation: $x – 0.2x = 72$; $0.8x = 72$; $x = 90$. Choice (C) is the answer.

110. **C.** (a) is 27, (b) is 16, and (c) is 16. Therefore, (a) > (b) = (c). Cross out Choices (B) and (D). 16 ≠ 2 × 16, which means Choice (A) is wrong, and Choice (C) is right.

111. **D.** The angles along a straight line equal 180°, and ∠A measures 90°. You don't know the individual measurements of the other two angles, but you do know that added together they equal 90°. That means the answer is Choice (D).

112. **C.** The equation for this question is $x = (\frac{3}{5} × 15) – 3$. Solve for x: $x = 9 – 3$; $x = 6$. Pick Choice (C).

Section 3: Reading

113. **C.** The author concludes the second paragraph by saying that legalizing some victimless crimes would save money. Consequently, you know that Choice (A) isn't right and that Choice (C) is probably the right answer. The author doesn't say anything about the ease of prosecuting crimes, which makes Choice (B) unlikely. The passage isn't about society's role in determining criminal behavior, so toss out Choice (D).

114. **C.** The last paragraph covers vocational training for inmates. Choice (A) is wrong because creating new jails isn't related to vocational training. The passage doesn't discuss white-collar crimes, so eliminate Choice (B). Decriminalizing victimless crimes is a separate issue from vocational training, which makes Choice (D) incorrect. If inmates don't get jobs, vocational training isn't valuable; Choice (C) is therefore the best answer.

115. **A.** Substitute the answer choices into the passage: Many legislators are advocating for *legalizing, declaring unconstitutional, outlawing,* or *prosecuting* some current crimes. The one that keeps the meaning is Choice (A), legalizing.

116. **A.** The middle paragraph says that the government spends $256 million on victimless crimes, which means $256 million is what could be saved, Choice (A).

117. **B.** Gainful employment would most likely reduce the rate of repeated criminal behavior (which is the definition of recidivism), Choice (B). The other options don't make sense.

118. **A.** This passage expresses an opinion about a current topic. It'd fit best in the editorial section of a newspaper, Choice (A). Clearly, it's not about biology or sports.

119. **C.** *Vocational* is used throughout the passage to describe the type of training proposed for inmates. The last paragraph says that vocational training prepares inmates for a career, which makes Choice (C), job, the best answer.

120. **D** The only answer not covered in the passage is Choice (D). The author doesn't propose a novel-writing program.

121. **D.** Eliminate Choices (A), (B), and (C) because they concern victimless crimes rather than vocational training. Choice (D) is best; if training doesn't decrease recidivism, it's not a worthwhile investment for taxpayers.

122. **B.** The passage doesn't mention confession or specify the kinds of positions inmates would be trained for; eliminate Choice (A). It doesn't compare the cost of imprisoning victimless criminals with other criminals, so Choice (C) is wrong. The passage does say that jobs may prevent repeat crimes, but that doesn't mean the repeat criminals will never get jobs. You don't have to assume too much to select Choice (B), which just so happens to be correct.

123. **C.** *Determined* appears in the second paragraph to describe the kinds of complaints neighbors make about recycle bins. The next sentence says that the neighbors' complaints are frequent. The word that fits best is Choice (C), resolute. The neighbors are unwavering in their complaining.

124. **C.** The last paragraph discusses successful recycling collection efforts on the behalf of Choice (C), entrepreneurs. The passage doesn't mention Choices (A) or (B), and it implies that the efforts of grocery stores are in fact unsuccessful.

125. **D.** *Contented* is used in the last paragraph to describe the customers of successful recycling efforts. These customers are satisfied, Choice (D).

126. **C.** The second paragraph says that the neighbors complain that the bins are unsightly, which means the bins are ugly, Choice (C).

127. **B.** To answer this question correctly, you need to know that a *lament* is a deep regret. Eliminate Choices (A), (C), and (D) because the author wouldn't deeply regret these positive statements. That bins have become trash cans, Choice (B), is regrettable.

128. **D.** The second paragraph includes tattered mattresses and TV dinners in its description of the kinds of trash that end up in recycle bins. Because at least two of the answers are right, Choice (D) must be the answer. Newspapers also end up in recycle bins.

129. **A.** The author is positive about the entrepreneurs described in the last paragraph. The only positive answer option is Choice (A), grateful.

130. **B.** Eliminate untrue answers. The first sentence suggests that people care about the environment, which makes Choice (A) untrue. The point of the second paragraph is that recycle bins are ineffective; cross out Choice (C). There's a monthly fee for recycle pickup, so Choice (D) is wrong. Given the first sentence, Choice (B) is the best answer.

131. **A.** The entrepreneurs pick up recycling; they don't provide drop-off bins. Choice (A) isn't one of their business practices and is, therefore, the correct answer.

132. **D.** Bedding, Choice (D), isn't included in the list of recyclable materials at the end of the second paragraph.

133. **B.** The first sentence of the last paragraph lists examples of trades. The answer that isn't included in this list is Choice (B), psychologist.

134. **D.** The last paragraph states that vocational grads often attend private trade schools, which makes Choice (D) the best answer.

135. **B.** Eliminate Choice (C) because it contains the debatable word *all*. Nothing in the passage justifies the statement that every single plumber, electrician, and mechanic has a trade school degree. Likewise, Choice (D) assumes too much by completely doing away with liberal arts programs. Choice (A) is wrong because there's no rule about who can work as a technician. Because unemployment rates for trade positions are low, demand for trade positions must be high, Choice (B).

Debatable words (such as *all, none,* and so on) are often clues that the answer option in question is incorrect.

136. **A.** The conclusion in the last sentence is that vocational education should receive more funding. This is the author's main point, so the best title is Choice (A). Choices (B) and (C) contain debatable language such as *only* and *useless*. Choice (D) is too broad for the topic.

137. **A.** Look at the second paragraph for the origins of the Bill of Rights. The only answer that's not included in the list is Choice (A), the U.S. Constitution.

138. **D.** The first paragraph tells you that the Fourteenth Amendment, Choice (D), is what applied the Bill of Rights to the states.

139. **C.** Incorporation, Choice (C), is defined in the first paragraph as the name of the process that applied the Bill of Rights to the states.

140. **D.** You discover in the second paragraph that 75 percent of the 14 states ratified the Bill of Rights. Seventy-five percent of 14 is about 11 states, Choice (D). Yes, you may encounter math in reading questions. Oh well.

141. **A.** The last paragraph lists all the rights in the answers except the one in Choice (A). A group can stage a protest as long as it's *not* violent.

142. **B.** In the first paragraph, you discover that the Bill of Rights consists of the first ten amendments to the Constitution, Choice (B). Choice (A) refers to the 30 liberties and rights it protects, and 14, Choice (D), is the number of states in existence when the Bill of Rights was ratified.

143. **B.** *Embedded* appears in the first sentence of the paragraph that describes how big a part the Bill of Rights plays in daily life. Because the Bill of Rights is deeply *rooted* in everyday life, Choice (B) is your answer.

144. **D.** The purpose of the passage is to instruct about the Bill of Rights, which is a part of the U.S. Constitution; Choice (D) sounds best. The passage isn't impassioned or opinionated, so Choices (A) and (B) can't be right. Nor is the passage about science, which means Choice (C) is incorrect.

145. **C.** Choice (A) isn't true because other inventors had tried and failed. Cut Choice (B) because the Wrights flew the aircraft in 1903, but the government didn't purchase it until 1908. The Wrights successfully flew and controlled the aircraft in 1903, so forget Choice (D). Choice (C) is right; the last sentence implies that the government had been considering the Wright brothers' proposals for more than four years.

146. **C.** The passage says that the first aircraft was an Army aircraft purchased by the War Department. The best answer is that the airplane was used by the military, Choice (C).

147. **A.** The passage uses *prevailing* to describe the current sentiments about the future of the balloon. The word that fits best is Choice (A), existing: *Existing* (not *triumphant, crushing,* or *minority*) sentiments held that the immediate future still belonged to the balloon.

148. **D.** The statement that's *not* true is Choice (D). The government bought the first airplane in 1908, which is less than six years after the first flight succeeded in 1903. If the future *still* belonged to the balloon, it must have already existed. Choice (B) is a paraphrase of the second sentence, and North Carolina is on the East Coast.

149. **D.** Choices (A), (B), and (C) are way too general for the one-paragraph topic. The paragraph is about the Wrights' aircraft, and its purchase is described as a "minor miracle."

150. **C.** The paragraph recounts a bit of American history, which makes a historian, Choice (C), the most logical author. Pilots probably discuss flying planes, and an Army officer may talk about war strategies. Nothing in the paragraph relates to senators.

151. **B.** The paragraph follows its mention of the "minor miracle" with an explanation that the government had refused to accept that man could fly in a heavier-than-air craft. Choice (B) paraphrases this explanation. The paragraph states that most people thought the future was in balloon travel, but it doesn't say that this was because of cost or effectiveness. The government wasn't interested in Langley's failed invention, but it must have needed an airplane, or else it wouldn't have invested in Langley at all.

152. **D.** Because the government waited so long to purchase the airplane and didn't believe a heavier-than-air craft could fly, its attitude must have been skeptical, Choice (D). It certainly wasn't confident or ecstatic. And Choice (B), agitated, is too strong an emotion.

153. **B.** You'd think the vocabulary questions in the Verbal Skills section would be enough for the HSPT people, but apparently they're not because the Reading section has about 20 more. A *paltry* sum is a small one. The best synonym is Choice (B), insignificant.

154. **B.** If something smells foul, it smells really gross. Another word that means "really gross" is *repulsive*, Choice (B).

155. **A.** Something *tedious* is boring, which means a state of *tedium* is a state of boredom, Choice (A).

156. **A.** *Zealous* fans are over the top, which means you can eliminate Choices (B) and (D). And Choice (C), continual, doesn't begin to express the enthusiasm a zealous fan feels. The best answer is Choice (A), ardent.

157. **C.** A *debilitating* disease is one that causes great suffering and weakness. It's devastating, Choice (C). Debilitating doesn't suggest length of time, which rules out Choices (A), (B), and (D).

158. **B.** To mind your manners is to pay attention or put your mind to them, Choice (B). It doesn't mean to ignore, object to, or worry about manners.

159. **D.** You usually hear a *eulogy* at a funeral where loved ones pay tribute, Choice (D), to the deceased.

160. **D.** Don't be tempted by Choice (B). To propose isn't to marry; it's to suggest getting married. To propose is to suggest, Choice (D).

161. **A.** A *commemorative* plaque is one that dedicates the memory of a person or event, which means the best synonym is Choice (A), dedicatory. Commemorative has nothing to do with how old the plaque is or what it's made of.

162. **C.** Delightful is a positive word; eliminate words with negative connotations, such as objectionable and dull. Choice (C) is an agreeable answer choice and the best synonym for delightful.

163. **B.** To *abhor* something is to hate it, and *abhorrent* means "hateful." A synonym for hateful is Choice (B), but if you're not familiar with the meaning of odious, you can at least eliminate positive choices such as likeable and pleasant.

164. **A.** A *realm* is the jurisdiction that those in power rule over. Its synonym is kingdom, Choice (A).

165. **B.** A *literal* interpretation is one based on the facts, Choice (B). Its opposites are symbolic or fictitious.

166. **B.** A person with a *congenial* disposition is outgoing and friendly. Sociable, Choice (B), is a good synonym, and it's the only positive answer choice of the four.

167. **C.** You may not know what vilify means, but because it's paired with enemy, it's probably not a positive verb. Cross out positive answer choices, such as compliment and justify. The answer is Choice (C). To *vilify* is to criticize or disparage.

168. **C.** Eliminate positive answer choices such as ally and companion because heckler is paired with discourteous. If you've seen standup comedy, you know that a heckler is an audience member who distracts the comedian. The answer is Choice (C), detractor.

169. **A.** *Cantankerous* sounds awful, and it means "crabby or grumpy," Choice (A).

170. **A.** Cosmo refers to world, and a cosmopolitan has experienced it all. The best synonym is Choice (A); a *sophisticate* is someone with experienced taste. Choice (D), *plebeian* means "commoner" and is an antonym.

171. **D.** To *discombobulate* is to confuse. The word even looks confusing! A synonym for confuse is Choice (D), confound.

172. **D.** An obvious truth is one that's known, which means you can eliminate Choices (A) and (B) because they're opposites. *Flimsy* means "weak," which isn't the same as known. By process of elimination, pick Choice (D). *Axiomatic* means "clear and obvious."

173. **B.** If an interloper is unwanted, he's probably not a citizen or an affiliate. A hermit likes to hide from people, so she wouldn't be around enough to make herself unwanted. The answer is Choice (B); an intruder and an interloper are both gatecrashers.

174. **C.** To *conjure* a memory is to call it up. Suppress and destroy are more opposite in meaning than similar. The most similar word is summon, Choice (C).

Section 4: Mathematics

175. **B.** The tenths place is the number to the right after the decimal point, which is 6 in this case. Round 6 to 7 because the number to the right of 6 is greater than 5. The answer is Choice (B), 54.7. Choice (D) improperly rounds the tenths place, and the other choices write the number to the incorrect place.

176. **C.** The only answer that describes a type of angle is Choice (C). An *obtuse angle* is one that's greater than 90°. The other choices describe a type of theorem, a kind of quadrilateral, and types of lines.

177. **A.** The order of operations tells you to solve the exponents first: $-5 \times -5 = 25$. Then multiply: $2 \times 25 = 50$, which is Choice (A).

178. **D.** The intersection sign means you look for the set of numbers that appears in both sets. Both sets contain 4 and 7, which is the answer in Choice (D).

179. **B.** *Consecutive numbers* are numbers that follow in sequence. The answer with two consecutive numbers is Choice (B) because 3 comes right after 2 on the number line. The numbers in Choice (D) are called *reciprocals* because one is the inverse of the other.

180. **A.** 0.23 is 23 hundredths, which means the number expressed as a fraction is $\frac{23}{100}$, Choice (A).

181. **D.** Move the decimal point to the right one place for every zero. 100 has two zeros, so you move the decimal point to the right two places, Choice (D).

182. **A.** The radius of a circle is ½ the diameter. $6 \times \frac{1}{2} = 3$, which is Choice (A).

183. **C.** $\frac{35}{3}$ written as a mixed fraction is $11\frac{2}{3}$. The integers between $11\frac{2}{3}$ and 17.4 are 12, 13, 14, 15, 16, and 17. That's a total of 6 numbers; the answer is Choice (C).

   Integers don't include decimals or fractions. Flip to Chapter 10 for a refresher on the various types of numbers.

184. **D.** 95 falls between the perfect squares of 81 and 100, but don't stop there and pick Choice (B). The question asks for the square root. 81 is 9^2, and 100 is 10^2. The square root of 95 is somewhere in between 9 and 10, Choice (D).

185. **C.** *Cent* means 100. A meter consists of 100 centimeters, Choice (C).

186. **A.** This question tests what you know about performing operations with negatives and positives. You probably know that Choices (B) and (C) are true, which means you can eliminate them. Choice (A), however, isn't true. When the absolute value of the positive number is greater than the absolute value of the negative number, the sum is positive. For example, $4 + (-2) = 2$, a positive number.

187. **B.** Create an equation and solve for x. Because the ratios of the two numbers is 4 to 1, you can express the two numbers as $1x$ and $4x$. The equation is $1x + 4x = 60$; $5x = 60$; $x = 12$. The smaller number is 12, and the larger number is 4(12), or 48, Choice (B).

188. **D.** The fraction that comes between ⅛ and ⅜ is 2/8, which reduces to ¼, Choice (D).

189. **B.** Examine each answer. Choice (A) isn't true; $3.5 \times 10 = 35$. $3.2 \times 10^3 = 3{,}200$, which means Choices (C) and (D) aren't true either. The answer must be Choice (B). Multiplying by $(\frac{1}{10})^2$ means you move the decimal point two places to the left.

190. **C.** The total number of degrees in a circle is 360. 40° of 360° is 40/360, which reduces to ⅑, Choice (C).

191. **A.** The equation for this word problem is $x = \$20 \times 0.30$. $x = \$6$, Choice (A).

192. **A.** Eliminate Choices (B) and (D) because they aren't prime. The remaining choices are 5 and 7. 7 isn't a factor of 30, which means the correct answer is Choice (A).

193. **B.** To find the percentage of nonvoters, subtract 27 + 43 (70) from 100: $100 - 70 = 30$. 30% means 30 per 100, or 30/100. Reduce to 3/10, Choice (B).

194. **C.** A quadrilateral has four sides. Octagons have eight sides, pentagons have five, and hexagons have six. The answer is Choice (C) because a rhombus has four sides.

195. **B.** Check the possible answers for the lowest number that both 3 and 5 go into evenly. 3 doesn't go into 5, and 5 doesn't go into 12. Therefore, the least common multiple of 3 and 5 is 15, Choice (B).

196. **D.** Because *XYZ* and *XVW* are similar, their corresponding sides are in the same proportions. The correct answer compares corresponding sides of each triangle. The ratios in Choices (A), (B), and (C) compare sides of the same triangle; the ratios in Choice (D) compare the sides of each triangle.

197. **A.** The associative property of addition states that you can add the same numbers in different orders and still get the same sum. Choice (A) demonstrates that this property is true. Choice (C) is straight addition, and Choices (B) and (D) aren't true.

198. **B.** Because they make up a straight line, the 120° angle and the angle next to it equal 180°. That means the bottom-left angle of the triangle equals 60° ($180° - 120° = 60°$). The angles in a triangle add up to 180°, which means that $60° + 60° + x = 180°$. $x = 60°$, Choice (B).

199. **A.** The equation for the word problem is $x = (8 \times \$4.35) + (5 \times \$3.78)$. Solve for x: $x = \$34.80 + \$18.90$; $x = \$53.70$, Choice (A).

200. **D.** A year consists of 12 months, which means Mr. Black spends an average of $\$630 \div 12$. The average per month is \$52.50, which rounds up to \$53, Choice (D).

201. **C.** Subtract x and 15 from both sides: $15 + 3x = 30$; $3x = 15$; $x = 5$, Choice (C).

202. **A.** Subtract to find the difference. First, make the fractions improper: 2½ = 5/2 and 1¾ = 7/4. The common denominator is 4, which makes the equation 10/4 − 7/4 = x. ¾ = x. Choice (A) is your answer.

203. **D.** $(-5) + (-4) = -9$, and $3 + 8 = 11$. $-9 + 11 = 2$. The correct answer is Choice (D).

When you have positive and negative numbers mixed together in an addition problem, add the negative numbers first and then the positive numbers. Then the problem becomes much easier to work with.

204. **C.** Substitute 10 for C in the formula and solve for F: $F = \frac{9}{5}(10) + 32$; $F = 18 + 32$; $F = 50°$. Choice (C) is the answer.

205. **B.** $(-6) + (-2) + (-2) = -10$; $-10 + 5 = -5$. Pick Choice (B).

206. **A.** Create an equation from the words. Let w = Wade's cards: $w = 3(106) - 5$; $w = 318 - 5$; $w = 313$. Looks like Wade has 313 cards, Choice (A).

207. **C.** Change $1\frac{2}{3}$ to an improper fraction: $\frac{5}{3}$. $\frac{5}{3} \times \frac{1}{2} = \frac{5}{6}$. Pick Choice (C).

208. **D.** Set up a ratio: $\frac{15}{1} = \frac{x}{5}$. Cross multiply: $x = 15 \times 5$; $x = 75$. Kathy can do 75 problems in 5 hours, Choice (D).

209. **B.** A pound is 16 ounces, which means 8 ounces is a half a pound. The cost for 1.5 pounds of meat is 3×1.5 pounds, which is \$4.50. Pick Choice (B).

210. **D.** Because 3 + the other number = N, the other number = $N - 3$. Three times the other number is $3(N - 3)$, Choice (D).

211. **C.** First, solve for x: $2x - 3 > 5$; $2x > 8$; $x > 4$. Then square both sides: $x^2 > 16$. The answer is Choice (C).

212. **A.** If $a + 3$ is the same number as $b + 8$, then a has to be greater than b. You can verify this by subtracting 3 and b from both sides of the equation: $a - b = 5$, which means that a must be 5 greater than b. The answer is therefore Choice (A).

213. **D.** Your equation looks like this: $K = 2(48) - 6$. $K = 96 - 6$; $K = 90$, Choice (D).

214. **B.** To find the price of the bike before tax, you need to figure out what number \$8.60 is 4% of: $8.60 = 0.04 \times x$; $215 = x$. The price of the bike is \$215, Choice (B).

215. **B.** Substitute the values for x and y in the equation and solve: $(4)^3 + 5(\frac{1}{2}) - 7$. $64 + 2.5 - 7 = 59.5$, or $59\frac{1}{2}$ — the answer in Choice (B).

216. **A.** The area of the carpet is length × width, which is 10×16, or 160 square feet. The total price is $160 \times \$5$, which is \$800. Choice (A) is your answer.

217. **D.** The formula for the volume of a rectangular solid is $V = l \times w \times h$. Substitute the values for the figure into the formula: $V = 6 \times 9 \times 4$; $V = 216$ cm^3. The answer is Choice (D).

218. **A.** Set up an equation and solve: $0.04 \times x = \$47.50$. The original loan amount, or x, was \$1,187.50 — Choice (A).

219. **B.** Substitute the values and solve: $3 \times 3 \times 5 \times 2 = 90$, Choice (B).

220. **C.** The sum is 7.129, Choice (C).

REMEMBER

When you're working with decimal problems, make sure you line up the decimal points before adding or subtracting the numbers.

221. **A.** Substitute 16 for a in the equation and solve for b: $4b - 8 = 16$; $4b = 24$; $b = 6$, Choice (A).

222. **D.** Add x to and subtract 6 from both sides: $6x = 3$; $x = \frac{3}{6}$, which reduces to $\frac{1}{2}$, Choice (D).

223. **B.** z is between -8 and -13. The integers between -8 and -13 are -9, -10, -11, and -12. Only -10 and -12 are even, and -10 isn't an answer choice. Pick Choice (B).

224. **B.** You don't have to completely multiply this problem to find the right answer. The number of places to the right of the decimal point in the product equals the total number of decimal places in the two multiplied values. The first number has two values after the decimal, and the second has three, which means the right answer will have five as long as the last number isn't 0. Choice (B) has five numbers after the decimal, and its last number isn't 0, so it's the correct answer.

225. **C.** It may be obvious to you that 30 days is 3 times 10 days, so Stan loses 3 times as many buttons in 30 days. To be sure, though, you can set up a proportion. Stan loses 3 buttons in 10 days ($\frac{3}{10}$) and x buttons in 30 days ($\frac{x}{30}$): $\frac{3}{10} = \frac{x}{30}$. Cross multiply: $10x = 3(30)$; $10x = 90$; $x = 9$. Choice (C) is your answer.

226. **A.** Multiply to find 30% of $40: $0.3 \times \$40 = \$12$. Jessie saves $12 per week. In four weeks, she saves $4 \times \$12$, or $48 — Choice (A).

227. **D.** The fastest way to solve this problem is to substitute answer choices. Because you're looking for the number that makes the left side *greater* than 17, start with the largest number in the answer choices, which is 8 in Choice (D). $3 \times 8 = 24$ and $24 - 5 > 17$. 8 is a possible value for x. Choice (D) is the answer; you don't have to try the others.

228. **A.** You know that 2.5455 goes into 4.31 at least once but not more than twice. Eliminate answers that are less than 1 and more than 2. The answer is Choice (A).

229. **B.** If four movies cost $23.40, the cost of two movies is half that much: $\$23.40 \div 2 = \$11.70$, Choice (B).

230. **D.** Solve for x: $\sqrt{x} + 6 = 11$; $\sqrt{x} = 5$. Square both sides to find that $x = 25$, Choice (D).

231. **A.** To divide the fraction, multiply both sides of the equation by the reciprocal: $x = 40 \times \frac{2}{1}$; $x = 80$. So the value of $\frac{3}{4}x = \frac{3}{4} \times 80$; $x = 60$, Choice (A).

232. **B.** Carefully multiply 436 and 42 to get a product of 18,312, Choice (B).

233. **D.** Figure out what you know. If Sally is 25 today, then 10 years ago she was 15 ($25 - 10 = 15$). Sally's mother was 3 times as old as Sally 10 years ago, meaning 10 years ago Sally's mother was 45 ($3 \times 15 = 45$). Don't stop there and pick Choice (C), though. The question asks you for Sally's mother's age today, 10 years later. $45 + 10 = 55$. Sally's mother is 55, Choice (D). If you picked Choice (A), you assumed that Sally's mother is still 3 times as old as Sally today, which isn't possible.

234. **B.** To find the ratio, divide the fractions: $\frac{3}{4} \div \frac{5}{8}$. Multiply by the reciprocal: $\frac{3}{4} \times \frac{8}{5} = \frac{24}{16}$, which simplifies to $\frac{3}{2}$, Choice (B).

235. **C.** Square both sides of the problem and solve for x: $x + 10 = 8^2$; $x + 10 = 64$; $x = 54$, Choice (C).

236. **D.** Let N stand for the money Andrew's sister has saved. Andrew's savings are $2N$. When Andrew gives his sister $5, his savings minus $5 will equal his sister's savings plus $5. Therefore, $2N - 5 = N + 5$. Solve for N: $2N = N + 10$; $N = 10$. Andrew's sister saved $10, and Andrew saved twice that. Andrew saved 2($10), or $20 — Choice (D).

237. **A.** Eliminate Choices (C) and (D) because they're odd numbers. y is either 6, Choice (A), or 8, Choice (B). y is less than 8, which means it can't equal 8. Choice (A) is your answer.

238. **B.** Find the area of the square and add it to the area of the four semicircles. The area of the square is s^2, which means this square is 8^2, or 64 m². The formula for finding the area of a circle is $A = \pi r^2$. The four semicircles are equal to two full circles with diameters of 8 (radii of 4). Figure out the area of one circle and times it by 2 to get the area of the four semicircles: $A = \pi(4)^2$; $A = 16\pi$. The area of two circles (four semicircles) is $2(16)\pi$, or 32π. Therefore, the area of the figure is $(64 + 32\pi)$ m², Choice (B).

Section 5: Language

239. **B.** Choice (B) has a capitalization error. The complete holiday name, Valentine's Day, should be capitalized.

240. **A.** The error is in the first word of Choice (A). "Him and Mary" is the subject of the sentence, which means the pronoun should be in the subjective form, "He and Mary." If you take "and Mary" out of the sentence, "him" doesn't sound right.

241. **C.** Choice (C) contains a usage error. People sit down; they don't set down.

242. **A.** The three verbs in Choice (A) are in different tenses. *Were growing* is past tense, so *tells* and *is* should also be past tense (*told* and *was*).

243. **D.** None of the answers contains a problem with usage, punctuation, or capitalization. Select Choice (D).

244. **A.** Choice (A) has a double negative (hardly never), which is a no-no in standard English. Changing *never* to *ever* corrects the problem.

245. **D.** The punctuation, capitalization, and usage are all fine in this question.

246. **B.** Dates require commas between the day and the year. Choice (B) should be "October 21, 1995."

247. **C.** *Nor* follows *neither*. Choice (C) should be "Neither my brother *nor* I. . . ."

248. **B.** When you compare more than two, you use the suffix *-est* rather than *-er*. In Choice (B), Matt is the youngest of five, not the younger.

249. **C.** Use *less* for nouns that can't be counted and *fewer* for nouns that are countable. You can count the flu cases, which means in Choice (C), there have been *fewer* cases, not less cases.

250. **B.** Choice (B) isn't a question; it's a statement that states what Gladys asked me. Consequently, it should end with a period rather than a question mark.

251. **D.** Nothing's wrong with any of the answers; Choice (D) is correct.

252. **D.** *Set* is proper for things like books. All is well in these answers. Pick Choice (D).

253. **A.** *They're* is a contraction for *they are*. The guys haven't waited all of *they are* lives in Choice (A). The proper form in this sentence is *their* because it shows possession.

254. **A.** Adverbs describe verbs. Computers run *efficiently,* not efficient; Choice (A) contains the error.

255. **B.** Choice (B) features the improper form of *to*. You use *too* to mean more than enough: Paul had eaten *too* much for dinner.

256. **B.** Choice (B) forms the possessive of father incorrectly. I have only one father, which means it's my father's coat. *Fathers'* means the coat belongs to many fathers.

257. **C.** The proper verb form in Choice (C) is *would have;* the phrase *would of* is never proper.

258. **C.** Because the dependent clause comes after the independent clause, the comma after *chocolate* in Choice (C) is incorrect.

259. **D.** The first three answer choices are constructed correctly. Go with Choice (D).

260. **A.** *It's* is a contraction of it is. The puppy didn't run with *it is* tail between *it is* legs. Use *its* to show possession.

261. **B.** Choice (B) has a capitalization error. The full name of the airport is Kennedy Airport.

262. **C.** In Choice (C), *who's* is a contraction of *who is*. You wouldn't say, "Do you know *who is* book this is?" The possessive form of who is *whose*.

263. **B.** There's a nasty double negative in Choice (B). It should read "don't tell anyone" or "tell no one" instead.

264. **D.** *Effects* in Choice (A) and *himself* in Choice (C) are used properly. Choice (B) is a question, which means the question mark at the end is okay. Choice (D) is right.

265. **C.** A company is a single entity, which means the pronoun that refers to company should be singular. *Their* in Choice (C) should be *its*.

266. **D.** The three sentences in this question are clean. Pick Choice (D) and move along.

267. **B.** Choice (B)'s use of an adjective to describe a verb is improper. The cat chased the mouse *quickly,* not quick.

268. **D.** Choices (A), (B), and (C) are fine as written. Choice (D) is your answer.

269. **C.** The past tense of *lie* is *lay,* not *lied.* Choice (C) contains the error.

270. **B.** The snowboards in Choice (B) belong to Carl and Cathy, which means the snowboards are *their* snowboards. *There* isn't the possessive form of *they.*

271. **C.** In Choice (C), *me* should be *I.* The idea is that Nellie is better than *I am.* So, Nellie is better than *I.*

272. **C.** *Circus* in Choice (C) is a general term, not a title; it shouldn't be capitalized.

273. **A.** The verbs in Choice (A) are in different tenses. They should both be past tense or present tense: The party *ends,* and they *wash* OR the party *ended,* and they *washed.*

274. **A.** Coney Island is the full name of the location in Choice (A). *Island* should be capitalized, too.

275. **B.** Choice (B) joins together two independent clauses with a comma and no conjunction, which makes it a comma splice. Changing the comma to a semicolon fixes the problem.

276. **B.** The comma separating the clauses in Choice (B) should be eliminated because the dependent clause "if I'm wrong" comes after the independent clause "correct me."

277. **D.** Choices (A), (B), and (C) are properly punctuated and constructed. Pick Choice (D).

278. **C.** As it's used in Choice (C), *east* is a direction and not a location. It shouldn't be capitalized.

279. **A.** *Recieved* in Choice (A) violates the *i*-before-*e*-except-after-*c* rule.

280. **B.** The stress in *examine* isn't on the last syllable, which means you don't double the *n* before adding *-ing.* Choice (B) has the spelling error.

281. **D.** Tricky words such as tournament and restaurant are spelled correctly in these sentences, which means the answer is Choice (D).

282. **A.** In Choice (A), you should drop the *ce* in science before adding *tist* to create *scientist.*

283. **D.** Traveling and humorous are spelled correctly, which means all three sentences are error free.

284. **B.** *Immediately* should have two *m*'s. Choice (B) contains the error.

285. **C.** Forefathers is spelled with an *e,* which means Choice (C) has the misspelling.

286. **C.** The problem with Choice (C) is that *independent* shouldn't contain any *a*'s.

287. **A.** *Equipment* doesn't have a *t* in it. Choice (A) has the error.

288. **B.** Don't skip over the error in Choice (B). *Columns* is properly spelled with an *mn.*

289. **B.** This sentence has a beginning phrase; choose an answer that clearly demonstrates that *I* am doing the gazing out the window. Choices (A) and (C) convey that the herds of deer are gazing out the window. Choice (D) contains redundant language; a herd is a group. Choice (B) is the best option.

290. **C.** Pick the transition word that makes the most sense. The second clause conveys a contrasting idea, and the answer that shows contrast is Choice (C), however.

291. **D.** College didn't graduate from high school; Sam did. Eliminate Choice (A). *Then* and *next step* convey similar ideas; using them both in the same sentence is redundant. Cross out Choices (B) and (C). Choice (D) is the best construction of the four options.

292. **D.** The paragraph is about using fantasy as a means to educate children. The last sentence, Choice (D), throws in science fiction stories out of the blue.

293. **A.** Find the answer that gives information that's relevant to finding a summer job. The resumes and interviewing skills mentioned in Choice (A) are relevant to finding a job. Drinking liquids and popular vacation times aren't.

294. **A.** The idea is that because Doug has done something in the past, he'll do the same thing in the future. Choose the transition word that shows a cause-and-effect relationship. Choice A, *therefore*, shows cause and effect; Choices (B) and (C) show contrast.

295. **D.** Choices (B) and (C) contain passive voice and other problems; cross them out. Choice (A) makes it sound like the meeting may be held on my desk. Choice (D) is clearer.

296. **C.** Eliminate Choices (A) and (B) because the "putting" and "hats and mittens" didn't hear about the weather. Choice (D) contains passive voice. The clearest sentence is Choice (C).

297. **C.** Choices (A) and (B) lack clarity because they separate the verb "cross" and its object "the river" with the phrase "without my waders and snorkel." Choice (D) is less clear than Choice (C) because it improperly makes "attempting to cross" the subject rather than "I."

298. **B.** The statement begins with *Therefore,* which means it comes after the idea that gives a reason for the government to permit private companies to take over transportation. So, it definitely doesn't work before the first sentence; you can cross out Choice (A). Eliminate Choice (D) also because the sentence is relevant to the paragraph. Sentences 2 and 3 talk about toll roads; it doesn't make sense to split these similar ideas with a sentence that talks about privatization. The best place for the sentence is in between Sentence 1 and Sentence 2, Choice (B). Private companies do a better job; therefore, they should be allowed to take over.

Answer Key for HSPT Practice Test 1

Section 1: Verbal Skills

1. B	13. B	25. A	37. D	49. A
2. A	14. C	26. B	38. B	50. A
3. D	15. B	27. A	39. A	51. C
4. A	16. B	28. A	40. C	52. C
5. A	17. A	29. C	41. B	53. B
6. D	18. C	30. B	42. C	54. A
7. C	19. D	31. A	43. A	55. D
8. B	20. C	32. C	44. B	56. B
9. D	21. B	33. B	45. D	57. D
10. D	22. B	34. D	46. A	58. D
11. A	23. C	35. D	47. D	59. A
12. A	24. B	36. C	48. B	60. C

Section 2: Quantitative Skills

61. C	72. D	83. A	94. C	105. D
62. C	73. C	84. C	95. A	106. B
63. B	74. A	85. B	96. A	107. C
64. D	75. C	86. D	97. D	108. D
65. B	76. D	87. D	98. C	109. C
66. A	77. B	88. B	99. A	110. C
67. A	78. A	89. B	100. C	111. D
68. A	79. C	90. D	101. A	112. C
69. D	80. D	91. B	102. B	
70. D	81. B	92. C	103. A	
71. B	82. A	93. D	104. C	

Section 3: Reading

113. C	126. C	139. C	152. D	165. B
114. C	127. B	140. D	153. B	166. B
115. A	128. D	141. A	154. B	167. C
116. A	129. A	142. B	155. A	168. C
117. B	130. B	143. B	156. A	169. A
118. A	131. A	144. D	157. C	170. A
119. C	132. D	145. C	158. B	171. D
120. D	133. B	146. C	159. D	172. D
121. D	134. D	147. A	160. D	173. B
122. B	135. B	148. D	161. A	174. C
123. C	136. A	149. D	162. C	
124. C	137. A	150. C	163. B	
125. D	138. D	151. B	164. A	

Section 4: Mathematics

175. B	188. D	201. C	214. B	227. D
176. C	189. B	202. A	215. B	228. A
177. A	190. C	203. D	216. A	229. B
178. D	191. A	204. C	217. D	230. D
179. B	192. A	205. B	218. A	231. A
180. A	193. B	206. A	219. B	232. B
181. D	194. C	207. C	220. C	233. D
182. A	195. B	208. D	221. A	234. B
183. C	196. D	209. B	222. D	235. C
184. D	197. A	210. D	223. B	236. D
185. C	198. B	211. C	224. B	237. A
186. A	199. A	212. A	225. C	238. B
187. B	200. D	213. D	226. A	

Section 5: Language

239. B	251. D	263. B	275. B	287. A
240. A	252. D	264. D	276. B	288. B
241. C	253. A	265. C	277. D	289. B
242. A	254. A	266. D	278. C	290. C
243. D	255. B	267. B	279. A	291. D
244. A	256. B	268. D	280. B	292. D
245. D	257. C	269. C	281. D	293. A
246. B	258. C	270. B	282. A	294. A
247. C	259. D	271. C	283. D	295. D
248. B	260. A	272. C	284. B	296. C
249. C	261. B	273. A	285. C	297. C
250. B	262. C	274. A	286. C	298. B

Chapter 19

HSPT Practice Test 2

You can never get too much practice. That's why we've included a second practice HSPT exam for your test-preparation pleasure.

We did our best to make this practice test similar to the real HSPT, but the test-makers may have tweaked the real thing slightly. Don't be surprised if the HSPT you take has a different number of questions in a section or slightly different time limits.

Your best bet when taking this practice test is to take it under conditions that are as much like real test conditions as possible by

- ✔ Finding a place where you won't be distracted. (Step away from the refrigerator! Practice test time isn't snack time.)
- ✔ Taking this test at approximately the same time of day as your HSPT is scheduled.
- ✔ Tearing out the answer sheet in this chapter and marking your answers on it by filling in the appropriate bubbles.
- ✔ Writing notes and computations in the margins of the test pages, except of course when you're required to estimate the answer.
- ✔ Timing yourself on each section. When the time is up for a particular section, move on to the next one.
- ✔ Giving yourself a 10- to 15-minute break between the Reading and Mathematics sections, which is probably when the HSPT proctor will let you have a little hiatus on test day.

After you complete this test, go on to Chapter 20. There you'll find the answers to each question, along with valuable explanations for each answer (trust us, you want to read them).

Answer Sheet for HSPT Practice Test 2

Section 1: Verbal Skills

1. Ⓐ Ⓑ Ⓒ Ⓓ
2. Ⓐ Ⓑ Ⓒ Ⓓ
3. Ⓐ Ⓑ Ⓒ Ⓓ
4. Ⓐ Ⓑ Ⓒ
5. Ⓐ Ⓑ Ⓒ Ⓓ
6. Ⓐ Ⓑ Ⓒ Ⓓ
7. Ⓐ Ⓑ Ⓒ Ⓓ
8. Ⓐ Ⓑ Ⓒ Ⓓ
9. Ⓐ Ⓑ Ⓒ Ⓓ
10. Ⓐ Ⓑ Ⓒ Ⓓ
11. Ⓐ Ⓑ Ⓒ Ⓓ
12. Ⓐ Ⓑ Ⓒ Ⓓ

13. Ⓐ Ⓑ Ⓒ
14. Ⓐ Ⓑ Ⓒ Ⓓ
15. Ⓐ Ⓑ Ⓒ Ⓓ
16. Ⓐ Ⓑ Ⓒ Ⓓ
17. Ⓐ Ⓑ Ⓒ Ⓓ
18. Ⓐ Ⓑ Ⓒ Ⓓ
19. Ⓐ Ⓑ Ⓒ Ⓓ
20. Ⓐ Ⓑ Ⓒ Ⓓ
21. Ⓐ Ⓑ Ⓒ Ⓓ
22. Ⓐ Ⓑ Ⓒ Ⓓ
23. Ⓐ Ⓑ Ⓒ
24. Ⓐ Ⓑ Ⓒ Ⓓ

25. Ⓐ Ⓑ Ⓒ Ⓓ
26. Ⓐ Ⓑ Ⓒ Ⓓ
27. Ⓐ Ⓑ Ⓒ
28. Ⓐ Ⓑ Ⓒ Ⓓ
29. Ⓐ Ⓑ Ⓒ Ⓓ
30. Ⓐ Ⓑ Ⓒ Ⓓ
31. Ⓐ Ⓑ Ⓒ Ⓓ
32. Ⓐ Ⓑ Ⓒ Ⓓ
33. Ⓐ Ⓑ Ⓒ Ⓓ
34. Ⓐ Ⓑ Ⓒ Ⓓ
35. Ⓐ Ⓑ Ⓒ Ⓓ
36. Ⓐ Ⓑ Ⓒ

37. Ⓐ Ⓑ Ⓒ Ⓓ
38. Ⓐ Ⓑ Ⓒ Ⓓ
39. Ⓐ Ⓑ Ⓒ Ⓓ
40. Ⓐ Ⓑ Ⓒ Ⓓ
41. Ⓐ Ⓑ Ⓒ Ⓓ
42. Ⓐ Ⓑ Ⓒ Ⓓ
43. Ⓐ Ⓑ Ⓒ
44. Ⓐ Ⓑ Ⓒ Ⓓ
45. Ⓐ Ⓑ Ⓒ Ⓓ
46. Ⓐ Ⓑ Ⓒ Ⓓ
47. Ⓐ Ⓑ Ⓒ Ⓓ
48. Ⓐ Ⓑ Ⓒ Ⓓ

49. Ⓐ Ⓑ Ⓒ Ⓓ
50. Ⓐ Ⓑ Ⓒ Ⓓ
51. Ⓐ Ⓑ Ⓒ Ⓓ
52. Ⓐ Ⓑ Ⓒ Ⓓ
53. Ⓐ Ⓑ Ⓒ
54. Ⓐ Ⓑ Ⓒ Ⓓ
55. Ⓐ Ⓑ Ⓒ Ⓓ
56. Ⓐ Ⓑ Ⓒ
57. Ⓐ Ⓑ Ⓒ Ⓓ
58. Ⓐ Ⓑ Ⓒ Ⓓ
59. Ⓐ Ⓑ Ⓒ Ⓓ
60. Ⓐ Ⓑ Ⓒ

Section 2: Quantitative Skills

61. Ⓐ Ⓑ Ⓒ Ⓓ
62. Ⓐ Ⓑ Ⓒ Ⓓ
63. Ⓐ Ⓑ Ⓒ Ⓓ
64. Ⓐ Ⓑ Ⓒ Ⓓ
65. Ⓐ Ⓑ Ⓒ Ⓓ
66. Ⓐ Ⓑ Ⓒ Ⓓ
67. Ⓐ Ⓑ Ⓒ Ⓓ
68. Ⓐ Ⓑ Ⓒ Ⓓ
69. Ⓐ Ⓑ Ⓒ Ⓓ
70. Ⓐ Ⓑ Ⓒ Ⓓ
71. Ⓐ Ⓑ Ⓒ Ⓓ

72. Ⓐ Ⓑ Ⓒ Ⓓ
73. Ⓐ Ⓑ Ⓒ Ⓓ
74. Ⓐ Ⓑ Ⓒ Ⓓ
75. Ⓐ Ⓑ Ⓒ Ⓓ
76. Ⓐ Ⓑ Ⓒ Ⓓ
77. Ⓐ Ⓑ Ⓒ Ⓓ
78. Ⓐ Ⓑ Ⓒ Ⓓ
79. Ⓐ Ⓑ Ⓒ Ⓓ
80. Ⓐ Ⓑ Ⓒ Ⓓ
81. Ⓐ Ⓑ Ⓒ Ⓓ
82. Ⓐ Ⓑ Ⓒ Ⓓ

83. Ⓐ Ⓑ Ⓒ Ⓓ
84. Ⓐ Ⓑ Ⓒ Ⓓ
85. Ⓐ Ⓑ Ⓒ Ⓓ
86. Ⓐ Ⓑ Ⓒ Ⓓ
87. Ⓐ Ⓑ Ⓒ Ⓓ
88. Ⓐ Ⓑ Ⓒ Ⓓ
89. Ⓐ Ⓑ Ⓒ Ⓓ
90. Ⓐ Ⓑ Ⓒ Ⓓ
91. Ⓐ Ⓑ Ⓒ Ⓓ
92. Ⓐ Ⓑ Ⓒ Ⓓ
93. Ⓐ Ⓑ Ⓒ Ⓓ

94. Ⓐ Ⓑ Ⓒ Ⓓ
95. Ⓐ Ⓑ Ⓒ Ⓓ
96. Ⓐ Ⓑ Ⓒ Ⓓ
97. Ⓐ Ⓑ Ⓒ Ⓓ
98. Ⓐ Ⓑ Ⓒ Ⓓ
99. Ⓐ Ⓑ Ⓒ Ⓓ
100. Ⓐ Ⓑ Ⓒ Ⓓ
101. Ⓐ Ⓑ Ⓒ Ⓓ
102. Ⓐ Ⓑ Ⓒ Ⓓ
103. Ⓐ Ⓑ Ⓒ Ⓓ
104. Ⓐ Ⓑ Ⓒ Ⓓ

105. Ⓐ Ⓑ Ⓒ Ⓓ
106. Ⓐ Ⓑ Ⓒ Ⓓ
107. Ⓐ Ⓑ Ⓒ Ⓓ
108. Ⓐ Ⓑ Ⓒ Ⓓ
109. Ⓐ Ⓑ Ⓒ Ⓓ
110. Ⓐ Ⓑ Ⓒ Ⓓ
111. Ⓐ Ⓑ Ⓒ Ⓓ
112. Ⓐ Ⓑ Ⓒ Ⓓ

Section 3: Reading

Comprehension

113. Ⓐ Ⓑ Ⓒ Ⓓ
114. Ⓐ Ⓑ Ⓒ Ⓓ
115. Ⓐ Ⓑ Ⓒ Ⓓ
116. Ⓐ Ⓑ Ⓒ Ⓓ
117. Ⓐ Ⓑ Ⓒ Ⓓ
118. Ⓐ Ⓑ Ⓒ Ⓓ
119. Ⓐ Ⓑ Ⓒ Ⓓ
120. Ⓐ Ⓑ Ⓒ Ⓓ

121. Ⓐ Ⓑ Ⓒ Ⓓ
122. Ⓐ Ⓑ Ⓒ Ⓓ
123. Ⓐ Ⓑ Ⓒ Ⓓ
124. Ⓐ Ⓑ Ⓒ Ⓓ
125. Ⓐ Ⓑ Ⓒ Ⓓ
126. Ⓐ Ⓑ Ⓒ Ⓓ
127. Ⓐ Ⓑ Ⓒ Ⓓ
128. Ⓐ Ⓑ Ⓒ Ⓓ

129. Ⓐ Ⓑ Ⓒ Ⓓ
130. Ⓐ Ⓑ Ⓒ Ⓓ
131. Ⓐ Ⓑ Ⓒ Ⓓ
132. Ⓐ Ⓑ Ⓒ Ⓓ
133. Ⓐ Ⓑ Ⓒ Ⓓ
134. Ⓐ Ⓑ Ⓒ Ⓓ
135. Ⓐ Ⓑ Ⓒ Ⓓ
136. Ⓐ Ⓑ Ⓒ Ⓓ

137. Ⓐ Ⓑ Ⓒ Ⓓ
138. Ⓐ Ⓑ Ⓒ Ⓓ
139. Ⓐ Ⓑ Ⓒ Ⓓ
140. Ⓐ Ⓑ Ⓒ Ⓓ
141. Ⓐ Ⓑ Ⓒ Ⓓ
142. Ⓐ Ⓑ Ⓒ Ⓓ
143. Ⓐ Ⓑ Ⓒ Ⓓ
144. Ⓐ Ⓑ Ⓒ Ⓓ

145. Ⓐ Ⓑ Ⓒ Ⓓ
146. Ⓐ Ⓑ Ⓒ Ⓓ
147. Ⓐ Ⓑ Ⓒ Ⓓ
148. Ⓐ Ⓑ Ⓒ Ⓓ
149. Ⓐ Ⓑ Ⓒ Ⓓ
150. Ⓐ Ⓑ Ⓒ Ⓓ
151. Ⓐ Ⓑ Ⓒ Ⓓ
152. Ⓐ Ⓑ Ⓒ Ⓓ

Vocabulary

153. Ⓐ Ⓑ Ⓒ Ⓓ   158. Ⓐ Ⓑ Ⓒ Ⓓ   163. Ⓐ Ⓑ Ⓒ Ⓓ   168. Ⓐ Ⓑ Ⓒ Ⓓ   173. Ⓐ Ⓑ Ⓒ Ⓓ
154. Ⓐ Ⓑ Ⓒ Ⓓ   159. Ⓐ Ⓑ Ⓒ Ⓓ   164. Ⓐ Ⓑ Ⓒ Ⓓ   169. Ⓐ Ⓑ Ⓒ Ⓓ   174. Ⓐ Ⓑ Ⓒ Ⓓ
155. Ⓐ Ⓑ Ⓒ Ⓓ   160. Ⓐ Ⓑ Ⓒ Ⓓ   165. Ⓐ Ⓑ Ⓒ Ⓓ   170. Ⓐ Ⓑ Ⓒ Ⓓ
156. Ⓐ Ⓑ Ⓒ Ⓓ   161. Ⓐ Ⓑ Ⓒ Ⓓ   166. Ⓐ Ⓑ Ⓒ Ⓓ   171. Ⓐ Ⓑ Ⓒ Ⓓ
157. Ⓐ Ⓑ Ⓒ Ⓓ   162. Ⓐ Ⓑ Ⓒ Ⓓ   167. Ⓐ Ⓑ Ⓒ Ⓓ   172. Ⓐ Ⓑ Ⓒ Ⓓ

Section 4: Mathematics

Concepts

175. Ⓐ Ⓑ Ⓒ Ⓓ   180. Ⓐ Ⓑ Ⓒ Ⓓ   185. Ⓐ Ⓑ Ⓒ Ⓓ   190. Ⓐ Ⓑ Ⓒ Ⓓ   195. Ⓐ Ⓑ Ⓒ Ⓓ
176. Ⓐ Ⓑ Ⓒ Ⓓ   181. Ⓐ Ⓑ Ⓒ Ⓓ   186. Ⓐ Ⓑ Ⓒ Ⓓ   191. Ⓐ Ⓑ Ⓒ Ⓓ   196. Ⓐ Ⓑ Ⓒ Ⓓ
177. Ⓐ Ⓑ Ⓒ Ⓓ   182. Ⓐ Ⓑ Ⓒ Ⓓ   187. Ⓐ Ⓑ Ⓒ Ⓓ   192. Ⓐ Ⓑ Ⓒ Ⓓ   197. Ⓐ Ⓑ Ⓒ Ⓓ
178. Ⓐ Ⓑ Ⓒ Ⓓ   183. Ⓐ Ⓑ Ⓒ Ⓓ   188. Ⓐ Ⓑ Ⓒ Ⓓ   193. Ⓐ Ⓑ Ⓒ Ⓓ   198. Ⓐ Ⓑ Ⓒ Ⓓ
179. Ⓐ Ⓑ Ⓒ Ⓓ   184. Ⓐ Ⓑ Ⓒ Ⓓ   189. Ⓐ Ⓑ Ⓒ Ⓓ   194. Ⓐ Ⓑ Ⓒ Ⓓ

Problem Solving

199. Ⓐ Ⓑ Ⓒ Ⓓ   207. Ⓐ Ⓑ Ⓒ Ⓓ   215. Ⓐ Ⓑ Ⓒ Ⓓ   223. Ⓐ Ⓑ Ⓒ Ⓓ   231. Ⓐ Ⓑ Ⓒ Ⓓ
200. Ⓐ Ⓑ Ⓒ Ⓓ   208. Ⓐ Ⓑ Ⓒ Ⓓ   216. Ⓐ Ⓑ Ⓒ Ⓓ   224. Ⓐ Ⓑ Ⓒ Ⓓ   232. Ⓐ Ⓑ Ⓒ Ⓓ
201. Ⓐ Ⓑ Ⓒ Ⓓ   209. Ⓐ Ⓑ Ⓒ Ⓓ   217. Ⓐ Ⓑ Ⓒ Ⓓ   225. Ⓐ Ⓑ Ⓒ Ⓓ   233. Ⓐ Ⓑ Ⓒ Ⓓ
202. Ⓐ Ⓑ Ⓒ Ⓓ   210. Ⓐ Ⓑ Ⓒ Ⓓ   218. Ⓐ Ⓑ Ⓒ Ⓓ   226. Ⓐ Ⓑ Ⓒ Ⓓ   234. Ⓐ Ⓑ Ⓒ Ⓓ
203. Ⓐ Ⓑ Ⓒ Ⓓ   211. Ⓐ Ⓑ Ⓒ Ⓓ   219. Ⓐ Ⓑ Ⓒ Ⓓ   227. Ⓐ Ⓑ Ⓒ Ⓓ   235. Ⓐ Ⓑ Ⓒ Ⓓ
204. Ⓐ Ⓑ Ⓒ Ⓓ   212. Ⓐ Ⓑ Ⓒ Ⓓ   220. Ⓐ Ⓑ Ⓒ Ⓓ   228. Ⓐ Ⓑ Ⓒ Ⓓ   236. Ⓐ Ⓑ Ⓒ Ⓓ
205. Ⓐ Ⓑ Ⓒ Ⓓ   213. Ⓐ Ⓑ Ⓒ Ⓓ   221. Ⓐ Ⓑ Ⓒ Ⓓ   229. Ⓐ Ⓑ Ⓒ Ⓓ   237. Ⓐ Ⓑ Ⓒ Ⓓ
206. Ⓐ Ⓑ Ⓒ Ⓓ   214. Ⓐ Ⓑ Ⓒ Ⓓ   222. Ⓐ Ⓑ Ⓒ Ⓓ   230. Ⓐ Ⓑ Ⓒ Ⓓ   238. Ⓐ Ⓑ Ⓒ Ⓓ

Section 5: Language

239. Ⓐ Ⓑ Ⓒ Ⓓ   251. Ⓐ Ⓑ Ⓒ Ⓓ   263. Ⓐ Ⓑ Ⓒ Ⓓ   275. Ⓐ Ⓑ Ⓒ Ⓓ   287. Ⓐ Ⓑ Ⓒ Ⓓ
240. Ⓐ Ⓑ Ⓒ Ⓓ   252. Ⓐ Ⓑ Ⓒ Ⓓ   264. Ⓐ Ⓑ Ⓒ Ⓓ   276. Ⓐ Ⓑ Ⓒ Ⓓ   288. Ⓐ Ⓑ Ⓒ Ⓓ
241. Ⓐ Ⓑ Ⓒ Ⓓ   253. Ⓐ Ⓑ Ⓒ Ⓓ   265. Ⓐ Ⓑ Ⓒ Ⓓ   277. Ⓐ Ⓑ Ⓒ Ⓓ   289. Ⓐ Ⓑ Ⓒ Ⓓ
242. Ⓐ Ⓑ Ⓒ Ⓓ   254. Ⓐ Ⓑ Ⓒ Ⓓ   266. Ⓐ Ⓑ Ⓒ Ⓓ   278. Ⓐ Ⓑ Ⓒ Ⓓ   290. Ⓐ Ⓑ Ⓒ Ⓓ
243. Ⓐ Ⓑ Ⓒ Ⓓ   255. Ⓐ Ⓑ Ⓒ Ⓓ   267. Ⓐ Ⓑ Ⓒ Ⓓ   279. Ⓐ Ⓑ Ⓒ Ⓓ   291. Ⓐ Ⓑ Ⓒ Ⓓ
244. Ⓐ Ⓑ Ⓒ Ⓓ   256. Ⓐ Ⓑ Ⓒ Ⓓ   268. Ⓐ Ⓑ Ⓒ Ⓓ   280. Ⓐ Ⓑ Ⓒ Ⓓ   292. Ⓐ Ⓑ Ⓒ Ⓓ
245. Ⓐ Ⓑ Ⓒ Ⓓ   257. Ⓐ Ⓑ Ⓒ Ⓓ   269. Ⓐ Ⓑ Ⓒ Ⓓ   281. Ⓐ Ⓑ Ⓒ Ⓓ   293. Ⓐ Ⓑ Ⓒ Ⓓ
246. Ⓐ Ⓑ Ⓒ Ⓓ   258. Ⓐ Ⓑ Ⓒ Ⓓ   270. Ⓐ Ⓑ Ⓒ Ⓓ   282. Ⓐ Ⓑ Ⓒ Ⓓ   294. Ⓐ Ⓑ Ⓒ Ⓓ
247. Ⓐ Ⓑ Ⓒ Ⓓ   259. Ⓐ Ⓑ Ⓒ Ⓓ   271. Ⓐ Ⓑ Ⓒ Ⓓ   283. Ⓐ Ⓑ Ⓒ Ⓓ   295. Ⓐ Ⓑ Ⓒ Ⓓ
248. Ⓐ Ⓑ Ⓒ Ⓓ   260. Ⓐ Ⓑ Ⓒ Ⓓ   272. Ⓐ Ⓑ Ⓒ Ⓓ   284. Ⓐ Ⓑ Ⓒ Ⓓ   296. Ⓐ Ⓑ Ⓒ Ⓓ
249. Ⓐ Ⓑ Ⓒ Ⓓ   261. Ⓐ Ⓑ Ⓒ Ⓓ   273. Ⓐ Ⓑ Ⓒ Ⓓ   285. Ⓐ Ⓑ Ⓒ Ⓓ   297. Ⓐ Ⓑ Ⓒ Ⓓ
250. Ⓐ Ⓑ Ⓒ Ⓓ   262. Ⓐ Ⓑ Ⓒ Ⓓ   274. Ⓐ Ⓑ Ⓒ Ⓓ   286. Ⓐ Ⓑ Ⓒ Ⓓ   298. Ⓐ Ⓑ Ⓒ Ⓓ

Section 1: Verbal Skills

Time: 16 minutes

Directions: Choose the best answer for Questions 1–60.

1. Which of these words does *not* belong with the others?

   (A) cake

   (B) pie

   (C) milk

   (D) cookies

2. Boat is to cruise ship as hotel is to

   (A) luggage

   (B) vacation

   (C) passport

   (D) resort

3. Which of these words does *not* belong with the others?

   (A) smug

   (B) superior

   (C) conceited

   (D) humble

4. Cats live longer than dogs. Dogs live longer than turtles. Turtles live longer than cats. If the first two statements are true, the third statement is

   (A) true

   (B) false

   (C) uncertain

5. Apparent most nearly means

   (A) uncertain

   (B) clear

   (C) doubtful

   (D) strict

6. Which of these words does *not* belong with the others?

   (A) creepy

   (B) incorrect

   (C) disturbing

   (D) eerie

7. Subordinate most nearly means

   (A) inferior

   (B) central

   (C) farthest

   (D) profound

8. Travel is to airport as shopping is to

   (A) sale

   (B) money

   (C) store

   (D) train station

9. Which of these words does *not* belong with the others?

   (A) intelligence

   (B) selfishness

   (C) wisdom

   (D) insight

10. Marginal most nearly means

    (A) written

    (B) crucial

    (C) minor

    (D) far

11. Ambassador is to represent as physician is to

    (A) heal

    (B) build

    (C) darn

    (D) live

Go on to next page

12. Which of these words does *not* belong with the others?

    (A) thoughtlessness

    (B) altruism

    (C) selflessness

    (D) philanthropy

13. Angela has a larger doll collection than Barbara. Barbara has a smaller doll collection than Cathy. Angela has a larger doll collection than Cathy. If the first two statements are true, the third statement is

    (A) true

    (B) false

    (C) uncertain

14. Bigotry most nearly means

    (A) tolerance

    (B) justice

    (C) bias

    (D) effort

15. A flamboyant display is

    (A) unnoticeable

    (B) unattractive

    (C) modest

    (D) showy

16. Forbid most nearly means

    (A) remember

    (B) pardon

    (C) excuse

    (D) ban

17. Scalding is to hot as diminutive is to

    (A) small

    (B) big

    (C) cold

    (D) large

18. Football is to pass as baseball is to

    (A) bat

    (B) pitch

    (C) run

    (D) score

19. Adversary most nearly means

    (A) ally

    (B) foe

    (C) neighbor

    (D) candidate

20. Which of these words does *not* belong with the others?

    (A) back

    (B) lock

    (C) support

    (D) approve

21. Which of these words does *not* belong with the others?

    (A) consider

    (B) cause

    (C) trigger

    (D) produce

22. Phillip gets better grades than Patrick. Carrie gets better grades than Patrick. Carrie gets better grades than Phillip. If the first two statements are true, the third statement is

    (A) true

    (B) false

    (C) uncertain

23. Ruth is the tallest girl in music class. Maggie is taller than Ruth. Maggie and Ruth are not in the same music class. If the first two statements are true, the third statement is

    (A) true

    (B) false

    (C) uncertain

24. Honesty is the *opposite* of

    (A) sincerity

    (B) respect

    (C) deception

    (D) privilege

Go on to next page

25. Which of these words does *not* belong with the others?

    (A) secluded

    (B) isolated

    (C) aloof

    (D) adjacent

26. Liberal is the *opposite* of

    (A) charitable

    (B) lenient

    (C) accurate

    (D) stingy

27. All dwaddles are lazy. Homer is lazy. Homer is a dwaddle. If the first two statements are true, the third statement is

    (A) true

    (B) false

    (C) uncertain

28. A glowering boss is

    (A) proud

    (B) angry

    (C) funny

    (D) tardy

29. Restore is the *opposite* of

    (A) rupture

    (B) fix

    (C) cleanse

    (D) transform

30. Pauper is the *opposite* of

    (A) employer

    (B) child

    (C) beggar

    (D) tycoon

31. Which of these words does *not* belong with the others?

    (A) dancer

    (B) comic

    (C) joker

    (D) jester

32. Fancy is the *opposite* of

    (A) decorate

    (B) impress

    (C) dislike

    (D) reveal

33. Garbage is to stench as cologne is to

    (A) smell

    (B) wrist

    (C) fragrance

    (D) bottle

34. Bloom is the *opposite* of

    (A) blossom

    (B) plan

    (C) mold

    (D) fade

35. Which word does *not* belong with the others?

    (A) hurt

    (B) injure

    (C) squander

    (D) wound

36. Brown River is wider than Cool River but narrower than White River. Deep River is wider than White River but narrower than Slimy River. Slimy River is the widest of all five rivers. If the first two statements are true, the third statement is

    (A) true

    (B) false

    (C) uncertain

37. Corrupt is the *opposite* of

    (A) sensible

    (B) decent

    (C) different

    (D) shady

Go on to next page

38. Which of these words does *not* belong with the others?
    (A) struggle
    (B) tussle
    (C) scuffle
    (D) expansion

39. A vital decision is
    (A) short-term
    (B) permanent
    (C) essential
    (D) unanimous

40. Which word does *not* belong with the others?
    (A) stout
    (B) obnoxious
    (C) plump
    (D) portly

41. Biology is to science as sculpture is to
    (A) art
    (B) clay
    (C) fashion
    (D) sculptor

42. Monastery is to monk as den is to
    (A) study
    (B) nest
    (C) desk
    (D) fox

43. All squirt fruit are green. Some green fruit tastes sweet. Some squirt fruit tastes sweet. If the first two statements are true, the third statement is
    (A) true
    (B) false
    (C) uncertain

44. Which of these words does *not* belong with the others?
    (A) fedora
    (B) bonnet
    (C) wrap
    (D) cap

45. A noxious fume is
    (A) toxic
    (B) aromatic
    (C) odorless
    (D) safe

46. Spirited most nearly means
    (A) ghostly
    (B) exhausting
    (C) annoying
    (D) lively

47. Psychology is to mind as zoology is to
    (A) zoos
    (B) animals
    (C) plants
    (D) science

48. Capitulate is the *opposite* of
    (A) surrender
    (B) resist
    (C) exhaust
    (D) save

49. Which of these words does *not* belong with the others?
    (A) slight
    (B) key
    (C) foremost
    (D) main

50. Which of these words does *not* belong with the others?
    (A) obliging
    (B) impractical
    (C) cooperative
    (D) accommodating

51. Fashioned is the *opposite* of
    (A) detected
    (B) blended
    (C) destroyed
    (D) styled

Go on to next page

52. Wretched most nearly means
    (A) determined
    (B) lazy
    (C) miserable
    (D) exultant

53. Jocelyn's birthday comes before Chloe's and after Randy's. Frank's birthday comes before Chloe's. Frank's birthday comes after Jocelyn's. If the first two statements are true, the third statement is
    (A) true
    (B) false
    (C) uncertain

54. Bleak is the *opposite* of
    (A) hopeless
    (B) spicy
    (C) weak
    (D) promising

55. Nuance most nearly means
    (A) newness
    (B) fine distinction
    (C) loud clamor
    (D) stillness

56. All swirls have blond hair and three toes. Chippy is a swirl. Chippy has blond hair. If the first two statements are true, the third statement is
    (A) true
    (B) false
    (C) uncertain

57. A wealthy aristocrat is
    (A) exotic
    (B) charming
    (C) youthful
    (D) privileged

58. Which of these words does *not* belong with the others?
    (A) starter
    (B) hors d'oeuvre
    (C) dessert
    (D) appetizer

59. Chess is to game as Cajun is to
    (A) cooking
    (B) Louisiana
    (C) bayou
    (D) catfish

60. Lochtown is north of Morristown. Noonville is south of Otisburg and north of Lochtown. Morristown is north of Otisburg. If the first two statements are true, the third statement is
    (A) true
    (B) false
    (C) uncertain

STOP DO NOT TURN THE PAGE UNTIL TOLD TO DO SO.
DO NOT RETURN TO A PREVIOUS TEST.

Section 2: Quantitative Skills

Time: 30 minutes

Directions: Choose the best answer for Questions 61–112.

61. What number is 3 more than 80% of 20?

    (A) 16

    (B) 18

    (C) 20

    (D) 19

62. What is the next number in this sequence: 4, 8, 12, . . . ?

    (A) 13

    (B) 16

    (C) 18

    (D) 24

63. Examine (a), (b), and (c) and choose the best answer.

    (a) three dimes and three nickels

    (b) two quarters

    (c) one quarter and two dimes

    (A) (a) is greater than (b) or (c).

    (B) (b) is less than (a).

    (C) (a) is less than (b) and equal to (c).

    (D) (a), (b), and (c) are equal.

64. What number times 3 is ½ of 12?

    (A) 6

    (B) 4

    (C) 2

    (D) 12

65. What is the next number in this sequence: 45, 50, 55, . . . ?

    (A) 56

    (B) 60

    (C) 65

    (D) 54

66. In the following figure, Line *BE* bisects the rectangle. Examine the figure and choose the best answer.

    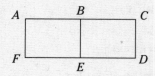

    (A) *AB* is equal to *ED*.

    (B) *AC* is equal to *CD*.

    (C) *BE* is equal to *FE*.

    (D) *BE* is greater than *CD*.

67. What number added to 42 is equal to the product of 8 and 6?

    (A) 6

    (B) 48

    (C) 8

    (D) 4

68. What is the square of 4 less the product of 3 and 4?

    (A) 4

    (B) 18

    (C) 14

    (D) 24

69. What are the next two numbers in this sequence: 33, 30, 35, 32, 37, . . . ?

    (A) 32, 35

    (B) 34, 37

    (C) 40, 35

    (D) 34, 39

Go on to next page

70. What is the missing number in this sequence: XIV, 17, XX, 23, _____, 29?

(A) 25

(B) XXV

(C) XXVI

(D) 26

71. What number is 3 times the average of 20, 5, 25, 10, and 10?

(A) 43

(B) 42

(C) 45

(D) 14

72. (a), (b), and (c) show shaded areas of the same pentagon, and each pentagon has equal side lengths. Examine (a), (b), and (c) and choose the best answer.

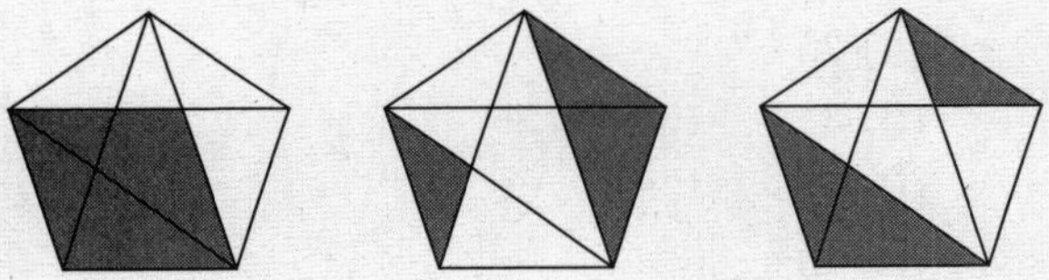

(a) (b) (c)

(A) (a) is less shaded than (b) or (c).

(B) (b) is less shaded than (a) and more shaded than (c).

(C) (c) is shaded equally to (b) and less shaded than (a).

(D) (a), (b), and (c) are shaded equally.

73. $\frac{5}{8}$ of what number is 5 more than 4 times 5?

(A) 25

(B) 45

(C) 40

(D) 20

74. Examine (a), (b), and (c) and choose the best answer.

(a) 25% of 80%

(b) 25% of 80

(c) 40% of 50

(A) (a) is greater than (b) or (c).

(B) (a) is equal to (b) and less than (c).

(C) (a) is equal to (b) and greater than (c).

(D) (c) is equal to (b).

75. What is the next number in this sequence: $\frac{1}{9}$, $\frac{1}{3}$, 1, . . . ?

(A) $\frac{3}{3}$

(B) 6

(C) $1\frac{1}{3}$

(D) 3

76. Examine (a), (b), and (c) and choose the best answer.

(a) $\frac{1}{2}$ of 66

(b) $\frac{2}{5}$ of 60

(c) $\frac{1}{3}$ of 72

(A) (b) is equal to (c) and less than (a).

(B) (a) is greater than (b) and less than (c).

(C) (c) is less than (a) and greater than (b).

(D) (a) is equal to (b) and less than (c).

77. What are the next two numbers in this sequence: 3, 10, 18, 27, 37, . . . ?

(A) 47, 57

(B) 48, 60

(C) 44, 51

(D) 44, 52

78. What number divided by $\frac{2}{3}$ is $\frac{3}{4}$?

(A) $\frac{1}{2}$

(B) 1

(C) $\frac{7}{8}$

(D) $\frac{5}{8}$

Go on to next page

79. Examine the graph and choose the best answer.

Sales by Employee

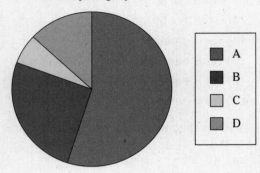

(A) The sales of C plus D are equal to A.

(B) D made more sales than B.

(C) B made more sales than D.

(D) The sales of B plus C plus D are greater than A.

80. What are the next two numbers in this sequence: 4, 6, 3, 5, 2, 4, . . . ?

(A) 1, 3

(B) 1, 5

(C) 5, 6

(D) 3, 1

81. ½ of what number is 7 times 8?

(A) 56

(B) 12

(C) 60

(D) 112

82. What fraction of the following figure is shaded?

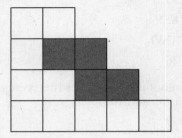

(A) ¼

(B) ⅓

(C) ½

(D) ⅔

83. What number is the quotient of 5 cubed divided by 5?

(A) 25

(B) 5

(C) 125

(D) 75

84. What is the next number in this sequence: 5, 3, 6, 4, 8, 6, 12, 10, . . . ?

(A) 8

(B) 20

(C) 14

(D) 16

85. Examine (a), (b), and (c) and choose the best answer.

(a) 70%

(b) 0.7

(c) ⁷⁄₁₀

(A) (b) and (c) are less than (a).

(B) (a) is greater than (c) and equal to (b).

(C) (b) is equal to (c) and less than (a).

(D) (a), (b), and (c) are equal.

Go on to next page

86. ¾ of what number is 5 times 15?

    (A) 56

    (B) 25

    (C) 75

    (D) 100

87. What is the next number is this sequence: 124, 62, 66, 33, . . . ?

    (A) 11

    (B) 37

    (C) 22

    (D) 29

88. Examine (a), (b), and (c) and choose the best answer.

    (a) 4^3

    (b) $(4 \times 3)(4 \times 3)(4 \times 3)$

    (c) 3^4

    (A) (a) is equal to (c).

    (B) (a) is equal to (b).

    (C) (c) is greater than (a) and less than (b).

    (D) (b) is less than (a) and greater than (c).

89. What is the next number in this sequence: 1¾, 9.25, 8½, 7.75, . . . ?

    (A) ⅝

    (B) 7.25

    (C) 7

    (D) ⅞

90. 20% of a number plus 60% of the same number equals 52. What is the number?

    (A) 65

    (B) 13

    (C) 39

    (D) 75

91. What is the missing number in this sequence: 17, 14, 28, 25, _____, 47, 94?

    (A) 50

    (B) 28

    (C) 39

    (D) 53

92. Examine this figure and choose the best answer.

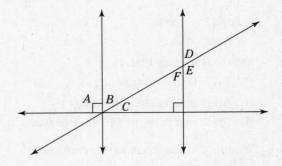

    (A) Angle B is equal to Angle C.

    (B) Angle B plus Angle C is equal to Angle D.

    (C) Angle B is equal to Angle D.

    (D) Angle E is equal to Angle C.

93. What is the next number in this sequence: 0, 1, –1, 2, –2, 3, –3, 4, . . . ?

    (A) –3

    (B) –4

    (C) 5

    (D) 4

94. What number is 4 less than twice the average of 60, 52, 43, 23, 60, and 38?

    (A) 544

    (B) 88

    (C) 42

    (D) 39

95. The number of sixths in the product of 10 times 3 is

    (A) 15

    (B) 18

    (C) 160

    (D) 180

Go on to next page

96. Examine (a), (b), and (c) and select the best answer.

    (a) $(5 \times 7) + 2$

    (b) $(5 + 7) \times 2$

    (c) $(5 - 7) \times 2$

    (A) (c) is greater than (a).

    (B) (b) is less than (a) and (c).

    (C) (a) is greater than (b) and (c).

    (D) (c) is less than (a) and greater than (b).

97. What is the next term in this sequence: C33, F44, I55, . . . ?

    (A) J66

    (B) K66

    (C) L4

    (D) L66

98. Examine (a), (b), and (c) and select the best answer.

    (a) ⅚

    (b) ⅙

    (c) ⅕

    (A) (a) > (b) > (c)

    (B) (b) + (c) > (a)

    (C) (a) > (c) > (b)

    (D) (c) < (a) < (b)

99. Examine this figure and select the best answer.

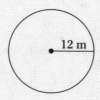

    (A) The diameter of the circle is 24 m.

    (B) The radius of the circle is 12π.

    (C) The circumference of the circle is 12π.

    (D) The radius plus the diameter equals 24 m.

100. What are the next three numbers in this sequence: 78, 79, 85, 86, 92, . . . ?

     (A) 93, 99, 100

     (B) 98, 99, 105

     (C) 98, 104, 105

     (D) 93, 94, 95

101. What is the missing number in this sequence: 76, 72, 36, 32, 16, _____, 6, 2?

     (A) 12

     (B) 28

     (C) 8

     (D) 10

102. The number that is 25 more than 191 is the cube of what number?

     (A) 216

     (B) 5

     (C) 6

     (D) 7

103. Examine (a), (b), and (c) and select the best answer.

     (a) $(17 + 32)(17 + 32)$

     (b) $(17 + 32)^2$

     (c) $2(17 + 32)$

     (A) (c) is greater than (b).

     (B) (a) is equal to (b) and greater than (c).

     (C) (b) is equal to (c) and less than (a).

     (D) (a), (b), and (c) are equal.

104. What number divided by 4 is 4 more than 32?

     (A) 123

     (B) 16

     (C) 36

     (D) 144

105. What are the next three numbers in this sequence: 45, 36, 36, 27, 27, 18, . . . ?

     (A) 18, 18, 9

     (B) 18, 9, 9

     (C) 18, 9, 0

     (D) 18, 9, 3

Go on to next page

106. Examine these three identical circles and select the best answer.

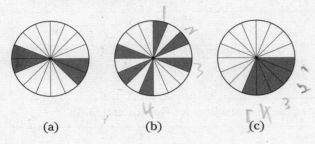

(a)   (b)   (c)

(A) The shaded area of (a) is equal to the shaded area of (c).

(B) The shaded area of (b) is less than the shaded area of (c).

(C) The shaded area of (c) is half the shaded area of (a) + (b).

(D) The shaded area of (c) is twice the shaded area of (a).

107. What are the next two numbers in this sequence: 33, 36, 33, 39, 33, 42, 33, . . . ?

(A) 33, 33

(B) 44, 55

(C) 45, 33

(D) 45, 48

108. What number when added to 23 results in a sum that is a perfect square?

(A) 144

(B) 100

(C) 20

(D) 98

109. What number increased by 30% of itself is 65?

(A) 40

(B) 25

(C) 95

(D) 50

110. Examine (a), (b), and (c) and select the best answer.

(a) 5^3

(b) 3^4

(c) 9^2

(A) (b) = (c)

(B) (a) > (b) > (c)

(C) (b) + (c) < (a)

(D) (a) > (c) > (b)

111. What number is 5 less than the quotient of 3^3 divided by 9?

(A) 3

(B) –3

(C) 2

(D) –2

112. Examine this figure and select the best answer.

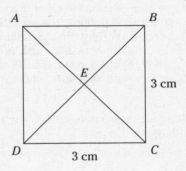

(A) The measure of $\angle EAB$ is ½ the measure of $\angle AEB$.

(B) Line *BD* is twice as long as Line *BC*.

(C) The measure of $\angle AEB$ is greater than the measure of $\angle CEB$.

(D) The measure of $\angle DEC$ is greater than 90°.

STOP DO NOT TURN THE PAGE UNTIL TOLD TO DO SO. DO NOT RETURN TO A PREVIOUS TEST.

Section 3: Reading

Time: 25 minutes

Comprehension

Directions: Read the following 5 passages and choose the best answers for Questions 113–152.

President Andrew Jackson signed the Indian Removal Act in 1830, which appropriated $500,000 for the U.S. military to force the Cherokee tribes to march from their homes in Florida and southern Georgia to Oklahoma. In 1832, the Native Americans won a victory supported by most Northern leaders in the U.S. Supreme Court case of *Worchester v. Georgia*. The decision held that Native American nations were independent and not subject to state regulation. However, after the case decision, President Jackson provokingly asserted that Chief Justice John Marshall had made his decision and "now let's see him enforce it." Although Jackson professed to having "the kindest feelings" toward the Cherokees, his actions and subsequent statements <u>belied</u> his words.

In 1835, Jackson entered into treaty negotiations with the Cherokees that ended up in the relinquishment of all of their land east of the Mississippi River. Jackson gave the Cherokees until 1838 to leave the area. Some left voluntarily, but most did not. Those who remained were forced by the U.S. military to walk the 1,200 mile "Trail of Tears" from Georgia to lands in Oklahoma, usually with only the clothes they were wearing. The brutal journey in 1838 to 1839 resulted in the deaths of about one-fourth of the Cherokee population from disease, starvation, exposure, and exhaustion.

113. Which party was successful in the case of *Worchester v. Georgia?*

   (A) settlers

   (B) Southern leaders

   (C) Native Americans

   (D) the U.S. Supreme Court

114. Which of the following is an appropriate title for this article?

   (A) The Power of the Supreme Court

   (B) Native American Policy in the 17th Century

   (C) The Indian Removal Act and the Trail of Tears

   (D) State Rights versus Federal Rights

115. For whom did President Jackson state that he had "the kindest feelings"?

   (A) Cherokees

   (B) Georgians

   (C) Oklahomans

   (D) the U.S. Supreme Court

116. According to the passage, President Jackson entered into treaty negotiations with which of the following parties?

   (A) the Comanche

   (B) the Cherokee

   (C) the Chickasaw

   (D) the Choctaw

Go on to next page

117. What did the *Worchester v. Georgia* decision provide?

   (A) that Native American tribes were independent

   (B) that Native American tribes were subject to state regulation

   (C) that the Cherokee were to march from Florida to Oklahoma

   (D) that President Jackson must enter into treaty negotiations with the Cherokee

118. As it is used in the passage, <u>belied</u> most nearly means

   (A) exaggerated

   (B) contradicted

   (C) supported

   (D) carried

Almost all great nations have composed myths. The Greek and Roman myths represent the most popular of these tales. These myths have extended their influence to virtually everyone from advertising agents to writers. It appears that we study myths primarily for four reasons.

First, as mentioned, Greek and Roman myths have profoundly inspired English and American literature. In fact, we can barely comprehend Shakespeare, Milton, Keats, or Lowell without familiarizing ourselves with the myths of Greece and Rome. Second, myths have greatly influenced our music, and many of the stories explain how musical instruments were first created. Many musical compositions have been inspired by the mythological characters, including the word "music" itself, which is derived from the Greek myth "Muses." Third, we study Greek and Roman myths because the stories are both beautiful and entertaining. These fables still appeal to our imagination. Finally, myths provide us with a <u>critical</u> link to the past. They are often our only source of knowledge regarding how our distant ancestors viewed the world around them.

Some of the most important mythological characters are Jupiter, Juno, and Mars. At the top of the mythological hierarchy is Jupiter, called the father of Roman gods and mortals. Jupiter is the founder of all kingly power, the supreme ruler, and the creator of law, order, and justice. All good and evil springs from Jupiter, who assigns his earthly share of sorrow and prosperity to all mortals. Armed with thunder and lightning, he causes storms by shaking his shield. Jupiter is the god of weather and is often associated with rain. A great eagle crouches before Jupiter, patiently waiting to be his messenger.

Sitting beside Jupiter in the heavens is his wife and <u>consort</u>, Juno. Juno knows all of Jupiter's secrets, and he listens to her with respect. However, Juno is less powerful than Jupiter and must obey him. Her domain is marriage, and she appears to be a beautiful and <u>majestic</u> woman in her middle ages who commands reverence but is not openly friendly. On Juno's head sits a crown with a veil hung behind her head. Iris, goddess of the rainbow is her constant attendant and companion.

Another important Roman god is Mars, the god of war and a son of Jupiter and Juno. He revels in conflict, and his war chariot races along at high speeds, pulled by four fiery steeds. Dogs and vultures follow Mars wherever he goes, and his symbols are a spear and a burning torch. His sons are known as Terror, Trembling, Panic, and Fear.

Go on to next page

119. Who carries Jupiter's words to others?

    (A) a great eagle

    (B) Juno

    (C) thunder and lightning

    (D) Mars

120. Which of the following would be an appropriate title for this passage?

    (A) Terror, Trembling, Panic, and Fear

    (B) The Families of Juno and Mars

    (C) The Impact of Greek and Roman Mythology on the Fall of Rome

    (D) The Importance of Mythology in Society

121. The author refers to myths as

    (A) scriptures

    (B) sermons

    (C) proverbs

    (D) fables

122. What does consort mean as it is used in the passage?

    (A) child

    (B) companion

    (C) nemesis

    (D) adversary

123. What does critical mean as it is used in the passage?

    (A) disapproving

    (B) irrelevant

    (C) dangerous

    (D) important

124. What animals pulled the war chariot that Mars traveled in?

    (A) greyhounds

    (B) donkeys

    (C) horses

    (D) lions

125. Majestic, as it is used in the passage, most nearly means

    (A) magnificent

    (B) modest

    (C) melodramatic

    (D) subservient

126. Jupiter is the god of what?

    (A) sorrow

    (B) good and evil

    (C) weather

    (D) prosperity

127. Which of the following is *not* a reason that modern students study myths?

    (A) Myths provide a link to past cultures.

    (B) Modern literature contains references to mythical tales.

    (C) Myths can tell students about the origins of some musical instruments.

    (D) Myths are hilariously funny.

128. Which of the following gods or goddesses oversees marriage?

    (A) Jupiter

    (B) Iris

    (C) Juno

    (D) Mars

Go on to next page

Many people believe that the existence of lawyers and lawsuits represent a relatively recent phenomenon. The opinion that many hold regarding lawyers, also known as attorneys, is that they are insincere and greedy. Lawyers are often referred to as "ambulance chasers" or other <u>pejorative</u> expressions.

Despite this negativity, lawyers are also known for their fights for civil rights, due process of law, and equal protection. Lawyers were instrumental in desegregating the institutions in our society and in cleaning up the environment. Most legislators at the local, state, and federal level of government are lawyers because they generally have a firm understanding of justice and the proper application of statutory and case law.

Lawyers are traditionally articulate public speakers, or orators, too. One of the finest legal orators was Marcus Tullius Cicero, who was an intellectually distinguished, politically savvy, and incredibly successful Roman lawyer. Cicero lived from 143–106 B.C. and was one of only a few Roman intellectuals credited with the flowering of Latin literature that largely occurred during the last decades of the Roman republic.

Cicero's compositions have been compared to the works of Julius Caesar. Their writings have customarily been included in the curriculum wherever Latin is studied. Cicero was a lifelong student of government and philosophy and a practicing politician. He was a successful lawyer whose voluminous speeches, letters, and essays tend to have the same quality that people usually associate with pleading a case. His arguments are well structured, eloquent, and clear. Cicero perfected the complex, balanced, and majestic sentence structure called "periodic," which was imitated by later writers from Plutarch in the Renaissance to Churchill in the 20th century.

129. Which of the following is *not* something that Cicero was involved in?

(A) politics

(B) law

(C) oration

(D) carpentry

130. What leader has Cicero been compared to?

(A) Caesar

(B) Socrates

(C) Aristotle

(D) Napoleon

131. Latin literature is the same as

(A) English literature

(B) Greek literature

(C) Roman literature

(D) Renaissance literature

132. To what does "the works of Julius Caesar" refer?

(A) Caesar's skilled carpentry

(B) Caesar's writings

(C) Caesar's paintings

(D) Caesar's culinary creations

133. Another name for "lawyer" is

(A) judge

(B) attorney

(C) writer

(D) intellectual

134. <u>Pejorative</u>, as it is used in the passage, most nearly means

(A) comic

(B) constructive

(C) simple

(D) uncomplimentary

Go on to next page

135. The author's attitude toward Cicero is

    (A) admiring

    (B) pejorative

    (C) unenthusiastic

    (D) disinterested

136. Which of the following statements is true?

    (A) Plutarch used some of Cicero's arguments in his writings.

    (B) Cicero studied under Julius Caesar.

    (C) Churchill's writings reflect Cicero's majestic sentence structure.

    (D) The public's view of Cicero was that he was insincere and greedy.

137. Which of these, according to the author, is a way that lawyers have positively contributed to society?

    (A) They have fought legislation designed to clean up the environment.

    (B) They have proposed laws to make "ambulance chasing" illegal.

    (C) They have taught public speaking skills to disadvantaged youth.

    (D) They have advocated for integration of public institutions.

138. Why are many politicians also lawyers?

    (A) because they are greedy

    (B) because they understand the idea of justice

    (C) because they clean up the environment

    (D) because they have studied Latin

Biomes are the major biological divisions of the earth. Biomes are characterized by an area's climate and the particular organisms that live there. The living organisms make up the "biotic" components of the biome, and everything else makes up the "abiotic" components. The density and diversity of a biome's biotic components is called its "carrying capacity." The most important abiotic aspects of a biome are the amount of rainfall it has and how much its temperatures vary. More rain and more stable temperatures means more organisms can survive. Usually, the wetter a biome is, the less its temperature changes from day to night or from summer to winter. Biomes include deserts, rain forests, forests, savannas, tundras, freshwater environments, and oceans.

Deserts are areas that get less than 10 inches of rain per year. Most deserts are hot (like the Sahara), but some are actually cold (like parts of Antarctica). Therefore, the thing that distinguishes deserts is their extreme dryness. The organisms that live in a desert need to be able to survive drastic temperature swings along with dry conditions, so the desert's carrying capacity is extremely low. Desert animals include reptiles, such as lizards and snakes, and some arachnids, like spiders and scorpions.

Conversely, tropical rain forests get lots of rain and have steady, mild temperatures, a combination that creates perfect living conditions for most terrestrial organisms. This means that the tropical rain forest has the greatest density and diversity of life. Tropical rain forests, like the ones in South America and southeast Asia, contain densely packed trees, plants, and vines that are home to millions of insect species, along with lots of rodents, reptiles, monkeys, birds, and just about every other kind of terrestrial animal there is.

There are two forest biomes: the temperate deciduous forest and the taiga. The first one exists in the eastern U.S. and in central Europe and gets more rain than the desert but less than the rain forest. Its temperature changes quite a bit from season to season, but not as dramatically as in the desert. Temperate biomes have a medium density and diversity of species, with big trees with leaves (that's what "deciduous" means) and lots of mammals, like rodents, deer, and many types of songbirds. The taiga has mostly evergreen trees, like

Go on to next page

pine and spruce, and animals like squirrels, deer, moose, wolves, bears, and birds. The taiga's carrying capacity is a little lower than that of the temperate deciduous forest because the taiga is a little colder and it usually gets less rain. The forests of northwestern North America and northern Europe and Asia are taigas.

The savanna is mostly grasslands with a few trees here and there. It has one good rainy season with long periods of drought every year, so its carrying capacity is below average. Because it has so much grass, this biome supports lots of grazing mammals, such as antelope, zebra, and bison, and feline predators, such as lions and cheetahs. The best-known savanna is in central Africa, but the central prairies of the U.S. count as well.

The main characteristic of the tundra is that the ground stays permanently frozen. The extreme tundras, like those near the North and South Poles, are too cold for almost anything to live there, so the carrying capacity is really low. The less extreme tundras can support lots of mosses, grasses, and hearty mammals, like caribou and bears.

Freshwater environments and oceans are also biomes. The freshwater biome includes elements such as rivers, lakes, and ponds. These areas are affected by temperature swings, the amount of available oxygen, and the speed of water flowing through them. All of these are affected by the larger climate area the freshwater biome is in, which also affects the biotic components. Algae, fish, amphibians, and insects are found in freshwater biomes. Oceans cover about 70 percent of the earth's surface, so they comprise the biggest biome. Temperature swings aren't nearly as wide in the oceans as they are on land, and there's plenty of water to go around. Therefore, the carrying capacity of the oceans is huge. The density and diversity of organisms isn't quite as high as in the tropical rain forest, but the total number of organisms in the oceans is much bigger than all the terrestrial biomes put together.

139. What is the definition of "carrying capacity" of biomes?

(A) the number and variety of living organisms it has

(B) the type of abiotic features it has

(C) its level of humidity

(D) how much its temperatures vary

140. What are the two forest biomes?

(A) the savanna and the tundra

(B) the tundra and the tropical rain forest

(C) the desert and the taiga

(D) the taiga and the temperate deciduous

141. What is the characteristic of "deciduous"?

(A) having a large diversity of species

(B) having leaves

(C) being filled with many mammals

(D) exhibiting extreme dryness

142. Which of these biomes has the lowest carrying capacity?

(A) desert

(B) tropical rain forest

(C) savanna

(D) taiga

Go on to next page

143. What is a characteristic of the tundra?

    (A) a high carrying capacity

    (B) ground that does not melt

    (C) a lack of mammals

    (D) mild temperatures

144. Which of these elements does *not* affect the quality of a freshwater biome?

    (A) oxygen levels

    (B) swings in temperature

    (C) the larger climate in which it exists

    (D) the policies of the country in which it exists

145. Which of the following lists the carrying capacity of some biomes from greatest to least?

    (A) ocean, tropical rain forest, taiga, savanna

    (B) tropical rain forest, ocean, desert, savanna

    (C) ocean, tropical rain forest, deciduous forest, desert

    (D) ocean, taiga, savanna, desert

146. What are examples of biotic components of a taiga?

    (A) evergreen trees and deer

    (B) pine, spruce, deer, and colder temperatures

    (C) spiders, snakes, and low humidity

    (D) deciduous trees, songbirds, and caribou

147. Where would one be most likely to find a desert?

    (A) in the rain forests of South America

    (B) in Antarctica

    (C) in a freshwater biome

    (D) in the northeastern United States

148. Which of these is a characteristic of a savanna?

    (A) lack of rainfall

    (B) many trees

    (C) grazing animals

    (D) average carrying capacity

Go on to next page

The Bible is about relationships. It explores the relationships between humans and nature and humans and other humans. Even though the Bible portrays other important relationships, these relationships are secondary to and contingent upon its primary focus: the relationship between God and humans. The story portrayed by the Bible is the story of God's unending desire to have an intimate relationship with the human beings He created. Throughout the Old and New Testaments, this message repeats itself: A good and merciful God reaches out to His rebellious creations in order to reconcile them to Himself.

The books of Genesis and Exodus embody all the pertinent information for understanding and interpreting the redemption message that permeates the entire Bible and <u>culminates</u> in the last book of Revelation. All the elements of the story are set up in these first two books. Genesis provides the background for God's desire to relate to human beings and the human choice to reject God's provision. Genesis further describes the measures God takes to set in motion His plan for the restoration of the God/human relationship. Exodus, by relating the story of Israel's physical redemption from bondage in Egypt through Moses, foretells God's plan for humans' spiritual redemption through the Messiah that is revealed in the New Testament.

149. This passage answers which of these questions?

(A) How many books are contained in the Bible?

(B) What is the Bible's primary focus?

(C) What exactly happens in the book of Revelation?

(D) How was Israel released from its bondage to Egypt?

150. As it is used in the passage, <u>culminates</u> most nearly means

(A) concludes

(B) commences

(C) disappears

(D) crumbles

151. Which of these is *not* a relationship that the passage mentions the Bible explores?

(A) between humans and nature

(B) between humans and God

(C) between humans and other humans

(D) between humans and a moral code

152. What background does the book of Genesis provide?

(A) the human choice to accept God's provision

(B) the story of Israel's redemption from Egypt

(C) God's attempt to reject rebellious humans

(D) a demonstration of God's longing to have a relationship with human beings

Go on to next page

Vocabulary

> **Directions:** For Questions 153–174, choose the answer that is closest in meaning to the underlined word.

153. to <u>excel</u> at an activity
    - (A) end
    - (B) shine
    - (C) stay
    - (D) work

154. an early <u>dismissal</u>
    - (A) glory
    - (B) meeting
    - (C) dawn
    - (D) discharge

155. a <u>frivolous</u> excuse
    - (A) silly
    - (B) satisfactory
    - (C) common
    - (D) cruel

156. to <u>introduce</u> a topic
    - (A) initiate
    - (B) evade
    - (C) support
    - (D) conclude

157. to <u>relish</u> an opportunity
    - (A) spread
    - (B) embellish
    - (C) loathe
    - (D) enjoy

158. a lasting <u>legacy</u>
    - (A) disadvantage
    - (B) inheritance
    - (C) flaw
    - (D) dominance

159. <u>insolent</u> behavior
    - (A) reverential
    - (B) excused
    - (C) rude
    - (D) caring

160. to seek <u>nirvana</u>
    - (A) paradise
    - (B) torment
    - (C) completion
    - (D) success

161. <u>unparalleled</u> genius
    - (A) accidental
    - (B) extraordinary
    - (C) scientific
    - (D) geometric

162. a <u>subtle</u> hint
    - (A) clear
    - (B) disapproving
    - (C) understated
    - (D) positive

163. unyielding <u>oppression</u>
    - (A) kindness
    - (B) power
    - (C) domination
    - (D) benevolence

164. cruel <u>indifference</u>
    - (A) hypocrisy
    - (B) spite
    - (C) unease
    - (D) unconcern

165. a <u>pessimistic</u> outlook
    - (A) gloomy
    - (B) positive
    - (C) suspicious
    - (D) confident

Go on to next page

166. to <u>wallow</u> in self-pity
     - (A) bask
     - (B) relapse
     - (C) proceed
     - (D) shrivel

167. a lengthy <u>tenure</u>
     - (A) outing
     - (B) speech
     - (C) term
     - (D) lesson

168. an unusual <u>phenomenon</u>
     - (A) location
     - (B) occurrence
     - (C) position
     - (D) arrangement

169. a <u>consuming</u> interest
     - (A) minor
     - (B) unnoticeable
     - (C) obvious
     - (D) intense

170. to <u>hoard</u> junk
     - (A) guard
     - (B) accumulate
     - (C) market
     - (D) scrap

171. a hopeless <u>miscreant</u>
     - (A) romantic
     - (B) realist
     - (C) troublemaker
     - (D) nomad

172. a <u>palpable</u> silence
     - (A) noticeable
     - (B) vague
     - (C) uncomfortable
     - (D) unpleasant

173. a <u>totalitarian</u> government
     - (A) complete
     - (B) democratic
     - (C) classless
     - (D) despotic

174. a compulsive <u>spendthrift</u>
     - (A) squanderer
     - (B) miser
     - (C) collector
     - (D) investor

STOP DO NOT TURN THE PAGE UNTIL TOLD TO DO SO.
DO NOT RETURN TO A PREVIOUS TEST.

Section 4: Mathematics

Time: 45 minutes

Directions: Choose the best answer for Questions 175–238.

Concepts

175. What is 34.467 rounded to the nearest tenth?

    (A) 34.5

    (B) 34

    (C) 34.47

    (D) 34.4

176. Which of the following is a type of angle?

    (A) right

    (B) obtuse

    (C) acute

    (D) all of the above

177. To divide a number by 100,000, move the decimal point _____.

    (A) three places to the left

    (B) four places to the left

    (C) five places to the right

    (D) five places to the left

178. $\{1, 2, 3, 4, 5, 6\} \cap \{2, 4, 5, 6, 8, 10\}$

    (A) $\{2, 4\}$

    (B) $\{6, 8, 10\}$

    (C) $\{2, 4, 5, 6\}$

    (D) $\{1, 3, 4\}$

179. The measure of Angle *B* is

    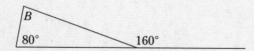

    (A) 45°

    (B) 80°

    (C) 90°

    (D) 65°

180. Simplify $5(-2)^3$

    (A) –40

    (B) 40

    (C) 20

    (D) –20

181. What is 0.55 written as a fraction?

    (A) $^{55}\!/_{1,000}$

    (B) $^1\!/_5$

    (C) $^{11}\!/_{20}$

    (D) $^{100}\!/_{55}$

182. What is the area of the circle?

    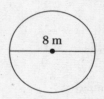

    (A) 8π m²

    (B) 12π m²

    (C) 4π m²

    (D) 16π m²

183. Which of the following best represents a pair of reciprocals?

    (A) $(3 \times 4), (4 \times 3)$

    (B) ¾, ⅘

    (C) ½, 0.5

    (D) 32, 23

Go on to next page

184. How many integers are between ⅝ and 3.5?

    (A) 1
    (B) 2
    (C) 3
    (D) 4

185. Which of the following is a perfect square?

    (A) 10
    (B) 54
    (C) 121
    (D) 135

186. What is the exact number of hundreds in 4,575?

    (A) 45.75
    (B) 475
    (C) 457.5
    (D) 0.4575

187. The ratio of two numbers is 5:7, and the sum of the two numbers is 24. What is the smaller integer?

    (A) 14
    (B) 12
    (C) 10
    (D) 5

188. What is the ratio of 36 inches to 3 yards?

    (A) 1 to 2
    (B) 1 to 3
    (C) 3 to 1
    (D) 2 to 1

189. Which of the following best represents a number written in scientific notation?

    (A) $2.45 \times 10^5 = 245$
    (B) $2.45 \times 10^4 = 245$
    (C) $0.0245 \times 10^3 = 245$
    (D) $2.45 \times 10^2 = 245$

190. A cafeteria serves milk in 8-ounce cups. How many servings of milk can be made from 4 gallons of milk?

    (A) 512
    (B) 55
    (C) 120
    (D) 64

191. What is the formula for the area of a rectangle?

    (A) A = (base)(width)(height)
    (B) A = (length)(width)
    (C) A = ½(length)(width)
    (D) A = (diameter)(π)

192. Janie sold 4 more boxes of chocolate chip cookies than sugar cookies. She sold 44 boxes of cookies. How many boxes of sugar cookies did she sell?

    (A) 20
    (B) 40
    (C) 35
    (D) 25

193. In an isosceles right triangle, what is the measurement in degrees of each of the acute angles?

    (A) 40
    (B) 35
    (C) 45
    (D) 90

194. What is the lowest common denominator of ¼ and ⅜?

    (A) 8
    (B) 4
    (C) 2
    (D) 16

195. What is the prime factorization of 8?

    (A) $2 \times 2 \times 2$
    (B) 2^5
    (C) 2×2
    (D) 4×2

Go on to next page

196. What is *not* equivalent to 25½%?

    (A) $^{51}\!/_{200}$

    (B) 25.5

    (C) 0.255

    (D) $^{25.5}\!/_{100}$

197. Triangles *ABC* and *XYZ* are similar. What is the length of *BC*?

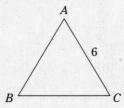

    (A) 4 units

    (B) 6 units

    (C) 8 units

    (D) 10 units

198. Which of the following is correct?

    (A) $a(b + c) = ab + ac$

    (B) $a + bc = abc$

    (C) $\dfrac{a+b+b}{c} = a(b+c)$

    (D) $3a + 3b + 3c = 3(abc)$

Problem Solving

199. $-3 + 2 + (-5) + (-7) =$

    (A) -18

    (B) 10

    (C) 13

    (D) -13

200. A building has a shadow that is 14 feet long. What is the height of the building if a 3-foot-tall child standing next to the building has a shadow of 2 feet?

    (A) 14 feet

    (B) 21 feet

    (C) 23 feet

    (D) 25 feet

201. A family went to the circus and bought 5 bags of peanuts for $3.75 each and 4 bags of cotton candy for $2.25 each. How much money did the family spend?

    (A) $27.75

    (B) $26.50

    (C) $24.25

    (D) $21.50

202. What is the difference between 3⅜ and 2¾?

    (A) 3⅔

    (B) 4½

    (C) 2¾

    (D) $^{11}\!/_{12}$

203. Solve for *x*: $2x + 7 = x + 12$

    (A) 2

    (B) 3

    (C) 4

    (D) 5

204. If the 6% tax on a used car totaled $600, what was the price of the used car without tax?

    (A) $10,000

    (B) $11,000

    (C) $12,000

    (D) $13,000

205. A bus traveled 1,525 miles last week. Approximately how many miles did it travel, on average, for each of those 7 days?

    (A) 173 miles

    (B) 200 miles

    (C) 218 miles

    (D) 242 miles

206. If $3a + 2 > 14$, then a^2 must be

    (A) equal to 9

    (B) greater than 16

    (C) less than 16

    (D) less than 9

Go on to next page

207. Alicia has $15 less than 3 times the amount her coworker has. If her coworker has $40, how many dollars does Alicia have?

    (A) $100

    (B) $103

    (C) $105

    (D) $108

208. A sales woman earns 6% commission on every set of tools she sells. If she sells 5 sets of tools at $60 each, what is her commission?

    (A) $18

    (B) $19

    (C) $20

    (D) $21

209. A high-end candy store charges $2 per ounce of candy. What is the cost of 1 pound, 8 ounces of candy?

    (A) $40

    (B) $44

    (C) $48

    (D) $50

210. If $x + 6 = y + 11$, then

    (A) $x = y$

    (B) $x < y$

    (C) $x > y$

    (D) $x = 5$

211. If the sum of two numbers is x and one of the numbers is 6, then four times the other number is what?

    (A) $4(x + 6)$

    (B) $4(x - 6)$

    (C) $4x + 6$

    (D) $4x(6)$

212. Solve: $1\frac{2}{3} + \frac{1}{2} + 3\frac{2}{6}$

    (A) $3\frac{1}{2}$

    (B) $\frac{3}{4}$

    (C) $\frac{1}{2}$

    (D) $5\frac{1}{2}$

213. Find the value of $2x^2 + 3y - 1$ if $x = \frac{1}{2}$ and $y = 3$.

    (A) $4\frac{1}{2}$

    (B) $8\frac{3}{4}$

    (C) $8\frac{1}{2}$

    (D) $5\frac{1}{2}$

214. If N% of 70 is 14, then $N =$

    (A) 5

    (B) 10

    (C) 15

    (D) 20

215. If Miguel paid $525 interest on a loan that had a 5% simple interest rate, how much did he borrow?

    (A) $10,500

    (B) $11,000

    (C) $11,500

    (D) $12,000

216. $0.453 + 6.7 + 0.45 =$

    (A) 6.603

    (B) 7.603

    (C) 8.543

    (D) 9.003

217. If $4x - 10 > 2$, then

    (A) $x^3 < 27$

    (B) $x^3 > 27$

    (C) $x^3 > 9$

    (D) $x^3 < 9$

218. $153.5 \times 0.041 =$

    (A) 2.245

    (B) 3.355

    (C) 5.4006

    (D) 6.2935

219. What is the volume of a cube solid with sides of 6 m?

    (A) 36 m^3

    (B) 54 m^3

    (C) 216 m^3

    (D) 300 m^3

Go on to next page

220. The tax rate at a certain car dealership is $2.76 per $100. How much are the taxes on a car valued at $40,000?

(A) $1,000

(B) $1,104

(C) $1,500

(D) $1,504

221. Danielle puts 6% of her salary into a savings account every month. If she earns $48,000 a year, how much does she put into the account each month?

(A) $240

(B) $360

(C) $1800

(D) $2,880

222. What is 638×18?

(A) 9,754

(B) 10,684

(C) 11,484

(D) 12,688

223. The product of 5 and 6 is 10 more than x. Solve for x.

(A) 35

(B) 30

(C) 25

(D) 20

224. $\sqrt{y-4}$ is equal to 3. What is y?

(A) 11

(B) 12

(C) 13

(D) 14

225. What is the ratio of $\frac{1}{2}$ and $\frac{6}{8}$?

(A) $\frac{1}{2}$

(B) $\frac{2}{3}$

(C) $\frac{1}{4}$

(D) $\frac{3}{4}$

226. What should be the next number in this sequence: 15, 15.02, 15.04, 15.06, . . . ?

(A) 15.80

(B) 15.10

(C) 16

(D) 15.08

227. What is the total area of this figure made up of a square and two isosceles triangles?

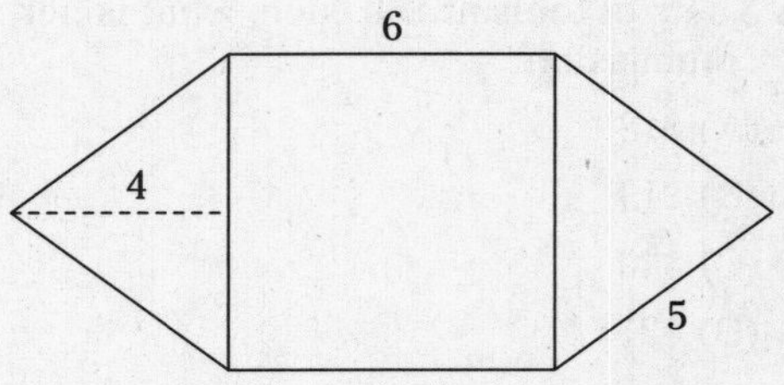

(A) 12

(B) 36

(C) 48

(D) 60

228. A 13-foot ladder is leaning against a wall, and the base of the ladder is 5 feet away from the building. How high up does the ladder reach?

(A) 12 feet

(B) 10 feet

(C) 8 feet

(D) 4 feet

229. What is the area of a rectangle with a width of 6 in and a length of 14 in?

(A) 24 in^2

(B) 36 in^2

(C) 64 in^2

(D) 84 in^2

230. $(\frac{1}{3} + \frac{3}{4}) - (\frac{2}{6} + \frac{9}{12}) = x$; solve for x.

(A) $\frac{2}{3}$

(B) $\frac{1}{6}$

(C) $\frac{3}{4}$

(D) 0

Go on to next page

231. Solve for x: $0.6x + 4.9 = 10.3$

    (A) 7

    (B) 8

    (C) 9

    (D) 10

232. During a road trip, Tyler drove 80 miles in one day, which was 20% of his planned mileage for that day. How many more miles did Tyler plan to drive that day?

    (A) 180

    (B) 320

    (C) 400

    (D) 450

233. Which of these is a multiple of 50?

    (A) 154

    (B) 250

    (C) 336

    (D) 402

234. The ratio of two acute angles of a right triangle is 5:1. What is the measure of the larger angle?

    (A) 15°

    (B) 30°

    (C) 65°

    (D) 75°

235. If $P\%$ of 80 is 4, then $P\% =$

    (A) 5

    (B) 10

    (C) 15

    (D) 20

236. $0.897 + 0.0092 + 5.7 =$

    (A) 6.4044

    (B) 6.6062

    (C) 7

    (D) 7.6062

237. Solve for x: $4x + 5 = 49$

    (A) 9

    (B) 10

    (C) 11

    (D) 12

238. $\frac{4}{5} \div \frac{5}{6} =$

    (A) $\frac{24}{25}$

    (B) $\frac{24}{36}$

    (C) $\frac{1}{3}$

    (D) $\frac{4}{5}$

STOP DO NOT TURN THE PAGE UNTIL TOLD TO DO SO.
DO NOT RETURN TO A PREVIOUS TEST.

Section 5: Language

Time: 25 minutes

Directions: For Questions 239–278, choose the answer with the sentence that has an error in punctuation, capitalization, or usage. If no sentence contains an error, choose Answer D.

239. (A) I set my alarm clock.
   (B) The morning arrived too quickly.
   (C) Josie stays in the top bunk when I got up.
   (D) No mistakes

240. (A) The truck weighed two tons.
   (B) My mom bought a new hamster for my brother and I.
   (C) Mary had a rather tiny lamb.
   (D) No mistakes

241. (A) The SUV progressed along the highway.
   (B) Professor Smith teaches history and economics.
   (C) Use black ink when signing contracts.
   (D) No mistakes

242. (A) The spaghetti sauce that Dad made was tasty.
   (B) The mayor's plan had no affect on the budget.
   (C) Do you know the answer to Josh's question?
   (D) No mistakes

243. (A) I paid 30 dollars for a paltry amount of gas.
   (B) Sue was charged with exceeding the speed limit.
   (C) The grocery store closes at 11:00 p.m. every night accept Sunday.
   (D) No mistakes

244. (A) Lynn excels at taking tests.
   (B) We live in a democratic society.
   (C) There were to many dogs in the animal shelter.
   (D) No mistakes

245. (A) Zoe won trophies in tennis track and wrestling.
   (B) Mary ran the mile in record time.
   (C) Pizza is Timothy's favorite food.
   (D) No mistakes

246. (A) Monkey's are fun to watch.
   (B) Barry was happy to receive the top score on his biology test.
   (C) Alison is an auto mechanic.
   (D) No mistakes

247. (A) Lee chews bubble gum all day long.
   (B) We are getting too old to run the marathon.
   (C) May we eat out tonight!
   (D) No mistakes

248. (A) The boat made its way across the river.
   (B) Roses are red; violets are blue.
   (C) The unemployment rate has reached a new high.
   (D) No mistakes

249. (A) My parents are moving into my house.
   (B) The soybean harvest was the best in over 11 years.
   (C) Todd and Natalie invited Heidi, Mark, and us for dinner.
   (D) No mistakes

Go on to next page

250. (A) The number of job seekers have increased over the past two months.
    (B) The game was postponed on account of rain.
    (C) Mary works 40 hours a week at the hardware store.
    (D) No mistakes

251. (A) The slump in travel has hurt hotel chains.
    (B) Paul has a variety of stocks in his retirement fund.
    (C) Jane won the Greater Denver area Spelling Bee.
    (D) No mistakes

252. (A) Joseph is an interior decorator with years of experience.
    (B) Stephanie is a lovely talented young lady.
    (C) Kevin broke his leg when he fell off the ladder.
    (D) No mistakes

253. (A) Zelda is allergic to ragweed and pollen.
    (B) Dan's pet cats have had there claws removed.
    (C) She was a cheerleader during her junior year of high school.
    (D) No mistakes

254. (A) Marco played in the intermediate checker tournament.
    (B) The ducks flew south for the winter.
    (C) Doris's chocolate chip cookie recipe one first place.
    (D) No mistakes

255. (A) Mother told us to mind our manners at grandma's house.
    (B) The city was under siege for months.
    (C) Brazil will host the upcoming Olympics.
    (D) No mistakes

256. (A) A clean environment is Vice President Morrison's top priority.
    (B) The brontosaur was my favorite dinosaur.
    (C) My Uncle owns a chicken farm.
    (D) No mistakes

257. (A) Atoms are components of all elements.
    (B) Onomatopoeia is a literary device used by many authors.
    (C) Jason's aunt lives like a hermit.
    (D) No mistakes

258. (A) Christina prefers to attend services on Saturday nights.
    (B) The quality of education in Newton City has increased over the last 20 years.
    (C) The governors office is not immune to charges of bribery.
    (D) No mistakes

259. (A) The Air Force's obstinate refusal to release its UFO records is proof that extra-terrestrials exist.
    (B) Elizabeth could of taken electives instead of courses in her major.
    (C) The newly elected president won the Nobel Peace Prize.
    (D) No mistakes

260. (A) Naomi takes notes in her chemistry class yesterday.
    (B) As they entered the anteroom, Cleo was quiet and reserved.
    (C) The airplane ride over the Rocky Mountains was turbulent.
    (D) No mistakes

261. (A) Zachary packed as if he were hiking up Mount Everest.
    (B) The Greek ruins in Athens, consisting of the Acropolis and other buildings, are very old.
    (C) Becca is a talented lacrosse player.
    (D) No mistakes

Go on to next page

262. (A) The reasons that I like Cleveland are: it has the Rock and Roll Hall of Fame, it's by the water, and it has a great basketball team.

    (B) The sofa is on sale at the nearby furniture store.

    (C) Jamie is known to drink cola instead of coffee for breakfast.

    (D) No mistakes

263. (A) Dora excelled at dance and received a scholarship to St. John's University.

    (B) Because it's snowing outside.

    (C) The flu is causing significant attrition at the local grade school.

    (D) No mistakes

264. (A) Leon learned to bake cookies from his mother.

    (B) Math hasn't always been easy for Chris.

    (C) The sauna was too hot for Mike.

    (D) No mistakes

265. (A) NASA was encouraged with the results of the rocket launch.

    (B) The soccer mom in the stands cheered for her daughter's team.

    (C) The U.S. Open was held at my grandfather's country club.

    (D) No mistakes

266. (A) Sustaining injuries from automobile accidents have decreased since wearing seat belts became mandatory.

    (B) Marvin plays fantasy football with his friends from high school.

    (C) Marianne was a successful class president.

    (D) No mistakes

267. (A) The new vaccine provided hope for people in developing countries.

    (B) The editorial in yesterday's newspaper had a conservative tone.

    (C) The priest's sermon last sunday enlightened the congregation.

    (D) No mistakes

268. (A) Mother Teresa may become a saint.

    (B) Ali refused to visit the local zoo because she didn't like to see caged animals.

    (C) The federal tax credit will enable Mark and Mindy to purchase they're first home.

    (D) No mistakes

269. (A) The church experienced a schism after the pastor resigned.

    (B) The United Nations successfully maintained peace in the Middle East.

    (C) Charlotte was the chair of her womens' club.

    (D) No mistakes

270. (A) Anne stated that her reign as Miss America made her very popular.

    (B) The orchestra was adept at playing chamber music.

    (C) Larry flew around the world in his new jet.

    (D) No mistakes

271. (A) Pete practiced needlepoint to relax before tests.

    (B) The dissidents' marched on the government as a show of support for the ousted leader.

    (C) We made a point of extending a helping hand to those in need.

    (D) No mistakes

272. (A) We must rehabilitate those whom we incarcerate.

    (B) Our class is studying the works of Jane Austen.

    (C) Her and I ride the bus to school every morning.

    (D) No mistakes

273. (A) The football game went into overtime.

    (B) Beauty isn't in the eye of the beholder.

    (C) Its' so cold outside that I had to wear a scarf to keep warm.

    (D) No mistakes

Go on to next page

274. (A) Many libertarians are opposed to further tax increases.

(B) The president discussed the advantages and disadvantages of public health insurance.

(C) Because the airline lost our luggage, it reimbursed my mother and me.

(D) No mistakes

275. (A) The novels of Charles Dickens' are often quite depressing.

(B) The birds fly north for the summer.

(C) The jets broke the speed of sound as they raced overhead.

(D) No mistakes

276. (A) The volleyball team's mascot is a badger.

(B) The colors of the flag are: red, white, and blue.

(C) The New York Yankees are perennial playoff contenders.

(D) No mistakes

277. (A) The intense drought has caused the decline of aspen groves.

(B) The automobile industry is finally beginning to manufacture electric cars.

(C) Each of the guests have visited the home several times.

(D) No mistakes

278. (A) My brother has played the guitar for two years, and now he is in a band.

(B) The bats flying in the dark caves.

(C) Out of habit, I eat seafood for dinner every Friday.

(D) No mistakes

Directions: For Questions 279–288, choose the answer that has the spelling error. If no sentence contains an error, choose Answer D.

279. (A) John asked many questions of his physician.

(B) Brenda biked over several mountain passes.

(C) I did not know that the gym was seperate from the main building.

(D) No mistakes

280. (A) Sara was pleased that her Wednesday schedule did not begin until 9:00.

(B) Lindsay celebrated her tennis victory at her favorite restaurant.

(C) The sailors were anxious to dock.

(D) No mistakes

281. (A) Jenny could not see why the extra math section was relevent.

(B) We have seen an abundance of horseflies in the barn this summer.

(C) Martin found it to be beneficial to study for a half hour every morning.

(D) No mistakes

282. (A) Mike did me the cortesy of calling before he came over.

(B) We decided to meet our parents at the barbecue after work.

(C) Never underestimate the power of a great smile.

(D) No mistakes

283. (A) The market reopened on the second weekend of May.

(B) Shoppers chatted about the return of warm temparatures.

(C) Sam could not wait to use the new picnic basket he received for his birthday.

(D) No mistakes

Go on to next page

284. (A) The prosecutor questioned the defendant.

(B) Raye's birthday is on the last weekend in February.

(C) Todd made a concious effort to complete the marathon.

(D) No mistakes

285. (A) We learned how to engage in proper hygiene in health class.

(B) Brian was the dominant player on the offense.

(C) Tracey tends to exaggerate about her accomplishments.

(D) No mistakes

286. (A) Chrissy's favorite class is psychology.

(B) Jim's actions may be unorthodox, but they are not sacreligious.

(C) We made sure that we bought souvenirs in every town we visited.

(D) No mistakes

287. (A) Which of these doctors would you recommend?

(B) Overseas travel is very effective against prejudice.

(C) I wish we had more tests and fewer quizzes.

(D) No mistakes

288. (A) There is no penalty for incorrect answers.

(B) What do you perceive to be the problem?

(C) Errors are more prevelent in work that is performed when one is tired.

(D) No mistakes

Directions: Follow the directions for Questions 289–298.

289. Choose the group of words that best completes the sentence.

    Before sitting down to write, _____.

(A) clearing and outlining his mind and head were the actions of the author

(B) clearing his mind and outlining his thoughts in his head were what the author did

(C) the author cleared his mind and outlined his thoughts in his head

(D) the author was clearing his mind and outlined in his head thoughts

290. Choose the word that provides a clear transition between the two thoughts in the sentence.

    The number of representatives from each state is based on population, _____ each state has at least one representative.

(A) because

(B) but

(C) or

(D) none of these

291. Which of these sentences expresses the idea best?

(A) Making friends at school is much more rewarding than to be antisocial.

(B) To make friends at school is much more rewarding than being antisocial.

(C) Making friends at school is more better than being antisocial.

(D) Making friends at school is much more rewarding than being antisocial.

292. Which answer provides the clearest sentence construction?

(A) The inspector solved the case within two weeks.

(B) The case, within two weeks, was solved by the inspector.

(C) Within two weeks, the case was solved by the inspector.

(D) The case, two weeks later, the inspector did solve.

Go on to next page

293. Which of these pairs of sentences fits best after this topic sentence?

> Scientists believe that a black hole is created when a supernova from a large star collapses on itself.

(A) Astronomy is a fascinating science. You can discover all sorts of interesting things by studying it.

(B) This collapse causes a gravitational field that grows more and more intense until nothing can escape from its pull, not even light. It's thought that the universe may end as a black hole.

(C) The sun is a star. The planets orbit around the sun.

(D) I was hoping to buy a telescope to view outer space. Maybe then I can see a supernova collapsing.

294. Choose the group of words that best completes the sentence.

> After hearing the verdict, _____.

(A) shouting was heard throughout the courtroom

(B) shouting is what the people in the courtroom did

(C) the courtroom spectators began shouting

(D) began the people in the courtroom to shout

295. Which of these sentences expresses the thought most clearly?

(A) Although Amanda hadn't finished her homework, she decided to go shopping with her friends.

(B) She decided to shopping with her friends even though Amanda hadn't finished her homework.

(C) Shopping with her friends is what Amanda decided to do even though she hadn't just yet finished her homework.

(D) After she hadn't finished her homework, Amanda went shopping with her friends as she had decided.

296. Which sentence does *not* belong in this paragraph?

> [1]Military customs and courtesies are proven traditions that explain what should and shouldn't be done in many situations. [2]They are acts of respect and courtesy when dealing with other people and have evolved as a result of the need for order, mutual respect, and a sense of fraternity that exists among military personnel. [3]The Air Force and the Navy are part of the military, too. [4]Customs and courtesies ensure proper respect for the chain of command and build the foundation for self-discipline.

(A) Sentence 1

(B) Sentence 2

(C) Sentence 3

(D) Sentence 4

297. Which of these sentences fits best under the topic of "The History of the Panama Canal"?

(A) Panama is a country in Central America.

(B) Ships transport cargo around the world.

(C) The Panama Canal is a ship canal that cuts through the Isthmus of Panama and connects the Atlantic and Pacific.

(D) Although several foreign companies tried to build the Panama Canal throughout the 19th century, none was successful.

298. Which of these sentences expresses the thought most clearly?

(A) The sound from outside being an alarming one, he scrambled out of bed and groped his way to the window.

(B) From outside came an alarming sound; therefore, out of bed he scrambled and to the window he groped his way.

(C) When he heard an alarming sound from outside, he scrambled out of bed and groped his way to the window.

(D) On his way to the window, he groped after he scrambled out of bed because he heard an alarming sound from outside.

STOP DO NOT TURN THE PAGE UNTIL TOLD TO DO SO. DO NOT RETURN TO A PREVIOUS TEST.

Chapter 20

Answers to HSPT Practice Test 2

The answer explanations in this chapter are full of tips and shortcuts that show you how to tackle HSPT questions more efficiently. We strongly encourage you to read all of them. Of course, if you're tight on time, you can always skip to the end of this chapter to check your answers using the abbreviated answer key.

Section 1: Verbal Skills

1. **C.** Cake, pie, and cookies are desserts. You can wash them down with milk, Choice (C), but milk isn't a dessert.

2. **D.** This analogy involves degrees. A boat that has extra amenities for a complete vacation is a cruise ship. A hotel that has extra amenities for a complete vacation is a resort. A hotel isn't luggage, a vacation, or a passport. Choice (D) is best.

3. **D.** Smug, superior, and conceited describe someone who's egotistical. Humble, Choice (D), is the opposite of egotistical, which means it doesn't belong.

4. **B.** Create a line diagram to help you visualize this logic question. Based on the information in the first two statements, the diagram that shows the order of life spans from longest to shortest looks like this: cats → dogs → turtles. The third statement, that turtles live longer than cats, is false, Choice (B).

   Never answer a logic question based on information you know. Your answer should be based solely on what you can logically conclude from the premises.

5. **B.** *Apparent* means "obvious" and so does Choice (B), clear. Choices (A) and (C) are opposites, and Choice (D) is unrelated.

6. **B.** Events that are creepy, disturbing, and eerie may make you really uneasy. Something incorrect, Choice (B), probably doesn't have that same effect on you, which means it's the word that doesn't belong.

7. **A.** The prefix *sub-* means "under or beneath." Therefore, *subordinate* means "lesser or lower." The best synonym is Choice (A), inferior.

8. **C.** Travel is a reason for going to the airport, and shopping is a reason for going to the store, Choice (C). If you're tempted to pick Choice (A), sale, keep in mind that an airport and a store are both places. A sale isn't a place.

9. **B.** Selfishness, Choice (B), doesn't fit with the other words. Intelligence, wisdom, and insight relate to having knowledge. Selfishness is all about you.

10. **C.** Something that's written in the margins probably isn't very important. *Marginal* means "trivial or insignificant" and so does minor, Choice (C).

11. **A.** This one's pretty easy. The job of an ambassador is to represent. The job of a physician is to heal, Choice (A).

12. **A.** *Altruism*, *selflessness*, and *philanthropy* are synonyms for self-sacrifice. Thoughtlessness, Choice (A), is the opposite and doesn't belong.

13. **C.** Create a line diagram from largest collection to smallest. There are two possibilities: Angela → Cathy → Barbara or Cathy → Angela → Barbara. You don't know whether Angela's collection is larger than Cathy's, which makes the third statement uncertain, Choice (C).

Just because a set of premises gives you more than one possible line diagram doesn't mean the third statement is automatically uncertain. You must analyze the information you're presented with; don't jump to conclusions.

14. **C.** *Bigotry* means "intolerance;" Choice (A) is obviously wrong. Justice and effort don't mean intolerance, which means the best answer has to be Choice (C), bias.

15. **D.** *Flamboyant* means "really, really noticeable," which makes showy, Choice (D), a good synonym. Choices (A) and (C) are opposites, and flamboyant doesn't describe whether something's attractive or not, making Choice (B) incorrect.

16. **D.** If you opted for Choices (B) or (C), you were thinking of the word *forgive* rather than *forbid*. To *forbid* is to prevent or ban something from happening, Choice (D).

17. **A.** Here's another degree analogy. Scalding is superhot, just like *diminutive* is supersmall, Choice (A). You can eliminate Choices (B) and (D) because they mean the same thing and can't both be right.

18. **B.** To throw a football is to pass, and to throw a baseball is to pitch. The best answer is Choice (B); the other answers don't relate to throwing.

19. **B.** An *adversary* is one who opposes you. An *ally*, one who sticks with you, is the opposite. Another word for someone who's against you is *foe*, Choice (B).

20. **B.** To back, support, and approve are verbs that mean to help or encourage. Lock, Choice (B) isn't an opposite, but it means something different and doesn't belong.

21. **A.** Used as verbs, cause, trigger, and produce mean to make something happen. Choice (A) is unrelated to creating action, which means it doesn't belong.

22. **C.** Line up the students from great grades to good. You have two options: Phillip → Carrie → Patrick or Carrie → Phillip → Patrick. Whether Carrie gets better grades than Phillip depends on which diagram you look at. Consequently, the truth of the third statement is uncertain, Choice (C).

23. **A.** If Ruth is the tallest girl in music class, then no other girl in music class is taller than she. So, Maggie can't be in music class with Ruth; if she were, Ruth wouldn't be the tallest girl in music class. The third statement is true, Choice (A).

24. **C.** This question asks you for the opposite meaning. Be sure to choose the word that's an antonym. The opposite of telling the truth is to hide the truth. The word that means the act of hiding the truth is Choice (C), deception.

25. **D.** The first three words have something to do with being separated or alone. Choice (D) means being next to, which isn't the same as being away from something.

26. **D.** Someone who's liberal gives freely and without restraint. Choices (A) and (B) are more similar in meaning than different, which means you can cut them. The opposite of giving freely is Choice (D), *stingy*, which is a good way to describe Scrooge.

27. **C.** Draw a Venn diagram of the first two statements in this logic question.

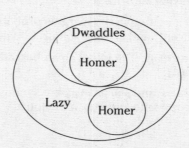

The diagram shows two possible places for Homer's circle. You know that Homer is lazy, but you don't know whether he's lazy just because he's lazy or whether he's lazy because he's a dwaddle. The premises don't give you enough information to say whether Homer is a dwaddle or not, so the third statement is uncertain, Choice (C).

28. **B.** Choices (C) and (D) don't seem to relate to boss; go ahead and eliminate them. If your boss is glowering, you may want to get out of the way because a glowering boss is an angry boss, Choice (B).

29. **A.** To *restore* is to make something like new again. Choices (B), (C), and (D) have similar meanings, but you need the answer that's opposite. *Rupture*, Choice (A), means "to come apart."

30. **D.** A pauper is poor, and a tycoon is rich. Choice (D) is the most opposite.

31. **A.** The goal of a comic, joker, and jester is to make people laugh. A dancer, Choice (A), isn't concerned with making jokes and doesn't belong with the other choices.

32. **C.** Not sure why the answer choices have nothing to do with fancy? That's because you're thinking of the word *fancy* as an adjective. Because all the answer choices are verbs, the question is actually about the verb form of *fancy*. To *fancy* something is to want it or like it. The answer that's opposite is Choice (C).

33. **C.** The scent emitted by garbage is a *stench* (a really bad smell). The scent emitted by cologne is a *fragrance* (a really good smell). Choice (C) is better than Choice (A) because it shows what *type* of smell is emitted, just like stench does.

34. **D.** The verb form of bloom means to blossom or grow. The opposite is to wither or fade, Choice (D). Choice (A) is a synonym, which means it can't be right.

35. **C.** Squander doesn't fit with the other answer choices because they mean to inflict injury or harm. Although squandering something may be harmful, it isn't the act of causing harm.

36. **A.** Draw a line diagram of the first premise: White River → Brown River → Cool River. The second premise adds Deep River before White River and Slimy River before Deep River like this: Slimy River → Deep River → White River → Brown River → Cool River. From that, you know that Slimy River is the widest. The third statement is therefore true, Choice (A).

37. **B.** *Corrupt* means "dishonest or shady;" you can eliminate Choice (D). The word that's most opposite is Choice (B), *decent*, which means "moral and honest."

38. **D.** The first three words are different ways to describe a fight. Expansion doesn't relate to fighting, which means Choice (D) doesn't belong.

39. **C.** A *vital* decision is an important one. Another word for important is essential, Choice (C). Vital doesn't have to do with time, so Choices (A) and (B) are incorrect.

40. **B.** Stout, plump, and portly are different ways of describing being heavy. Obnoxious, Choice (B), has nothing to do with weight, which means it doesn't belong.

41. **A.** Biology is a type of science, and sculpture is a type of art. Sculpture isn't a type of clay, fashion, or sculptor. Choice (A) is the best answer.

42. **D.** A monastery is where a monk lives, and a den is where a fox lives. Choice (D) is the only answer that fits the analogy.

43. **C.** Here's another chance to draw a Venn diagram.

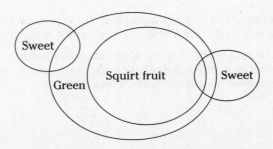

The diagram shows that you know all squirt fruit are green, but that you don't know whether all green fruit are squirt fruit. The two options for tasting sweet show that it could include squirt fruit, but it could also not, which means the last statement is uncertain, Choice (C).

44. **C.** Fedora, bonnet, and cap are names for types of hats. A wrap, Choice (C), is a large scarf or cape, which means it isn't specifically meant for covering the head the way the other answers are.

45. **A.** A *noxious* fume can kill you; it's toxic, Choice (A). Some noxious fumes (such as carbon monoxide) can be odorless, but noxious doesn't mean odorless.

46. **D.** *Spirited* means "full of life, or lively," Choice (D). Ghostly means like a ghost, which is more opposite in meaning than similar.

47. **B.** Psychology is the science that studies the mind. Zoology is the science that studies animals, Choice (B). Don't go for zoos just because that's part of the word *zoology*.

48. **B.** To *capitulate* is to surrender, which means Choice (A) isn't opposite and you can eliminate it. The opposite of to surrender is to resist giving in; Choice (B) is best.

49. **A.** Three words that mean important or primary are key, foremost, and main. Slight, Choice (A), is the opposite; it means unimportant or minor.

50. **B.** Obliging, cooperative, and accommodating show a willingness to get along. Not being practical is unrelated to getting along; impractical, Choice (B), doesn't belong.

51. **C.** Something that has been *fashioned* has been created or styled, which means you have to cross out Choice (D). The opposite of created is destroyed, Choice (C).

52. **C.** To be *wretched* is to be miserable, Choice (C). Choice (D), exultant, is the opposite.

53. **C.** List the birthdays in order of first to last based on the first premise: Randy → Jocelyn → Chloe. The second premise gives you several options: Randy → Jocelyn → Frank → Chloe, Randy → Frank → Jocelyn → Chloe, or Frank → Randy → Jocelyn → Chloe. Clearly it's uncertain whether Frank's birthday comes before or after Jocelyn's — Choice (C).

54. **D.** If things look bleak, the outlook is pretty much hopeless. Eliminate Choice (A) because it's a synonym. The opposite of hopeless is promising, Choice (D).

55. **B.** Although *nuance* sounds sort of like newness, it doesn't mean newness. It means "hint or slight degree of difference." The best answer is fine distinction, Choice (B).

56. **A.** It may be obvious to you without a diagram that Chippy has blond hair because he's a swirl. In case it isn't, here's a Venn diagram that shows you the relationship.

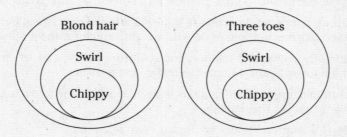

Because all swirls fit into the blond hair circle and Chippy belongs in the swirl circle, you must conclude that Chippy does indeed have a blond head of hair, Choice (A).

57. **D.** An aristocrat enjoys high social standing. A wealthy aristocrat has high social standing and lots of money and is, therefore, quite privileged, Choice (D). Wealthy aristocracy doesn't guarantee youth or charm, however.

58. **C.** Starter, hors d'oeuvre, and appetizer are names for foods that you eat before the main meal. Dessert, Choice (C), comes at the end of the meal, so it doesn't belong.

59. **A.** Chess is a type of game, and Cajun is a type of cooking. It's not a type of Louisiana, bayou, or catfish; Choice (A) is the best answer.

60. **B.** Draw a line diagram of the list of cities from north to south. The first premise gives you this: Lochtown → Morristown. Add Noonville and Otisburg in relation to Lochtown: Otisburg → Noonville → Lochtown → Morristown. Morristown is south of Otisburg, which means the third statement is false, Choice (B).

Section 2: Quantitative Skills

61. **D.** Create a mathematical equation from the words in the problem. Let x mean "what number," let *is* mean =, let *more than* mean +, and let *of* mean multiply. Then solve for x: $x = 3 + (0.8 \times 20)$; $x = 3 + 16$; $x = 19$. The answer is Choice (D).

62. **B.** Going from 4 to 8 requires an operation of either +4 or ×2. Because the next number is 12, the operation must be +4. The next number is $12 + 4 = 16$, Choice (B).

63. **C.** Write down the value of (a), (b), and (c). Three dimes and three nickels is $3(10) + 3(5)$, which means (a) is 45, (b) is 50, and (c) is 45. Go ahead and write down the relationships, too: (b) > (a) = (c). (b) is greater than (a), which means you can eliminate Choices (A), (B), and (D). Choice (C) correctly describes the relationship among the values.

64. **C.** $3x = \frac{1}{2} \times 12$. Solve for x: $3x = 6$; $x = 2$. The answer is Choice (C).

65. **B.** The numbers in this sequence increase by 5. $55 + 5 = 60$, which is Choice (B).

66. **A.** If BE bisects the rectangle, the resulting quadrilaterals are exactly the same. So, $AB = EF$ and $EF = ED$, meaning $AB = ED$, Choice (A). You can't assume the quadrilaterals are square because you don't know the original line lengths. So, you don't know whether Choice (C) is true. The other choices must be false.

67. **A.** Create an equation and solve: $x + 42 = 8 \times 6$; $x + 42 = 48$; $x = 6$, Choice (A).

68. **A.** $x = 4^2 - (3 \times 4)$. Do the operation in parentheses first: $x = 4^2 - 12$. Then tackle the exponent: $x = 16 - 12$. So $x = 4$, Choice (A).

69. **D.** As you read through the sequence, say the operations to yourself: −3, +5, −3, +5. The next number is 3 less than 37, or 34, which means the answer is either Choice (B) or (D). Moving forward in the pattern, you find that $34 + 5$ is 39, which is the second number in Choice (D).

70. **C.** The missing number is probably a Roman numeral because the sequence appears to alternate Roman numerals. The answer is therefore either Choice (B) or Choice (C). The operation is +3, and $23 + 3$ is 26. Choice (C) is the Roman numeral for 26.

71. **B.** An *average* is the sum of the set of numbers divided by the amount of numbers in the set. The equation looks like this: $x = 3[(20 + 5 + 25 + 10 + 10) \div 5)]$. Follow the order of operations: $x = 3(70 \div 5)$; $x = 3 \times 14$; $x = 42$, Choice (B).

72. **C.** The three figures are pentagons with equal side lengths, which means the larger shaded triangles in (b) and (a) are equal, and the shaded areas of (b) and (c) are equal. The shaded area in (a) is greater than the shaded area of (b) or (c). So, (a) > (b) = (c). The only answer that presents the correct relationship is Choice (C).

73. **C.** Put the question into equation format: $\frac{5}{8} \times x = 5 + (4 \times 5)$. Then solve for x: $\frac{5}{8} \times x = 5 + 20$. $\frac{5}{8} \times x = 25$; $x = 25 \times \frac{8}{5}$. You can factor 5 from 25 and 5 to simplify the multiplication: $x = 5 \times 8$; $x = 40$. The answer is Choice (C).

74. **D.** (a) and (b) aren't the same. 25% of 80% is less than 25% of 80. Therefore, Choices (A), (B), and (C) must be wrong, and the answer has to be Choice (D). You don't have to consider the value of (c) to answer this one, but if you did, you'd find that (b) and (c) are equal. Both of them are 20.

75. **D.** The numbers in this sequence are multiples of 3. $\frac{1}{9} \times 3 = \frac{1}{3}$, and $\frac{1}{3} \times 3 = 1$. $1 \times 3 = 3$, which is the next number in the sequence.

76. **A.** Half of 66 is 33, $\frac{2}{5}$ of 60 is 24, and $\frac{1}{3}$ of 72 is 24. The order is (a) > (b) = (c), which is exactly what Choice (A) says.

77. **B.** This sequence is achieved by adding consecutive numbers. The next operation is +11, and 37 + 11 is 48. Only Choice (B) begins with 48.

TIP

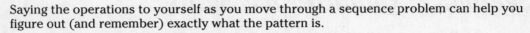

Saying the operations to yourself as you move through a sequence problem can help you figure out (and remember) exactly what the pattern is.

78. **A.** Solve for x: $x \div \frac{2}{3} = \frac{3}{4}$; $x = \frac{2}{3} \times \frac{3}{4}$; $x = \frac{6}{12}$, which is $\frac{1}{2}$, Choice (A).

79. **C.** Based on the graph, the sales by employee look like this: A > B > D > C. The answer that reflects this relationship is Choice (C). Because A's sales are more than half the graph, the sales of the other three combined are less than A's sales.

80. **A.** The operations go like this: +2, –3, +2, –3, +2, and so on. The next number is 4 – 3, which is 1. Cross out Choices (C) and (D) because they don't start with 1. Now add 2 to 1 to get the next number, 3; the answer that fits the pattern is Choice (A).

81. **D.** Make an equation and solve: $\frac{1}{2} \times x = 7 \times 8$; $\frac{1}{2} \times x = 56$; $x = 56 \times \frac{2}{1}$; $x = 112$, Choice (D).

82. **D.** Count the squares carefully. There are a total of 14, 4 of which are shaded. The fraction of the shaded area is $\frac{4}{14}$, which simplifies to $\frac{2}{7}$, Choice (D).

83. **A.** The equation is $x = 5^3 \div 5$. Dividing a cube by its cube root is like taking away one of the roots. So, $5^3 \div 5$ is the same as 5^2, or 25, Choice (A).

84. **B.** The operations in the sequence alternate –2 and ×2. 5 – 2 = 3. 3 × 2 = 6. 6 – 2 = 4. 4 × 2 = 8. 8 – 2 = 6. 6 × 2 = 12. 12 – 2 = 10. The next number is 10 × 2, which is 20 — Choice (B).

85. **D.** 70% written as a decimal is 0.7, which means (a) and (b) are equal. 70% written as a fraction is $\frac{70}{100}$, or $\frac{7}{10}$. So, (a), (b), and (c) are equal, Choice (D).

86. **D.** Solve $\frac{3}{4} \times x = 5 \times 15$: $\frac{3}{4} \times x = 75$; $x = 75 \times \frac{4}{3}$. Factor 3 from 3 and 75 to make the multiplication easier: $x = 25 \times 4$; $x = 100$, Choice (D).

87. **D.** The difference between the first two numbers is either –62 or ÷2. The next operation is –4. The next operation is ÷2. So, the pattern is probably ÷2, –4, which makes the next operation –4. 33 – 4 = 29, Choice (D).

88. **C.** Change (b) to a base and exponent: 4 × 3 is 12, which tells you that (b) is equal to 12^3. Now that you know (b) is greater than (a), you can eliminate Choices (B) and (D). You know that $4^3 \neq 3^4$; you can eliminate Choice (A) and pick Choice (C) without ever figuring out the exact value of (c).

89. **D.** The sequence alternates fractions with decimals, which means the next number must be a fraction. Scrap Choices (B) and (C). The sequence decreases by 0.75, or $\frac{3}{4}$. 7.75 – 0.75 = 7, which, when expressed as a fraction, is Choice (D). ***Note:*** Even though Choices (C) and (D) represent a value of 7, Choice D is the better answer because it expresses the value as a fraction.

90. **A.** Here's the equation: $0.2x + 0.6x = 52$; $0.8x = 52$; $x = 65$, Choice (A).

91. **A.** The operations seem to be –3, ×2. 25 × 2 = 50, which makes Choice (A) the missing number.

92. **C.** The figure displays parallel lines and a couple transversals, which means the corresponding and opposing angles are equal to each other. So $\angle B$ and $\angle D$ are equal,

Choice (C). Cross out Choices (A) and (B) because you know that $\angle B + \angle C = 90°$, but you don't know the angles' individual measurements. Choice (D) is wrong because $\angle E = \angle C +$ the angle next to $\angle C$, which means $\angle E$ can't $= \angle C$.

93. **B.** The operations in the sequence are +1, –2, +3, –4, +5, –6, +7, and so on. The next operation is –8. 4 – 8 = –4, Choice (B).

94. **B.** The equation is $x = 2[(60 + 52 + 43 + 23 + 60 + 38) \div 6] - 4$. Solve for x: $x = 2(276 \div 6) - 4$; $x = 2(46) - 4$; $x = 92 - 4$; $x = 88$, Choice (B). If you picked Choice (C), you didn't multiply the average by 2 before you subtracted 4.

95. **D.** The number of sixths in 10 times 3 could be written like this: $x \times \frac{1}{6} = 10 \times 3$; $x \times \frac{1}{6} = 30$; $x = 30 \times \frac{6}{1}$, or 180 — Choice (D).

96. **C.** Look at the three values. (c) has to be less than (b) or (a) because (c) is a negative number, and the others are positive. Eliminate Choices (A), (B), and (D). You know the answer has to be Choice (C) without actually calculating the values.

97. **D.** The numbers in each set increase by 11, which means the next number ends in 66; eliminate Choice (C). Each set skips two letters in the alphabet, so the next set begins with the letter L because L is the third letter after I (I, J, K, L). Choice (D) is correct.

98. **C.** Without doing calculations, you know that the value of (b) is less than (a), which means you can cross out Choice (D). You also know that $\frac{1}{6}$ is less than $\frac{1}{5}$, which means (c) > (b) and you can eliminate Choice (A). (a) > (b); pick Choice (C). $\frac{5}{6} = \frac{25}{30}$, which is greater than $\frac{6}{30}$ (the equivalent of $\frac{1}{5}$).

99. **A.** The circumference is $2\pi r$, or 24π, which rules out Choice (C). The radius of the circle is 12 m, which means its diameter is 24 m, Choice (A).

100. **A.** The pattern is +1, +6. 92 + 1 = 93. Toss out Choices (B) and (C) because they don't start with 93. The next operation in Choice (D) is +1 rather than +6, which means Choice (A) must be right.

101. **A.** Say the operations as you move along the sequence: –4, ÷2, –4, ÷2. . . . The missing number is 16 – 4 = 12, Choice (A).

102. **C.** $25 + 191 = x^3$. Solve for x: $216 = x^3$. The cube root of 216 is 6, Choice (C).

103. **B.** $(17 + 32)(17 + 32)$ and $(17 + 32)^2$ are two ways of saying the same thing, which means (a) = (b). The only number that has a squared value that's not greater than twice its value is 2; so, (c) has to be < (a) or (b). The relationship of the values is (a) = (b) > (c). Choice (B) is your answer.

104. **D.** Create an equation and solve for x: $x \div 4 = 4 + 32$; $x \div 4 = 36$; $x = 144$, Choice (D).

105. **B.** The numbers seem to repeat twice and then decrease by 9. The next three numbers after 18 should be 18, 9, 9, which is Choice (B).

106. **C.** The circles are divided into 16 equal sections. (a) is shaded $\frac{4}{16}$, (b) is shaded $\frac{6}{16}$, and (c) is shaded $\frac{5}{16}$. The relationship is (b) > (c) > (a). Eliminate Choices (A), (B), and (D). Choice (C) has to be right: $\frac{4}{16} + \frac{6}{16}$ is $\frac{10}{16}$. Half of $\frac{10}{16} = \frac{5}{16}$, which is the value of (c).

107. **C.** 33 appears as every other number in the sequence, which means you can cut Choices (B) and (D). The other numbers increase by 3, proving Choice (C) to be the answer.

108. **D.** $x =$ a perfect square – 23. Add 23 to each of the answer choices to see which one produces a perfect square. 98 + 23 = 121, which is 11^2. The answer is Choice (D).

109. **D.** Write out the equation and solve: $x + 0.3x = 65$; $1.3x = 65$; $x = 50$ — Choice (D).

110. **A.** Multiply the values to compare them. (a) = 125; (b) = 81; (c) = 81. The correct answer is Choice (A); 81 = 81.

111. **D.** Create the equation and solve for x: $x = (3^3 \div 9) - 5$; $x = (27 \div 9) - 5$; $x = 3 - 5$; $x = -2$, Choice (D).

112. **A.** You know the figure is a square because its length and width are the same number. Therefore, its diagonals form right angles where they cross, and the triangles they form are equal to each other (which makes Choice (D) wrong). The diagonals cut the square in half and therefore bisect the right angles at the corners of the square, making Choice (A) correct. The measure of the angle created by the diagonal is half that of the original angle. The diagonal isn't equal to 2 times the side length, so toss out Choice (B). The angles in Choice (C) are equal; cut Choice (C).

Section 3: Reading

113. **C.** The case is mentioned in the first paragraph, where it tells you that the Native Americans, Choice (C), won.

114. **C.** This passage is about Jackson's treatment of Native Americans, specifically Cherokees, in the early 19th century. Choices (A) and (D) have nothing to do with that topic. Choice (B) relates to the topic, but it refers to the wrong century. The best answer is Choice (C).

Title questions ask you to identify the main point of the passage.

115. **A.** The last sentence of the first paragraph says that Jackson professed to having "the kindest feelings" toward the Cherokees, Choice (A).

116. **B.** The beginning of the second paragraph informs you that Jackson negotiated with the Cherokee, Choice (B). The other answers aren't mentioned in the passage at all.

117. **A.** In the first paragraph, you discover that the decision "held that Native Americans were independent and not subject to state regulation." Choice (B) provides a contradictory statement, and Choices (C) and (D) are unrelated. Choice (A) is best.

118. **B.** *Belied* is in the last sentence of the first paragraph. The sentence begins with *although,* which shows contrast. Substitute the answers into the sentence to see which one expresses the contrasting idea: Although Jackson said he had kind feelings, his actions *contradicted* his words. His actions didn't *exaggerate, support,* or *carry* his words.

119. **A.** This passage talks about Jupiter in the third paragraph. The last sentence says that a great eagle is his messenger. A messenger carries words to others, so the answer must be Choice (A). Thunder and lightning are Jupiter's weapons, not his message carriers.

120. **D.** Choose a title that expresses the main idea of the passage and is neither too specific nor so general as to be off topic. Terror, Trembling, Panic, and Fear are mentioned only in the last sentence, which means Choice (A) can't be right. The passage doesn't talk about Mars's family; Choice (B) is wrong too. It doesn't mention the fall of Rome, so Choice (C) isn't the main point. The passage begins by explaining why people study myths and focuses on their impact on society. Although you can probably think of a better title, Choice (D) is the best answer out of the four.

121. **D.** The second paragraph refers to myths as fables, Choice (D).

122. **B.** *Consort* appears in the fourth paragraph to describe the role of Juno, Jupiter's wife. The paragraph states that Jupiter respects Juno and tells her his secrets. Therefore, she is his companion, Choice (B). You can cross out Choices (C) and (D) because they mean pretty much the same thing.

A question can't have two right answers. When you see more than one answer choice that means the same thing, toss those aside and zero in on the remaining choices.

123. **D.** *Critical* has several meanings; make sure you pick the definition that fits in the passage. You find *critical* in the second paragraph, where it describes what type of link myths give to the past. The last sentence in the paragraph states that myths may be the only source of information about how people in the past saw their world, which means that myths

provide an important link to the past, Choice (D). Choices (A) and (C) are other definitions of critical, but they don't make good replacements for the way critical is used in the passage.

124. **C.** The sixth paragraph states that steeds pull the chariot. *Steeds* is a name for horses, Choice (C).

125. **A.** *Majestic* is used in the second-to-last paragraph to describe Juno, the wife of Jupiter. The paragraph says that Juno commands reverence, or respect. The adjective that best fits the quality of gaining respect is Choice (A), magnificent.

126. **C.** The third paragraph mentions all the answer choices in relation to Jupiter, but it specifically states that Jupiter is known as the god of weather, Choice (C).

127. **D.** Cross out reasons that appear in the passage. The fourth reason expressed in the second paragraph is that myth links us to the past. The first reason is about references in modern literature. The second reason points out the link to musical instruments. Choice (D) must be the answer. Although the passage says that myths are entertaining, it doesn't state that they're hilariously funny.

128. **C.** The fourth paragraph says that Juno's domain is marriage. Iris is Juno's companion and goddess of the rainbow, and the passage doesn't mention marriage in relation to Jupiter or Mars. Go with Choice (C).

129. **D.** The only activity that the passage doesn't tell you that Cicero engaged in is carpentry, Choice (D). He was a politician, lawyer, and public speaker.

130. **A.** The last paragraph touches on the comparison of Cicero's writings to those of Caesar, Choice (A). The other choices aren't mentioned in the passage.

131. **C.** The second paragraph states that Roman intellectuals created Latin literature in the Roman republic, which makes the most logical answer Choice (C).

132. **B.** Caesar's works are compared to Cicero's compositions, and the next sentence references "their writings." "Caesar's works" refers to writings, Choice (B).

133. **B.** In the first sentence, the passage tells you that attorney, Choice (B), is another name for lawyer.

134. **D.** An example of a pejorative expression in the first paragraph is "ambulance chaser," and the author refers to pejorative expressions as "this negativity." Therefore, *pejorative* must have a negative connotation. The most negative of the answers is Choice (D). Pejorative expressions are uncomplimentary expressions.

135. **A.** The author is very complimentary toward Cicero and praises his accomplishments. The best answer is Choice (A). None of the other choices conveys the author's positivity.

136. **C.** Examine each answer to determine its truth. The last paragraph says that Plutarch imitated Cicero's sentence structure, but it doesn't say he used Cicero's arguments. Cicero's works have been compared to Caesar's, but the passage doesn't say they knew each other. The author says that some people think lawyers in general are insincere and greedy, but that view isn't attributed specifically to Cicero. The only true answer is Choice (C). The last paragraph states that Churchill imitated Cicero's sentence structure.

137. **D.** The author covers the positive attributes of lawyers in the second paragraph, which mentions their contributions to cleaning up the environment and promoting integration. Nothing is said about making "ambulance chasing" illegal or teaching public speaking, which means you can cut Choices (B) and (C). Choice (A) is a little tricky if you don't read it carefully. Because Choice (A) says that attorneys have fought rather than promoted cleaning up the environment, the best answer has to be Choice (D).

138. **B.** The second paragraph says that most legislators (who are politicians) are lawyers because they understand justice and the application of the law. Choice (B) is the only answer that supports the author's statement.

139. **A.** The first paragraph defines *carrying capacity* as "the density and diversity of a biome's components." Choice (A) paraphrases this definition as number and variety of organisms. The other answers refer to other characteristics of a biome.

140. **D.** The passage covers forest biomes in the fourth paragraph. The two kinds of forest biomes are the temperate deciduous forest and the taiga, which is Choice (D).

141. **B.** The parentheses in the fourth paragraph tell you that deciduous trees have leaves, Choice (B).

142. **A.** The tropical rain forest has the greatest carrying capacity; scrap Choice (B). The second paragraph says that deserts have "extremely low" carrying capacities. The capacity of the taiga is medium, and the savanna is below average. Therefore, among the answer choices, the desert, Choice (A), has the lowest carrying capacity.

143. **B.** The tundra paragraph tells you that the main characteristic of the tundra is that the ground stays frozen. It has a low carrying capacity, extreme temperatures, and a few hearty mammals. Choice (B) is the best answer.

144. **D.** The last paragraph says that freshwater biomes are affected by temperature swings, the amount of available oxygen, and the speed of water flowing through them, which means you can eliminate Choices (A), (B), and (C). The passage doesn't cover issues that are unrelated to the natural environment; Choice (D)'s your answer.

145. **D.** The passage says that the tropical rainforest has the greatest carrying capacity, which makes Choices (A) and (C) wrong because they list the rainforest after the ocean. Choice (D) is better than Choice (B) because it lists the extremely low desert after the below-average savanna. The desert has a lower carrying capacity than the savanna. Choice (D) is best.

146. **A.** Because biotic components are living organisms, you can eliminate Choices (B) and (C). The taiga is a forest biome and has evergreen trees and forest animals. Choice (D) lists caribou, which live in the tundra rather than the taiga. Choice (A) is the best answer.

147. **B.** The second paragraph mentions Antarctica, Choice (B), as a place to find a desert.

148. **C.** Refer to the fifth paragraph. The savanna has a good rainy season, which means Choice (A) isn't right. It's known for its grasslands rather than its trees, and it has a below-average carrying capacity. Toss out Choices (B) and (D). The grasslands of the savanna provide food for lots of grazing animals, Choice (C).

149. **B.** The first paragraph says that the primary purpose of the Bible is to explore the relationship between God and humans, which suggests that Choice (B) is the right answer. You can eliminate Choice (A) because nowhere does the passage reveal the number of books in the Bible. Although the passage mentions the book of Revelation and Israel's exit from Egypt, it doesn't go into detail on either subject. Choice (B) is the best answer.

150. **A.** Because the passage says that the message culminates in the last book of the Bible, the best definition of *culminates* is Choice (A), concludes.

151. **D.** The first paragraph mentions the relationships between humans and nature, humans and other humans, and God and humans. It doesn't say anything about the relationship between humans and a moral code. Pick Choice (D).

152. **D.** The passage discusses Genesis in the second paragraph. It says that the book provides the background for God's desire to relate to humans and humans' choice to reject God's provision. Choices (A) and (C) are contrary to the statement in the passage, and Choice (B) isn't related to what the passage says is the background provided by Genesis. The best answer is Choice (D), which paraphrases part of the statement in the first paragraph.

153. **B.** For this question and the rest of the section, you have to switch gears a bit and focus on vocabulary. To *excel* at an activity is to be excellent at it, to be a star. Stars shine, so the best synonym for excel is Choice (B), shine.

154. **D.** You'd probably be happy to receive an early dismissal from school. It means to be let out early. Another word that means to be let go is Choice (D), discharge.

155. **A.** A frivolous excuse for being late probably wouldn't convince your parents. *Frivolous* means "trivial or silly," Choice (A).

156. **A.** When you introduce a topic, you bring it up or initiate it, Choice (A). *Evade* means "to avoid," which is more opposite than similar.

157. **D.** To *relish* an opportunity is to delight in it. Thus, the best answer is Choice (D), enjoy. You may have picked Choice (B) because you were thinking that pickle relish embellishes a hot dog, but now you know that relish means to really, really, really like something.

158. **B.** A legacy is something that's passed down for generations. An inheritance, Choice (B), is also passed down from one generation to another.

159. **C.** If you don't know for sure that *insolent* means "rude," you may be familiar enough with it to know that it has a negative connotation, which means you can eliminate positive answer choices such as reverential and caring. The best answer is Choice (C).

160. **A.** *Nirvana* is another name for utopia or paradise, Choice (A).

161. **B.** Unparalleled genius has no parallel; there's nothing like it. It's unusually remarkable or extraordinary, Choice (B).

162. **C.** A *subtle* hint isn't obvious; it's understated, Choice (C).

163. **C.** You probably know that oppression isn't a positive word, which means you can eliminate Choices (A) and (D) because they're positive. Choices (B) and (C) are similar in meaning, but oppression is more than just power; it's total domination, Choice (C).

164. **D.** Having the quality of indifference means to be unconcerned, Choice (D).

165. **A.** A pessimistic outlook is a negative one. The best synonym for pessimistic is gloomy, Choice (A).

166. **A.** To *wallow* in self-pity is sort of like wallowing in mud. It means "to immerse yourself or get caught up in a feeling or state of mind." The best synonym is Choice (A), bask. The other choices aren't related to getting caught up in something.

167. **C.** *Tenure* is a period of time or term, Choice (C).

168. **B.** A *phenomenon* is something that happens. Occurrence, Choice (B), is a synonym.

169. **D.** A consuming interest is one that involves every part of your life. It's overwhelming. Choices (A) and (B) have more opposite meanings. The best synonym is intense, Choice (D).

170. **B.** To *hoard* is to (sometimes obsessively) save or accumulate stuff, Choice (B). A hoarder may guard what she has, but the act of hoarding is in the accumulating, not the guarding.

171. **C.** Miscreant just sounds negative, and it is. The most negative word in the bunch is Choice (C), troublemaker, and it fits; a *miscreant* is a wrongdoer.

172. **A.** A *palpable* silence is a silence you can feel. Something that's palpable is easily experienced using your senses. Palpable doesn't have a negative connotation, which means Choices (C) and (D) are incorrect. The best answer is Choice (A), noticeable.

173. **D.** A *totalitarian* government is a dictatorship. The best synonym is Choice (D), *despotic*, which also refers to authoritarian and dictatorial rule.

174. **A.** Spendthrift is a confusing word. It has *spend* in it, but it also contains *thrift*. You may think it means a thrifty spender, but it doesn't. The *spend* part of the word rules. A *spendthrift* is one who spends money to the point of wasting it, a squanderer — Choice (A).

Section 4: Mathematics

175. **A.** The *tenths* place is the number to the right of the decimal point, which is the second 4. Round the 4 to 5 because the number to the right of the 4 is greater than 5. The answer is Choice (A), 34.5. Choice (D) improperly rounds the tenths place, and the other choices write the number to the incorrect place.

176. **D.** All three are types of angles, Choice (D).

    A *right angle* is 90°, an *obtuse angle* is greater than 90°, and an *acute angle* is less than 90°.

177. **D.** When you divide a number by a multiple of 10, you move the decimal point one place to the left for every zero in the multiple. 100,000 has five zeros, which means you move the decimal point five places to the left, Choice (D).

178. **C.** The intersection sign means you must look for the set of numbers that appears in both sets. Both sets contain 2, 4, 5, and 6, which is the answer in Choice (C).

179. **B.** The value of the angle next to the 160° angle is 20°. You know that because the angles along a straight line add up to 180° (180 – 160 = 20). The angles inside a triangle also add up to 180 degrees. Subtract the sum of the other two angles in the triangle to find the measure of $\angle B$: $\angle B = 180 - (20 + 80)$; $\angle B = 180 - 100$; $\angle B = 80°$, Choice (B).

180. **A.** The cube of a negative number is negative, which means the final answer is negative. Eliminate Choices (B) and (C). $-2 \times -2 \times -2 = -8$. $5 \times -8 = -40$, Choice (A).

181. **C.** 0.55 is 55 hundredths, which looks like $\frac{55}{100}$ when expressed as a fraction. Simplified, that reduces to $\frac{11}{20}$, Choice (C).

182. **D.** The formula for the area of a circle is $\pi \times r^2$. The radius of this circle is half of 8, or 4. $4^2 = 16$, which means the area of the circle is 16π m^2, Choice (D).

    The radius of a circle is half the diameter.

183. **B.** You have to know what a reciprocal is to answer this question correctly. Fortunately, you're aware that a *reciprocal* is the inverse of a fraction; in other words, it's the numerator and denominator flipped. An example is Choice (B).

184. **B.** $\frac{15}{8}$ as a mixed number is $1\frac{7}{8}$. The two integers between $1\frac{7}{8}$ and 3.5 are 2 and 3, which makes Choice (B) the answer.

185. **C.** The only perfect square among the choices is 121, Choice (C); it's 11^2.

186. **A.** To find the number of hundreds, create a fraction; 4,575 hundreds is $\frac{4575}{100}$. Divide to get 45.75, Choice (A).

187. **C.** Answer this question by adding multiples of 5 and 7 to see which ones equal 24; $5 + 7 \neq 24$, but $10 + 14 = 24$. If you prefer an algebra approach, you can set up an equation like this one to find what multiplier results in the sum of 24: $5x + 7x = 24$; $12x = 24$; $x = 2$. Take $2 \times$ the smaller value in the ratio to find the smaller number: $2 \times 5 = 10$. In either case, the smaller number is 10, which is Choice (C). Choice (A) is the larger number.

188. **B.** Convert the values so that you're comparing like units of measure. 36 inches is the same as 1 yard. The ratio is 1 to 3, Choice (B).

189. **D.** The first value must be written with only one digit to the left of the decimal point, which means Choice (C) can't be right. The exponent is the number of places you move the decimal point to the right to produce the complete number. The scientific notation that actually equals 245 is Choice (D). Choice (A) equals 245,000, and Choice (B) equals 24,500.

190. **D.** One gallon equals 4 quarts, which means that 4 gallons is 16 quarts. A quart is 32 ounces, so each quart of milk produces four 8-ounce cups. If there are 16 quarts, then $16 \times 4 = 64$ 8-ounce cups of milk, Choice (D).

191. **B.** This question is a memory exercise, plain and simple. To find the area of a rectangle, you multiply its length by its width, Choice (B).

192. **A.** Let x = the number of boxes of sugar cookies and create an equation: $x + x + 4 = 44$; $2x + 4 = 44$; $2x = 40$; $x = 20$ boxes of sugar cookies, Choice (A).

193. **C.** An isosceles right triangle has a 90° angle, and the other two angles are equal to each other. Because the other two angles add up to 90°, each one is 45° — Choice (C).

194. **A.** The lowest number that both 4 and 8 go into evenly is 8, Choice (A).

195. **A.** Eliminate Choice (D) because 4 isn't a prime number. Then toss out answers that don't equal 8; 2^5 is 32, and 2×2 is 4, which means Choices (B) and (C) are wrong. The answer is Choice (A).

196. **B.** 25½% is equal to $^{25.5}/_{100}$, which is 0.255. If 0.255 is equal to 25½%, then 25.5 can't be equal to 0.255. The correct answer is Choice (B).

197. **D.** The side lengths of similar triangles are proportional, which means the ratio of AC to BC is equal to the ratio of XZ to YZ. You know the value of AC, XZ, and YZ, so you can set up a proportion and solve for x: $^6/_x = ^3/_5$. Cross multiply: $3x = 30$; $x = 10$. The length of BC is 10 units, Choice (D).

198. **A.** Choice (A) is an example of the distributive property and is correct. Because the distributive property doesn't apply to division, Choice (C) can't be right. Addition and multiplication aren't the same, so Choice (B) is wrong too. Choice (D) would be correct if the variables in the parentheses were added rather than multiplied.

199. **D.** $-3 + 2 = -1$. $-1 + (-5) = -6$. $-6 + (-7) = -13$. The answer is Choice (D).

200. **B.** Set up a proportion of the heights to the shadows, cross multiply, and solve for x: $^3/_x = ^2/_{14}$; $2x = 3 \times 14$; $2x = 42$; $x = 21$. The shadow is 21 feet tall, Choice (B).

201. **A.** Let x equal the total amount spent and set up an equation: $x = (5 \times \$3.75) + (4 \times \$2.25)$; $x = \$18.75 + 9$; $x = \$27.75$, which is Choice (A).

202. **D.** First things first: Change the mixed numbers to improper fractions: $3^2/_6 = ^{22}/_6$, and $2^3/_4 = ^{11}/_4$. Then find the least common denominator: 4 and 6 go evenly into 12. $^{22}/_6 = ^{44}/_{12}$, and $^{11}/_4 = ^{33}/_{12}$. Finally, subtract: $^{44}/_{12} - ^{33}/_{12} = ^{11}/_{12}$, Choice (D).

203. **D.** Subtract x and 7 from both sides: $2x + 7 = x + 12$; $x = 5$ — Choice (D).

204. **A.** Set up an equation for $600 is 6% of what number and solve: $\$600 = 0.06x$; $10,000 = x$. The price of the car before tax was $10,000, Choice (A).

205. **C.** $1,525 \div 7 = 217.857$; the answer becomes 218 miles, Choice (C), when you round to the nearest mile.

206. **B.** Find the value of a: $3a + 2 > 14$; $3a > 12$; $a > 4$. Square both sides to find that $a^2 > 16$, Choice (B).

207. **C.** Let x equal Alicia's dollars and create an equation: $x = (3 \times 40) - 15$; $x = 120 - 15$; $x = 105$. Alicia has $105, Choice (C).

208. **A.** The saleswoman earns 6% of $60 for each tool set, which means she earns $3.60 per tool set ($0.06 \times \$60 = \$3.60$). For 5 tool sets, she earns $18 ($5 \times \$3.60$), Choice (A).

209. **C.** A pound is 16 ounces, which added to 8 ounces is a total of 24 ounces of candy. The candy costs $2 per ounce, and 2×24 is $48, Choice (C).

210. **C.** Subtract y and 6 from both sides of the equation: $x - y = 5$. If $x - y$ is a positive number, x must be greater than y, which is what's stated in Choice (C).

211. **B.** If the sum of two numbers is x and one of the numbers is 6, then the other number has to be $x - 6$. So, 4 times the other number is $4(x - 6)$, which is Choice (B).

212. **D.** Convert the mixed fractions to improper fractions: $1\frac{2}{3} = \frac{5}{3}$, and $3\frac{2}{6} = \frac{20}{6}$. The lowest common denominator of the fractions is 6; the resulting equation is $\frac{10}{6} + \frac{3}{6} + \frac{20}{6} = \frac{33}{6}$. Convert to a mixed fraction and simplify: $5\frac{1}{2}$, Choice (D). Another way to solve is to reduce $3\frac{2}{6}$ to $3\frac{1}{3}$. $1\frac{2}{3} + 3\frac{1}{3} = 5$. Add $\frac{1}{2}$ to 5 to get $5\frac{1}{2}$.

213. **C.** Substitute the values for x and y in the equation and solve: $2(\frac{1}{2})^2 + 3(3) - 1 = ?$; $2(\frac{1}{4}) + 9 - 1 = ?$; $\frac{1}{2} + 8 = 8\frac{1}{2}$, Choice (C).

214. **D.** $N\% \times 70 = 14$; $N\% = 0.2$; $N = 20$, Choice (D).

215. **A.** $0.05x = \$525$; $x = \$10,500$. Miguel borrowed \$10,500, Choice (A).

216. **B.** Line up the decimal points and add to get 7.603, Choice (B).

217. **B.** Isolate the x on the left side: $4x > 12$; $x > 3$. The answer choices are cubed, so cube both sides: $x^3 > 27$. The answer is Choice (B).

218. **D.** Because the multiplied values have a total of four digits to the right of their decimal points, the answer should have four digits to the right of the decimal point. The answer is either Choice (C) or (D). You know that the last number is a 5 because the last numbers of the multiplied values are 1 and 5 and $1 \times 5 = 5$. Choice (D) is therefore your answer.

219. **C.** Recall the formula for the volume of a cube: s^3. $s = 6$, and s^3 is 6^3, or 216 m^3, Choice (C).

220. **B.** *Per 100* is another way of saying *percent*, which means the tax is 2.76%. $0.0276 \times \$40,000 = \$1,104$. The taxes on \$40,000 are \$1,104, Choice (B).

221. **A.** Per month, Danielle makes $\$48,000 \div 12$, or \$4,000. 6% of \$4,000 is $0.06 \times \$4,000$, or \$240. Danielle saves \$240 per month, Choice (A).

222. **C.** The answer to this basic multiplication problem is 11,484, Choice (C).

223. **D.** The equation is $(5 \times 6) = 10 + x$. So, $30 = 10 + x$, and $20 = x$, Choice (D).

224. **C.** Square both sides of the equation to eliminate the square root sign: $y - 4 = 3^2$. Solve for y: $y = 9 + 4$; $y = 13$. Choice (C)'s your answer.

225. **B.** A ratio is really just a division problem, which means the question is $\frac{1}{2} \div \frac{5}{6} = x$. Multiply by the reciprocal: $\frac{1}{2} \times \frac{6}{5} = x$; $\frac{6}{12} = x$; $\frac{3}{5} = x$. Choice (B) wins!

226. **D.** The operation for the sequence is +0.02. $15.06 + 0.02 = 15.08$, Choice (D).

227. **D.** Find the areas of each of the three figures and add them together to find the total area. The area of the square is easy: $s^2 = 6^2$, or 36. The area of one triangle is $\frac{1}{2}bh$. The base is 6, and the height is 4. So, $A = \frac{1}{2}(6)(4)$, which is 12. Add the areas: $36 + 12 + 12 = 60$, Choice (D). The other answers give you the partial area.

228. **A.** Create a right triangle with a base of 5 ft and a hypotenuse of 13 ft, like this one.

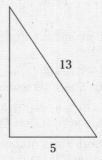

Because one side measures 5 and the hypotenuse measures 13, this is one of those special right triangles with proportionate side lengths of 5-12-13. That makes the height 12 ft. ***Note:*** If you didn't remember the proportion, you could use the Pythagorean theorem to calculate the length of the other side instead: $a^2 + b^2 = c^2$; $5^2 + b^2 = 13^2$; $25 + b^2 = 169$; $b^2 = 144$; $b = 12$. Either way, go with Choice (A).

229. **D.** Apply the formula for the area of a rectangle ($A = lw$). $A = 6 \times 14$, or 84 in^2 — Choice (D).

230. **D.** The lowest common denominator for the fractions is 12. Convert each fraction and solve: $(\frac{6}{12} + \frac{9}{12}) - (\frac{4}{12} + \frac{9}{12}) = x$; $\frac{13}{12} - \frac{13}{12} = x$; $0 = x$, which is Choice (D).

231. **C.** You can multiply both sides by 10 to eliminate the decimal points: $6x + 49 = 103$; $6x = 54$; $x = 9$. Pick Choice (C).

232. **B.** First, set up an equation to figure out how many total miles Tyler planned to drive that day: $0.2x = 80$; $x = 400$ total miles. You're not finished, so don't pick Choice (C). Tyler drove 80 miles of the 400, which means the number of miles he has left to drive to reach his planned total miles is $400 - 80$, or 320, which is Choice (B).

233. **B.** A multiple of 50 must end in a zero; the only answer that ends in zero is 250, Choice (B).

234. **D**. Because the angles in a right triangle total 180°, and one angle is 90°, the sum of the remaining two acute angles must be 90°. Set up an equation given the ratio of the unknown angles: $5x + 1x = 90$; $6x = 90$; $x = 15$. The smaller angle is 15°, but the question asks for the larger angle. Multiply 15 by 5. The larger angle is 75°, Choice (D).

235. **A.** Solve for P: $P\% \times 80 = 4$; $P\% = \frac{4}{80}$; $P\% = 0.05$; $P\% = 5$.

236. **B.** Add the numbers, making sure you line up the decimal points: $0.897 + 0.0092 + 5.7 = 6.6062$, Choice (B).

237. **C.** Subtract 5 from both sides: $4x = 44$; $x = 11$, Choice (C). Not too shabby!

238. **A.** For fractions, the word *divide* means multiply by the reciprocal: $\frac{4}{5} \div \frac{5}{6} = \frac{4}{5} \times \frac{6}{5}$, which is $\frac{24}{25}$ — Choice (A).

Section 5: Language

239. **C.** Choice (C) has a verb tense error. *Stays* is present tense, and *got* is past tense. The verbs should both be past or both be present, but not one of each.

240. **B.** In Choice (B), the pronoun *I* is the object of the preposition *for,* which means it should be in objective form rather than subjective form: . . . for my brother and *me.* If you eliminate *my brother* from the sentence, the correct form is obvious: My mom bought a new hamster for me.

241. **D.** The sentences in this question are all properly constructed, punctuated, and capitalized; pick Choice (D).

242. **B.** Choice (B) contains a word usage error. *Affect* is a verb, not a noun. The wording should be that the plan had no *effect* on the budget.

243. **C.** Choice (C) uses *accept* to mean *except.* It closes every night *except* Sunday.

244. **C.** *To* in Choice (C) is supposed to mean more than enough. The proper form is *too,* as in there were *too* many dogs.

245. **A.** Choice (A) lacks punctuation in its sequence. There should be two commas: tennis, track, and wrestling.

246. **A.** The first word in Choice (A) uses a possessive form for a plural noun. The apostrophe is incorrect. The sentence should say that "monkeys are fun to watch."

247. **C.** Choice (C) is a question. The proper ending punctuation for questions is a question mark, not an exclamation point.

248. **D.** These sentences are great just the way they're written; opt for Choice (D).

249. **D.** All is well in these sentences. The pronoun *us* in Choice (C) is proper. It's used as an object, and the objective form is right: They invited us. Pick Choice (D).

250. **A.** Choice (A) has a subject-verb agreement error. Its subject is number, and number is singular. The verb *have increased* is plural. The proper wording is "the number has increased."

251. **C.** The complete title of the contest in Choice (C) should be capitalized: Greater Denver Area Spelling Bee.

252. **B.** The two descriptive adjectives (*lovely* and *talented*) that precede *young lady* in Choice (B) should be separated by a comma, as in "lovely, talented young lady."

253. **B.** In Choice (B), the claws belong to the cats, which means you must use the possessive form of *they* (their) before claws.

254. **C.** *One* and *won* sound alike, but they mean very different things. The recipe in Choice (C) should have *won* first place.

255. **A.** *Grandma* in Choice (A) should be capitalized because it's used as a proper name.

256. **C.** In Choice (C), *uncle* isn't used as a name, which means it should be lowercase.

257. **D.** The sentences in these answers are fine as written; go with Choice (D).

258. **C.** The office in Choice (C) belongs to the one governor, which means *governors* needs an apostrophe to be in the possessive form (as in *governor's*).

259. **B.** *Could of* in Choice (B) is never proper. The verb form is *could have*.

260. **A.** Because Naomi's note-taking occurred yesterday, the verb in Choice (A) should be in the past tense: Naomi *took* notes yesterday.

261. **D.** The sentences are fine as is. The use of *were* in Choice (A) is okay because it's contained in an if-clause that conveys an idea that's contrary to fact. There's no comma between *talented* and *lacrosse* in Choice (C) because *talented* describes *lacrosse player*, not just *player* alone.

262. **A.** The colon in Choice (A) incorrectly separates the verb *are* from the rest of the sentence. The clause before the colon should be a complete sentence, something like "I like Cleveland for three reasons: it has the Rock and Roll Hall of Fame, . . ."

263. **B.** Choice (B) is an incomplete sentence. It's a dependent clause and needs to include another idea in order to form a complete thought. For instance, "We are cold because it's snowing outside."

264. **D.** The sentences in this question are constructed properly. Choice (D)'s the winner!

265. **D.** All three sentences are error free; select Choice (D).

266. **A.** The subject of Choice (A) is *sustaining*, which is singular. The verb *have decreased* is plural. It should be changed to *has decreased*.

267. **C.** Days of the week, including Sunday, are always capitalized. Choice (C) contains the problem.

268. **C.** The home in Choice (C) belongs to Mark and Mindy, which means you use the possessive form of they. It's *their* home. *They're* is a contraction of *they are*.

269. **C.** *Women* is a plural noun that's formed without an ending *s*. To properly form the possessive of women in Choice (C), you'd add *'s* to get *women's*.

270. **D.** There are no problems with the sentences in this question. Pick Choice (D).

271. **B.** *Dissidents* is the subject of the sentence in Choice (B) and, therefore, shouldn't be in possessive form.

272. **C.** "Her and I" is the subject of the sentence in Choice (C). So, both pronouns should be in the subjective form: She and I ride the bus. . . .

273. **C.** Contrary to what Choice (C) thinks, the construction *its'* never appears in the English language. The way to express *it is* as a contraction is *it's*.

274. **D.** The usage, punctuation, and construction are proper in these sentences. The pronoun *me* in Choice (C) is a direct object, which means the objective form is correct.

275. **A.** The proper way to express the possessive in Choice (A) is "the novels of Charles Dickens." The apostrophe after Dickens is unnecessary and incorrect.

276. **B.** The colon in Choice (B) is used improperly and should be eliminated.

277. **C.** The subject of the sentence in Choice (C), *each,* is singular and should have a singular verb. *Have visited* is plural and should be changed to *has visited.*

278. **B.** Choice (B) has no verb and is therefore an incomplete sentence. Simply adding *were* before *flying* fixes the problem.

279. **C.** In Choice (C), the word *separate* should be spelled with an *a* in the second syllable rather than an *e*.

280. **D.** None of these sentences contains a misspelled word; select Choice (D).

281. **A.** In Choice (A), *relevant* should be spelled with an *a* in the last syllable.

282. **A.** Choice (A) incorrectly spells *courtesy* without a *u*.

283. **B.** The last word of Choice (B) has *temper* in it; it's spelled *temperatures.*

284. **C.** In Choice (C), *conscious* should be spelled with an *s* after the *n*.

285. **D.** *Hygiene, dominant, offense, exaggerate,* and *accomplishments* are all spelled correctly. Pick Choice (D).

286. **B.** Strangely enough, *sacrilegious* in Choice (B) doesn't have the word *religious* in it.

287. **D.** All the words in this question are spelled correctly. Choice (D) it is!

288. **C.** In Choice (C), *prevalent* should have an *a* in the second syllable rather than an *e*.

289. **C.** This sentence has a beginning phrase; choose an answer that clearly demonstrates that *he* is the one sitting down to write. Eliminate Choices (A) and (B) because they say that "clearing and outlining" are sitting down to write, and they use passive voice. Choice (D) lacks parallel construction and just sounds really weird. Choice (C) is the best answer.

290. **B.** Pick the transition word that makes the most sense. The second clause conveys a contrasting idea, and the answer that shows contrast is Choice (B). Choice (C) changes the meaning of the sentence, and Choice (A) incorrectly conveys a cause-and-effect relationship between the two ideas in the sentence.

291. **D.** The choice that expresses the idea using parallel construction is Choice (D). Choices (A) and (B) lack parallel construction, and Choice (C) uses improper comparison language. *More better* is redundant; it should simply be *better*.

292. **A.** The clearest answer is Choice (A). The other choices use passive rather than active voice or employ awkward sentence construction.

293. **B.** The topic sentence describes how a black hole is created. Pick sentences that continue this idea. Choice (A) is about astronomy and is too general for the topic. Choices (C) and (D) discuss unrelated topics. The best answer is Choice (B) because it builds on the information in the topic sentence.

294. **C.** The only answer that says that the people in the courtroom heard the verdict is Choice (C). Choices (A) and (B) have *shouting* hearing the verdict, and Choice (D) implies that *began* heard the verdict.

295. **A.** Choice (B) doesn't make clear who *she* is. Choices (C) and (D) are awkward and use too many words to convey simple ideas. The clearest sentence is Choice (A).

296. **C.** The paragraph is about military customs and courtesies. That the Air Force and Navy are part of the military is irrelevant to the purpose of the paragraph. Therefore, Sentence 3, Choice (C), doesn't belong. All the other sentences supply information about the topic.

297. **D.** Choice (A) would be good for introducing an essay on the country of Panama but not for a piece on the Panama Canal. Choice (B) about ships is far too broad to relate to the Panama Canal. Both Choices (C) and (D) discuss the Panama Canal, but Choice (C) just describes it. Because Choice (D) provides information about the canal's history, it's the best answer.

298. **C.** Choice (C) states the idea in the clearest way. In simple terms, it describes what he did and why. The beginning phrase in Choice (A) doesn't properly describe the subject of the sentence, which is *he*. Choice (B) separates prepositional phrases from the verbs they describe, and Choice (D) is wordy and awkward.

Answer Key for HSPT Practice Test 2

Section 1: Verbal Skills

1. C	13. C	25. D	37. B	49. A
2. D	14. C	26. D	38. D	50. B
3. D	15. D	27. C	39. C	51. C
4. B	16. D	28. B	40. B	52. C
5. B	17. A	29. A	41. A	53. C
6. B	18. B	30. D	42. D	54. D
7. A	19. B	31. A	43. C	55. B
8. C	20. B	32. C	44. C	56. A
9. B	21. A	33. C	45. A	57. D
10. C	22. C	34. D	46. D	58. C
11. A	23. A	35. C	47. B	59. A
12. A	24. C	36. A	48. B	60. B

Section 2: Quantitative Skills

61. D	72. C	83. A	94. B	105. B
62. B	73. C	84. B	95. D	106. C
63. C	74. D	85. D	96. C	107. C
64. C	75. D	86. D	97. D	108. D
65. B	76. A	87. D	98. C	109. D
66. A	77. B	88. C	99. A	110. A
67. A	78. A	89. D	100. A	111. D
68. A	79. C	90. A	101. A	112. A
69. D	80. A	91. A	102. C	
70. C	81. D	92. C	103. B	
71. B	82. D	93. B	104. D	

Section 3: Reading

113. C	126. C	139. A	152. D	165. A
114. C	127. D	140. D	153. B	166. A
115. A	128. C	141. B	154. D	167. C
116. B	129. D	142. A	155. A	168. B
117. A	130. A	143. B	156. A	169. D
118. B	131. C	144. D	157. D	170. B
119. A	132. B	145. D	158. B	171. C
120. D	133. B	146. A	159. C	172. A
121. D	134. D	147. B	160. A	173. D
122. B	135. A	148. C	161. B	174. A
123. D	136. C	149. B	162. C	
124. C	137. D	150. A	163. C	
125. A	138. B	151. D	164. D	

Section 4: Mathematics

175. A	188. B	201. A	214. D	227. D
176. D	189. D	202. D	215. A	228. A
177. D	190. D	203. D	216. B	229. D
178. C	191. B	204. A	217. B	230. D
179. B	192. A	205. C	218. D	231. C
180. A	193. C	206. B	219. C	232. B
181. C	194. A	207. C	220. B	233. B
182. D	195. A	208. A	221. A	234. D
183. B	196. B	209. C	222. C	235. A
184. B	197. D	210. C	223. D	236. B
185. C	198. A	211. B	224. C	237. C
186. A	199. D	212. D	225. B	238. A
187. C	200. B	213. C	226. D	

Section 5: Language

239. C	251. C	263. B	275. A	287. D
240. B	252. B	264. D	276. B	288. C
241. D	253. B	265. D	277. C	289. C
242. B	254. C	266. A	278. B	290. B
243. C	255. A	267. C	279. C	291. D
244. C	256. C	268. C	280. D	292. A
245. A	257. D	269. C	281. A	293. B
246. A	258. C	270. D	282. A	294. C
247. C	259. B	271. B	283. B	295. A
248. D	260. A	272. C	284. C	296. C
249. D	261. D	273. C	285. D	297. D
250. A	262. A	274. D	286. B	298. C

Chapter 21

TACHS Practice Test 1

· ·

*H*ere's a chance to show what you know! The following practice test features the kinds of reading, language, math, and ability questions you can expect to find on the TACHS. Completing all the questions takes about two hours with breaks.

This test is very similar to the real TACHS, but the test-makers always have the option of changing the test slightly, so the one you take could have a different number of questions, different time limits, or even slightly different question formats.

To make the most of this practice test, make your practice time as similar to real test conditions as possible by doing the following:

- ✔ Find a place where you won't be distracted (preferably as far as possible from your neighbor's drum practice).

- ✔ Try to take this test at approximately the same time of day your actual TACHS test is scheduled (probably early morning).

- ✔ Rip out the answer sheet and mark your answers on it by filling in the appropriate bubbles.

- ✔ Use the margins of the test pages to scribble down notes and calculations, unless of course a particular question wants you to estimate the answer.

- ✔ Use a timer to time each section. When your time is up, stop answering questions in that section and move on. If you finish a section early, go back and check your work, but don't work ahead.

- ✔ Give yourself a short break between each of the sections. On test day, you'll probably receive at least one 10- to 15-minute break midway into the exam.

When you're finished with this practice test, go ahead and check your answers by flipping to Chapter 22. It features answer explanations to help you identify why right answers are right and wrong answers are wrong so you can understand the strategy for answering each question type when you take your exam.

Answer Sheet for TACHS Practice Test 1

Reading Section

Part 1

1. (A) (B) (C) (D) 3. (A) (B) (C) (D) 5. (A) (B) (C) (D) 7. (A) (B) (C) (D) 9. (A) (B) (C) (D)
2. (J) (K) (L) (M) 4. (J) (K) (L) (M) 6. (J) (K) (L) (M) 8. (J) (K) (L) (M) 10. (J) (K) (L) (M)

Part 2

11. (A) (B) (C) (D) 15. (A) (B) (C) (D) 19. (A) (B) (C) (D) 23. (A) (B) (C) (D) 27. (A) (B) (C) (D)
12. (J) (K) (L) (M) 16. (J) (K) (L) (M) 20. (J) (K) (L) (M) 24. (J) (K) (L) (M) 28. (J) (K) (L) (M)
13. (A) (B) (C) (D) 17. (A) (B) (C) (D) 21. (A) (B) (C) (D) 25. (A) (B) (C) (D) 29. (A) (B) (C) (D)
14. (J) (K) (L) (M) 18. (J) (K) (L) (M) 22. (J) (K) (L) (M) 26. (J) (K) (L) (M) 30. (J) (K) (L) (M)

Language Section

Part 1

1. (A) (B) (C) (D)   9. (A) (B) (C) (D)   17. (A) (B) (C) (D)   25. (A) (B) (C) (D)   33. (A) (B) (C) (D)
2. (J) (K) (L) (M)   10. (J) (K) (L) (M)   18. (J) (K) (L) (M)   26. (J) (K) (L) (M)   34. (J) (K) (L) (M)
3. (A) (B) (C) (D)   11. (A) (B) (C) (D)   19. (A) (B) (C) (D)   27. (A) (B) (C) (D)   35. (A) (B) (C) (D)
4. (J) (K) (L) (M)   12. (J) (K) (L) (M)   20. (J) (K) (L) (M)   28. (J) (K) (L) (M)   36. (J) (K) (L) (M)
5. (A) (B) (C) (D)   13. (A) (B) (C) (D)   21. (A) (B) (C) (D)   29. (A) (B) (C) (D)   37. (A) (B) (C) (D)
6. (J) (K) (L) (M)   14. (J) (K) (L) (M)   22. (J) (K) (L) (M)   30. (J) (K) (L) (M)   38. (J) (K) (L) (M)
7. (A) (B) (C) (D)   15. (A) (B) (C) (D)   23. (A) (B) (C) (D)   31. (A) (B) (C) (D)   39. (A) (B) (C) (D)
8. (J) (K) (L) (M)   16. (J) (K) (L) (M)   24. (J) (K) (L) (M)   32. (J) (K) (L) (M)   40. (J) (K) (L) (M)

Part 2

41. (A) (B) (C) (D) 43. (A) (B) (C) (D) 45. (A) (B) (C) (D) 47. (A) (B) (C) (D) 49. (A) (B) (C) (D)
42. (J) (K) (L) (M) 44. (J) (K) (L) (M) 46. (J) (K) (L) (M) 48. (J) (K) (L) (M) 50. (J) (K) (L) (M)

Math Section

Part 1

1. Ⓐ Ⓑ Ⓒ Ⓓ
2. Ⓙ Ⓚ Ⓛ Ⓜ
3. Ⓐ Ⓑ Ⓒ Ⓓ
4. Ⓙ Ⓚ Ⓛ Ⓜ
5. Ⓐ Ⓑ Ⓒ Ⓓ
6. Ⓙ Ⓚ Ⓛ Ⓜ
7. Ⓐ Ⓑ Ⓒ Ⓓ

8. Ⓙ Ⓚ Ⓛ Ⓜ
9. Ⓐ Ⓑ Ⓒ Ⓓ
10. Ⓙ Ⓚ Ⓛ Ⓜ
11. Ⓐ Ⓑ Ⓒ Ⓓ
12. Ⓙ Ⓚ Ⓛ Ⓜ
13. Ⓐ Ⓑ Ⓒ Ⓓ
14. Ⓙ Ⓚ Ⓛ Ⓜ

15. Ⓐ Ⓑ Ⓒ Ⓓ
16. Ⓙ Ⓚ Ⓛ Ⓜ
17. Ⓐ Ⓑ Ⓒ Ⓓ
18. Ⓙ Ⓚ Ⓛ Ⓜ
19. Ⓐ Ⓑ Ⓒ Ⓓ
20. Ⓙ Ⓚ Ⓛ Ⓜ
21. Ⓐ Ⓑ Ⓒ Ⓓ

22. Ⓙ Ⓚ Ⓛ Ⓜ
23. Ⓐ Ⓑ Ⓒ Ⓓ
24. Ⓙ Ⓚ Ⓛ Ⓜ
25. Ⓐ Ⓑ Ⓒ Ⓓ
26. Ⓙ Ⓚ Ⓛ Ⓜ
27. Ⓐ Ⓑ Ⓒ Ⓓ
28. Ⓙ Ⓚ Ⓛ Ⓜ

29. Ⓐ Ⓑ Ⓒ Ⓓ
30. Ⓙ Ⓚ Ⓛ Ⓜ
31. Ⓐ Ⓑ Ⓒ Ⓓ
32. Ⓙ Ⓚ Ⓛ Ⓜ

Part 2

33. Ⓐ Ⓑ Ⓒ Ⓓ
34. Ⓙ Ⓚ Ⓛ Ⓜ
35. Ⓐ Ⓑ Ⓒ Ⓓ
36. Ⓙ Ⓚ Ⓛ Ⓜ

37. Ⓐ Ⓑ Ⓒ Ⓓ
38. Ⓙ Ⓚ Ⓛ Ⓜ
39. Ⓐ Ⓑ Ⓒ Ⓓ
40. Ⓙ Ⓚ Ⓛ Ⓜ

41. Ⓐ Ⓑ Ⓒ Ⓓ
42. Ⓙ Ⓚ Ⓛ Ⓜ
43. Ⓐ Ⓑ Ⓒ Ⓓ
44. Ⓙ Ⓚ Ⓛ Ⓜ

45. Ⓐ Ⓑ Ⓒ Ⓓ
46. Ⓙ Ⓚ Ⓛ Ⓜ
47. Ⓐ Ⓑ Ⓒ Ⓓ
48. Ⓙ Ⓚ Ⓛ Ⓜ

49. Ⓐ Ⓑ Ⓒ Ⓓ
50. Ⓙ Ⓚ Ⓛ Ⓜ

Ability Section

1. Ⓐ Ⓑ Ⓒ Ⓓ Ⓔ
2. Ⓙ Ⓚ Ⓛ Ⓜ Ⓝ
3. Ⓐ Ⓑ Ⓒ Ⓓ Ⓔ
4. Ⓙ Ⓚ Ⓛ Ⓜ Ⓝ

5. Ⓐ Ⓑ Ⓒ Ⓓ Ⓔ
6. Ⓙ Ⓚ Ⓛ Ⓜ Ⓝ
7. Ⓐ Ⓑ Ⓒ Ⓓ Ⓔ
8. Ⓙ Ⓚ Ⓛ Ⓜ Ⓝ

9. Ⓐ Ⓑ Ⓒ Ⓓ Ⓔ
10. Ⓙ Ⓚ Ⓛ Ⓜ Ⓝ
11. Ⓐ Ⓑ Ⓒ Ⓓ Ⓔ
12. Ⓙ Ⓚ Ⓛ Ⓜ Ⓝ

13. Ⓐ Ⓑ Ⓒ Ⓓ Ⓔ
14. Ⓙ Ⓚ Ⓛ Ⓜ Ⓝ
15. Ⓐ Ⓑ Ⓒ Ⓓ Ⓔ
16. Ⓙ Ⓚ Ⓛ Ⓜ Ⓝ

17. Ⓐ Ⓑ Ⓒ Ⓓ Ⓔ
18. Ⓙ Ⓚ Ⓛ Ⓜ Ⓝ
19. Ⓐ Ⓑ Ⓒ Ⓓ Ⓔ
20. Ⓙ Ⓚ Ⓛ Ⓜ Ⓝ

Reading Section

Part 1

Time: 5 minutes

Directions: Questions 1–10 contain an underlined word. Find the answer choice that has the most similar meaning to the underlined word. Mark the answer sheet by filling in the bubble that corresponds with your choice.

1. a <u>dejected</u> spirit
   - (A) cheerful
   - (B) supportive
   - (C) awkward
   - (D) gloomy

2. an <u>onerous</u> task
   - (J) effortless
   - (K) important
   - (L) arduous
   - (M) confusing

3. to <u>brood</u> about a problem
   - (A) fret
   - (B) console
   - (C) communicate
   - (D) gossip

4. high <u>aspirations</u>
   - (J) hopes
   - (K) ascents
   - (L) views
   - (M) dives

5. to rejoice <u>heartily</u>
   - (A) softly
   - (B) angrily
   - (C) wholeheartedly
   - (D) sympathetically

6. <u>reckless</u> actions
   - (J) irresponsible
   - (K) exciting
   - (L) cautious
   - (M) deliberate

7. to <u>squander</u> money
   - (A) hoard
   - (B) conserve
   - (C) waste
   - (D) worship

8. <u>amicable</u> agreements
   - (J) solid
   - (K) flimsy
   - (L) official
   - (M) friendly

9. to <u>foresee</u> a conflict
   - (A) create
   - (B) anticipate
   - (C) break up
   - (D) reconcile

10. to seek <u>serenity</u>
   - (J) activity
   - (K) gratification
   - (L) tranquility
   - (M) success

Go on to next page

Part 2

Time: 25 minutes

Directions: The following four selections ask questions that pertain to their respective content. Choose the best answer for each of the questions and mark it on the answer sheet.

Questions 11–14 pertain to the following passage.

The present level of sugar consumption in America is a historically new phenomenon that rivals the increasing rise in drug dependency in our society. In 1821, Americans annually consumed an average of 10 pounds of sugar per person. In the years since then, annual per person sugar consumption has risen at least thirteen-fold, reaching 126 pounds in 2006, the last full year for which data is available. In fact, the 2006 figure reveals an increase of 13 percent just since 1990, when the corresponding figure was 111.2 pounds. The Department of Agriculture's estimate for 2009 was that annual <u>per capita</u> consumption of sugar rose another 2 pounds since 2006 to a new high of 128.1 pounds. At this rate, Americans presently consume in excess of 130 pounds of sugar per person annually.

These figures may sound implausible to anyone who still thinks of sugar as a commodity that is bought in bags at the grocery store and then added to foods in one's own home. As recently as 1920, 65 percent of the sugar used in this country was consumed in that fashion. But by 1976, only 24 percent of the sugar consumed in the country was sold for home use. Over 70 percent of it went into manufactured or processed foods and beverages. Added sugar now appears in a wide range of foods not commonly thought of as being sweet or sweetened, such as bouillon cubes, frozen vegetables, and bologna.

11. The passage mainly deals with

   (A) the types of processed foods, like frozen vegetables and bologna, that contain sugar

   (B) the Department of Agriculture's estimates of food consumption

   (C) how much sugar consumption has risen in the United States over the past years

   (D) how sugar is sold at the grocery store

12. What is true according to the passage?

   (J) Sugar consumption is as bad for you as drug dependency.

   (K) Americans are consuming more sugar in processed foods than they used to.

   (L) Grocery stores have stopped selling sugar in bags for home use.

   (M) You can tell which processed foods have sugar in them by how sweet they taste.

13. <u>Per capita</u> consumption refers to

   (A) consumption per person

   (B) consumption per country

   (C) consumption per state capital city

   (D) consumption per year

14. The author's attitude toward sugar consumption in America seems to be

   (J) optimistic

   (K) indifferent

   (L) accepting

   (M) concerned

Go on to next page

Questions 15–18 pertain to the following passage.

Persons accused of crimes have an absolute right to be tried by a jury of their peers, and parties to a civil lawsuit may choose to have their cases decided by a jury. In the end, though, it's the judge who decides the fate of the accused and the verdict in a civil dispute. Judges have numerous tools at their disposal to reverse the decisions of juries.

To begin with, in most states, the jury's decision to convict someone of a crime must be unanimous. If the jury has reasonable doubt to believe that the accused committed the crime, then the jury must acquit, which means it finds the accused not guilty of the alleged charges. But no matter what the jury's decision, the judge can overrule the verdict by granting the losing party's motion for judgment notwithstanding the verdict, which essentially throws out the jury's decision. Or the judge can exercise discretion in giving out a sentence.

The judge's omnipotence rules in civil cases, too. The judge can decide that a jury's award to a plaintiff is either too high or too low and decrease it by granting the defendant's motion for remittitur or increase it by granting the plaintiff's motion for additur.

15. Which of the following is *not* a judicial tool that the author says judges use to change jury decisions?

(A) remittitur

(B) additur

(C) omnipotence

(D) motion for judgment notwithstanding the verdict

16. The author's purpose in writing this passage is to

(J) thoroughly explain the elements of the American jury system

(K) confirm that the American jury system is the fairest system in the world

(L) prove that the jury system should be abolished

(M) show that judges have the power to overturn decisions made by juries

17. According to the passage, which of the following is true about persons accused of crimes?

(A) They have the right to a jury trial.

(B) They have no right to a jury trial.

(C) They must file a motion of additur.

(D) They must file a motion of remittitur.

18. Which of the following statements would the author most likely agree with?

(J) Judges should always reverse the decisions of juries.

(K) Judges have more power than juries do.

(L) Juries have the power to reverse a judge's decision.

(M) Judges should grant every motion for judgment notwithstanding the verdict.

Go on to next page

> *Questions 19–21 pertain to the following poem, "Stars" by Robert Frost.*

How countlessly <u>they</u> congregate
O'er our tumultuous snow,
Which flows in shapes as tall as trees
When wintry winds do blow!

As if with keenness for our fate,
Our faltering few steps on
To white rest, and a place of rest
Invisible at dawn,

And yet with neither love nor hate,
Those stars like some snow-white
Minerva's snow-white marble eyes
Without the gift of sight.

19. <u>They</u> in the first line refers to what?

   (A) stars

   (B) snowflakes

   (C) trees

   (D) people

20. The poet presents what simile in the last stanza?

   (J) Trees are like wintry winds.

   (K) Stars are like eyes that do not see.

   (L) Minerva is like a gift.

   (M) Stars are like snow.

21. What rhyming scheme does the poet apply in this poem?

   (A) He rhymes the last words of the first and third lines of each stanza.

   (B) He rhymes the last words of the first lines of each stanza.

   (C) The only words that rhyme are the last words of the second and fourth lines in each stanza.

   (D) The poem has no rhyming scheme.

Go on to next page

Questions 22–26 pertain to the following passage.

One important facet of colonial America's early development was the role played by slave artisans from Africa. Slave art rose from slavery as a skilled handicraft, an art that descended from African imagery and later became a functional aesthetic in the form of wrought-iron balconies in New Orleans and magnificent ornamentation on the mansions of Charleston, South Carolina. Although they received little credit for their labor, slave artisans accomplished necessary work in preindustrial America and became one of the first classes of technical experts in the New World.

Afro-American arts and crafts originated on the west coast of Africa. Many Africans were master artisans, demonstrating various skills and great proficiency in the fashioning of ivory, wood, and bone in weaving, pottery making, and the creation of clothes, tools, and other implements. There is also strong evidence that some African groups were skilled in the building trades, while others proved skillful in developing exquisite sculptured objects of bronze through new casting techniques.

As producers of goods, contributors to the building trades, manufacturers of furniture, and designers of household objects and décor, slave artisans also aided America in its aesthetic development. Their creativity and cleverness laid the foundation for furthering the development of the African American artist.

22. The author's primary concern is to
(J) describe the slave artisans' response to the limited opportunities for creative expression in colonial America
(K) show how the specific talents of slave artisans in the areas of decoration and design contributed to the aesthetic of colonial America
(L) note that contemporary African American art emerged from the work of slave artisans
(M) praise the long history of the artistic tradition of Africa

23. Slave artisans were important to colonial America because they
(A) helped meet the needs of its preindustrial society
(B) persuaded the colonists to diversify in farming and industry
(C) recognized the need for new and more complex manufacturing procedures
(D) taught other slaves skills to give them greater freedom

24. Which of the following is an example of the contribution of slave artisans in colonial America?
(J) metal balconies
(K) bronze tools
(L) weavings with bone detail
(M) clothes with wooden buttons

25. The author would most likely agree that slave artisans
(A) were well-respected
(B) were rewarded for their contributions to colonial America
(C) created primarily manufactured goods
(D) received little recognition from the local community

26. The skilled handicrafts of slave artisans were most likely influenced by
(J) builders of mansions in South Carolina
(K) artisans from the west coast of Africa
(L) modern African American artists
(M) colonial American aristocrats

Go on to next page

Questions 27–30 pertain to the following passage.

It's seven in the morning, and I reach over to hit the snooze button on my alarm clock for the last time. Climbing out of bed, I turn on the TV to see that an early episode of a popular sitcom is on. I doodle around and put myself together while periodically glancing at the TV and laughing. On the elevator, I make small talk with some of my friends who live on the floor above. Getting on the bus, I sit next to the girl from my Spanish class, and we talk about our weekend. When I finally get to class, the teacher starts to lecture . . . another boring Monday. This seems like a normal Monday morning, right? For a blue-eyed white girl like me, it is. At no point in the morning do I notice that all the main characters in the popular sitcom are white. I never feel out of place on the elevator because everyone I come in contact with looks like me. I do not think twice about talking to my friend from class on the bus because I am afraid of her judging me. My teacher does not <u>intimidate</u> me because of his skin color. These are just some examples of white privilege that I experience living in America, and it is not yet eight in the morning.

27. The author's objective in this passage is to

   (A) explain a typical morning in her life

   (B) compare the teaching styles of her teachers

   (C) demonstrate how early she has to wake up in the morning

   (D) show some of the advantages she has because of her race

28. Based on information in the passage, which of the following is most likely true about the author?

   (J) She almost missed the bus because she "doodled" around before school.

   (K) She rides the bus to get to school.

   (L) She is completely unaware of the privileges she has.

   (M) She has blond hair.

29. The word <u>intimidate</u> as it is used in the passage most nearly means

   (A) banish

   (B) frighten

   (C) indulge

   (D) analyze

30. This passage is most likely

   (J) a response to an assignment on the existence of racial privilege in America

   (K) an article in a professional trade magazine that reports statistics on racial discrimination

   (L) a letter written to a close friend who has recently moved far away

   (M) an e-mail to a potential employer who wants the author to provide information about why she would be a good employee

STOP DO NOT TURN THE PAGE UNTIL TOLD TO DO SO. DO NOT RETURN TO A PREVIOUS TEST.

Language Section

Part 1

Time: 20 minutes

Directions: This section tests how well you recognize usage, mechanics, capitalization, punctuation, and spelling errors in writing. Each of the following 40 questions contains three parts of a complete sentence. Pick the answer choice that corresponds with the part of the sentence that contains an error. If none of the sentence parts has an error, pick the last answer choice. Mark your answer on the answer sheet.

Check for usage and mechanics errors in Questions 1–10.

1. (A) The human resources department's recent report
    (B) reveals that it hopes to gain support for
    (C) their new policy on employee uniforms.
    (D) *(No mistakes)*

2. (J) The student's essay
    (K) borrowed heavy from
    (L) the magazine article in the library.
    (M) *(No mistakes)*

3. (A) The team played the basketball game
    (B) aggressively, emotionally,
    (C) and reckless.
    (D) *(No mistakes)*

4. (J) Matters are clearer now
    (K) than they were back in June
    (L) when the summer had just begun.
    (M) *(No mistakes)*

5. (A) Jane had a hard time choosing between
    (B) a pink flamingo, picnic table, chaise lounge, and
    (C) bird bath for her parents' anniversary gift.
    (D) *(No mistakes)*

6. (J) As the fighting in the Middle East escalates,
    (K) so do the cost of basic staples,
    (L) like bread, milk, and meat.
    (M) *(No mistakes)*

7. (A) In his biography of the life
    (B) of the well-known comic, George
    (C) revealed the comic's personality quite well.
    (D) *(No mistakes)*

8. (J) Finding a job is getting so difficult
    (K) that one empathizes with those
    (L) which are unemployed.
    (M) *(No mistakes)*

9. (A) When Leon received a score of 32 on the ACT,
    (B) he knew that he would be excepted
    (C) at almost any college that he wanted to attend.
    (D) *(No mistakes)*

10. (J) The debate team suffered its first loss ever
    (K) when it faced its rival, the Cougars, in the
    (L) annual city debate event last January.
    (M) *(No mistakes)*

Go on to next page

Check for capitalization errors in Questions 11–20.

11. (A) My Uncle is the
    (B) chairman of a large corporation
    (C) called the ABC Company.
    (D) *(No mistakes)*

12. (J) Professor Stone has been
    (K) teaching at Colgate university
    (L) for almost three decades.
    (M) *(No mistakes)*

13. (A) Steve read his favorite book,
    (B) *The Red Badge of Courage,*
    (C) three times this summer.
    (D) *(No mistakes)*

14. (J) The Jensen family
    (K) travels East to New York to visit
    (L) relatives every Christmas.
    (M) *(No mistakes)*

15. (A) The Marshall County Fair
    (B) is the largest fair north of the
    (C) Walden river.
    (D) *(No mistakes)*

16. (J) Percy Graves, md, is
    (K) the finest surgeon
    (L) at Stevens Point General Hospital.
    (M) *(No mistakes)*

17. (A) Mandy Esteves shouted to me
    (B) from across the street, "where is
    (C) the entrance to the bookstore?"
    (D) *(No mistakes)*

18. (J) Every Halloween my
    (K) mother, father, sister, brother,
    (L) and I sing several pumpkin carols
       around the fireplace.
    (M) *(No mistakes)*

19. (A) Ms. Anderson is my English teacher,
    (B) but she also teaches spanish
    (C) and history at our school.
    (D) *(No mistakes)*

20. (J) Timothy mouse is just one
    (K) of many mouse characters
    (L) in a group of recent animated movies.
    (M) *(No mistakes)*

Check for punctuation errors in Questions 21–30.

21. (A) Jennifer is really smart; she
    (B) received a grade of 95
    (C) on her last math test.
    (D) *(No mistakes)*

22. (J) My YMCA membership
    (K) will expire tomorrow,
    (L) if I do not renew it.
    (M) *(No mistakes)*

23. (A) Mike went to the store and
    (B) bought: apples, cherries,
    (C) plums, and marshmallows.
    (D) *(No mistakes)*

24. (J) When Jacob comes home. We
    (K) will have a party and
    (L) invite the neighbors.
    (M) *(No mistakes)*

25. (A) Sammie has studied art for seven
    (B) months and now she is ready
    (C) to enter one of her works in the county
       fair.
    (D) *(No mistakes)*

26. (J) I proposed this plan for
    (K) example, because I am interested
    (L) in helping the environment.
    (M) *(No mistakes)*

Go on to next page

27. (A) I used everything I could find,

    (B) like tape, glue, tacks,

    (C) etc to get the poster to stick to the wall.

    (D) *(No mistakes)*

28. (J) The payment is due before

    (K) the end of the month, but you should

    (L) send it in by May, 25, 2010.

    (M) *(No mistakes)*

29. (A) Angel walked past the public

    (B) library, which is on Third Street,

    (C) on his way to the grocery store.

    (D) *(No mistakes)*

30. (J) No one knew why Des Moines,

    (K) Iowa was not included

    (L) on the list of best cities.

    (M) *(No mistakes)*

Check for spelling errors in Questions 31–40.

31. (A) It is important to study

    (B) commonly mispelled words

    (C) to excel on the TACHS.

    (D) *(No mistakes)*

32. (J) The calender on John's

    (K) desk is neither from this

    (L) year nor last.

    (M) *(No mistakes)*

33. (A) It's true that the puppy

    (B) spent hours and hours

    (C) chasing it's tail.

    (D) *(No mistakes)*

34. (J) Charlie was greatful

    (K) that his summer internship included

    (L) travel to foreign countries.

    (M) *(No mistakes)*

35. (A) The new soldiers had

    (B) to register their belongings

    (C) before they reported to the kernel.

    (D) *(No mistakes)*

36. (J) The principal opened up

    (K) the assembly with an admonition

    (L) to obey the school rules.

    (M) *(No mistakes)*

37. (A) Drums preceed horns

    (B) in the marching band procession

    (C) to the football field.

    (D) *(No mistakes)*

38. (J) Students must pass a

    (K) particular number of classes

    (L) before they can recieve diplomas.

    (M) *(No mistakes)*

39. (A) Jackie and Sheila tried to

    (B) separate the dark and white items

    (C) before they did thier wash.

    (D) *(No mistakes)*

40. (J) We've had better weather

    (K) than we've had in

    (L) over ten years.

    (M) *(No mistakes)*

Go on to next page

Part 2

> **Time:** 10 minutes
>
> **Directions:** For Questions 41–50, choose the best answer based on the paragraphs.

> *Questions 41 and 42 pertain to the following paragraph.*

(1)Ethics come into play almost every day in a <u>lawyers</u> working life. (2)Making moral decisions and then acting on them <u>basically</u> is an everyday occurrence for a lawyer. (3)The code states that lawyers are not only responsible for themselves but also for the actions of their associates. (4)This is why lawyers have a difficult time choosing cases. (5)Some lawyers might choose a case that they do not morally agree with. (6)Whether ethical decisions come into play when defending a client or picking and choosing cases, lawyers are faced with this dilemma every day.

41. What is the best way to write the underlined word in Sentence 1?

    (A) lawyers'

    (B) lawyer's

    (C) lawyer

    (D) *(No change)*

42. Where is the best place for <u>basically</u> in Sentence 2?

    (J) It should come after *an*.

    (K) It should come after *lawyer*.

    (L) It should be eliminated from the sentence.

    (M) It should stay where it is.

> *Questions 43 and 44 pertain to the following paragraph.*

(1)*The Burial of Conde Orgaz* by El Greco uses the burial of an esteemed and religious Spanish count as a means of portraying the relationship between the heavens and the earth. (2)The brilliantly colored oil-on-canvas painting, measuring 16 feet high and almost 12 feet wide, adorns one wall of the Church of San Tome in Toledo. (3)The painting contains two main settings. (4)The lower scene depicts an ornately robed Saint Stephen and Saint Augustine gently lowering the armored body of Conde Orgaz into an unseen grave. (5)Surrounding the saints is a group of clergy and noblemen in varying states of worship and mourning. (6)Above this scene hovers the inhabitants of heaven.

43. What is the best way to begin Sentence 5?

    (A) However,

    (B) Therefore,

    (C) Nevertheless,

    (D) *(No change)*

44. Which word in Sentence 6 is incorrect?

    (J) Above

    (K) hovers

    (L) heaven

    (M) *(No incorrect words)*

Go on to next page

Questions 45–47 pertain to the following paragraph.

(1)As a child I read every night before going to sleep, and *Little Women* remains in my memory as the novel that most captured my heart. (2)I became caught up in the lives of the four March girls, and, like Laurie, dreamed that I could join their club. (3)I settled for membership through the expressive storytelling of Louisa May Alcott. (4)Robin Swicord's adaptation for the screen of this enduring novel quickly swept me into their world once again. (5)The screenplay provides a delicious rendering of the essence of Alcott's novel without declining into moral discourse or a bland presentation. (6)Highlighting the character of each girl, <u>the strength of women and importance of family is emphasized by Swicord.</u>

45. Which of the commas in Sentence 2 should be eliminated?

    (A) the comma after *girls*

    (B) the comma after *and*

    (C) the comma after *Laurie*

    (D) *(None)*

46. Which word in Sentence 4 is an adverb?

    (J) swept

    (K) quickly

    (L) enduring

    (M) world

47. What is the best way to write the underlined part of Sentence 6?

    (A) the strength and importance of women and family is emphasized by Swicord.

    (B) Swicord emphasizes the strength of women and the importance of family.

    (C) the strength of women and importance of family are emphasized by Swicord.

    (D) *(No change)*

Questions 48–50 pertain to the following paragraph.

(1)Philosophy is the desire to seek knowledge, gain insight, and improve judgment. (2)Socrates, one of the greatest Philosophers, contended that the beginning of wisdom comes from self-knowledge. (3)His belief has transcended the ages: "The unexamined life is not worth living." (4)Knowledge, insight, and judgment results from careful scrutiny of our beliefs in all issues. (5)How we perceive ourselves determines how we perceive the world, decide what is true, and act as a result. (6)Philosophy peels away at the layers of preconceived notions and assumptions to reach the core of human understanding. (7)Exposing our beliefs about core issues reveals the basis of our notions of truth.

48. Which word in Sentence 4 is incorrect?

    (J) judgment

    (K) results

    (L) scrutiny

    (M) beliefs

49. Which sentence contains a capitalization error?

    (A) Sentence 2

    (B) Sentence 3

    (C) Sentence 5

    (D) Sentence 6

50. Which is true about Sentence 5?

    (J) It contains an error in parallel structure.

    (K) It contains a punctuation error.

    (L) It is a run-on sentence.

    (M) It contains no error.

STOP DO NOT TURN THE PAGE UNTIL TOLD TO DO SO. DO NOT RETURN TO A PREVIOUS TEST.

Math Section

Part 1

Time: 35 minutes

Directions: For Questions 1–20, choose the best answer from the four choices and mark it on your answer sheet.

1. Which of the following is a prime number?
   (A) 37
   (B) 22
   (C) 35
   (D) 63

2. $\frac{1}{2} \div \frac{3}{4}$ is equal to _____?
   (J) $\frac{3}{8}$
   (K) $\frac{2}{3}$
   (L) $\frac{1}{3}$
   (M) $\frac{3}{2}$

3. 1.3 written as a fraction is _____?
   (A) $1\frac{3}{10}$
   (B) $1\frac{3}{100}$
   (C) $3\frac{1}{10}$
   (D) $\frac{1}{30}$

4. Bryan uses 6 pieces of cloth to make 1 hat. If he already has 10 pieces of cloth, how many more pieces of cloth will he need to make 5 hats?
   (J) 5
   (K) 20
   (L) 15
   (M) 10

5. The least common denominator of $\frac{1}{2}$, $\frac{5}{8}$, and $\frac{3}{4}$ is _____?
   (A) 8
   (B) 12
   (C) 16
   (D) 24

6. 35% =
   (J) $\frac{1}{5}$
   (K) $\frac{2}{5}$
   (L) $\frac{3}{20}$
   (M) $\frac{7}{20}$

7. A sports store needs to hang up 138 jerseys for display. If each hanger holds 6 jerseys, how many hangers are needed to hang up all the jerseys?
   (A) 12
   (B) 16
   (C) 20
   (D) 23

8. 14^2 =
   (J) 28
   (K) 70
   (L) 196
   (M) 182

9. Joe earned $60 waiting tables at a restaurant one night. If $10 of his total is tip, what is Joe's hourly wage if he worked 5 hours?
   (A) $10
   (B) $12
   (C) $13
   (D) $14

10. What is the greatest common factor of 14 and 21?
    (J) 3
    (K) 4
    (L) 7
    (M) 21

Go on to next page

11. The decimal equivalent of ⅜ is _____?

    (A) 0.3

    (B) 0.375

    (C) 2.66

    (D) 0.4

12. 1– (–6) =

    (J) 7

    (K) 5

    (L) –7

    (M) –5

13. Jessica decided to try a new route to work that John told her was a shortcut. The new route is 4.38 miles shorter than if she took the normal route. If the distance to her work is 19.75 miles using the shortcut, how far is it to work if she doesn't use the shortcut?

    (A) 4.38 miles

    (B) 10.5 miles

    (C) 15.37 miles

    (D) 24.13 miles

14. Becca's parents make her save 20% of her allowance each month. If Becca saves $10.50 one month, how much was Becca's total allowance for the month?

    (J) $35.75

    (K) $42.00

    (L) $52.50

    (M) $63.00

15. 0.0000035 written in scientific notation is _____?

    (A) 3.5×10^6

    (B) 3.5×10^{-4}

    (C) 3.5×10^4

    (D) 3.5×10^{-6}

16. Zach bought two cases of soda at the store. One case cost $6.95, and the other did not have a price on it. If the total cost was $15.50, how much did the second case cost? (Assume there was no sales tax.)

    (J) $6.95

    (K) $8.00

    (L) $8.55

    (M) $22.45

17. Stacey puts ¼ of every paycheck she gets into savings and uses the rest to fix up her car. If she earns $40 this paycheck, how much of the paycheck does she have to use on her car?

    (A) $30

    (B) $35

    (C) $40

    (D) $50

18. A local jewelry store is having a sale where everything is 40% off. How much would a necklace cost if the original price is $85?

    (J) $34

    (K) $40

    (L) $50

    (M) $51

19. If candy sells for $1.75 a pound, how much does 3.4 pounds cost?

    (A) $3.00

    (B) $4.20

    (C) $5.95

    (D) $6.25

20. Amy worked 120 math problems between the hours of 3 p.m. and 7 p.m. If it takes her the same amount of time to do each problem, how many problems does she do per hour?

    (J) 45

    (K) 25

    (L) 40

    (M) 30

Go on to next page

Directions: Answer Questions 21–32 based on the corresponding graph or chart and mark your answers on the answer sheet.

Use the following chart to answer Questions 21 and 22.

Burrito Menu			
Burrito Type	**Half**	**Full**	**Extra Ingredients, add $0.65 ea.**
Chicken	$4.35	$6.25	Guacamole
Steak	$4.55	$6.45	Sour cream
Pork	$4.65	$6.85	Queso dip

21. According to the menu chart, how much does a full chicken burrito with guacamole and sour cream cost?

    (A) $5.65

    (B) $6.90

    (C) $7.55

    (D) $8.20

22. Given the information in the menu chart, how much does it cost to purchase a half pork burrito with extra queso dip?

    (J) $4.65

    (K) $5.30

    (L) $5.95

    (M) $6.00

23. The following chart records the amount of sales made in one day by four employees of a large department store. How much more in sales did Alan make than Diane?

Total Sales for Tuesday by Employee

    (A) $1,000

    (B) $1,500

    (C) $2,000

    (D) $2,500

Go on to next page

24. Over the course of a season, three hockey teams (1, 2, and 3) kept track of how many goals were scored per month. Which month was the only month where Team 1 outscored Team 3?

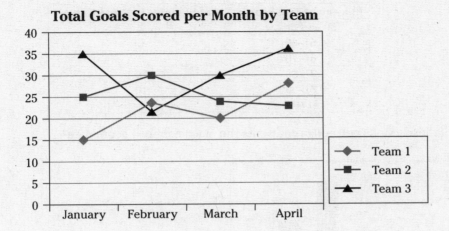

Total Goals Scored per Month by Team

(J) January

(K) February

(L) March

(M) April

25. John, Dan, Mike, and Jill pooled their money together to buy raffle tickets. They all agreed that if they won the raffle, they would split the prize money up among themselves as shown in the following chart. What fraction of the prize money would John and Jill keep if John and Jill combined their percentages?

Raffle Participant	Fraction of Total Prize Money to Be Received
John	0.11
Dawn	0.60
Mike	0.15
Jill	0.14

(A) ¾

(B) ½

(C) ¹⁷⁄₂₀

(D) ¼

Go on to next page

26. Fifty students took a placement test to determine which math class they should take the following semester. The distribution of the placement test scores appears in this chart.

Placement Test Scores	# of Students in Score Range
50 and below	2
51–60	5
61–70	8
71–80	20
81–90	10
91–100	5

Which of these graphs correctly represents the placement test score data?

(J)

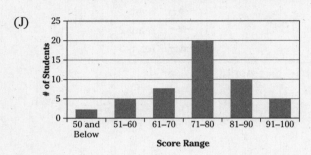

(K)

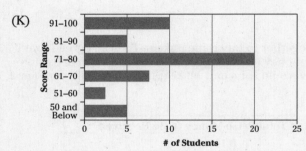

(L)

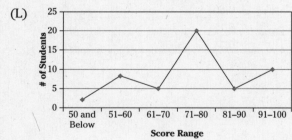

(M)

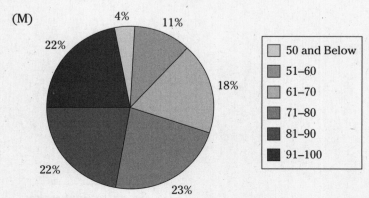

Go on to next page

27. Percentages of students in different age groups at several high schools are shown in the following stacked bar graph. Which two schools have the largest percentage of students in the 19+ age group?

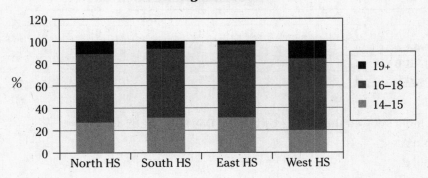

Percentage Age Distribution at Area High Schools

(A) South and East

(B) North and West

(C) East and West

(D) North and East

28. Using the following chart, Jennifer kept track of how many home runs she hit per month in her softball league.

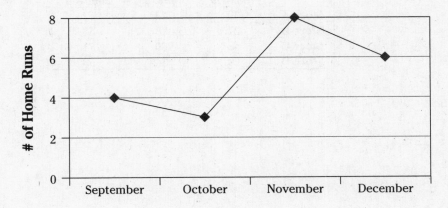

How many more home runs did she hit in November than October?

(J) 2

(K) 3

(L) 4

(M) 5

Go on to next page

29. Scott wanted to see how water affected mold growth on a rotting apple over a nine-day period. He used three separate rotting apples. He did not spray the mold on Apple A. He sprayed the mold on Apple B with a small amount of water. He sprayed the mold on Apple C with large amounts of water. The following table displays his findings.

Growth of Diameter in Centimeters								
Day								
1	**2**	**3**	**4**	**5**	**6**	**7**	**8**	**9**
Mold A 1	1	1	2	2	3	4	5	6
Mold B 1	2	2	3	5	5	7	8	9
Mold C 1	2	4	5	7	8	10	12	14

Which mold showed the most growth from Day 6 to Day 8?

(A) Mold A

(B) Mold B

(C) Mold C

(D) Not enough information

30. According to the following table, how many more employees did Store C have than Store B between 1980 and 1989?

Number of Employees by Decade 1980–2009			
	1980–89	**1990–99**	**2000–09**
Store A	30	44	62
Store B	27	38	55
Store C	48	60	71
Store D	20	34	53

(J) 10

(K) 21

(L) 16

(M) 22

31. The following graph shows test scores for the first two math tests of several students in an Algebra II course. Which two students did better on the second test than they did on the first?

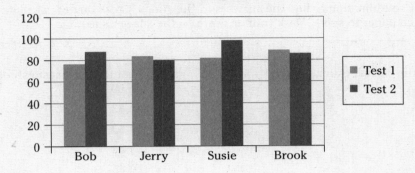

Test Scores for Algebra II

(A) Bob and Susie

(B) Jerry and Brook

(C) Bob and Jerry

(D) Brook and Susie

32. Three branches of an international office supply company are competing to see which branch can bring in the most revenue in a three-month period. Based on the information found in this chart, how much more revenue did the Appleton branch take in than did the Brockton and Carelton branches combined?

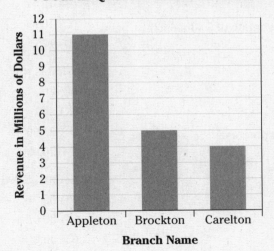

Fourth Quarter Branch Revenues

(J) $1,000,000

(K) $2,000,000

(L) $3,000,000

(M) $4,000,000

Go on to next page

Part 2

Time: 10 minutes

Directions: Use estimation to find the answers to Questions 33–50. Do not calculate exact answers or use scratch paper to solve. Mark your answers on the answer sheet.

33. What is the closest estimate of 561 + 420?
    (A) 900
    (B) 1,000
    (C) 1,100
    (D) 1,200

34. What is the closest estimate of 723 ÷ 9?
    (J) 8
    (K) 80
    (L) 800
    (M) 8,000

35. What is the closest estimate of 31 + 34 + 42?
    (A) 90
    (B) 95
    (C) 100
    (D) 110

36. What is the closest estimate of 5.43 × 6.52?
    (J) 35
    (K) 30
    (L) 36
    (M) 40

37. What is the closest estimate of
    26,828 − 20,420?
    (A) 7,000
    (B) 6,000
    (C) 5,000
    (D) 4,000

38. 5.543 rounded to the nearest tenths place
    is _____?
    (J) 4
    (K) 4.5
    (L) 5.5
    (M) 6

39. What is the closest estimate of
    $15.00 − $12.38?
    (A) $2
    (B) $3
    (C) $4
    (D) $5

40. $4.73 + $3.43 + $5.34 rounded to the nearest
    dollar is _____?
    (J) $10
    (K) $11
    (L) $12
    (M) $13

41. What is the closest estimate of
    (592 + 933) ÷ 30?
    (A) 50
    (B) 75
    (C) 100
    (D) 125

42. What is the closest estimate of 49 × 42?
    (J) 20
    (K) 200
    (L) 2,000
    (M) 20,000

43. Round 35.008 to the nearest tenths place.
    (A) 35.01
    (B) 35.0
    (C) 40.0
    (D) 35.1

Go on to next page

44. What is the closest estimate of 6,434 − 3,942?

    (J) 2,000

    (K) 3,000

    (L) 4,000

    (M) 5,000

45. What is the closest estimate of 34,544 ÷ 7?

    (A) 5

    (B) 50

    (C) 500

    (D) 5,000

46. What is 122.566 rounded to the nearest hundredths place?

    (J) 123.00

    (K) 122.00

    (L) 122.60

    (M) 122.57

47. What is the closest estimate of 20.93 − 4.43?

    (A) 16

    (B) 17

    (C) 18

    (D) 19

48. What is 3,708 rounded to the nearest hundreds place?

    (J) 4,000

    (K) 3,000

    (L) 3,700

    (M) 3,710

49. What is the closest estimate of 222 × 253?

    (A) 40,000

    (B) 50,000

    (C) 60,000

    (D) 70,000

50. A hat that Matt buys costs $7.74 with tax. If Matt gives the cashier a $20 bill, what is the closest estimate of the amount of change that Matt receives?

    (J) $12

    (K) $13

    (L) $14

    (M) $15

STOP DO NOT TURN THE PAGE UNTIL TOLD TO DO SO. DO NOT RETURN TO A PREVIOUS TEST.

Ability Section

Time: 10 minutes

Directions: For Questions 1–7, find the figure in the answer choices that is most similar to the initial three provided figures. Mark your answer on the answer sheet.

1.

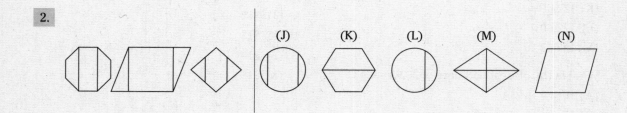

2.

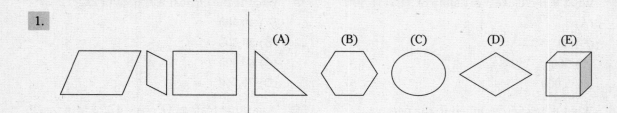

3.

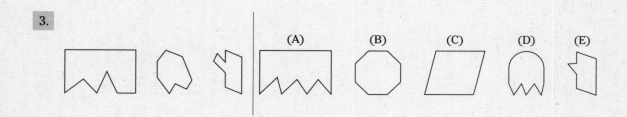

4.

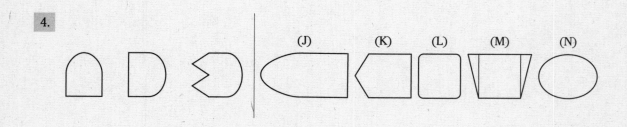

Go on to next page

5.

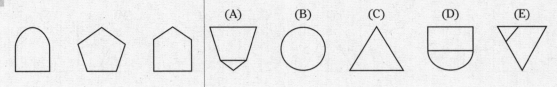

6.

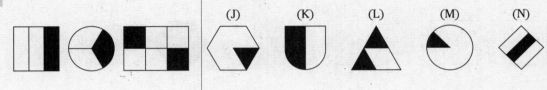

7.

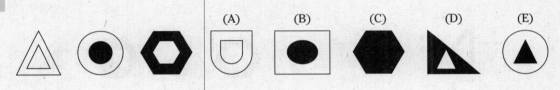

Directions: Determine the relationship between the first two figures in Questions 8–14. Observe the third figure in each question and choose an answer that creates the same relationship with the third figure as the relationship between the first two figures. Mark your answer on the answer sheet.

8.

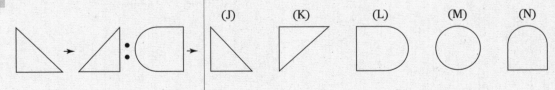

9.

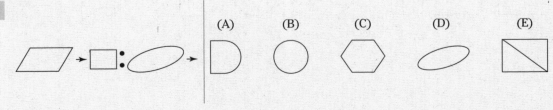

Go on to next page

10.

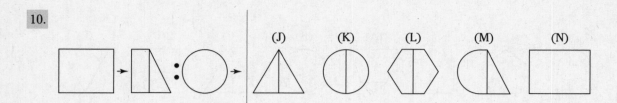

11.

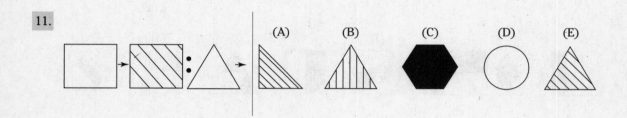

12.

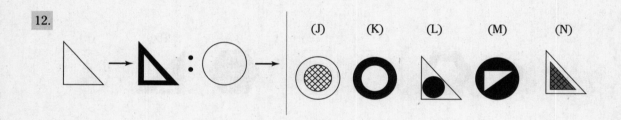

13.

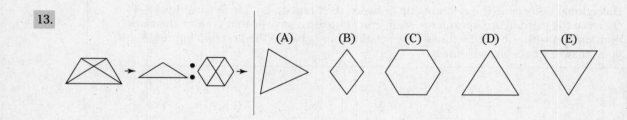

14.

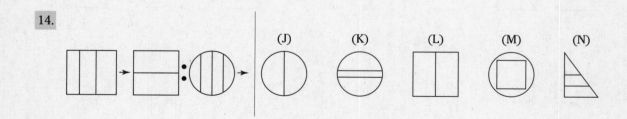

Go on to next page

Directions: The top row in Questions 15–20 shows the direction that a square piece of paper is folded and then punched. Choose the answer choice that shows how the same piece of paper appears after it has been unfolded. Mark your answer on the answer sheet.

15.

(A)   (B)   (C)   (D)   (E)

16.

(J)   (K)   (L)   (M)   (N)

17.

(A)   (B)   (C)   (D)   (E)

18.

(J)   (K)   (L)   (M)   (N)

19.

(A)   (B)   (C)   (D)   (E)

20.

(J)   (K)   (L)   (M)   (N)

STOP   DO NOT TURN THE PAGE UNTIL TOLD TO DO SO.
DO NOT RETURN TO A PREVIOUS TEST.

Chapter 22

Answers to TACHS Practice Test 1

● ●

*Y*ou may have finished taking TACHS Practice Test 1 in Chapter 21, but you're not done yet. Now it's time to review your answers. Read through all the explanations contained in this chapter, even the ones for the questions you answered correctly. You may just find enlightening information that'll help you answer similar questions on the real TACHS. (*Note:* If you don't have the time to read the answer explanations, check your work using the abbreviated answer key found at the end of this chapter.)

Reading Section

1. **D.** You probably know that *dejected* means "sad or down," so look for words that mean the same thing. You can eliminate Choice (C) right away because having an awkward spirit just doesn't make sense. Supportive and cheerful are positive words, so cross out Choices (A) and (B). The best answer is Choice (D); *gloomy* means "down in the dumps."

2. **L.** You may not know that *onerous* means "difficult," and it isn't a word that's easily broken down. You do have at least one clue, though. Onerous is paired with task, so you can probably eliminate Choice (J), effortless. Tasks aren't likely to be effortless. *Arduous* also means "difficult," so Choice (L) is the best answer.

3. **A.** Eliminate Choices (B) and (C) because it doesn't make sense to console or communicate about a problem. To *brood* is to dwell on or worry. To *fret* also means "to worry," so the best answer is Choice (A).

4. **J.** When you aspire toward something, you hope to achieve it. *Aspirations* are hopes, so the answer is Choice (J). Choice (M) is more opposite in meaning than similar. Choice (K), *ascents,* means "climb or rise," and views, Choice (L), doesn't relate to hopes at all.

5. **C.** A big clue to this one is that Choice (C) has the same root, *heart,* as the given word. The suffix -*y* means "full of." Whole also means full or complete, so you can deduce that heartily and wholeheartedly have similar meanings; they both mean to do something with a full heart. Softly and angrily don't have anything to do with heart (except that getting angry too often may harm your heart!), and there's nothing in sympathy to convey fullness of heart.

6. **J.** A reckless driver drives irresponsibly. The correct answer is Choice (J). Although reckless driving may be exciting for some, being reckless doesn't necessarily mean being exciting; Choice (K) is wrong. Choices (L) and (M) have opposite meanings, so they're not right either.

7. **C.** Someone who *squanders* money wastes it, so Choice (C) is the correct answer. Choices (A) and (B) are opposites, and Choice (D) is pretty irrelevant.

8. **M.** If you've ever studied Spanish, you may recognize the root *ami* in the words *amor,* which translates to love, and *amigo,* which translates to friend. So an *amicable* agreement would be a positive or friendly one, Choice (M). The other choices don't convey love or friendship.

9. **B.** To *foresee* literally means "to see something before it happens." If you see that something is going to happen, you anticipate it. Choice (B) is the best answer. The other answer choices don't relate to seeing, so they can't be correct.

10 **L.** *Serenity* means "peacefulness or calmness," and so does *tranquility*. Choice (L) is therefore the best answer. The other choices don't have anything to do with peace or calm, so you can have the serenity of mind to eliminate Choices (J), (K), and (M).

11. **C.** The first sentence of the passage tells you that the main point is that sugar consumption has risen greatly in the last several years. Choice (C) conveys that message best. The information in Choices (A) and (D) is covered only in the last paragraph, and Choice (B)'s point is found only in the first paragraph.

The answers to main-point questions should include information covered in most of the passage, not just one part of it.

12. **K.** The answer to this details question comes from the second paragraph. In 1920, 65 percent of sugar was consumed from home use (not processed foods). In 1976, only 24 percent of sugar was consumed from home use. Because home use consumption decreased, sugar consumption from processed foods must have risen a bunch (from 35 percent to more than 70 percent), which is the answer in Choice (K). Choices (J) and (L) present exaggerations that aren't stated in the passage, and Choice (M) contradicts the passage, which says that sugar is present in foods that don't taste sweet.

13. **A.** You know Choice (A) is the answer because the author uses both *per capita* and *per person* in the same way throughout the passage. Nothing in the passage talks about how much sugar each country or state capital consumes. And if Choice (D) were correct, the second-to-last sentence of the first paragraph would be silly and repetitive. It'd read, ". . . the annual consumption per year. . . ."

14. **M.** Well, the author definitely isn't positive about rising sugar consumption, so you can eliminate Choices (J) and (L). In the first sentence, the author compares the rise in sugar consumption to the rise in drug dependency, which tells you that the author is concerned and not indifferent about increased sugar consumption, so Choice (M) is the best answer.

15. **C.** The passage says that the judge's *omnipotence* (exclusive power) rules in civil cases, but omnipotence isn't an actual judicial tool, so Choice (C) is the answer. All the other answer choices are actual tools (or ways) that the passage says a judge can use to change decisions.

16. **M.** Although the author explains one aspect of the jury system, he or she doesn't give a thorough explanation, so Choice (J) is wrong. Choices (K) and (L) exaggerate with phrases such as "fairest system in the world" and words such as *abolished*. Choice (M) expresses the author's purpose the best without resorting to exaggeration.

17. **A.** The correct answer is right there in the first sentence of the passage, which says that persons accused of crimes have an absolute right to a jury trial, Choice (A). Choice (B) contradicts this statement, and Choices (C) and (D) deal with elements of a civil trial rather than a criminal trial.

18. **K.** The author doesn't seem too pleased with the power judges have to change jury decisions, so Choices (J) and (M) are out. The passage doesn't talk about whether juries can change judges' decisions, so Choice (L)'s no good. The best answer is Choice (K).

19. **A.** First off, the poem doesn't even mention people, so you can cut Choice (D) right away. Also, the poem only brings up trees to let you know what the snow shapes look like, which means Choice (C) can't be right either. Now you have to decide whether *they* in the first line refers to stars or snowflakes. The poem doesn't mention snowflakes, but it does talk about stars in the third stanza and refers to them as *those stars*. This language indicates that the author has alluded to stars before the third stanza, probably in the first line where he talks about *they*. Another clue is the poem's title, "Stars," which means it's all about the twinkling lights. Pick Choice (A).

20. **K.** A *simile* tells you what something is like. Check out the third stanza. It tells you that stars are like something, and the only answers that compare stars to something else are Choices (K) and (M). The poem says that stars are like "some snow-white Minerva's snow-white marble eyes." When you cut through all of those adjectives, you discover that stars

are like eyes (rather than snow). "Without the gift of sight" tells you the eyes don't see. So, stars are like eyes that can't see, Choice (K).

21. **B.** Rhyming schemes usually involve the last word of each line, so focus on the last words. *Snow* and *blow* rhyme in the first stanza, *on* and *dawn* rhyme in the second, and *sight* and *white* rhyme in the last. The last words of the second and fourth lines of each stanza definitely rhyme, so you may be tempted to pick Choice (C). But watch out for the debatable word *only*. Is this really the only rhyming pattern in the poem? Look at the last words of the first lines of each stanza. *Congregate, fate,* and *hate* also rhyme, which means Choice (C) is wrong because the poem has two rhyming patterns, and Choice (A) is wrong because the last words of the first and third lines of each stanza don't rhyme. Choice (D) is wrong too because the poem definitely has some sort of rhyming scheme. Choice (B) is your best bet because it mentions a correct rhyming scheme, but it doesn't tell you that it's the only one.

22. **K.** From the first sentence of the passage, you know that the topic is the role slave artisans played in colonial America. Choice (K) expresses this idea best. Choices (L) and (M) are obviously wrong because the passage isn't primarily about African art. Also, the passage states that slaves did indeed express their creativity, so Choice (J) is incorrect.

23. **A.** The last sentence of the first paragraph states that "slave artisans accomplished necessary work in preindustrial America." Choice (A) paraphrases this statement, so it's the best answer. The passage doesn't talk about farming, complex manufacturing processes, or slaves teaching other slaves, so Choices (B), (C), and (D) are out.

24. **J.** The first paragraph mentions that slave artisans created wrought-iron balconies, so the best answer is Choice (J). Choices (K), (L), and (M) all describe work done by African artists rather than slave artisans.

25. **D.** The passage states in the first paragraph that the artisans received little credit for their labor, so you can eliminate Choices (A) and (B), which imply that slave artisans received respect and reward for their efforts. The passage suggests that artisans manufactured furniture, but it doesn't say that manufactured goods were their primary products; Choice (C) is wrong. The best answer is Choice (D).

26. **K.** The first sentence of the second paragraph states that American slave crafts originated on the west coast of Africa, which is the answer in Choice (K). It doesn't mention mansion builders or colonial aristocrats, so Choices (J) and (M) don't work. Modern African Americans can't really influence those who came before them, so Choice (L) is also out.

27. **D.** The concluding sentence explains that the passage contains examples of white privilege, so the passage is probably about white privilege. Consequently, the answer that best states the author's purpose is Choice (D). All the other choices mention specific parts of the passage but not the overall point.

The main point or objective of a reading comprehension passage usually appears in its first or last few sentences.

28. **K.** The author says she rides the bus with a fellow student and then goes to class, so you can reasonably assume she rides the bus to class, Choice (K). The author says she has blue eyes but doesn't mention her hair color, so Choice (M) is wrong. Also, the author gives no indication that she was late for the bus, and the concluding sentence shows that she's aware of her privileges, so Choices (J) and (L) are incorrect as well.

29. **B.** To answer this question, just substitute the answer choices for *intimidate* in the passage and see which one makes the most sense. *Indulge* and *analyze* don't bear out the meaning of the sentence, and *banish* is too strong a word for the subject. The best answer is Choice (B): My teacher does not *frighten* me because of his skin color.

30. **J.** Because the passage is written in the first person and has a casual tone, it isn't likely an article in a professional trade magazine; eliminate Choice (K). The message definitely doesn't address the author's qualifications for employment, so cross out Choice (M). The subject matter isn't quite what you'd expect in a letter from a friend, so forget about Choice (L). The best answer is Choice (J); the passage is likely part of a class assignment.

Language Section

1. **C.** The error is in the third part, Choice (C). This sentence has two pronouns, the singular *it* and the plural *their*. Both rename "human resources department," which is a singular noun because there's only one department. You need to use the singular pronoun *it* to refer to the singular noun *department*. Choice (C) should read "its new policy on employee uniforms."

2. **K.** The problem in this sentence is a word-choice issue. *Heavy* is used as an adverb; it shows *how* the essay borrowed. But heavy is an adjective, not an adverb. The adverb form is *heavily*. So the second part of the sentence should be "borrowed heavily from."

3. **C.** A descriptive series like the one in this sentence should maintain the same form for each element. *Aggressively* and *emotionally* are both properly stated as adverbs that show how the team played. *Reckless* is an adjective; the part of speech is wrong, and the series lacks parallel structure. Reckless should be *recklessly* in Choice (C).

4. **M.** No problems here. The verb tenses are just fine. The present tense is used for now, the past tense for back in June, and the past perfect for showing an action that happened before another in the past (summer had begun before). Pick Choice (M).

5. **A.** Choice (A) uses improper language. Use *between* for two entities and *among* for three or more. So Jane actually chooses among four items, not between them.

6. **K.** There's a subject-verb agreement problem in this sentence. Look at the second part. The cost of staples *does* (not do) escalate. Cost is a singular subject that needs a singular verb. Choice (K) should read "so does the cost of basic staples."

7. **A.** Did you recognize the repetitive language in this sentence? It's kind of tricky to spot. A biography, by definition, is a story of one's life. So saying "biography of the life" is redundant. The phrase "of the life" should be eliminated from Choice (A).

8. **L.** *Which* refers to people in this sentence, specifically the people who are unemployed. You use *who* to refer to people, not *which*. Choice (L) should read "who are unemployed."

9. **B.** You probably noticed the word-choice error in Choice (B). Leon wouldn't want to be *excepted* at his college choices. After all, to *except* is to exclude! Leon would hope to be *accepted* instead.

10. **M.** Here's another question that's perfectly fine as is. Pick Choice (M) and move on.

11. **A.** You only capitalize family relationships when you use them like a proper name. So you'd capitalize Uncle Jack because *Uncle* is part of your uncle's name. When you simply refer to the relationship, like "my uncle is the" in Choice (A), you don't capitalize it.

12. **K.** *University* in Choice (K) is part of the proper name of Colgate University, so it must be capitalized. When you make a general reference to a university, you don't capitalize the word.

13. **D.** Everything in this sentence is capitalized perfectly. The main words in a book title are capitalized just like they're presented in this question. Go with Choice (D).

14. **K.** The only time you capitalize directions is when you use them as proper names for areas of the country. Choice (K) should be written as "travels east to New York to visit."

15. **C.** Because the word *river* in Choice (C) is part of the name of Walden River, it should be capitalized. *North* is properly presented in lowercase because it's a direction, not the name of a location.

16. **J.** Degrees and distinctions are capitalized, and MD stands for a medical degree. So Choice (J) should read "Percy Graves, MD, is."

17. **B.** You always capitalize the first word of a quote that's a full sentence. So, *where* in Choice (B) should really be *Where*.

18. **M.** This sentence is free of capitalization errors. Halloween is a properly capitalized holiday, and the family relationships here aren't used as proper names, so they're correctly placed in lowercase. The phrase *pumpkin carols* is a general description of a type of song and not an actual song title, so it shouldn't be capitalized either.

19. **B.** Languages, like Spanish and English, are capitalized. Most other course names, like history and philosophy, aren't capitalized. Choice (B) has the error.

20. **J.** In this sentence, Timothy Mouse is the name of a character, so the name should be completely capitalized in Choice (J).

21. **D.** This sentence is punctuated perfectly. The only punctuation present is the semicolon, which joins two independent clauses. It's doing its job just fine!

22. **K.** Focus on the comma in Choice (K). You only use a comma to separate a dependent clause from the rest of the sentence when the dependent clause comes at the beginning. So the comma in this sentence is entirely unnecessary and should be eliminated.

23. **B.** This sentence has four punctuation marks. The commas in Choices (B) and (C) properly separate the items in a series, but Choice (B) also contains a colon that's used incorrectly. You don't have to fix the sentence for the test, but if you did make a change, you'd either eliminate the colon altogether or add something (like "and bought these items:") to make a complete sentence before the colon.

The words that lead up to a colon should be a complete sentence.

24. **J.** That period in Choice (J) creates a sentence fragment, and fragments just won't do. "When Jacob comes home" contains a subject (Jacob) and a verb (comes), but it doesn't express a complete thought because you don't know what happens when Jacob comes home.

25. **B.** This sentence has no punctuation marks, which means you need to evaluate it to make sure nothing's missing. The sentence contains the conjunction *and,* and the groups of words on either side of *and* are complete sentences (or independent clauses), which means you need a comma to separate them. Choice (B) should read "months, and now she is ready. . . ."

26. **J.** *For example* is an expression that isn't necessary for the sentence to make sense, which means it should be set apart from the rest of the sentence with a comma before and after it. The second comma is there in Choice (K), but the first one between *plan* and *for* is missing in Choice (J).

27. **C.** This sentence has two punctuation problems, and both are contained in Choice (C). The abbreviation *etc* should end with a period and be enclosed in commas. That means Choice (C) should look like this: "etc., to get the poster to stick to the wall."

28. **L.** The proper way to punctuate a complete date is to enclose the year in commas. You don't use a comma to separate the month and day. Therefore, the date in Choice (L) should be punctuated like this: May 25, 2010. The comma in Choice (K) is proper because it separates two independent clauses joined by the conjunction *but.*

29. **D.** The commas in Choice (B) are placed correctly. They surround the nonrestrictive clause "which is on Third Street." This clause provides additional info that isn't essential to the meaning of the sentence, which is why you put commas before and after it.

30. **K.** A comma appears in Choice (J), but the problem is actually with the part of the sentence in Choice (K). When you list a city and a state name, you should set off the state name with commas. That means you need one comma after Iowa and one before it. If the part in Choice (K) were punctuated properly, it'd look like this: Iowa, was not included.

31. **B.** Ironically, the misspelled word in this sentence is *mispelled* in Choice (B). It should have two *s*'s.

32. **J.** *Calendar* is spelled with a final *a* rather than *e.*

33. **C.** To create the possessive form of *it,* you simply add an *s* without an apostrophe. *It* with an apostrophe *s* is the contraction of *it is.* So Choice (C) really says that the puppy was "chasing it is tail." That just doesn't make sense! The tail belongs to *it,* so the proper construction of Choice (C) is "chasing its tail."

34. **J.** Did this error slip past you? *Greatful* in Choice (J) should be spelled *grateful.* Choice (L) is just fine. *Foreign* is one of those words that's an exception to the *i*-before-*e* rule.

35. **C.** *Kernel* in Choice (C) refers to a seed, like a kernel of corn. Because the sentence deals with soldiers, the correct spelling is *colonel.*

36. **M.** The proper spelling for the head administrator of a school is *principal.* (You can remember this fact by telling yourself that the principal of your school is your pal — even though you may not truly believe it.) Choice (M) is your answer because none of the words are misspelled.

37. **A.** Here's another tricky one. The proper spelling of *preceed* is really *precede,* which means Choice (A) contains the misspelled word. In the word precede, the *d* precedes the *e* just like it does in the alphabet.

38. **L.** Choice (L) contains the classic violation of the *i*-before-*e*-except-after-*c* rule. *Receive* has a *c* before the long *e* sound, which must be followed by an *e,* not an *i.*

39. **C.** The error in this sentence may have been pretty obvious to you. *Their* is an exception to the *i*-before-*e* rule, and Choice (C) misspells it.

40. **M.** If you couldn't find an error anywhere in this sentence, that's because there isn't one! Choice (M) is correct.

41. **B.** The underlined word in Sentence 1 is *lawyers;* because it's preceded by *a,* you know the noun is singular. Therefore, that *s* on the end can't mean the noun's plural, so Choice (D) must be wrong. The noun must be possessive, and the proper construction of a singular possessive noun is *'s.* Choice (A) is the possessive of a plural noun, so it's wrong. Choice (B) is the proper construction.

42. **L.** *Basically* doesn't add anything relevant to the sentence, so it doesn't belong anywhere. Choice (L) is the best answer.

43. **D.** Sentence 5 simply provides another description of the painting. It doesn't contradict the information that precedes it, so Choices (A) and (C) aren't correct. There's no cause-and-effect relationship between Sentences 5 and 4, so Choice (B) is wrong too. Sentence 5 is fine the way it is; pick Choice (D).

44. **K.** This one's tricky because the plural subject of the sentence (inhabitants) comes after the verb. Therefore, noticing that the singular verb *hovers* doesn't match it is tough. Try rearranging the sentence: Inhabitants hover above the scene. Now you can tell that the verb form is wrong. It should be *hover,* not hovers.

45. **A.** You only put a comma before a conjunction if the words before and after the conjunction are complete sentences. The phrase "like Laurie, dreamed that I could join their club" isn't a complete sentence, which means the comma after *girls* is unnecessary. "Like Laurie" is a nonrestrictive clause, so you need the comma before *like* and after *Laurie.* Choice (A) is correct.

46. **K.** Adverbs answer the questions "how," "when," "where," and "why" in a sentence. *Quickly,* Choice (K), addresses how the author was swept, so it's an adverb. (By the way, Choice (J) is a verb, Choice (L) is an adjective, and Choice (M) is a noun.)

47. **B.** The underlined part of the last sentence is phrased in passive voice, which is rarely the best option, and it pairs a plural subject (strength and importance) with a singular verb (is). Choice (C) corrects the subject-verb agreement issues but keeps the problem of passive voice. Choice (A) doesn't correct either error. The best answer is Choice (B), which makes the underlined part active voice and doesn't introduce a new error.

48. **K.** The subject of Sentence 4 (knowledge, insight, and judgment) is plural. *Results* is a singular verb. The plural form is *result,* so Choice (K) is the problem word. Choice (J), judgment, is spelled correctly, and there's nothing wrong with the other two words.

49. **A.** *Philosophers* in Sentence 2 shouldn't be capitalized because it's not a proper name. None of the other sentences have words that are improperly capitalized, so the answer is Choice (A).

50. **M.** Sentence 5 is fine; go with Choice (M). The series is presented with parallel construction and is punctuated properly, so you can say bye-bye to Choices (J) and (K). Choice (L) is out because the sentence doesn't contain a bunch of independent clauses running on and on without proper punctuation.

Math Section

1. **A.** A prime number has two and only two factors, itself and 1. The only even prime number is 2, so you can eliminate Choice (B) right away. The only prime number that ends with a 5 is the number 5, so Choice (C) isn't prime. Choice (D) can't be prime because it has factors of 7 and 9. Choice (A) is the only answer divisible by only 1 and itself.

2. **K.** Dividing fractions is simple. You just invert the second fraction from $\frac{3}{4}$ to $\frac{4}{3}$ and multiply: $\frac{1}{2} \times \frac{4}{3} = \frac{4}{6}$. To simplify, divide the numerator and denominator by 2: $\frac{4}{6} = \frac{2}{3}$, which is Choice (K).

3. **A.** The answer will be a mixed number because 1.3 is greater than 1. You'd read 1.3 as "one and three tenths." That means the whole number is 1 and the fraction is $\frac{3}{10}$, as in Choice (A). If you picked Choice (B), you mistakenly figured that the 3 was in the hundredths place rather than the tenths place.

4. **K.** Each hat takes 6 pieces of cloth, so Bryan needs a total of 30 pieces of cloth to make 5 hats ($6 \times 5 = 30$). But Bryan already has 10 pieces of cloth, so you need to subtract what he already has to find out what he still needs: $30 - 10 = 20$, Choice (K).

5. **A.** The least common denominator is the smallest number that each of the denominators (2, 8, and 4) divides evenly into in this problem. Find the multiples of the largest number, 8, until you land on one that's divisible by 2 and 4. Start with 8. Because both 2 and 4 go into 8, Choice (A) is the least common denominator. 2 and 4 go into 12, Choice (B), but 8 doesn't. Choices (C) and (D) are common denominators of all three fractions but not the smallest denominator possible.

6. **M.** A glance at the answer choices lets you know that you're looking for the fraction that's the same as 35%. *Percent* means per 100, so put the 35 over 100 and reduce: $\frac{35}{100} = \frac{7}{20}$.

7. **D.** This word problem is a division problem. You can get 6 jerseys on a hanger, and there's a total of 138 jerseys. Divide 138 by 6 to find out the number of hangers you need: $138 \div 6 = 23$, Choice (D).

8. **L.** 14^2 is the same thing as 14×14, which equals 196, Choice (L). If you picked Choice (J), you added instead of multiplying.

9. **A.** First, you need to figure out how much Joe earned without the tip: $60 - $10 is $50. $50 was Joe's total wage for the night. Joe worked 5 hours for $50, so divide $50 by 5 to get $10. Joe made $10 per hour, Choice (A). If you selected Choice (B), you forgot to subtract the tip.

10. **L.** List out all the factors for 14 and 21 and find the largest number that they have in common. The factors of 14 are 1, 2, 7, and 14; the factors of 21 are 1, 3, 7, and 21. You can eliminate Choices (J) and (K) immediately because neither goes into 14. The greatest common factor is 7, Choice (L).

The greatest common factor of two whole numbers is the largest whole number that goes evenly into both numbers.

11. **B.** To change a fraction into a decimal, you divide the numerator by the dominator: $3 \div 8 = 0.375$, Choice (B). If you picked Choice (C), you incorrectly divided the denominator by the numerator.

12. **J.** Subtracting a negative number is easy. Change the negative to a positive and add: $1 + 6 = 7$, which is Choice (J). If you picked Choice (M), you changed 6 to a positive but subtracted rather than added. Choice (L) results from ($-6 - 1$), which is a totally different problem.

13. **D.** The normal route is longer than the shortcut, so you need to add 4.38 to the number of miles that the shortcut spans: $19.75 + 4.38 = 24.13$ miles, which is Choice (D). If you subtracted 4.38 instead of adding it, you got Choice (C).

14. **L.** To find Becca's total allowance, you must calculate what number $10.50 is 20% of. The equation looks like this: $n \times 20\% = \$10.50$. Divide both sides by 0.2 (which is the same as 20%): $n = \$10.50 \div 0.2$; $n = \$52.50$, Choice (L). If you picked Choice (M), you added $10.50 to $52.50; Choice (K) subtracts $10.50 from $52.50.

15. **D.** To solve this problem, you move the decimal point until it lands before the tenths place (3.5). Then you count the number of spaces you moved to determine the exponent (6). Because you moved to the right, the exponent is negative. To express the number in scientific notation, show the new decimal number multiplied by 10 to the exponent, like this: 3.5×10^{-6}, which is the answer in Choice (D).

16. **L.** If one case costs $6.95 and the total price is $15.50, all you have to do is subtract the one case from the total price to find the price of the second case: $15.50 - 6.95 = \$8.55$, the answer in Choice (L). Choice (M) results from adding $6.95 to $15.50.

17. **A.** First, multiply $40 by ¼ to see how much money Stacey puts into savings: $¼ \times \$40 = \$10$. Then subtract the savings from the total amount of money she made: $\$40 - \$10 = \$30$, Choice (A). If you added the savings instead of subtracting them, you wound up with Choice (D).

18. **M.** To determine the discount, multiply $85 by 40%: $0.4 \times \$85 = 34$. Don't pick Choice (J) yet, though; $34 is just the discount, not the new price. Subtract $34 from $85 to find the new price: $\$85 - \$34 = \$51$, Choice (M).

19. **C.** Figure the total cost by multiplying the price per pound ($1.75) by the total weight (3.4): $\$1.75 \times 3.4 = \$5.95$, Choice (C).

20. **M.** Amy worked problems for 4 hours (from 3 p.m. to 7 p.m.). To find the number of problems she worked per hour, divide the number of hours by the number of problems: $120 \div 4 = 30$, Choice (M). You got Choice (L) if you miscalculated the number of hours Amy worked.

21. **C.** You know from the chart that a full chicken burrito costs $6.25. Each extra ingredient costs $0.65 extra, so add two extra ingredients (guacamole and hot sauce) to the cost of the burrito: $\$0.65 + \$0.65 + \$6.25 = \$7.55$, Choice (C).

22. **K.** A half pork burrito costs $4.65. Add the queso dip, which costs $0.65, and you get a total cost of $5.30: $\$4.65 + \$0.65 = \$5.30$. The answer is Choice (K).

23. **A.** The graph shows that Alan made $4,000 in sales and Diane made $3,000. Subtract to find out how much more Alan made: $\$4,000 - \$3,000 = \$1,000$, Choice (A).

24. **K.** Use the legend to determine which line corresponds with which team. Analyze the lines to discover that Team 3 has more goals than Team 1 in all months except February, Choice (K).

25. **D.** Add up John and Jill's percentages to find what percentage they'd win together: $14\% + 11\% = 25\%$. To change the decimal to a fraction, use 25 as the numerator and 100 as the denominator: $^{25}/_{100}$. Reduce the fraction by dividing the numerator and denominator by 25 to get ¼, Choice (D). (If you combined Dan and Mike's winnings, you got Choice (A).)

26. **J.** Examine the data to find a trend. You can eliminate Choice (M) because pie charts aren't good for showing trends. The number of students with lower scores is small and slowly

increases as scores increase to a peak in the 71–80 range. Then the numbers start dropping off as scores get higher. Look for a chart that shows a steady increase to a peak and then a gradual decrease. The only option is Choice (J). Choices (K) and (L) show a series of peaks and valleys that aren't justified by the data.

27. **B.** The legend tells you that the darkest area shows the figures for the 19+ age group. The black area for all high schools is on the top of each graph. Focus on only this section of the graph to answer the question. The two schools with the biggest dark sections are North and West, Choice (B). If you selected Choice (A), you focused on the wrong age group.

28. **M.** To find out how many more home runs Jennifer hit in November than October, find the value for November (8) and the value for October (which is 3 because the value falls directly between 2 and 4). Subtract the two values to get your answer: 8 − 3 = 5, Choice (M).

29. **C.** First, find the values of each mold on Day 6 and Day 8. Then subtract Day 6 from Day 8 to see which mold grew the most. The chart gives you everything you need to accomplish this, so eliminate Choice (D) right off the bat. Mold A grew 2 cm (5 − 3), Mold B grew 3 cm (8 − 5), and Mold C grew 4 cm (12 − 8). Obviously Mold C, Choice (C), grew the most.

30. **K.** Look at the first column on the chart, which represents the period from 1980–1989. The values for Stores C and B show you that Store C had 48 employees and Store B had 27 during this time frame. Subtract the two values to find the difference: 48 − 27 = 21 employees, Choice (K). If you chose any other answer, you looked at the wrong column.

31. **A.** Determine which students have higher bars for the second test than they do for the first. The chart shows that Bob and Susie are the only two students who received higher scores on the second test, Choice (A).

32. **K.** To find the combined total revenue for Brockton and Carelton, add the values you see on the chart: $5 million + $4 million = $9 million. The chart shows that Appleton had $11 million in revenue. Subtract to find the difference: $11 million − $9 million = $2 million, Choice (K).

33. **B.** Because you can't use scratch paper on this part of the Math section, look at the answer choices to see what place you should round to. All the options are rounded to the hundreds place. To round 561 to the hundreds place, look at the number to the right of the hundreds place, 6. Because 6 is greater than 5, you round the number in the hundreds place up one value and add zeros to get 600. The number to the right of the hundreds place in 420 is 2. 2 is less than 5, so round down to 400. Add 600 and 400 to get 1,000, Choice (B). If you chose any other answer, you rounded incorrectly.

34. **K.** Round 723 to a number you can divide in your head by 9 with no remainder. Thanks to that mean ol' teacher who made you memorize multiplication tables, you know that 72 ÷ 9 = 8. Round 723 to 720; 9 goes into 720 80 times, so the answer is Choice (K).

35. **C.** Round each number to the nearest tens place. 31 rounds to 30 (because 1 < 5), 34 becomes 30 (because 4 < 5), and 42 rounds to 40 (because 2 < 5). Add the rounded numbers together (30 + 30 + 40 = 100) to get Choice (C).

> **TIP** For TACHS estimation questions, round the numbers *before* you perform the operation instead of rounding the final answer. The idea is to make the problem easy enough to do in your head, and it's much easier to perform operations with rounded numbers.

36. **J.** The answer choices are whole numbers, so round the two numbers in the problem to the nearest whole number. 5.43 rounds to 5 because the number to the right of the decimal (4) is less than 5. 6.52 rounds up to 7 because the number to the right of the decimal (5) is 5 or greater. Multiply the rounded whole numbers 5 and 7 to get 35, Choice (J). Rounding errors lead to picking either Choice (K) or Choice (L).

37. **A.** Round each number to the nearest thousands place. 26,828 rounds up to 27,000 (8 ≥ 5), and 20,420 becomes 20,000 (4 < 5). 27,000 − 20,000 = 7,000, Choice (A). Rounding errors, such as rounding up both numbers, gets you Choice (B).

38. **L.** The *tenths place* is the number directly to the right of the decimal, which is the second 5 in the number 5.543. The number to the right of the second 5 (4) is less than 5, so the number is properly rounded to 5.5. Choice (M) is incorrectly rounded to the ones place.

39. **B.** Round $12.38 to the nearest dollar without any cents. The number to the right of the decimal is 3, which is less than 5. $12.38 rounds to $12. $15 is already in whole dollars, so just subtract: $15 – $12 = $3, Choice (B). Incorrectly rounding $12.38 to $13 would result in Choice (A).

40. **M.** Look at the number directly to the right of the decimal to round each value to the nearest dollar. $4.73 rounds up to $5 (7 ≥ 5), $3.43 rounds to $3 (4 < 5), and $5.34 rounds to $5 (3 < 5). Add the new amounts together ($5 + $3 + $5 = $13) to get Choice (M). Choices (K) and (L) result from improper rounding.

41. **A.** First, round the numbers inside the parentheses to the hundreds place. 592 rounds up to 600 (9 ≥ 5), and 933 rounds to 900 (3 < 5). Add the rounded numbers: 600 + 900 = 1,500. Then divide by 30 to get Choice (A): 1,500 ÷ 30 = 50.

42. **L.** Round each number. 49 becomes 50 because 9 ≥ 5; 42 becomes 40 because 2 < 5. Now multiply the rounded numbers: 50 × 40 = 2,000 (to do this in your head, calculate 5 × 4 = 20 and add two zeros). The answer is Choice (L).

43. **B.** The number to the right of the tenths place is 0, which means the number in the tenths place doesn't change. Fill the rest of the decimal places with zeros and delete the numbers to the right of the tenths place. The answer is 35.0, Choice (B). Choice (A) is rounded to the hundredths place, and Choice (C) is incorrectly rounded up.

44. **J.** Start this problem by rounding each number to the nearest thousands place, which is the number directly to the right of the comma. 6,434 rounds to 6,000 because 4 < 5, and 3,942 rounds up to 4,000 because 9 ≥ 5. Now subtract the rounded numbers to get the answer: 6,000 – 4,000 = 2,000. Choice (J) is your answer.

45. **D.** 7 goes into 35 evenly, and if you round 34,544 to the nearest thousand, you get 35,000 because 5 ≥ 5. Divide 35,000 by 7 in your head by dividing 35 by 7 to get 5 and adding three zeros. The answer is Choice (D), 5,000.

46. **M.** The number in the hundredths place in this problem is 6, and the number to the right of the hundredths place is 6, which is greater than 5. This means the number is rounded up to 122.57, which is Choice (M). If you chose any other answer, you rounded to the wrong decimal place.

The *hundredths place* is the second number to the right of the decimal point. Don't confuse it with the *hundreds place,* which is three places to the left of the decimal point.

47. **B.** Round each number to the nearest whole number. 20.93 rounds up to 21 (9 ≥ 5), and 4.43 rounds to 4 (4 < 5). Subtract the rounded numbers: 21 – 4 = 17, Choice (B).

48. **L.** The number in the hundreds place is 7. The number directly to the right of 7 is 0, which means the number is rounded to 3,700, Choice (L). The other answer choices are rounded to the wrong decimal place.

49. **C.** To solve this one, round each number to the nearest hundreds place. 222 rounds to 200 because 2 < 5, and 253 rounds up to 300 because 5 ≥ 5. Multiply the two rounded numbers. To do that in your head, just take 2 × 3 to get 6 and add four zeros. Choice (C), 60,000, is correct.

50. **J.** First, round $7.74 to the nearest dollar. $7.74 rounds up to $8. Subtract this amount from $20 to get the answer: $20 – $8 = $12, Choice (J).

Ability Section

1. **D.** Each of the three given figures is two-dimensional and has four sides. The diamond in Choice (D) is the only two-dimensional figure with four sides.

2. **J.** Examine the given figures. They all have two lines, so you can cross out Choices (K), (L), and (N) because they don't have two lines. The lines in Choice (M) cross, but the lines in the given figures are all parallel. Choice (J) is the best answer.

3. **B.** These weird-looking figures have something in common, but what? Start by counting the sides. Each figure has eight sides. Even though Choice (B) doesn't look much like the given figures, it too has eight sides, so it's the right answer. The other choices have neither eight sides nor another feature that's like those of the given figures.

4. **J.** If this question seems tricky at first, focus on what makes the three figures similar. Each of the three figures has a curved portion, so eliminate answers that don't contain a curve, specifically Choices (K) and (M). Each of the three figures also contains a right angle. Choices (L) and (N) don't have right angles. Choice (J) has both a curved part and a right angle, so it's the best answer.

5. **C.** The feature that all three figures share is a straight bottom line. Choices (A), (D), and (E) have straight lines on their tops, but they lack straight lines on their bottoms. All of these choices also contain an inner line, which isn't a feature of the three figures in the question set. Choice (B) contains no straight lines at all, so it can't be right. This leaves Choice (C) as the only answer with a straight line on its bottom.

6. **N.** Each given figure is ⅓ shaded. Choice (N) is the only figure with ⅓ shaded. Choices (K) and (L) are ½ shaded, Choice (M) is ⅛ shaded, and Choice (J) is ⅙ shaded.

7. **A.** The shading isn't similar on the given figures, but the shape within a shape is. Each figure contains another shape that's the same as the outside shape. Choice (C) has no shape within a shape, so it's wrong. The remaining choices, except for Choice (A), have different shapes inside and outside.

8. **L.** The big triangle in the first set of figures becomes a smaller triangle that faces the other direction. To complete the analogy, find the smaller rounded-side figure that faces the opposite direction. Choices (J), (K), and (M) aren't the right shape, and Choice (N) faces the wrong direction. Choice (L) is best.

9. **B.** The stretched rectangle becomes a smaller, nonstretched rectangle, so the stretched circle should become a smaller, nonstretched circle, like Choice (B).

10. **M.** The second figure halves the first and adds a triangle. Choice (M) also halves the figure and adds a triangle. None of the other choices follows the pattern.

11. **E.** The unshaded rectangle becomes a rectangle shaded with diagonal lines. The unshaded triangle should become a triangle shaded with diagonal lines. Choices (A), (C), and (D) aren't the same shape, and Choice (B) shades the triangle with vertical lines.

12. **K.** The right triangle becomes a shaded right triangle with another right triangle inside, so you're looking for a shaded circle with another circle inside. Only Choice (K) gives you this option. The other choices are the wrong shape or the wrong shading.

13. **D.** This tricky analogy gives you a figure with crossed lines and then relates it to the shape that those lines create at the bottom of the figure. The shape that the crossed lines create at the bottom of the third figure in the question appears to be an equilateral triangle that points up. The triangles in Choices (A) and (E) are positioned incorrectly, so the triangle you're looking for is the one that points up — Choice (D).

14. **K.** The first square has two vertical lines; the second square has one horizontal line. To move from one to the other, you must eliminate a line and make the remaining line horizontal. Find the answer that does the same for the circle with three vertical lines. Remove one line, leaving two, and make them horizontal, Choice (K).

15. **A.** The number of holes in the correct answer will be twice the number of original holes if the paper is folded once. Therefore, the right answer will have only two holes; eliminate Choices (B) and (E). The hole is at the bottom and the fold is vertical, so when you open the paper, both holes will appear at the bottom, like in Choice (A).

16. **J.** You can cross out Choice (L) because the answer must have four holes. Notice that the paper is folded horizontally. When you unfold it, you'll have a hole in the top-right corner and the bottom-right corner. Choice (J) is the only option with holes in both right corners.

17. **C.** Your answer must have four holes, so toss out Choices (D) and (E). There isn't a hole in the corner of the folded paper, so Choices (A) and (B) can't be right. Choice (C) is the best answer.

18. **N.** This paper is folded twice, so you end up with four times the number of holes (eight total). Choices (K), (L), and (M) don't have eight holes. The difference between the two remaining choices is that Choice (N) has four holes in the middle of the unfolded page and Choice (J) has holes that line its right and left side. The hole in the lower-right corner of the original folded page would result in four center holes in the unfolded page, which is what you see in Choice (N).

19. **E.** The answer will have 12 holes (3 holes $\times$ 4 = 12). Only Choices (B) and (E) have 12 holes. Choice (B) has holes in the corners, though, and there are no corner holes in the folded paper. Choice (E) has to be right because its holes appear in the middle of the page.

20. **L.** The paper has one fold and five holes, so the answer must have ten holes. The only choice with ten holes is Choice (L). You can cross out all the other options.

Answer Key for TACHS Practice Test 1

Reading Section

1. D	7. C	13. A	19. A	25. D
2. L	8. M	14. M	20. K	26. K
3. A	9. B	15. C	21. B	27. D
4. J	10. L	16. M	22. K	28. K
5. C	11. C	17. A	23. A	29. B
6. J	12. K	18. K	24. J	30. J

Language Section

1. C	11. A	21. D	31. B	41. B
2. K	12. K	22. K	32. J	42. L
3. C	13. D	23. B	33. C	43. D
4. M	14. K	24. J	34. J	44. K
5. A	15. C	25. B	35. C	45. A
6. K	16. J	26. J	36. M	46. K
7. A	17. B	27. C	37. A	47. B
8. L	18. M	28. L	38. L	48. K
9. B	19. B	29. D	39. C	49. A
10. M	20. J	30. K	40. M	50. M

Math Section

1. A	11. B	21. C	31. A	41. A
2. K	12. J	22. K	32. K	42. L
3. A	13. D	23. A	33. B	43. B
4. K	14. L	24. K	34. K	44. J
5. A	15. D	25. D	35. C	45. D
6. M	16. L	26. J	36. J	46. M
7. D	17. A	27. B	37. A	47. B
8. L	18. M	28. M	38. L	48. L
9. A	19. C	29. C	39. B	49. C
10. L	20. M	30. K	40. M	50. J

Ability Section

1. D	6. N	11. E	16. J
2. J	7. A	12. K	17. C
3. B	8. L	13. D	18. N
4. J	9. B	14. K	19. E
5. C	10. M	15. A	20. L

Chapter 23

TACHS Practice Test 2

• •

The TACHS really isn't so bad if you take the time to prepare. That's why we include a second practice test that's chock-full of the kinds of reading, language, math, and ability questions you can expect to see on the real TACHS test.

This practice test is quite similar to the real TACHS, but the test-makers always have the option of changing the test slightly, so the one you take may have slightly different question formats, a different number of questions, and/or different time limits.

Completing this practice test takes about two hours, with a break. We suggest you make your practice time as similar to actual test conditions as possible by

- ✔ Setting yourself up somewhere you won't be distracted (preferably as far as possible from your little brother who's watching cartoons like they're oxygen).

- ✔ Trying to take the practice test at approximately the same time of day as the time your TACHS is scheduled (that's probably early morning).

- ✔ Removing the answer sheet from this chapter and marking your answers on it by filling in the appropriate bubbles.

- ✔ Writing notes and calculations on the test pages, except where you're supposed to estimate answers.

- ✔ Using a timer to time yourself on each section. Stop when time is up and move on — even if you're not done yet. (You won't get the luxury of finishing a section past the allotted time on test day.)

- ✔ Giving yourself a 10- to 15-minute break. On exam day, you'll probably be given a quick break between the Language and Math sections.

After completing the practice test, mosey on over to Chapter 24 to check your answers.

Answer Sheet for TACHS Practice Test 2

Reading Section

Part 1

1. Ⓐ Ⓑ Ⓒ Ⓓ   3. Ⓐ Ⓑ Ⓒ Ⓓ   5. Ⓐ Ⓑ Ⓒ Ⓓ   7. Ⓐ Ⓑ Ⓒ Ⓓ   9. Ⓐ Ⓑ Ⓒ Ⓓ
2. Ⓙ Ⓚ Ⓛ Ⓜ   4. Ⓙ Ⓚ Ⓛ Ⓜ   6. Ⓙ Ⓚ Ⓛ Ⓜ   8. Ⓙ Ⓚ Ⓛ Ⓜ   10. Ⓙ Ⓚ Ⓛ Ⓜ

Part 2

11. Ⓐ Ⓑ Ⓒ Ⓓ   15. Ⓐ Ⓑ Ⓒ Ⓓ   19. Ⓐ Ⓑ Ⓒ Ⓓ   23. Ⓐ Ⓑ Ⓒ Ⓓ   27. Ⓐ Ⓑ Ⓒ Ⓓ
12. Ⓙ Ⓚ Ⓛ Ⓜ   16. Ⓙ Ⓚ Ⓛ Ⓜ   20. Ⓙ Ⓚ Ⓛ Ⓜ   24. Ⓙ Ⓚ Ⓛ Ⓜ   28. Ⓙ Ⓚ Ⓛ Ⓜ
13. Ⓐ Ⓑ Ⓒ Ⓓ   17. Ⓐ Ⓑ Ⓒ Ⓓ   21. Ⓐ Ⓑ Ⓒ Ⓓ   25. Ⓐ Ⓑ Ⓒ Ⓓ   29. Ⓐ Ⓑ Ⓒ Ⓓ
14. Ⓙ Ⓚ Ⓛ Ⓜ   18. Ⓙ Ⓚ Ⓛ Ⓜ   22. Ⓙ Ⓚ Ⓛ Ⓜ   26. Ⓙ Ⓚ Ⓛ Ⓜ   30. Ⓙ Ⓚ Ⓛ Ⓜ

Language Section

Part 1

1. Ⓐ Ⓑ Ⓒ Ⓓ   9. Ⓐ Ⓑ Ⓒ Ⓓ   17. Ⓐ Ⓑ Ⓒ Ⓓ   25. Ⓐ Ⓑ Ⓒ Ⓓ   33. Ⓐ Ⓑ Ⓒ Ⓓ
2. Ⓙ Ⓚ Ⓛ Ⓜ   10. Ⓙ Ⓚ Ⓛ Ⓜ   18. Ⓙ Ⓚ Ⓛ Ⓜ   26. Ⓙ Ⓚ Ⓛ Ⓜ   34. Ⓙ Ⓚ Ⓛ Ⓜ
3. Ⓐ Ⓑ Ⓒ Ⓓ   11. Ⓐ Ⓑ Ⓒ Ⓓ   19. Ⓐ Ⓑ Ⓒ Ⓓ   27. Ⓐ Ⓑ Ⓒ Ⓓ   35. Ⓐ Ⓑ Ⓒ Ⓓ
4. Ⓙ Ⓚ Ⓛ Ⓜ   12. Ⓙ Ⓚ Ⓛ Ⓜ   20. Ⓙ Ⓚ Ⓛ Ⓜ   28. Ⓙ Ⓚ Ⓛ Ⓜ   36. Ⓙ Ⓚ Ⓛ Ⓜ
5. Ⓐ Ⓑ Ⓒ Ⓓ   13. Ⓐ Ⓑ Ⓒ Ⓓ   21. Ⓐ Ⓑ Ⓒ Ⓓ   29. Ⓐ Ⓑ Ⓒ Ⓓ   37. Ⓐ Ⓑ Ⓒ Ⓓ
6. Ⓙ Ⓚ Ⓛ Ⓜ   14. Ⓙ Ⓚ Ⓛ Ⓜ   22. Ⓙ Ⓚ Ⓛ Ⓜ   30. Ⓙ Ⓚ Ⓛ Ⓜ   38. Ⓙ Ⓚ Ⓛ Ⓜ
7. Ⓐ Ⓑ Ⓒ Ⓓ   15. Ⓐ Ⓑ Ⓒ Ⓓ   23. Ⓐ Ⓑ Ⓒ Ⓓ   31. Ⓐ Ⓑ Ⓒ Ⓓ   39. Ⓐ Ⓑ Ⓒ Ⓓ
8. Ⓙ Ⓚ Ⓛ Ⓜ   16. Ⓙ Ⓚ Ⓛ Ⓜ   24. Ⓙ Ⓚ Ⓛ Ⓜ   32. Ⓙ Ⓚ Ⓛ Ⓜ   40. Ⓙ Ⓚ Ⓛ Ⓜ

Part 2

41. Ⓐ Ⓑ Ⓒ Ⓓ   43. Ⓐ Ⓑ Ⓒ Ⓓ   45. Ⓐ Ⓑ Ⓒ Ⓓ   47. Ⓐ Ⓑ Ⓒ Ⓓ   49. Ⓐ Ⓑ Ⓒ Ⓓ
42. Ⓙ Ⓚ Ⓛ Ⓜ   44. Ⓙ Ⓚ Ⓛ Ⓜ   46. Ⓙ Ⓚ Ⓛ Ⓜ   48. Ⓙ Ⓚ Ⓛ Ⓜ   50. Ⓙ Ⓚ Ⓛ Ⓜ

Math Section

Part 1

1. Ⓐ Ⓑ Ⓒ Ⓓ
2. Ⓙ Ⓚ Ⓛ Ⓜ
3. Ⓐ Ⓑ Ⓒ Ⓓ
4. Ⓙ Ⓚ Ⓛ Ⓜ
5. Ⓐ Ⓑ Ⓒ Ⓓ
6. Ⓙ Ⓚ Ⓛ Ⓜ
7. Ⓐ Ⓑ Ⓒ Ⓓ

8. Ⓙ Ⓚ Ⓛ Ⓜ
9. Ⓐ Ⓑ Ⓒ Ⓓ
10. Ⓙ Ⓚ Ⓛ Ⓜ
11. Ⓐ Ⓑ Ⓒ Ⓓ
12. Ⓙ Ⓚ Ⓛ Ⓜ
13. Ⓐ Ⓑ Ⓒ Ⓓ
14. Ⓙ Ⓚ Ⓛ Ⓜ

15. Ⓐ Ⓑ Ⓒ Ⓓ
16. Ⓙ Ⓚ Ⓛ Ⓜ
17. Ⓐ Ⓑ Ⓒ Ⓓ
18. Ⓙ Ⓚ Ⓛ Ⓜ
19. Ⓐ Ⓑ Ⓒ Ⓓ
20. Ⓙ Ⓚ Ⓛ Ⓜ
21. Ⓐ Ⓑ Ⓒ Ⓓ

22. Ⓙ Ⓚ Ⓛ Ⓜ
23. Ⓐ Ⓑ Ⓒ Ⓓ
24. Ⓙ Ⓚ Ⓛ Ⓜ
25. Ⓐ Ⓑ Ⓒ Ⓓ
26. Ⓙ Ⓚ Ⓛ Ⓜ
27. Ⓐ Ⓑ Ⓒ Ⓓ
28. Ⓙ Ⓚ Ⓛ Ⓜ

29. Ⓐ Ⓑ Ⓒ Ⓓ
30. Ⓙ Ⓚ Ⓛ Ⓜ
31. Ⓐ Ⓑ Ⓒ Ⓓ
32. Ⓙ Ⓚ Ⓛ Ⓜ

Part 2

33. Ⓐ Ⓑ Ⓒ Ⓓ
34. Ⓙ Ⓚ Ⓛ Ⓜ
35. Ⓐ Ⓑ Ⓒ Ⓓ
36. Ⓙ Ⓚ Ⓛ Ⓜ

37. Ⓐ Ⓑ Ⓒ Ⓓ
38. Ⓙ Ⓚ Ⓛ Ⓜ
39. Ⓐ Ⓑ Ⓒ Ⓓ
40. Ⓙ Ⓚ Ⓛ Ⓜ

41. Ⓐ Ⓑ Ⓒ Ⓓ
42. Ⓙ Ⓚ Ⓛ Ⓜ
43. Ⓐ Ⓑ Ⓒ Ⓓ
44. Ⓙ Ⓚ Ⓛ Ⓜ

45. Ⓐ Ⓑ Ⓒ Ⓓ
46. Ⓙ Ⓚ Ⓛ Ⓜ
47. Ⓐ Ⓑ Ⓒ Ⓓ
48. Ⓙ Ⓚ Ⓛ Ⓜ

49. Ⓐ Ⓑ Ⓒ Ⓓ
50. Ⓙ Ⓚ Ⓛ Ⓜ

Ability Section

1. Ⓐ Ⓑ Ⓒ Ⓓ Ⓔ
2. Ⓙ Ⓚ Ⓛ Ⓜ Ⓝ
3. Ⓐ Ⓑ Ⓒ Ⓓ Ⓔ
4. Ⓙ Ⓚ Ⓛ Ⓜ Ⓝ

5. Ⓐ Ⓑ Ⓒ Ⓓ Ⓔ
6. Ⓙ Ⓚ Ⓛ Ⓜ Ⓝ
7. Ⓐ Ⓑ Ⓒ Ⓓ Ⓔ
8. Ⓙ Ⓚ Ⓛ Ⓜ Ⓝ

9. Ⓐ Ⓑ Ⓒ Ⓓ Ⓔ
10. Ⓙ Ⓚ Ⓛ Ⓜ Ⓝ
11. Ⓐ Ⓑ Ⓒ Ⓓ Ⓔ
12. Ⓙ Ⓚ Ⓛ Ⓜ Ⓝ

13. Ⓐ Ⓑ Ⓒ Ⓓ Ⓔ
14. Ⓙ Ⓚ Ⓛ Ⓜ Ⓝ
15. Ⓐ Ⓑ Ⓒ Ⓓ Ⓔ
16. Ⓙ Ⓚ Ⓛ Ⓜ Ⓝ

17. Ⓐ Ⓑ Ⓒ Ⓓ Ⓔ
18. Ⓙ Ⓚ Ⓛ Ⓜ Ⓝ
19. Ⓐ Ⓑ Ⓒ Ⓓ Ⓔ
20. Ⓙ Ⓚ Ⓛ Ⓜ Ⓝ

Reading Section

Part 1

Time: 5 minutes

Directions: Questions 1–10 contain an underlined word. Find the answer choice that has the most similar meaning to the underlined word. Mark the answer sheet by filling in the bubble that corresponds with your choice.

1. to <u>dissolve</u> a partnership
   - (A) soften
   - (B) break up
   - (C) solidify
   - (D) construct

2. a deep <u>chasm</u>
   - (J) gap
   - (K) association
   - (L) pain
   - (M) joy

3. an important <u>diplomat</u>
   - (A) slave
   - (B) astronaut
   - (C) ambassador
   - (D) nonentity

4. to come to a <u>solution</u>
   - (J) resolution
   - (K) crisis
   - (L) combination
   - (M) outline

5. an <u>eccentric</u> old man
   - (A) conventional
   - (B) popular
   - (C) lovely
   - (D) unusual

6. to <u>augment</u> the supply
   - (J) contaminate
   - (K) increase
   - (L) adjust
   - (M) reduce

7. a <u>somber</u> mood
   - (A) boring
   - (B) solemn
   - (C) cheerful
   - (D) mercurial

8. an <u>impromptu</u> meeting
   - (J) organized
   - (K) brief
   - (L) spontaneous
   - (M) lengthy

9. an <u>innocuous</u> remark
   - (A) offensive
   - (B) silly
   - (C) important
   - (D) harmless

10. a <u>fleeting</u> moment
    - (J) enduring
    - (K) amusing
    - (L) unpleasant
    - (M) passing

Go on to next page →

Part 2

Time: 25 minutes

Directions: The following four passages ask questions that pertain to their respective content. Choose the best answer for each of the questions and mark it on the answer sheet.

Questions 11–15 pertain to the following passage.

Elizabeth awaited the gathering of her followers for the bimonthly get-together in her exclusive London Arms flat. Elizabeth, or "Liz" as her friends commonly called her, was awaiting her guests in the parlor, which she preferred to her master suite, and she hoped that each would bring a monetary gift to fill her dwindling campaign chest.

Her constituents were seemingly visiting for social reasons, but Liz had other intentions. Her popularity was waning, and her hold on the general electorate was loosening. Never before had she worried about elections, but now the climate had changed. How she wished that the peasants could vote! Only they realized the agony of having only a few thousand pounds with which to dine. The days of caviar, nectar, and roses may be all but over, and she dreaded the thought of having to trade her wealth for votes.

Once the session began in Liz's glorious living chamber, the guests received some tea and crumpets — but without sugar. Sugar was too precious a commodity to serve to such a large group. Liz's speech was condescending as she appealed for votes with the promise of reward in exchange. She aimed to maintain the status quo as long as that boosted her own power and pocketbook. Liz took pleasure in her presentation. As her captive audience looked on and their contributions increased, she bathed in the glory of the moment. If the election were held tomorrow, surely she would prevail.

11. The events in this passage most likely take place where?

   (A) a large auditorium
   (B) a luxury apartment
   (C) a church hall
   (D) the boardroom of a corporation

12. The author's tone is

   (J) serious
   (K) objective
   (L) sarcastic
   (M) admiring

13. Elizabeth is most likely which of the following?

   (A) a politician who does not care much about her followers
   (B) a political science professor
   (C) the owner of a small business
   (D) a community volunteer

14. For what reason did the refreshments not contain sugar?

   (J) Sugar was fattening.
   (K) Sugar was expensive.
   (L) The group did not like sugar.
   (M) The cook had run out of sugar.

15. What is Elizabeth most concerned about?

   (A) that her followers will not receive an adequate amount of tea
   (B) that sugar is more precious than caviar, nectar, and roses
   (C) that only peasants can vote
   (D) that she will lose her power and money

Go on to next page

Questions 16–20 pertain to the following passage.

One aspect of high school that freshmen find challenging and confusing is the abundance of facts they must sort through for each class. Incoming students are flooded with countless facts about history, psychology, biology, economics, and so on. Many students unquestionably accept these facts to be true; others do not. The question becomes how a student determines whether information is true or not.

Determining truth is the goal of scientific research, which attempts to establish laws of cause and effect to help students predict and explain facts. Students usually depend on authority, instruction, and logic to establish facts. However, since each of these methods can lead to subjective or false conclusions, scientists have developed their own method for establishing facts called the scientific method. When applied correctly, the scientific method validates facts and attempts to establish a clear cause-and-effect relationship between events.

It is not always easy to find out the exact causes of events. The elements of establishing cause and effect include association, time priority, rationale, and nonspurious (or genuine) relationship. First, there must be an association, or relationship, between two variables. For instance, if there is no relationship between levels of education and crime, one cannot say that a lack of education causes one to commit a crime.

Time priority is also important. This means that if one event happens before another, there may be reason to deduce that the first event had something to do with the other one. For example, smoking may cause cancer because it happens before the cancer occurs.

Another factor to consider in establishing cause and effect is rationale. Rationale comes from observation and experimentation. One proposes a hypothesis that one event causes another and then sets up a series of measureable experiments to test the validity of the hypothesis.

Finally, the association between two events should not be able to be explained by another variable. If another variable is not responsible, one can say that the relationship between the cause and the effect is nonspurious, or genuine. This step is hard to accomplish because one cannot always control other variables well enough to determine whether they are part of the relationship or not.

16. What method do students usually use if they do not use the scientific method?

(J) association

(K) time priority

(L) rationale

(M) logic

17. The tone of the passage is

(A) objective

(B) disapproving

(C) aggressive

(D) depressing

18. What is the test of a nonspurious relationship?

(J) One event happens before another.

(K) There is no other variable that could cause the event.

(L) The relationship does not relate to history or biology.

(M) One determines the relationship by relying on authority.

Go on to next page

19. Rationale primarily involves which of these?

    (A) observation and experimentation

    (B) history and psychology

    (C) subjective and false conclusions

    (D) time priority

20. According to the passage, what is the primary goal of scientific research?

    (J) to reach subjective conclusions

    (K) to determine truth

    (L) to show that it is easy to prove a cause-and-effect relationship

    (M) to overwhelm high school students with a bunch of facts

---

Questions 21–25 pertain to the following passage.

I get in my car and drive 70 mph down the interstate to "Lee's Studio." I get out of my car, walk to the garage, and open it. I already know the code. I open the front door and proceed to walk through the kitchen and down the stairs to the band room. I am greeted with warm hellos from my fellow band members. We chat for a while about our day. Then, about 15 minutes later, we set up our instruments.

All I have to do is tune my drums by tightening the heads until I get the sound I want. While I involve myself in this task, Jake extracts his Shecter Red Sunburst from its case, plugs the custom-made cord into his Crate Amplifier, flips up the on switch, and proceeds to tune his guitar. Mark opens up his case and takes out his BC Rich bass and begins the tuning process. Meanwhile, Bryan removes his Les Paul guitar from its case and proceeds to add the sounds of his tuning to the mix. When we complete our warmup, the rest of us plug ourselves in and set up the microphones.

After a little discussion about the practice list, we decide to go with our favorites: "Impatient Love," "Let's Change the World," and "Valentine's Day." Lately, we have been playing some of our newer material and practicing for our May 6th performance in front of three judges representing three different record labels, including Columbia Records! This opportunity presents us with a new level of commitment to our nightly practice session.

21. "Lee's Studio" is most likely a

    (A) large professional music studio in a downtown office building

    (B) room in the basement of a private home

    (C) back room at an automotive dealership

    (D) small, family-owned restaurant

22. The Shecter Red Sunburst is most likely

    (J) an amplifier

    (K) a drum set

    (L) a custom-made cord

    (M) a guitar

23. "Impatient Love" is probably

    (A) the title of a romantic short story

    (B) the title of a song

    (C) the name of a perfume

    (D) the name of a music studio

24. What instrument does the author of the passage play?

    (J) guitar

    (K) bass

    (L) drums

    (M) flute

Go on to next page

25. Why is the band particularly motivated for the practice session described in the passage?

    (A) because it is the first time they have practiced in "Lee's Studio"

    (B) because Mark is playing a new bass for the first time

    (C) because it is the first time the band has practiced "Valentine's Day" together

    (D) because it will be playing soon for representatives from three different record labels

---

Questions 26–30 pertain to the following passage.

At the conclusion of the Seven Years' War, England's national debt doubled, and the need for new revenue became extremely important for maintaining England's position as a world superpower. A statesman named George Greenville sought to solve this problem through taxation on American colonists. Greenville initially tested the success of taxation in 1764 by creating a bill that would increase English revenue through enforcement of customs duties. The revenue and success that came through this initial bill opened the door for Greenville's next piece of legislation that would later be called the Sugar Act.

The Sugar Act was designed to lower the duty on foreign molasses to threepence while raising the penalties for smuggling. The Sugar Act accomplished Greenville's goals of raising money for England, but the money raised was not enough. The most significant aspect of the Sugar Act is that reactions from American colonists raised questions about Britain's right to tax America.

American colonists argued that taxation was a way of taking property without consent. Edmund S. Morgan claimed that whatever threatened the security of property threatened liberty. So, liberty was directly threatened by England's decision to tax colonists without American representation in Parliament. The Connecticut Assembly came to the conclusion that Parliament's authority in America was limited to legislation, and therefore Parliament had no right to tax the colonists.

26. Who was George Greenville?

    (J) an English politician

    (K) an American colonist

    (L) a British explorer

    (M) a member of the Connecticut Assembly

27. What motivated England to implement the Sugar Tax?

    (A) It wanted to protest the creation of the Connecticut Assembly.

    (B) It wanted to increase the smuggling of foreign molasses.

    (C) It wanted to lower the national debt caused by the Seven Years' War.

    (D) It wanted America to become a world superpower.

Go on to next page

28. According to the passage, what was the most important consequence of the Sugar Act?

    (J) England raised sufficient funds to take care of the national debt.

    (K) The French no longer exported molasses.

    (L) The American colonists questioned England's right to tax them.

    (M) America was given representation in Parliament.

29. How did the American colonists react to the Sugar Act?

    (A) The colonists accepted the Act as necessary to improve England's economy.

    (B) The colonists understood that the Act would improve their freedom.

    (C) The colonists thought the Act would secure their representation in Parliament.

    (D) The colonists viewed the act as a threat to their liberty.

30. What conclusion did the Connecticut Assembly come to?

    (J) Parliament did not have the right to tax American colonists.

    (K) Parliament did not have the right to pass any legislation that would affect the American colonists.

    (L) The American colonists had no choice but to declare war on England.

    (M) The American colonists would no longer export molasses to England.

STOP DO NOT TURN THE PAGE UNTIL TOLD TO DO SO.
DO NOT RETURN TO A PREVIOUS TEST.

Language Section

Part 1

Time: 20 minutes

Directions: This section, which consists of 40 questions, tests how well you recognize usage, mechanics, capitalization, punctuation, and spelling errors in writing. Follow the specific directions before each group of questions. Mark your answer on the answer sheet.

Directions: In Questions 1–10, choose the answer that contains the misspelled word. If there are no misspelled words, choose the last answer.

1. (A) excellent
    (B) embarass
    (C) effort
    (D) *(No mistakes)*

2. (J) guaranty
    (K) warranty
    (L) threats
    (M) *(No mistakes)*

3. (A) popular
    (B) explode
    (C) experiance
    (D) *(No mistakes)*

4. (J) shove
    (K) begining
    (L) disappear
    (M) *(No mistakes)*

5. (A) tongue
    (B) sensible
    (C) comment
    (D) *(No mistakes)*

6. (J) receipt
    (K) recipe
    (L) restarant
    (M) *(No mistakes)*

7. (A) catagory
    (B) stunning
    (C) neighbor
    (D) *(No mistakes)*

8. (J) twelfth
    (K) judgment
    (L) intelligence
    (M) *(No mistakes)*

9. (A) relevent
    (B) spinning
    (C) miniature
    (D) *(No mistakes)*

10. (J) library
    (K) leisure
    (L) lisence
    (M) *(No mistakes)*

Go on to next page

Directions: Questions 11–35 contain three parts of a complete sentence. Pick the answer choice that corresponds with the part of the sentence that contains an error. If none of the sentence parts has an error, pick the last answer choice. Mark your answer on the answer sheet.

Check for capitalization errors in Questions 11–20.

11. (A) My favorite band,
    (B) The Eternal flames, plays
    (C) at the theatre on May 7th.
    (D) *(No mistakes)*

12. (J) Travis phoned his uncle
    (K) to find out what time the
    (L) Boston Red Sox team plays.
    (M) *(No mistakes)*

13. (A) Jill Thomas, phd,
    (B) is a professor at Lawrence University
    (C) in Appleton, Wisconsin.
    (D) *(No mistakes)*

14. (J) Every time I go
    (K) to the grocery store,
    (L) I pick up some Corn flakes.
    (M) *(No mistakes)*

15. (A) For my sixteenth birthday party,
    (B) my Father is
    (C) hiring a live band.
    (D) *(No mistakes)*

16. (J) Rachel was raised in the south,
    (K) but now she lives
    (L) in the Rocky Mountains.
    (M) *(No mistakes)*

17. (A) The head administrator
    (B) of the High School
    (C) is Sister Margaret.
    (D) *(No mistakes)*

18. (J) Timothy has not decided
    (K) what he should
    (L) give up for lent.
    (M) *(No mistakes)*

19. (A) Mr. Janney has read
    (B) *War and Peace,* by Leo
    (C) Tolstoy, four times!
    (D) *(No mistakes)*

20. (J) Whenever aunt Eleanor
    (K) comes to our house for a visit,
    (L) we take her to the art museum.
    (M) *(No mistakes)*

Check for punctuation errors in Questions 21–30.

21. (A) Agnes and Andy have lived on my
    (B) street for many years, in fact, they
    (C) were my first friends.
    (D) *(No mistakes)*

22. (J) Michael asked, "Can
    (K) we get ice cream."
    (L) "No," his mother replied.
    (M) *(No mistakes)*

23. (A) My family travels every summer
    (B) and visits many cities, but my favorite
    (C) is Orlando Florida.
    (D) *(No mistakes)*

24. (J) Before you take a walk,
    (K) take out the trash and,
    (L) lock the back door.
    (M) *(No mistakes)*

Go on to next page ⇨

25. (A) If I don't get enough sleep,
    (B) eat a good breakfast, or take a quick jog
    (C) I cannot function well at school.
    (D) *(No mistakes)*

26. (J) Jenny took a long hard look
    (K) at her brother before she told him
    (L) that she knew he was lying.
    (M) *(No mistakes)*

27. (A) Efforts to save the historical
    (B) building from demolition were thwarted
    (C) by powerful developers from Kansas City.
    (D) *(No mistakes)*

28. (J) Mary Anne and Emily went
    (K) shopping but neither girl
    (L) made a purchase.
    (M) *(No mistakes)*

29. (A) Although the Bulldogs faced their
    (B) opponents with determination, grit, and
    (C) persistence they lost by two points in overtime.
    (D) *(No mistakes)*

30. (J) The meeting will be held
    (K) in the old warehouse building
    (L) which is right next to the large park.
    (M) *(No mistakes)*

Check for usage errors in Questions 31–35.

31. (A) Before you assemble the furniture,
    (B) one has to read through all of the directions
    (C) and make sure you have the proper tools.
    (D) *(No mistakes)*

32. (J) It is easier for him and I to go
    (K) into town than it is for
    (L) her and Peter.
    (M) *(No mistakes)*

33. (A) Since arriving in town last week,
    (B) Susan has not seen anything
    (C) particularly unusual or surprising.
    (D) *(No mistakes)*

34. (J) The band played less songs
    (K) at its summer concert than it
    (L) played at the winter one.
    (M) *(No mistakes)*

35. (A) Much of the planning initiated last July by
    (B) the dedicated committee members never
    (C) results in any real action.
    (D) *(No mistakes)*

Go on to next page

Directions: For Questions 36–40, choose the best way to express the idea.

36. (J) The forest blanketed by a refreshing morning dew.

    (K) The forest was blanketed by a refreshing morning dew.

    (L) A refreshing morning dew blanketed the forest.

    (M) Blanketed by a refreshing morning dew was the forest.

37. (A) Flying through the windy March skies with a colorful tail, I saw the most beautiful kite ever.

    (B) Flying through the windy March skies with a colorful tail, the most beautiful kite was seen by me.

    (C) Flying through the windy March skies, I saw the most beautiful kite ever with a colorful tail.

    (D) I saw the most beautiful kite with a colorful tail flying through the windy March skies.

38. (J) I think that they, as a rule, are much more conniving than us.

    (K) I think that they are as a rule much more conniving than us.

    (L) As a rule, I think that they are much more conniving than us.

    (M) As a rule, I think that they are much more conniving than we.

39. (A) Of the two candidates for class president, Andie is the better qualified.

    (B) Andie is the best qualified of the two candidates for class president.

    (C) Of the two candidates for class president, Andie is the best qualified.

    (D) Andie is the best qualified class president candidate of the two.

40. (J) Crossing the bridge, a glimpse of the islands was caught by us.

    (K) Crossing the bridge, we caught a glimpse of the islands.

    (L) Crossing the bridge, the islands were caught by a glimpse.

    (M) Crossing the bridge, a view of the islands was glimpsed by us.

Go on to next page

Part 2

Time: 10 minutes

Directions: Choose the best answer to the following 10 questions based on the paragraph they follow.

Questions 41 and 42 pertain to the following paragraph.

(1)What is a writer for children to do? (2)Can the writer present evil as an unsolvable problem that no one, not even an adult, can do anything about? (3)Painting a picture of cruelty with no solution is surely unethical. (4)Excepting that, if you suggest that horrible situations like famine and brutality are easily solved, you are just lying. (5)It is immoral to insist that there is no solution to the problem of evil. (6)Children need protection and shelter. (7)They also need to hear the truth. (8)One way of presenting truth about evil in a moral way is to use fantasy in your stories.

41. What is the best way to write the underlined words in Sentence 4?

    (A) However

    (B) And

    (C) But that

    (D) *(No change)*

42. Which of the following sentences provides repetitive information and should be eliminated?

    (J) Sentence 2

    (K) Sentence 4

    (L) Sentence 5

    (M) Sentence 8

Questions 43 and 44 pertain to the following paragraph.

(1)Johnson focuses on the changing political agenda in hip-hop. (2)Another author, Sanders, argues that hip-hop's commercialization has overshadowed hip-hop's mainstream political agenda. (3)She blames the increased use of hip-hop culture in mainstream advertising for creating a business element that overshadows political protest. (4)Due to rap's commercial success and the severe lack of jobs for African American youth, some African Americans are willing to embrace rap's money-making side and ignore political consciousness in order that they become wealthy. (5)Sanders sees the potential for a hip-hop political agenda. (6)But she argues for unity between the business and political agendas. (7)Unity of these two areas is crucial to produce a political hip-hop agenda.

43. What is the best way to write the underlined words in Sentence 2?

    (A) hip-hop's-commercialization

    (B) Hip-Hop Commercialization

    (C) Hip Hop commercialization

    (D) *(No change)*

44. What is the best way to write the underlined words in Sentence 4?

    (J) to

    (K) on account of they want to

    (L) due to the fact that they

    (M) *(No change)*

Go on to next page

Questions 45–47 pertain to the following paragraph.

(1)Over the last two decades, college tuition rates have increased at a higher <u>rate, then</u> the rate of inflation. (2)Over a two-year period, tuition at four-year universities increased an average of 26 percent. (3)The Bureau of Labor Statistics published a report stating that <u>rising college tuition fees</u> have gone up more than the rate of inflation for every year since 1982. (4)Throughout the past generation, tuition fees have risen faster than family incomes, a situation that is not maintainable on a long-term basis. (5)Federal financial assistance in higher education during this period has increased. (6)In the 1983–1984 school year, American college students received $28.4 billion in financial assistance from all sources. (7)Twenty years later, that aid had grown to $122 billion. (8)<u>However</u>, two-thirds of this was provided by the federal government.

45. What is the best way to write the underlined words in Sentence 1?

    (A) rate then

    (B) rate, than

    (C) rate than

    (D) *(No change)*

46. What is the best way to write the underlined portion of Sentence 3?

    (J) growing college tuition fees

    (K) rising college tuition

    (L) college tuition fees

    (M) *(No change)*

47. What is the best way to write the underlined word in Sentence 8?

    (A) But,

    (B) Because

    (C) Omit the underlined part and begin the sentence with "Two-thirds."

    (D) *(No change)*

Questions 48–50 pertain to the following paragraph.

(1)Jody's current production process consists of many different steps that <u>takes up lots</u> of time and decrease efficiency. (2)Jody has a problem with organization in her inventory room, <u>to</u>. (3)A good business consultant would resolve Jody's production problems. (4)The first problem that could easily be changed is the lack of efficiency. (5)Jody's business wastes time when bundles have to be assembled and disassembled; a new production scheme should be implemented that would reduce the number of steps in the production process. (6)The next problem the business consultant should address would be to hire an <u>Inventory Manager</u> to organize the inventory room to run more efficiently. (7)Solving these two problems would dramatically improve Jody's company.

48. What is the best way to write the underlined words in Sentence 1?

    (J) takes up much

    (K) take up a lot

    (L) takes up huge amounts

    (M) *(No change)*

49. What is the best way to write the underlined portion of Sentence 2?

    (A) additionally

    (B) too

    (C) two

    (D) *(No change)*

50. What is the best way to write the underlined portion of Sentence 6?

    (J) Inventory manager

    (K) inventory manager

    (L) inventory Manager

    (M) *(No change)*

STOP DO NOT TURN THE PAGE UNTIL TOLD TO DO SO.
DO NOT RETURN TO A PREVIOUS TEST.

Math Section

Part 1

Time: 35 minutes

Directions: For Questions 1–19, choose the best answer from the four choices and mark it on your answer sheet.

1. Which of the following numbers is <u>not</u> prime?

   (A) 7

   (B) 37

   (C) 43

   (D) 55

2. $3^3 - 2(3) = ?$

   (J) 0

   (K) 21

   (L) –21

   (M) 18

3. $\frac{3}{8} + \frac{1}{4} = ?$

   (A) $\frac{5}{8}$

   (B) $\frac{1}{2}$

   (C) 1

   (D) $\frac{1}{4}$

4. Bob decided to put 65% of his Christmas money in the bank. If he had $70 left after he put money in the bank, how much money did he get for Christmas?

   (J) $24.50

   (K) $50.00

   (L) $70.00

   (M) $200.00

5. Twenty friends decided to rent a limo to take them to the football game. If it costs $12 for each friend, how much money will the limo driver collect?

   (A) $200

   (B) $240

   (C) $300

   (D) $325

6. Brittney spent $23.46 and had $8.34 left. How much money did Brittney start off with?

   (J) $15.12

   (K) $25.50

   (L) $31.80

   (M) $33.00

7. Jane ordered two tacos, one with all the regular ingredients and one with extra cheese and extra beans. A taco costs $13.00 plus $0.50 for each extra ingredient. How much will Jane's order cost?

   (A) $26.50

   (B) $27.00

   (C) $28.50

   (D) $29.00

8. What is the value of x if $x + 23 = -53$?

   (J) 76

   (K) 30

   (L) –30

   (M) –76

9. What is the greatest common factor of 25, 65, and 110?

   (A) 5

   (B) 10

   (C) 20

   (D) 25

Go on to next page

10. One soda costs $0.76. What would be the total cost for 100 sodas?

    (J) $1.76

    (L) $7.60

    (K) $76.00

    (M) $760.00

11. What is $(-4)(2)(-2)$?

    (A) 8

    (B) -8

    (C) -16

    (D) 16

12. Bob went through 4 crates of fruit juice at a graduation party. If each crate contained 14 cups of fruit juice, how many cups of fruit juice did Bob go through?

    (J) 45

    (K) 56

    (L) 60

    (M) 63

13. Amy has $34.57 in her wallet. If her mom gives her $7.87, how much will she have total?

    (A) $40.00

    (B) $42.44

    (C) $45.37

    (D) $47.44

14. Tim got ¼ of the problems wrong on his last test. The test had 60 problems on it. How many problems did Tim get wrong?

    (J) 30

    (K) 25

    (L) 20

    (M) 15

15. List the following fractions in order from least to greatest: ⅑, ⅗, and ¾.

    (A) ⅑, ⅗, ¾

    (B) ⅗, ⅑, ¾

    (C) ⅑, ¾, ⅗

    (D) ¾, ⅗, ⅑

16. Michelle bought two shirts for $15 each and one pair of jeans for $30. If she gives the cashier $70, how much change will she receive? (Assume there is no sales tax.)

    (J) $10

    (K) $12

    (L) $14

    (M) $16

17. ⅜ ÷ ⅔ = ?

    (A) ¾

    (B) ¼

    (C) ⁹⁄₁₆

    (D) ⅜

18. Solve $|x| + 3y$, if $x = -3$ and $y = 2$.

    (J) -3

    (K) 3

    (L) -9

    (M) 9

19. The perimeter of this octagon is 40 meters. If x is the missing length, what is the length in meters of side x?

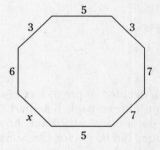

    (Figure not drawn to scale.)

    (A) 4

    (B) 5

    (C) 6

    (D) 7

Directions: Answer Questions 20–32 based on the corresponding graph or chart and mark your answers on the answer sheet.

20. Sophie surveyed students at her school to discover the most popular colors for T-shirts. The following table shows her findings. What are the three most popular colors for T-shirts at her school?

Shirt Color	Gray	Blue	Green	Black	White	Red	Purple
Number	17	21	19	27	15	20	17

(J) black, blue, red

(K) green, red, black

(L) black, red, green

(M) blue, green, purple

Use the following chart to answer Questions 21 and 22.

Welch Inc. Monthly Expenses

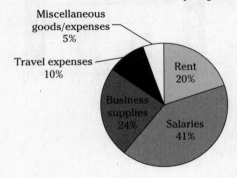

21. Welch Inc. recorded its expenses for the month on this pie chart. What fraction of expenses does the company spend on rent?

(A) ⅖

(B) ½

(C) ⅕

(D) ¾

22. What fraction of Welch Inc.'s expenses goes toward miscellaneous goods and expenses?

(J) ⅕

(K) ¹⁄₂₀

(L) ½

(M) ¾

23. The following graph shows the number of ice cream cones sold in one day according to flavor. If chocolate, mint, and vanilla were the only flavors sold, what percent of the ice cream cones sold was mint?

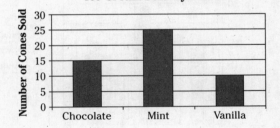

(A) 25%

(B) 30%

(C) 45%

(D) 50%

Go on to next page

24. Three students kept track of their test scores over the course of three tests. According to this chart, which student made the most improvement?

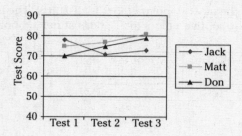

(J) Jack

(K) Don

(L) Matt

(M) Not enough information

25. The following chart shows the total number of home runs hit by three teams over the course of three months. During which month did the Dawgs hit more home runs than the Hawks and Cougars combined?

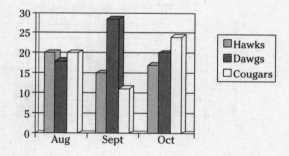

(A) August

(B) September

(C) October

(D) Not enough information

26. Luke put 15 marbles into a bag. Based on this chart, what is the probability that Luke will pull out a solid red marble?

Marble Color	Solid	Striped
Red	5	2
Blue	3	4
White	1	0

(J) ½

(K) ¼

(L) ⅕

(M) ⅓

27. The following chart records the number of freshmen girls with the same first name. How many more girls were named Sarah than Bre in the freshmen class?

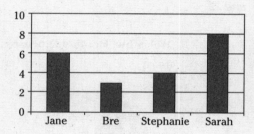

(A) 2

(B) 3

(C) 4

(D) 5

Go on to next page

Use the following chart to answer Questions 28 and 29.

Item	Price
Turkey sandwich	$8.50
Steak (12 oz.)	$12.75
Entree salad	$4.00
Large bowl of soup of the day	$3.00
Sides (chips, baked potato, small salad, small bowl of soup, corn)	$0.75 each

28. This menu shows the price of four entrees and side orders at a local diner. What would the total price be if someone ordered a 12-oz. steak and one baked potato?

(J) $8.50

(K) $10.00

(L) $13.50

(M) $14.00

29. Based on the same menu, how much would an entree salad and two small bowls of soup cost?

(A) $4.50

(B) $5.00

(C) $5.50

(D) $6.00

30. According to this graph, what fraction of the students chose black as their favorite car color?

Results of Car Color Survey

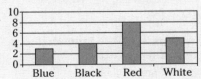

(J) ⅕

(K) ½

(L) ⅓

(M) ¼

31. The following table shows types of cars, the number in stock, and the price for each car type at Crazy Al's Car Lot. How much in dollars are 3 minivans and 1 sports car worth at Crazy Al's?

Car Type	Number of Cars on the Lot	Price
Sports car	2	$50,000
SUV	10	$37,000
Minivan	5	$28,000
Four-door sedan	8	$20,000

(A) $125,000

(B) $134,000

(C) $140,000

(D) $142,000

32. Eighth graders at Myron Middle School surveyed a science class to determine which pets were students' favorites. They recorded their findings in the following chart. According to the chart, how many more students prefer dogs to fish?

Favorite Pet

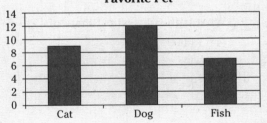

(J) 3

(K) 4

(L) 5

(M) 6

Go on to next page

Part 2

Time: 10 minutes

Directions: Use estimation to find the answers to Questions 33–50. Do not calculate exact answers or use scratch paper to solve. Mark your answers on the answer sheet.

33. What is the closest estimate of 11.7×99.8?

    (A) 120

    (B) 1,200

    (C) 2,000

    (D) 2,100

34. What is the closest estimate of 8,011 − 7,210?

    (J) 4,000

    (K) 3,000

    (L) 2,000

    (M) 1,000

35. What is the closest estimate of 6.32×10.44?

    (A) 77

    (B) 70

    (C) 60

    (D) 66

36. What is the closest estimate of 433 + 578?

    (J) 1,000

    (K) 900

    (L) 800

    (M) 700

37. What is the closest estimate of 42 + 56 + 47 + 63?

    (A) 190

    (B) 200

    (C) 210

    (D) 220

38. What is the closest estimate of $16.32 − $3.43?

    (J) $13

    (K) $14

    (L) $15

    (M) $16

39. What is the closest estimate of 2,356 ÷ 54?

    (A) 50

    (B) 40

    (C) 400

    (D) 4,000

40. What is 20.9433 rounded to the nearest hundredths place?

    (J) 21

    (K) 20.9

    (L) 20.94

    (M) 20.95

41. What is 2,534 rounded to the nearest thousand?

    (A) 1,000

    (B) 2,000

    (C) 2,500

    (D) 3,000

42. What is 34,574.361 rounded to the nearest tenths place?

    (J) 35,000

    (K) 34,574.4

    (L) 34,570

    (M) 34,574.36

Go on to next page

43. What is 344.533 rounded to the nearest whole number?

    (A) 345

    (B) 340

    (C) 344.5

    (D) 350

44. What is the closest estimate of $20(10 + 1)$?

    (J) 100

    (K) 150

    (L) 200

    (M) 250

45. If a race car travels at 242 mph and a remote control car travels at 23 mph, approximately how many times faster is the race car than the remote control car?

    (A) 10

    (B) 15

    (C) 20

    (D) 25

46. What is 2,543 rounded to the nearest hundred?

    (J) 3,000

    (K) 2,500

    (L) 2,540

    (M) 2,000

47. Ashleigh works 12 hours at $8.24 an hour. What is the closest estimate of how much money she will make for the 12-hour shift?

    (A) $80

    (B) $90

    (C) $96

    (D) $106

48. Vance rode his bike a total of 1,344 miles this year. Last year he rode his bike 1,566 miles. Estimate how many more miles Vance rode last year than this year.

    (J) 300 miles

    (K) 400 miles

    (L) 500 miles

    (M) 600 miles

49. Bananas cost $0.78 per pound, and soda is $3.20 for a case. If you need 5 pounds of bananas and 1 case of soda, approximately how much money will you need?

    (A) $5

    (B) $6

    (C) $7

    (D) $8

50. What is the closest estimate of $(3,534 - 1,422) \div 30$?

    (J) 10

    (K) 100

    (L) 1,000

    (M) 10,000

STOP DO NOT TURN THE PAGE UNTIL TOLD TO DO SO.
DO NOT RETURN TO A PREVIOUS TEST.

Ability Section

Time: 10 minutes

Directions: For Questions 1–7, find the figure in the answer choices that is similar to the initial three provided figures. Mark your answer on the answer sheet.

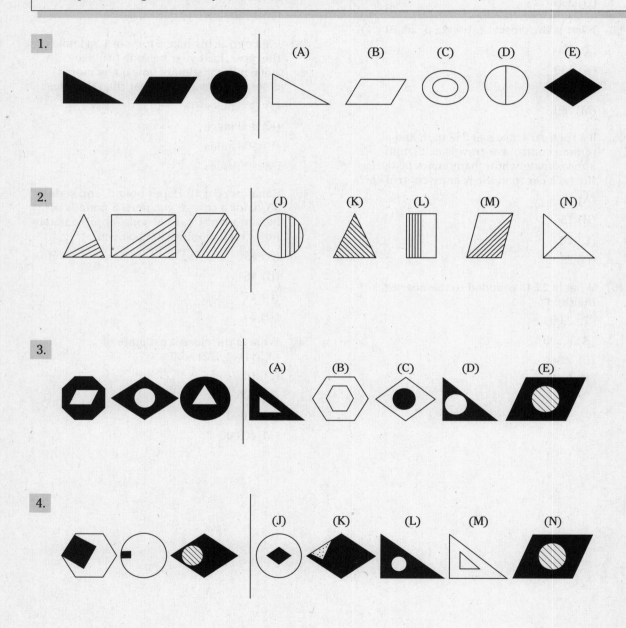

Go on to next page

5.

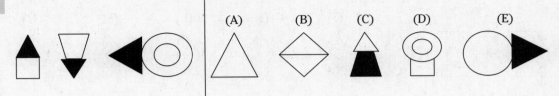

       (A)   (B)   (C)   (D)   (E)

6.

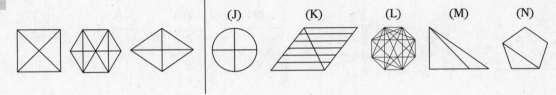

       (J)   (K)   (L)   (M)   (N)

7.

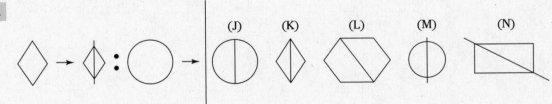

       (A)   (B)   (C)   (D)   (E)

Directions: Determine the relationship between the first two figures in Questions 8–14. Observe the third figure in each question and choose an answer that creates the same relationship with the third figure as the relationship between the first two figures. Mark your answer on the answer sheet.

8.

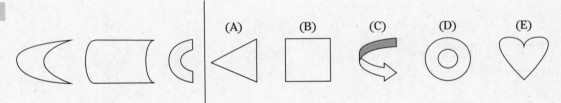

       (J)   (K)   (L)   (M)   (N)

9.

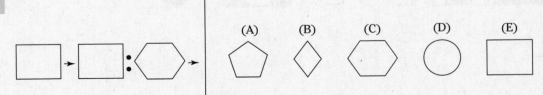

       (A)   (B)   (C)   (D)   (E)

Go on to next page

10.

(J) (K) (L) (M) (N)

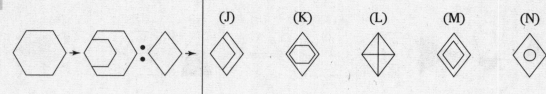

11.

(A) (B) (C) (D) (E)

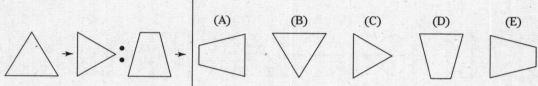

12.

(J) (K) (L) (M) (N)

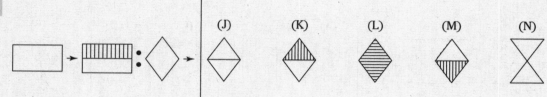

13.

(A) (B) (C) (D) (E)

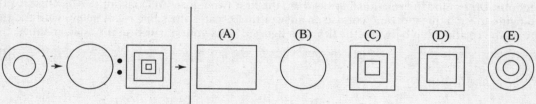

14.

(J) (K) (L) (M) (N)

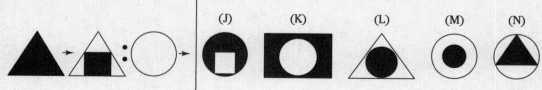

Go on to next page

Directions: The top row in Questions 15–20 shows the direction that a square piece of paper is folded and then punched. Choose the answer choice that shows how the same piece of paper appears after it has been unfolded. Mark your answer on the answer sheet.

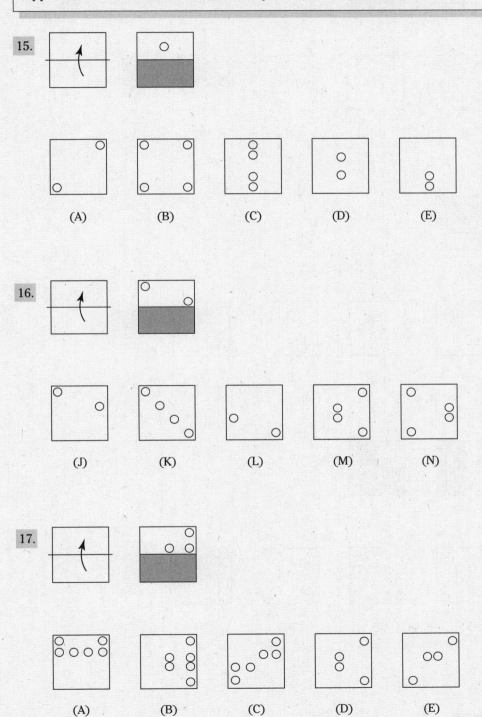

15.

(A)   (B)   (C)   (D)   (E)

16.

(J)   (K)   (L)   (M)   (N)

17.

(A)   (B)   (C)   (D)   (E)

Go on to next page

18.

(J)   (K)   (L)   (M)   (N)

19.

(A)   (B)   (C)   (D)   (E)

20.

(J)   (K)   (L)   (M)   (N)

STOP DO NOT TURN THE PAGE UNTIL TOLD TO DO SO.
DO NOT RETURN TO A PREVIOUS TEST.

Chapter 24

Answers to TACHS Practice Test 2

• •

Get ready to dive into detailed answer explanations for every question featured on the second TACHS practice test (found in Chapter 23). Reading the explanations will help reinforce what you've discovered about answering TACHS questions and help you become even more familiar with how to approach the typical and not-so-typical question types. (Don't have time for more reading? Head to the end of this chapter for a list of question numbers and answers — nothing more, nothing less.)

Reading Section

1. **B.** When you think of something dissolving, you may picture a sugary substance that melts in water. How does this picture relate to a partnership? Well, a melted partnership is one that breaks up, Choice (B). Choices (C) and (D) have more opposite meanings, and you can soften your skin, but you can't soften a partnership.

2. **J.** *Chasm* isn't easily broken down, so you really need to know that it means "a deep crack in the earth." The word with the closest meaning to crack is Choice (J), gap. The other three choices don't relate to characteristics of the earth, so cross them out.

3. **C.** A *diplomat* is an international negotiator; an *ambassador*, Choice (C), is also an international negotiator. Problem solved! Choices (A) and (B) don't relate to negotiation. A *nonentity*, Choice (D), is a nobody, and there's no such thing as an important nobody.

4. **J.** Resolution, Choice (J), actually has the word *solution* in it. Both words describe what happens when you solve a problem. Choice (K) is an opposite, and Choices (L) and (M) are completely unrelated.

5. **D.** You can break up eccentric into its prefix, *ec-*, which means "outside," and root, *cent,* which relates to center. So, generally, you're looking for an answer that means the same thing as being outside of the center. The best answer is Choice (D), unusual.

6. **K.** *Augment* means "to add to," so the best answer is Choice (K), increase. Choice (M) is an opposite, and Choice (L), adjust, doesn't tell you that the change in supply is an addition.

7. **B.** A *somber* mood is a serious or sad one. You wouldn't describe a mood as boring, so eliminate Choice (A). Choice (C) is the opposite of somber. Finally, a *mercurial* mood is one that changes frequently; like mercury in a thermometer, it goes up and down. Eliminate Choice (D). The best answer is Choice (B), *solemn*, which also means "serious or sad."

8. **L.** If you do something *impromptu*, you do it at the spur of the moment. Choice (L), *spontaneous*, also means "without a plan." Impromptu has nothing to do with length of time, so eliminate Choices (K) and (M). Choice (J) is more of an antonym than a synonym.

9. **D.** Perhaps you don't know what innocuous means, but you notice it sounds a little bit like innocent. The answer choice that's most like innocent is Choice (D), harmless, which is a good synonym for innocuous. Choice (A) has the opposite meaning, and the other two choices aren't related at all.

10. **M.** A *fleeting* moment doesn't last very long, so eliminate Choice (J). Choices (K) and (L) don't have anything to do with length of time, so they aren't right. The best answer is Choice (M), passing. A passing moment is there and gone quickly, just like a fleeting one.

11. **B.** The first paragraph of this passage tells you that Elizabeth is in her *flat* (the British name for an apartment). Later the passage comments on her "glorious living chamber." These clues tell you that the passage most likely takes place in a luxury apartment, Choice (B). Nothing in the passage suggests any of the other choices are appropriate.

When it comes to reading comprehension passages, always look for clues in the passages to answer the questions.

12. **L.** You know the author isn't admiring because the passage describes Elizabeth as condescending, so eliminate Choice (M). The author isn't serious, Choice (J), or objective, Choice (K); he or she has a definite opinion about Elizabeth that's presented in a sort of goofy way. The best answer is Choice (L); the author uses sarcasm in the second paragraph when discussing how "Liz" relates to peasants because she can no longer afford caviar.

13. **A.** Find the answer to this question through the process of elimination. Elizabeth doesn't have enough compassion to be a community volunteer, so Choice (D) is out. The passage doesn't talk about employees, so she's not a small business owner, Choice (C). Nor does it mention students, so cut Choice (B), a professor. Elizabeth is likely a politician, Choice (A).

14. **K.** The third paragraph says that sugar is a precious commodity, which means it's either scarce or expensive, Choice (K). The passage doesn't give you enough detail to choose any of the other answers.

15. **D.** You can eliminate Choice (C) right off the bat because the passage says that peasants *can't* vote. Elizabeth isn't really concerned about the needs of others, so Choice (A) can't be right. And the passage says that sugar is precious but not more precious than caviar and roses. In every paragraph, the passage mentions that Elizabeth is either worried about losing her position of power or losing her money, Choice (D).

16. **M.** The second paragraph of the passage states that "students usually depend on authority, instruction, and logic to establish facts." Choice (M), logic, is the best answer. The other choices present elements of the scientific method.

17. **A.** The author of this passage states facts without emotion, which means the tone of the passage is objective, Choice (A). The other three choices convey strong emotion that isn't present in the passage.

18. **K.** The passage talks about a nonspurious relationship in the last paragraph. The main point of the paragraph is that you have to show that no other variables caused a result to happen. This point is summarized in Choice (K).

19. **A.** The author discusses rationale in the second-to-last paragraph. In the second sentence of the paragraph, he or she states that "rationale comes from observation and experimentation," which is the exact wording of Choice (A).

20. **K.** The first sentence of the second paragraph clearly states that "determining truth is the goal of scientific research," which is Choice (K).

21. **B.** Because the author describes entering through a garage and going down a flight of stairs, you can reasonably conclude that the studio is in the basement of a home, Choice (B). Nothing in the passage suggests that it's in a professional building, automotive dealership, or restaurant.

22. **M.** In the second paragraph, Jake takes the Shecter Red Sunburst from a case. You don't take a drum set out of a case, so Choice (K) is wrong. The author then describes Jake plugging a cord into an amplifier, suggesting that the cord and amplifier are different from the Sunburst. Toss Choices (J) and (L). The Sunburst has to be a guitar, Choice (M).

23 **B.** The band plays music, and "Impatient Love" is on its practice list, so it must be a song title, Choice (B).

24. **L.** In the first sentence of the second paragraph, the author refers to "my drums," which tells you that the drums, Choice (L), are the author's instrument.

25. **D.** In the last paragraph, the author mentions that the band will soon be playing before representatives from record labels and states that this gives the band a "new level of commitment" to its practice session. Consequently, the best answer is Choice (D).

26. **J.** You may have to look at several clues to answer this question. The first paragraph describes Greenville as a statesman, so he's probably a political figure. Eliminate Choice (L) right away. Next, find out whether Greenville is American or English. The second paragraph says that Greenville wanted to raise money for England, so he's probably English. Forget Choice (K). He wanted to tax colonists, so he wasn't a member of the Connecticut Assembly, Choice (M). Choice (J) is the best answer.

27. **C.** The passage says that England wanted to remain a superpower, but it doesn't say that England wanted the American colonies to be a superpower; cross out Choice (D). In the second paragraph, you discover that England raised the penalty for smuggling, so Choice (B) doesn't make sense. The passage doesn't discuss how England felt about the Connecticut Assembly, so Choice (A) is wrong. The best answer is Choice (C). The war increased England's national debt, and it needed to raise money through taxes.

28. **L.** You can find the answer to this question in the last sentence of the second paragraph, which says that the Sugar Act "raised questions about Britain's right to tax America" — the idea stated in Choice (L). The second paragraph directly states that the Sugar Act didn't raise enough revenue, so Choice (J) is wrong. The third paragraph tells you that American colonists didn't have representation in Parliament, which eliminates Choice (M). Choice (K) isn't even covered in the passage, so it can't possibly be right.

29. **D.** American colonists had a negative reaction to the Sugar Act, so toss out all the answer choices that suggest a positive reaction. The only option left is Choice (D).

30. **J.** The last sentence of the passage clearly states that the conclusion of the Connecticut Assembly was that "Parliament had no right to tax the colonists." This is the answer in Choice (J). Choices (L) and (M) aren't dealt with in the passage, and you know Choice (K) can't be right because the passage says the assembly saw that Parliament had a role in legislation.

Language Section

1. **B.** Don't be embarrassed if you didn't know that embarrass has a double *r*. Choice (B) is misspelled; effort and excellent are spelled properly.

2. **J.** Guarantee and warranty have similar-sounding endings, but they're spelled differently. Warranty, Choice (K), is spelled correctly, but guaranty, Choice (J), ends with *ee*, not *y*.

3. **C.** Experience ends with *ence* rather than *ance*, so Choice (C) is the misspelled word. Popular and explode are fine just as they appear in Choices (A) and (B).

4. **K.** Noticing that begining, Choice (K), is misspelled may be difficult at first glance, but it should have a double *n* before the *ing*. You may have picked Choice (L) thinking that disappear has a double *s*, but just one *s* does the trick in disappear.

5. **D.** All the words in this question are spelled correctly. Pick Choice (D) and move along.

6. **L.** You may have been tempted to pick Choice (J) here, but remember that the rule is "*i* before *e* except after *c*." The *ei* in receipt comes after a *c*, so it's spelled correctly. Choice (L) is the problem; restarant should contain a silent *u* after the first *a*.

7. **A.** Although category sounds like it's spelled with an *a* in the second syllable, the proper spelling is with an *e,* so Choice (A) is misspelled. The *ei* in neighbor, Choice (C), is an exception to the *i*-before-*e* rule because the *ei* makes a long *a* sound.

8. **M.** None of the words is misspelled. The *f* in twelfth, Choice (J), is proper even though you can't really hear it. You toss out the *e* in judge when you add on *ment* to make judgment, so Choice (K) is okay. Intelligence has a double *l* and ends in *ence,* just like it appears in Choice (L). Choice (M) is the right answer!

9. **A.** The problem word in this question is Choice (A), relevent. It should end with *ant,* not *ent.* Even though you don't really hear the *a* in miniature, Choice (C), including it is proper. To keep the short *i* sound in spin, Choice (B), you must double the *n* before adding *ing.*

10. **L.** License is hard to spell for many people. The first *s* sound is made with a *c,* and the second *s* sound is made with an *s,* so it's not spelled right in Choice (L). The *ei* combination in leisure, Choice (K), is proper (it's one of those tricky exceptions to the rule). Choice (J), library, is just fine the way it appears.

11. **B.** In Choice (B), The Eternal Flames is the name of the band, so every important word in the name should be capitalized.

12. **M.** This sentence is free of capitalization problems, so you can safely pick Choice (M).

13. **A.** Titles that follow proper names are capitalized, which means Choice (A) should be written like this: Jill Thomas, PhD.

14. **L.** The phrase *corn flakes* in this sentence isn't the proper name of a cereal. You know that because it talks about "some corn flakes." Even if it were the proper name, both words in the name would have to be capitalized. Choice (L) is capitalized incorrectly.

15. **B.** In Choice (B), *father* isn't used as a proper name, so it shouldn't be capitalized. You know this because the sentence refers to "*my* father" rather than "Father."

16. **J.** *South* in Choice (J) refers to an area of the country rather than a direction, so it should be capitalized: Rachel was raised in the South. Rocky Mountains in Choice (L) is the name of a region, so it's properly capitalized.

17. **B.** *High school* isn't the proper name of the school that Sister Margaret administers, so Choice (B) should be written as "of the high school."

18. **L.** *Lent* is the name of a specific religious period; it should be capitalized in Choice (L).

19. **D.** Hooray! No capitalization errors in this sentence.

20. **J.** *Aunt* in Choice (J) is part of Aunt Eleanor's proper name, so it needs to be capitalized. The art museum in Choice (L) is a general term rather than the name of a place, which means writing it in lowercase is correct.

21. **B.** A sentence formed by two independent clauses (in this case, "Agnes and Andy have lived on my street for many years" and "in fact, they were my first friends") joined only by a comma and no conjunction is a *comma splice.* The two clauses need to be punctuated differently in Choice (B). Something like this would be more appropriate: Agnes and Andy have lived on my street for many years. In fact, they were my first friends.

22. **K.** "Can we get ice cream" is a question, so Choice (K) should have a question mark after *cream* rather than a period.

23. **C.** A comma separates a city name from a state name. Choice (C) should be "is Orlando, Florida." The comma in Choice (B) properly separates two independent clauses with a conjunction.

24. **K.** You don't place a comma after a conjunction, so the ending comma in Choice (K) is wrong. Choice (J) properly puts a comma after *walk* to separate a beginning dependent clause (before you take a walk) from an independent clause (take out the trash and lock the back door.) Choice (K) is your answer.

25. **B.** There should be a comma after *jog* to separate the beginning dependent clause (If I don't get enough sleep, eat a good breakfast, or take a quick jog) from the independent clause (I cannot function well at school). The other commas in this sentence properly punctuate the series. Choice (B) is the right answer.

26. **J.** Two or more adjectives that come before and refer to the same noun should be separated by commas, which means Choice (J) should be written like this: Jenny took a long, hard look.

27. **D.** There's no need for any punctuation marks in this sentence other than the ending period. The correct answer is Choice (D).

28. **K.** The conjunction *but* joins two independent clauses ("Mary Anne and Emily went shopping" and "neither girl made a purchase"). Because a comma is necessary before a conjunction in order to join two independent clauses, Choice (K) is the obvious answer.

29. **C.** "Although the Bulldogs faced their opponents with determination, grit, and persistence" is a beginning dependent clause, so you need a comma after *persistence* in Choice (C) to separate the clause from the remaining independent clause. The other commas are proper for the series.

30. **K.** *Which* is used to begin nonrestrictive clauses, and nonrestrictive clauses provide nonessential information, so there should be a comma after *building* in Choice (K).

31. **B.** This sentence incorrectly switches between second person (you) and third person (one) throughout. Because *you* appears in both Choice (A) and Choice (C), you must change *one* to *you* and the verb *has* to *have* in Choice (B) so that it reads like "you have to read through all of the directions."

32. **J.** Most of the pronouns in this sentence are objects of the preposition *for*. Therefore, you need to use the objective form (me, him, her, them, us). Choice (J) should be written like this: It is easier for him and me to go.

Figuring out which form of pronoun to use is easier if you consider each pronoun separately. For instance, in the phrase "It is easier for him and I to go," if you take away *him*, you clearly see that *me* is better than *I*.

33. **D.** This sentence is a-okay as is. Pick Choice (D) and move on.

34. **J.** The proper word for showing a reduction of countable items (such as songs) is *fewer*. Choice (J) should be written like this: The band played fewer songs.

35. **C.** The first part of the sentence is in past tense, so the verb in Choice (C) should be in past tense also (meaning *results* should be *resulted*).

36. **L.** Choice (J) is a sentence fragment because it doesn't have a verb, Choice (K) is in passive voice, and Choice (M) puts the main subject (forest) in the predicate of the sentence rather than the subject. Choice (L) is the best way to phrase the idea. It's a complete sentence, it's in active voice, and it puts the subject in its proper place in the sentence.

37. **D.** Choices (A) and (C) make it seem like I is flying through the windy March skies, which is downright silly! Choice (B) has the kite flying through the March skies, but it uses passive voice. Choice (D) makes sense and is in active voice.

38. **M.** The only answer that applies the proper form of the ending pronoun is Choice (M). The full thought is that they're much more conniving than *we are*. Therefore, *we* rather than *us* is the proper form of the pronoun in this sentence.

39. **A.** When you compare two things or people, you use *better* rather than *best*. The only sentence that suggests Andie is the better qualified candidate is Choice (A). All the other options improperly use best to compare the two candidates.

40. **K.** The constructions of Choices (J), (L), and (M) suggest that either a glimpse or view crosses the bridge. Now that'd be an unusual sight! Choice (K) is the only sentence that has people crossing the bridge.

41. **A.** Sentence 4 presents an idea that's opposite to the idea expressed in Sentence 3, so you need a transition word that shows contrast. Choice (B), and, shows similarity rather than contrast, so it's wrong. Choices (C) and (D), excepting that and but that, are improper constructions. However, Choice (A), is a proper way of showing contrast.

42. **L.** Consider each of the answer choices to determine which one repeats an idea that's already stated in the paragraph. Sentence 2 isn't the same as Sentence 1, so Choice (J) is wrong. Sentence 4, Choice (K), provides a contrasting idea to Sentence 3, so it's not repetitive. Sentence 8 introduces using fantasy in stories, which is completely new. Therefore Choice (M) isn't right. The idea that it's immoral to show that there's no solution to evil is stated in both Sentence 3 and Sentence 5. Choice (L) is correct.

43. **D.** You need the possessive form of *hip-hop* in this sentence because it's talking about the commercialization of hip-hop, or *hip-hop's commercialization*. Eliminate Choices (B) and (C). And although you put a hyphen between hip and hop, you can't connect *hip-hop's* as an adjective to the noun *commercialization* with a hyphen like Choice (A) does. Choice (D) is correct.

44. **J.** Clear writing expresses an idea in the simplest way possible. *To* in Choice (J) states in one word what all the other answer choices do with a confusing mumbo jumbo of too many words.

45. **C.** The underlined part of Sentence 1 has two problems. First, there's no reason to put a comma after *rate,* so you can cross out Choices (B) and (D). Second, the proper comparison word is *than,* not *then.* Choice (C) is the best answer.

46. **L.** Saying that rising college tuition fees have gone up is redundant. If fees are rising, then they're going up. Choose the answer that states the idea of rising fees only once. Because *going up* isn't underlined, you have to find the answer that eliminates *rising,* which is Choice (L). Choice (K) still has rising in it, and Choice (J) just changes rising to a different word.

47. **C.** Sentence 8 emphasizes the idea that federal financial assistance is increasing, so words that show contrast rather than continuation aren't appropriate. *But* in Choice (A) and *however* in Choice (D) show contrast, so they can't be right. *Because* shows cause and effect, not continuation, so Choice (B) isn't right either. The best answer is Choice (C), which continues the thought without a transition word.

48. **K.** The subject of the verb *takes* in the underlined part of Sentence 1 is plural, and a plural subject needs a plural verb. The plural form of takes is *take.* Eliminate Choices (J), (L), and (M) because they contain takes rather than take. Choice (K) is the only answer that has the plural form of the verb.

TIP

Compare answer choices to see what makes each one different. If only one out of four possible answers uses, say, *take* rather than *takes,* that may be a clue that the verb is the problem.

49. **B.** The underlined part uses the wrong form of *to* to mean *also.* The proper construction is Choice (B), too.

50. **K.** Inventory manager isn't a proper name, so it shouldn't be capitalized. The answer that properly presents both words in lowercase is Choice (K).

Math Section

1. **D.** You're looking for the answer that *isn't* a prime number, so all you have to do is find the answer that has more factors than 1 and itself. Choice (D) should stand out because it ends in a 5. Any two-digit number that ends in a 5 has a factor of 5 and can't be prime. Choice (D) is the answer.

2. **K.** Follow the order of operations (PEMDAS). You don't have any operations in parentheses, so solve the exponent first: $3^3 = 27$. The next step is to multiply: $2 \times 3 = 6$. Then subtract: $27 - 6 = 21$, Choice (K).

3. **A.** Find the least common denominator: 4 goes into 8 twice, so 8 works. Change the second fraction from ¼ to ⅜ by multiplying the numerator and denominator by 2. Now that the denominators are the same, add the numerators and place the sum over 8: ⅜ + ⅜ = ⅝. The answer is Choice (A).

   You can only add fractions together when they have the same denominator.

4. **M.** Believe it or not, you don't need to make any calculations to figure this one out. If Bob has already put his savings in the bank and still has $70 left, he must have received more than $70 for Christmas. Guess what. You can safely eliminate the first three choices because none is greater than $70. (If you really want to calculate Bob's gift, consider that because Bob saved 65%, the part he didn't save, $70, must be 35% of the total. Just divide $70 by 35%: $70 ÷ 0.35 = $200.)

5. **B.** This is a simple multiplication problem. 20 limo riders × $12 each is $240, Choice (B). What a deal!

6. **L.** To discover the original amount of money Brittney had, just add what she spent to what she had left: $23.46 + $8.34 = $31.80. Choice (L) is the answer. If you subtracted rather than added, you got Choice (J).

7. **B.** You can figure out what Jane spent on lunch by first calculating how much she spent on two basic tacos: $13 × 2 = $26. Then add on the cost of the two extra ingredients she bought for the second taco: $26 + $0.50 + $0.50 = $27.00, Choice (B).

8. **M.** To solve for x, subtract 23 from both sides of the equation: $x = -53 - 23$. When you subtract a number from a negative number, you add the numbers and keep the negative sign: $-53 - 23 = -76$. The answer is Choice (M). If you picked any of the other answers, you subtracted the numbers incorrectly.

9. **A.** You know Choices (B) and (C) are wrong because 10 and 20 are only factors of numbers that end in 0. So the factor is either 5 or 25. Because 25 doesn't go into 65 or 110, Choice (A) must be the answer.

10. **K.** To multiply by 100, just move the decimal point two places to the right. 100 sodas at $0.76 each cost $76.00, Choice (K). If you picked Choices (L) or (M), you moved the decimal the wrong number of places.

11. **D.** A multiplication problem with an even number of negative signs has a positive answer. This problem has two negative signs, so eliminate any negative answer options, namely Choices (B) and (C). $4 × 2 × 2 = 16$, Choice (D).

12. **K.** Multiply the number of crates (4) by the number of cups per crate (14) to find out the total number of cups consumed at the party: $4 × 14 = 56$, which is Choice (K).

13. **B.** This problem requires simple addition. Add how much Amy has to the amount her mom gives her: $34.57 + $7.87 = $42.44. Choice (B) is the answer.

14. **M.** *Of* means multiply, so multiply 60 by ¼. ⁶⁰⁄₁ × ¼ = ⁶⁰⁄₄. 60 ÷ 4 = 15, Choice (M).

15. **C.** Sure, you can solve this problem by changing each fraction to a decimal and then placing them in order — but you don't need to. You already know that 2/4 is the same as ½. Tell yourself that 4/9 is less than ½ because half of 9 is 4.5 and 4 is less than 4.5. 3/5 is more than ½ because 2.5 is half of 5 and 3 is more than 2.5. The order is 4/9, 2/4, 3/5, Choice (C).

16. **J.** Add up Michelle's purchase. Two shirts at $15 each cost $30 total. Add to that another $30 for a pair of pants to get $60. Subtract $60 from $70 to find out how much change she gets: $70 − $60 is $10. Mark Choice (J) on your answer sheet.

17. **C.** Apply the rule for dividing fractions to this problem and you get this equation: ⅜ × 3/2. Multiply the numerators, $3 × 3 = 9$, and the denominators, $8 × 2 = 16$. The answer is 9/16, Choice (C).

   When you divide fractions, flip the numerator and denominator of the second fraction and multiply.

18. **M.** To solve this problem, just substitute the values for x and y into the equation, like this: $|-3| + 3(2)$. Those parallel lines on either side of the –3 mean absolute value. Absolute value is always positive, so now you have 3 + 3(2). $3 \times 2 = 6$, and 3 + 6 = 9. The answer is Choice (M). If you went with Choice (K), you forgot that absolute value is positive.

19. **A.** You figure out the perimeter of a polygon by adding up the length of each side. This octagon has a perimeter of 40 meters, so you can set up an equation that looks like this: 40 = 5 + 3 + 3 + 6 + 5 + 7 + 7 + x. Now solve: 40 = 36 + x; subtract 36 from both sides: 4 = x. The answer is Choice (A).

20. **J.** On the chart, find the colors with the largest numbers to determine the most popular ones. The most popular color is black with 27 shirts. Next is blue with 21 shirts, and third is red with 20 shirts. The answer that lists these top three colors is Choice (J).

21. **C.** The pie chart displays Welch's rent expense as 20 percent of total expenses, but all the answer choices are fractions. To convert 20 percent to a fraction, put 20 over 100 and simplify. Divide both the numerator and denominator by 20: $^{20}/_{100} = ^{1}/_{5}$. The answer is Choice (C).

22. **K.** A total of 5 percent (or $^{5}/_{100}$) of Welch's expenses goes to miscellaneous goods and expenses. Reduce the fraction by dividing the numerator and denominator by 5: $^{5}/_{100} = ^{1}/_{20}$. Choice (K) is the correct answer.

23. **D.** You may be tempted to pick Choice (A), but 25 is the *number* of mint ice cream cones sold, not the *percentage* of mint cones sold. To find the percentage, you first have to figure out the total number of ice cream cones sold. 15 chocolate cones, 10 vanilla cones, and 25 mint cones were sold; that's 50 total cones (15 + 10 + 25 = 50). The fraction of mint cones sold is $^{25}/_{50}$, or $^{1}/_{2}$. You probably know that $^{1}/_{2}$ is the same as 50%, Choice (D), but if you don't, you can find the answer by dividing: 1 ÷ 2 = 0.50, and 0.50 is 50%.

24. **K.** Use the chart to compare the students' first scores to their last. Jack's score decreased from 79 to 71, so Choice (J) isn't right. Compare Don and Matt's scores. Matt's score went from 75 to 82, a change of 7. Don's score increased from 70 to 79, an improvement of 9. The student who improved the most is Choice (K), Don.

25. **B.** The chart shows that September is the only month when the Dawgs hit more home runs than the other two teams did, so Choice (B) is probably the answer. The Dawgs hit about 28 home runs in September. The Hawks hit 15 home runs, and the Cougars hit around 12. 12 + 15 = 27, which is fewer than the 28 home runs hit by the Dawgs.

26. **M.** The chart shows that there are 5 solid red marbles in the bag of 15 marbles, so Luke has a 5 in 15 ($^{5}/_{15}$) chance of pulling out a solid red marble. $^{5}/_{15}$ reduces to $^{1}/_{3}$, Choice (M).

27. **D.** The bar for Sarah goes up to the 8 mark. The bar for Bre ends between 2 and 4, which means 3 girls were named Bre. 8 – 3 = 5; there are 5 more girls named Sarah than girls named Bre in the class. The answer is Choice (D).

28. **L.** According to the table, a steak costs $12.75. A baked potato on the side would be an extra $0.75. The total cost is $13.50 ($12.75 + $0.75 = $13.50), Choice (L).

29. **C.** An entree salad costs $4.00. Two small side bowls of soup cost a total of $1.50 ($0.75 + $0.75). Add to find the total of all three purchases: $4.00 + $1.50 = $5.50, Choice (C).

30. **J.** To find the fraction of students who like black cars, you must first know the total number of students in the survey. Using the information in the chart, add up the number of students who like blue, black, red, and white cars: 3 + 4 + 8 + 5 = 20. Four students prefer black cars, so the fraction of students whose favorite car color is black is 4 out of 20, or $^{4}/_{20}$. Reduce the fraction by dividing the numerator and denominator by 4: $^{4}/_{20} = ^{1}/_{5}$, Choice (J).

31. **B.** This problem requires you to do a little multiplication and addition. The chart states that minivans sell for $28,000 each. Three of them would cost $84,000: $3 \times$ $28,000 = $84,000. A sports car is $50,000. Add $50,000 to $84,000 to find the total cost of all four cars: $50,000 + $84,000 = $134,000, Choice (B).

32. **L.** Use the chart to determine how many students like dogs and how many students like fish. The bar for dogs goes up to 12, so 12 students prefer dogs. The bar for fish ends exactly between 6 and 8, so 7 students prefer fish. To find out the difference, subtract 7 from 12: 12 − 7 = 5. The answer is Choice (L).

33. **B.** The most obvious way to estimate the answer to this problem in your head is to get rid of the decimal points for both numbers by rounding to the nearest whole number. Because the numbers to the right of the decimal points in both numbers are greater than 5, you round up for each number. 11.7 rounds up to 12, and 99.8 rounds up to 100. The problem then becomes 12 × 100. To multiply 12 × 100, multiply 12 × 1 and add two zeros to get 1,200. You can eliminate Choices (C) and (D) because the product of 12 and 1 doesn't begin with a 2! The difference between Choice (A) and Choice (B) is the number of zeros. Choice (B) is the correct answer.

34. **M.** All of the choices provided are rounded to the thousands place, which means you round the original numbers to the thousands place to estimate the difference. The number to the right of the thousands place in each number is less than 5, so you keep the existing number in the thousands place and add three zeros to get 8,000 − 7,000. Subtracting is easy now; the answer is Choice (M).

You can use the given answer choices to determine what place you should round to.

35. **C.** The answer choices are whole numbers, so round each number to the nearest whole number. The number to the right of the decimal point in each number is less than 5, so 6.32 rounds to 6, and 10.44 rounds to 10. 6 × 10 = 60, which is Choice (C).

36. **J.** The answer choices are rounded to the hundreds place. 433 rounded to the nearest hundred is 400 because the number to the right of the 4 is 3, which is less than 5. The number 578 rounds up to 600 because the number to the right of the 5 is greater than 5. Add the rounded numbers: 400 + 600 = 1,000, Choice (J).

37. **C.** Round each number to the nearest ten. 42 rounds to 40 (2 < 5), 56 becomes 60 (6 ≥ 5), 47 rounds up to 50 (7 ≥ 5), and 63 becomes 60 (3 < 5). 40 + 60 = 100, 100 + 50 = 150, and 150 + 60 = 210. Choice (C) is correct.

38. **J.** Round to whole dollars. $16.32 rounds to $16 because 3 < 5. $3.43 rounds to $3 because 4 < 5. $16 − $3 is $13, Choice (J). If you picked Choices (K) or (L), you incorrectly rounded up.

39. **B.** Round the numbers to something that's easy to work in your head. You can only round 54 to the tens place; 4 < 5, so 54 rounds to 50. 2,356 rounds to 2,000. Now do the division in your head. Eliminate one zero from both 50 and 2,000; when you do that, the problem becomes 200 ÷ 5. You know that 20 ÷ 5 is 4, so just add a zero to get 40, Choice (B). If you selected Choice (A), you rounded improperly. Choices (C) and (D) result from dividing incorrectly.

40. **L.** You can eliminate Choices (J) and (K) because neither is rounded to the hundredths place. Choice (M) rounds the 4 up to 5, but the digit next to the 4 is 3, which is less than 5. That means the 4 in the hundredths place stays a 4; the answer is Choice (L).

41. **D.** Choice (C) is rounded to the hundreds place, so it's wrong. The 2 is in the thousands place. The number to the right of the 2 is 5, which is ≥ 5, so round up to 3,000, Choice (D).

42. **K.** You find the tenths place directly to the right of the decimal point. In this large number (34,574.361), that number is a 3. The number to the right of that 3 is a 6. Because 6 ≥ 5, you round the 3 up to 4, just like Choice (K). All the other choices are rounded to the wrong place.

43. **A.** Choice (C) isn't a whole number, so it's wrong. Because the number to the right of the decimal point is 5, you round up. The number therefore becomes 345, Choice (A).

44. **L.** The order of operations tells you to add the parentheses first. 10 + 1 is 11. 11 rounds to 10, and 20 is already rounded. Multiply: 20 × 10 = 200, Choice (L).

45. **A.** The race car's estimated rate is 200 mph; the remote car travels at an estimated rate of 20 mph. The race car is about 10 times faster than the remote control car: 200 ÷ 20 is 10. Choice (A) is your answer.

46. **K.** Choices (J) and (M) are rounded to the nearest thousand. Choice (L) is rounded to the nearest ten. The only answer rounded to the nearest hundred is Choice (K).

47. **C.** You can round the dollar amount to the nearest whole dollar, which is $8. Ashleigh therefore makes about $8 an hour. In 12 hours, Ashleigh makes about $96, Choice (C), because 8 × 12 is 96. If you picked Choice (A), you rounded the number of hours too. The question specifically asks for the amount of money Ashleigh makes in 12 hours, which means you don't round the hours. Choice (C) is the best answer.

48. **J.** The answer choices are rounded to the nearest hundred, so round each mileage number to the nearest 100. 1,344 rounds to 1,300 because 4 < 5; 1,566 rounds to 1,600 because 6 ≥ 5. Subtract: 1,600 − 1,300 = 300. Vance rode about 300 more miles last year than this year, Choice (J).

49. **D.** Round the prices to the nearest whole dollar. Bananas are about $1 per pound, and soda is about $3 a case. Five pounds of bananas are about $5 (5 × $1). Add $5 to the $3 case of soda to find the total spent. Choice (D), $8, is correct.

50. **K.** Round the numbers in parentheses to the nearest thousand. 3,534 rounds up to 4,000, and 1,422 rounds to 1,000. Subtract: 4,000 − 1,000 = 3,000. To divide 3,000 by 30 in your head, eliminate a zero from both numbers to get 300 ÷ 3. You know that 3 ÷ 3 is 1, so add two zeros to get Choice (K), 100.

Ability Section

1. **E.** The common characteristic among the three figures is that each is shaded. Choices (A), (B), (C), and (D) aren't shaded, so Choice (E) must be the answer.

2. **M.** The three figures are half shaded with diagonal lines. Choices (K) and (N) aren't half shaded; Choices (J) and (L) are half shaded with vertical lines. The best answer is Choice (M).

3. **D.** Examine the three figures. Each has a shaded outer figure with an inner unshaded figure. Choices (B) and (C) don't have a shaded outer figure, and Choice (E) doesn't have an unshaded inner figure. Eliminate them. All of the given figures have different inner and outer figures, but the inner figure in Choice (A) is the same shape as the outer figure, so it can't be right. The best answer is Choice (D).

4. **K.** The similarities among the three figures may escape you at first. But notice that all of them have a different-shaped and -shaded inner figure stuck to the left side of the outer figure. The only answer with an inner figure stuck to the left side of its outer figure is Choice (K). All the other choices have floating inner figures.

5. **E.** Each given figure contains a shaded black triangle. The only answer with a shaded black triangle is Choice (E).

6. **L.** The given figures are different shapes, but each one has inner lines that connect each of its angles. The only figure in the answer choices that has lines attaching all of its angles is Choice (L). What a tangled web that figure weaves!

7. **C.** Although the given figures are different shapes, each of them has a convex left side that curves out and a concave right side that curves in. The figure with this similar characteristic is the arrow in Choice (C). None of the other figures have the same curved sides.

8. **M.** The second figure in the first set bisects the first figure with a vertical line that extends past the figure on either end. Because the first figure of the second set is a circle, the answer should be a circle with a vertical line that bisects it and extends in both directions. You find that figure in Choice (M).

9. **C.** The figures in the first set are exactly the same! The answer must be the figure that's exactly the same as the hexagon in the second set — Choice (C).

10. **J.** The second figure in the first set of figures adds an inner figure that's the same shape as the first. The only answers that add a similar inner figure to the diamond in the second set of figures are Choices (J) and (M). However, Choice (J) is the better answer because its inner figure is flush to the left, just like the one in the first set of given figures.

11. **E.** The second figure in the first set of figures is the same shape as the first but it's tipped 90 degrees to the right. Eliminate Choices (B) and (C) because they aren't the same shape as the first figure in the second set. The answer that tips the quadrilateral 90 degrees to the right is Choice (E).

12. **K.** The second figure in the first set shades the top half of the first figure with vertical lines. The first figure of the second set is a diamond, so look for the answer that's a diamond with a top half shaded in vertical lines. Only Choice (K) meets this requirement.

13. **C.** You may be tempted to pick Choice (A) for this analogy, but although the shape in Choice (A) is a quadrilateral like the first figure in the second set, it doesn't have the same dimensions. Go back and examine the first set of figures carefully. The second figure results from removing the inner circle from the outer circle. The answer that removes one of the inner squares from the outer square is Choice (C).

14. **J.** Examine the first set of figures; the first one is a shaded triangle, and the second is an unshaded triangle with a shaded square inside. To make the first figure into the second, you must change the shading (but not the shape) and add an inner figure that's shaded differently from the outer figure. Apply this pattern to the next figure, an unshaded circle. Choices (K) and (L) change the third figure's shape, so forget about 'em. The remaining choices keep the circle's shape, but Choices (M) and (N) don't change the shading; both have unshaded outer circles just like the unshaded circle in the question. The answer has to be Choice (J). It has a circle with different shading, and (wonder of wonders!) that circle contains the required unshaded square.

15. **D.** You know the number of holes in the unfolded paper will be twice the number of original holes if the paper is folded once. Therefore, the right answer can't be Choice (B) or Choice (C). Choice (A) puts the holes in the corner, which can't be right either because the original hole is in the middle of the fold. Both of the resulting holes in Choice (E) appear below the fold line, but one of the holes should be above the line, and the other should be below it. Choice (D) is the answer you're looking for.

16. **N.** Eliminate Choices (J) and (L) because the answer must have four holes. When you unfold the paper, there's a hole in the upper- and bottom-left corners. The only answer with this configuration is Choice (N).

17. **B.** When you eliminate any answer choices that don't have six holes, you're left with Choices (A), (B), and (C). Choice (A) would result if the paper were folded vertically, but Choice (C) isn't even possible because all the holes must be on the same side. The answer is Choice (B).

18. **J.** When a paper is folded twice, the end result has four times the number of holes, so the answer will have four holes (which means you can toss out Choices (K) and (M)). The hole is in the middle of the page, and Choice (J) is the only remaining answer with holes in the middle.

19. **D.** Look for an answer with four holes; Choices (A) and (E) obviously don't fit the bill. The original holes aren't in the middle of the page, so Choice (C) is out. And two holes have to appear on either side of the diagonal fold, so Choice (B) doesn't work. Choice (D) is correct.

20. **L.** The paper has two folds and 4 holes, so the answer must have 16 holes. The only option with 16 holes is Choice (L). That was pretty easy for the last question!

Answer Key for TACHS Practice Test 2

Reading Section

1. B	7. B	13. A	19. A	25. D
2. J	8. L	14. K	20. K	26. J
3. C	9. D	15. D	21. B	27. C
4. J	10. M	16. M	22. M	28. L
5. D	11. B	17. A	23. B	29. D
6. K	12. L	18. K	24. L	30. J

Language Section

1. B	11. B	21. B	31. B	41. A
2. J	12. M	22. K	32. J	42. L
3. C	13. A	23. C	33. D	43. D
4. K	14. L	24. K	34. J	44. J
5. D	15. B	25. B	35. C	45. C
6. L	16. J	26. J	36. L	46. L
7. A	17. B	27. D	37. D	47. C
8. M	18. L	28. K	38. M	48. K
9. A	19. D	29. C	39. A	49. B
10. L	20. J	30. K	40. K	50. K

Math Section

1. D	11. D	21. C	31. B	41. D
2. K	12. K	22. K	32. L	42. K
3. A	13. B	23. D	33. B	43. A
4. M	14. M	24. K	34. M	44. L
5. B	15. C	25. B	35. C	45. A
6. L	16. J	26. M	36. J	46. K
7. B	17. C	27. D	37. C	47. C
8. M	18. M	28. L	38. J	48. J
9. A	19. A	29. C	39. B	49. D
10. K	20. J	30. J	40. L	50. K

Ability Section

1. E	5. E	9. C	13. C	17. B
2. M	6. L	10. J	14. J	18. J
3. D	7. C	11. E	15. D	19. D
4. K	8. M	12. K	16. N	20. L

Chapter 25

COOP Practice Test 1

*T*aking the COOP? Here's your chance to practice. This test gets you ready for all seven sections of the exam so you won't be surprised on test day.

We've designed this practice test to be similar to the actual COOP, but the exam you take may be a little different because the test-makers like to periodically change things up (such as the numbers of questions in each section and the time limits).

Try to take this practice test under conditions that are as close to the real thing as possible. Here are our suggestions:

- ✔ Find a place where you won't be distracted. (Hide your cellphone in the closet!)
- ✔ Take this test at approximately the same time of day as the time your COOP is scheduled (which means you have to start around 8 or 9 a.m.).
- ✔ Remove the answer sheet and mark your answers on it by filling in the appropriate bubbles.
- ✔ Use the space in the margins around the test questions for notes and computations.
- ✔ Use a timer to time yourself on each section. When your time is up, stop answering questions in that section and move on.
- ✔ Take a short (10- to 15-minute) break between the fourth and fifth tests; this is likely when you'll receive a break on the day of the COOP.

After you finish the test, review the answer explanations in Chapter 26 (yes, even if you got every question right; you just might pick up something you didn't know).

Answer Sheet for COOP Practice Test 1

Test 1: Sequences

1. Ⓐ Ⓑ Ⓒ Ⓓ	5. Ⓐ Ⓑ Ⓒ Ⓓ	9. Ⓐ Ⓑ Ⓒ Ⓓ	13. Ⓐ Ⓑ Ⓒ Ⓓ	17. Ⓐ Ⓑ Ⓒ Ⓓ
2. Ⓕ Ⓖ Ⓗ Ⓙ	6. Ⓕ Ⓖ Ⓗ Ⓙ	10. Ⓕ Ⓖ Ⓗ Ⓙ	14. Ⓕ Ⓖ Ⓗ Ⓙ	18. Ⓕ Ⓖ Ⓗ Ⓙ
3. Ⓐ Ⓑ Ⓒ Ⓓ	7. Ⓐ Ⓑ Ⓒ Ⓓ	11. Ⓐ Ⓑ Ⓒ Ⓓ	15. Ⓐ Ⓑ Ⓒ Ⓓ	19. Ⓐ Ⓑ Ⓒ Ⓓ
4. Ⓕ Ⓖ Ⓗ Ⓙ	8. Ⓕ Ⓖ Ⓗ Ⓙ	12. Ⓕ Ⓖ Ⓗ Ⓙ	16. Ⓕ Ⓖ Ⓗ Ⓙ	20. Ⓕ Ⓖ Ⓗ Ⓙ

Test 2: Analogies

1. Ⓐ Ⓑ Ⓒ Ⓓ	5. Ⓐ Ⓑ Ⓒ Ⓓ	9. Ⓐ Ⓑ Ⓒ Ⓓ	13. Ⓐ Ⓑ Ⓒ Ⓓ	17. Ⓐ Ⓑ Ⓒ Ⓓ
2. Ⓕ Ⓖ Ⓗ Ⓙ	6. Ⓕ Ⓖ Ⓗ Ⓙ	10. Ⓕ Ⓖ Ⓗ Ⓙ	14. Ⓕ Ⓖ Ⓗ Ⓙ	18. Ⓕ Ⓖ Ⓗ Ⓙ
3. Ⓐ Ⓑ Ⓒ Ⓓ	7. Ⓐ Ⓑ Ⓒ Ⓓ	11. Ⓐ Ⓑ Ⓒ Ⓓ	15. Ⓐ Ⓑ Ⓒ Ⓓ	19. Ⓐ Ⓑ Ⓒ Ⓓ
4. Ⓕ Ⓖ Ⓗ Ⓙ	8. Ⓕ Ⓖ Ⓗ Ⓙ	12. Ⓕ Ⓖ Ⓗ Ⓙ	16. Ⓕ Ⓖ Ⓗ Ⓙ	20. Ⓕ Ⓖ Ⓗ Ⓙ

Test 3: Quantitative Reasoning

1. Ⓐ Ⓑ Ⓒ Ⓓ	5. Ⓐ Ⓑ Ⓒ Ⓓ	9. Ⓐ Ⓑ Ⓒ Ⓓ	13. Ⓐ Ⓑ Ⓒ Ⓓ	17. Ⓐ Ⓑ Ⓒ Ⓓ
2. Ⓕ Ⓖ Ⓗ Ⓙ	6. Ⓕ Ⓖ Ⓗ Ⓙ	10. Ⓕ Ⓖ Ⓗ Ⓙ	14. Ⓕ Ⓖ Ⓗ Ⓙ	18. Ⓕ Ⓖ Ⓗ Ⓙ
3. Ⓐ Ⓑ Ⓒ Ⓓ	7. Ⓐ Ⓑ Ⓒ Ⓓ	11. Ⓐ Ⓑ Ⓒ Ⓓ	15. Ⓐ Ⓑ Ⓒ Ⓓ	19. Ⓐ Ⓑ Ⓒ Ⓓ
4. Ⓕ Ⓖ Ⓗ Ⓙ	8. Ⓕ Ⓖ Ⓗ Ⓙ	12. Ⓕ Ⓖ Ⓗ Ⓙ	16. Ⓕ Ⓖ Ⓗ Ⓙ	20. Ⓕ Ⓖ Ⓗ Ⓙ

Test 4: Verbal Reasoning—Words

1. Ⓐ Ⓑ Ⓒ Ⓓ	5. Ⓐ Ⓑ Ⓒ Ⓓ	9. Ⓐ Ⓑ Ⓒ Ⓓ	13. Ⓐ Ⓑ Ⓒ Ⓓ
2. Ⓕ Ⓖ Ⓗ Ⓙ	6. Ⓕ Ⓖ Ⓗ Ⓙ	10. Ⓕ Ⓖ Ⓗ Ⓙ	14. Ⓕ Ⓖ Ⓗ Ⓙ
3. Ⓐ Ⓑ Ⓒ Ⓓ	7. Ⓐ Ⓑ Ⓒ Ⓓ	11. Ⓐ Ⓑ Ⓒ Ⓓ	15. Ⓐ Ⓑ Ⓒ Ⓓ
4. Ⓕ Ⓖ Ⓗ Ⓙ	8. Ⓕ Ⓖ Ⓗ Ⓙ	12. Ⓕ Ⓖ Ⓗ Ⓙ	16. Ⓕ Ⓖ Ⓗ Ⓙ

Test 5: Verbal Reasoning—Context

1. Ⓐ Ⓑ Ⓒ Ⓓ   5. Ⓐ Ⓑ Ⓒ Ⓓ   9. Ⓐ Ⓑ Ⓒ Ⓓ   13. Ⓐ Ⓑ Ⓒ Ⓓ   17. Ⓐ Ⓑ Ⓒ Ⓓ
2. Ⓕ Ⓖ Ⓗ Ⓙ   6. Ⓕ Ⓖ Ⓗ Ⓙ   10. Ⓕ Ⓖ Ⓗ Ⓙ   14. Ⓕ Ⓖ Ⓗ Ⓙ   18. Ⓕ Ⓖ Ⓗ Ⓙ
3. Ⓐ Ⓑ Ⓒ Ⓓ   7. Ⓐ Ⓑ Ⓒ Ⓓ   11. Ⓐ Ⓑ Ⓒ Ⓓ   15. Ⓐ Ⓑ Ⓒ Ⓓ   19. Ⓐ Ⓑ Ⓒ Ⓓ
4. Ⓕ Ⓖ Ⓗ Ⓙ   8. Ⓕ Ⓖ Ⓗ Ⓙ   12. Ⓕ Ⓖ Ⓗ Ⓙ   16. Ⓕ Ⓖ Ⓗ Ⓙ   20. Ⓕ Ⓖ Ⓗ Ⓙ

Test 6: Reading and Language Arts

1. Ⓐ Ⓑ Ⓒ Ⓓ   11. Ⓐ Ⓑ Ⓒ Ⓓ   21. Ⓐ Ⓑ Ⓒ Ⓓ   31. Ⓐ Ⓑ Ⓒ Ⓓ
2. Ⓕ Ⓖ Ⓗ Ⓙ   12. Ⓕ Ⓖ Ⓗ Ⓙ   22. Ⓕ Ⓖ Ⓗ Ⓙ   32. Ⓕ Ⓖ Ⓗ Ⓙ
3. Ⓐ Ⓑ Ⓒ Ⓓ   13. Ⓐ Ⓑ Ⓒ Ⓓ   23. Ⓐ Ⓑ Ⓒ Ⓓ   33. Ⓐ Ⓑ Ⓒ Ⓓ
4. Ⓕ Ⓖ Ⓗ Ⓙ   14. Ⓕ Ⓖ Ⓗ Ⓙ   24. Ⓕ Ⓖ Ⓗ Ⓙ   34. Ⓕ Ⓖ Ⓗ Ⓙ
5. Ⓐ Ⓑ Ⓒ Ⓓ   15. Ⓐ Ⓑ Ⓒ Ⓓ   25. Ⓐ Ⓑ Ⓒ Ⓓ   35. Ⓐ Ⓑ Ⓒ Ⓓ
6. Ⓕ Ⓖ Ⓗ Ⓙ   16. Ⓕ Ⓖ Ⓗ Ⓙ   26. Ⓕ Ⓖ Ⓗ Ⓙ   36. Ⓕ Ⓖ Ⓗ Ⓙ
7. Ⓐ Ⓑ Ⓒ Ⓓ   17. Ⓐ Ⓑ Ⓒ Ⓓ   27. Ⓐ Ⓑ Ⓒ Ⓓ   37. Ⓐ Ⓑ Ⓒ Ⓓ
8. Ⓕ Ⓖ Ⓗ Ⓙ   18. Ⓕ Ⓖ Ⓗ Ⓙ   28. Ⓕ Ⓖ Ⓗ Ⓙ   38. Ⓕ Ⓖ Ⓗ Ⓙ
9. Ⓐ Ⓑ Ⓒ Ⓓ   19. Ⓐ Ⓑ Ⓒ Ⓓ   29. Ⓐ Ⓑ Ⓒ Ⓓ   39. Ⓐ Ⓑ Ⓒ Ⓓ
10. Ⓕ Ⓖ Ⓗ Ⓙ   20. Ⓕ Ⓖ Ⓗ Ⓙ   30. Ⓕ Ⓖ Ⓗ Ⓙ   40. Ⓕ Ⓖ Ⓗ Ⓙ

Test 7: Mathematics

1. Ⓐ Ⓑ Ⓒ Ⓓ   9. Ⓐ Ⓑ Ⓒ Ⓓ   17. Ⓐ Ⓑ Ⓒ Ⓓ   25. Ⓐ Ⓑ Ⓒ Ⓓ   33. Ⓐ Ⓑ Ⓒ Ⓓ
2. Ⓕ Ⓖ Ⓗ Ⓙ   10. Ⓕ Ⓖ Ⓗ Ⓙ   18. Ⓕ Ⓖ Ⓗ Ⓙ   26. Ⓕ Ⓖ Ⓗ Ⓙ   34. Ⓕ Ⓖ Ⓗ Ⓙ
3. Ⓐ Ⓑ Ⓒ Ⓓ   11. Ⓐ Ⓑ Ⓒ Ⓓ   19. Ⓐ Ⓑ Ⓒ Ⓓ   27. Ⓐ Ⓑ Ⓒ Ⓓ   35. Ⓐ Ⓑ Ⓒ Ⓓ
4. Ⓕ Ⓖ Ⓗ Ⓙ   12. Ⓕ Ⓖ Ⓗ Ⓙ   20. Ⓕ Ⓖ Ⓗ Ⓙ   28. Ⓕ Ⓖ Ⓗ Ⓙ   36. Ⓕ Ⓖ Ⓗ Ⓙ
5. Ⓐ Ⓑ Ⓒ Ⓓ   13. Ⓐ Ⓑ Ⓒ Ⓓ   21. Ⓐ Ⓑ Ⓒ Ⓓ   29. Ⓐ Ⓑ Ⓒ Ⓓ   37. Ⓐ Ⓑ Ⓒ Ⓓ
6. Ⓕ Ⓖ Ⓗ Ⓙ   14. Ⓕ Ⓖ Ⓗ Ⓙ   22. Ⓕ Ⓖ Ⓗ Ⓙ   30. Ⓕ Ⓖ Ⓗ Ⓙ   38. Ⓕ Ⓖ Ⓗ Ⓙ
7. Ⓐ Ⓑ Ⓒ Ⓓ   15. Ⓐ Ⓑ Ⓒ Ⓓ   23. Ⓐ Ⓑ Ⓒ Ⓓ   31. Ⓐ Ⓑ Ⓒ Ⓓ   39. Ⓐ Ⓑ Ⓒ Ⓓ
8. Ⓕ Ⓖ Ⓗ Ⓙ   16. Ⓕ Ⓖ Ⓗ Ⓙ   24. Ⓕ Ⓖ Ⓗ Ⓙ   32. Ⓕ Ⓖ Ⓗ Ⓙ   40. Ⓕ Ⓖ Ⓗ Ⓙ

Test 1: Sequences

Time: 20 minutes

Directions: For Questions 1–20, choose the answer that best continues the pattern.

1.

				(A)	(B)	(C)	(D)
??!?	!!?!	???!	! __	??!	!!?	!??	?!!

2.

3.

4.

5.

6.

Go on to next page

7. 2 6 10 14 18 22 _____
   - (A) 26
   - (B) 25
   - (C) 24
   - (D) 28

8. 45 40 35 30 25 20 _____
   - (F) 22
   - (G) 15
   - (H) 10
   - (J) 5

9. 12 15 18 35 38 41 80 83 _____
   - (A) 88
   - (B) 87
   - (C) 86
   - (D) 90

10. 2 4 8 10 20 40 7 _____ 28
    - (F) 9
    - (G) 12
    - (H) 14
    - (J) 16

11. 3 9 15 5 15 21 10 30 _____
    - (A) 50
    - (B) 35
    - (C) 36
    - (D) 40

12. 60 56 8 18 14 2 _____ 21 3
    - (F) 26
    - (G) 30
    - (H) 27
    - (J) 25

13. 27 9 3 125 25 5 48 8 _____
    - (A) 16
    - (B) 12
    - (C) 4
    - (D) 6

14. X2Y3Z4 X3Y4Z5 X4Y5Z6 _____
    - (F) X5Y6Z7
    - (G) X1Y2Z3
    - (H) X4Y3Z2
    - (J) Z5Y6Z7

15. C F I L O R _____
    - (A) S
    - (B) U
    - (C) T
    - (D) V

16. CBA FED _____ LKJ
    - (F) HIJ
    - (G) IHG
    - (H) GHI
    - (J) JIH

17. rst uvw _____ abc
    - (A) def
    - (B) zyx
    - (C) xyz
    - (D) abc

18. ABBB CBDB EBFB _____
    - (F) GHHH
    - (G) GBJB
    - (H) GBHB
    - (J) HBIB

19. ABCE BCDF _____ DEFH
    - (A) CDEG
    - (B) CDEF
    - (C) DEFG
    - (D) CDEH

20. ABC XYZ DEF _____ GHI
    - (F) XYZ
    - (G) FGH
    - (H) EFG
    - (J) HIJ

STOP DO NOT TURN THE PAGE UNTIL TOLD TO DO SO.
DO NOT RETURN TO A PREVIOUS TEST.

Test 2: Analogies

Time: 15 minutes

Directions: For Questions 1–20, choose the answer that belongs in the empty box so that the bottom two pictures relate in the same way as the top two pictures.

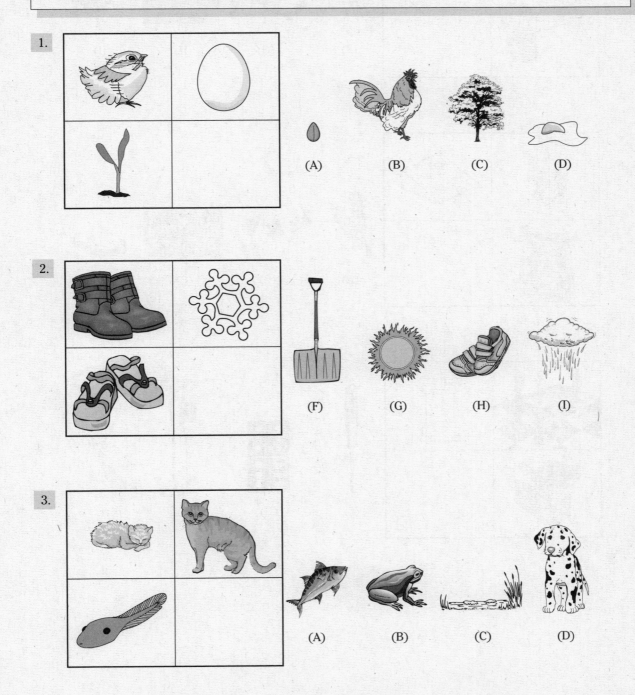

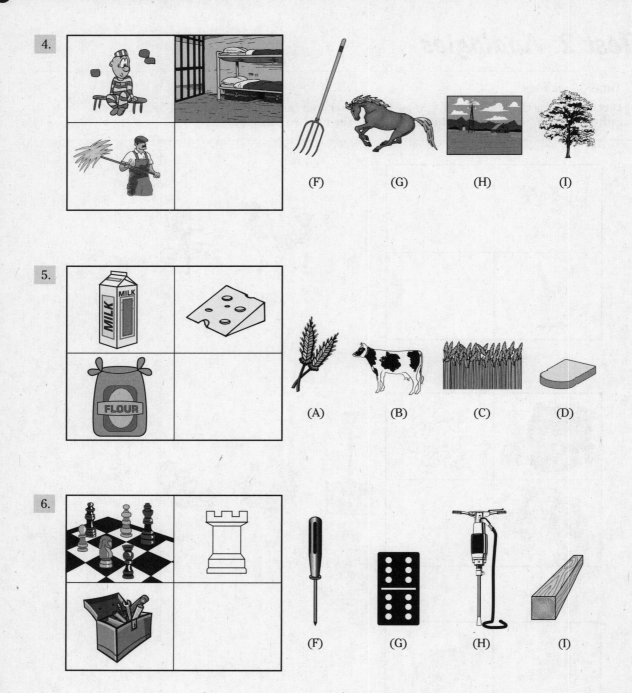

4.

(F) (G) (H) (I)

5.

(A) (B) (C) (D)

6.

(F) (G) (H) (I)

Go on to next page

7.

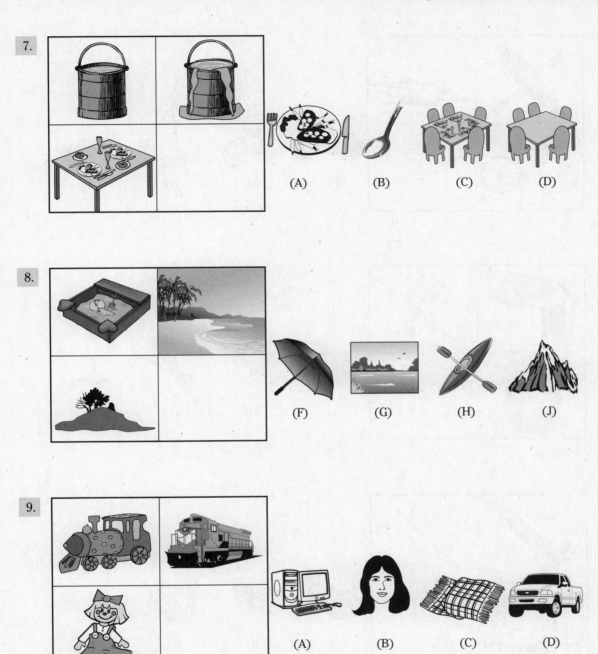

(A)   (B)   (C)   (D)

8.

(F)   (G)   (H)   (J)

9.

(A)   (B)   (C)   (D)

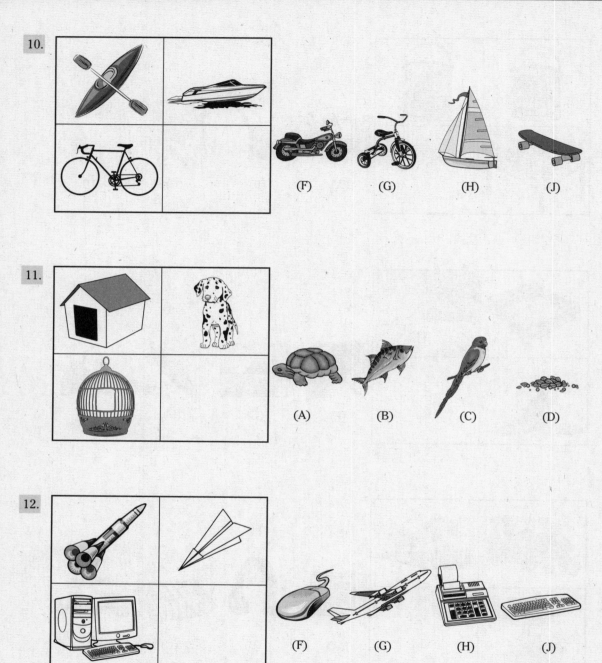

10.

(F)   (G)   (H)   (J)

11.

(A)   (B)   (C)   (D)

12.

(F)   (G)   (H)   (J)

Go on to next page

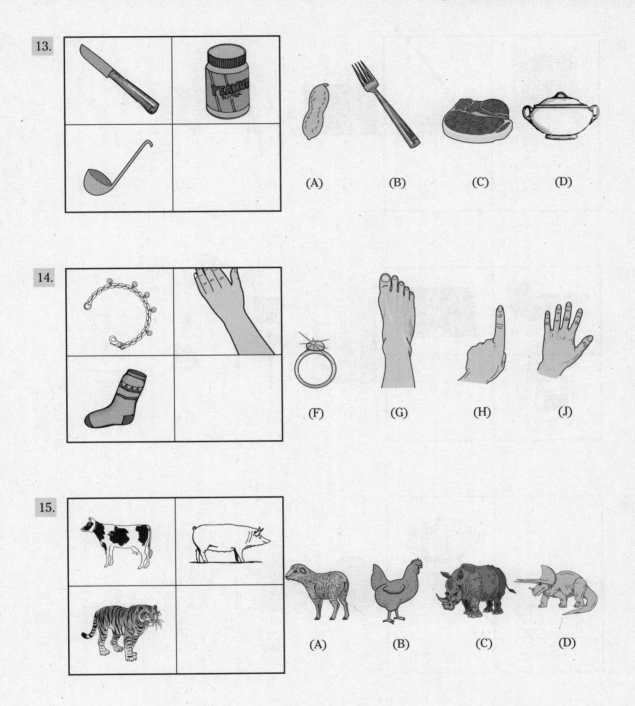

13.

(A) (B) (C) (D)

14.

(F) (G) (H) (J)

15.

(A) (B) (C) (D)

Go on to next page

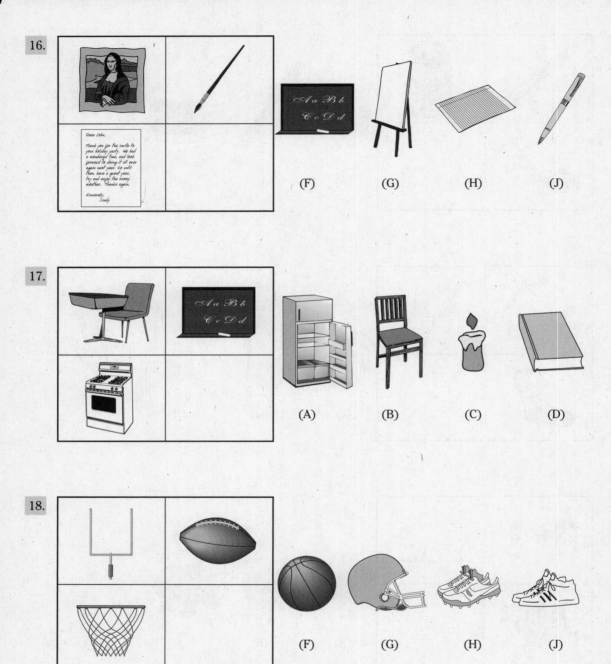

16.

(F)   (G)   (H)   (J)

17.

(A)   (B)   (C)   (D)

18.

(F)   (G)   (H)   (J)

Go on to next page

19.

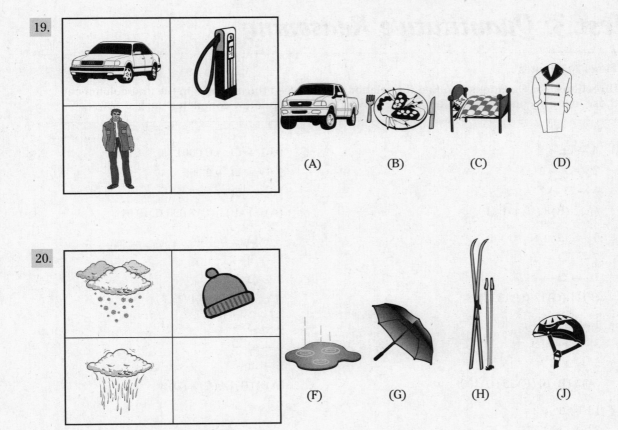

(A)   (B)   (C)   (D)

20.

(F)   (G)   (H)   (J)

STOP DO NOT TURN THE PAGE UNTIL TOLD TO DO SO.
DO NOT RETURN TO A PREVIOUS TEST.

Test 3: Quantitative Reasoning

Time: 20 minutes

Directions: For Questions 1–7, find the relationship between the numbers in the first column and those in the second column. Choose the answer that appropriately completes the last row.

1. $4 \rightarrow \square \rightarrow 2$
    $2 \rightarrow \square \rightarrow 1$
    $6 \rightarrow \square \rightarrow ?$
    (A) 2 (B) 3 (C) 4 (D) 1

2. $5 \rightarrow \square \rightarrow 8$
    $7 \rightarrow \square \rightarrow 10$
    $10 \rightarrow \square \rightarrow ?$
    (F) 11 (G) 12 (H) 13 (J) 14

3. $1 \rightarrow \square \rightarrow 5$
    $3 \rightarrow \square \rightarrow 15$
    $5 \rightarrow \square \rightarrow ?$
    (A) 5 (B) 10 (C) 25 (D) 100

4. $16 \rightarrow \square \rightarrow 2$
    $32 \rightarrow \square \rightarrow 4$
    $56 \rightarrow \square \rightarrow ?$
    (F) 8 (G) 7 (H) 42 (J) 6

5. $0.01 \rightarrow \square \rightarrow 0.0001$
    $0.6 \rightarrow \square \rightarrow 0.006$
    $10 \rightarrow \square \rightarrow ?$
    (A) 0.1 (B) 1 (C) 1,000 (D) 0.01

6. $\frac{1}{3} \rightarrow \square \rightarrow \frac{2}{3}$
    $\frac{2}{3} \rightarrow \square \rightarrow 1$
    $3 \rightarrow \square \rightarrow ?$
    (F) $\frac{2}{3}$ (G) $3\frac{2}{3}$ (H) 4 (J) $3\frac{1}{3}$

7. $\frac{1}{4} \rightarrow \square \rightarrow \frac{1}{2}$
    $\frac{1}{3} \rightarrow \square \rightarrow \frac{2}{3}$
    $\frac{3}{8} \rightarrow \square \rightarrow ?$
    (A) $\frac{5}{8}$ (B) $1\frac{1}{8}$ (C) $\frac{5}{6}$ (D) $\frac{3}{4}$

Go on to next page

Directions: For Questions 8–14, find the fraction of the shape that is shaded.

8.

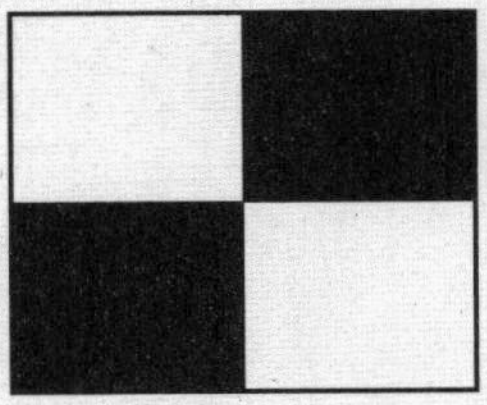

(F) $\frac{1}{2}$ (G) $\frac{3}{4}$ (H) $\frac{1}{4}$ (J) $\frac{1}{8}$

9.

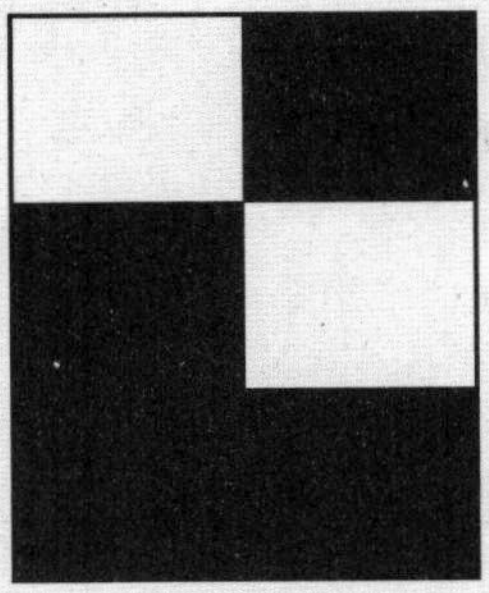

(A) $\frac{1}{2}$ (B) $\frac{1}{3}$ (C) $\frac{2}{3}$ (D) $\frac{3}{5}$

10.

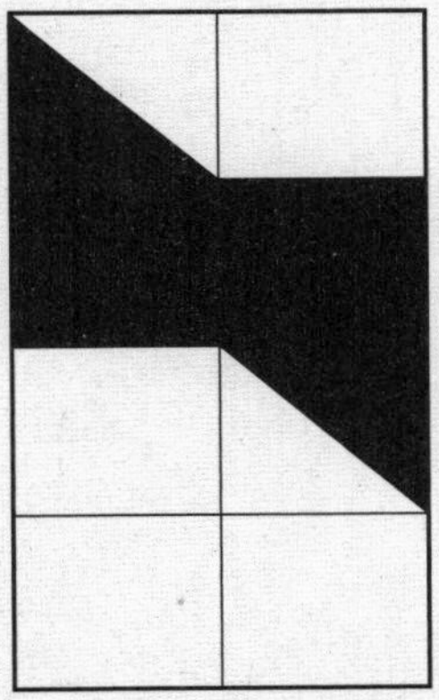

(F) $\frac{5}{8}$ (G) $\frac{3}{8}$ (H) $\frac{1}{2}$ (J) $\frac{3}{4}$

11.

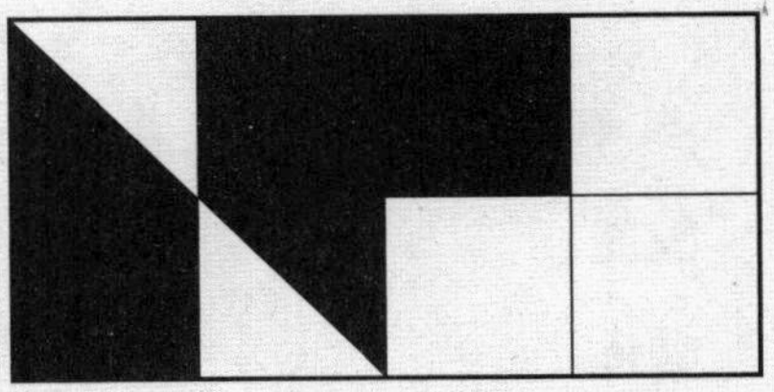

(A) $\frac{3}{4}$ (B) $\frac{1}{2}$ (C) $\frac{3}{8}$ (D) $\frac{7}{8}$

12.

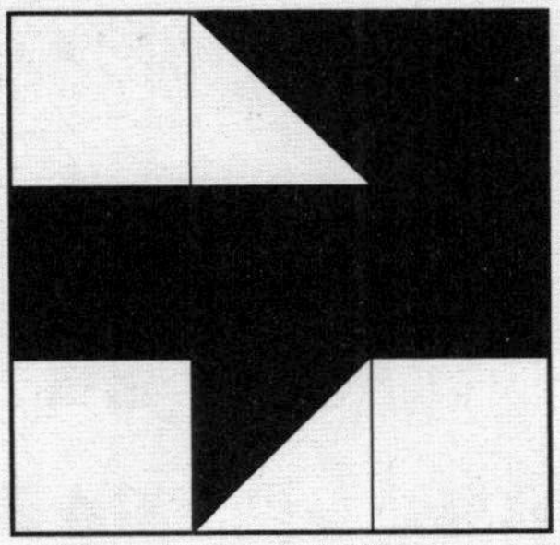

(F) $\frac{4}{9}$ (G) $\frac{1}{3}$ (H) $\frac{2}{3}$ (J) $\frac{5}{9}$

13.

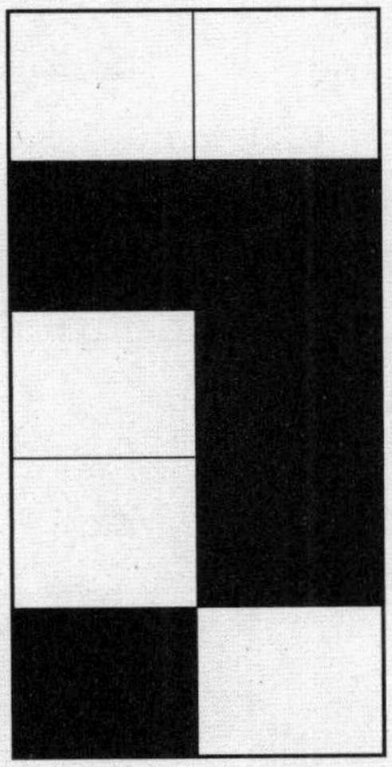

(A) $\frac{1}{2}$ (B) $\frac{5}{8}$ (C) $\frac{4}{9}$ (D) $\frac{3}{5}$

14.

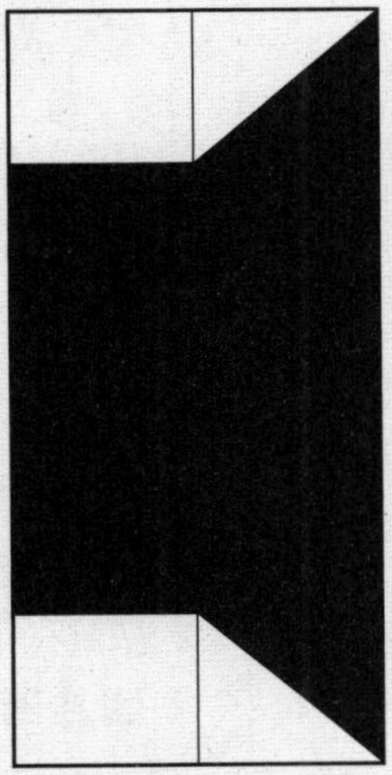

(F) $\frac{1}{2}$ (G) $\frac{3}{5}$ (H) $\frac{7}{10}$ (J) $\frac{4}{5}$

Go on to next page

Directions: The scales in Questions 15–20 show combinations of shapes in equal weights. Find an answer with a pair of shape sets that also balances the scale.

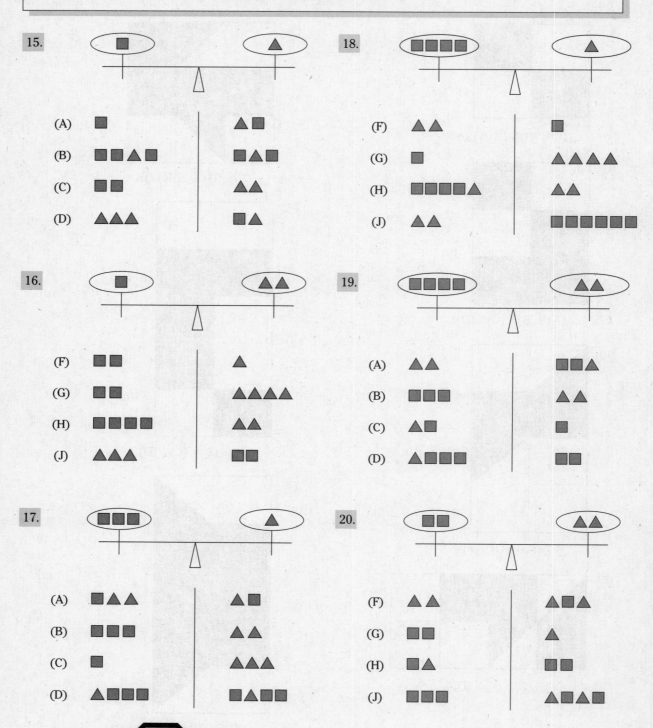

Test 4: Verbal Reasoning—Words

Time: 15 minutes

Directions: For Questions 1–4, find the word that identifies an essential part of the underlined word.

1. <u>sink</u>
   - (A) water
   - (B) food
   - (C) cold
   - (D) cloth

2. <u>skin</u>
   - (F) cleanliness
   - (G) protection
   - (H) paleness
   - (J) heat

3. <u>holiday</u>
   - (A) Christmas
   - (B) celebration
   - (C) fireworks
   - (D) cake

4. <u>spaghetti</u>
   - (F) tomatoes
   - (G) cheese
   - (H) meatballs
   - (J) noodles

Directions: For Questions 5–8, find the answer that is most similar to the underlined words.

5. <u>hate</u> <u>detest</u> <u>loathe</u>
   - (A) abhor
   - (B) like
   - (C) condemn
   - (D) adore

6. <u>narrow</u> <u>thin</u> <u>slender</u>
   - (F) broad
   - (G) slim
   - (H) spacious
   - (J) varied

7. <u>stick</u> <u>pole</u> <u>rod</u>
   - (A) flag
   - (B) glue
   - (C) staff
   - (D) ball

8. <u>rose</u> <u>violet</u> <u>daisy</u>
   - (F) leaf
   - (G) stem
   - (H) garden
   - (J) pansy

Go on to next page

Directions: Three of the words in the answer choices in Questions 9–12 belong together. Choose the answer that does not belong with the other three words.

9. (A) surrender
   (B) yield
   (C) submit
   (D) persevere

10. (F) sleepy
    (G) drowsy
    (H) somnolent
    (J) aware

11. (A) bat
    (B) goal
    (C) base
    (D) glove

12. (F) computer
    (G) refrigerator
    (H) stove
    (J) dishwasher

Directions: In Questions 13–16, the words in the bottom row are related to each other in the same way that the words in the top row are related to each other. Find the answer that completes the missing word in the bottom row.

13. house   roof   wall
    box   cover
    (A) cardboard
    (B) side
    (C) shingle
    (D) paint

14. aunt   uncle   cousin
    mother   sibling
    (F) grandparent
    (G) brother
    (H) father
    (J) sister

15. sour   sweet   cloying
               spicy   blistering
    (A) mild
    (B) sugary
    (C) unpleasant
    (D) nice

16. purse   suitcase trunk
    armchair   loveseat
    (F) table
    (G) sofa
    (H) lamp
    (J) door

STOP DO NOT TURN THE PAGE UNTIL TOLD TO DO SO.
DO NOT RETURN TO A PREVIOUS TEST.

Test 5: Verbal Reasoning—Context

Time: 20 minutes

Directions: For Questions 1–20, choose the answer that must be true given that the information in the question is true.

1. When it snows all day, we go skiing. It has snowed all day.
   (A) It has snowed two feet.
   (B) We will go skiing.
   (C) The ski conditions are excellent.
   (D) It will snow tomorrow.

2. Rover is a dog. Mickey owns two pets, a mouse and a cat.
   (F) Mickey's cat chases his mouse.
   (G) Mickey does not like birds.
   (H) Rover does not belong to Mickey.
   (J) Mickey wishes he had more pets.

3. Eric drew an illustration of a boy. This book is a book of illustrations.
   (A) Eric's illustration is in this book.
   (B) This book contains an illustration of a boy.
   (C) Eric knows how to draw illustrations.
   (D) Eric is an excellent artist.

4. Betsy watches the Iguanas play football every Sunday. This Sunday the Iguanas play football against the Salamanders.
   (F) The Iguanas will win the game on Sunday.
   (G) This Sunday is the only time the Iguanas will play the Salamanders.
   (H) Betsy wants the Salamanders to lose the football game.
   (J) Betsy will watch the Salamanders play football this Sunday.

5. When Fenn earns at least $5, he buys a plastic animal for his collection. Today Fenn earned $8.
   (A) Fenn earned more today than he has in the past.
   (B) Fenn has a large collection of plastic animals.
   (C) Plastic animals are expensive.
   (D) Fenn will buy a plastic animal for his collection.

6. Chrissy and Ellen are twins. Ellen was born on a Monday.
   (F) Chrissy and Ellen have the same parents.
   (G) Ellen is older than Chrissy.
   (H) Chrissy has only one sister.
   (J) Chrissy was born before Ellen.

7. Sean eats a banana with his cereal in the morning. He puts milk on his cereal.
   (A) Sean eats cereal every morning.
   (B) When Sean eats a banana with his cereal, he also has milk.
   (C) Sean does not like to have eggs for breakfast.
   (D) Bananas are Sean's favorite fruit.

8. The Great Wall is in China. Mavis has never seen the Great Wall.
   (F) Mavis has never been to China.
   (G) Mavis does not like to travel.
   (H) If Mavis wants to see the Great Wall, she must go to China.
   (J) Mavis does not want to see the Great Wall.

Go on to next page

9. Neil jogs more often than he walks. Yesterday, Neil rode his bike for ten miles.

    (A) Neil prefers biking to jogging.

    (B) Neil engages in different types of physical activity.

    (C) Jogging is a better form of exercise than walking.

    (D) When Neil bikes, he travels farther than when he jogs.

10. Bridget bought a dress, skirt, and shirt from Greenmart. Greenmart is located in a mall downtown.

    (F) Greenmart is a grocery store.

    (G) Bridget went downtown.

    (H) Bridget has a job.

    (J) Greenmart has good deals on clothing.

11. Peggy works puzzles in her spare time. Peggy has finished four puzzles in the last week.

    (A) Working puzzles is Peggy's favorite pastime.

    (B) Peggy is unemployed.

    (C) Peggy has had spare time in the last week.

    (D) Four is the most puzzles Peggy can finish in one week.

12. Elizabeth belongs to a quilting bee. Everyone in the quilting bee works on each quilt. The quilting bee entered one of its quilts in a contest and won first place.

    (F) Quilts take a long time to make.

    (G) Making a quilt requires the work of more than one person.

    (H) The quilting bee enters all of its quilts in contests.

    (J) Elizabeth worked on the quilt that won first prize in the contest.

13. Whenever Molly goes on vacation, her mother picks up her mail and leaves it on Molly's kitchen table. Molly's mother put Molly's mail on the kitchen table on Monday.

    (A) Molly's mother has access to Molly's house when Molly is on vacation.

    (B) Molly was on vacation on Monday.

    (C) Molly goes on vacation often.

    (D) Molly's mother is sad that she cannot travel with Molly.

14. Deer like to eat pansies and daisies. The flowers in Mr. McDonald's flower bed had been nibbled off their stems on Saturday morning.

    (F) The flowers in Mr. McDonald's flower bed were pansies and daisies.

    (G) Deer ate Mr. McDonald's flowers on Saturday morning.

    (H) Something has eaten Mr. McDonald's flowers.

    (J) Mr. McDonald will not grow flowers next summer.

15. Clayton and Courtney took a train from Stockholm, Sweden, to Oslo, Norway, in Scandinavia. The train ride lasted for 12 hours.

    (A) The train is the fastest way to get from Stockholm to Oslo.

    (B) Clayton and Courtney could have reached Oslo faster if they had taken a bus.

    (C) Clayton and Courtney traveled overnight in the train from Stockholm to Oslo.

    (D) Clayton and Courtney have visited Scandinavia.

Go on to next page

16. This season the Madison track team has won five meets in a row. Throughout the season, Paula has brought home five first-place ribbons in the javelin throw. Paula is on the Madison track team.

    (F) Every time Paula wins first place in the javelin throw, the Madison track team wins the meet.

    (G) Paula competes in the javelin throw for the Madison track team.

    (H) The javelin throw is the only event that Paula competes in.

    (J) The Madison track team is the best team in the league.

17. Brad takes piano lessons every Thursday and sings in the choir on Sundays. He plays tennis three times a week and volunteers at the community center on Saturdays and Mondays. Brad does not participate in more than one activity each day.

    (A) Brad plays tennis on Tuesdays, Wednesdays, and Fridays.

    (B) Brad is involved in too many activities.

    (C) Brad likes to play tennis more than he likes to play the piano.

    (D) Brad spends more time volunteering at the community center than he does singing in the choir.

18. Becky has been working at the Burger Barn for three months. Lynn has worked at the Burger Barn longer than Becky but for less time than Andy.

    (F) Andy has worked at the Burger Barn for more than three months.

    (G) Lynn has worked at the Burger Barn longer than any other employee.

    (H) Andy is a better employee than Becky.

    (J) Lynn has worked at the Burger Barn for four months.

19. Wolves have not been seen in Colorado for 60 years. Last week Larry spotted a wolf in Rocky Mountain National Park in Colorado.

    (A) The wolf that Larry saw is over 60 years old.

    (B) Wolves have not lived in Colorado for 60 years.

    (C) There is at least one wolf in Colorado.

    (D) The only wolf in Colorado is in Rocky Mountain National Park.

20. Mr. Wilson teaches English to high school freshmen, coaches the high school boys' soccer team, and advises the yearbook committee. This afternoon the soccer team completed its tenth consecutive winning season.

    (F) Mr. Wilson spends more time coaching the soccer team than he does advising the yearbook committee.

    (G) Mr. Wilson has been coaching the boys' soccer team for at least ten years.

    (H) Coaches of high school athletics must also teach at the high school.

    (J) Mr. Wilson has coached the boys' soccer team during at least one winning season.

STOP DO NOT TURN THE PAGE UNTIL TOLD TO DO SO. DO NOT RETURN TO A PREVIOUS TEST.

Test 6: Reading and Language Arts

Time: 40 minutes

Directions: Read this passage about photosynthesis and answer Questions 1–7.

Photosynthesis is the process that plants go through to use light and water to make glucose, which is sugar. Photosynthesis creates sugar in the green parts of plants, which is a substance that every animal on earth depends on. The process also causes plants to give off the oxygen that animals need to survive.

The "photo" in photosynthesis means that this process uses light as its energy source. "Synthesis" refers to how the process synthesizes, or creates, glucose. Plants absorb an ordinary gas from the air called carbon dioxide. This, combined with the water they pull up through their roots and the light from the sun, makes sugar. Plants use the sugar to grow, and the green parts of plants make the sugar and oxygen. Without plants, humans would have no food to eat or oxygen to breathe.

Here is what the photosynthesis reaction looks like: $6\ CO_2$ (carbon dioxide) + $6\ H_2O$ (water) + light energy $\rightarrow C_6H_{12}O_6$ (glucose) + $6\ O_2$ (oxygen).

The overall reaction in photosynthesis is accomplished in many small steps. The leaves of plants act like big solar panels, soaking up as much light energy as they can. Leaves contain something called chlorophyll, which is the molecule that actually absorbs the incoming energy. Have you ever asked yourself why grass is green? Plants are green because of chlorophyll. Perhaps you learned in science class that the white light from the sun is actually a blend of many different colors of light like you see in a rainbow. Chlorophyll absorbs all colors of light except green. Since it isn't absorbed, the green light bounces off of the leaves and enters our eyes, making us see green.

The light energy that is absorbed by the chlorophyll is used to break apart the water molecules, and some electrons from the H_2O are fed into an electron transport chain. The electrons get passed down the chain, and this ends up breaking up the H_2O molecules, which results in the production of O_2. The oxygen is released into the atmosphere so that creatures like us can breathe it in and use it for ourselves.

1. The O_2 produced in photosynthesis results from the breakup of which molecules?

    (A) glucose molecules

    (B) CO_2 molecules

    (C) chlorophyll molecules

    (D) H_2O molecules

2. Which color of light would be least likely to help a plant perform photosynthesis?

    (F) blue

    (G) red

    (H) white

    (J) green

3. Which substance is created by photosynthesis?

    (A) carbon dioxide

    (B) water

    (C) sugar

    (D) chlorophyll

4. What is the probable definition of "photo" in the word "photosynthesis"?

    (F) picture

    (G) light

    (H) camera

    (J) creation

Go on to next page

5. What step is missing in the basic photosynthesis process below?

carbon dioxide + water + _____ →
glucose + oxygen

(A) oxygen

(B) sugar

(C) light energy

(D) color

6. Which of the following statements is a fact about photosynthesis?

(F) The only color that chlorophyll absorbs is green.

(G) It uses oxygen and gives off carbon dioxide.

(H) The plant's roots soak up the light used in the process.

(J) It produces sugar in the green parts of the plant.

7. Which of the following is the best title for this passage?

(A) "How Plants Keep Animals Alive"

(B) "The Basic Process of Photosynthesis"

(C) "The Importance of Glucose"

(D) "Everything Plants Can Do with Light and Water"

Directions: Look for the mistakes in this story about plants and answer Questions 8–10.

---

(1)When I was nine, my mom decided it would be a good idea for me to plant my own garden. (2)Me and my mom went to the local nursery to pick out flowers. (3)I chose only pink flowers at first, but then I noticed the brilliant yellow blooms of the daisies and the cute faces on the purple pansies. (4)By the time we left the store, I had a rainbow of blossoms with less pink flowers than any other color. (5)I couldn't wait to get them into the ground. (6)I lovingly dug holes for each of my flowers and made sure they had the right amount of food and water. (7)I ended up with a garden that was more lovelier than any I had ever seen.

8. Which is the best way to write Sentence 2?

(F) My mom and I went to the local nursery to pick out flowers.

(G) My mom and me went to the local nursery to pick out flowers.

(H) I and my mom went to the local nursery to pick out flowers.

(J) Best as is.

9. Which is the best way to write Sentence 4?

(A) By the time we left the store, I had a rainbow of blossoms with fewer pink flowers than any other color.

(B) I had a rainbow of blossoms, by the time we left the store, with less pink flowers than any other color.

(C) By the time we left the store, I had a rainbow of flower blossoms with a lesser amount of pink flowers than any.

(D) Best as is.

10. Which is the best way to write Sentence 7?

(F) I ended up with a garden that was the most loveliest I had ever seen.

(G) I ended up with a garden that was the loveliest I had ever seen.

(H) I ended up with a garden that was more lovely as any I had ever seen.

(J) Best as is.

Go on to next page

Directions: Read this essay about Frederick Douglass and answer Questions 11–18.

Frederick Douglass was an African American abolitionist and civil rights leader in the 1800s. Although Frederick Douglass had a negative view of slaveholders, he blamed the system of slavery rather than the individuals. In his autobiography, Douglass talked about his first slaveholder, Captain Anthony. He stated that the system of slavery affected slaveholders as well as slaves. Douglass believed that slaveholders would not have acted in such cruel ways if they had not been influenced by the slavery system.

The way that Douglass portrayed slaveholders helped gain support for the abolitionist movement. Since Douglass placed blame on the system of slavery rather than on slaveholders, it was easier for white Americans to become attracted to the abolitionist movement. It was easier to justify the abolition of a system than the abolition of persons. White abolitionists were able to identify the system of slavery rather than individual slaveholders as the problem. If Douglass were to condemn whites and argue that whites were the problem, he probably would not have gained as much support from white abolitionists. Therefore, Douglass's portrayal of slaveholders opened up the issue of abolition to whites in America.

Douglass was able to express his ideas of abolition to a larger audience when he founded the newspaper *North Star* in December of 1847, which by 1851 became *Frederick Douglass's Paper*. Douglass had 3,000 subscriptions and a large audience in the North to voice his opinions to about slavery and abolition. Douglass's willingness to work with whites showed that he was committed to ending slavery without blaming whites. Douglass's ability to recognize slavery as the main problem encouraged Northerners and allowed them to feel more comfortable to join the struggle to end slavery.

Douglass was able to cement a place in history as the voice of the abolitionist movement through his carefully argued views on slavery. His work in the fight against slavery and racism allowed for support from Northerners and paved the way for emancipation after the Civil War. One of the most progressive persons of his era and perhaps of all time, Douglass served as an inspiration to many and helped fuel later civil rights thinkers such as W.E.B. Dubois.

11. What is the author's attitude toward Frederick Douglass?

    (A) Douglass was a great person, but he had little influence on American history.

    (B) Douglass could have influenced the course of slavery more if he had blamed slaveholders rather than the institution of slavery.

    (C) Douglass was a great leader who was a major contributor to the end of slavery in America.

    (D) Douglass used his experience as a slaveholder to change Northerners' opinions about slavery.

12. The information in this essay could help you answer which of these questions?

    (F) When did the Civil War end?

    (G) In what year did slavery end in America?

    (H) What newspapers did Douglass use to express his views about slavery?

    (J) What are the names of several influential Northern abolitionists?

Go on to next page

13. During what era was Frederick Douglass an abolitionist?

(A) the 18th century

(B) the 1900s

(C) the 1700s

(D) the 19th century

14. What was a method that the essay says Douglass used to get support for the abolitionist movement?

(F) He voiced his opinions about slavery in a newspaper he founded.

(G) He condemned whites so that they would feel guilty about slavery.

(H) He attacked the people involved in slavery rather than the system of slavery.

(J) Although he blamed whites for slavery, he allowed them to join the abolitionist movement.

15. Which of the following statements is true according to the essay?

(A) It took a long time for Northerners to join the abolitionist movement.

(B) Douglass was an African American slave.

(C) Northerners never would have joined the abolitionist movement if not for the influence of Douglass.

(D) Very few people read *Frederick Douglass's Paper*.

16. The last paragraph says that Douglass was able to "cement" a place in history. Which of the following words has a similar meaning to "cement" as it is used in the essay?

(F) separate

(G) cover

(H) weaken

(J) secure

17. Here are two sentences related to the essay:

Douglass was an abolitionist. He founded a newspaper and influenced Northerners to join the cause against slavery.

Choose the answer that best makes one sentence out of the two.

(A) Douglass was a newspaper-founding abolitionist, and influencing Northerners to join the cause against slavery.

(B) Douglass's founding a newspaper and influencing Northerners to join the cause against slavery caused him to be an abolitionist.

(C) Founding a newspaper, Douglass was an abolitionist and influencing Northerners to join the cause against slavery.

(D) Douglass was an abolitionist who founded a newspaper and influenced Northerners to join the cause against slavery.

18. Choose the sentence that is written correctly.

(F) Douglass's sympathetic portrayal of slaveholders being victims of the system, too.

(G) Based on Douglass's newspaper editorials, different views on slavery were held by many Northerners.

(H) Douglass's depiction of the problem of slavery was compassionate, powerful, and persuasive.

(J) The views Northerners had toward slavery were more fairer after listening to Douglass.

Go on to next page

Directions: Read this paragraph that relates to the essay and answer Questions 19 and 20.

Narrative of the Life of Frederick Douglass is an autobiographical account of African American abolitionist and civil rights leader Frederick Douglass. In this book, Douglass tells stories about his life growing up as a slave. He tells how he gained his freedom and became a powerful voice in the struggle to end slavery. Through his story, Douglass gives a unique portrayal of slaveholders that was effective in attracting Northerners to the American abolitionist movement.

19. Which is the best introductory sentence for this paragraph?

    (A) One can learn much about the abolition movement from reading about its leaders.

    (B) Other cultures practiced slavery, too.

    (C) Slaves are not the only people who influenced the abolitionist movement.

    (D) When will we ever learn?

20. What is a logical topic for the paragraph that comes after the one above?

    (F) the autobiography of a famous race car driver

    (G) how Douglass portrayed slaveholders

    (H) an overview of the history of slavery in England

    (J) a summary of the battles in the Civil War

Directions: Read the following article about ice hockey and answer Questions 21–26.

Ah, the coolness of the ice rink, the hum of the Zamboni . . . it can mean only one thing; it's hockey time! And all signs point toward a successful season for the Clement Cougars.

Clement's hockey team is not just made up of Clement players. Rounding out the team are players from St. Thomas High School and Our Lady High School, too. Though three schools are represented, the vast majority of the players are from Clement. Returning to Clement for his senior year is goalie Brendan Sanchez. For the past two years Brendan has been playing hockey in a special league in Washington State. Sanchez's unmatched skills will be an excellent addition to an already great Clement team. Sanchez is surrounded by a great supporting cast that includes such star players as Clement center Taylor Poldale, St. Thomas senior Don Silver, Our Lady senior Nick Woodson, and Clement junior Justin Frank. Look for the upperclassmen to step up and take over the roles vacated by graduated players Brad Hunt and Steve Wilson.

Some of the players have been preparing for the rigorous season by joining fall hockey teams. Poldale and Sanchez are currently playing for local AA league teams. It is hoped that this extra practice will give the team the edge to overcome its rival, Apple River High School. Last year, the Clement Cougars went 9-5 and were good enough to make the playoffs. Unfortunately, they were dealt a devastating 2-1 loss in the final seconds at the hands of coach Jim Quinlan and the Apple River team. The Cougars hope to rebound this season and take home the state championship.

This year will be an exciting one. So grab your jackets, buy your tickets, and come support the Cougars on their way to high school hockey stardom.

Go on to next page

21. The Clement Cougars are most likely
    (A) a high school hockey team
    (B) an AA league hockey team
    (C) a college basketball team
    (D) a professional hockey team

22. The Cougars have players from each of these schools EXCEPT
    (F) Clement
    (G) Our Lady
    (H) St. Thomas
    (J) Apple River

23. Which of the Clement team members is the goalie?
    (A) Jim Quinlan
    (B) Taylor Poldale
    (C) Brendan Sanchez
    (D) Steve Wilson

24. How many games did the Clement team play last year?
    (F) 9
    (G) 5
    (H) 14
    (J) 15

25. This article probably appeared in which publication?
    (A) a national sports magazine
    (B) a high school newspaper
    (C) a book about the history of ice hockey
    (D) the athletics page of a college Web site

26. The author writes the article in a way that creates a feeling of
    (F) excitement
    (G) sadness
    (H) anger
    (J) fear

Go on to next page

Directions: Look for mistakes in this paragraph related to the article. Then answer Questions 27–29.

(1)Some of the reasons that kids play sports are to have fun, learn new skills, being with friends, and it's good to get physically fit. (2)Kids can get these benefits and more from playing sports. (3)They can get a sense of accomplishment and respect while improving their bodies and overall coordination. (4)Studies have shown that kids who participate in organized sports perform better in school, are better team players, and are more healthier. (5) Kids in sports learn how to follow rules and handle winning and losing.

27. Choose the best way to write Sentence 1.

(A) Some of the reasons that kids play sports are to have fun, learn new skills, be with friends, and get physically fit.

(B) Some of the reasons that kids play sports are to have fun, learning new skills, be with friends, and you want to get physically fit.

(C) Kids play sports to: have fun, learn new skills, be with friends, and get physically fit.

(D) Best as is.

28. Sentence 2 is best written in which way?

(F) Kids getting these benefits from playing sports and more.

(G) Kids can get more than just these benefits on playing sports.

(H) If kids play sports, than they can get these benefits and more.

(J) Best as is.

29. Which is the best way to write Sentence 4?

(A) Studies have shown that kids who participate in organized sports perform better in school, they are better team players, and are more healthier.

(B) Studies have shown that kids who participate in organized sports perform better in school, they are better team players and are healthier.

(C) Studies have shown that kids who participate in organized sports perform better in school, are better team players, and are healthier.

(D) Best as is.

Go on to next page

Directions: Read this essay on El Greco and Beuys and answer Questions 30–36.

El Greco painted *The Burial of Conde Orgaz* in Toledo, Spain, between the years of 1586–88. Almost 400 years later, Joseph Beuys, a post-World War II German artist, began his artistic creations of mixed media drawings, one of which he entitled *Kadmon*. Although the two artists painted different subjects, in different time periods, in different countries, with different media, and in different styles, they convey a common meaning. Both works demonstrate the relationship between the spiritual and material world and explore the human position within these worlds.

The backgrounds of both El Greco and Beuys prepared them for expressing the links and divisions between the spiritual world and the material world. Their personal experiences and formal art training promoted their interest in mysticism and earthliness, and their art attempted to portray the qualities of both.

El Greco received his formal art training in Crete and Italy, but he created his masterworks in Spain, a country known for both spirituality and reality. His formal training was a blend of Byzantine mysticism and Italian Mannerism. Not only did El Greco receive varied artistic training, but he also received a well-rounded spiritual, historical, literary, and scientific education from his early schooling and his diverse group of friends in cosmopolitan Toledo. His paintings combined his artistic and intellectual influences to portray the interaction between the spiritual world and the material world.

Like El Greco, Joseph Beuys experienced a variety of personal and artistic influences that inspired him to portray spiritual and material themes in his works. Beuys grew up in the tiny German town of Kleve, and his youth was influenced by the small community's predominant Catholicism and its rural natural setting. According to Christopher Lyon, Beuys's art came from his attempts to deal with the chaotic aftermath of World War II, and his early drawings portray both the personal and political disruption created by the war's devastation. *Kadmon,* one of Beuys's earliest works, portrays his fascination with the relationship between the spiritual and the material.

El Greco and Beuys chose different subjects to portray the relationship between the heavens and the earth. Because his art was commissioned by churches and because art before the advent of photography served not only aesthetic purposes but also as a record of history, El Greco most often recreated specific religious events. Unobstructed by the limitations of church sponsorship and freed by modern artistic exploration, Beuys chose more primitive subject matter for his interpretations.

30. How are the works of El Greco and Beuys similar?

(F) They both use mixed media.

(G) They both explore the interplay between the spiritual and the material worlds.

(H) Both artists have German influences in their works.

(J) The artists painted the same subjects.

31. In what century did Beuys begin creating works of art?

(A) the 1500s

(B) the 1800s

(C) the 1900s

(D) the 2000s

Go on to next page

32. In which country did El Greco create his masterworks?

    (F) Spain

    (G) Crete

    (H) Germany

    (J) Italy

33. What would be a good title for this essay?

    (A) "A Comparison of the Works of El Greco and Beuys"

    (B) "How El Greco's Artistic Style is Superior to that of Beuys"

    (C) "El Greco and Beuys: A Tale of Two Friends"

    (D) "How to Study Art"

34. Which of these events was a major influence on Beuys?

    (F) World War I

    (G) The Seven Years' War

    (H) The Gulf War

    (J) World War II

35. What was the primary subject matter of El Greco's art?

    (A) fruit, tableware, and other tangible objects

    (B) nature scenes

    (C) primitive objects

    (D) specific religious events

36. Which of the following statements is NOT true about El Greco?

    (F) He did not receive formal training.

    (G) His work was commissioned by churches.

    (H) His art served as a record of history.

    (J) His paintings often portrayed the interaction between the spiritual world and the material world.

37. Here are two sentences related to the passage:

    Beuys and El Greco painted different subjects. They painted in different styles and used different media.

    Which answer best combines the two sentences into one?

    (A) Beuys painted different subjects than El Greco, different styles and media, too.

    (B) Beuys and El Greco painted different subjects in different styles with different media.

    (C) Beuys and El Greco painted different subjects, they painted using different styles and media.

    (D) El Greco and Beuys painted differently, using different subjects, they painted with different media and styles.

38. Choose the sentence that is written correctly.

    (F) El Greco was an artist which painted in the sixteenth century.

    (G) When Beuys set out to create works of art, he chose between drawing, painting, and mixing the two.

    (H) Some people cannot see the similarity between the works of El Greco and those of Beuys.

    (J) The spiritual themes in El Greco's painting emerges in the portrayal of specific religious events.

Go on to next page ⟶

Directions: Read this paragraph related to the essay and answer Questions 39 and 40.

The artist uses the burial of an esteemed and religious Spanish count, who had died over 250 years before its painting, as a means of portraying the relationship between the heavens and the earth. The brilliantly colored oil-on-canvas painting, measuring 16 feet high and almost 12 feet wide, adorns one wall of the Church of San Tome in Toledo. The painting contains two main settings.

39. What would be the best topic sentence for this paragraph?

(A) Oil paintings are better than watercolors.

(B) Some paintings are larger than others.

(C) Toledo, Spain, has many tourist attractions.

(D) *The Burial of Conde Orgaz* is an example of a painting that depicts a specific religious event.

40. What subject would you expect to follow this paragraph?

(F) a description of how Conde Orgaz died

(G) an explanation of the two main settings in the painting

(H) a comparison of the churches in Toledo

(J) a clarification of why the painting hangs in the Church of San Tome

STOP DO NOT TURN THE PAGE UNTIL TOLD TO DO SO.
DO NOT RETURN TO A PREVIOUS TEST.

Test 7: Mathematics

Time: 35 minutes

Directions: Choose the response that best answers Questions 1–40.

1. $5.4 - 0.2 =$
   (A) 5.2
   (B) 3.4
   (C) 4.8
   (D) 3

2. 0.03% is equivalent to
   (F) 3
   (G) 0.3
   (H) ³⁄₁₀,₀₀₀
   (J) ⅓

3. $2^2 \times 2^3 =$
   (A) 18
   (B) $2 \times 2 \times 2 \times 2$
   (C) 210
   (D) 2^5

4. What is ⅜ greater than?
   (F) ⅝
   (G) ½
   (H) ¼
   (J) ⅞

5. What is the value of the digit 1 in the number 316,322?
   (A) 1
   (B) 10
   (C) 100
   (D) 10,000

6. ⅜ + 4.75 =
   (F) 3.5
   (G) 4
   (H) 4.75
   (J) 5

7. $0.4 \times 14.45 =$
   (A) 5.78
   (B) 5.87
   (C) 0.578
   (D) 57.8

8. A pizza is sliced into 8 equal pieces. What percent of the whole pizza is 2 slices?
   (F) 20%
   (G) 25%
   (H) 0.25%
   (J) 30%

9. $0.975 - 0.463 =$
   (A) 0.495
   (B) 0.500
   (C) 0.510
   (D) 0.512

10. Alyssa commutes to work every day. It takes her 30 minutes. If her average speed is 65 miles per hour, how far is her home from work?
    (F) 300 miles
    (G) 30 miles
    (H) 32.5 miles
    (J) 19.5 miles

11. $-5(4 - 2 \times 6) =$
    (A) 40
    (B) −40
    (C) −60
    (D) 60

Go on to next page

12. Gomez, Inc. developed a budget for each division of the company. 40% went to salaries, 30% to expenses, 15% to advertising, and the rest to research and product development. What fraction of the budget went to research and product development?

    (F) ¹⁄₂₀

    (G) ³⁄₂₀

    (H) ⅓

    (J) ¹⁄₇₅

13. Zoe earns $200 a week plus a 5% commission on her clothing sales. If she sells $3,500 worth of clothing this week, what are her total earnings for the week?

    (A) $175

    (B) $425

    (C) $400

    (D) $375

14. "Four hundred twenty five thousand forty five" is equal to

    (F) 425,045

    (G) 400,045

    (H) 400,025

    (J) 4,025

15. An arcade has 5 pinball machines, 13 action games, and 2 air hockey tables. When ⅕ of all the games are being played, how many games are in use?

    (A) 20

    (B) 15

    (C) 12

    (D) 4

16. A cafeteria serves 48 slices of pizza a day. If ⁵⁄₁₂ of the slices are cheese, how many slices of cheese pizza are served?

    (F) 42

    (G) 30

    (H) 36

    (J) 45

17. Which set of numbers can equal x in this sentence: $3 > x > -1$?

    (A) {3, 2, 1, 0, –1}

    (B) {2, 1, 0, –1}

    (C) {3, 2, 1, 0}

    (D) {2, 1, 0}

18. What is equal to x in this sentence: $3(4x) + 7 = 43$?

    (F) 3

    (G) 4

    (H) 6

    (J) 10

19. One inch is what part of one foot?

    (A) ¹⁄₁₂

    (B) ¹⁄₂₄

    (C) ¹⁄₃₆

    (D) ⅓

20. What is the area of a triangle with a base of 14 inches and a height of 8 inches?

    (F) 56 inches square

    (G) 42 inches square

    (H) 36 inches square

    (J) 112 inches square

21. What is the set of common factors for 50 and 125?

    (A) {5, 10, 25, 50}

    (B) {5, 25}

    (C) {2, 5, 10}

    (D) {2, 5, 10, 25}

22. Paul's Used Car Lot made $96,520 last month. Three of the five salespeople made 50 percent of the sales. How much in total sales did the other two salespeople make?

    (F) $24,500

    (G) $35,575

    (H) $48,260

    (J) $52,324

Go on to next page

23. A pentagon always has how many sides?

    (A) 4

    (B) 5

    (C) 6

    (D) 8

24. If $-2 < x < 2$, which of the following must NOT be true?

    (F) $x < 2$

    (G) $x = 1$

    (H) $x = -1$

    (J) $x < -2$

25. If one hat costs y dollars and x cents, how much do 4 hats cost?

    (A) $4x(y)$

    (B) $4(y + x)$

    (C) $4y(x)$

    (D) $4(yx)$

26. The product of two negative integers is?

    (F) 1

    (G) negative

    (H) positive

    (J) 0

27. What is 4×10^2?

    (A) 40

    (B) 400

    (C) 4,000

    (D) 40,000

28. Pat owns a shoe store and pays $20 for each pair of shoes he imports. To make a profit, Pat sets the price of a pair of shoes to be 200% of the price he pays. For how much does Pat sell each pair of shoes?

    (F) $50

    (G) $40

    (H) $60

    (J) $35

29. Which coordinates best show the location of Bluebird Mall on this map?

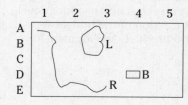

    (A) C4

    (B) E3

    (C) D4

    (D) A1

30. Jack and Jill have different ideas about how to solve this problem: $5 + 3 \times (3 + 3 + 6)$. Jack believes that the numbers 5 and 3 should be added first and then multiplied by the sum in the parentheses. Jill thinks that the operations inside the parentheses should be completed first, then the multiplication step, followed by the addition. Who is correct?

    (F) Only Jack is correct.

    (G) Only Jill is correct.

    (H) Neither Jack nor Jill is correct.

    (J) Both Jack and Jill are correct.

31. What is the measurement of a right angle?

    (A) 120 degrees

    (B) 45 degrees

    (C) 180 degrees

    (D) 90 degrees

32. Solve for x: $3(x + 3) = 36$

    (F) 9

    (G) 10

    (H) 12

    (J) 15

33. Which of the following is a quadrilateral?

    (A) a pentagon

    (B) a triangle

    (C) a square

    (D) an octagon

Go on to next page

34. Find the circumference of a circle with a radius of 3 units.

    (F) 12π units

    (G) 9π units

    (H) 6π units

    (J) 3π units

35. Which of these sets contains *all* the values that satisfy both x and y if x and y are integers and $x > -2$ and $y < 3$?

    (A) $\{-1, 0, 1, 2, 3\}$

    (B) $\{0, 1\}$

    (C) $\{-1, 0, 1, 2\}$

    (D) $\{0\}$

36. Alexis took out a bank loan for $13,000 to pay for a new car. The interest is 10%. What is the total amount of money Alexis owes the bank?

    (F) $13,000

    (G) $13,130

    (H) $14,000

    (J) $14,300

37. Bob grew a total of 6 inches this year, which is 3 more inches than he grew last year. What is the average number of inches he grew per month this year?

    (A) $6 + \frac{3}{12}$ inches

    (B) $\frac{1}{2}$ inches

    (C) $\frac{3}{12}$ inches

    (D) $\frac{6}{12} + \frac{3}{12}$ inches

38. Which of the following is a prime factorization of 45?

    (F) $3^2, 5$

    (G) $2, 3$

    (H) $3^3, 3$

    (J) $9, 5$

39. Which coordinates represent the location of Point A on the graph?

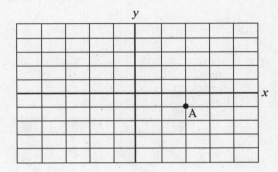

    (A) $(2, -1)$

    (B) $(2, 1)$

    (C) $(-2, 1)$

    (D) $(-1, 2)$

Go on to next page ➡

40. Which chart best represents the fraction of total expenses that a local cable company spends on paying its employees?

(F)

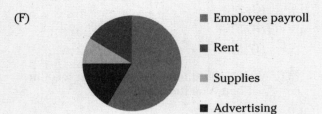

- Employee payroll
- Rent
- Supplies
- Advertising

(G)

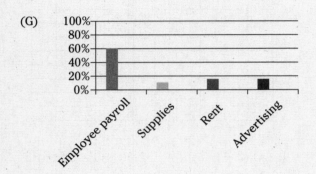

(H)

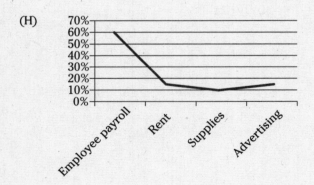

(J)

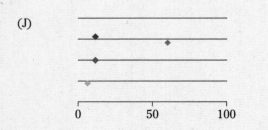

Chapter 26

Answers to COOP Practice Test 1

This chapter not only gives you the answers to COOP Practice Test 1 (in Chapter 25) but it also explains why those answers are what they are. Try to read through each explanation. After all, figuring out which answers are wrong (and why) can be just as important as determining which answers are correct. *Note:* If you don't have time for this, skip ahead a few pages to check your work against the short 'n' sweet answer key.

Test 1: Sequences

1. **B.** The sequence is made up of a series of ?s and !s. The first set in the sequence is two ?s, a !, and a ?. The next set is the same basic pattern with the sequence of the two symbols reversed. The third set is a different pattern: three ?s and a !. The next set is likely the same pattern with the symbols reversed because it begins that way. All you have to do is add two more ! and a ? — Choice (B). The other choices don't complete a pattern with the other sets in the sequence.

2. **H.** The four symbols that appear in this sequence are a small shaded circle (SS), a small unshaded circle (SU), a large shaded circle (LS), and a large unshaded circle (LU). The second set is merely the reverse of the first set. The third is similar to the first except that the circles demonstrate a pattern of reverse shading. Rather than LS, SU, SS, the pattern in the third set is LU, SS, SU. You can reasonably assume that the fourth set is a reverse of the third, especially because the first two circles demonstrate that pattern. The reverse of LU, SS, SU is SU, SS, LU — Choice (H).

3. **A.** Note the consistencies. Each set begins with a heart (h). Additionally, no set contains more than one of the same symbol. Each set also has a diamond (d), but the diamond appears only in either the second or last place. The club (c) appears in two sets, but the spade (s) appears only once. Therefore, you can safely assume that the last symbol in the last set is a spade, Choice (A), because that completes the pattern. (The first two sets are the same except the spade takes the place of the club. The addition of the spade in the fourth set makes the last two sets the same except the spade takes the place of the club.)

4. **J.** The pattern in this sequence of four sets of four symbols contains only two different symbol types. Each set decreases the number of squares at the beginning of the set by one and adds a circle to the end of the set. To create the fourth set, you take away a square from the beginning of the third set and add a circle to the end to get a square and three circles. The last three symbols in the set should be three circles, Choice (J).

5. **C.** Focus on a pattern. The third set reverses the pattern of the second: Smile, frown, smile, frown becomes frown, smile, frown, smile. Because set reversal occurs in the sequence, it's possible that the fourth set reverses the first. The first set is two frowns followed by two smiles, which would mean the fourth set is two smiles followed by two frowns, Choice (C). Every other choice introduces new patterns that aren't justified by the rest of the sets in the sequence.

6. **G.** This sequence appears random, but consistencies do exist. The arrows alternate up and down, and the two consecutive arrows display the same shading before a new shading is introduced. Because the direction of the arrows alternates, the last arrow in the last set

must be pointing up, so cross out Choices (F) and (J). The first two arrows in the last set exhibit the same shading, so the next arrow in the set should have a new type of shading. The shading type of the arrow in Choice (H) has already appeared in the third set. There's nothing in the pattern to suggest that a shading type should repeat, which means Choice (G) is the best answer because it introduces a new shading type.

7. **A.** The numbers in this sequence increase by 4. 22 + 4 is 26, which is Choice (A).

8. **G.** This sequence diminishes by 5 each time, so the last number is 15, Choice (G).

9. **C.** Each set contains three numbers that increase by 3. The last number of the last set should be 3 more than 83, which is 86 — Choice (C).

10. **H.** At first you may think the numbers in each set increase by 2 because 2 + 2 = 4. However, 4 + 2 ≠ 8. Turns out you find the next number in each set by *multiplying* by 2, not adding. Multiply 7 by 2 to get 14, Choice (H).

11. **C.** You may assume the pattern is to multiply by 3, which would make the last number in the sequence 90. However, 90 isn't an answer choice. Perhaps the pattern is to increase by 6: 3 + 6 is 9, and 9 + 6 is 15. Sounds good, but if you look at the last set of numbers, you see 10 followed by 30, and 30 isn't 6 more than 10. To find the pattern, examine the second set. Yes, 15 is 3 times 5, but 21 is only 6 more than 15. You must have to multiply the first number in the set by 3 to get the second number and then add 6 to get the third, which means you add 6 to 30 to get 36, Choice (C).

12. **J.** The numbers in each set of this sequence decrease, and you're looking for the number that fits into the beginning of the last set. Concentrate on the relationship between the first two numbers in the first two sets to find it. The difference between 60 and 56 is 4, and 14 is 4 less than 18. So the number that begins the last set is 4 more than 21, which is 25, Choice (J).

When the missing number is the first one in a set, don't waste your time determining how the last two numbers in each set are related. Just focus on the first two.

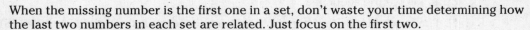

13. **D.** Based on the first set, the pattern in this sequence seems to be dividing the previous number by 3. 27 ÷ 3 = 9; 9 ÷ 3 = 3. But when you look at the second set, you find that 3 doesn't figure into the pattern at all. Examine the sets again. In both cases the last two numbers of the sets are factors of the first number in each set. 9 × 3 = 27; 5 × 25 = 125. So the correct answer is the number that equals 48 when it's multiplied by 8. 8 × 6 = 48; Choice (D) is right.

14. **F.** This sequence adds a few letters to the mix. Notice that each set begins with an X, not a Z; eliminate Choice (J). The numbers in each set are consecutive and start with a number that's 1 more than the beginning number in the previous set. The first number in the set that comes before the missing set is a 4. 5 is 1 more than 4, and the only remaining option with a first number of 5 is Choice (F).

15. **B.** This sequence is a little different from the ones in the previous questions. It doesn't have separate sets, and all of the components are letters. Keep the order of the alphabet in mind for letter sequences. If you've written out the alphabet in your test booklet as we suggest in Chapter 14, you can see that C is the third letter. You jump over two letters to get to F and another two letters to reach I. The pattern consists of every third letter of the alphabet. When you skip two letters from R, you land on U, so Choice (B) is the answer.

16. **G.** For this question, you must find the third set of four. To determine the pattern in each set, concentrate on the sets that appear before and after the blank. Referring to your alphabet, you see that F is the letter right after E and that D comes before E. The same is true for the last set: LKJ is the reverse of the alphabetical order of JKL. Eliminate Choices (F) and (H) because they don't reverse the order of the alphabet. Each set in the original sequence begins with a letter that's three letters from the first letter in the previous set. The letter that's three from F is I, so the third set must begin with I. The answer must be Choice (G) because it's the only one that begins with I.

17. **C.** The three letters in each set of this sequence are in consecutive alphabetical order, as are the sets themselves. The three letters that come after uvw are xyz, Choice (C), which ends the alphabet. The last set begins the alphabet again.

18. **H.** Focus on what you know when looking at this tricky pattern. Each set ends with a B, which means Choice (F) is wrong because it ends with an H. The first letter of each of the given sets is A, C, E. You skip one letter to get from A to C, and you skip one letter to get from C to E. When you skip the letter after E, you get G, which means the first letter of the last set must be G. Cross out Choice (J). The only difference between the remaining choices is the third letter of the set. The pattern of the third letters of each set is B, D, F. Again, the letters skip a letter in alphabetical order. The next letter in this pattern would be H (B, D, F, H). Choice (H) has an H in the third spot and is the right answer.

19. **A.** The first three letters of each set are in consecutive order, but that doesn't help you much because all the answer choices begin with consecutive letters. Focus your attention on the last letter of each set. The last letters are E, F, __, and H. To maintain the consecutive pattern of the last letter in each set, the missing set should end with G, which means you can cut Choices (B) and (D). You can also eliminate Choice (C) because the first letters of each set progress in consecutive alphabetical order (A, B, __, D), which means the first letter of the third set should be a C. The answer is Choice (A).

20. **F.** The first, third, and fifth sets are in strict alphabetical order: ABC DEF GHI. The second set interjects letters from the end of the alphabet. The only answer choice that maintains the pattern is Choice (F).

Test 2: Analogies

1. **A.** The relationship between a baby chick and an egg is probably physical development. Baby chicks come from eggs. Apply the relationship to a plant sprout. A plant sprout comes from a seed, Choice (A), not a rooster, large tree, or fried egg.

2. **G.** Snow boots are what you wear on your feet when there are snowflakes. Apply this sentence for the second relationship: Sandals are what you wear on your feet when. . . . You know the answer isn't Choice (F) or Choice (H) because neither a snow shovel nor a tennis shoe is a reason to wear sandals. The remaining options depict the weather, but sandals are more appropriate for a sunny day, Choice (G), than a rain shower.

3. **B.** A kitten grows into a cat, and a tadpole grows into a frog, Choice (B). Easy, huh?

4. **H.** The question shows you a picture of a convict and a jail cell. A convict lives in a jail cell. Apply this relationship to the second picture. A farmer doesn't live on a pitchfork, horse, or tree. He does, however, live on a farm, Choice (H).

5. **D.** The relationship between milk and cheese is that milk is the chief ingredient in cheese. Flour isn't the chief ingredient in a wheat stalk, cow, or field, but it *is* the main ingredient in bread, Choice (D).

6. **F.** A rook is one part of a chess game, so find the answer that's a part of a tool chest. Neither a domino nor a jackhammer belongs in a tool chest. A board doesn't belong there either. Choice (F), screwdriver, is the best answer.

7. **C.** This is a way that the COOP may portray a degree relationship. The first picture shows a full pail of water, and the second picture shows a pail that's overflowing. Overflowing is a greater degree of fullness. The third picture shows a table with an adequate amount of food. The picture that shows a table with a greater abundance of food than the original table is Choice (C). Choices (A) and (D) can't be right because they show lesser rather than greater amounts of food.

8. **J.** What does a sandbox have in common with the beach? Sand! The beach has a lot more sand than a sandbox does, though. Likewise, a mountain has a lot more height than a hill does, so Choice (J) is the best answer.

9. **B.** The toy train is the toy version of the real locomotive. A doll is a toy version of a real person. The only choice that shows a real person is Choice (B), the woman.

10. **F.** A kayak and a motorboat are both vessels for moving along the water, but the motorboat has a motor, and the kayak doesn't. The motorized version of a bicycle is the motorcycle in Choice (F).

11. **C.** A doghouse houses a dog, and a birdcage houses a bird, Choice (C).

12. **H.** A rocket and a paper airplane both fly in the air, but the rocket is a much more technologically advanced version of the paper airplane. Similarly, a computer is a much more technologically advanced version of an adding machine. Choice (H) is the best answer.

13. **D.** You use a knife to get peanut butter out of a jar, and you use a ladle to get soup out of a tureen, the object pictured in Choice (D).

14. **G.** A bracelet is worn on a wrist, but a sock isn't worn on a ring. Just because Choice (F) is a piece of jewelry doesn't mean it's the right answer. Choice (G), foot, is correct here.

15. **C.** A cow and a pig are mammals. See whether this relationship works for the second set of images. A tiger is a mammal, but so are sheep and rhinos. Look at the primary relationship again to see whether you can narrow your options. Cows and pigs usually live together on farms. Tigers live in the wild. Sheep are domesticated mammals. The better answer is Choice (C), rhino, because rhinos, like tigers, are wild animals.

16. **J.** A paintbrush is a tool used to create a painting. Likewise, you use a pen to handwrite a letter, making Choice (J) the best answer. A piece of paper is also involved in creating a letter, but it's not the tool for creating the letter.

17. **A.** A desk and a blackboard are both items that belong in a classroom. Both a stove and a refrigerator are appliances that belong in a kitchen. Choice (A) is your answer.

18. **F.** To score points in football, you propel a football through goal posts. To score points in basketball, you propel a basketball, Choice (F), through a net.

19. **B.** A car is powered by fuel, and a person is powered by food, Choice (B).

20. **G.** You wear a hat to protect your head during a snow shower, and you use an umbrella, Choice (G), to protect your head during a rain shower. See? These COOP analogies aren't too tough!

Test 3: Quantitative Reasoning

1. **B.** Examine the first line. The operation that takes you from 4 to 2 could be –2, but that operation doesn't apply to the second line. $2 - 2 \neq 1$, which means there must be another operation that fits into the boxes. Another way to go from 4 to 2 is by dividing by 2, an operation that also works for the second line. $2 \div 2 = 1$. Apply the operation of $\div 2$ to the third line: $6 \div 2 = 3$, Choice (B).

2. **H.** You get from 5 to 8 by adding 3. +3 also works for moving from 7 to 10 in the second line. Add 3 to 10 in the third line, and you get 13, Choice (H). Easy as pie!

3. **C.** The operation for the box in the first line could be +4 or ×5. When you consider the second line, you realize it has to be ×5 because $3 \times 5 = 15$. Apply ×5 to the third line, and you get Choice (C), 25.

4. **G.** The possible operations for the first line are –14 or ÷8. ÷8 works for the second line: $32 \div 8 = 4$. The answer is Choice (G), 7, because $56 \div 8 = 7$.

5. **A.** Figuring out the operation for this question may be a little trickier because you're dealing with decimals. Notice that the decimal point moves two spaces to the left when you go from 0.01 to 0.0001. It does the same on the second line. Move the decimal point two places to the left for 10 in the third line to get 0.1, Choice (A).

6. **J.** Consider the first line of this fraction-focused question. The operations that change ⅓ to ⅔ are ×2 or +⅓. Which one works for the second line? ⅔ × 2 = ⁴⁄₃, not 1. So the operation has to be +⅓. Add ⅓ to 3 to get Choice (J), 3⅓.

7. **D.** This question is similar to the last one. ½ is the result of either 2 × ¼ or ¼ + ¼. ⅔ is 2 times greater than ⅓, so the operation must be ×2. ⅜ × 2 is ⁶⁄₈, which becomes ¾, Choice (D), when reduced.

8. **F.** This square has a total of four boxes. Two of the boxes are shaded, which means the shaded area is ²⁄₄. When you reduce ²⁄₄ you get ½, Choice (F).

9. **C.** This figure is made up of six equal boxes; four of them are shaded. The shaded area is therefore ⁴⁄₆, or ⅔ — Choice (C).

10. **G.** This figure has a total of eight equal-sized boxes. Two full boxes and two half boxes are shaded, which equals three fully shaded boxes. The shaded area is therefore ⅜, Choice (G).

 Recall that two half-shaded boxes equal one fully shaded box. Be sure not to count each individual half-shaded box as a fully shaded box on these types of questions.

11. **B.** This figure also has eight equal-sized boxes. Three of them are fully shaded, and two are half shaded. So you have up to four fully shaded boxes out of eight for a ratio of ⁴⁄₈, which reduces to ½, Choice (B).

12. **J.** You can count nine equal-sized boxes in this figure. Four are fully shaded, and two are half shaded, totaling five fully shaded boxes. The shaded area is therefore ⁵⁄₉, Choice (J).

13. **A.** This figure contains ten equal-sized boxes, five of which are shaded. The proportion of shaded boxes to total boxes is ⁵⁄₁₀, or ½ — Choice (A).

14. **H.** This figure has ten equal-sized boxes, just like the one in the previous question. Six of these boxes are fully shaded, and two of 'em are half shaded, which means there are seven fully shaded boxes. The answer is Choice (H), ⁷⁄₁₀. Don't you wish all the COOP questions were this easy?

15. **C.** At first the scale questions may seem foreign to you, but the more you practice them, the easier they'll become. This one tells you that the value of a square equals the value of a triangle. For every square on one side of the answer choices, there must be the equivalent of a triangle on the other side. Eliminate Choices (A), (B), and (D) because each of these has more figures on one side than the other. The only answer with an equal number of squares and triangles on both sides is Choice (C).

16. **G.** The figure tells you that for every square you must have two triangles. Choices (F) and (J) violate this rule. Two triangles equal one square, not four squares, so Choice (H) is clearly wrong. The answer is Choice (G): Two squares equal four triangles.

17. **D.** Every time you see a triangle on one side of the scale, you must see three squares on the other side. The two triangles on a side in Choices (A) and (B) aren't balanced by six squares on the other side, so they're not right. And just because one triangle equals three squares doesn't mean one square equals three triangles. Cross out Choice (C) and pick Choice (D), where both sides have an equal number of squares and triangles.

18. **H.** A triangle on one side means there must be four squares on the other side. So to balance the two triangles in Choice (F), you need eight squares on the other side, not just one. The four triangles in Choice (G) need 16 squares to balance them! Choice (J) is wrong too, because it provides only six squares rather than eight to balance out the two triangles. Choice (H) is correct because it balances one triangle with four squares and the other triangle with one triangle.

19. **A.** Four squares equaling two triangles is really the same as two squares equaling one triangle. So for every triangle on one side, there must be two squares on the other, which makes Choice (B) obviously wrong because two triangles equal four squares, not three. Choice (C) doesn't balance the one triangle on one side with two squares on the other. Choice (D) balances the triangle with two squares but doesn't compensate for the additional three squares next to the triangle. The answer is Choice (A): The first triangle is balanced by another triangle, and the second triangle is balanced by two squares.

20. **H.** If two squares equal two triangles, then one square equals one triangle. Each shape is equal, so pick the answer that has equal numbers of either shape on both sides. The only answer that matches this qualification is Choice (H), which has two shapes on both sides.

Test 4: Verbal Reasoning—Words

1. **A.** What makes a sink a sink? Well, sinks are primarily designed to catch the water that comes out of the faucet, which means the best answer is Choice (A). Cold is a necessary element of a refrigerator, not a sink, and you don't need food or a cloth to use a sink.

2. **G.** The purpose of skin is to protect the inside of the body from the outside elements, which means the best answer is Choice (G). Skin may be clean, pale, or hot, but it doesn't have to be any of those three things to be skin.

3. **B.** Not all holidays are Christmas, only a few are commemorated with fireworks, and cake isn't always on the holiday menu. But the purpose of holidays is always to celebrate an event. The best answer is Choice (B).

4. **J.** Examine each answer choice and ask yourself whether spaghetti would be spaghetti without it. You can have spaghetti with clam sauce, so tomatoes, Choice (F), aren't essential. Cheese and meatballs aren't necessary either, so Choices (G) and (H) are out. Spaghetti is a type of noodle, and noodles, Choice (J), are absolutely essential to the idea of spaghetti.

5. **A.** The three words in the question are synonyms for extreme dislike. Eliminate answers that are opposites — Choices (B) and (D). Condemn is a negative term, but it isn't as similar to hate as abhor is. Pick Choice (A).

6. **G.** Narrow, slender, and thin suggest slimness. The perfect answer, also known as Choice (G), is right in front of you. Choices (F) and (H), broad and spacious, are opposites, and Choice (J), varied, is unrelated to slimness.

7. **C.** The given words are other names for long, straight objects. Choice (D), a ball, is neither long nor straight. Glue, Choice (B), has nothing to do with sticks. A flag may hang on a pole, but it's not a pole; Choice (A) is wrong. Choice (C), staff, is the only choice that's another word for stick.

8. **J.** Each of the words in the question is the name of a flower. Every answer choice is somewhat related to a flower, but only Choice (J), pansy, is the name of a flower. A leaf and a stem, Choices (F) and (G), are parts of a flower but not the specific names of flowers. You can find flowers in a garden, Choice (H), but, again, garden isn't the name of a flower.

9. **D.** Pick out the word that isn't the same as the others. Choices (A), (B), and (C) are words that mean to give in or give up. Choice (D) means to stick it out; it doesn't belong.

10. **J.** Choices (F), (G), and (H) mean tired. Choice (J) is the opposite (and correct!) answer.

You can sometimes find the word that doesn't belong even if you don't know what one of the words means. Just look at the words you do know the meaning of. If three of 'em mean roughly the same thing, you've found your answer.

11. **B.** Choices (A), (C), and (D) are related to the game of baseball. Baseball doesn't have goals, which means Choice (B) is your answer.

12. **F.** Choices (G), (H), and (J) are all kitchen appliances. The oddball is Choice (F); a computer isn't considered a kitchen appliance.

13. **B.** Take a few seconds to think about how the words in the first row are related. The first word, house, is a structure covered by the second word, roof, and for which the third word, wall, is a side. The first and second word in the second row name a structure, box, and its top, cover. Which answer choice names the side of a box? Hmm, Choice (B), perhaps? Yes, a side is indeed a side of a box.

14. **H.** The top row names some relatives. An aunt is a female, an uncle is a male, and the cousin is their child. The second row begins with a female, mother, and ends with sibling. The answer choice that completes the group is the male counterpart to mother and the parent of the sibling. That'd be a father, Choice (H).

15. **A.** The three words in the top row describe degrees of flavor. Sour is the opposite of sweet, and *cloying* is excessively sweet. The last two words in the second row are varying degrees of spiciness, from spicy to excessively spicy. The word that begins the row should be the opposite of spicy. The best answer is Choice (A), mild. Choice (B) isn't related to spiciness, and Choices (C) and (D) aren't opposites of spicy (they actually provide unwarranted judgments about whether spicy is good or bad).

16. **G.** A purse is used to carry things, a suitcase is a larger carrying case, and a trunk is a really big way to carry things. The related words increase in size as they move from left to right. An armchair is smaller than a loveseat, which is smaller than a sofa, Choice (G). Choices (F) and (J) may be larger than a loveseat, but they're not similar to a loveseat, which makes Choice (G) the best answer.

Test 5: Verbal Reasoning—Context

1. **B.** The first premise tells you that snowing all day equals skiing. Because the second premise says it has snowed all day, you know that we will go skiing, Choice (B). There isn't enough information in the premises to make the assumptions in Choices (A), (C), or (D).

2. **H.** Because Mickey has two pets and neither pet is a dog, you can conclude that Rover the dog doesn't belong to Mickey, Choice (H). You can't make judgments about Mickey's likes or wishes or whether his cat chases mice; eliminate the other answers.

3. **C.** The premises don't tell you whether Eric's illustration is in the book of illustrations, so you can't draw the conclusions in Choices (A) and (B). You don't know anything about the quality of Eric's work either, so cross out Choice (D). The best answer is Choice (C). Because Eric has drawn an illustration, he must know how to draw.

4. **J.** You can safely conclude that Betsy will watch the game between the Iguanas and Salamanders on Sunday because Betsy watches the Iguanas every Sunday. Choice (J) is the best answer. You don't know future game schedules, who'll win the game, or how Betsy feels about the Salamanders, so the rest of the options are wrong.

5. **D.** Because Fenn has earned at least $5, you can conclude that he buys a plastic animal, Choice (D). You don't know anything about Fenn's earning history or the size of his collection. Whether or not the animals are expensive is a value judgment that isn't supported by the statements.

6. **F.** Twins share the same parents, which means Chrissy and Ellen have the same parents, Choice (F). You have no information about who was born first, so Choices (G) and (J) are definitely wrong. The twins could have other siblings, so forget about Choice (H) too.

7. **B.** The premises tell you that Sean has milk and a banana with his cereal in the morning. They don't tell you that he eats cereal every morning; cross out Choice (A). Nor do the premises tell you what Sean does and doesn't like. Choice (B) is the only possible correct answer.

When you're dealing with logic questions, you can't make conclusions about someone's likes or dislikes based on his or her actions. You can only go by the information stated in the premises.

8. **H.** As far as you know, Mavis went to China without visiting the Great Wall; Choice (F) is wrong. Choices (G) and (J) make unsupported judgments about what Mavis likes and wants, so cross them out too. Because the Great Wall is in China, Mavis has to travel to China if she wants to see the Great Wall, Choice (H).

9. **B.** The premises tell you what's stated in Choice (B) — that Neil engages in three different types of physical activity (jogging, walking, and biking). They don't say what his preferences are, and they don't compare his miles jogged to his miles biked; cut Choices (A) and (D). Choice (C) is unrelated to Neil, so eliminate that one too.

10. **G.** Bridget bought clothing at Greenmart, which means she must have gone there. Because Greenmart is downtown, Bridget must have gone downtown, Choice (G). You don't know whether Greenmart sells food, what Bridget paid for the clothing, or whether Bridget has a job, which means you can toss out Choices (F), (H), and (J).

11. **C.** If Peggy finished four puzzles last week, she must have had spare time, Choice (C). You can't assume that puzzles are Peggy's favorite pastime, Choice (A), just because she does them in her spare time; the premises don't tell you that. Given more spare time, Peggy may be able to finish more than four puzzles in a week; cross out Choice (D). And because you don't know why Peggy has spare time, you can't assume Choice (B).

12. **J.** You know that the bee entered one quilt in a contest, but you don't know whether it entered all of its quilts. Choices (F) and (G) require you to know more about making quilts than is given by the premises. Elizabeth is a member of the bee, and all members work on each quilt. Therefore Elizabeth must have worked on the quilt that won first place, Choice (J).

An answer choice containing a debatable word (such as *all, every, none,* and so on) is rarely correct.

13. **A.** The premises tell you that Molly's mother picks up her mail when Molly goes on vacation, but they don't indicate that's the *only* time her mother picks up her mail; toss Choice (B). You don't know how often Molly goes on vacation or her mother's feelings, so eliminate Choices (C) and (D). If Molly's mother can get into her house to put her mail in the kitchen, she must have access to the house, Choice (A).

14. **H.** You know the flowers were eaten, but you can't conclude from the premises that the deer did it. Neither Choice (F) nor Choice (G) can logically be true. You don't know what Mr. McDonald will do next year, so the best answer is Choice (H).

15. **D.** The most you can say is that Clayton and Courtney have been to Scandinavia, Choice (D). You don't know anything that allows you to compare travel speed among types of transportation between Stockholm and Oslo. Nor do you know what time of day the train travels. Chuck the other answer options.

16. **G.** You know that Paula is on the Madison track team and that she has won five javelin throws this season. You don't know whether those five wins occurred in the five consecutive meets that Madison won; toss Choice (F). Other teams may have won more meets than Madison, and Paula may compete in more than just the javelin throw, which means Choices (J) and (H) are also wrong. Stick with Choice (G).

17. **A.** You may need to draw a chart like this one to keep track of Brad's activities:

S	M	T	W	T	F	S
Choir	Com Ctr	Tennis	Tennis	Piano	Tennis	Com Ctr

The premises don't tell you that Brad plays tennis on Tuesdays, Wednesdays, and Fridays, but that has to be true because Brad plays three times a week and doesn't participate in more than one activity per day. Choices (B), (C), and (D) require you to make unwarranted and subjective judgments about how Brad spends his time.

18. **F.** The ranking of length of employment from longest to shortest is Andy, Lynn, and Becky. Because Andy has worked longer than Becky and Becky has worked for three months, you know that Andy has worked longer than three months, Choice (F). Choice (G) simply isn't true, and Choice (H) is an unfounded value judgment. Although you know that Lynn has worked longer than Becky, you don't know exactly how much longer; consequently, Choice (J) is also wrong.

19. **C.** According to the premises, Larry is the first person to spot a wolf in Colorado in 60 years. If Larry saw the wolf, the wolf must exist; Choice (C) is the answer. Just because people haven't seen wolves in Colorado for 60 years doesn't mean wolves haven't existed in Colorado during that time. Likewise, there could be other wolves in Colorado that nobody has spotted. None of the other answer choices work.

20. **J.** Just because Mr. Wilson coaches and teaches doesn't mean that all coaches have to teach; eliminate Choice (H). You don't know how long Mr. Wilson has coached soccer, so cross out Choice (G). Choice (F) has to be wrong because the time Mr. Wilson spends on each activity is never mentioned. If Mr. Wilson currently coaches the soccer team and that soccer team just completed a winning season, then Mr. Wilson has coached the soccer team during a winning season, Choice (J).

Test 6: Reading and Language Arts

1. **D.** The last paragraph tells you that H_2O is broken up in photosynthesis to produce O_2, which makes Choice (D) correct. Photosynthesis produces glucose, but it doesn't break it up. Therefore, the answer can't be Choice (A). Chlorophyll and CO_2 are involved in the process of photosynthesis, but they're not broken up to produce O_2.

2. **J.** This inference question may seem a little tricky at first. The fourth paragraph covers light absorption, so focus your attention there. It tells you that leaves appear green because all the colors in white light are being absorbed by the plant except green, which bounces off the leaves and makes it to your eyes. Because plants are bouncing off green light rather than absorbing it, you can assume that they don't use green light as an energy source for photosynthesis. The best answer is Choice (J).

3. **C.** The first sentence states that photosynthesis creates glucose, which is sugar. The right answer is Choice (C). The other choices are substances used in the process of photosynthesis to create sugar.

4. **G.** The first sentence of the second paragraph states that *photo* means that the process uses light as its energy source. The only answer choice that appears in this explanation is Choice (G), light. Therefore, you can infer that *photo* means light.

5. **C.** The equation in the question paraphrases the equation in the middle of the passage. The third element in the equation is Choice (C), light energy. Choices (A) and (B) are already listed in the equation, and Choice (D) isn't part of the photosynthesis process.

6. **J.** To answer this question correctly, you must read through all the answer choices and cut those that aren't true. Choice (H) doesn't make sense because a plant's roots aren't exposed to light. The photosynthesis equation shows that the process is opposite to that stated in Choice (G); it uses CO_2 and gives off O_2. According to the end of the fourth paragraph, the only color chlorophyll *doesn't* absorb is green, which means Choice (F) is wrong. According to the second paragraph, the green parts of the plant make sugar. Photosynthesis produces sugar, Choice (J).

7. **B.** Title questions ask for the passage's main point. The primary purpose of this passage is to describe the process of photosynthesis, which makes the best answer Choice (B). The passage isn't about plants or glucose in general, so Choices (A) and (C) are obviously wrong. The debatable word *everything* in Choice (D) should prompt you to cross it out, too.

8. **F.** The subject of Sentence 2 is "me and my mom." *Me* is an objective form and can't be used in the subject of a sentence. The proper form is *I*. (You wouldn't say "Me went to the nursery," so you can't say "Me and my mom went to the nursery.") Choice (J) is wrong, and Choice (G) doesn't change *me* to *I*. That leaves Choices (F) and (H). Putting another before yourself is standard English, which means it's better to say "My mom and I" than "I and my mom." Choice (F) is the best answer.

9. **A.** Sentence 4 contains a usage problem. You use *less* for nouns that can't be counted and *fewer* for nouns that can. Because you can count flowers, scratch Choices (B), (C), and (D).

10. **G.** Using two qualifiers, such as "more lovelier," is improper word usage. Both *more* and the suffix *-er* demonstrate the idea of *greater* just like both *most* and the suffix *-est* demonstrate *greatest*. Cross out Choices (F) and (J). Choice (H) eliminates one of the qualifiers, but it has an improper comparison construction. You don't say that something is more lovely *as* something else; it's more lovely *than*. Choice (G) is the only answer that corrects the qualifier problem without adding a new issue.

11. **C.** You need to know the author's tone in order to answer this question. In the last sentence, the author describes Douglass as "a true American hero, whose vision and views live on today." From that statement, you know the author admires Douglass and his influence. The answer that best reflects this admiration is Choice (C). Choice (A) is partially right; the author does think Douglass is a great person, but he or she wouldn't agree that Douglass had little influence. Choice (B) contradicts information in the second paragraph, and Choice (D) is wrong because although it's true that Douglass changed opinions about slavery, he wasn't a slaveholder.

12. **H.** The passage doesn't give ending dates for the Civil War or slavery. Nor does it provide the names of abolitionists other than Douglass. The best answer is Choice (H). The third paragraph provides the names of the newspapers.

13. **D.** The first sentence of the passage states that Douglass was an abolitionist in the 1800s. The 1800s made up the 19th century, Choice (D).

14. **F.** The passage makes a point of stating that Douglass attacked the institution of slavery rather than the people involved in it. Knowing this fact allows you to eliminate Choices (G), (H), and (J). The second paragraph supports Choice (F); it states that Douglass used his newspaper to express his ideas about slavery to a large audience.

15. **B.** The first paragraph mentions Douglass's slaveholder. If Douglass had a slaveholder, he must have been a slave, Choice (B). You know Choice (D) is wrong because the third paragraph says that the newspaper had a large audience. Choice (A) is wrong because the answer doesn't define "long time," and the passage doesn't suggest that the movement was slow. The second paragraph seems to suggest that Douglass's influence paved the way for a quicker Northern response to the abolitionist movement. Choice (C) contains one of those pesky debatable words. Although Douglass was a major influence on the North, the passage doesn't suggest that he was the *only* influence.

16. **J.** This vocabulary-in-context question asks for a synonym of *cement*. Substitute each answer choice for *cement* in the sentence to see which one fits best. Douglass didn't *separate, cover,* or *weaken* a place in history. The best answer is Choice (J); Douglass did *secure* a place in history.

17. **D.** This written composition question wants to see how well you combine sentences. The best way to join the two sentences is Choice (D), which mentions Douglass just once and clearly includes all the information about him that appears in both sentences. The other choices either construct the combined sentence in a way that lacks parallel construction, Choices (A) and (C), or changes the meaning, Choice (B).

18. **H.** Eliminate sentences that are poorly constructed. Choice (F) is an incomplete sentence without a verb, Choice (G) uses passive voice, and Choice (J) has an improper qualifier (more fairer). The best answer is Choice (H); it's constructed clearly and contains no usage errors.

19. **A.** Choose a sentence that leads into the specific topic of abolitionist leader Frederick Douglass. Choice (D) is way too general. Choice (B) is off topic; the paragraph doesn't talk about the practice of slavery in other cultures. Choice (C) doesn't work because it suggests that the paragraph will discuss abolitionists who weren't former slaves, but the paragraph's topic is Douglass, who was in fact a former slave. The best answer is Choice (A) because it leads into the topic of a particular abolitionist leader.

20. **G.** The points of the last sentence are that Douglass gives a unique portrayal of slaveholders and that this portrayal attracted Northerners. Choice (G) addresses one of these issues, Douglass's portrayal of slaveholders; it's probably the best answer. The rest of the answers are off topic and way too general.

The last sentence of a paragraph often contains clues as to what could or should come after it. Read it carefully, and you'll have an easier time answering questions that want to know what happens next.

21. **A.** The passage mentions hockey and high school players, which makes it pretty likely that the Cougars are a high school hockey team, Choice (A).

22. **J.** The second paragraph describes the Clement players. The only school not mentioned in this paragraph is Apple River, Choice (J), which is the name of a rival team mentioned in the third paragraph.

23. **C.** The second paragraph contains the answer to this straightforward details question. It states that the goalie is Brendan Sanchez, Choice (C).

24. **H.** The third paragraph lists last year's team record. Because the Cougars' record was 9-5 (9 wins and 5 losses), the team must have played 14 games, Choice (H).

25. **B.** The subject matter (hockey at Clement High School) and casual tone of this passage suggest that it was probably written for a high school newspaper, Choice (B).

26. **F.** You can tell the author is excited about the hockey season in the opening paragraph. The use of exclamation points and the positive language support picking Choice (F) as the best description of the author's tone. The other choices are too negative.

27. **A.** Sentence 1 lacks parallel construction; eliminate Choice (D). Choice (B) doesn't correct the problem. Although Choice (C) repairs the parallel construction problem, it introduces a new error by incorrectly separating objects from their prepositions. Choice (A) fixes the parallel construction problem without creating additional errors.

28. **J.** Sentence 2 seems fine as is, but check the other answers just to be sure. Choice (F) is an incomplete sentence, and Choice (G) contains improper usage (the phrase should be *benefits of,* not *benefits on*). The proper construction for Choice (H) is *if . . . , then,* not *if . . . , than.* Choice (J) is the best answer.

29. **C.** Sentence 4 contains improper usage; *more healthier* should be just plain *healthier*. Choice (A) doesn't help. It contains the same improper usage issues, punctuation errors, and construction problems. Choice (B) is a comma splice; the comma after *school* should be a semicolon. The best answer is Choice (C).

30. **G.** The last sentence of the first paragraph says that both works "demonstrate the relationship between the spiritual and material world." The answer that paraphrases this idea is Choice (G). Only Beuys used mixed media and had German influences, and the first paragraph states that the artists' subject matters were different.

31. **C.** The first paragraph says that Beuys painted almost 400 years after El Greco painted *The Burial of Conde Orgaz* in the late 1500s, which means Beuys began painting in the 1900s. Choice (C) is your answer.

32. **F.** The third paragraph tells you that El Greco painted his masterworks in Spain, Choice (F). He trained in Crete and Italy but apparently didn't paint his masterworks there.

33. **A.** The main point of the passage is to compare El Greco and Beuys, which makes Choice (A) the winning answer. Choice (D) is too general a title for the passage. Choice (B) is wrong because the author doesn't make judgments about which artist is better, and Choice (C) is absurd because the two artists lived in completely different centuries and therefore couldn't have been friends.

34. **J.** The fourth paragraph tells you that World War II, Choice (J), greatly influenced Beuys. None of the other choices is even mentioned in the passage.

35. **D.** In the last paragraph, you read that El Greco "most often recreated specific religious events." Choice (D) is therefore the best answer. Choice (C) was the subject matter of Beuys.

36. **F.** You're looking for what's *not* true, so eliminate true statements. El Greco's work was commissioned by churches (see Paragraph 5), his art recorded history (also in Paragraph 5), and his painting portrayed interaction between the spiritual and material (Paragraphs 1, 2, and 5). He received formal training in Crete and Italy, which means Choice (F) isn't true and is therefore the right answer.

37. **B.** Choice (B) combines the sentences in the clearest way. Choice (A) is awkward, Choice (C) is a comma splice, and Choice (D) lacks parallel construction.

38. **H.** You can't use *which* to refer to people, so Choice (F) is wrong. Also, you choose between two things and among three or more, so throw out Choice (G). The verb *emerges* in Choice (J) should be plural because the subject (themes) is plural. The sentence without any errors is Choice (H).

39. **D.** The paragraph describes a specific painting, which means the topic sentence should introduce that painting. Choices (A) and (B) introduce painting in general and are too broad for this paragraph. With Choice (C), you'd expect a paragraph on the city of Toledo rather than a painting. Choice (D) introduces the painting and provides its name, which is missing from the rest of the paragraph; it's the best answer.

40. **G.** Because the paragraph ends by stating that the painting has two main settings, it makes sense that the next paragraph would talk more about those settings. The other answer choices reference topics that aren't justified by the end of the paragraph.

Test 7: Mathematics

1. **A.** This subtraction problem is pretty easy. Just make sure you line up the decimal points before you subtract:

$$\begin{array}{r} 5.4 \\ -\ 0.2 \\ \hline 5.2 \end{array}$$

2. **H.** *Percent* is equivalent to per 100, which means you show 0.03% as a fraction by placing 0.03 over 100, like this: $^{0.03}/_{100}$. To get rid of the decimal point, move it to the right two places for both the numerator and the denominator. The fraction then becomes $^{3}/_{10,000}$, which is Choice (H).

3. **D.** To multiply like numbers with exponents, you keep the base the same and add the exponents. The base in this problem is 2, and the sum of the exponents is 5. Therefore your answer is 2^5, Choice (D).

4. **H.** Look carefully at all the answer choices. A couple of 'em are easy to eliminate because ⅜ shares the same denominator with Choices (F) and (J). You know that ⅞ and ⅝ are greater than ⅜, which means you can eliminate both of those choices. ⁴⁄₈ is equal to ½, which means ⅜ is less than ½; Choice (G) is wrong. The answer is Choice (H).

5. **D.** The number 1 in this problem is in the ten thousand's place, which means its value is 10,000, Choice (D).

6. **J.** All the answer choices are decimals. ²⁄₈ simplifies to ¼, which you know is 0.25. Therefore, 4.75 + 0.25 is 5, Choice (J).

Adding a fraction to a decimal (or vice versa) is easier if both values are in the same form. See Chapter 10 for help converting one to the other.

7. **A.** Multiply the two numbers and make sure you put the decimal point in the proper place. Because there are three total digits to the right of the decimal points in the numbers being multiplied, the product must have three digits to the right of the decimal point:

$$\begin{array}{r} 14.45 \\ \times\ \ 0.4 \\ \hline 5.780 \end{array}$$

Dropping the zero gives you Choice (A). If you picked Choice (C), you probably thought it was correct because it had three digits to the right of the decimal, but you didn't take into consideration that the original answer had an ending zero that took one of the places to the right of the decimal.

8. **G.** The fraction of two pieces of pizza in an eight-piece pizza is ²⁄₈, or ¼. ¼ expressed as a percentage is 25%, Choice (G).

9. **D.** Line up the decimals and subtract:

$$\begin{array}{r} 0.975 \\ -\ 0.463 \\ \hline 0.512 \end{array}$$

The answer is 0.512, Choice (D).

10. **H.** The formula for finding distance is Rate × Time = Distance. The rate is 65 miles per hour, and 30 minutes is a half hour, or 0.5. To find the distance, multiply 65×0.5, which is 32.5 miles — Choice (H).

11. **A.** Follow the order of operations (PEMDAS). Parentheses are first, but there are two operations in the parentheses — subtraction and multiplication. The order of operations dictates that you multiply before you subtract. Do that to get $2 \times 6 = 12$. Now subtract 12 from 4: $4 - 12 = -8$. The remaining operation is to multiply -5 and -8: $-5 \times -8 = 40$, Choice (A). If you picked Choice (C), you subtracted within the parentheses before you multiplied. If you went with Choice (B) or Choice (D), you mixed up your positives and negatives.

12. **G.** Figure out what percentage of the budget goes to research and product development (R&D) by adding up the percentages of the other expenditures and subtracting that number from 100% (total expenditures): R&D = 100% − (40% + 30% + 15%). R&D = 100% − 85%, so R&D = 15%. To change that percentage to a fraction, put 15 over 100 and reduce: $^{15}/_{100} = ^{3}/_{20}$, Choice (G).

13. **D.** Zoe's total earnings consist of her salary of $200/week + her commission. Here's how you can set up the equation: E = $200 + ($3,500 × 5%). $3,500 × 5% is $175. $175 + $200 is $375. Zoe earns a total of $375 for the week, Choice (D).

14. **F.** Four hundred twenty five thousand looks like this: 425,000. Add 45 and the answer is 425,045, Choice (F).

15. **D.** There are 20 total games (5 + 13 + 2). Don't stop there and pick Choice (A), though. ⅕ of 20 is 4. The answer is Choice (D).

16. **H.** This question asks you to find 9⁄12 of 48. *Of* means multiply, so the equation is $x = \frac{9}{12} \times 48$. If multiplying 9 by 48 and dividing by 12 takes too long, you can make the problem easier by dividing 12 and 48 by the common factor of 12. Doing so leaves you with ¾ × 4⁄1 = 36, Choice (H).

17. **D.** The correct answer must be a set of numbers that's less than 3 and greater than –1. Choice (D) is the only option that doesn't contain either of these numbers.

18. **F.** Solve for x: 3(4x) + 7 = 43; 12x + 7 = 43; 12x = 36; x = 3. The answer is Choice (F).

19. **A.** Twelve inches are in a foot, so an inch is ¹⁄12 of a foot, Choice (A).

20. **F.** This one's easy as long as you know that the formula for the area of a triangle is ½*bh*. Start plugging away: A = ½ × 14 × 8. A = 7 × 8, which is 56 inches square, Choice (F).

21. **B.** 10 doesn't go into 125, so eliminate Choices (A), (C), and (D). You want Choice (B).

22. **H.** If three of the salespeople made 50 percent of the sales, the other two made the other 50 percent. Just find out what 50% of $96,520 is, and you're home free! You don't have to fully divide $96,520 by 2 to choose the right answer; just estimate: $96,520 rounds up to $100,000. Half of $100,000 is $50,000, so scratch Choices (F) and (G) because they're way under that amount. Given that you rounded up, you know the answer must be less than $50,000, which means the answer is Choice (H).

23. **B.** This one's more like a vocabulary question than a math question. A *pentagon* is a five-sided figure, Choice (B).

24. **J.** You know that x is any number between –2 and 2. It's less than 2, so Choice (F) is true. Choices (G) and (H) could be true, so forget about 'em. The false statement is Choice (J); x can't be less than –2.

> When faced with an exception question (one that asks what's *not* true), rephrase the question so you know for sure you're looking for an answer that must be false.

25. **B.** For this question, you create an equation, but you don't have to solve it. *And* means add, so a hat is $y + x$. 4 hats would be 4 times that: 4($y + x$). Choice (B) is the answer.

26. **H.** A negative times a negative is always positive; Choice (H) is correct.

27. **B.** 10^2 = 10 × 10, which = 100. 4 × 100 is 400, Choice (B).

28. **G.** Because *of* means *multiply,* 200% of the price Pat pays ($20) is the same as 2 × 20. Pat sells each pair for $40, Choice (G).

29. **C.** Put your finger on Bluebird Mall on the map. Move your finger to the left to determine that the mall's vertical coordinate is D. Move your finger up to find that 4 is the horizontal coordinate. The coordinate pair is D4, Choice (C).

30. **G.** Jill follows the proper order of operations (PEMDAS) by solving the information in the parentheses first, multiplying next, and adding last. Pick Choice (G).

31. **D.** Right angles are always 90°. The answer is Choice (D).

32. **F.** First, distribute the 3: 3x + 9 = 36. Then subtract 9 from both sides of the equation. Finally, solve for x: 3x = 27, and x = 9, Choice (F).

33. **C.** A quadrilateral has four sides. The only answer choice with four sides is Choice (C), a square. A pentagon has five sides, a triangle has three, and an octagon has eight.

34. **H.** The formula for circumference is $2r\pi$. So a circle with a radius of 3 has a circumference of $2(3)\pi$, or 6π units — Choice (H).

35. **C.** To solve this problem you have to figure out what numbers meet all the possible values for both x and y. Possible values for x are –1, 0, 1, 2, 3, and so on. Possible values for y are 2, 1, 0, –1, –2, and so on. The values in common are –1, 0, 1, and 2. Choices (B) and (D) contain some of these possible values, but the best answer option is Choice (C) because it contains all the possible values. Choice (A) contains a value that's incorrect.

36. **J.** The total amount Alexis owes is the original loan amount plus the interest: $x = \$13,000 +$ ($\$13,000 \times 10\%$). First, figure out the interest: $\$13,000 \times 0.1 = \$1,300$. Then add that to $\$13,000$: $\$13,000 + \$1,300 = \$14,300$, which is Choice (J).

37. **B.** The question asks only about average inches grown this year, so the fact that Bob grew more this year than last is irrelevant. Bob grew 6 inches this year, and there are 12 months in a year. Consequently, the average number of inches Bob grew per month was $\frac{6}{12}$, or $\frac{1}{2}$, Choice (B).

38. **F.** The factors of 45 are 5 and 9. The number 5 is already prime, so you should list it as one of the prime factors. Eliminate Choices (G) and (H) because they don't contain 5. The other factor, 9, contains the factors of 3×3. Because 3 is prime, the prime factors of 45 are $5 \times 3 \times 3$, or 5×3^2 — Choice (F). Eliminate Choice (J) because 9 isn't prime.

39. **A.** Figure out the point on the x-axis first. Start at the point where the x-axis and y-axis cross and count the spaces to the right until you reach Point A. Point A is 2 spaces to the right, which means it's a +2. Point A on the y-axis is 1 space below the x-axis, which means it's –1. Thus, the correct answer is Choice (A). Choice (B) would be above the x-axis, and Choices (C) and (D) would be to the left of the y-axis and above the x-axis.

40. **F.** The chart that gives the best visual of the relationship among fractions of a whole is the pie chart, Choice (F). If you didn't get this one right, refer to Chapter 13 for a refresher on which charts are best for showing specific types of information.

Answer Key for COOP Practice Test 1

Test 1: Sequences

1. B	5. C	9. C	13. D	17. C
2. H	6. G	10. H	14. F	18. H
3. A	7. A	11. C	15. B	19. A
4. J	8. G	12. J	16. G	20. F

Test 2: Analogies

1. A	5. D	9. B	13. D	17. A
2. G	6. F	10. F	14. G	18. F
3. B	7. C	11. C	15. C	19. B
4. H	8. J	12. H	16. J	20. G

Test 3: Quantitative Reasoning

1. B	5. A	9. C	13. A	17. D
2. H	6. J	10. G	14. H	18. H
3. C	7. D	11. B	15. C	19. A
4. G	8. F	12. J	16. G	20. H

Test 4: Verbal Reasoning—Words

1. A	5. A	9. D	13. B
2. G	6. G	10. J	14. H
3. B	7. C	11. B	15. A
4. J	8. J	12. F	16. G

Test 5: Verbal Reasoning—Context

1. B	5. D	9. B	13. A	17. A
2. H	6. F	10. G	14. H	18. F
3. C	7. B	11. C	15. D	19. C
4. J	8. H	12. J	16. G	20. J

Test 6: Reading and Language Arts

1. D	9. A	17. D	25. B	33. A
2. J	10. G	18. H	26. F	34. J
3. C	11. C	19. A	27. A	35. D
4. G	12. H	20. G	28. J	36. F
5. C	13. D	21. A	29. C	37. B
6. J	14. F	22. J	30. G	38. H
7. B	15. B	23. C	31. C	39. D
8. F	16. J	24. H	32. F	40. G

Test 7: Mathematics

1. A	9. D	17. D	25. B	33. C
2. H	10. H	18. F	26. H	34. H
3. D	11. A	19. A	27. B	35. C
4. H	12. G	20. F	28. G	36. J
5. D	13. D	21. B	29. C	37. B
6. J	14. F	22. H	30. G	38. F
7. A	15. D	23. B	31. D	39. A
8. G	16. H	24. J	32. F	40. F

Chapter 27

COOP Practice Test 2

*J*ust what you always wanted — another opportunity to practice for the COOP. Contain your excitement, please.

This practice test is very similar to the actual COOP, but the exam you take on test day may have a different number of questions or slightly different time limits. Blame the discrepancy on those dastardly test-makers.

You'll get the most out of this practice experience if you try to make it as much like the real thing as you can. Following are some suggestions for doing just that:

- ✔ Find a place where you won't be distracted (which means you may want to tell your friends you won't be available for a few hours).

- ✔ Aim to take this test at about the same time of day — likely pretty early in the morning — as the time of your scheduled COOP.

- ✔ Tear out the answer sheet in this chapter and mark your answers on it by filling in the appropriate bubbles.

- ✔ Scribble notes and computations in the margins of the test questions.

- ✔ Time yourself on each section. When the time is up, move on to the next section. (**Remember:** As much as you may want to, you can't go back to a section to answer any skipped questions.)

- ✔ Give yourself about 10 to 15 minutes to relax between the fourth and fifth tests. You'll probably be given a similar break on test day.

When you're all done with this practice test, head to Chapter 28 to check your answers.

Answer Sheet for COOP Practice Test 2

Test 1: Sequences

1. Ⓐ Ⓑ Ⓒ Ⓓ	5. Ⓐ Ⓑ Ⓒ Ⓓ	9. Ⓐ Ⓑ Ⓒ Ⓓ	13. Ⓐ Ⓑ Ⓒ Ⓓ	17. Ⓐ Ⓑ Ⓒ Ⓓ
2. Ⓕ Ⓖ Ⓗ Ⓙ	6. Ⓕ Ⓖ Ⓗ Ⓙ	10. Ⓕ Ⓖ Ⓗ Ⓙ	14. Ⓕ Ⓖ Ⓗ Ⓙ	18. Ⓕ Ⓖ Ⓗ Ⓙ
3. Ⓐ Ⓑ Ⓒ Ⓓ	7. Ⓐ Ⓑ Ⓒ Ⓓ	11. Ⓐ Ⓑ Ⓒ Ⓓ	15. Ⓐ Ⓑ Ⓒ Ⓓ	19. Ⓐ Ⓑ Ⓒ Ⓓ
4. Ⓕ Ⓖ Ⓗ Ⓙ	8. Ⓕ Ⓖ Ⓗ Ⓙ	12. Ⓕ Ⓖ Ⓗ Ⓙ	16. Ⓕ Ⓖ Ⓗ Ⓙ	20. Ⓕ Ⓖ Ⓗ Ⓙ

Test 2: Analogies

1. Ⓐ Ⓑ Ⓒ Ⓓ	5. Ⓐ Ⓑ Ⓒ Ⓓ	9. Ⓐ Ⓑ Ⓒ Ⓓ	13. Ⓐ Ⓑ Ⓒ Ⓓ	17. Ⓐ Ⓑ Ⓒ Ⓓ
2. Ⓕ Ⓖ Ⓗ Ⓙ	6. Ⓕ Ⓖ Ⓗ Ⓙ	10. Ⓕ Ⓖ Ⓗ Ⓙ	14. Ⓕ Ⓖ Ⓗ Ⓙ	18. Ⓕ Ⓖ Ⓗ Ⓙ
3. Ⓐ Ⓑ Ⓒ Ⓓ	7. Ⓐ Ⓑ Ⓒ Ⓓ	11. Ⓐ Ⓑ Ⓒ Ⓓ	15. Ⓐ Ⓑ Ⓒ Ⓓ	19. Ⓐ Ⓑ Ⓒ Ⓓ
4. Ⓕ Ⓖ Ⓗ Ⓙ	8. Ⓕ Ⓖ Ⓗ Ⓙ	12. Ⓕ Ⓖ Ⓗ Ⓙ	16. Ⓕ Ⓖ Ⓗ Ⓙ	20. Ⓕ Ⓖ Ⓗ Ⓙ

Test 3: Quantitative Reasoning

1. Ⓐ Ⓑ Ⓒ Ⓓ	5. Ⓐ Ⓑ Ⓒ Ⓓ	9. Ⓐ Ⓑ Ⓒ Ⓓ	13. Ⓐ Ⓑ Ⓒ Ⓓ	17. Ⓐ Ⓑ Ⓒ Ⓓ
2. Ⓕ Ⓖ Ⓗ Ⓙ	6. Ⓕ Ⓖ Ⓗ Ⓙ	10. Ⓕ Ⓖ Ⓗ Ⓙ	14. Ⓕ Ⓖ Ⓗ Ⓙ	18. Ⓕ Ⓖ Ⓗ Ⓙ
3. Ⓐ Ⓑ Ⓒ Ⓓ	7. Ⓐ Ⓑ Ⓒ Ⓓ	11. Ⓐ Ⓑ Ⓒ Ⓓ	15. Ⓐ Ⓑ Ⓒ Ⓓ	19. Ⓐ Ⓑ Ⓒ Ⓓ
4. Ⓕ Ⓖ Ⓗ Ⓙ	8. Ⓕ Ⓖ Ⓗ Ⓙ	12. Ⓕ Ⓖ Ⓗ Ⓙ	16. Ⓕ Ⓖ Ⓗ Ⓙ	20. Ⓕ Ⓖ Ⓗ Ⓙ

Test 4: Verbal Reasoning—Words

1. Ⓐ Ⓑ Ⓒ Ⓓ	5. Ⓐ Ⓑ Ⓒ Ⓓ	9. Ⓐ Ⓑ Ⓒ Ⓓ	13. Ⓐ Ⓑ Ⓒ Ⓓ
2. Ⓕ Ⓖ Ⓗ Ⓙ	6. Ⓕ Ⓖ Ⓗ Ⓙ	10. Ⓕ Ⓖ Ⓗ Ⓙ	14. Ⓕ Ⓖ Ⓗ Ⓙ
3. Ⓐ Ⓑ Ⓒ Ⓓ	7. Ⓐ Ⓑ Ⓒ Ⓓ	11. Ⓐ Ⓑ Ⓒ Ⓓ	15. Ⓐ Ⓑ Ⓒ Ⓓ
4. Ⓕ Ⓖ Ⓗ Ⓙ	8. Ⓕ Ⓖ Ⓗ Ⓙ	12. Ⓕ Ⓖ Ⓗ Ⓙ	16. Ⓕ Ⓖ Ⓗ Ⓙ

Test 5: Verbal Reasoning—Context

1. Ⓐ Ⓑ Ⓒ Ⓓ	5. Ⓐ Ⓑ Ⓒ Ⓓ	9. Ⓐ Ⓑ Ⓒ Ⓓ	13. Ⓐ Ⓑ Ⓒ Ⓓ	17. Ⓐ Ⓑ Ⓒ Ⓓ
2. Ⓕ Ⓖ Ⓗ Ⓙ	6. Ⓕ Ⓖ Ⓗ Ⓙ	10. Ⓕ Ⓖ Ⓗ Ⓙ	14. Ⓕ Ⓖ Ⓗ Ⓙ	18. Ⓕ Ⓖ Ⓗ Ⓙ
3. Ⓐ Ⓑ Ⓒ Ⓓ	7. Ⓐ Ⓑ Ⓒ Ⓓ	11. Ⓐ Ⓑ Ⓒ Ⓓ	15. Ⓐ Ⓑ Ⓒ Ⓓ	19. Ⓐ Ⓑ Ⓒ Ⓓ
4. Ⓕ Ⓖ Ⓗ Ⓙ	8. Ⓕ Ⓖ Ⓗ Ⓙ	12. Ⓕ Ⓖ Ⓗ Ⓙ	16. Ⓕ Ⓖ Ⓗ Ⓙ	20. Ⓕ Ⓖ Ⓗ Ⓙ

Test 6: Reading and Language Arts

1. Ⓐ Ⓑ Ⓒ Ⓓ	9. Ⓐ Ⓑ Ⓒ Ⓓ	17. Ⓐ Ⓑ Ⓒ Ⓓ	25. Ⓐ Ⓑ Ⓒ Ⓓ	33. Ⓐ Ⓑ Ⓒ Ⓓ
2. Ⓕ Ⓖ Ⓗ Ⓙ	10. Ⓕ Ⓖ Ⓗ Ⓙ	18. Ⓕ Ⓖ Ⓗ Ⓙ	26. Ⓕ Ⓖ Ⓗ Ⓙ	34. Ⓕ Ⓖ Ⓗ Ⓙ
3. Ⓐ Ⓑ Ⓒ Ⓓ	11. Ⓐ Ⓑ Ⓒ Ⓓ	19. Ⓐ Ⓑ Ⓒ Ⓓ	27. Ⓐ Ⓑ Ⓒ Ⓓ	35. Ⓐ Ⓑ Ⓒ Ⓓ
4. Ⓕ Ⓖ Ⓗ Ⓙ	12. Ⓕ Ⓖ Ⓗ Ⓙ	20. Ⓕ Ⓖ Ⓗ Ⓙ	28. Ⓕ Ⓖ Ⓗ Ⓙ	36. Ⓕ Ⓖ Ⓗ Ⓙ
5. Ⓐ Ⓑ Ⓒ Ⓓ	13. Ⓐ Ⓑ Ⓒ Ⓓ	21. Ⓐ Ⓑ Ⓒ Ⓓ	29. Ⓐ Ⓑ Ⓒ Ⓓ	37. Ⓐ Ⓑ Ⓒ Ⓓ
6. Ⓕ Ⓖ Ⓗ Ⓙ	14. Ⓕ Ⓖ Ⓗ Ⓙ	22. Ⓕ Ⓖ Ⓗ Ⓙ	30. Ⓕ Ⓖ Ⓗ Ⓙ	38. Ⓕ Ⓖ Ⓗ Ⓙ
7. Ⓐ Ⓑ Ⓒ Ⓓ	15. Ⓐ Ⓑ Ⓒ Ⓓ	23. Ⓐ Ⓑ Ⓒ Ⓓ	31. Ⓐ Ⓑ Ⓒ Ⓓ	39. Ⓐ Ⓑ Ⓒ Ⓓ
8. Ⓕ Ⓖ Ⓗ Ⓙ	16. Ⓕ Ⓖ Ⓗ Ⓙ	24. Ⓕ Ⓖ Ⓗ Ⓙ	32. Ⓕ Ⓖ Ⓗ Ⓙ	40. Ⓕ Ⓖ Ⓗ Ⓙ

Test 7: Mathematics

1. Ⓐ Ⓑ Ⓒ Ⓓ	9. Ⓐ Ⓑ Ⓒ Ⓓ	17. Ⓐ Ⓑ Ⓒ Ⓓ	25. Ⓐ Ⓑ Ⓒ Ⓓ	33. Ⓐ Ⓑ Ⓒ Ⓓ
2. Ⓕ Ⓖ Ⓗ Ⓙ	10. Ⓕ Ⓖ Ⓗ Ⓙ	18. Ⓕ Ⓖ Ⓗ Ⓙ	26. Ⓕ Ⓖ Ⓗ Ⓙ	34. Ⓕ Ⓖ Ⓗ Ⓙ
3. Ⓐ Ⓑ Ⓒ Ⓓ	11. Ⓐ Ⓑ Ⓒ Ⓓ	19. Ⓐ Ⓑ Ⓒ Ⓓ	27. Ⓐ Ⓑ Ⓒ Ⓓ	35. Ⓐ Ⓑ Ⓒ Ⓓ
4. Ⓕ Ⓖ Ⓗ Ⓙ	12. Ⓕ Ⓖ Ⓗ Ⓙ	20. Ⓕ Ⓖ Ⓗ Ⓙ	28. Ⓕ Ⓖ Ⓗ Ⓙ	36. Ⓕ Ⓖ Ⓗ Ⓙ
5. Ⓐ Ⓑ Ⓒ Ⓓ	13. Ⓐ Ⓑ Ⓒ Ⓓ	21. Ⓐ Ⓑ Ⓒ Ⓓ	29. Ⓐ Ⓑ Ⓒ Ⓓ	37. Ⓐ Ⓑ Ⓒ Ⓓ
6. Ⓕ Ⓖ Ⓗ Ⓙ	14. Ⓕ Ⓖ Ⓗ Ⓙ	22. Ⓕ Ⓖ Ⓗ Ⓙ	30. Ⓕ Ⓖ Ⓗ Ⓙ	38. Ⓕ Ⓖ Ⓗ Ⓙ
7. Ⓐ Ⓑ Ⓒ Ⓓ	15. Ⓐ Ⓑ Ⓒ Ⓓ	23. Ⓐ Ⓑ Ⓒ Ⓓ	31. Ⓐ Ⓑ Ⓒ Ⓓ	39. Ⓐ Ⓑ Ⓒ Ⓓ
8. Ⓕ Ⓖ Ⓗ Ⓙ	16. Ⓕ Ⓖ Ⓗ Ⓙ	24. Ⓕ Ⓖ Ⓗ Ⓙ	32. Ⓕ Ⓖ Ⓗ Ⓙ	40. Ⓕ Ⓖ Ⓗ Ⓙ

Test 1: Sequences

Time: 20 minutes

Directions: For Questions 1–20, choose the answer that best continues the pattern.

1.

(A) ☆ (B) ☺ (C) ★ (D) 🚫

2.

(F) (G) (H) (J)

3.

(A) $ $ (B) Ƨ Ƨ (C) Ƨ $ (D) $ Ƨ

4.

(F) □ □ (G) △ △ (H) □ △ (J) △ □

5.

(A) △◇ (B) △△ (C) ◇⬠ (D) ◇△

6.

(F) (G) (H) (J)

Go on to next page

7. 3 6 9 12 15 _____
   (A) 16
   (B) 17
   (C) 18
   (D) 20

8. 100 80 60 40 20 _____
   (F) 0
   (G) 10
   (H) 30
   (J) 5

9. 3 5 7 6 8 10 40 42 _____
   (A) 50
   (B) 44
   (C) 47
   (D) 46

10. 7 14 28 5 10 20 _____ 12 24
    (F) 9
    (G) 3
    (H) 6
    (J) 4

11. 2 3 6 5 3 15 6 _____ 12
    (A) 2
    (B) 3
    (C) 6
    (D) 4

12. 1 4 5 5 5 10 6 _____ 9
    (F) 6
    (G) 3
    (H) 7
    (J) 5

13. 25 5 0 50 10 5 45 9 _____
    (A) 10
    (B) 15
    (C) 6
    (D) 4

14. A4B3C2 A5B4C3 A6B5C4 _____
    (F) A7B6C5
    (G) A1B2C3
    (H) A7B8C9
    (J) D3E2F1

15. $C_1B^2A_3$ $F^2E_3D^4$ $I_3H^4G_5$ _____
    (A) $L^4K_5J^6$
    (B) $J^4K_5L^6$
    (C) $J_3K^4L_5$
    (D) $L_4K^5J_6$

16. P R T _____ X Z
    (F) Y
    (G) U
    (H) V
    (J) S

17. o n m l k j _____
    (A) l
    (B) h
    (C) d
    (D) i

18. ABCE FGHJ KLMO _____
    (F) QRTV
    (G) PQRT
    (H) OPQR
    (J) PQRS

19. AZBY CXDW _____ GTHS
    (A) DWEV
    (B) EVFU
    (C) ABCZ
    (D) EHFI

20. ZYX AAA WVU BBB _____
    (F) CCC
    (G) XWV
    (H) RQP
    (J) TSR

STOP DO NOT TURN THE PAGE UNTIL TOLD TO DO SO.
DO NOT RETURN TO A PREVIOUS TEST.

Test 2: Analogies

Time: 15 minutes

Directions: For Questions 1–20, choose the answer that belongs in the empty box so that the bottom two pictures relate in the same way as the top two pictures.

1.

(A)   (B)   (C)   (D)

2.

(F)   (G)   (H)   (J)

3.

(A)   (B)   (C)   (D)

Go on to next page

4.

(F)   (G)   (H)   (J)

5.

(A)   (B)   (C)   (D)

6.

(F)   (G)   (H)   (J)

Go on to next page

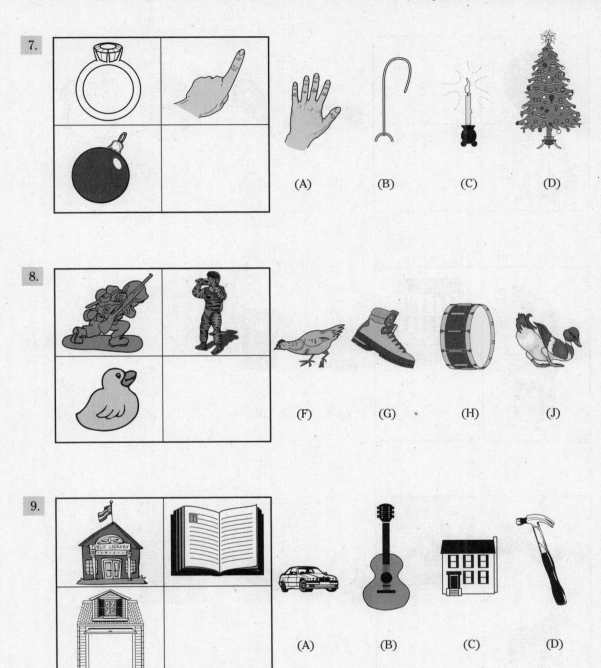

7.

(A) (B) (C) (D)

8.

(F) (G) (H) (J)

9.

(A) (B) (C) (D)

Go on to next page

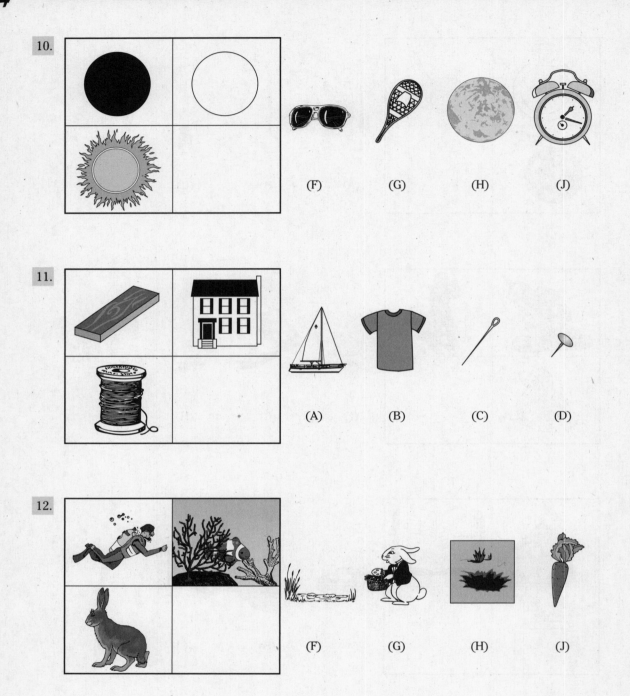

10.

(F)   (G)   (H)   (J)

11.

(A)   (B)   (C)   (D)

12.

(F)   (G)   (H)   (J)

Go on to next page

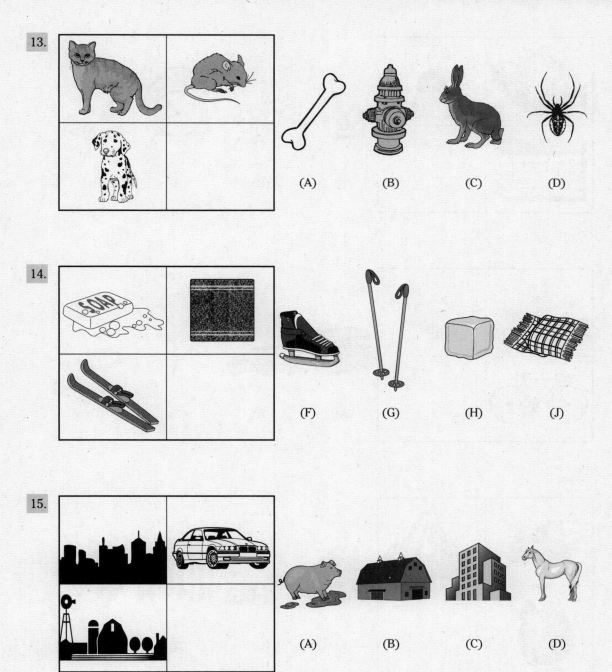

13.

(A) (B) (C) (D)

14.

(F) (G) (H) (J)

15.

(A) (B) (C) (D)

Go on to next page

16.

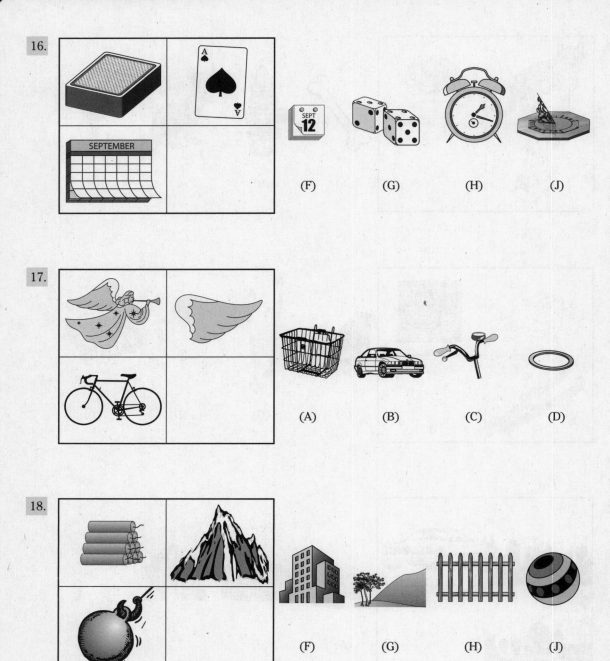

(F) (G) (H) (J)

17.

(A) (B) (C) (D)

18.

(F) (G) (H) (J)

Go on to next page

19.

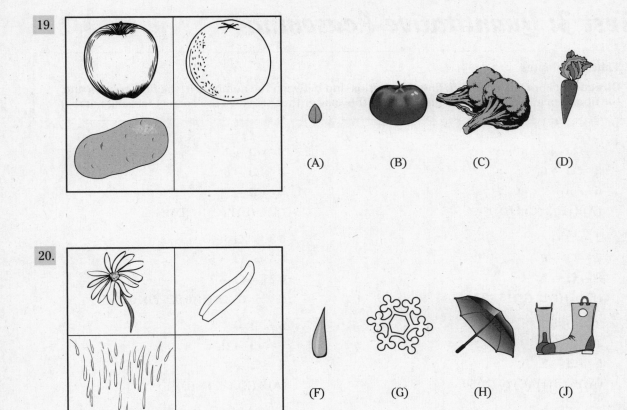

(A) (B) (C) (D)

20.

(F) (G) (H) (J)

Test 3: Quantitative Reasoning

Time: 20 minutes

Directions: For Questions 1–7, find the relationship between the numbers in the first column and the numbers in the second column. Choose the answer that provides the correct missing number.

1. $4 \rightarrow \square \rightarrow 2$
    $8 \rightarrow \square \rightarrow 6$
    $6 \rightarrow \square \rightarrow ?$
    (A) 2 (B) 3 (C) 4 (D) 1

2. $2 \rightarrow \square \rightarrow 4$
    $7 \rightarrow \square \rightarrow 9$
    $8 \rightarrow \square \rightarrow ?$
    (F) 10 (G) 12 (H) 13 (J) 14

3. $3 \rightarrow \square \rightarrow 9$
    $4 \rightarrow \square \rightarrow 12$
    $5 \rightarrow \square \rightarrow ?$
    (A) 15 (B) 11 (C) 20 (D) 50

4. $25 \rightarrow \square \rightarrow 5$
    $50 \rightarrow \square \rightarrow 10$
    $100 \rightarrow \square \rightarrow ?$
    (F) 25 (G) 20 (H) 15 (J) 50

5. $\frac{1}{2} \rightarrow \square \rightarrow 1$
    $3 \rightarrow \square \rightarrow 6$
    $\frac{2}{3} \rightarrow \square \rightarrow ?$
    (A) ⅓ (B) 1 (C) 1⅔ (D) 1⅓

6. $0.3 \rightarrow \square \rightarrow 3$
    $0.5 \rightarrow \square \rightarrow 5$
    $0.25 \rightarrow \square \rightarrow ?$
    (F) 25 (G) 2.5 (H) 0.025 (J) 10.25

7. $\frac{5}{8} \rightarrow \square \rightarrow \frac{3}{4}$
    $1 \rightarrow \square \rightarrow 1\frac{1}{8}$
    $\frac{3}{8} \rightarrow \square \rightarrow ?$
    (A) ⅛ (B) ½ (C) ⅝ (D) ¼

Go on to next page

Directions: For Questions 8–14, find the fraction of the shape that is shaded.

8. 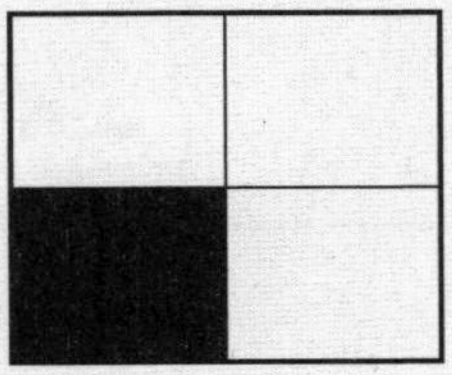

(F) ½ (G) ¾ (H) ¼ (J) ⅛

9. 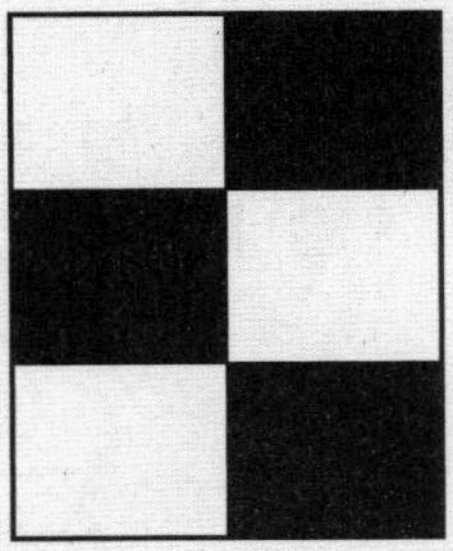

(A) ½ (B) ⅓ (C) ⅔ (D) ¾

10. 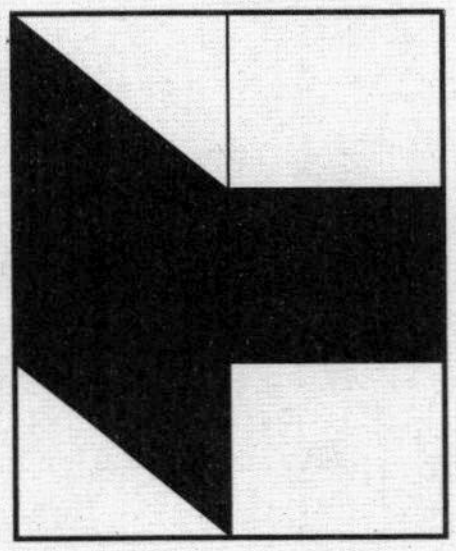

(F) ⅓ (G) ⅔ (H) ½ (J) ¾

11. 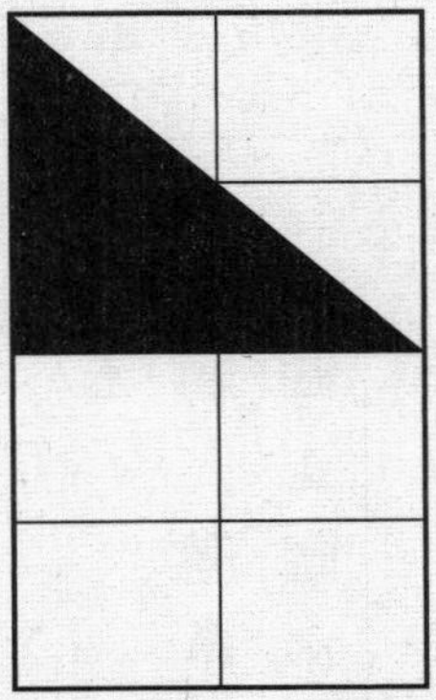

(A) ¾ (B) ¼ (C) ⅜ (D) ⅛

12. 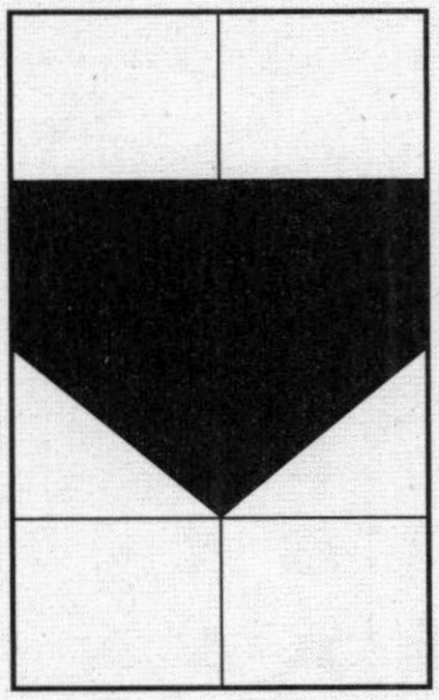

(F) ⅜ (G) ⅓ (H) ½ (J) ¼

13. 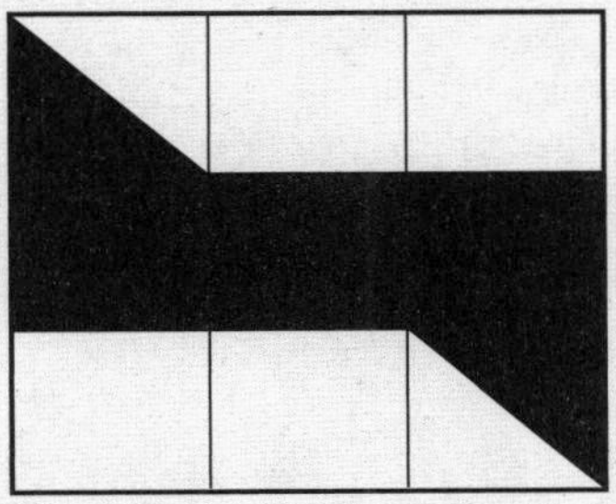

(A) ⅓ (B) ½ (C) $\frac{4}{9}$ (D) $\frac{5}{9}$

14. 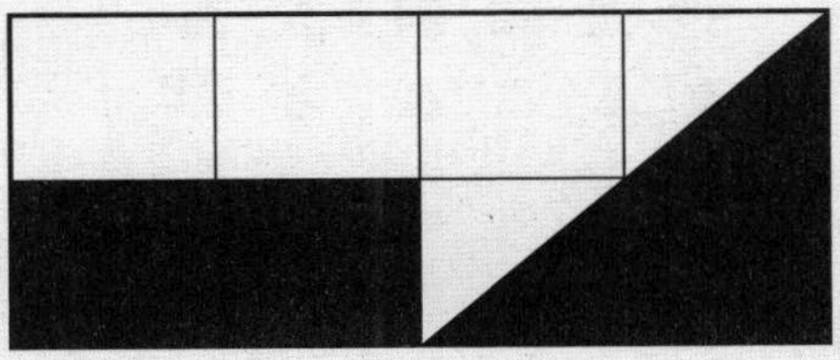

(F) ½ (G) ¼ (H) ⅖ (J) ⅜

Go on to next page

Directions: The scales in Questions 15–20 show combinations of shapes in equal weights. Find an answer with a pair of shape sets that also balances the scale.

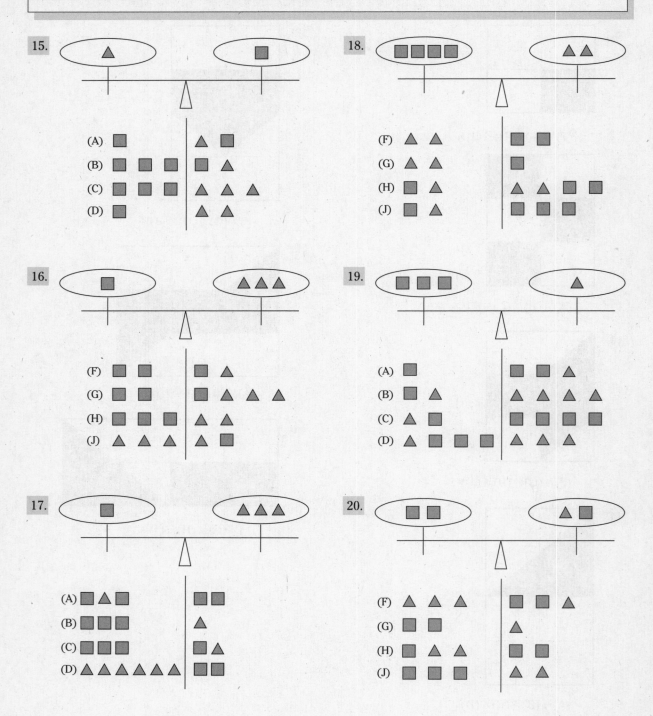

Test 4: Verbal Reasoning—Words

Time: 15 minutes

Directions: For Questions 1–4, find the word that identifies an essential part of the underlined word

1. <u>ocean</u>
   (A) water
   (B) beach
   (C) rain
   (D) palm

2. <u>pizza</u>
   (F) anchovy
   (G) pepperoni
   (H) crust
   (J) tomato

3. <u>forest</u>
   (A) sun
   (B) foliage
   (C) grass
   (D) picnic

4. <u>mammal</u>
   (F) hair
   (G) egg
   (H) scales
   (J) legs

Directions: For Questions 5–8, find the answer that is most similar to the underlined words.

5. <u>carpenter</u> <u>hammer</u> <u>nails</u>
   (A) paper
   (B) wood
   (C) jackhammer
   (D) puppy

6. <u>geology</u> <u>biology</u> <u>chemistry</u>
   (F) English
   (G) rocks
   (H) physics
   (J) history

7. <u>cuff</u> <u>sleeve</u> <u>collar</u>
   (A) shirt
   (B) cotton
   (C) button
   (D) blouse

8. <u>flames</u> <u>blaze</u> <u>conflagration</u>
   (F) camp
   (G) hydrant
   (H) match
   (J) inferno

Go on to next page

Directions: Three of the words in the answer choices for Questions 9–12 belong together. Choose the answer that does not belong with the other three words.

9. (A) Jupiter
    (B) Saturn
    (C) Mercury
    (D) moon

10. (F) sedan
    (G) truck
    (H) car
    (J) motorcycle

11. (A) frog
    (B) hamster
    (C) mammal
    (D) shark

12. (F) ruler
    (G) mile
    (H) yardstick
    (J) compass

Directions: In Questions 13–16, the words in the bottom row are related to each other in the same way that the words in the top row are related to each other. Find the answer that completes the missing word in the bottom row.

13. | paint | artist | painting |
    |-------|--------|----------|
    | clay | potter | |

    (A) pot
    (B) kiln
    (C) photograph
    (D) camera

14. | morning | noon | night |
    |---------|--------|-------|
    | | middle | end |

    (F) day
    (G) beginning
    (H) time
    (J) date

15. | infant | adolescent | adult |
    |---------|------------|--------|
    | boulder | | gravel |

    (A) geology
    (B) pebble
    (C) tree
    (D) quarry

16. | planet | solar system | galaxy |
    |--------|--------------|--------|
    | stem | | garden |

    (F) root
    (G) soil
    (H) flower
    (J) rake

STOP DO NOT TURN THE PAGE UNTIL TOLD TO DO SO.
DO NOT RETURN TO A PREVIOUS TEST.

Test 5: Verbal Reasoning—Context

Time: 20 minutes

Directions: For Questions 1–20, choose the answer that must be true given that the information in the question is true.

1. Jeffrey likes to eat chicken noodle soup. Steve likes to eat tomato soup.

    (A) Jeffrey does not like tomato soup.

    (B) Steve does not like chicken noodle soup.

    (C) Both Jeffrey and Steve like to eat soup.

    (D) Jeffrey and Steve eat lunch together.

2. Jenny is older than Sammy Jo. Sammy Jo is older than Dave.

    (F) Dave is older than Jenny.

    (G) Jenny is older than Dave.

    (H) Jenny is taller than Sammy Jo.

    (J) Sammy Jo and Jenny are sisters.

3. Karen rides her bike to school. Melanie rides the bus to school.

    (A) Karen and Melanie go to different schools.

    (B) Karen does not like to ride the bus.

    (C) Melanie does not have a bike.

    (D) Karen and Melanie go to school.

4. Pauline plays on a Little League softball team. Her team scored nine runs last Saturday.

    (F) Pauline's team won the game last Saturday.

    (G) Pauline's softball team had a score of 9 last Saturday.

    (H) Every player on her team scored a run on Saturday.

    (J) Pauline must have scored a run last Saturday.

5. A grocery store sells apples, bread, and milk. An apple is a fruit.

    (A) The grocery store sells fruit.

    (B) The grocery store is small.

    (C) People do not usually shop at this grocery store.

    (D) Apples are the only fruit the grocery store sells.

6. Agnes takes her dog for a walk every day. Agnes's dog does not like to be in the rain.

    (F) Agnes does not take her dog for a walk on rainy days.

    (G) On days that it rains, Agnes's dog does not like to go on walks.

    (H) Agnes likes to take walks in the rain.

    (J) Agnes puts a coat on her dog on rainy days.

7. Mama Tina's Italian Eatery is a restaurant that specializes in serving Italian food. The restaurant serves recipes created by its owner. There is a large Italian population in the city where the restaurant is located.

    (A) Mama Tina owns the restaurant.

    (B) The restaurant serves dishes from the recipes of Mama Tina's family.

    (C) Mama Tina's Italian Eatery is one of many Italian restaurants in the city where it is located.

    (D) The people in the city where Mama Tina's Italian Eatery is located have access to Italian food.

Go on to next page

8. Mary is using her college education in her career. Mary works as a biologist. The college Mary attended had a strong biology curriculum.

    (F) Mary will return to college to seek an advanced degree in biology.

    (G) Mary received an "A" grade in her college biology classes.

    (H) Mary earned a college degree in the sciences.

    (J) Mary took at least one biology class in college.

9. Rob plays the guitar and sings in the school choir. The school choir sings in the spring musical.

    (A) Rob would rather sing than play the guitar.

    (B) Rob is a good actor.

    (C) Rob sings in the spring musical.

    (D) Rob plays the guitar in the spring musical.

10. Greg has a coin collection with many silver coins and one gold coin. Gold coins are worth $100 each.

    (F) Gold coins are worth more than silver coins.

    (G) Greg should sell his coin collection.

    (H) Greg's collection is worth more than $100.

    (J) Greg is rich.

11. The waiting room in a dentist's office has seating for eight people. All the seats are occupied except one. Jeff sits in one of the chairs.

    (A) The dentist has at least seven patients.

    (B) There is a seat for one more person in the dentist's waiting room.

    (C) The dentist never sees more than eight patients at one time.

    (D) Jeff is one of the dentist's patients.

12. Aspen trees do not grow at low altitudes. The aspen trees in Sherry's yard have green leaves.

    (F) It is June.

    (G) Sherry's aspen trees are not healthy.

    (H) Sherry does not live at sea level.

    (J) It is not fall.

13. The train from Salt Lake City to San Francisco leaves just once a day at 6 a.m. Morgan lives in Salt Lake City and wants to travel to San Francisco on Monday.

    (A) Morgan must awaken early on Monday morning.

    (B) San Francisco is Morgan's favorite travel destination.

    (C) The train is the best way for Morgan to travel to San Francisco.

    (D) If Morgan wants to travel to San Francisco by train, she must leave at 6 a.m.

14. The Corner Deli opens at 6:30 a.m. and closes at 3:00 p.m. every day. Joe works at The Corner Deli. Dinner is considered to be any meal that is eaten after 4:00 p.m.

    (F) Joe works from 6:30 a.m. to 3:00 p.m. every day.

    (G) The Corner Deli serves sandwiches and egg dishes for dinner.

    (H) Joe does not work during the evenings.

    (J) The Corner Deli is not open for dinner.

15. Everyone who works for a large corporation must be on a health insurance plan. Dave and his family have not been on a health insurance plan for over six months.

    (A) Dave currently does not work for a large corporation.

    (B) Dave must be unemployed.

    (C) Large corporations spend more than half their earnings on health insurance plans for their employees.

    (D) Dave wants to work for a large corporation.

Go on to next page

16. The varsity football team has 34 members. No player plays on both the defense and the offense. Josh plays on the defense. During every play of a varsity football game, exactly 11 defensive players are on the field.

    (F) Some members of the varsity football team do not play on the defense.

    (G) The varsity team has exactly 17 offensive players and 17 defensive players.

    (H) When he is not playing defense, Josh plays on the offense.

    (J) Josh plays in every varsity football game.

17. The City Zoo has two families of monkeys, one family of gorillas, and one family of orangutans. A family consists of an adult male, an adult female, and at least one infant under the age of three.

    (A) The City Zoo has at least four animal infants under the age of three.

    (B) Each animal family is housed together in the same cage.

    (C) The City Zoo has only four families of animals.

    (D) The City Zoo is the only zoo in town where one can see a family of orangutans.

18. Dan owns a lawn service. He mows someone's yard every day. He does not mow the same yard more than once a week. He mows the Petersons' yard on Tuesdays, the Davidsons' yard on Friday, and the Stevensons' yard on Saturday.

    (F) Dan spends more time mowing the Stevensons' yard than he does mowing the Petersons' yard.

    (G) Dan spends the same amount of time mowing the Petersons' yard as he does mowing the Davidsons' yard.

    (H) Dan has other customers in addition to the Petersons, Davidsons, and Stevensons.

    (J) Dan enjoys mowing lawns.

19. Oceans cover about 71 percent of the earth's surface. There are five oceans. The Pacific is the largest ocean. The Indian Ocean separates Africa and Australia.

    (A) The Pacific Ocean covers more than half of the earth's surface.

    (B) The Indian Ocean covers less than three-quarters of the earth's surface.

    (C) The Indian Ocean is the smallest of the five oceans.

    (D) The Indian Ocean is the only ocean that touches Australia.

20. Only students who have completed three years of high school Spanish may go on the school trip to Costa Rica. Julie has completed four years of high school Spanish, and Rhiannon has completed two and half years of high school Spanish.

    (F) Julie is eligible to go on the school trip to Costa Rica.

    (G) Rhiannon does not want to go on the school trip to Costa Rica.

    (H) Neither Julie nor Rhiannon may go on the school trip to Costa Rica.

    (J) Both Julie and Rhiannon want to go to Costa Rica, but only one of them is allowed to.

STOP DO NOT TURN THE PAGE UNTIL TOLD TO DO SO. DO NOT RETURN TO A PREVIOUS TEST.

Test 6: Reading and Language Arts

Time: 40 minutes

Directions: Read this passage about a story in the Old Testament and answer Questions 1–7.

The Old Testament book of Ruth follows the book of Judges and is generally considered to take place during the time of Judges, which was a low point in Israel's moral, political, and religious history. As opposed to the largely dark and pessimistic tone of the historical book of Judges, the tone of Ruth's story is uplifting and bright. Its unknown author has fashioned a remarkably balanced and beautifully written Hebrew short story that provides an intimate look into the private life of a young Moabite girl and the Israelite family she chooses to adopt as her own.

During a period of famine in Judah, an Israelite family travels to Moab to find provisions. Moabites and Israelites have had a history of hostility toward each other, and the Moabites worship gods other than Yahweh. However, the two sons in the family find Moabite wives, and all goes well until all the male members of the family die, leaving the mother, Naomi, alone with her two Moabite daughters-in-law, named Ruth and Orpah. Embittered and desolate because of the death of her husband and sons, Naomi decides to return to Judah. Ruth chooses to devote herself to Naomi and Naomi's God, the God of Israel, and accompanies Naomi back to Bethlehem to live with and care for her there.

It is the spring harvest in Bethlehem, and Ruth <u>gleans</u> the fields to provide food for her and her mother-in-law. Boaz, a goodly owner of one of the fields and a relative of Naomi's late husband, sees Ruth and encourages her to pick only from his fields so that she might avoid the harassment of men at the other fields.

According to Hebrew custom, the nearest relative of a deceased husband is required to marry his widow to provide the deceased with an heir. Naomi encourages Ruth to approach Boaz on the threshing floor in the traditional manner to show that she is willing to be his bride. Trusting Naomi and her God, Ruth does so. Boaz honors Ruth's request by covering her with his cloth, but he must first make sure that another, closer relative does not wish to use his right to marry Ruth. The other relative refuses his right. Boaz marries Ruth, and they have a son. Therefore, Naomi's fullness is restored; she is well cared for, and her family line is reestablished through the obedience and loyalty of Ruth.

1. Where is Ruth from originally?

   (A) Moab

   (B) Israel

   (C) Judah

   (D) Bethlehem

2. Who is Naomi?

   (F) Ruth's mother-in-law

   (G) Ruth's sister-in-law

   (H) Boaz's mother

   (J) Ruth's mother

3. As it is used in the first sentence of the third paragraph, what does <u>gleans</u> mean?

   (A) glows from

   (B) burns up

   (C) shines on

   (D) picks from

Go on to next page

4. What adjective best describes the character of Boaz?

(F) mean

(G) inconsiderate

(H) indifferent

(J) kind

5. Who is Boaz related to?

(A) Naomi's late husband

(B) Ruth's father

(C) Naomi's father

(D) Orpah

6. What does Boaz do before he marries Ruth?

(F) He travels to Moab.

(G) He makes sure a closer relative does not want to marry her.

(H) He tells Ruth to gather grain in fields other than his.

(J) He sells his field.

7. How does the passage describe Naomi after Ruth and Boaz marry?

(A) sad

(B) embittered

(C) resigned

(D) provided for

Directions: Look for the mistakes in this paragraph about the story of Ruth and answer Questions 8–10.

(1)Each person in the story make their position better by caring for others. (2)Naomi, through a concern and love for Ruth, finds a family. (3)Boaz, through his compassion for Ruth and concern for the laws of his community, secures his future with a wife and son. (4)Ruth, through love and devotion to Naomi, gains marital happiness, she gets a son, too. (5)The story of Ruth is a hopeful depiction of the power of human love to overcome cultural differences and personal hardships.

8. Which is the best way to write Sentence 1?

(F) Each person in the story make their position better by caring for others.

(G) The characters in the story make their positions better by caring for others.

(H) Each person in the story makes their position better by caring at others.

(J) Best as is.

9. Which is the best way to write Sentence 4?

(A) Ruth, through love and dedication to Naomi, gets marital happiness, she gets a son, too.

(B) Ruth, through love and devotion to Naomi, gains marital happiness and has a son.

(C) Ruth, through love and dedication to Naomi, gains marital happiness, and she also gets a son, too.

(D) Best as is.

10. Which is the best way to write Sentence 5?

(F) The book of Ruth is a hopeful, depiction of the power of human love to overcome cultural differences and personal hardships.

(G) The Story Of Ruth is a hopeful depiction of the power of human love to overcome cultural differences and personal hardships.

(H) The book of Ruth is a hopeful depiction of the power of human love, to overcome cultural differences, and personal hardships.

(J) Best as is.

Go on to next page

Directions: Read this story and answer Questions 11–18.

Zoe and her friends enjoyed figure skating on ponds close to their homes in Winthrop, Maine. They all dreamed of becoming good enough skaters that they would be able to compete in the junior division preliminaries in Portland during next month's winter break.

The junior division tryouts brought skaters from around New England to compete on an indoor ice skating rink. Zoe and her friends had never skated on an indoor rink, and they were very uneasy. The competition on the indoor rink was fierce, but after three full days of competitive routines, Zoe was one of the top six finalists, which entitled her to compete one month later at the regionals in Albany, New York.

During the days leading up to the event in Albany, Zoe practiced her routines on the local pond and got some help from a coach at an indoor rink in Augusta about a half hour away. Every afternoon when the school bell rang, Zoe ran out to the parking lot and hopped in the passenger side of the family's 1992 pickup truck to drive to the rink. Her younger brother was squeezed in between her father and her. Zoe drowned out his nonstop chattering to concentrate on what she would be working on with her coach that day.

Her brother was still jabbering incessantly when he, Zoe, and their father set out for the six-hour drive to the competition in Albany. During the entire drive, Zoe had butterflies in her stomach. Then waiting for her turn on the ice was excruciating. She was so nervous when she stepped out onto the ice that she tripped a bit as she was striking her initial pose. She regained her composure, though, and felt more and more exhilarated as she completed each jump and turn. She felt that she should have won the skating competition, but the judges chose otherwise. "You have to earn your stripes," her father told her as they left the rink. "Judges don't usually place first-timers." On the long road home, Zoe's disappointment slowly changed to excited anticipation as she realized that next year she wouldn't be a "first-timer" anymore.

11. Which word best describes the feeling that Zoe and her friends had about skating on an indoor rink?

(A) comfortable

(B) confident

(C) anxious

(D) excited

12. In what city was the regional figure skating event held?

(F) New York

(G) Augusta

(H) Portland

(J) Albany

13. Which of the following is true about Zoe's brother?

(A) He also skated in the regional competition.

(B) He is younger than Zoe.

(C) He never talks.

(D) He refused to watch Zoe skate.

14. On the day of the regionals, Zoe

(F) slept late and missed the competition

(G) wanted to go home

(H) forgot her routine

(J) was nervous

Go on to next page

15. Which of the following statements is true according to the story?

    (A) It gets cold enough in Maine to freeze the ponds.

    (B) Zoe will win the regional ice skating competition next year.

    (C) Zoe's friends are not good enough skaters to skate on an indoor rink.

    (D) Zoe has only one sibling.

16. According to Zoe's dad, what was one reason that Zoe did not place in the regional competition?

    (F) She tripped as she was getting into her initial pose.

    (G) She was too nervous to concentrate.

    (H) She was skating in the competition for the first time.

    (J) Her skates were too loose.

17. Here are two sentences related to the story:

    Zoe did not win the figure skating competition. She was disappointed.

    Choose the answer that best makes one sentence out of the two.

    (A) Zoe did not win the figure skating competition, she was disappointed.

    (B) Zoe was disappointed, she did not win the figure skating competition.

    (C) Zoe was disappointed that she did not win the figure skating competition.

    (D) Zoe was a figure skater, who was disappointed, that she did not win.

18. Choose the sentence that is written correctly.

    (F) Zoe's dad was glad that him and Zoe's brother were able to see Zoe compete.

    (G) Zoe's dad was glad that he and Zoe's brother were able to see Zoe compete.

    (H) That him and Zoe's brother were able to see Zoe compete made Zoe's dad glad.

    (J) Zoe's dad and brother were able to see Zoe compete, and that made him glad.

Directions: Read this paragraph that relates to the essay and answer Questions 19 and 20.

Their daily practice routines consisted of an hour of practice at the local pond that Zoe's father cleared after significant snowfall accumulations. Zoe's father wasn't able to clear the ice until he returned home from work. He usually ended his workday at 3 p.m., and it took him about an hour to clear the ice. Therefore, on days that it snowed, Zoe and her friends were not able to skate on the pond until 4 p.m. It became dark at 5 p.m., and, because Zoe wasn't allowed to skate after dark, on days that it snowed heavily, Zoe only skated for one hour.

19. Which is the best introductory sentence for this paragraph?

    (A) Maine has many ponds that freeze over in the winter.

    (B) Some figure skaters are good enough to win skating competitions.

    (C) Zoe's father was very busy.

    (D) Zoe and her friends loved to figure skate.

20. Which of the following topics most logically follows this paragraph?

    (F) a biography of a famous figure skater

    (G) a description of how to create a figure eight on skates

    (H) an account of how Zoe tried to get in more skating time on snowy days

    (J) an overview of the history of figure skating

Go on to next page

Directions: Read the following passage about silent films and answer Questions 21–26.

What silent films lack in subtlety, they make up for in exaggeration. Without assistance from dialogue, silent films have to use other means to get their points across. One-dimensional characters, exaggerated movements, ceaseless action, and expressive musical scores compensate for the lack of words.

Because characters cannot be developed through conversation, silent film personalities are essentially one-dimensional. Bad guys are all bad, and good guys are all good. Supporting characters are often stereotypes included just to show the theme or add humor.

Silent film characters cannot tell the audience what they are thinking, so they must show it. Therefore, physical actions and gestures are exaggerated far beyond normal movement. For example, a character could demonstrate puzzlement by aggressively scratching his head. Without the use of words, silent film stars must talk with their bodies.

To maintain the attention of its audience, the silent film is a frenzy of perpetual activity. Scenes change by the second, and the transition between them is choppy. Silent films may contain car chases, foot chases, jail breaks, roller skating escapades, and dance numbers, all occurring in a matter of minutes. When action cannot clarify the story, placards expressing dialogue, thoughts, and the passage of time fill the void.

Complementing this <u>frenetic</u> motion is an expressive musical score. Unlike modern film, the musical score provides much more than background accompaniment. The music plays as large a role in the silent film as dialogue does in the "talkies." Ominous chords signal danger, fast-paced jingles heighten chase scenes, and singing violins encourage romance. In the absence of words, silent films employ creativity and ingenuity to tell their stories.

21. Which is the best title for this passage?

    (A) "Musical Scores Play a Big Role in Silent Films"

    (B) "How Silent Films Tell Their Stories"

    (C) "The Evolution of Film in the Twentieth Century"

    (D) "Why Films Contain Car Chases"

22. Which of the following is NOT a means that silent films use to communicate their stories?

    (F) larger-than-life gestures

    (G) constant action

    (H) dialogue

    (J) stereotypical characters

23. Why do actors in silent films use exaggerated motions?

    (A) because they do not know how to act

    (B) because they cannot use words to tell what they are thinking

    (C) because they do not want to bore the audience

    (D) because they have not read the script

24. Which of the following is NOT a use for placards in silent films?

    (F) They make up for the lack of music.

    (G) They state what a character is saying.

    (H) They state what a character is thinking.

    (J) They tell the audience how much time has passed.

Go on to next page

25. The word <u>frenetic</u> in the first sentence of the last paragraph most nearly means

(A) mellow

(B) calm

(C) lively

(D) muggy

26. According to the passage, what do ominous chords in silent films convey?

(F) romance

(G) danger

(H) creativity

(J) delight

Directions: Look for mistakes in this paragraph related to the article. Then answer Questions 27–29.

---

(1)In the early 1930s, "talkies" emerged. (2)Suddenly characters could talk, and movies that relied on dialogue to advance character and storyline became possible. (3)Through conversation, actors expressed nuance of personality; characters changed and grew. (4)Characters were less stereotypical and more complex. (5)Facial expressions and signals were toned down and are more realistic. (6)With the advent of words, filmmakers no longer had to step up the action to hold the audiences attention. (7)Characters had ample opportunity to sit and chat.

27. Choose the best way to write Sentence 3.

(A) Through conversation, actors expressed nuance of personality, characters changed and grew.

(B) Through conversation actors, expressed nuance of personality characters changed and grew.

(C) Through conversation actors expressed nuance of personality, and characters changed and grow.

(D) Best as is.

28. Sentence 5 is best written in which way?

(F) Facial expressions and signals are toned down and were more realistic.

(G) Facial expressions and signals were toned down and are getting more and more realistic.

(H) Facial expressions and signals were toned down and more realistic.

(J) Best as is.

29. Which is the best way to write Sentence 6?

(A) With the advent of words, filmmakers no longer had to step up the action to hold the audiences' attention.

(B) With the advent of words, filmmakers no longer had to step up the action to hold the audiences's attention

(C) With the advent of words, filmmakers no longer had to step up the action to hold the audience's attention.

(D) Best as is.

Go on to next page

Directions: Read this essay on the digestive system and answer Questions 30–38.

The purpose of the digestive system is to break down food into nutrients and absorb nutrients. This process starts with the mouth. Some animals suck in their food whole and send it right to the stomach. Others use their teeth to slice, grind, or crush their food before they swallow. Teeth are specialized for the typical diet of the animal, so if teeth are wide and flat, the animal is probably an herbivore that needs to grind up leaves and other plant material. On the other hand, if an animal's teeth are sharp and pointy, it is probably a carnivore that needs to kill its food and slice it up into manageable chunks.

After coming in through the mouth, food goes down a tube called the esophagus and ends up in the stomach. Muscles lining the esophagus help push the food down to the stomach. Most animals have a very acidic stomach that starts breaking down food and kills off some of the bacteria that the food could contain. Stomach acid is very good at breaking down proteins and dissolving minerals and sugars.

After the stomach, the food goes to the small intestine, which is where most of the breakdown occurs. The longer the food stays in the small intestine, the more time it has for digestion. That's why the small intestine in humans is about six feet long! Digestive enzymes are produced in the pancreas and then sent to the small intestine where they systematically break down all the proteins, carbohydrates, lipids, and nucleic acids. The liver also helps out by producing a nasty green substance called bile that is sent to the small intestine. Bile helps to break up fats and oils. The lining of the small intestine absorbs nutrients and sends them into the bloodstream where they are delivered to the rest of the body.

After the small intestine comes the large intestine, which is mostly just a storage area. Whatever is left over after digestion in the small intestine is kept in the large intestine until the animal can find a convenient time to eliminate it.

30. Which of the following is a purpose of the digestive system?

    (F) It breaks down food into nutrients.

    (G) It moves the blood through the body

    (H) It helps animals perceive their world.

    (J) It protects the body from external danger.

31. If an animal has teeth that are wide and flat, the animal is probably what?

    (A) a carnivore

    (B) a bird

    (C) a dinosaur

    (D) an herbivore

32. What happens after the food leaves the mouth?

    (F) It moves into the small intestine.

    (G) It sits in the large intestine.

    (H) It stays in the stomach until the animal eliminates it.

    (J) It moves down the esophagus.

33. Which of the following is NOT a function of the small intestine?

    (A) It uses digestive enzymes to break down food.

    (B) It absorbs nutrients from broken-down food.

    (C) It uses acids to kill bacteria and fungus.

    (D) It receives bile from the liver.

Go on to next page

34. Why is the stomach very acidic?

    (F) The stomach uses acid to produce bile.

    (G) Stomach acid is good at breaking down protein.

    (H) The acid in the stomach helps move the food down the esophagus.

    (J) Acid makes the stomach a good storage area.

35. What is the role of the pancreas?

    (A) It produces and delivers bile to the stomach.

    (B) It produces and delivers bile to the small intestine.

    (C) It breaks down food and absorbs nutrients.

    (D) It produces and delivers digestive enzymes to the small intestine.

36. Where is bile produced?

    (F) in the liver

    (G) in the esophagus

    (H) in the large intestine

    (J) in the small intestine

37. Here are two sentences related to the passage:

    Animals use a digestive system. They use their digestive systems to break down food and absorb nutrients.

    Which answer best combines the two sentences into one?

    (A) Animals use a digestive system, they break down food and absorb nutrients.

    (B) Animals use their digestive systems to break down food and absorb nutrients.

    (C) To break down food, animals use a digestive system to absorb nutrients.

    (D) A digestive system serves two purposes, to break down food and absorb nutrients, and animals use it.

38. Choose the sentence that is written correctly.

    (F) If the appendix ruptures, it would be really bad news, when someone develops an appendicitis they need to get it fixed right away.

    (G) A ruptured appendix is dangerous; therefore, when someone develops appendicitis, he needs to get it fixed right away.

    (H) If the appendix ruptures, bad news results which means you have to get it fixed right away.

    (J) If the appendix ruptures, then it would be really dangerous and when anyone develops an appendicitis they need to get it fixed right away.

Go on to next page →

Directions: Read this paragraph related to the essay and answer Questions 39 and 40.

The large intestine has a little dead-end area called the vermiform appendix. This part of the organ does not appear to serve any function at all. Sometimes excess bacteria builds up inside the appendix, which makes it swell up and causes appendicitis. A ruptured appendix may be deadly if it is not treated properly.

39. What is the best topic sentence for this paragraph?

   (A) Some body parts are very useful.

   (B) The human body contains many kinds of bacteria.

   (C) Some useful organs are dangerous.

   (D) The large intestine has a peculiar feature.

40. What subject would you expect to follow this paragraph?

   (F) a description of how to properly treat appendicitis

   (G) an explanation of how the stomach digests food

   (H) a comparison of how cows chew their food and how tigers chew their food

   (J) a critique of modern medical practices

STOP DO NOT TURN THE PAGE UNTIL TOLD TO DO SO. DO NOT RETURN TO A PREVIOUS TEST.

Test 7: Mathematics

Time: 35 minutes

Directions: Choose the response that best answers Questions 1–40.

1. 4% =
   (A) $^{0.4}\!/_{100}$
   (B) ¼
   (C) $^{4}\!/_{100}$
   (D) $^{40}\!/_{100}$

2. 3(–2) – 2 =
   (F) –8
   (G) 4
   (H) 8
   (J) –4

3. $\sqrt{1300}$ =
   (A) $10 + \sqrt{13}$
   (B) $\sqrt{10} + 13$
   (C) 10×13
   (D) $10\sqrt{13}$

4. $\dfrac{13 \times 5 \times 10}{5 \times 10 \times 2}$
   (F) $^{5}\!/_{2}$
   (G) 13½
   (H) $^{2}\!/_{5}$
   (J) 6½

5. $-3^3(2 - 3)^2 + (-3)^2$
   (A) 5
   (B) 18
   (C) –18
   (D) none of the above

6. What is the value of the digit 7 in the number 167,456?
   (F) 700
   (G) 7,000
   (H) 7
   (J) 70,000

7. 14.565 – 2.35 =
   (A) 12.565
   (B) 13.35
   (C) 12.215
   (D) 10.215

8. $3^3 \times 3^5$ =
   (F) 3×8
   (G) 3^7
   (H) 729
   (J) $3 \times 3 \times 3 \times 3 \times 3 \times 3 \times 3 \times 3$

9. A small county fair has 15 rides. When people are on ⅗ of the rides, how many rides are being ridden?
   (A) 6
   (B) 9
   (C) 3
   (D) 12

10. 10,000 is equivalent to
    (F) 10^2
    (G) 10^3
    (H) 10^4
    (J) 10^5

11. A recent poll of moviegoers asked whether or not they had liked the movie they had just seen. Of those polled, 13 percent did not like the movie, 37 percent liked it, and 12 percent were undecided. The rest of those polled did not answer at all. What is the ratio of people who answered the poll to those who did not answer?
    (A) ⅗
    (B) $^{31}\!/_{19}$
    (C) 62%
    (D) ⅕

Go on to next page

12. What best represents {4, 5, 8, 10, 12} ∩ {3, 4, 6, 7, 11, 12}?

    (F) {4}

    (G) {2, 3, 4, 5}

    (H) {4, 12}

    (J) {10, 11, 12}

13. If a birthday cake is cut into 15 equal pieces and ⅞ of the pieces are consumed, approximately what percent of the cake was consumed?

    (A) 30%

    (B) 44%

    (C) 47%

    (D) 52%

14. Natasha took a train to her friend Dylan's house. They live 142 miles apart, and the train ride took 2 hours. How fast was the train traveling?

    (F) 65 mph

    (G) 71 mph

    (H) 75 mph

    (J) 58 mph

15. What best represents {10, 11, 13, 15, 17} ∩ {6, 8, 10, 11, 14}?

    (A) {14}

    (B) {10, 15}

    (C) {13, 14, 15}

    (D) {10, 11}

16. An equilateral triangle must have which of the following?

    (F) equal sides

    (G) angles with a sum that equals 180 degrees

    (H) equal angles

    (J) all of the above

17. Which is the complete set of integers that could be placed in the sentence below to make it true?

    9 > _____ > 4

    (A) {5}

    (B) {5, 6, 7}

    (C) {5, 6, 7, 8}

    (D) {6, 7, 8}

18. What is equivalent to "two million five hundred forty-five thousand twenty-two"?

    (F) 2,545,022

    (G) 2,522,045

    (H) 2,455,022

    (J) 2,540,022

19. What are prime factors of 222?

    (A) 2

    (B) 2, 3

    (C) 2, 3, 11

    (D) 2, 3, 10, 11

20. Sales people at Lamps for Less do not earn a base salary. They instead receive commission. The commission they receive is 8% on all their sales. How many dollars worth of lamps must a salesperson sell in order to make $500 a week?

    (F) $500

    (G) $2,500

    (H) $6,250

    (J) $7,250

21. What is the set of all the common factors of 32 and 64?

    (A) {1, 2, 4, 8, 16, 32}

    (B) {1, 2, 6, 8, 16, 32}

    (C) {4, 8}

    (D) {6, 8}

Go on to next page

22. Finish the following statement:

$4(2 \times _____) + 12 = 2{,}012$

(F) 425

(G) 300

(H) 250

(J) 150

23. What is the area of a triangle with a base of 15 m and a height of 12 m?

(A) 80 m^2

(B) 90 m^2

(C) 95 m^2

(D) 100 m^2

24. A group of nine friends raised $1,200 for a charity. Four of the friends raised 85% of the money. How much did the other five friends raise together?

(F) $100

(G) $180

(H) $1,020

(J) $1,080

25. What is the perimeter of a clothing store that is 15 yards wide by 25 yards long?

(A) 90 yards

(B) 85 yards

(C) 80 yards

(D) 75 yards

26. A plumber charged Casey $125 to repair a broken pipe plus $55 for each hour she worked. The total charge was $290. About how long did the plumber work on the broken pipe?

(F) 3 hours

(G) 4 hours

(H) 5 hours

(J) 6 hours

27. Which point on the line best represents 3×10^3?

A	B	C	D
300	3,000	30,000	300,000

(A) Point A

(B) Point B

(C) Point C

(D) Point D

28. $-5 < x < -3$

Which of the following could be a value of x?

(F) 4

(G) 0

(H) –1

(J) –4

29. One kilogram equals about 2.2 pounds. If a piece of metal weighs 25 pounds, about how many kilograms is that piece of metal? (Round your answer to the nearest whole number.)

(A) 15 kg

(B) 5 kg

(C) 11 kg

(D) 13 kg

30. What set of numbers is written in ascending order with the smallest number first?

(F) $\frac{5}{6}$, $\frac{1}{2}$, $\frac{3}{6}$

(G) 40%, $\frac{1}{4}$, 0.44

(H) $\frac{3}{1000}$, 30%, $\frac{3}{5}$

(J) $\frac{1}{5}$, 20%, 0.2

31. A 12-ounce steak costs x dollars; a 6-ounce steak costs $4 less. What is the cost of two 6-ounce steaks?

(A) $4x$

(B) $2x - 4$

(C) $4x - 2$

(D) $2(x - 4)$

Go on to next page

32. Which of these is an example of the distributive property?

    (F) $a(b - c) = ab - c$

    (G) $a(b - c) = ab - ac$

    (H) $a(b - c) = abc$

    (J) $a(bc) = {}^{ab}\!/\!_c$

33. A soccer team won 16 games and tied 4, which made up 40% of its season. How many games did the soccer team lose?

    (A) 20

    (B) 25

    (C) 28

    (D) 30

34. Rico has $50 to spend at the mall. He wants to buy as many shirts as he can with his money. Each shirt costs $15, and there is a 6% sales tax on each shirt. What is the maximum number of shirts he can buy with his $50?

    (F) 3

    (G) 4

    (H) 5

    (J) 6

35. What is the circumference of a wheel that has 20-inch spokes?

    (A) 20π inches

    (B) 30π inches

    (C) 40π inches

    (D) 50π inches

36. One centimeter is what part of two meters?

    (F) $\frac{1}{100}$

    (G) $\frac{1}{1,000}$

    (H) $\frac{1}{200}$

    (J) $\frac{1}{10}$

37. According to the chart, what percent of the T-shirt sales was Maria responsible for?

	Jeans	Collared shirts	T-shirts	Tank tops
Maria	$400	$350	$125	$100
Bill	$325	$470	$130	$78
Justine	$775	$525	$140	$95
Nate	$1,100	$300	$105	$105

    (A) 20%

    (B) 25%

    (C) 30%

    (D) 35%

38. Reference the chart in Question 37 to determine the average price of jeans if 26 pairs were sold.

    (F) $35

    (G) $75

    (H) $95

    (J) $100

Go on to next page

39. If a store manager wants to make a graph to show what fraction of the total revenue each item makes up, what would be the best graph to use?

(A)

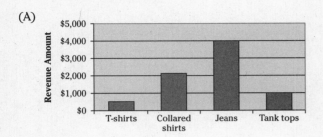

(B)

Sales by Item

Jeans	Collared shirts	T-shirts	Tank tops
‖‖‖	‖‖	‖‖‖ ‖‖‖	‖‖

(C)

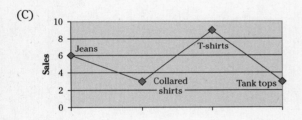

(D)

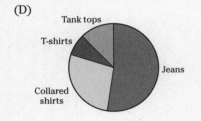

40. A teacher wants to see whether or not it is true that students who play one sport often play another sport as well. What would be the best way to display the information the teacher receives?

(F)

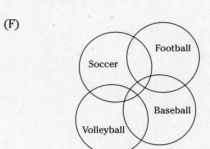

(G)

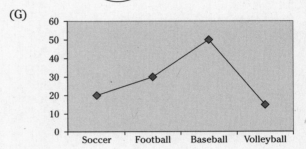

(H)

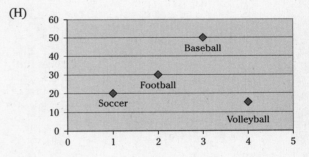

(J)

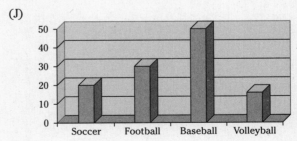

STOP DO NOT TURN THE PAGE UNTIL TOLD TO DO SO.
DO NOT RETURN TO A PREVIOUS TEST.

Chapter 28

Answers to COOP Practice Test 2

∙∙∙

*Y*ou've finished taking the second COOP practice test, but you're not done yet. Now it's time to check your answers. We strongly encourage you to read through all the answer explanations, even for those questions you answered correctly. You may pick up an additional helpful tidbit that'll help you on the real test. Of course, if you don't have the time or just plain aren't interested in reading delightful explanations, you can check your work using the abbreviated answer key at the end of this chapter.

Test 1: Sequences

1. **C.** Notice that the shaded star in Choice (C) appears in each of the first three sets. It's likely that the last set needs a shaded star, too. Examine the pattern of the sequence to see whether putting the shaded star at the end makes sense. The second set in the sequence is the reverse of the first. With Choice (C) placed at the end, the fourth set is the reverse of the third. Choice (C) is correct.

2. **H.** The sets add a figure as they progress. Each set alternates unshaded right-facing right triangles with shaded left-facing right triangles. The third set has four symbols ending with a shaded triangle, so it makes sense that the last set would contain five symbols and end with an unshaded triangle, much like the set in Choice (H).

3. **B.** All three of the full sets contain four of the same symbol. To complete the pattern, the last set should contain four of the same symbol. Choice (B) completes the set.

4. **J.** The second set is the reverse of the pattern in the first set: three of one symbol and one of the other. The pattern of the third set is one symbol, two of the other symbol, and one of the first symbol. The answer that creates the same pattern with the symbols switched in the fourth set is Choice (J): ❑△△❑.

5. **D.** The last symbol of the first set is the same as the first symbol of the second set. To maintain that pattern, find an answer with a first symbol that's the same as the last symbol of the second set and a last symbol that's the same as the first symbol of the last set. Choice (D) begins with the second set's diamond and ends with the last set's triangle.

6. **G.** All the answer choices are double-pointed arrows, so focus on the shading. The shading pattern in the first two sets is the same: three unshaded arrows and one shaded arrow. The shading of the arrows in the fourth set begins in the same way as the arrows in the third set. So you can choose the answer with the arrows that are shaded in the same way as the last two arrows in the third set (which are unshaded). Therefore, the option with two unshaded arrows, Choice (G), is the answer that completes the pattern.

7. **C.** The numbers in this sequence increase by 3. 15 + 3 = 18, Choice (C).

8. **F.** The numbers in this sequence decrease by 20. The last number is 20 less than 20, which is 0 — Choice (F).

9. **B.** Each set contains three numbers that increase by 2. The last number of the last set should be 2 more than 42, which is 44 — Choice (B).

10. **H.** The second number in each set is twice the first number. To find the first number in the last set, divide 12 by 2 to get 6, Choice (H).

11. **A.** The last number in each set is the product of the first two numbers in the set. $12 \div 6 = 2$. The second number in the last set must be 2, Choice (A).

12. **G.** The third number in each set is the sum of the first two numbers. Because $6 + 3 = 9$, the answer that completes the pattern is 3, Choice (G).

13. **D.** The numbers in each set decrease in value, so Choices (A) and (B) are wrong because they're greater than 9. Focus on the last two numbers in each set. $5 - 5 = 0$, and $10 - 5 = 5$. Because the last number is 5 less than the second number, the answer is $9 - 5 = 4$, Choice (D).

14. **F.** Each set contains the letters ABC; eliminate Choice (J) because it doesn't contain ABC. The first number in each set increases by 1 as the sets progress. Choice (G) doesn't follow this pattern, so it's wrong. The numbers within each set decrease rather than increase, which means the correct answer is Choice (F).

15. **A.** Here's where knowing your alphabet (and jotting it down in your test booklet) comes in handy. Each set lists the letters of the alphabet in reverse order, and the last letter of the following set is the letter that comes alphabetically right after the first letter in the preceding set. What does this mean to you? That the last letter in the missing set should be J because J comes after I (which is the first letter in the third set). Confused? Hang in there! Eliminate Choices (B) and (C) because their last letters aren't Js. Now focus on the numbers. All the even numbers in the sets are superscript, and the odds are subscript. Choice (D) has subscript even numbers and superscript odds, which means it can't be the right answer. Choice (A) follows the pattern properly all the way around.

16. **H.** This sequence skips every other letter in the alphabet. Refer to the alphabet you've written in your test booklet. Start at T, skip over U, and select V — Choice (H).

17. **D.** These letters are in reverse alphabetical order. Choice (D), i, comes before j.

18. **G.** The first three letters in each set are in alphabetical order. Then you skip a letter to get the fourth. Toss out Choice (F) because it doesn't begin with letters that are in alphabetical order. Cut Choices (H) and (J) too because they don't skip a letter to get to the fourth letter in their sets. Choice (G) is the only set that follows the pattern.

19. **B.** The first and third letters in each set follow the order of the alphabet. The second and fourth letters move in reverse order from the end of the alphabet. The third set should begin with an E; Choices (A) and (C) are wrong. The letter that comes before W is V, so the second letter of the third set should be V, as in Choice (B).

20. **J.** The first and third sets follow reverse alphabetical order. The fifth set should maintain that reverse order. The letter that comes before U is T, which means the fifth set should begin with T. The only answer that begins with T is Choice (J).

Test 2: Analogies

1. **A.** A bird lives in a nest. A bat lives in a cave, Choice (A), not your house (we hope!).

2. **H.** A bow is used to shoot an arrow in the same way that a slingshot is used to shoot a stone, Choice (H).

3. **C.** The fruit of an apple tree is an apple. The fruit of a coconut palm tree is a coconut, Choice (C). Palm trees grow palm leaves, but the leaves aren't their fruit.

4. **G.** A pew belongs in a church just as a desk belongs in a school, Choice (G).

5. **B.** A pebble is a smaller version of a boulder; a cottage is a smaller version of a mansion. The answer is Choice (B).

6. **J.** Create a sentence out of the relationship between cloud and rain: A cloud produces rain. Apply that sentence to chicken: A chicken produces eggs, Choice (J).

7. **D.** A ring belongs on a finger, and an ornament belongs on a Christmas tree, Choice (D). However, using that sentence you may have logically thought an ornament belongs on a hook, Choice (B). Try making your sentence as specific as possible: A ring adorns a finger like an ornament adorns a Christmas tree. Tada! No confusion with that one.

8. **J.** A toy soldier is the toy version of a real soldier. The rubber ducky in Choice (J) is the toy version of a real duck (but not a chicken, so you can't pick Choice (F)).

9. **A.** The purpose of a library is to house books. The purpose of a garage is to house a car. Choice (A) is the best answer.

10. **H.** The shaded circle is the opposite of the unshaded circle, and the sun is the opposite of the moon (because they appear in the sky at different times). Choice (H) is correct.

11. **B.** A piece of wood is a component of a house like thread is a component of a shirt, Choice (B).

12. **H.** A scuba diver belongs in the ocean, and a rabbit belongs in a hole, Choice (H).

13. **C.** A cat chases a mouse, and a dog chases a rabbit, Choice (C). You may have been tempted to pick Choice (A), but a dog doesn't chase a bone the way a cat chases a mouse.

14. **G.** You use soap and a cloth to wash, and you use skis and poles, Choice (G), to ski.

15. **D.** In the city, you use a car for transportation. On a farm, you use a horse for transportation. The best answer is Choice (D).

16. **F.** A deck of cards is a group that one card is a member of. A month is a group of days that one day is a member of. Choice (F) is your answer.

17. **C.** A necessary part of an angel is its wings, and a necessary part of a bicycle is its handlebars, Choice (C). A basket can be a part of a bicycle, but it's not a necessary part.

18. **F.** Dynamite is used to break up a mountainside like a wrecking ball is used to break up an old building, Choice (F).

19. **D.** An apple and an orange are fruits that grow on trees. A potato and a carrot, Choice (D), are foods from the root of a plant (called *tubers*). A tomato is a fruit, and broccoli is the stem and flower; neither is a root. Also, a seed may be underground, but it isn't a tuber.

20. **F.** A small part of a daisy is a petal, and a small part of a rain shower is a raindrop, Choice (F).

Test 3: Quantitative Reasoning

1. **C.** The operation that takes you from 4 to 2 could be either –2 or ÷2. To go from 8 to 6, though, you must subtract 2. 6 – 2 = 4, Choice (C).

2. **F.** The operation in the first line could be either +2 or ×2. A glance at the second line tells you it's +2: 8 + 2 = 10, Choice (F).

3. **A.** The operation could be +6 or ×3. When you consider the second line, you realize it must be ×3 because 4 × 3 = 12. Apply ×3 to the third line, and you get Choice (A), 15.

4. **G.** The possible operations for the first line are –20 or ÷5. The second option, ÷5, works for the second line. The answer is Choice (G) because 100 ÷ 5 = 20.

5. **D.** The operation in the first line could be ×2 or +½. However, you know it's ×2 when you look at the second line. ⅔ × 2 = ⁴⁄₃, which simplifies to 1⅓, Choice (D).

6. **G.** To go from 0.3 to 3, move the decimal point one place to the right. This move works for the second line, too. Move the decimal point in the same way for 0.25, and you wind up with 2.5, Choice (G).

7. **B.** Figuring out the operation in this problem is easier if you just look at the second line. Going from 1 to 1⅛ means the operation must be +⅛. ⅜ + ⅛ = ⁴⁄₈, or ½ — Choice (B).

8. **H.** This square has a total of four boxes. One box is shaded, which means the shaded area is ¼, Choice (H).

9. **A.** This figure is made up of six equal-sized boxes, three of which are shaded. The shaded area is therefore ³⁄₆, or ½ — Choice (A).

10. **H.** This figure has a total of six equal-sized boxes. Two full boxes and two half boxes are shaded, which equals three fully shaded boxes altogether. The shaded area is therefore ³⁄₆, or ½, which is Choice (H). If you picked Choice (G), you incorrectly counted each half-shaded box as a fully shaded box.

Don't fall for the COOP's dirty tricks in the Quantitative Reasoning section. Keep in mind that two half-shaded boxes equal one fully shaded box, and you're set.

11. **B.** This figure has eight equal-sized boxes. One of them is fully shaded, and two are half shaded. This adds up to two fully shaded boxes out of eight, or ²⁄₈, which reduces to ¼ — Choice (B).

12. **F.** This figure has eight equal-sized boxes. Two are fully shaded, and two are half shaded, creating three fully shaded boxes. The shaded area is therefore ³⁄₈, Choice (F).

13. **C.** This figure contains nine equal-sized boxes, three of which are fully shaded and two of which are half shaded. That means you have four shaded boxes out of nine total boxes. The answer is ⁴⁄₉, Choice (C).

14. **F.** Looks like you have eight equal-sized boxes, three of which are fully shaded and two of which are half shaded. You therefore have four fully shaded boxes, which makes the answer ⁴⁄₈, or ½ — Choice (F).

15. **C.** This scale question tells you that the value of a square equals the value of a triangle. For every square on one side of the answer choices, there must be a triangle on the other side. Eliminate Choices (A), (B), and (D) because each of these has more figures on one side than the other. The only answer with an equal number of squares and triangles on both sides is Choice (C).

16. **G.** You must have three triangles or one square on one side of the scale for every square on the other side. The answer that meets this requirement is Choice (G); it balances the two squares on the left side with one square and three triangles on the right side.

17. **D.** This is the same scale you see in Question 16, which means every square has to be balanced by another square or three triangles. Choice (D) balances the two squares on the right side with six triangles on the left side.

18. **J.** Four squares equaling two triangles is the same thing as two squares equaling one triangle. So, for every triangle on one side, there has to be the equivalent of two squares on the other side. Choice (F) is wrong because a triangle and a square aren't equal. Also, two squares equal one triangle, not the other way around, so Choice (G) is wrong too. To balance the triangle and square in Choice (H), you'd need three squares on the other side, which is what you see in Choice (J), the correct answer.

19. **C.** For every triangle, there must be three squares or another triangle on the other side of the scale. The square and triangle on the left side of Choice (C) are nicely balanced by the four squares on the right side.

20. **F.** This scale may seem a bit complicated at first, but think about it for a moment. If two squares equal one square and one triangle, then one square equals one triangle. You just need to find the answer that has the same number of symbols on each side. The answer that meets this requirement is Choice (F), with a total of three symbols on each side.

Test 4: Verbal Reasoning—Words

1. **A.** Without water, Choice (A), there'd be no ocean. Period.

2. **H.** You can have a pizza without anchovy, pepperoni, or tomato, but not without a crust, Choice (H).

3. **B.** If you were expecting trees to be among the options, get over your shock that they aren't and start cutting any answers that aren't necessary. Sun isn't a requirement for a forest; consider the rain forest. Picnics are fun, but they're not a necessary element to a forest. A forest may have grass, but it doesn't have to have grass to be a forest. It does have to contain some plant life, though. Foliage, Choice (B), is the best answer.

4. **F.** One of the traits that makes mammals mammals is hair/fur, Choice (F). Mammals don't typically lay eggs or have scales, and animals other than mammals have legs.

5. **B.** The last two words are tools used by the first word, carpenter. Wood, Choice (B), is another element carpenters use in their trade. They don't need paper, puppies, or jackhammers.

6. **H.** The three words in the question are different kinds of sciences, and Choice (H) is another kind of science. Choices (F) and (J) are courses but not science courses. Finally, rocks relate to geology but not to the other listed sciences.

7. **C.** Cuff, sleeve, and collar are parts of a shirt. The answer that's also a part of a shirt is Choice (C). Choices (A) and (D) are items of clothing that contain cuffs, sleeves, and collars, but they don't name parts of a shirt.

8. **J.** The given words list different names for a fire. Inferno, Choice (J), is another name for a fire. Choices (G) and (H) are related to fire, but they aren't synonyms for fire.

9. **D.** Pick out the word that's different from the others. Choices (A), (B), and (C) are all planets. The moon isn't a planet, which makes Choice (D) your answer.

10. **J.** A sedan, a truck, and a car are all four-wheeled vehicles. Choice (J), a motorcycle, is different because it's a two-wheeled vehicle.

11. **C.** Choices (A), (B), and (D) are names of particular animals. Choice (C) is a general category of animal; therefore, it's the one that doesn't belong.

12. **G.** A ruler, yardstick, and compass are concrete tools you use to measure length or direction. A mile, Choice (G), is an intangible term for a measurement.

13. **A.** You can make a sentence with the words in the top row: Paint is what an artist uses to create a painting. Try it with the second row: Clay is what a potter uses to create _____. Potters create pots, Choice (A). They use kilns, but they don't create them.

14. **G.** The morning is the start of the day, noon is the middle, and night is the end. Need we say more? Choice (G) completes the theme of beginning, middle, and end.

15. **B.** The words in the top row show stages of human development: An infant becomes an adolescent who becomes an adult. Keep the development process in mind as you examine the second row. A boulder eventually breaks down to become gravel. The answer choice that best describes the stage in between a boulder and gravel is Choice (B). A boulder breaks down into smaller pieces such as pebbles, which break down into gravel.

16. **H.** A planet is a smaller part of the larger solar system, which is a part of the entire galaxy. A stem is a part of _____, which is a part of a garden. A stem isn't part of a root, soil, or rake. The answer has to be Choice (H); a stem is a part of a flower.

Test 5: Verbal Reasoning—Context

1. **C.** Because Jeffrey likes to eat soup and Steve likes to eat soup, you can conclude that both guys like to eat soup, Choice (C). You know what they like, but you don't know what they don't like; eliminate Choices (A) and (B). Choice (D) is completely off topic.

2. **G.** You can draw a line diagram to show the relationship from oldest to youngest: Jenny → Sammy Jo → Dave. Choice (F) isn't true, and nothing in the premises gives you enough information to pick Choices (H) or (J). Choice (G) is right.

3. **D.** The best answer here is Choice (D). Because Karen and Melanie ride to school, you can conclude that they go to school. You don't know anything about what Melanie doesn't own or what Karen doesn't like, so Choices (B) and (C) are wrong. And just because they use different types of transportation doesn't mean they go to different schools.

4. **G.** Because Pauline's team scored nine runs on Saturday, the most you know is that her team had a score of nine. You don't know that nine runs were enough to win the game or who scored the nine runs. Choice (G) is the best answer.

5. **A.** The store sells apples, and apples are fruit; therefore, the store sells fruit, Choice (A). You know nothing about the size of the store, what else it sells, or who shops there.

6. **G.** The first premise tells you that Agnes walks her dog every day. That means the weather doesn't affect whether she walks her dog. Because the dog doesn't like to be in the rain, you can conclude that the dog isn't fond of walks on rainy days. You don't know what Agnes likes or whether she dresses her dog. Choice (G) is the best answer.

7. **D.** You can't assume that Mama Tina owns the restaurant based on its name. Heck, you don't even know that Mama Tina is a real person! Scrap Choices (A) and (B). You don't know how may Italian restaurants exist other than Mama Tina's. All you know is that there's at least one Italian restaurant in the city, which means people there can get Italian food, Choice (D).

8. **J.** Mary must have taken a course on biology in college, Choice (J), because she works as a biologist and is using what she learned in college in her career as a biologist.

9. **C.** Because Rob sings in the choir and the choir sings in the musical, you can logically conclude that Rob sings in the spring musical, Choice (C).

In the face of logic questions, avoid answer choices that require you to make value judgments about a person's abilities or assumptions about what a person likes or dislikes.

10. **H.** Choices (G) and (J) are personal judgments; eliminate them. You don't know how much silver coins are worth, so you can't assume that Choice (F) is true. Because you know that Greg has a gold coin worth $100 and some silver coins of some value, you can conclude that Greg's collection is worth more than $100, Choice (H).

11. **B.** Eight seats are available, and one isn't taken, which means there's room for one more person to sit in the waiting room, Choice (B). You can't assume that everyone sitting in the waiting room is a patient; they could be friends and/or family members of patients. Forget about Choices (A) and (D). And just because the waiting room has seats for only eight people doesn't mean that the dentist never sees more than eight patients at one time. The presence of the debatable word *never* is a good clue that Choice (C) is wrong.

12. **H.** If aspen trees don't grow at low altitudes and Sherry has aspen trees in her yard, then Sherry must not live at sea level, Choice (H), because that's a low altitude.

13. **D.** Don't be tempted by Choice (A). The premise says that Morgan wants to travel to San Francisco on Monday, but it doesn't say she has to travel by train. Maybe if she travels by car, she won't have to leave until the afternoon. Choice (D) is more precise; if Morgan travels by train, she'll have to leave early in the morning. Choices (B) and (C) make unjustified judgments about Morgan's likes and the best way to travel, so they're wrong.

14. **J.** You can't assume that Joe works every hour the deli's open, nor can you assume that working at the deli is Joe's only job. Cross out Choices (F) and (H). Because the premises tell you that the deli isn't open during the hours when dinner would be served, you can safely pick Choice (J).

15. **A.** Because Dave isn't on a health insurance plan and employees of large corporations must be on a health insurance plan, Dave must not work for a large corporation, Choice (A). He doesn't have to be unemployed; maybe he just works for a small company.

16. **F.** Eliminate Choice (H) because it contradicts the premise that no player plays both defense and offense. You can't make the assumption that half the players play offense and half play defense, nor can you assume that Josh plays in every game. The best answer is Choice (F): The members of the team that play offense don't play defense.

17. **A.** The premises don't give information about other zoos or the zoo's housing policies, which means you can cut Choices (B) and (D). Because the premises mention four animal families and tell you that each family has at least one infant, you know for sure that the zoo has at least four infants, Choice (A).

18. **H.** The premises don't tell you how much time Dan spends on the lawn, which means you can cross out Choices (F) and (G). Choice (J) requires you to make assumptions about what Dan likes. If Dan mows every day, he has at least four customers in addition to the Petersons, Davidsons, and Stevensons. Choice (H) is the logical answer.

19. **B.** The premises tell you that the Pacific is the largest ocean, but they don't tell you how big it is or anything about the relative sizes of the other oceans; cross out Choices (A) and (C). You also don't know about other oceans that lap up on Australia's shores; eliminate Choice (D). You know that oceans cover about 71 percent of the earth, which is less than 75 percent. There's no way the Indian Ocean could cover more of the earth than all the oceans combined; it has to cover less than 75 percent of the earth. Choice (B) is right.

Don't use your knowledge about a subject to answer logic questions. Rely only on the information in the premises (if you don't, you may miss a relatively easy question).

20. **F.** You can conclude from the premises that Julie has the qualifications to go to Costa Rica and Rhiannon doesn't; Choice (F) is therefore the best answer.

Test 6: Reading and Language Arts

1. **A.** The answer is in the second paragraph. Naomi meets Ruth while she is in Moab, and Ruth is referred to as a Moabite. The answer is Choice (A).

2. **F.** The second paragraph tells you that Ruth is Naomi's daughter-in-law, which means Naomi must be Ruth's mother-in-law, Choice (F).

3. **D.** Substitute the answers for *gleans* in the passage. The sentence is: It is the spring harvest in Bethlehem, and Ruth *gleans* the fields to provide food for her and her mother-in-law. Ruth doesn't *glow from* or *shine on* the fields. Nor does she *burn up* the fields to provide food. The best answer is Choice (D). She *picks from* the fields to provide food.

4. **J.** The third paragraph describes Boaz as goodly and tells how he's kind to Ruth, which means you can eliminate Choices (F), (G), and (H). The answer is Choice (J), kind.

5. **A.** The third paragraph states that Boaz is related to Naomi's late husband, Choice (A).

6. **G.** In the last paragraph, you discover that Boaz makes sure another relative doesn't want to exercise his right to marry Ruth, Choice (G). Don't be fooled by Choice (H); Boaz tells Ruth to gather grain in *his* field, not the fields of others.

7. **D.** The last paragraph says that Naomi is well cared for. Although she was bitter before Ruth and Boaz marry, she's content and cared for at the end of the passage. Toss out the first three answers and pick Choice (D).

8. **G.** Sentence 1 has two problems. The subject is *person,* which is singular, but the verb *make* is plural, and the pronoun *their* that refers to person is also plural. Toss any choices that don't correct the subject-verb agreement — specifically Choices (F) and (J). Choice (G) makes the subject plural so that the plural verb is okay; it's better than Choice (H) because Choice (H) doesn't correct the problem with the pronoun *their.*

9. **B.** In Sentence 4, the comma between *happiness* and *she* is used to join two independent clauses without a conjunction. Choice (A) just changes the first verb without correcting the punctuation problem. Choice (C) corrects the comma splice by introducing a conjunction, but it creates needless repetition with the use of *also* and *too.* The best answer is Choice (B); it eliminates the problem comma without creating a new error.

10. **J.** The sentence seems fine as is, but check the answers to be sure. Choice (F) adds an improper comma between *hopeful* and *depiction,* Choice (G) improperly capitalizes the story of Ruth, and Choice (H) features improper punctuation. Choice (J) it is!

11. **C.** The second paragraph says that Zoe and her friends were "very uneasy." Choice (C), anxious, is a synonym for very uneasy. The other choices are antonyms.

12. **J.** Paragraph 2 tells you that the regionals are held in the city of Albany, Choice (J).

13. **B.** The passage mentions Zoe's brother in the last two paragraphs. It refers to him as her "younger" brother, so you know that Choice (B) is correct.

14. **J.** The regionals are touched on in the last paragraph, which says that Zoe had butterflies in her stomach (meaning she was nervous, Choice (J)).

15. **A.** The reasoning you use to answer this question is similar to the logic you use to answer questions in the Verbal Reasoning—Context section. You can't assume Zoe will win next year, and just because the passage doesn't mention other siblings doesn't mean they don't exist. The passage implies that Zoe's friends skated on the indoor rink, so Choice (C) is wrong. The best answer is Choice (A): Zoe skates on frozen ponds in Maine.

16. **H.** Zoe's dad's comments in the last paragraph suggest that he thought she didn't win because it was her first time in the regional competition, Choice (H). He didn't mention any of the reasons offered by the other options.

17. **C.** The answer that joins the two ideas best is Choice (C). Choices (A) and (B) are comma splices, and Choice (D) contains improper punctuation. You can't place a comma before a restrictive clause such as "that she did not win."

18. **G.** The objective form of the pronoun *him* is improper in Choices (F) and (H); it should be "he and Zoe's brother were able to see Zoe compete." Choice (J) contains an unclear pronoun reference because *him* could refer to either Zoe's dad or her brother.

19. **D.** Find the sentence that transitions well into the first sentence and that addresses the specific topic of the paragraph. The first word of the first sentence is *their;* it'd be good to know who that refers to. Choice (C) talks about one person, so *their* doesn't make sense. Choice (A) is all about ponds, and ponds don't have daily practice routines that we know about. *Their* could refer to "some figure skaters" in Choice (B), but the rest of the paragraph is about Zoe and her friends, not skaters in general. Choice (D) fits best.

20. **H.** Pick Choice (H) because it talks more about Zoe, who's the main character in the paragraph, and builds on information provided in the paragraph.

21. **B.** As you discover in the first paragraph, the purpose of the passage is to describe the means silent films use to get their points across. Choice (B) paraphrases this purpose. Choice (A) is too specific; the musical score is just one element of silent films that the author describes. Choices (C) and (D) are too general. The main purpose of the passage isn't to show how film in general has changed over a century, nor is it mostly concerned with explaining why all types of films have car chases.

22. **H.** Eliminate the answers that *are* covered in the passage. Paragraphs 2 and 3 mention exaggerated gestures and stereotypical characters, and Paragraph 4 references perpetual activity, which means you can cross out Choices (F), (G), and (J). Silent films don't contain dialogue, so it makes sense that the answer is Choice (H).

23. **B.** Paragraph 3 explains that actors in silent films must show their feelings with exaggerated gestures because they can't say how they feel, Choice (B).

24. **F.** According to the last line of the fourth paragraph, placards express dialogue, thoughts, and passage of time. The answer that isn't included is Choice (F).

25. **C.** The first sentence of the last paragraph refers to the descriptions of car chases, jail breaks, and skating scenes in the prior paragraph as "frenetic motion." These antics aren't mellow or calm, and muggy motion doesn't make sense. The best answer is lively, Choice (C).

26. **G.** The answer is stated clearly in the last paragraph: Ominous chords signal danger, Choice (G).

27. **D.** Nothing's wrong with Sentence 3, but you should check the other answer choices just to make sure another one isn't better. Choice (A) is a comma splice. Choice (B) incorrectly puts a comma between its subject (actors) and verb (expressed). Choice (C) uses inconsistent verb tenses; *changed* is past tense, and *grow* is present tense. The best answer is still Choice (D).

28. **H.** The verbs in Sentence 5 are in different tenses; *were* is past tense, and *are* is present. The rest of the paragraph is in the past tense, so the present tense *are* is incorrect. Choices (F) and (G) don't solve the problem. The best answer is Choice (H).

29. **C.** Sentence 6 looks pretty good at first glance, but it contains an error that you may miss if you read it too quickly. In Sentence 6, the attention belongs to the audience; it's the audience's attention. Choice (A) incorrectly puts the apostrophe after the *s,* which implies there's more than one audience. Choice (B) really messes things up by putting the apostrophe after the *s* and adding another *s.* Choice (C) correctly places the apostrophe before the *s.*

30. **F.** The first line of the passage describes the purposes of the digestive system as breaking down food and absorbing nutrients. Choice (F) states one of these purposes, breaking down food. The other choices describe purposes of other bodily systems.

31. **D.** The first paragraph explains that wide, flat teeth belong to herbivores, Choice (D).

32. **J.** According to Paragraph 2, food goes down the esophagus, Choice (J), after it passes through the mouth. It hits the esophagus before it reaches the rest of the organs involved in the digestion process.

33. **C.** The question asks you to choose something the small intestine *doesn't* do, so you need to find where the passage describes what it *does* do. Paragraph 3 suggests that the small intestine breaks down food, absorbs nutrients, and receives bile from the liver. It doesn't claim that it uses acids to kill bacteria, Choice (C).

34. **G.** The liver produces bile, so you can cross out Choice (F). Choices (H) and (J) are wrong because muscles, not acid, work to move food down the esophagus and the stomach isn't designed to store food. Its purpose is to break down food, Choice (G).

35. **D.** The passage only mentions the pancreas once, and it's to say that it produces and sends digestive enzymes, Choice (D).

36. **F.** Paragraph 3 explains that bile is produced in the liver, Choice (F).

37. **B.** Both sentences contain the idea of using the digestive system, so pick the answer that best gets rid of that duplication. Choice (A) is a comma splice that doesn't eliminate the duplication of *animals* and *they,* which refers to animals. Choice (C) alters the meaning, and Choice (D) changes the sentence's focus. Choice (B) is best.

38. **G.** Choice (F) is a comma splice; cut it. Choice (H) is awkward and contains an unclear pronoun reference; you don't know what *it* refers to. Choice (J) is a mess; it has unclear and faulty pronoun references and punctuation problems. Choice (G) is your best bet because it clearly states what's dangerous and, using proper punctuation and construction, tells you what to do about the dangerous situation.

39. **D.** The paragraph describes the appendix and what causes it to rupture. Choose a topic sentence that introduces the primary characteristic of an appendix. Choices (A) and (C) are wrong because the appendix isn't useful. Choice (B) addresses the whole body and would be good for introducing a discussion of bacteria. Choice (D) is the best answer because it focuses on the peculiar nature of the appendix.

40. **F.** The question paragraph ends by telling you that appendicitis is dangerous if it's not treated properly. It wouldn't be fair to you if the next paragraph didn't then tell you how to treat appendicitis properly to avoid this danger. The best answer is therefore Choice (F). Choices (G) and (H) bring up unrelated topics, and Choice (J) is far too general to follow the specific topic of appendicitis.

Test 7: Mathematics

1. **C.** 4% is 4 per (or divided by) 100. You can express this number as either a decimal or a fraction, but all the answer are fractions, which means you must create a fraction: $\frac{4}{100}$, Choice (C).

2. **F.** Multiply before you subtract: $3 \times -2 = -6$; $-6 - 2 = -8$, Choice (F).

   Don't forget to follow the order of operations (PEMDAS) when faced with problems involving multiple operations.

3. **D.** The best way to simplify a square root problem is to consider a number's factors and look for perfect squares. 100 is a factor of 1,300 ($100 \times 13 = 1,300$), and 100 is a perfect square. So, $\sqrt{100 \times 13} = \sqrt{100} \times \sqrt{13} = 10\sqrt{13}$, which is Choice (D).

4. **J.** You can simplify your approach to this problem by canceling out common factors in the numerator and denominator. Strike through 5 and 10 on both the top and bottom, and you get $\frac{13}{2}$, which simplifies to $6\frac{1}{2}$ — Choice (J).

5. **C.** Follow the order of operations. Parentheses go first: $-3^3(-1)^2 + (-3)^2$. Exponents next: $-27 \times 1 + 9$. Then multiply and add to get -18, Choice (C).

   The value of a negative number with an odd-numbered exponent is negative; one with an even-numbered exponent is positive.

6. **G.** The 7 is in the thousands place, which means its value is 7,000, Choice (G).

7. **C.** Line up the decimal points and subtract:

   $$\begin{array}{r} 14.565 \\ -\ \ 2.35 \\ \hline 12.215 \end{array}$$

8. **J.** Because the bases are the same, you can just add the exponents. $3 + 5 = 8$, which means the answer is 3^8, which is the same as Choice (J).

9. **B.** To find $\frac{3}{5}$ of 15, multiply. *Note:* This is easier if you eliminate the common factors before you begin. Because 5 goes into both 15 and 5, $\frac{15}{1} \times \frac{3}{5} = \frac{3}{1} \times \frac{3}{1}$. The answer is 9, Choice (B).

10. **H.** The easiest way to solve this problem is to count the zeros in the number. The number of zeros is the value of the exponent. 10,000 has 4 zeros, so the answer is 10^4, Choice (H).

11. **B.** To find the percentage of people who didn't answer the poll, add the percentages of those who did and subtract from 100: x = 100% – (13% + 37% + 12%); x = 100% – 62%; x = 38%. The ratio of those who answered to those who didn't is 62:38, or $\frac{62}{38}$, which reduces to $\frac{31}{19}$, Choice (B).

12. **H.** The intersection symbol tells you that you're looking for the numbers that are common to both sets of numbers. Both sets have 4 and 12 in common, Choice (H).

13. **B.** This question is really just asking for the percentage that $\frac{4}{9}$ represents. $\frac{4}{9}$ of the pieces is 0.4444 . . . , or approximately 44%, which is Choice (B).

14. **G.** This problem looks for how fast the train traveled, which is the rate. Use the distance formula: Distance = Rate × Time. The distance was 142 miles, and the time was 2 hours. Plug that into the equation: 142 = r × 2; 71 = r. The train traveled 71 mph, Choice (G).

15. **D.** The numbers that appear in both sets are 10 and 11, Choice (D).

16. **J.** An *equilateral triangle* is a triangle with equal sides and equal angles, and the angles of all triangles add up to 180°. Because the first three options are true, the answer must be Choice (J).

17. **C.** All of the integers that are less than 9 and greater than 4 are 5, 6, 7, and 8 — Choice (C).

18. **F.** Two million is 2,000,000; five hundred-forty-five thousand looks like 545,000; and twenty-two is 22. Add them together, and you get 2,545,022 — Choice (F).

19. **B.** 10 isn't prime, so scratch Choice (D). Now all you have to do is figure out whether 3 and 11 are factors of 222. 3 × 74 = 222, which means 3 is a factor; cross out Choice (A). 11, however, isn't a factor of 222. The answer is Choice (B).

20. **H.** The other way to phrase the question is "$500 is 8% of what," which looks like this when expressed as an equation: $500 = 0.08 × x. Looks like x = $6,250, Choice (H).

21. **A.** Both numbers are even, so 2 must be a common factor. Cut Choices (C) and (D) because they don't include 2. Choices (A) and (B) are the same except that Choice (A) includes 4 and Choice (B) includes 6. Choice (A) is the answer because 6 isn't a factor of 64.

22. **H.** You can substitute x for the missing number: 4(2x) + 12 = 2,012. Now solve for x: 8x + 12 = 2,012; 8x = 2,000; x = 250, Choice (H).

23. **B.** The formula for the area of a triangle is A = ½bh. Substitute the base and height measurements into the formula: A = ½ × 15 × 12 = 90 m², Choice (B).

24. **G.** The other five friends raised 15% of the money (100% – 85% = 15%). 15% of $1,200 means 0.15 × 1,200, which equals $180, Choice (G).

25. **C.** The *perimeter* is the sum of the sides. Two of the sides are 15 yards, which is a total of 30 yards. The other two sides are 25 yards each, which totals 50 yards. The answer is Choice (C) because 30 + 50 = 80.

26. **F.** Create an equation for the problem and make x the number of hours worked: $290 = $125 + 55x$. Solve for x: $165 = 55x$; 3 = x. Choice (F), 3 hours, is your answer.

27. **B.** 10³ = 1,000, and 3 × 1,000 is 3,000, which is Point B on the line.

28. **J.** According to the parameters, x can be any value that's greater than –5 and less than –3. Only –4, Choice (J), meets these requirements.

29. **C.** There are 2.2 pounds in a kilogram, which means you divide 25 by 2.2 to find out how many kilograms are in 25 pounds. 25 ÷ 2.2 = 11.3636 . . . , which rounds to 11 kg, Choice (C).

30. **H.** First, eliminate obviously incorrect answers. You know that Choice (F) is wrong because $\frac{5}{6}$ is greater than $\frac{3}{4}$. ¼ is 25%, which means Choice (G) isn't ordered properly. The values in Choice (J) are equal, so they can't be arranged in ascending order. The correct answer is Choice (H).

31. **D.** If a 6-ounce steak costs $4 less than a 12-ounce steak, which is x dollars, the price of a 6-ounce steak is $x - 4$. Two of them would cost twice that, $2(x - 4)$, which is Choice (D).

32. **G.** Choice (G) demonstrates the distributive property because it multiplies a by both b and c to get $ab - ac$.

The distributive property states that the value being multiplied by values within parentheses must be distributed to each of the values inside the parentheses.

33. **D.** The number of games the team won and tied is 20 ($16 + 4 = 20$). 20 games make up 40% of the team's season. Therefore, 20 games = $0.4 \times$ all games played (x). $20 \div 0.4 = x$, which means x equals 50. If the team played a total of 50 games, then it lost 30 games ($50 - 20 = 30$), Choice (D).

34. **F.** One shirt costs $15 + (6\% \times \$15)$, which is $15.90. $15.90 rounds up to $16. Rico has $50, which divided by $16 is 3.125. That means Rico can buy three shirts and have a few dollars left over. The correct answer is Choice (F).

35. **C.** The formula for finding the circumference of a circle is $2r\pi$. The spokes coming out from the center of a wheel are its radii. So the radius of the wheel is 20 inches. Apply this value to the formula, and you have your answer: $C = 2(20)\pi$, or 40π — Choice (C).

36. **H.** To answer this question, you have to know that 1 meter equals 100 centimeters. This means that 2 meters contain 200 centimeters. Therefore, 1 centimeter is $\frac{1}{200}$ of 2 meters, which is Choice (H).

37. **B.** Use the information in the chart to calculate the total dollar amount of T-shirt sales: $125 + \$130 + \$140 + \$105 = \$500$. Maria sold $125 of the $500 in T-shirt sales, or $\frac{125}{500}$, which reduces to ¼, or 25%, Choice (B).

38. **J.** The average price of the jeans is their total cost divided by the number sold. You know how many were sold; you just need to figure out the total cost. Add up the information in the jeans column of the chart: $400 + \$325 + \$775 + \$1,100 = \$2,600$. $2,600 \div 26 = \$100$. The average price of the jeans is $100, Choice (J).

39. **D.** The pie chart, Choice (D), is the best chart to show fractions of a whole. (For the full scoop on how to use charts, head to Chapter 13.)

40. **F.** A Venn diagram, Choice (F), is the best way to display the desired data because it shows the intersection of students who play more than one sport. The other charts don't reveal any information about how many students are involved in more than one sport.

Answer Key for COOP Practice Test 2

Test 1: Sequences

1. C	5. D	9. B	13. D	17. D
2. H	6. G	10. H	14. F	18. G
3. B	7. C	11. A	15. A	19. B
4. J	8. F	12. G	16. H	20. J

Test 2: Analogies

1. A	5. B	9. A	13. C	17. C
2. H	6. J	10. H	14. G	18. F
3. C	7. D	11. B	15. D	19. D
4. G	8. J	12. H	16. F	20. F

Test 3: Quantitative Reasoning

1. C	5. D	9. A	13. C	17. D
2. F	6. G	10. H	14. F	18. J
3. A	7. B	11. B	15. C	19. C
4. G	8. H	12. F	16. G	20. F

Test 4: Verbal Reasoning—Words

1. A	5. B	9. D	13. A
2. H	6. H	10. J	14. G
3. B	7. C	11. C	15. B
4. F	8. J	12. G	16. H

Test 5: Verbal Reasoning—Context

1. C	5. A	9. C	13. D	17. A
2. G	6. G	10. H	14. J	18. H
3. D	7. D	11. B	15. A	19. B
4. G	8. J	12. H	16. F	20. F

Test 6: Reading and Language Arts

1. A	9. B	17. C	25. C	33. C
2. F	10. J	18. G	26. G	34. G
3. D	11. C	19. D	27. D	35. D
4. J	12. J	20. H	28. H	36. F
5. A	13. B	21. B	29. C	37. B
6. G	14. J	22. H	30. F	38. G
7. D	15. A	23. B	31. D	39. D
8. G	16. H	24. F	32. J	40. F

Test 7: Mathematics

1. C	9. B	17. C	25. C	33. D
2. F	10. H	18. F	26. F	34. F
3. D	11. B	19. B	27. B	35. C
4. J	12. H	20. H	28. J	36. H
5. C	13. B	21. A	29. C	37. B
6. G	14. G	22. H	30. H	38. J
7. C	15. D	23. B	31. D	39. D
8. J	16. J	24. G	32. G	40. F

Part V
The Part of Tens

The 5th Wave · By Rich Tennant

Jimmy spent all day concentrating on his up-coming HSPT. This proved an excellent study habit up until he tried milking his father's prize bull.

In this part . . .

This part summarizes in a nice, neat list some of the pitfalls to avoid as you prepare for and take your Catholic high school entrance exam. It also outlines ways your parents can participate in your exam-preparation efforts to help you do your best on test day. Share Chapter 30 with them and take some of the pressure off of yourself.

Chapter 29

Ten Test-Taking Traps to Avoid

The majority of this book focuses on what you should do to perform your best on test day, but this chapter highlights ten equally helpful *don'ts* you ought to know about.

Don't Try to Cram the Night Before

All three Catholic high school entrance exams test you on skills you've learned throughout your life. Pulling an all-nighter doesn't give you ample study time. Start studying at least two weeks before exam day so you can sleep well the night before.

Don't Lose Your Focus

Shock of shocks, but tackling 300 multiple-choice questions can get a little boring. Don't use test boredom as an excuse to let your mind wander. Keep your perspective, focus on the task at hand, and reward yourself when it's all over.

Don't Stew Over Questions on Prior Sections

Focus on doing your best in the current moment. Don't let what you think may have been a poor performance on an earlier section affect the rest of your test.

Don't Pay Attention to Other Test-Takers

Seeing others put down their pencils while you're still slaving away can be alarming. Just remember that some people work more quickly than others and that speed doesn't equal stellar performance. If you compare yourself to those around you, you can psych yourself into thinking that you're a loser, and feeling like a loser doesn't do much for your test score.

Don't Waste Your Time on Hard Questions

An easy question is worth the same amount of points as a hard one. So, discipline yourself to know when to move on. You may miss out on a simple question at the end of the test because you've stubbornly tried to answer an earlier difficult one.

Don't Read Questions Too Quickly

You shouldn't be so concerned about answering some 200 or 300 questions in a couple hours that you fly through the test. You don't get points if you don't answer questions correctly. Reading carefully makes you more likely to mark the correct answers.

Don't Lose Track of the Answers on Your Sheet

Keep the sections straight on your answer sheet and make sure you mark the answer to Question 6 in the bubble for Question 6 and not the bubble for Question 5. If you mess up one question, you could mess up your answer sheet from that point forward.

Get in the habit of checking your answer sheet about every fifth question to make sure you're on track. It helps to transfer your answers to the sheet five at a time. Also, always circle the right answer in your test booklet so that if you discover you've messed up your answer sheet, you won't have to reread the questions to figure out the right answers.

Don't Blow Off Extra Time

If you finish your exam before the time is up, use those last few minutes wisely instead of twiddling your thumbs. Return to tough questions and double-check your answers.

Don't Bring Electronic Devices with You

Cellphones, calculators, watches that contain calculators, and MP3 players aren't allowed in the testing room. Having any of these devices on you (even if they're in your pocket or purse) is grounds for dismissal from the test. Make sure you leave all electronic devices at home so you don't accidentally forget you have one on you and risk getting kicked out of the testing site.

Don't Cheat, Duh

It's a no-brainer, but we still have to say it: Cheating isn't the right thing to do, and it's also just plain illogical. Your hand isn't big enough to hold all the info you need to master the entrance exam, and the person next to you may know less than you do. This book gives you everything you need to do your best on the exam, so don't risk messing things up by cheating.

Chapter 30

Attention, Parents! Ten Ways You Can Help Your Child Succeed on the Exam

....

In This Chapter

▶ Discovering constructive ways to help your son or daughter prepare for the HSPT, TACHS, or COOP

▶ Pointing out your role the day of the test

....

As a parent, you're probably wondering what you can do to help your child study for his or her Catholic high school entrance exam. Well, wonder no longer! This chapter has ten action steps you can take to help your student do his or her best.

Give Him Awesome Test Prep Materials

If you bought this book for your child, you did him a huge favor. Reading this book and taking the practice tests within it will give your child an edge over other eighth-graders who haven't prepared. Nicely done!

Encourage Her to Study

Possessing this book is one thing; actually using it is another. Help your child work out a study schedule and give her incentives to stick to it, such as picking out the family's dinner menu for one week or allotting her a larger share of the family's cellphone minutes.

Supply Him with a Good Study Environment

Make sure your student has a quiet study area where he can concentrate without being disturbed by siblings, pets, friends, TV, the computer, or his cellphone. Quality study time is time spent without distractions.

Take Practice Tests with Her

You'll be better able to discuss the questions and answers with your child if you take the practice tests, too. Pretend you're a test proctor and be the official timer for your student when she takes the full-length practice tests. Afterward, read through the answer explanation chapters with her and help her discover which question types she may need to focus on improving. Then look up those particular topics earlier in the book for a refresher on the rules that govern them.

Model Good Grammar for Him

Help your child recognize mistakes in English-usage questions by speaking properly with him and *gently* correcting his grammar mistakes in your conversations. Before you know it, he'll be correcting you!

Quiz Her on Spelling Words

Assist your student in developing a list of commonly misspelled words (see Chapter 6 for tips on how) and encourage her to spell them for you. In fact, why not hold a spelling bee for family game night?

Help Him Memorize Math Formulas

The online Cheat Sheet for this book has a list of formulas your student should memorize for the test. Quiz him to make sure he remembers them.

Flash Her Vocabulary Notecards

Encourage your student to write unfamiliar words from the practice tests on index cards. Have her look up their definitions and write them on the backs of the cards. Then work with her for several minutes each day to help improve her vocabulary. Also, use the words in your conversations with her; repetition aids word retention.

Get Him to the Test Site on Time

Take a test drive a day or two before the exam date to make sure you don't get lost on the way there or encounter unexpected roadwork on the morning of the test. That day, make sure your kid's alarm is set properly so he rises with plenty of time to get dressed, eat a healthy breakfast, and make sure he has the items he needs to take with him to the exam.

Help Her Keep a Proper Perspective

Remind your student that, although the entrance exam is important, it isn't more important than her schoolwork or being good to her family. Her exam score isn't a reflection of her worth (or your parenting skills). It's just a tool Catholic high schools use to assess students' skills and place them in classes.

Index

● **X** ●

● **Y** ●

● **Z** ●

Notes

Notes

Notes

Notes

Notes

Business/Accounting & Bookkeeping
Bookkeeping For Dummies
978-0-7645-9848-7

eBay Business
All-in-One For Dummies,
2nd Edition
978-0-470-38536-4

Job Interviews
For Dummies,
3rd Edition
978-0-470-17748-8

Resumes For Dummies,
5th Edition
978-0-470-08037-5

Stock Investing
For Dummies,
3rd Edition
978-0-470-40114-9

Successful Time
Management
For Dummies
978-0-470-29034-7

Computer Hardware
BlackBerry For Dummies,
3rd Edition
978-0-470-45762-7

Computers For Seniors
For Dummies
978-0-470-24055-7

iPhone For Dummies,
2nd Edition
978-0-470-42342-4

Laptops For Dummies,
3rd Edition
978-0-470-27759-1

Macs For Dummies,
10th Edition
978-0-470-27817-8

Cooking & Entertaining
Cooking Basics
For Dummies,
3rd Edition
978-0-7645-7206-7

Wine For Dummies,
4th Edition
978-0-470-04579-4

Diet & Nutrition
Dieting For Dummies,
2nd Edition
978-0-7645-4149-0

Nutrition For Dummies,
4th Edition
978-0-471-79868-2

Weight Training
For Dummies,
3rd Edition
978-0-471-76845-6

Digital Photography
Digital Photography
For Dummies,
6th Edition
978-0-470-25074-7

Photoshop Elements 7
For Dummies
978-0-470-39700-8

Gardening
Gardening Basics
For Dummies
978-0-470-03749-2

Organic Gardening
For Dummies,
2nd Edition
978-0-470-43067-5

Green/Sustainable
Green Building
& Remodeling
For Dummies
978-0-4710-17559-0

Green Cleaning
For Dummies
978-0-470-39106-8

Green IT For Dummies
978-0-470-38688-0

Health
Diabetes For Dummies,
3rd Edition
978-0-470-27086-8

Food Allergies
For Dummies
978-0-470-09584-3

Living Gluten-Free
For Dummies
978-0-471-77383-2

Hobbies/General
Chess For Dummies,
2nd Edition
978-0-7645-8404-6

Drawing For Dummies
978-0-7645-5476-6

Knitting For Dummies,
2nd Edition
978-0-470-28747-7

Organizing For Dummies
978-0-7645-5300-4

SuDoku For Dummies
978-0-470-01892-7

Home Improvement
Energy Efficient Homes
For Dummies
978-0-470-37602-7

Home Theater
For Dummies,
3rd Edition
978-0-470-41189-6

Living the Country Lifestyle
All-in-One For Dummies
978-0-470-43061-3

Solar Power Your Home
For Dummies
978-0-470-17569-9